MEMOIRS

OF

ALLEGHENY COUNTY

PENNSYLVANIA

PERSONAL AND GENEALOGICAL

WITH PORTRAITS

VOLUME I

MADISON, WIS.
NORTHWESTERN HISTORICAL ASSOCIATION
1904

INDEX, VOLUME I

A

	PAGE
Abbott, August	325
Abernathey, Samuel	213
Ackerman, Nick	311
Albrecht, Nicholas	262
Alderson, William	548
Allebrand, Charles W	553
Allman, John G	242
Anderson, Charles A	206
Anderson, Charles F	108
Armstrong, Elmer	156
Armstrong, John H	76
Armstrong, William B	442
Arnold, William A	474
Aston, Walter	417

B

	PAGE
Bailey, Samuel G	462
Bair, David F	559
Baird, George H	546
Baker, Millard F	419
Barker, Olin G. A	127
Barnett, James E	502
Barr, Francis X	77
Battles, John	430
Beale, George W	483
Beck, Robert	347
Bedell, Milton	253
Behen, Dennis Æ	502
Beinhauser, Louis	424
Bekavac, Bosiljko	220
Bellingham, Uriah	84
Benham, William M	112
Benner, Thomas M	146
Berkenbush, John	558
Bernhard, Charles P	430
Best, William E	505
Bickerton, James	286
Black, Alexander	82
Black, Howard L	515
Black, Walter R	121
Bleichner, John A	64
Boden, Daniel	494
Boden, George W	538
Bohlander, John P	539
Bollman, Edward W	421
Bolster, Peter	228
Boothe, Willis A	465
Borgmann, William	542
Bost, Frank	385
Bost, William	277
Botkin, Lester H	320
Bowes, S. Cameron	383
Boyd, Samuel F	245
Bradley, John	82
Brady, Nicholas H	89
Brierley, Robert	264
Brinker, Addison J	215
Brown, J. A. A	54
Brown, J. O	412
Brown, John L	219
Brown, John T	327
Brown, John W	113
Brown, Michael J	233
Browne, William R	436
Buckley, Jeremiah D	95
Buente, Henry H	310
Bullion, John J	160
Burgoon, J. A	373
Burkert, Philip C	392
Burns, Simon	30
Burroughs, Hamilton S	57
Byrne, Patrick C	90

C

	PAGE
Cahen, Alfred	138
Cahill, John	451
Caldwell, John	32
Callery, James D	438
Calvert, George H	415
Campbell, Joseph	343
Campbell, W. J	345
Campbell, William W	130
Carnahan, Thomas D	36
Carney, Jeremiah	111
Carney, John	103
Carter, Charles G	116
Chalmers, George B	94
Chaplin, James C	370
Chaplin, J. Crossan	364
Chaplin, John H	359
Chaplin, John M	366
Chaplin, William C	360
Clark, James A	55
Clark, Robert W	525
Cluley, Robert E	458

	PAGE.		PAGE.
Cochrane, Robert K	226	Englehart, William F	175
Cole, Orange S	185	Erskine, W. H	535
Collingwood, David F	78	Evans, William	519
Conlin, Milo G	271	Evert, Henry C	441
Connor, James R	422	Ewing, Robert M	136
Cook, Lawrence B	511	Eynon, Henry	71
Cooper, Charles A	176		
Corlett, Edward S	110		
Coulter, Samuel	459	**F**	
Cox, John F	497		
Craig, Hugh S	509	Faidley, Elijah P	296
Craig, Isaac	357	Fair, D. O	382
Craig, Robert C	326	Fairfield, John	402
Crump, Stephen S	552	Fairman, John A	214
Cunningham, Finley R	485	Fawcett, William G	337
Cunningham, Robert J	130	Fife, Jared B	535
		Fife, Joseph P	486
		Filcer, William J	312
D		Fisher, John A	287
		Fisher, Mary	128
Dabbs, Benjamin L. H	75	Fisher, William	128
Daggette, Alvin St. C	179	Fite, John	204
Daube, Henry	548	Flood, Edward H	133
Davidson, Henry M	205	Flowers, George W	134
Davis, Carroll P	489	Ford, Cornelius F	108
Davis, Charles	37	Ford, William A	217
Davis, David L	163	Fording, Thomas	42
Davis, Frank B	470	Forrester, William G	299
Davis, Lewis E	524	Forsyth, Andrew W	115
Davis, Ralph C	491	Forsythe, George B	334
Davis, Thomas G	92	Foster, George M	437
Demmel, Philip	432	Francies, William H	450
Deverts, Charles O	421	Franenheim, Edward J	80
Dickson, A. B	199	Frederick, Frank H	232
Dickson, James	199	Fullerton, James M	86
Dickson, James W	150		
Dierstein, Frederick	282		
Dilworth, Linford L	461	**G**	
Dodds, William	92		
Dolan, Patrick	111	Gabler, Thomas C	518
Dorrington, John K	109	Gailey, Oliver A	249
Dorsey, William J	295	Gaub, Otto C	258
Downey, John	76	Gerdts, Fred	507
Doyle, Joseph A	288	Gever, William	257
Doyle, Paul B	190	Gilchrist, Joseph J	248
Dublin, David B	316	Glenn, William J	448
Duff, Davidson	398	Glojnaric, Francis	224
Duff, John M	251	Goldstrohm, Charles F	304
Duff, Josiah S	235	Gosser, George W	97
Duffner, John B	221	Gottfried, Julius	371
Dunn, J. C	528	Grabe, George A	418
Duvall, Samuel M	91	Graebing, John, Jr.	225
		Graham, Thomas	508
		Granger, Thomas S	280
E		Gray, Alexander	210
		Gray, James W	208
Eckbreth, William C	272	Gray, William	559
Edgar, Thomas	463	Gregg, Edward R	527
Edlis, Adolph	53	Green, James H	395
Edwards, Frederick W	53	Grelle, Henry	59
Eickemeyer, W. E	530	Grenet, Samuel J	244
Elicker, Jacob	512	Grierson, Malcolm	98
Elphinstone, James A	52	Griscom, William A	492

INDEX

	PAGE.
Groetzinger, John	423
Guffey, James M	46
Guffey, Wesley S	20
Guiler, William G	513

H

Hamilton, Amelia	393
Hamilton, Charles A	557
Hamilton, Charles W	151
Hamilton, James B	33
Hanlon, Matthew A	88
Harkins, Frank B	220
Harper, James G	425
Harvey, George H	397
Harvey, Thomas W	227
Harvey, William H	493
Haslett, Edwin C	375
Hauser, Henry	218
Hays, George L	261
Hays, Joseph	123
Heath, Robert H	317
Heisel, William	536
Henderson, John H	35
Henderson, Robert L	352
Henry, John	159
Henry, John C	456
Hepline, George W	148
Hering, Frederick	387
Hershberger, Thomas P	90
Hill, Lucius L	125
Hill, William	478
Hilldorfer, Joseph P	411
Hock, John	229
Hogg, George	529
Holliday, George L	18
Holozsnyay, Alex	281
Holtzman, Louis F	301
Hope, William A	504
House, George L	451
House, Jesse M	501
Hunter, John M	118

I

Imbrie, Addison M	495
Irwin, James H., Sr	260

J

Jastrzembski, Stanley	196
Jenkins, Edwin B	212
Johns, Harry E	292
Johnson, George A	140
Johnston, Edward P	349
Johnston, George C	526
Johnston, John A	402
Jones, Evan	518
Jones, Jenkin	48
Jordan, William	184

K

	PAGE.
Kambach, George J	125
Kane, James F	138
Kappeler, Herman	237
Kaufman, William	114
Keane, John H	230
Kelly, A. J., Jr	489
Kelly, James L	418
Kennedy, Joseph	305
Kennedy, Robert	487
Kennedy, Robert B	376
Keyes, John A	344
Kimberlin, John C	289
Kimberlin, William E	234
Kimmey, Edson	107
King, Henry L	472
King, William D	439
Kintner, Joseph J	498
Kirkbride, George T	541
Kirschler, Charles F	70
Kistler, Jonas M	313
Klaus, Nicholas G	425
Klumpp, Frank J	173
Knoderer, Charles F	557
Kraus, Jacob W	491
Kuhn, Arthur J	499
Kuhn, John E	198

L

Lambie, John S	24
Lang, William	424
Lantz, Jesse S	303
Latimore, Willmer A	259
Latshaw, Henry B	389
Lawrence, E. A	412
Lawry, James	276
Lawson, Lindley S	279
Lawson, Oscar P	323
Layton, Robert D	444
Lea, William H. H	183
Leadbeater, John	283
Leader, William J	521
Leslie, A. H	34
Leslie, Millard F	79
Leuschner, Albert F	543
Levy, Isaac A	428
Lewis, Charles A	513
Lightenheld, Gustavus J	333
Lighthill, Charles W	211
Lindsay, Robert H	433
Lindsey, William T	69
Linsley, William H	466
Livingston, Charles L	457
Lobingier, Chauncey	509
Locke, Charles A	124
Logan, William H	155
Lohrey, Henry	427
Lowe, Harry W	87
Lowry, John K	510
Lutz, Anton	39
Lynch, Humphrey	434

M

Name	Page
MacBroom, William	314
MacCloskey, Thomas D	149
MacMath, Joseph	381
Magee, Christopher, Jr	106
Malarkey, Andrew J	341
Malone, Robert J. H	101
Manning, William G	223
Marks, Ulysses G	151
Marshall, William T	433
Martin, Charles E	470
Martin, John A	436
Martin, J. B	336
Martin, Robert S	478
Mattern, Robert G	141
Maurer, George	346
Maxey, William S	144
McAlinney, John J	102
McCabe, Francis J	222
McCabe, James H	182
McCabe, Joseph E	481
McCall, Elliot	238
McCandless, J. Guy	38
McCann, Alonzo N	469
McCarthy, Daniel J	121
McClarin, John A	473
McClelland, Robert W	522
McClure, Thomas G	63
McCormick, Richard	231
McCurdy, Steward LeRoy	164
McDermott, Thomas	480
McElhiney, Samuel	315
McFail, Charles B	100
McGarey, David J	41
McGeary, Jesse M	56
McGovern, Charles C	85
McGrogan, John	378
McGunnegle, Daniel K	51
McIlvain, Edward J	208
McKee, Joseph H	321
McKelvy, William H	537
McKenna, Charles F	64
McKinley, William C	58
McLain, Theodore R	109
McMasters, James V	443
McNally, John	234
McPartland, Frank J	302
Mead, Morris W	47
Means, William A	74
Mercer, J. Carson	55
Merriman, Thomas	560
Metcalf, George H	208
Meyer, Albert P	115
Meyer, Edward	462
Miller, Andrew S	120
Miller, Harold A	522
Miller, Harry W	249
Miller, Henry A	520
Miller, Jacob Jay	374
Mitchell, David E	116
Mitchell, Joseph, Jr	429
Mohney, Coursin L	239
Molamphy, John M	263
Monahan, Lawrence P	145
Montgomery, John	269
Montgomery, Nathaniel	162
Moore, G. Wash	43
Moore, John W	391
Moreland, Thomas B	81
Morris, Walter	147
Morrow, James E	401
Morrow, John	338
Morton, Edward	545
Muehlbronner, Charles A	44
Mueller, F. W	73
Mueller, Gustave A	256
Mueller, Michael F	307
Murphy, James P	431
Murphy, Marion H	126
Murray, William W	436
Mustin, William I	40

N

Name	Page
Naylor, Henry B	531
Negley, Henry H	447
Nesbit, John W	68
Neu, Emil W	306
Neville, John	355
Newlin, William E	139
Noble, William V	335

O

Ober, John P	73
Obey, Gustavus B	468
Obushkevich, Theofan A	202
O'Donnell, Simon	240
O'Leary, Timothy	50
Omslaer, John	340
Orbin, Frank	442
Orris, John M	284
Orzechowski, M. J	550
Ostermaier, Robert	49
Oyer, Christian F	119

P

Pagan, Robert B	388
Painter, Josiah	353
Palen, Gilbert	270
Palmer, Robert	496
Parker, George B	122
Parker, William J	413
Patterson, Fred W	201
Patterson, Isaac N	455
Pearson, Frank C	434
Pedder, Charles J	85
Peebles, George E	497
Perrine, J. K. M	166
Perry, Thomas	45
Petty, John M	500
Philips, James F	186
Phillips, John	384

INDEX

	PAGE
Phillips, Mrs. Robert	384
Phillis, Clarence L.	104
Phipps, Henry	17
Pierce, John	103
Pirl, Frederick W.	308
Pitcairn, Andrew J.	458
Pitcock, D. M.	412
Pitts, Arthur B.	319
Prestley, John I.	137
Prosser, Thomas	532
Pruett, Abner B.	246

Q

Quaill, George H.	476
Queck, Harry P. H.	297

R

Radcliffe, John N.	482
Ralston, Benedict S.	268
Ralston, Samuel H.	266
Ramage, R. H.	471
Randolph, E. N.	437
Reed, James H.	423
Reel, Charles C.	324
Reel, David, Jr.	403
Renshaw, Thomas	464
Reukauf, Christian	379
Richards, George W.	551
Ridgway, Frank	60
Riehl, Leonard	547
Rinehart, A. Walter	99
Rinehart, C. C.	255
Ritter, Horace S.	181
Roberts, George L.	116
Robinson, William	440
Rodgers, Arthur D.	117
Rook, Charles A.	21
Ross, Mansfield A.	169
Ross, William S.	250
Rott, Louis	273
Rowe, William R.	46
Rowley, Thomas A.	83
Ruhlandt, Charles J.	440
Ruoff, Frederick	454
Russell, James A.	291
Russell, John M.	480

S

Sachs, Charles H.	97
Samson, Hudson	27
Sarver, William H.	453
Saupp, Frank D.	96
Scandrett, Thomas B.	197
Schell, John E.	394
Schellman, Frank J.	254
Schleich, Simon	243
Schmitt, Charles	267
Schoults, James M.	540
Schreiner, Edward	508
Schroedel, Justus	416
Schroeder, Adolph H.	503
Schulz, Charles A.	278
Schulz, Rudolph	281
Schulz, Victor H.	318
Scott, William	490
Scott, William M.	158
Seibel, Harry J.	165
Seifried, Frank J.	157
Shaffer, Theodore J.	31
Shaw, William C.	177
Sheasley, Jesse H.	241
Sherran, James	59
Sherrard, R. M.	533
Shields, James W.	330
Shoemaker, James K P.	293
Shroyer, William F.	332
Siebert, Peter W.	26
Simon, Charles W.	420
Sloan, John	556
Smail, Edward J.	152
Smalley, Robert E.	545
Smith, Albert Y.	78
Smith, William U.	188
Snaman, George W.	348
Sneathen, Frank F.	467
Snee, Sylvester J.	473
Soffel, Jacob	93
Sparr, Emil	520
Spicer, Charles A.	247
Staab, Anthony	486
Staley, John A.	493
Steel, Christian D.	172
Steen, William J.	57
Steffy, Walter E.	285
Stengel, George H.	96
Stevenson, William M.	460
Stewart, Joseph	339
Stewart, William A.	524
Stone, Stephen P.	75
Stork, Adam	212
Stottler, Sylvester	328
Stouffer, Benjamin W.	67
Stowe, Edwin H.	19
St. Peter, Paul	51
Strang, John Y.	332
Subasic, Joseph	309
Suter, James A.	171
Sutkaitis, John	209
Sutter, George L.	196
Szabo, John	193

T

Thein, George	400
Theis, George W.	88
Theobald, Charles E.	133
Thompson, James H.	153
Thompson, William E.	29
Thomson, Henry D.	555
Tonnele, Theo.	414
Toole, Stephen J.	119

INDEX

	PAGE
Torrance, Francis J	445
Torrence, David R	25
Trautman, Jacob	506
Treacy, James R	479
Tredway, William T	167
Tressel, Jacob	380
Tschume, Frederick	399
Tunstall, William	350

V

Vernon, Joseph A	550
Vierheller, Edward C	77
Voegtly, Jacob J	443
Voegtly, Nicholas H	443
Vogt, Aug. A	198
Vogt, William	534
Vokolek, William	516
Vondera, Charles H	517
Vondera, Christian F	377
Von Moss, Charles	294

W

Wachter, John	396
Waite, Thomas C	252
Walker, Huston Q	135
Walker, James D	71
Walker, John J	452
Wallace, Clarence E	142
Wallace, John I	426
Walsh, William F	100
Walter, Labanna H	174
Walton, William L	52
Watson, Robert L	544

	PAGE
Watson, William M	475
Weber, Joseph A	322
Weir, Albert	549
Weis, Joseph	236
Weller, John S	123
Wiggins, Hubert P	274
Wilcox, Fred F	195
Will, Silas A	488
Williams, Edward J	390
Willock, Curtis M	143
Wills, Lafayette	224
Wilson, George W	435
Wilson, John A	484
Wilson, John M	154
Wilson, Lewis W	526
Wilson, Thomas J	132
Winters, Anna T	554
Wolfe, William W	191
Wright, Jesse H	463
Wylie, Daniel W	189

Y

Young, Annie L	351
Young, Hugh	66
Young, Robert C	351
Young, Robert O	511

Z

Zahniser, William J	67
Zimmerman, George H	386
Zinsser, Louis	162
Zoeller, William F	203

INDEX, VOLUME II

A

	PAGE
Abbott, Edward	410
Abbott, Walter S	444
Aber, Robert E	341
Adams, Thomas B	267
Addenbrook, Thomas	107
Alperman, Frederick	38
Alter, W. B.	300
Alter, William S	177
Ambrose, Parks A	490
Anderson, John T	220
Arthurs, Charles	60
Atkins, George T	374
Atwater, Harry	276
Auld, David W	476
Auld, V. Arthur	30
Austen, John T	498
Ayers, J. Bucher	468

B

	PAGE
Baehr, George	280
Bailey, Charles M	23
Baird, Thomas W	307
Baldwin, Edward I	241
Bame, Jacob E	355
Bard, Edward	471
Barker, Thomas W	315
Barndollar, William L	230
Barnhart, Charles K	198
Barr, L. O.	440
Bash, Elmer J	425
Baxter, R. H	321
Beattie, Jeremiah A	458
Beatty, Robert	335
Beck, Calvin	385
Beck, John J	487
Bedell, J. J	72
Beedle, Evan	298
Belsmeyer, August	497
Bennett, William	108
Berg, Henry	194
Bert, Peter	174
Bestwick, Jacob	21
Bew, William	327
Bickel, Christ L	504
Biehl, Charles	213
Bishoff, Lowery H	471
Black, Abram H. S	495
Black, Francis B	429
Black, R. L	443
Blackburn, James P	79
Blackley, Hamilton Mael	130
Blayney, John S	287
Blind, Henry L	357
Blose, Daniel P	38
Blumenthal, Maximilian	211
Boax, Charles F	472
Bock, John N	450
Bollje, Theodore	57
Boots, E. W	464
Boss, Gustav A	524
Bowman, Daniel	394
Boyd, David S	219
Boyle, Andrew J	206
Boyle, John C	266
Bradshaw, William P	283
Brandt, Herman P	522
Brassert, Herman A	485
Braun, Jacob J	134
Brennan, John	272
Briney, S. A	363
Brinker, William M	400
Brinton, Samuel McG	251
Brockman, Thomas W	193
Brooks, Lawrence A	488
Brown, James, Jr	40
Brown, J. Wilbert	35
Bruner, Harry E	333
Brush, F. S.	463
Bryce, Charles K	119
Burkman, John	197
Burtner, George	423
Butler, Robert	264

C

	PAGE
Calhoun, David K	135
Calhoun, John F	61
Cameron, Lewis O	365
Camp, Oliver C	413
Campbell, Anson B	65
Campbell, James	88
Campbell, Joseph L	112
Campbell, William O	390
Campbell, William V	95
Carnegie Free Library, The	244
Carney, David K	337

	PAGE
Carothers, Joseph C	494
Carothers, Robert T	41
Carson, James	233
Carter, John	37
Chambers, M. W	493
Clark, Samuel D	427
Clay, Rachel A	243
Clay, William H	316
Clifford, John M	273
Clifford, Joseph B	90
Clinton, William J	450
Coe, John S	414
Cole, George H	282
Coleman, Andrew	501
Conkle, Robert F	525
Conner, Alfred D	212
Conway, David M	406
Conwell, Stephen C	158
Conwell, William	418
Cook, Robert H	391
Coursin, B. L	469
Coursin, Frederick H	82
Craft, William A	489
Crawford, E. R	24
Crawford, Harry B	39
Crawford, John Jay	216
Cribbs, Fielding D	116
Cribbs, Hyatt M	115
Cribbs, Oliver L	181
Croft, J. A	439
Crosby, George A	469
Cross, John C	254
Crossland, William	277
Crouch, William H	319
Crusan, William A	526
Crytzer, George W	416
Cunningham, David H	361
Cunningham, Joseph	361
Cunningham, William H	386
Cunningham, William P	352
Curry, William L	464
Czepananis, Stephen J	147

D

	PAGE
Dahlstrom, Charles F	26
Datt, Charles T	351
Daum, Adam	350
Day, Joseph R	172
Dean, E. W	465
Debolt, George S. T	138
De Long, Charles F	63
Denny, John	152
Dersam, John N	62
Dexter, Emery E	54
Dick, George A	526
Dick, John A	432
Dick, William	434
Dieterich, Jacob	245
Dinsmore, Samuel W. S	200
Dithrich, W. J	202
Dittmer, Emil F. A	204

	PAGE
Donaghy, Joseph F	195
Donnell, John H	192
Dougan, Howard G	501
Dougherty, Oscar R	100
Douglass, Wm. L	289
Duerr, George H	228
Duncan, Archibald	42
Duncan, George	57
Duncan, James W	86
Dunlap, David D	261
Dunn, Joseph C	437
Duster, John	164
Duwell, Charles	514

E

	PAGE
Eckert, Ferdinand C	523
Edmundson, George L	20
Edwards, Elmer M	236
Einsporn, Albert	342
Ellerman, Christian	209
Ellison, Ellwood W	380
Elwarner, Charles C	380
Elwell, John D	409
Elwood, Robert D	238
Emmert, Peter F	104
Engelhardt, J. A	150
Erhard, Ernest L	505
Etheridge, Harry	447
Euwer, Joseph E	252
Evans, Oliver	506
Evans, William	74
Everett, Frank M	443

F

	PAGE
Falkenstein, George J. F	442
Faulk, Philip	364
Fawcett, Christopher C	92
Fawcett, John W	97
Fawcett, Thomas R	321
Fawcett, William D	84
Fawcett, William L	464
Fell, Charles	479
Ferguson, John A	160
Ferguson, Thomas	339
Ferree, Harry W	529
Fidler, Joseph	32
Fiedler, Charles P	459
Fink, Frederick	509
Finney, Edward C	507
Fisher, John W	58
Fisher, Julius K	467
Firestone, Henry	66
Forsythe, George W	274
Forsythe, Lewis	271
Foss, John M	504
Foster, David A	77
Friedman, Henry	29
Fryer, Amos	301
Fulton, Joseph K., Sr	186

G

	PAGE
Gardner, Samuel L	157
Gardner, Thomas D	199
Geeting, John A	73
German, William J	55
Gibson, Robert M	346
Giles, John	41
Gillen, John H	133
Gillespie, Andrew	170
Givins, Albert J	483
Glover, Anthony W	479
Goeddel, Charles	123
Goldsmith, Louis J	137
Goodwin, Herman W	176
Gordon, Ezekiel, Jr	485
Gordon, Robert W., Jr	94
Gorzynski, John S	98
Graham, Norman R	490
Granger, William L	513
Gray, G. E. Frank	231
Gray, H. W	448
Greene, Bennett P	332
Greer, D. Newton	109
Griffin, Hezekiah C	460
Griffith, Joseph	248
Griffith, Joshua N	155
Griffith, McKinstry	34
Gross, Michael	63
Gross, Otto J	178
Gundy, Thomas S	161
Guttridge, Charles B	115

H

Haber, Louis	481
Hallam, F. F	440
Hamilton, James B	329
Hamilton, Samuel	371
Hammer, Michael	214
Hammitt, J. Lewis	458
Hanna, John W	234
Hardt, Henry	349
Hardt, John	438
Hardwick, Walter	478
Hardy, Daniel M	50
Hardy, William	442
Harper, Cassius M. C	253
Harrison, George	121
Harrison, Richey C	120
Harrison, William R	388
Hart, George B	210
Hartig, Anton	234
Hauer, George I	247
Hayes, John	128
Hazlett, James E	345
Heath, William H	370
Heckert, William H	348
Heidenkamp, Joseph	397
Heile, Peter	328
Held, Fred	90
Hemphill, John W	404
Henderson, Harry E	285
Herwick, George B	456
Herwig, William K	457
Hezlep, William W	238
Hickey, John	313
Hieber, Charles J	375
Hill, Jabez J	61
Hinkel, Fred C	377
Hitchens, George E	55
Hodgson, Jesse	144
Hoffman, Philip L., Jr	78
Hoffmeyer, Charles K	508
Holinger, Emil F	462
Holland, Paul R	217
Holtzheimer, Joseph G	218
Horner, Samuel J	398
Howat, William	106
Huey, Daniel	385
Huggins, Raleigh R	314
Hughes, Benjamin W	431
Hughes, John A	438
Hultz, John	405
Humphrey, Walter N	242
Hundhausen, Herman	138
Hunter, Orlando M	70
Hunter, William L	432
Hunter, William L	484
Hutchison, Henry F	179
Hutchison, Peter	208
Huth, Conrad	311
Hynes, Bernard J	506

I

Irvin, James A	91
Irvine, J. Q. A	210
Irwin, Benjamin C	196
Ivory, Peter	362

J

Jackel, John, Sr	71
Jackman, Andrew	353
Jackman, William	354
Jacobs, George	127
Janda, Valerian J	142
Jaquay, Gideon H	258
Johnstin, U. Grant	503
Johnston, George R	451
Johnston, James L	383
Johnston, William E	278
Jones, John B	229
Jones, John O	140
Jones, Richard L	168
Jones, Thomas C	52

K

Kapteina, John	326
Karns, James E	250
Karns, James E	302
Katchmar, Anton J	225
Kazinczy, Albert	477

	PAGE
Kelly, Henry E	499
Kelly, Matthew F	89
Kemp, James F	99
Keppel, John N	455
Kerr, Henry M	492
Kerr, John	215
Kerruish, John R	513
Kidd, Walter S	167
King, William	303
Kirkpatrick, Allen	474
Kirkpatrick, Joseph O	263
Kline, Alpha K	473
Klingensmith, Barkley J	399
Knorr, Victor C	118
Knox, William J	105
Koch, Peter	22
Koehler, Charles D	447
Koehler, George A	256
Kola, Frank	481
Kooser, Henry C	515
Kovats, Kalman	85
Krauth, Frederick	122
Krigbaum, Conard G	446
Krogmann, Clement	500
Kunkel, Frank C	448
Kuntz, Peter P	263

L

	PAGE
Lamb, George H	470
Lane, Dilla A	495
Lang, Adam	498
Langsdorf, Peter S	28
Larimer, Thomas McM	487
Lashell, George A	250
Lauck, John E	33
Laughner, Perry O	209
Lawson, Chalmers M	54
Lee, Caleb, Jr	395
Lee, Henry E	436
Lenhart, David G	507
Lewis, John F	466
Lewis, Thomas J	52
Lippert, Ernest T	151
Little, David B	478
Little, John C	322
Loeb, Milton	389
Loeffert, John	270
Logan, George W	507
Lohman, Henry J	22
Lonabaugh, Albert	236
Long, James N	36
Loucks, William L	408
Lourey, William P	165
Love, Thomas J	491
Lowers, John F	125
Luckert, John	466
Lynch, David H	452
Lynch, Madison B	271
Lyon, Florence M	291
Lyon, William R	294

M

	PAGE
McAlpin, William	417
McBride, Herman J	133
McCaffrey, Samuel P	511
McCarthy, Maurice	320
McCarty, R. Lee	25
McCaw, William J	103
McClinton, William	401
McClure, Andrew F	516
McClure, Daniel R	141
McClure, John C	493
McClure, Matthew L	126
McCormick, S. C	222
McCullough, William	435
McCune, D. P	453
McCune, W. C	47
McDermott, Congal A	441
McDowell, James A	304
McElroy, Archibald D	76
McFarland, George L	258
McFetridge, George H	166
McFetridge, William	171
McGeary, George H	480
McGinley, John S	392
McGinley, Neil	476
McGinniss, Thomas A	433
McLaughlin, H. A	136
McMahon, Joseph M	415
McMullen, P. S	260
McPherson, J. Clyde	336
McWilliams, George A	418
MacDougall, Duncan	98
Madden, Francis J	524
Marshall, Henry L	338
Marshall, William S	356
Martin, Harry R	412
Martin, John	480
Martin, J. Will	279
Martin, Taylor McI	262
Masters, Frank R	229
Maurhoff, Emil E	188
Meckel, Gustave A	156
Medvetzky, Julius	475
Meeds, Harrison P	163
Melhorn, John K	295
Mellon, James A	412
Metcalf, Orlando	402
Mettler, J. W	284
Metzler, J. H	310
Meyers, Charles A	454
Meyer, William C	139
Miller, J. Clyde	189
Miller, Samuel D	275
Millheim, John H	334
Milligan, J. Knox	474
Milliken, Samuel	462
Mills, Isaac	243
Mills, James K	468
Mills, Stephen D	467
Miner, F. B	377
Monnier, Henry	350
Montgomery, John R	257

	PAGE.
Montgomery, Samuel P	232
Moore, Charles	423
Moore, George H	143
Morgan, John T	191
Morgan, Lewis N	124
Moore, Thomas	68
Morressey, P. J	59
Morrison, James	445
Mullet, Samuel	344
Murphey, Harry O	96
Murphy, Patrick J	101
Murray, John H	528
Muth, Frederick L	226
Myers, Samuel M	488
Myers, W. Harvey	430

N

Naudler, John S	44
Needling, August J	504
Nicholas, William	182
Nicol, John F	457
Nimmo, Alexander A	45
Norman, Thomas, Jr	153

O

O'Brien, J. E	446
O'Brien, Leo F	53
O'Donovan, Michael C	185
Oeffner, Peter J	207
Oertel, Frank L	120
Oncken, John P	325
O'Shea, Cornelius	396
Overy, Joseph	162
Owens, George T	411

P

Painter, John W	36
Pancoast, George W	290
Parker, Charles	105
Parry, Thomas L	117
Pastre, George F	93
Patterson, James H	247
Patterson, Peter	48
Patterson, Peter C	453
Patterson, William H	222
Peairs, Andrew F	502
Penney, James L	460
Petty, A. Lewis, Jr	24
Pfaub, George N	482
Pfeifer, Edward J	486
Pfordt, Charles C	419
Phillips, Charles A	486
Philips, O. H	113
Poundstone, John A	146
Power, John H	367
Powers, Edward W	201
Pratt, Frank W	461
Price, B. Frank	149
Pugh, E. J	378

Q

	PAGE.
Quaill, David R	358
Quaill, Elizabeth (Reel)	358
Quaill Family, The	358
Quaill, George	358

R

Rankin, Charles A	80
Rankin, John I	494
Rankin, John W	502
Rea, Thomas R	456
Reed, William A	227
Reel, Wiley G	398
Reel, William H	373
Reese, William S	434
Reinhart, Joseph	499
Rickenbaugh, John R	197
Rhoades, Peter F	286
Rhoades, Sylvester E	522
Riblet, Harry L	369
Richards, Arthur J	56
Richards, Wm. Henry	59
Riethmiller, George W	491
Riggs, Robert L	17
Rinard, John	111
Robb, John D	312
Roche, Joseph T	94
Romine, John R	75
Roose, Arthur E	129
Roseborough, William J	475
Rosenberg, David	49
Rosensteel, Thomas W	221
Roth, Jacob	31
Roth, Joseph	30
Rotharmel, John P	103
Rotzsch, Louis E	67
Rowley, Daniel G	318
Rudert, Paul	420
Russell, W. F	305
Ryan, John M	529

S

Sargeant, W. A	183
Schmidt, Aristide J	316
Schmitt, John	512
Schopp, Lawrence	517
Schrandt, Frederick W	265
Schuetz, Elmer A	299
Schwarz, George	422
Schwitter, Fred	366
Scott, Alexander M	114
Scott, David	340
Scott, George H	175
Scott, Harry C	317
Scott, John	403
Sefton, Frank	343
Seifert, Edward O	78
Serena, John E	20
Shaffer, J. O	424
Shale, Jacob B	43

	PAGE
Shaner, James	497
Shanks, John I	376
Sheets, William L	28
Shields, John	312
Shields, Robert J	503
Shultz, Herman	496
Sieber, William	70
Simons, Hugh	387
Sinn, Charles J	409
Skelly, John K	86
Smith, Albert G	281
Smith, Duane P	77
Smith, Samuel B	224
Snyder, Daniel A	246
Snyder, George W	124
Sober, Craig M	429
Soles, Anderson	81
Soles, Clarence E	68
Soles, Wesley C	75
Spence, David	159
Spencer, Daniel B	448
Sproat, H. H	463
Stahl, James W	470
Staley, William J	154
Stamm, Henry	435
Stanton, William M	255
Stark, Christ	427
Starke, Emil C	368
Starke, Richard H	118
Stebick, Edward J	102
Stein, John	518
Stephens, Louis M	240
Stevens, Joseph D	100
Stewart, John W	180
Stewart, Samuel E	145
Stitt, Meredith C	324
Stone, George R	27
Stone, William A	40
Street, George T	472
Sullivan, J. Bailey	386
Sullivan, N. K	407
Sutter, Charles	173

T

Taylor, Dos	205
Taylor, Francis A	514
Taylor, Samuel	520
Thompson, George W	267
Thompson, Harvey	331
Thompson, Lloyd F	393
Thompson, Matthew J	265
Tibby, William C	269
Tinstman, Abraham O	239
Todd, L. Lewis	473
Trich, Edward M	45

U

Uhlinger, Charles	180

V

	PAGE
Van Kirk, Herbert S	446
Van Sciver, William K	131
Verner, Thomas H	80
Vogel, Adam	436
Vogeley, Jacob G	308
Vogt, John J	187
Volkay, Eugene	392

W

Walker, Clarence A	46
Walker, James	379
Walsh, Charles H	96
Wampler, James N	461
Warner, Herbert L	422
Warren, George B	51
Weaver, George P	226
Weigle, Charles R	382
Weigle, Philip	382
Weigle, William	207
Wellinger, John G	213
Wernke, F. W	67
Wertz, J. George	232
Westwood, Howard H	483
Wheatley, John C	518
Wheeler, Hiram J	249
White, D. M	72
White, Thomas W	47
White, William B	190
Wiggins, Samuel L	64
Wilkins, John	379
Williams, Ulysses G	237
Wilson, William F	388
Wise, John	527
Wise, William E	510
Wittman, John M	235
Wittman, Joseph J	203
Wolf, David	426
Wolf, Melchior, Sr	519
Wolfe, Frank	451
Wolferd, William	428
Wolff, Frank	223
Wolff, John A	132
Woodside, Samuel P	309
Woodward, James F	42

Y

Yates, William E	383
Yochum, A. M	381
Yost Bros	449
Young, Clyde F	444
Young, John F	169

Z

Zenn, Philip	26
Zimmermann, Henry	421

MEMOIRS

OF

ALLEGHENY COUNTY, PENNSYLVANIA

VOLUME I

HENRY PHIPPS. Among the men prominent in the history of Pittsburg, and among those who are loved and honored for their public spirit and true philanthropy, is Henry Phipps. He is a native of Pennsylvania, and was born in Philadelphia in 1839. His father, Henry Phipps, Sr., and mother, Hannah (Franks) Phipps, came to America from Shropshire, England, in 1832, settling in the east, and twelve years later settling in Allegheny city. Of the three sons and one daughter in the family, only two are living—Henry Phipps and Rev. William H. Phipps—both residing in Pittsburg. Mr. Henry Phipps was educated in the schools of Allegheny city, but left at an early age to enter the employ of the firm of J. J. Gillespie & Co., and after a short time became bookkeeper for the firm of D. W. C. Bidwell & Co. During this time Mr. Phipps attended night school for several years, and supplemented this by private study, and has become a man of broad culture and sympathies. While in the employ of the latter company, he so won the confidence of his employers that he became a partner, continuing as such until the early sixties, when he engaged in the iron business in Pittsburg with Andrew Kloman, who had organized the Cyclops iron works, and shortly afterwards the firm took in Andrew and Thomas M. Carnegie. The firm underwent many changes in name, culminating in the Edgar Thompson steel works, the first plant west of the Allegheny mountains to manufacture steel rails. Mr. Phipps was in active charge of the financial department of these different enterprises until 1888, when ill health forced him to resign. A few years spent in travel in foreign countries proved to be both a benefit and pleasure, for his taste for travel had not been satisfied on account of pressing business cares. Mr. Phipps led to the altar Annie Childs Shaffer, daughter of Mr. and Mrs. John S. Shaffer, one of the best known of the early Pittsburg families. Five children came to bless their home—three sons, John Shaffer, Henry Carnegie and Howard, and two daughters, Amy and Helen. The first public benefaction of Mr. Phipps was the Allegheny conservatories, which were given to the city on the condition that they should be open to the public at all times. Shortly after this followed the gift to Pittsburg of the conservatory and botanical school, which are the finest of the kind in the country and complete in every detail. In making his gifts to the public and in all charitable work, Mr. Phipps has been anxious to escape public notice, and believes that one should not "let the right hand know what the left hand doeth." Mr. Phipps has earned for himself a reputation as one of the ablest financiers of the country, and numbers among his friends all of the leading financial men of the United States.

GEORGE L. HOLLIDAY, postmaster of Pittsburg, has been for many years prominently before the public. He was first elected to the city council in 1873, on the republican ticket, and served in that body for twenty-five years, being for about fifteen years president of the council. By virtue of being president of the council, he was a member of the library commission and of the building committee of that body when the main library building was erected, and took a special interest in the location and erection of the branch libraries. When appointed postmaster, he resigned from the office of president of the council and library commission. He was appointed postmaster of Pittsburg on April 16, 1898, by President McKinley and was reappointed by President Roosevelt on May 2, 1902. Mr. Holliday was born in Perth, Ontario Co., Canada, May 19, 1845, and is descended from Scotch ancestors. His paternal grandfather, John Holliday, was sent by the English government to Canada as a teacher in the pioneer government schools. Francis Holliday, son of John and father of George L., was born in Great Britain, came to Canada when a lad, and was educated in Perth. Subsequently he learned the harness-makers' trade, which he followed for several years, and, in 1857, moved to Logan county, Ohio, where he engaged in general farming until his death, which occurred in May, 1896. He married Mrs. Margaret Hamilton McEwan, daughter of John McEwan, of Carleton, Ont., and became the father of nine children. George L. Holliday had acquired the rudiments of his education in his native town, when, at the age of twelve, he moved with his parents to their new home in Ohio. Here his schooling was for several years limited to a few months in the winter season, and then, when he had reached the age of eighteen, he began to attend the academy at Northwood, two miles distant. He completed his education at the normal school at Lebanon, Ohio, being graduated from the classical department in 1866. He accepted a position with Harper Brothers, being stationed in Ohio until 1869, when he came to Pittsburg and continued to be the firm's representative until 1880. He was for a time employed by Ivison, Blakeman & Co., of Pittsburg, but, upon the organization of the American book company, became its active representative. On Sept. 7, 1870, Mr. Holliday was united in marriage to Miss Mary T. Pringle, daughter of Dr. George W. Pringle, of New Concord, Ohio, and is the father of seven children, viz.: George A., Harry C., Grace W., Mary E., Edna M., Samuel P. and Francis M. Mr. Holliday and wife are members of the Second Presbyterian church, and Mr. Holliday belongs to the Masonic fraternity. He was one of the original promoters and is now president of the Duquesne inclined plane company.

EDWIN H. STOWE, ex-judge of the court of common pleas, and for many years a resident of Pittsburg, was born in Beaver county, Pa., Jan. 2, 1826, where he spent his boyhood. He was educated in Washington college. After being admitted to the bar, he spent many years in the successful practice of his profession, and was then elected to his present office. Judge Stowe has the distinction of being the oldest judge in commission in the State of Pennsylvania. He has been re-elected to his position a number of times, and, although in politics a republican, his election has several times received the indorsement of both parties, showing the high esteem in which he is held in Pittsburg.

WESLEY S. GUFFEY, capitalist and oil magnate.  Out of the depths of his wisdom, Carlyle wrote, "History is the essence of innumerable biographies," and Macaulay has said, "The history of a nation is best told in the lives of its people." It is therefore fitting that mention of this distinguished citizen should be made in this publication. History was at one time almost entirely a record of wars, a tale of conquest in which armed hosts went forth to capture, pillage and destroy, but with advancing civilization it has become a very different chronicle, being now more particularly the story of the onward march of progress, the upbuilding of cities and the establishing of enterprises and interests which contribute to man's happiness and welfare. A man's reputation is the property of the world. The laws of nature have forbidden isolation. As every human being submits to the controlling influence of others, or as a master wields a power for good or evil on the masses of mankind, there can be no impropriety in justly scanning the acts of any man as they affect his public, social and business relations. If he be honest and successful in his chosen fields of endeavor, investigation will brighten his fame and point the paths along which others may follow. Mr. Guffey is a son of Alexander Guffey, a direct descendant of William Guffey, who came to this country in 1738. This pioneer joined the expedition under Gen. John Forbes against the French at Fort Duquesne, and afterwards settled at Loyalhanna Creek, where was established by his aid the first English-speaking settlement in Westmoreland county. In 1886 occurred a reunion of the Guffey family, attended by five generations, aggregating 293 persons. Mr. Wesley S. Guffey was born in Madison, Westmoreland county, Feb. 22, 1842, and his career has been a busy and successful one from the beginning. He is the senior member of Guffey & Queen, one of the most prominent, successful and progressive oil, coal and mineral producing firms in the country. This firm is one of the heralds of advancing civilization, recognizing that into the bosom of the earth the hand of nature had placed rich deposits that had been lying dormant for centuries, only waiting for progressive men to open the way that the more timid might follow. Their bold, progressive and successful operations in oil, coal, gas, gold, silver and copper mining have not been confined to narrow limits, but have covered every State in the Union where minerals were to be found. The life-record of Mr. Guffey may be chronicled in this brief sentence: Success comes not to the man who idly waits, but to the faithful toiler whose labor is characterized by force and intelligence. It comes only to the man who has the keenness of mental vision to know when, where and how to exert his energies, and thus it happens that but a small proportion of those who enter the "world's broad field of battle" come off victorious in the struggle for wealth and position. His career has been an honorable and upright one, and now, in the evening of life, he can look back over the past without regret. He has performed a noble work for himself and his fellow-man, has left the impress of his individuality upon this community, and has inscribed his name high on the roll of Pittsburg's eminent and honored citizens.

CHARLES ALEXANDER ROOK, president of the Dispatch publishing company, was born at Pittsburg in 1861, the eldest son of Alexander W. and Harriet L. (Beck) Rook. He was educated at the Western University of Pennsylvania. When nineteen years of age he entered the publication office of the Pittsburg Dispatch, and has spent practically all his life in the service of that journal in various capacities, rising from one position to another until he has become the proprietor and editor of one of the most famous and influential dailies of the United States. Mr. Rook is well and favorably known to the members of the newspaper fraternity throughout the country. He has exceptional executive ability, his pleasantness of manner compelling more than force of command. He was married, in 1884, to Miss Anna Wilson. Three children have been born to them, viz.: Helen Emma, Charles Alexander, Jr., and Florence Anna.

Alexander W. Rook, father of the subject of this sketch, was one of the pioneer printers and publishers of Pittsburg, a man beloved by his employes, in which respect the son has followed in his father's footsteps. This was appropriately illustrated when Mr. Rook became the president of the Dispatch publishing company, the members of the Dispatch chapel uniting in a series of cordial and happily-worded resolutions of congratulation, emphasizing the good wishes of the Dispatch force for the new owner. Mr. Rook is broad-gauge in character, liberal in his treatment of persons and subjects He has an ample realization of the responsibilities of the direction of a great and influential newspaper. The Dispatch is never actuated by any petty considerations, its power being always used to foster the best interests of the community and to bring forth the fittest men for public office. As a journal, it was one of the first in the country to stand upon a platform of absolute independence upon all questions of politics or capital and labor. The wisdom of such a course has been exemplified within the last few years by the great majority of other journals which have been forced to disregard their hide-bound partisan predilections Some evidence of the worth of the paper as conducted under the regime which Mr. Rook represents may be found in the fact that the Dispatch was responsible for the agitation that resulted in the movement to secure pure water for Pittsburg, for which a large appropriation was made in the recent bond issue; the improvement of the public roads not only in Allegheny county, but throughout western Pennsylvania; the campaign of education which succeeded in having the survey made for a navigable waterway between the great lakes and the Ohio river, and the stupendous movement of the last few months which has brought before the people, the congress and president of the United States the enormous importance of having a nine-foot stage in the Ohio river the year around in order that full advantage might be taken of the commercial possibilities resulting from the acquisition and construction of the isthmian canal.

The Dispatch has, also, under the management of Mr. Rook, succeeded in establishing a national and international reputation through its possession of an up-to-date London bureau by means of which it has been enabled to secure the exclusive publication of some of the most startling items of international news for the past several months.

This spirit of enterprise, however, is characteristic of the history of the Dispatch. Founded in 1846 by Col. J. Heron Foster, the stirring news of the Mexican war presented an opportunity for the display of energy in securing and imparting intelligence of which the publishers made the most. Special efforts were made to obtain the news at the earliest moment, and one of these resulted in the first issue of a Sunday edition. Brownsville was then the distributing center for the Pittsburg mail which came by stage over the national turnpike. The Dispatch organized a daily express for the purpose of bringing the latest advices to its office, where they were immediately issued to the public. Upon the last day of May, 1846, the Brownsville boat was delayed, and the important news of the crossing of the Rio Grande by the American army under Gen. Zachary Taylor was carried by the Dispatch express from Elizabeth, Sunday morning. An extra edition was at once issued, the first Sunday edition of a newspaper in Pittsburg. It was not until thirty-five years later that the Sunday issue of the Dispatch was undertaken as a regular edition, one of the strongest in excellence and circulation in the country. A feature of the Sunday Dispatch is the fact that it prints a larger number of wants, help and agents' advertisements than any other paper in the United States, and more classified advertisements than all other Pittsburg Sunday papers together. In a recent test, out of 280 leading American papers, only 9 brought more than 200 answers each, and the Dispatch led them all with 274. The explanation of the success of the Dispatch as an advertising medium is no doubt to be found in the policy, inaugurated during Mr. Rook's tenure as business manager, of seeking to bring good returns to its advertising customers.

The modern development of the Dispatch dates from the purchase of a half interest in it by Alexander W. Rook and Daniel O'Neill, in 1865. Mr. O'Neill was a strong and original writer. Mr. Rook was one of the foremost of his time in all that related to the mechanical and typographical department of newspaper-making. His qualifications were long experience, remarkable executive ability and sound judgment. Under the new management the paper was remodeled and enlarged, and its price increased to three cents to meet the greater expenses consequent upon the war.

But the most notable change was the announced determination that, while continuing to support the principles and national candidates of the republican party, the Dispatch would be absolutely free from the control of politicians and from the suspicion of being the organ of any political party. Two years later, when Colonel Foster died, Messrs. O'Neill and Rook purchased the other half interest, the partnership continuing until the death of Mr. O'Neill, in 1877. Mr. Rook survived him but two and a half years, his death occurring Aug. 14, 1880. The ownership was continued in the families, Eugene M. O'Neill, brother of Daniel O'Neill, becoming president of the company, and C. A. Rook treasurer and business manager, with Florence O'Neill, secretary and manager of circulation.

On March 12, 1902, Mr. Rook bought the controlling interest

of E. M. O'Neill, succeeding him as president of the corporation and editor. Under his direction there have been liberal and rapid improvements dictated by his personal thorough knowledge of every department of newspaper-making. While retaining the excellencies of the past, the Dispatch has expanded under the genial influences of Mr. Rook's control, adding new and popular features, and exhibiting renewed and inspiring devotion to the public interest, and the dissemination of the news and views of the day without prejudice or favor.

JOHN S. LAMBIE, attorney, of Pittsburg, and for twenty-six consecutive years a member of the select council and for six years president of that body, was born in Pittsburg, Nov. 1, 1843. His father, William Lambie, a native of Scotland, died when forty-three years old, in 1858. His mother, Aimee (Sioussa) Lambie, a native of Washington, D. C., was a daughter of John P. Sioussa, a Frenchman who came to Washington about 1812, and lived there the rest of his life, having a position in the White House under President Madison. John P. Sioussa was a sailor in the French navy, and took part in the battle of the Nile. During the War of 1812, when the British came to devastate Washington, he saved Sir Joshua Reynolds' portrait of Washington, and in appreciation of that act received a personal letter from President Madison. John S. Lambie was reared and educated in Pittsburg, graduating from the high school in 1862. During the Civil war he served several times for short terms; was corporal of Company F, 193d Pennsylvania volunteer infantry, for 100 days, in 1864; and, prior to that time, served ninety days in the Pennsylvania militia as corporal of Company F, 15th regiment. After the war he studied law with Thomas M. Marshall and A. M. Brown; was admitted to the bar April 16, 1865, and has been very successful in his practice. He was elected to the council in 1877, and has served ever since, representing the eighth ward. For the past six years he has been president of the select council. In January, 1902, on the twenty-fifth anniversary of his election to the council, Mr. Lambie was presented by that body with a magnificent hall clock, as a mark of appreciation of his long and faithful service.

Mr. Lambie was married, in 1865, to Miss Agnes Cunningham, daughter of John Cunningham, and had by this marriage one daughter, Elizabeth, now the wife of Dr. Edward H. Wiggins, of Philadelphia. In 1870 he took as his second wife Anna, daughter of Thos. Robertson, and had by this marriage eight children, of whom seven survive, as follows: Jeanette R., wife of Louis F. Ross; Louis F., editor of the McKeesport Daily News; Aimee S., wife of Dr. David Beggs; Charles S., a civil engineer on the Wabash railroad; John S., Thomas A. and Marguerite McCandless. Mr. Lambie is a member of Post No. 3, G. A. R., of which he has been commander. He belongs to the United Presbyterian church.

DAVID REECE TORRENCE, city treasurer of Pittsburg, is a native of Pittsburg, born April 10, 1847. He was reared and educated in his native city, and has been an honored resident most of his life. When fifteen years old he left school, and was for two years employed in his father's grocery, then he entered the employ of the P. C. C. & St. L. R. R. company, as a clerk in the South Side office. He remained with this company about eight years, then resigned and went to Paducah, Ky. He was appointed local freight and ticket agent of the Elizabethtown & Paducah railroad company, which later became the Louisville, Paducah & Southwestern. In 1876 Mr. Torrence returned to Pittsburg, and was for two years employed by the coal firm of Negley & Co. He entered the office of the city treasurer in 1878, as clerk, where his career has been brilliant and eventful. In the same year that he became an employe in the city treasurer's office, Mr. Torrence was made cashier, and, in 1885, he was made chief clerk. In 1896 he was elected treasurer, was re-elected in 1899, and, in 1902, was appointed to fill the office for a third term, under the famous "Ripper bill." Mr. Torrence served the thirty-second ward, Pittsburg, for eighteen years as a member of the school board, and for fifteen years of that time represented his ward on the Central school board. During his service on the Central board he was one of its most prominent members, and was chairman of the committee which introduced industrial education into the public schools, and chairman of the committee which built the Fifth Avenue high school and the South Side high school. Mr. Torrence is an enthusiastic Mason, a Knight Templar and Mystic Shriner. He is a member of the Episcopal church.

PETER WILLIAM SIEBERT, register of deeds of Allegheny county, was born Jan. 25, 1849, on a farm in Shaler township, Allegheny Co., Pa. In 1854 he removed with his father, Christian Siebert, to Pittsburg, where his father engaged in the leather business until the year 1883, becoming one of the largest dealers in that line. The son also was engaged with his father from 1866 to 1881, obtaining a thorough business experience. P. W. Siebert was educated in the public schools; at Witherspoon institute at Butler, Pa.; at the military academy at West Chester, Pa., and at Western university in Pittsburg. Upon arriving at the age of twenty-one years, he was chosen to represent the eighteenth ward, Pittsburg, in the common council, and, removing to the seventeenth ward, was chosen to represent this ward first in the common branch, then in the select branch. He served as councilman for over fourteen years, he and his father sitting side by side for two terms in the city council from different wards. He also took a prominent part in military affairs, having enlisted in the service of the United States at the age of sixteen. He enlisted in March, 1864, in Gordon's West Virginia battery, light artillery, and served until mustered out, in Wheeling, W. Va., in May, 1865. During this time he took part in the movements up and down the Shenandoah valley, and was slightly wounded in the leg in an engagement near Winchester, Va. Afterwards he joined the "Duquesne Grays," of Pittsburg, in which he was promoted to first lieutenant. The "Grays" were later organized into the 18th regiment, Pennsylvania national guard, and were thrice called upon by the State authorities to quell riots. Retiring from the leather business, the subject of this sketch became, in 1882, bookkeeper for the Third National bank of Pittsburg, and later became cashier for the Transverse street railway company, serving this company until it consolidated with the Citizens' traction company, and afterwards entered the office of the county commissioners of

Allegheny county as chief clerk. When the department of registering of deeds was established, in October, 1901, Mr. Siebert was chosen, on account of his experience, as register of deeds, and superintendent of transferring and plotting property. Mr. Siebert has been secretary of the Ewalt Street bridge company since 1868, a director of that company since 1874, and, in 1893, upon the death of his father, Christian Siebert, succeeded him as treasurer of the concern, still retaining this position. He has also been a director in the German National bank of Pittsburg since 1893, taking the place of his father, who was one of its founders before the Civil war. Mr. Siebert is also actively engaged in church work, having been superintendent of St. Paul's Reformed church, Pittsburg, for over thirty years, and having served his church in the higher councils of the same on many occasions. He was also a manager of an orphans' home for several years. He is now the supreme representative from Pennsylvania in the Royal Society of Good Fellows, and is a member of the Independent Order of Heptasophs, Royal Arcanum, A. O. U. W. and the Odd Fellows. He was married, in 1874, to Sarah O'Brien, of Burlington, Iowa. They have four sons, Wm. C., J. F., Paul T. and George E., and one daughter, Sarah M. In politics Mr. Siebert is a stanch republican.

HUDSON SAMSON (deceased), for many years one of the leading funeral directors of Pittsburg, was born in Pulaski, Oswego Co., N. Y., April 29, 1840. His parents were Jonathan M. and Elizabeth (Draper) Samson, of an old New England Quaker family. There were four children in the family—two daughters, who died when young; Hudson Samson (deceased), and Dexter M. Samson, who is still living in Los Angeles, Cal. The father died in Pittsburg, Jan. 3, 1894, at an advanced age. Mr. Samson was educated in the common schools of Pulaski, and prepared for college at the old Pulaski academy. On account of ill health he did not attend college, but came to Pittsburg in December, 1859, when nineteen years old. On Feb. 14, 1862, Mr. Samson married Miss Susan Gilmore, of Utica, N. Y. They had six children, four of whom died in infancy, while one daughter, Miss Cora L., died Feb. 1, 1898. In 1859 Mr. Samson entered the undertaking business in Pittsburg, and was probably the oldest undertaker in the city, in point of service, at the time of his death. In 1861 he took Robert Fairman as a partner, and the business was successfully conducted under the firm name of Fairman & Samson, until 1875. During the last fifteen years of his life he was ably assisted by his son, Harry G. Samson, who now succeeds his father in the business. In 1884 Mr. Samson erected a beautiful funeral chapel at No. 433 Sixth Ave., which was considered at the time it was built to be the finest and most complete in the United States. He early considered the idea of erecting a crematory, and, in 1885, built a model establishment. It was the second of its kind in the United States, and soon became famous. It first came into prominence in 1891, when the body of Emma Abbott, the famous opera singer, was cremated there. Mr. Samson was perhaps the most conspicuous layman of the Methodist Episcopal church in western Pennsylvania, and was one of the bulwarks of the Pittsburg church union, being its president for many years. He was deeply interested in city evangelization, and was an officer, for a long time, of the National union. It was his custom for a number of years past to build a church each year. This he accomplished through the Church Extension society of the Methodist Episcopal church, and, as a result, many frontier town congregations are happy in their modest and comfortable little buildings, not knowing where the money came from that made them possible. Mr. Samson guarded this pet way of doing good very jealously, and few, even of his most intimate friends, knew that he had followed it for nearly a score of years. Mr. Samson was president of the National city evangelization union of the Methodist Episcopal church. He was also a trustee of the Young Men's Christian association, a member of the advisory board of the Young Women's Christian association, a member of the board of the Methodist Episcopal deaconesses' home, and a member of the board of the Pittsburg free dispensary. He was a member of the board of trustees of Allegheny college, Meadville, Pa., and of Beaver college, Beaver, Pa. He was treasurer of the Anti-saloon league of Allegheny county, and for the past ten years had been one of the most consistent members of the Oakland Methodist Episcopal church. He was a delegate to the general conference of the Methodist Episcopal church, held in Chicago, Ill., in 1900. For several terms he was president of the National and State funeral directors' associations, and was one of the most progressive and widely-known men in his profession. Mr. Samson was a thirty-second degree Mason, and a member of

Franklin lodge, No. 221, also of Tancred commandery, Knights Templars. During Mr. Samson's business career in Pittsburg he had been fortunate in his investments, and thereby had amassed a considerable fortune. After a long and useful career he died, July 14, 1903. Thus, we have briefly incorporated in this sketch of the life of one of Pittsburg's leading citizens, a summary worthy the emulation of all who aspire to the nobler aims of true and beneficent citizenship.

WILLIAM EMERY THOMPSON, controller of Allegheny county, was born in Fredericktown, Washington Co., Pa., Jan. 31, 1850. When six years old he moved with his parents to Elizabeth, Allegheny county, and lived there until 1885. Mr. Thompson received only a limited education, and left school at the age of thirteen, being employed at first in a boat yard, and later in a sawmill. In 1868 he went into his father's wagon shop in Elizabeth, and was engaged with his father for several years in making wagons. Afterwards he ran the business himself for a time, until 1876, when he became a clerk in the office of the county recorder. He has since been prominent in public life, and, after some six years' service in the recorder's office, was elected, in 1882, to the State legislature, where he remained for two two-year terms. While a resident of Elizabeth, he was one of the leading citizens of that place, serving his city as a justice of the peace from 1880 to 1883, and as burgess in 1881 and 1882. After his service as legislator, he was engaged for a time in the office of register of wills. He was made mercantile appraiser of Allegheny county in 1893, was elected controller in 1896, and re-elected in 1899. On Sept. 1, 1885, Mr. Thompson moved to McKeesport, where he was for some years chairman of the republican city committee, and, in 1891, acted as secretary of the McKeesport board of education. Mr. Thompson entered the State militia service in 1868, as a private, and has risen by reason of ability and faithful service through minor positions to the office of colonel of the 14th regiment, Pennsylvania national guards, which position he has held since 1899. He served at Johnstown from June 4 to June 30, 1889, during the terrible times following the flood. He served as senior major of the 14th regiment, Pennsylvania volunteer infantry, during the Spanish-American war. Colonel Thompson is a past master of Stephen Bayard lodge, F. and A. M.; a member of Shiloh chapter, No. 257, and of Ascalon commandery, No. 59, Knights Templars, and is also past exalted ruler of Lodge No. 136, B. P. O. E. He was married, on Oct. 7, 1872, to Miss Mary F. Applegate. Eight children have blessed this union, namely: Harvey A., Malinda Y., Mary F., Lillian B., Jean M., Sarah A., Lila L. and William E., Jr.

SIMON BURNS, president of the Window glass workers, local assembly No. 300, Knights of Labor, and ex-general master workman of the Knights of Labor, was born at La Salle, Ill., in 1856, son of James Burns, a native of Ireland and a riverman by vocation, who died in 1857. The subject of this sketch received a limited education at La Salle, and then began to work in a glass factory there, where he remained two years, later moving to Rock Island, Ill. He followed his trade as a glass worker in Rock Island until 1874, rising to the position of gatherer, and, in 1894, went to Marion, Ind., where he was employed in a window glass factory. He remained there from March to October, then went to Gas City, Ind., staying there until January, 1895. He came to Pittsburg to assume the duties of president of the Window glass workers, local assembly No. 300, to which office he had been previously elected, receiving in the election a majority over some half dozen competitors. He has been re-elected every year since then, on all but two occasions on the first ballot, and has proved himself a capable and efficient official. Since his election as president, Mr. Burns has, in every year except one, secured for the glass workers an advance of ten per cent. in wages. He is an aggressive leader, and possesses that rare brand of courage which has the singular charm of being admired by others besides his friends and associates. In November, 1900, Mr. Burns was elected general master workman of the Knights of Labor. He held this position one year, and then declined a unanimous re-election, which was tendered him at the convention held in Indianapolis, in November, 1901. Mr. Burns is a member of the Modern Woodmen of America. He belongs to the Catholic church.

THEODORE J. SHAFFER, president of the Amalgamated association of iron, steel and tin workers of the United States and Canada, was born in Pittsburg in 1856, raised there, and educated in the public schools. He began selling papers when eight years old, and left school at the age of twelve, but afterwards, when nineteen years old, resumed his studies under the private tutorship of Prof. L. M. Eaton, and later attended the Western university in Pittsburg. When fourteen years old he began work in the iron mill of Moorhead, McLean & Co., of Pittsburg. remaining there a year and a half, and then worked until 1872 at the Penn forge (Everson, Preston & Co.) iron mill on Second avenue. He was employed by the same company for a time in a new mill at Scottdale, Pa., but returned and again worked at the Penn forge. He next spent three years in the employ of Bradley, Rice & Co., returning a second time to the Penn forge. While at this last employment, he studied at odd times under Rev. Dr. W. P. Turner, a Methodist minister, now presiding elder in the Pittsburg conference. After three months' preparation, Mr. Shaffer went before the conference committee and was ordained to preach the gospel. Although he was making fifteen dollars a day at his trade, he cheerfully gave up his position and began his ministerial labors at Confluence, Somerset Co., Pa., at a salary of $500 a year. In this mountainous country he struggled for two years, walking thirty-four miles a day in all kinds of weather and preaching three times. This life was so disastrous to his health that he was compelled to give up the charge, and even now he suffers from the effects of these early hardships. He spent two years each in Washington and Butler counties, holding two charges in each and preaching on alternate Sundays. He was then taken from the circuit, and was given charge of a church at Brownsville, Pa., for two years, and, in 1888, went to Johnstown, Pa., where he remained only six months, being compelled to give up his work on account of ill health. He went to Pittsburg, a dangerously sick man, but, after a short time, his inherent energy asserted itself, so he opened a small grocery and notion store. After about four months of this work, Mr. Shaffer's health was so far improved that he was again able to do a man's work, and, giving up the ministry for good, he returned to the iron mills, and has since devoted himself to the work of bettering the condition of his fellow-workmen. From August, 1889, to October, 1894, he was employed as a rougher and roller in the Demmler mill of the United States sheet steel and tin plate company, and, after an idleness of eleven months, became roller in the tin mill of Oliver Bros. in Pittsburg, working there until April, 1897, part of the time as acting manager. In April, 1897, Mr. Shaffer was placed in his present position by the advisory board of the association, was elected to the position a month later, and has been re-elected every year since then. Mr. Shaffer is a member of the Junior Order of American Mechanics, Royal Arcanum, B. P. O. Elks, and the Amalgamated association of iron, steel and tin workers. In politics he is a republican, and in religious belief a Methodist. In 1902 he was appointed a member of the municipal improvement committee by Recorder Brown. Both of Mr. Shaffer's parents are living in the East End, Pittsburg, his father at the age of ninety and his mother about ten years younger. The father, Mathias F. Shaffer, is a native of Carlsruhe, Germany, and came to America in early manhood, in 1847.

JOHN CALDWELL, alderman from the twenty-fourth ward, Pittsburg, was born in County Donegal, Ireland, in 1842. He came to America with his parents in 1855, locating in Pittsburg, where he attended the parochial schools. Leaving school when fourteen years old, he started to learn the saddlers' trade, and, in August, 1861, enlisted as a private in Company G, 4th Pennsylvania cavalry. Mr. Caldwell's career in the Civil war is a most creditable one. His first term expiring in February, 1864, he re-enlisted, and was mustered out on July 12, 1865, although the papers bear the date, July 1, 1865. He fought with distinction in the great battles of Antietam and Fredericksburg, and later at second Cold Harbor and the Wilderness. In a skirmish with Stuart's cavalry, Feb. 25, 1863, he received a wound in the left ankle, which disabled him until October of that year. On June 24, 1864, he was captured and confined a long time in the rebel prisons. He was first taken to Richmond, to Libby prison, thence to Lynchburg, Va., and from there marched to Danville, Va. From Danville he was sent by train to Andersonville, and held in this famous prison from July to October. After this he was taken to Blackshear, then to Charleston, and from Charleston was moved to Florence, S. C., where he was held in a stockade until Dec. 13, 1864, being then paroled, exchanged and sent to Annapolis. He rejoined his regiment at Lynchburg, Va., in April, 1865. Shortly after enlistment he was made corporal, and came out with the rank of sergeant. The war over, Mr. Caldwell became a street car conductor, and was employed thus for twelve years with the exception of two years, from 1870 to 1872, when he worked in a foundry at West Point. In November, 1880, he entered the employ of the Lake Erie railroad company, remaining with them but a short time, and later went to work for Jones & Laughlin. Mr. Caldwell was elected alderman in February, 1891, and has been twice re-elected. In politics he is a democrat, and in religious belief a Catholic. He is a member of Union Veteran legion, No. 1, of Pittsburg.

JAMES BURNETT HAMILTON, a prominent republican politician of Pittsburg, was born in Elizabeth, Allegheny Co., Pa., March 12, 1849, and has lived in Elizabeth most of his life. He came to Pittsburg when five years old, but afterwards returned to Elizabeth, where he was educated at Elizabeth academy, from which he graduated. He then learned the carpenters' trade, at which he was engaged until 1880, doing most of his work in Elizabeth. In that year he entered the prothonotary's office, in which his ability and faithfulness won him promotion to chief clerk. In the last election he was chosen to the office of prothonotary. Mr. Hamilton became a member of the State militia in 1869, enlisting as a private in Company A, 19th regiment, Pennsylvania national guard, and served until mustered out in 1874, having risen in the meantime to the position of first sergeant of his company. In 1880 he enlisted as a private in Company I of the same regiment, later became captain of Company L, and, in October, 1898, was made major of the regiment. On April 28, 1898, the 14th regiment was ordered to report at Camp Hastings, Pa., for service in the Spanish-American war. Mr. Hamilton went there with his regiment, following it thence to various forts, and finally to Charleston, S. C., where he remained until mustered out, Feb. 28, 1899, and later returned to his place in the prothonotary's office. Mr. Hamilton is a member of the F. and A. M., B. P. O. E., I. O. O. F. and Encampment, K. of P., and Jr. O. U. A. M. He is a member of the Methodist Episcopal church. He has long been prominent in Allegheny county politics, has been a member of the republican county executive committee for the past twenty years, and was for five years prior to 1901 secretary of the committee. He was a member of the Elizabeth board of education for fifteen years, serving for twelve years of that time as its president.

A. H. LESLIE, director of the department of public safety, of Pittsburg, was born in Westmoreland county, Pa., in 1853, and spent his early life there, attending the common schools. His father, Malichie Leslie, dying in 1868, the son came to Pittsburg, went to school for about two months and then started to learn the carpenters' trade. He served a three-year apprenticeship at this vocation, and finding it too severe for his health, entered the employ of the Allegheny Valley railroad company, where he worked first as a brakeman, then as flagman, and finally as freight conductor. In 1872 Mr. Leslie gave up railroading and went into the fire insurance business, also taking up real estate after a time. In 1880 he was elected alderman from the seventeenth ward for a five-year term, and in this position his ability and attention to duty won him re-election three times. When there were still four years to serve on his last term, Mr. Leslie resigned, Aug. 1, 1896, to accept the office of superintendent of police, serving in this position until Oct. 1, 1901, and was then thrown out of office by the provisions of the Ripper bill. He was appointed to his present office on Nov. 26, 1901, by Recorder J. O. Brown, and has proved a faithful and capable official. Mr. Leslie belongs to the Masonic fraternity, Knights Templars and Mystic Shrine, the I. O. O. F., Jr. O. U. A. M. and Knights of the Mystic Chain. He was for two years, 1886-1888, grand chief templar of Pennsylvania. He is a member of the Methodist Episcopal church, of which he is a trustee.

JOHN H. HENDERSON, a prominent lawyer of Allegheny county, was born in Meadville, Pa., Sept. 9, 1866. He was educated at Carrier institute, Clarion, Pa., and at Allegheny college, Meadville. He read law with his father, Harvey Henderson, and was admitted to the bar of Allegheny county in March, 1889, since which time he has been engaged, with his father, in the practice of his profession. For several years he has taken an active part in the work of the republican party. He was a delegate to the State convention of 1896, and the following year was elected to the Allegheny city council. In 1898 he was elected a member of the State house of representatives, and again in the year 1900. The ancestor of the Henderson family who first settled in America was Robert, a Scotch-Irishman, who emigrated from County Cavan, Ireland, in 1795; landed at Philadelphia, and came westward to Pittsburg, where he remained until 1799. He removed with his family, who were then adults, to Worth township, Mercer county, where he settled and where many of his descendants still reside. Robert Henderson's son, John, who served in the War of 1812, was married to Mary Carroll, and to them was born a son, in 1801, whom they named William Carroll. This son afterwards became a minister in the Methodist Episcopal church, and was a constituent member of the Pittsburg conference of that church, formed in 1825. He was an active member of this conference until 1853, when, to enable him more readily to educate his children, he was transferred to the Erie conference, of which he was a member at his death, in 1882. William C. Henderson was married to Eliza Fawcett, born in South Fayette township, Allegheny county, in 1813, daughter of Joseph, who was born in the same neighborhood in 1748, and whose father, John Fawcett, emigrated from near Belfast, Ireland, in 1769; was married to Ann Fawcett, at Winchester, Va., and removed to Cecil township, Washington Co., Pa., in 1772, where he died, in 1810. William C. Henderson and his wife, Eliza, had five children, one of whom, Anna, died in early life. Harvey, the father of the subject of this sketch, was born in Ross township, Allegheny county; educated at Allegheny college, Meadville; read law; was admitted to the bar, and practiced his profession in Meadville ten years. During this time he served a term as district attorney, and held other public offices. He has resided in Allegheny county, and practiced law there, during the last twenty-one years. He was married to Harriet J. Hogeboom, of Rochester, N. Y., who descended from one of the families who emigrated from Holland and settled in Columbia county, N. Y., soon after the discovery of the Hudson river. This family has produced a number of men of note in the history of the State of New York. Jeremiah Hogeboom was colonel of the first regiment raised in Columbia county for service in the Revolution, John T. was a judge in the county just named, and Henry served with distinction on the bench of the court of appeals of his State. Harvey Henderson's three brothers reside in Meadville. Edward H. (retired) and John J. served through the Civil war. John J. is now one of the judges of the superior court of this State. William W. is a lawyer. Harvey Henderson's other surviving children are: Gertrude H., wife of Archibald G. Hamilton, and Miss Grace Henderson, all of Allegheny city.

THOMAS DORRINGTON CARNAHAN, city solicitor of Pittsburg, was born on the South Side, Pittsburg, and there was reared and received his early education. Subsequently he attended the Western university at Pittsburg, graduating in 1872. After graduation, he became a reporter on the Pittsburg Evening Chronicle, and was connected with this paper from the fall of 1872 to the spring of 1881. Mr. Carnahan was admitted to the bar in 1876, and was associated with his father, Robert B. Carnahan, in the practice of law until the death of the latter, which occurred in 1890. He devoted his attention at first to office work, but has since 1881 been actively engaged in the practice of law in the civil courts, where he has met with marked success. Mr. Carnahan was appointed assistant city solicitor in 1888, and served in this capacity until January, 1902, when he was appointed city solicitor by Recorder J. O Brown. Mr. Carnahan is a member of the Royal Arcanum. He belongs to the Third Presbyterian church. He is a trustee of the Western University of Pennsylvania, of which he is an honored alumnus.

CHARLES DAVIS, county engineer for Allegheny county, Pa., was born at Bridgetown, Bucks Co., Pa., in 1837, and spent the first nineteen years of his life in that part of Pennsylvania. After the usual preparation, he entered Jefferson college, but gave up his books in his junior year to enlist in the Union army as a private in Company D, 10th regiment, Pennsylvania reserve volunteer corps. He served three years, until June, 1864, being promoted to second lieutenant in 1862, and in command of his company the latter part of the last year of his term of service. He was captured at the battle of Spottsylvania Court House, but was recaptured a few days later by Sheridan's cavalry at Beaver Dam Station. During the war he took part in the following engagements: the seven days' battles on the peninsula, also South Mountain, Antietam, Fredericksburg, Gettysburg, Bristoe Station, the Wilderness, Spottsylvania and Bethesda church. His war service completed, Mr. Davis took up engineering for a livelihood, and has been successful in his chosen vocation. He was first engaged as transitman on railroad surveys in Lawrence county, Pa., and then, for two years, was employed as assistant engineer by the Pennsylvania railroad company, under Antes Snyder, on the Western Pennsylvania railroad. From 1867 to 1876, inclusive, he was city engineer of Allegheny city. During his term of office as city engineer he designed the sewerage system and superintended the construction of the parks of Allegheny. On his recommendation, the city council secured the passage of an act of the legislature authorizing the present lot registry system. This system has since been extended to Pittsburg. While city engineer he was made consulting engineer on the construction of the Point bridge at the mouth of the Monongahela river. After this he was engaged in the preliminary surveys and construction of the Pittsburg & Lake Erie railroad, and while there he made the preliminary survey for its extension to Connellsville, then known as the Pittsburg & Youghiogheny river railroad; then for a year a resident engineer on the construction of buildings of the Pittsburg Bessemer steel company, which is now a part of the Homestead steel works. Following this, he was made engineer for the Monongahela bridge company, which was then reconstructing its suspension bridge at the end of Smithfield street. Before the work had progressed very far, the ownership changed, and plans were adopted under which the present Smithfield street bridge was constructed by Mr. Lindenthal. Mr. Davis was retained as an assistant engineer on this work for some time. In 1881 he was made county engineer of Allegheny county, and has held this responsible position ever since. During his long career Mr. Davis has gained many honors. He has been breveted first lieutenant and captain of the United States volunteers, was made commissioner to the Vienna exposition in 1873, under appointment by President Grant, and, in 1887, was given the degree of A. M. by Washington and Jefferson college. He is a member of the American society of civil engineers and the Engineers' society of western Pennsylvania, and the Pittsburg academy of science and art. He is also prominent among the veterans of the Civil war, is a member of the Loyal Legion; Post No. 1, Union Veteran legion, and Post No. 88, G. A. R. He is a Knight Templar in Masonry, a republican in politics, and a Presbyterian in religion, being a member of the North Presbyterian church of Allegheny city.

J. GUY McCANDLESS, director of the department of public works, Pittsburg, and one of the oldest and most prominent physicians of the city of Pittsburg, was born in Ferryville, Allegheny county, Jan. 1, 1839. He is descended on both his father's and mother's side from early settlers of Allegheny county. His great-grandfather, William McCandless, came to America in a very early day, and died in Washington county, Pa. William's son, Archibald, born in Allegheny county in 1756, was for half a century elder in the Presbyterian church. Alexander G. McCandless, father of the subject of this sketch, was born in Allegheny county, Jan. 15, 1816, being one of the thirteen children of Archibald McCandless. He was for many years a practicing physician in Pittsburg, and died Feb. 24, 1875. His wife, Margaret A. (Guy) McCandless, whom he married on Feb. 15, 1838, was descended from settlers who came to Allegheny county in the old days when the Indians infested the district. Dr. J. Guy McCandless received a common-school education in Pittsburg, attended the Cleveland medical college a year and was graduated from the Jefferson medical college in 1863. He also taught school for a time. Dr. McCandless served three years in the Civil war, enlisting as assistant surgeon of the 52d Pennsylvania volunteer infantry. He was afterwards made surgeon in charge of the Cotton Factory hospital at Harrisburg, and lived there until the close of the war, ranking as major. During his service he was under fire in the Peninsular campaign, at Fair Oaks, the Wilderness and Yorktown. Returning after the war to Pittsburg, he has since successfully engaged in the practice of medicine there. He has also a long and creditable career in the public service, and has taken great interest in republican politics. Dr. McCandless has served on the school board as member and also as president of the Franklin board, and has represented his ward in both the common and select councils of Pittsburg, acting as president of each. He is a member of the Masonic fraternity and the G. A. R., and was formerly, for fourteen years, surgeon of the 14th regiment, Pennsylvania national guard. He is a prominent member of the Sixth Presbyterian church, of which he has been an elder since 1875. Dr. McCandless has been twice married. By his first marriage, to Emma Jones, he has one son, Guy, now engaged in the men's furnishing business. In 1876 he married Margaret E. Cluley, daughter of John F. Cluley, and has by this union three children, Walter C., Ida May and Alexander Wilson.

ANTON LUTZ, of the firm of D. Lutz & Son brewing company, brewers, of Allegheny city, was born in Pittsburg, Pa., in 1853. He was reared in Allegheny city and attended school there, afterwards pursuing his studies in the classical school in Pittsburg, taught by Professor Hoontz. When seventeen years old, he left school and entered his father's brewery in Allegheny city, and has been, since 1879, a member of the firm. The D. Lutz & Son brewery is an old and well-established concern and is doing a flourishing business. Mr. Lutz was a school director from 1881 to 1891. He was for many years interested in the Third National bank, and is now director of the Allegheny trust company. He is a member of the B. P. O. E. In religious belief Mr. Lutz is a Catholic.

WILLIAM I. MUSTIN, a prominent Pittsburg business man and former president of the Pittsburg stock exchange, comes from a long line of distinguished ancestors. On his father's side he is descended from French Huguenots, who were forced by religious persecution to emigrate to England, where the family name was changed from Moustain to the present form of spelling. The great-grandfather of the subject of this sketch and the first of the family to emigrate to America, became a merchant in Philadelphia, and his son, Anthony Mustin, was the first to establish in Philadelphia what is known as a "trimming store." James G. Mustin, son of Anthony and father of William I., was a native of Philadelphia, and for some years engaged there in the trimming business. He came to Pittsburg in 1840, became connected with the Logan-Gragg hardware company, and continued in the hardware business until his death, which occurred in March, 1864. His wife, Frances (Irwin) Mustin, died in Pittsburg, Feb. 24, 1897. She was a granddaughter of John Irwin, who was born in Ireland, and came to America in 1772, residing for a number of years in Carlisle, Pa., and then, in 1790, came to the village of Pittsburg. Here he opened the first dry-goods store, located at the corner of Fourth and Market streets, and continued in that business up to the time of his death, which occurred in April, 1830. A son of John Irwin, William Wallace, grandfather of William I. Mustin, was for many years prominent in Pittsburg politics, at first as a whig and later as a democrat. He was a member of congress, mayor of Pittsburg in 1839, and, by appointment of President Tyler, served as United States minister to Denmark. He died in Pittsburg, in September, 1856. William I. Mustin, the subject of this article, was one of five children, of whom two besides himself are living: Caroline Denny, wife of George W. Nicholson, of Pittsburg, and Edwin T., a commercial traveler. Mr. Mustin was born in Pittsburg, June 8, 1860, and was educated at home, under the direction of his mother. He began to learn the printers' trade at an early age, and, on Oct. 9, 1871, entered the employ of George B. Hill. In 1881 he was admitted to partnership, which relationship continued until Mr. Hill died, in 1900. In political belief he is an ardent republican, and has long been a prominent factor in Pittsburg politics. He was, from 1898 to 1902, a member of the select council of Pittsburg; councilmanic trustee of the Carnegie library and Carnegie institute from April, 1900, to April, 1902; president of the Americus club from 1894 to 1898; has been vice-president of the Mozart club since 1890; served five years as president of the stock exchange, and it is largely by his efforts that the exchange owns and occupies its present building. He is past eminent commander of Tancred commandery, No. 48, Knights Templars, and a member of the Mystic Shrine, and belongs to the following clubs: Monongahela, Duquesne, Americus, Masonic country, Browning and Fishing, all of Pittsburg. He is a member of the Art society, and is a patron of the Pittsburg orchestra. He also belongs to the Manufacturers' club, of Philadelphia, and the New York athletic club, of New York. On April 12, 1883, Mr. Mustin married Miss Sarah Isabel Dorrington, daughter of John and Sarah Dorrington, and has three children, Burton Hill, Eleanor Dorrington and Agnes Mahon.

DAVID J. McGAREY, police magistrate and alderman from the twenty-sixth ward, Pittsburg, is a well-known and prominent politician. He was born in Pittsburg, Aug. 16, 1859, reared there and educated in the public schools. In 1872 he left school and went to work in the tack factory of Chess, Cook & Co., and remained for seventeen years in the employ of this firm. He has been for many years prominent in public life, as alderman and police magistrate. Judge McGarey was elected alderman from the twenty-sixth ward in 1889, and has been three times re-elected. His career as a police magistrate began in 1896. He was appointed to this position by Mayor H. P. Ford and Mayor W. J. Diehl, reappointed by Recorder A. M. Brown, and, after the latter's removal, by Recorder J. O. Brown. Judge McGarey is a member of the I. O. O. F., Jr. Order of United American Mechanics, Birmingham Turnverein, Odd Fellows, Leider Tafel and the Lotus club. Judge McGarey is now engaged in the mantel and tile business at No. 1211 Carson St., as the president of the Central mantel and tile company. He is also secretary of the Central brick company, of Pittsburg, Pa.

THOMAS FORDING, superintendent of the bureau of water assessment, of Pittsburg, was born in what is now Pittsburg, and has spent most of his life within the present city limits. He was born in 1841, and taken, in infancy, by his parents to what was then called Elliott's Delight, later Temperanceville, and now thirty-sixth ward, Pittsburg. Here Mr. Fording was reared and given a limited education. His father was killed by a boiler explosion, so the boy left school at ten years of age, and was employed first for a year in an ax factory, and then in a nail factory. In August, 1862, he enlisted to fight for his country in the Civil war, as a private in Battery E, Mississippi marine brigade, light artillery, where he served with distinction throughout the war. After the engagement at Vicksburg, he was promoted for bravery in battle to the position of first duty sergeant, in accordance with the following order issued by Capt. D. P. Walling, commanding the battery:

VICKSBURG, MISS.,
Headquarters Light Battery, M. M. B.,
Copy   July 22, 1863.
Battery Order, No. 5.

Promotion—Corporal Thomas Fording to be sergeant for gallantry in action on De Soto Point, opposite Vicksburg, June 21st and 22nd, 1863, vice James A. Nevin, dead.—To rank from July 1st, 1863.   D. P. WALLING,
Capt. Com'g Battery, M. M. B.

Mr. Fording served in this capacity until February, 1865, when he was mustered out at Vicksburg. During the war, he fought in the Red river campaign, on the Black river, at Vicksburg and in many minor engagements. The war over, he returned to Pittsburg and resumed his work in the nail factory. In 1867 he went to Wheeling, W. Va., where he worked about two years. Returning to Pittsburg, he worked in the nail factory again until 1873, when he was appointed inspector of the board of health. He served in this capacity until 1878, and then the council elected him street commissioner. This position Mr. Fording filled most creditably for fifteen years, the title being changed, in 1888, to assistant superintendent of streets. In 1893 he was appointed to his present office, where he has made an enviable record as an able and faithful public servant. Mr. Fording is a member of Garfield post, No. 215, G. A. R., of which he was commander for five consecutive years, 1895 to 1900. He is at present treasurer of the G. A. R. association of Allegheny county. He is a member of the Knights Templars and Mystic Shrine and the Jr. O. U. A. M., and has been for the past twenty-one years treasurer of St. Clair lodge, No. 362, I. O. O. F. Mr. Fording is a member of the Methodist Episcopal church.

G. WASH MOORE, superintendent of the bureau of city property, Pittsburg, was born in Pittsburg in 1847, and there reared and educated in the common schools. When twelve years old, he left school and spent two years working in a machine shop, and then learned the carpenters' trade. In 1868 he began a long and eventful career in the public service, as hose-man in the volunteer fire department of Lawrenceville. This suburb was made a part of Pittsburg the same year, and, in 1870, Mr. Moore became hose-man in the Pittsburg fire department. After about five years' service in this capacity he was promoted to the position of captain, and acted as such for about twelve years. In 1885 he was elected member of the State legislature from the fourth, now the fifth, district and, in 1887, was re-elected. Between his terms in the legislature he was elected assistant chief engineer of the Pittsburg fire department and served about a year. After his second term in the legislature, Mr. Moore filled the position of sanitary officer in the bureau of health, and, in 1893, was appointed wharfmaster, but resigned thirty days later to accept the position of superintendent of the bureau of city property. In 1901 he was thrown out of office by the Ripper bill, but was reinstated five months later by Recorder J. O. Brown. Mr. Moore has been connected with the city service for thirty-three years, excepting the two years in the State legislature, and has an enviable record for faithful and efficient service. At present he is superintendent of the bureau of health, his appointment dating April 1, 1903. He is a member of the Knights of Honor, and in religious belief is a Methodist.

CHARLES A. MUEHLBRONNER, the leading produce merchant of Pittsburg, was born in Philadelphia, Pa., May 10, 1857. His parents moved, when Mr. Muehlbronner was a baby, to La Grange, Ohio, thence to Richmond, Ky, and afterwards, in 1865, came to Pittsburg, where their son attended the public schools until his fifteenth year. At this time he started to learn painting, and was thus engaged for about eighteen months, afterwards spending four years as a clerk in a grocery in Allegheny city. He went to San Francisco, remaining there as a painter for about a year and a half, and then returned to Allegheny city, where he sold grocers' supplies for two and a half years. He then started a poultry business in Pittsburg, later adding vegetables to his stock, and from this humble beginning he has built up the Iron City produce company, now the largest house of its kind in Pittsburg, occupying a large four-story building at No. 623 Liberty Ave., and handling about $600,000 worth of produce annually. This immense business is carried on entirely by correspondence, no traveling salesmen being employed, yet the better class of trade send in orders by mail, knowing that they will receive prompt and careful attention. Over 21,000 carloads of produce were handled by the firm in 1902, besides a large amount that was received and shipped by boat, the river trade being an important factor in the growing business of the company. In all his dealings Mr. Muehlbronner has been fair and honorable, and he has an enviable reputation for unimpeachable integrity in his business life. Besides his vast produce interests, he is a director in the Western savings and deposit bank, a director in the German National bank of Pittsburg and the Central savings and trust company and a stockholder in the German-American savings and trust company. His political career has been such as reflects great credit upon himself. For three years he was tax collector for the seventh ward of Allegheny city, and while serving in this capacity, he was elected to the school board and afterwards to the common council, so that at the same time he held three public offices, discharging the duties of each with great care and fidelity. His ability and attention to the public welfare won him a re-election to the common council, and then a place in the select council. While serving in the latter body, he was elected to the State legislature, in 1890, and he therefore resigned his seat in the council after serving two years. He served four terms of two years each in the legislature, and, in 1898, was elected to the State senate for a four-year term. In all this long political service he has ever had the welfare of his constituents at heart, and his political opponents have never been able to attack his standing or character. Mr. Muehlbronner is prominent in the social life of Pittsburg, being a member of the Teutonia and the Turners, as well as other social organizations. He is a thirty-second degree Mason, and a noble of the Mystic Shrine. He is also a member of the Independent Order of Odd Fellows, the Knights of Pythias, the B. P. O. Elks, and several other fraternal orders, and is a contributing member to the German Lutheran church.

THOMAS PERRY, superintendent of the bureau of public lighting, Pittsburg, has for years been prominent in republican politics, and has held many positions of responsibility in the public service. He was born in Pittsburg, in 1858, and there reared and educated, attending the public schools and later the Western university, where he studied for four years. He left the university in June, 1877, and, in 1879, entered the office of the county sheriff as clerk, under Sheriff Thomas H. Hunter, remaining there three years. After this he was clerk in the county treasurer's office for two years, and for two and a half years clerk in the postoffice. In 1885 Mr. Perry went into the grocery business, was engaged in this business for three years, and again returning to the postoffice, served as clerk for two and a half years longer. In 1893 he resigned this position to accept the office of wharfmaster, being employed in this capacity for seven years. In July, 1900, he was appointed to his present position, and was deposed, June 1, 1901, by Recorder E. M. Bigelow. He was then employed for six months in the office of the county commissioner as inspector of county roads, and, on Dec. 1, 1901, was reappointed to his old position as superintendent of the department of public lighting by Dr. J. Guy McCandless, director of the department of public works. In religious belief Mr. Perry is a Methodist.

WILLIAM R. ROWE, general manager of the Pittsburg Gazette and Chronicle-Telegraph, Pittsburg, was born at Confluence, Pa., in 1872, and, in 1874, came to Pittsburg, where he was reared, and educated in the common schools. Beginning at the age of fourteen, he worked until he reached the age of eighteen in the drug business, and then became assistant bookkeeper in the office of the Pittsburg Press. He remained with the Press ten years, rising to the position of advertising manager, and, in 1900, was made business manager of the Gazette, and, early in 1901, became business manager of the Chronicle-Telegraph, when that paper was acquired by Mr. George T. Oliver. In September, 1902, he was made general manager of both these papers. Mr. Rowe is a rising young business man, who has in the few years of his service exhibited great ability in his line of work. He is a member of the Masonic fraternity, and in religious belief is a Presbyterian.

JAMES McCLURG GUFFEY, the Pittsburg oil and gas king, and the largest individual producer of oil and natural gas in this country, was born in Westmoreland county, Pa., in 1839. He is of Scotch descent, and his ancestors were among the early settlers of western Pennsylvania, where they located in colonial times, probably about 1750. James M. Guffey attended the public schools, and later the Iron City college, from which he graduated, and at the age of eighteen obtained a clerkship in the office of the superintendent of the Louisville & Nashville railroad company, at Louisville, Ky. He was employed by this company several years, for a time at Nashville, Tenn., by the Adams southern express company, and, in 1870, returned to Pennsylvania to engage in the petroleum business as a producer. Mr. Guffey acquired large interests at St. Petersburg, in Clarion county, and subsequently made Bradford the base of his operations. He also opened the Grapeville gas field and controlled it until it was taken by a corporation. This was the greatest of all the gas fields and brought vast wealth to the enterprising operator, who also acquired large interests in the Murraysville field. Mr. Guffey is a man of sound judgment and wonderful executive ability. In politics he is an ardent democrat, firm in his loyalty to the principles of his party and always ready to make personal sacrifices for the party's benefit. Mr. Guffey came to Pittsburg about fifteen years ago. He is married and lives in the East End.

MORRIS W. MEAD, superintendent of the bureau of electricity, Pittsburg, was born at Underhill, Vt. (now New Burlington), Oct. 28, 1854. He is a son of the late Daniel C. and Naomie E. (Terrel) Mead, and a grandson of Josiah Mead, a farmer of Underhill and a member of one of the old Vermont families. Daniel C. Mead, born in Underhill in 1828, was a prominent man in his day, and was an early oil prospector and promoter of manufacturing enterprises. He died in 1874, and his wife in 1875. Morris W. Mead, whose name heads this article, received his education in the public schools of the fourteenth ward, Pittsburg, and at the Pittsburg high school, graduating from the high school in 1873. He also attended the University of Underhill. He read law two years with J. H. Baldwin, then, after his father's death, spent two years in the oil business, and returning to Pittsburg in 1877, became head salesman in the establishment of J. R. & A. Murdoch. Shortly after this Mr. Mead entered the city fire alarm office as operator, was made chief operator a year later, and two years after that was appointed superintendent of the Fire Alarm telegraph While holding this last position he was also made secretary of the fire commission, and for two years held both offices. It was Mr. Mead who introduced the police telephone system of the department of public safety. When the new city charter went into effect in 1887, Mr. Mead became head of the newly established bureau of electricity, a bureau which has charge of all the electrical interests of Pittsburg, including the control of electric railroads, safety arrangements for electrical propulsion, inspections of all electric power and light wires, and so forth. In performing the duties of his office, Mr. Mead has shown such rare judgment and unusual ability that he has won the confidence of the public. Under his supervision there has been installed in Pittsburg as fine a system of police and fire alarm and electrical inspection as can be found in the United States. He is also the inventor of a scheme for protecting underground wires by means of a rubber covering. Mr. Mead married Johanna E. Ecker, sister of H. P. Ecker, city organist of Allegheny, and lives with his wife in Oakland, East End. They are members of the Bellefield Presbyterian church. Mr. Mead is an enthusiastic member of the Masonic fraternity, in which he has attained the thirty-second degree, and is a Shriner, a member of the I. O. O. F., Knights of Pythias, B. P. O. Elks, Jr. O. U. A. M. and a past master of the A. O. U. W. He was, in 1900, chairman of the board of directors of the International association of municipal electricians, was president of the association in 1901 and is still a member of the board of directors of the organization. He is also an honorary member of the National electric light association, and of the electrical committee of the International association of chief engineers of fire departments. In 1893 he was one of the three assistants to the manager of the electrical department of the World's Fair at Chicago.

JENKIN JONES, a citizen of Pittsburg for sixty-four years, was born in Cardiganshire, South Wales, in 1835. His parents brought him to America when he was four years old, and located at Pittsburg, where Mr. Jones received a limited education. He went to work at the age of twelve in a glass factory, and, in 1863, started in the business for himself, under the name of Campbell, Jones & Co. This combination continued until 1886, when Mr. Jones organized another company for the manufacture of glass, the new concern being known as Jones, Cauff & Co. (limited). This firm was discontinued in 1892, and Mr. Jones has since devoted his time to the public service. He has held many positions of responsibility and trust during his long and eventful career. He was from 1868 to 1870 councilman for the borough of East Birmingham, Allegheny county, and was then elected to the office of burgess of that borough, but a change of residence necessitated his resigning this position before his term expired. His next office was that of school director from the twenty-seventh ward, Pittsburg, where he served three years. He was also elected a member of the central board of education, where he served for a similar period. In 1873 he was elected for one three-year term as a member of the board of fire commissioners of Pittsburg. He has held his present position as wharfmaster since December, 1901. Mr. Jones has long been a prominent republican, and has taken an important part in party affairs. He was a delegate to the State convention held at Harrisburg in 1878, and also to the State convention in 1881 which nominated Silas M. Bailey for State treasurer. In 1881 he was chairman of the finance committee of the republican county central committee of Allegheny county. In religious belief Mr. Jones is a Congregationalist and a member of that church. He is a member of the I. O. O. F. and Royal Arcanum.

ROBERT OSTERMAIER, delinquent tax collector for the city of Pittsburg, was born in Pittsburg, Jan. 2, 1857, and is a son of John and Katherine Ostermaier, both of whom were natives of Germany. Robert Ostermaier attended the public schools when a lad, graduating later from the Iron City commercial college, and at the age of sixteen became a clerk in the Pittsburg postoffice. Here he filled every position except postmaster, and was assistant postmaster during President Cleveland's first term, fulfilling the duties of that responsible post most admirably. Upon retiring from the postoffice, he became clerk in the office of Mayor McCollin, later filling a similar position for three years under Mayor H. I. Gourley. He then became assistant superintendent of highways and sewers, resigned this position three months later, and was elected secretary of the republican city committee, an office which he has held since that time and one which he has filled with conspicuous success. In 1896 he became police magistrate under Mayor H. P. Ford, and held this position from April, 1896, to May 1, 1897. Then, on May 17, 1897, he undertook the duties of collecting the delinquent city taxes. This position he has since held, with the exception of two months, from October to December, 1901, when he was temporarily thrown out of office by the provisions of the Ripper bill. He is a member of the Junior Order of United American Mechanics, the Heptasophs, Royal Arcanum and Knights of the Mystic Chain, and also belongs to the Young Men's tariff club and the John Dalzell republican club of the seventeenth ward. Mr. Ostermaier is a director of the Metropolitan National bank of Pittsburg. He is a member of the Methodist Episcopal church.

TIMOTHY O'LEARY, special agent of the Pittsburg brewing company, was born in County Cork, Ireland, Dec. 28, 1848. His parents came to America in 1849, locating in Pittsburg, and there Mr. O'Leary was reared and received his education in the public schools. Leaving school when fifteen years old, he went to work as messenger for the Pennsylvania railroad, and was made clerk after being messenger only two months. In July, 1864, he was transferred to the Allegheny Valley railroad as transfer clerk, and acted in this capacity until 1869, when he became clerk in the office of the treasurer of the Valley railroad. Two years later he was employed in the auditor's office, and, in 1874, entered the employ of the Baltimore & Ohio railroad as voucher clerk. After a year in this position, he resigned and went to Harrisburg, Pa., where he was for four years employed as clerk in the department of internal affairs. Returning to Pittsburg, he worked in the city assessor's office for a short time, and later engaged in the manufacture of window glass, under the firm name of O'Leary Bros., continuing in this business until 1893. Since 1893 he has been employed in his present position, that of special agent for the Pittsburg brewing company. From 1886 to 1889 Mr. O'Leary held the position of city viewer of Pittsburg, appointed by the court. Mr. O'Leary has had a varied and eventful career, and has won his present standing in the community by merit alone. In politics he is a democrat, and has attended every national democratic convention since 1872. He was a delegate to the national democratic convention in St. Louis, in 1888, and has always taken an active interest in party politics. Mr. O'Leary belongs to no secret order. He is a member of the Roman Catholic church.

DAVID KENNEDY McGUNNEGLE, chief clerk in the office of the clerk of courts of Allegheny county, was born in Robinson township, Allegheny Co., Pa., on a farm, July 3, 1849. His parents moved later to Chartiers township, where Mr. McGunnegle was reared, and received his early education in the public schools. Later he attended the Western university, of Pittsburg. In 1869 he entered the office of the clerk of courts, and remained there until elected clerk of courts, in 1885. This position he held for three terms, nine years in all, receiving each time the largest majority on the ticket. His term of office expired in 1894, and he was then appointed chief clerk, and has held this position continuously since that time. Since 1899 he has also been burgess of Estlin borough. Mr. McGunnegle belongs to no secret orders. He is a member of the Episcopal church.

PAUL ST. PETER, secretary of the Window glass workers, local assembly No. 300, Knights of Labor, was born in Montreal, Canada, in May, 1858. He is a son of Albert W. St. Peter, who was born at Three Rivers, Canada, and a grandson of Paul St. Peter, a native of France. The subject of this sketch came to the United States with his parents, in infancy, the family locating at Blossburg, Pa., and was reared and educated in that city. He began his apprenticeship as a glass worker in Blossburg, and, in 1877, removed to Jeannette, Pa., where he worked at his trade in a glass factory until 1896. Mr. St. Peter was then elected secretary of the Window glass workers, and has been re-elected to the position every year since. He has proved a careful and competent official, and has earned the popularity which he has attained. Mr. St. Peter was married, in 1882, at Blossburg, Pa., to Miss Nellie E. Kelly, and has five children, Helen C., Mary A., Gertrude U., Pauline and Alice M. He is a member of the Knights of Maccabees, and belongs to the Catholic church.

JAMES A. ELPHINSTONE, merchandise broker, of Pittsburg, was born in Baltimore, Md., Feb 1, 1849, and lived in Baltimore until 1863, attending the public schools. Coming then to Pittsburg, he continued his studies until he reached the age of eighteen, when he left school and engaged in the wholesale cracker and confectionery business for a period of about five years. He then entered the employ of Reymer & Bros., wholesale and retail confectioners, and remained with this firm until 1886, when he began his present business as a merchandise broker, at which he has been most successful. Mr. Elphinstone has attained the thirty-second degree in Masonry, and is a Mystic Shriner and Knight Templar. He is a member of the I. O. O. F., Knights of Honor and Royal Arcanum, and belongs to the Americus club. In religious belief he is a Presbyterian.

WILLIAM L. WALTON, merchandise broker, of Pittsburg, was born in Pittsburg in 1864, and there reared and educated in the public schools. When seventeen years old, he left school and went to work for his uncle, James McClurg, a crockery manufacturer, remaining in his employ eight years. At the end of that time he started in at his present business, and has devoted his attention to it continuously ever since. He is also engaged in the real estate and insurance business with offices in the Smith building, Pittsburg, under the firm name of Braun, Walton & Euwer. In his professional life he has been as honorable in his dealings as he has been successful. Says a friend, in speaking of Mr. Walton: "He is a successful business man and a manly fellow, whose character is above reproach." Mr. Walton is an enthusiastic member of the Masonic fraternity, in which he has attained the thirty-second degree, and is a Shriner, a member of the I. O. O. F., American Mechanics, Heptasophs and Royal Arcanum. In religious belief he is a Presbyterian.

ADOLPH EDLIS, dealer in barbers' supplies, Pittsburg, was born in Hungary, in 1859, and educated in his native country. He came to America in 1880, remained in New York until 1888, and then moved to Pittsburg, where he has since resided. In Pittsburg Mr. Edlis has been engaged as a dealer in barbers' supplies, and has built up a lucrative business in this line. In politics he is a republican, and was elected, in 1897, a member of the common council from the seventh ward to fill an unexpired term caused by the election of Harvey Lowry to the position of sheriff. Mr. Edlis has been chairman of the seventh ward republican executive committee for three years. Mr. Edlis is a prominent member of the I. O. O. F. and K. of P. He also belongs to three benevolent societies—the Home of Shelter, the Benevolent society and the Hospital society. He is a member of the Orthodox Hebrew church.

FREDERICK W. EDWARDS, register of wills and ex-officio clerk of the Orphans' court of Allegheny county, is a native of South Wales, Great Britain, where he was born Oct. 2, 1861. He received a good common-school education in his youth, and then was employed for some time as engineer at the Edgar Thompson steel works, but for many years he has held various official positions in Allegheny county. He has successively been tax collector, justice of the peace, clerk in the treasurer's office, deputy register, and register of Allegheny county. During his whole official career, he has conducted his office in a capable and efficient manner. While many of the duties of his office require a legal training, and although not a lawyer, still he has fulfilled these duties with entire satisfaction, and his record as an obliging and painstaking officer is one to be proud of. In 1883 he was married to Alice L. Lightner, daughter of Daniel Lightner, and they have the following children: Mary Winona and Vurse Dalzell Edwards.

Mr. Edwards is a stanch republican, and in a campaign he may always be counted on to do his full share of hustling. He has been a resident of Allegheny county for the last twenty-five years, and, at the present time, resides in North Braddock, where he is held in high esteem by all who know him.

J. A. A. BROWN, superintendent of the bureau of building inspection, of Pittsburg, is a native of Pittsburg. He was born in 1847, and attended school when a boy, but left school at the age of thirteen. His first position was in the shipyard, on the Monongahela river, near Pittsburg, where he worked one day, heating rivets to be used in the construction of the gunboat "Sandusky," and then got a place as messenger boy in a dry-goods store in Pittsburg. Here he was soon promoted to the position of clerk, later entered the employ of William B. Hays & Co., wholesale pork dealers, remaining in this position about two years. Captain Brown then learned the carpenters' trade and followed this vocation successfully for about fifteen years. In 1870 he went into the grocery and feed business, and was engaged thus until 1888, when he was appointed chief clerk in the office of the building inspector. The following year he was appointed assistant building inspector, and, in March, 1896, when the bureau of building inspection was formed, under the new law, he was made superintendent of the bureau, and still holds that position. Captain Brown's long experience in the practical side of building construction has made him a valuable man in his present position, and his career has been a most creditable one. In 1869 Captain Brown enlisted as a private in the Washington infantry, State militia, and served for almost twenty years, resigning Nov. 15, 1888. He was given the rank of captain five years before. Although he has not been actively connected with the militia since 1888, yet he takes an active interest in military affairs, and has been for almost fifteen years drill-master of the Pittsburg police force Captain Brown is a member of the A. O. U. W. and the Heptasophs. He is also a member of the Sixth Presbyterian church.

J. CARSON MERCER, county commissioner of Allegheny county, was born in Pittsburg, Pa., in 1848. He was reared in Pittsburg and received a common-school education, leaving at the age of fifteen. He went to work in an iron and steel mill, continuing at this employment until 1879, when he was appointed superintendent of the Allegheny county courthouse. Since that time he has devoted himself to the public service. He held his position of superintendent of the courthouse until 1894, when he was appointed county commissioner to fill an unexpired term. In 1896 he was elected to the same position for a three-year term, and, in 1899, his faithful services won him a re-election, with the largest majority ever given a candidate for that office in Allegheny county. In 1902 he was again elected, being the only successful candidate on the republican ticket. In 1880 Mr. Mercer was chosen as a member of the select council of Pittsburg, from the twenty-fifth ward, and was three times re-elected, serving eight years in all. He is a member of the Independent Order of Odd Fellows, and belongs to the Methodist Protestant church. In politics he is a republican.

JAMES A. CLARK, county commissioner of Allegheny county, was born at Barnesville, Belmont Co., Ohio, in 1860. In 1861 his parents moved to Altoona, Pa., and four years later came to Pittsburg, where their son was reared and received a common-school education. Mr. Clark's schooling stopped at the age of sixteen, when he went to spend a year in the oil fields of Pennsylvania. He then learned the hammer trade in the steel works in Pittsburg, and was engaged in this work for about six years, after which he was for about the same length of time employed as utility man in the East End stockyards, Pittsburg. In 1888 Mr. Clark was appointed railway postal clerk, and a year later was chosen by Governor Pattison as assistant gas inspector of Pittsburg.

After this he held the position of secretary and treasurer of the Keystone paint and color company, and was then employed by the Iron City brewing company for about a year and a half in the capacity of general superintendent. In 1896 he was elected county commissioner for a three-year term, was re-elected in 1899, and again, in 1902. Mr. Clark is one of the most prominent young men of Allegheny county, and the future promises him even more success than has fallen to his lot in the past. He is a member of the B. P. O. E., and was a delegate to the national convention in Kansas City, July 5, 1900.

JESSE M. McGEARY, coroner of Allegheny county, was born on a farm in Windfield township, Butler Co., Ohio, and spent his early life in that county. His parents were Giffen and Susan M. (Brown) McGeary. In 1870 he moved to Pittsburg, where he remained two years, and, in 1872, located in the sixth ward of Allegheny city, where he has since resided, and has long been considered one of its prominent and influential citizens. Mr. McGeary served in the Allegheny common council for twelve years, but, on Dec. 1, 1898, he resigned to accept the office of county coroner, to which he had been elected on Nov. 8, 1898. His efficient services as coroner won him re-election in 1901. As evidence of Mr. McGeary's interest in his party's welfare, will state that he served as a member of the Allegheny county republican executive committee for twenty-two years, and for twenty years was secretary of the committee on speakers and meetings. Besides his interest in political affairs, Mr. McGeary affiliates with several prominent secret orders, viz.: Davage lodge, No. 374, F. and A. M., Allegheny; Zion lodge, No. 1057, I. O. O. F.; Standard council, No. 62, Jr. O. U. A. M.; Manchester castle, No. 212, K. of G. E.; Allegheny lodge, No. 339, B. P. O. Elks; Allegheny council, No. 445, Royal Arcanum; Allegheny council, No. 63, Loyal additional benefit association, and Allegheny assembly, No. 103, Royal Society of Good Fellows.

WILLIAM JOHN STEEN, jury commissioner of Allegheny county, was born in Pittsburg, Pa., Sept. 6, 1841, and is of Irish descent. He was reared in Pittsburg, where he attended the public schools, and afterwards the Iron City commercial college, graduating from the latter institution in 1860. In August, 1862, Mr. Steen enlisted in the Civil war as a private in Company G, 136th Pennsylvania volunteer infantry, and served ten months, being honorably discharged at the end of that time. While in the service he fought with distinction at Antietam, Fredericksburg and Chancellorsville, and escaped injury and capture. After the war he went into the coal-producing business with his father in Allegheny county, and was so engaged until 1898, when he sold out and was for one term director of the poor of Allegheny county. He has also served one term as burgess of Chartiers, now Carnegie. Mr. Steen was appointed to his present position in May, 1902, and has given good service. He is a member of the Knights Templars, and G. A. R. post, No. 153, of Carnegie. In politics he is a republican. He affiliates in religion with the Presbyterian church, in which he holds the position of trustee.

HAMILTON S. BURROUGHS, M. D., of Pittsburg, Pa., a prominent general practitioner of medicine, was born in Greene county, near Waynesburg, Pa., and is the son of Talmage Burroughs, a retired farmer, and of his wife, Jane Scott, both natives of Pennsylvania. His paternal grandfather, Samuel Burroughs, was also a native of the Keystone State, having been born in Brownsville, Pa., about 1800. Young Burroughs attended the public schools of Waynesburg, Pa., and Waynesburg college. He matriculated at the Jefferson medical college, of Philadelphia, and was graduated from that noted school in 1879, with the degree of doctor of medicine. On graduation, Dr. Burroughs began the practice of his profession at Waynesburg, where he met with much success, and, in 1891, he removed to Pittsburg, and since has prospered as a general practitioner in the metropolis of western Pennsylvania. He is medical examiner for the Equitable and the Metropolitan life insurance companies, and is a member of the Allegheny county, the Pennsylvania State and the American medical associations. He is prominently identified with the Masonic fraternity, having taken the thirty-second degree, and is a member of the Odd Fellows, the Pittsburg alumni association of Jefferson medical college, the republican party, and a member and deacon of the Shady Avenue Baptist church. Dr. Burroughs was married, in 1882, to Margaret A., daughter of Samuel and Martha (Millikin) Hopkins, of Waynesburg, Pa., her father being a prosperous farmer and her mother a descendant of the early settlers of Greene county. They have one child, Samuel Gross, attending the Margaretta public school of East End, Pittsburg.

WILLIAM CLAVER McKINLEY, sheriff of Allegheny county, Pa., was born in Pittsburg, March 29, 1859, and was educated in the public schools. Leaving school at the age of fifteen, he was employed for five years in the glass works in Pittsburg, at the end of which time he began his long and successful career in the public service as clerk in the office of the city assessor. He remained there three years, and then spent two years as clerk in the county treasurer's office. He became deputy sheriff under Sheriff Alexander E. McCandless, and after that served under three successors in that office—Sheriffs McCleary, Richards and Lowry. Mr. McKinley served, in all, twelve years as deputy, and, in 1900, was elected sheriff for a three-year term, a position for which his twelve years of experience as deputy had well fitted him. He has held the office of sheriff for four years, being one year longer than the office was ever held by any other official in the same capacity. Sheriff McKinley is a member of the F. and A. M. and the Knights of the Golden Eagle. He is a regular attendant upon the services of the Presbyterian church. He was married, in 1891, to Dora, daughter of Charles F. Hilger, and has one son, William Hilger McKinley.

HENRY GRELLE, alderman from the thirty-eighth ward, Pittsburg, was born in Brunswick, Germany, in 1853, and came to America in 1869. Mr. Grelle attended school in Wheeling, W. Va., leaving at fifteen years of age to work in an iron mill. He came to Pittsburg in 1874, where he has since resided. Mr. Grelle was employed as an iron worker until 1892, at that time receiving the appointment of assistant superintendent of the Metropolitan insurance company of New York. In 1897 he was elected alderman for a five-year term, and rewarded by re-election, in February, 1902. In politics he is a republican. Mr. Grelle is a member of the Knights of Pythias, Heptasophs and Independent Order of Red Men. He is a member of the Methodist Episcopal church.

JAMES SHERRAN, alderman from the twenty-eighth ward, Pittsburg, was born in that city in 1840. He is a son of Daniel Sherran, who was, however, commonly known as Dan, son of Daniel Sherran, of London, England. Daniel Sherran, father of the subject of this sketch, came to America in the early twenties, when eight years old, and died in Pittsburg in 1854. Alderman James Sherran was raised in Pittsburg, and went to school until his father's death made it necessary for him to go to work. From that time until 1888 he worked in various iron mills, when he was elected constable for the twenty-eighth ward. Mr. Sherran held this position until June 20, 1901, when he was appointed alderman by Governor Stone. He was appointed to fill a vacancy, and succeeded in so pleasing his constituents that they elected him to the position in February, 1902, for a five-year term. Mr. Sherran was married, in 1869, to Jane A., daughter of David Thomas. They have no children living. Mr. Sherran is a member of the Senior Order of United American Mechanics and the Ancient Order of United Workmen.

FRANK RIDGWAY, the local forecaster of the United States weather bureau at Pittsburg, Pa., comes of a family which, for many years, was distinguished on both sides of the Atlantic. This family, alias Peacock (alluding to which the old bearing of arms was three peacocks, heads erased), had been in Devon from a very early period, as manifested by the collection of Sir William Pole, the best antiquary of that county The name may be presumed to have been local, there being two places so called in the shire, one near Plymouth, the other in the parish of Owlscomb, near Honiton. The first who advanced the family was Stephen Ridgway, who was one of the stewards of the city of Exeter in the sixth year of the reign of Edward IV., and mayor thereof in the seventh year of the reign of Henry VII. (1466), and the next was John Ridgway, a son or a grandson of Stephen Ridgway, who purchased from the Mohuns of Dunster the Manor of Tor, in Devon, and was elected one of the representatives of the city of Exeter in the first two parliaments called by Queen Mary. He married Elizabeth, daughter of John Wentford, and was succeeded by his son, Thomas Ridgway, Esq., who purchased, in 1599, from Sir Edward Seymour, the site of the Abbey of Tor in Devon. He married Mary, daughter of Thomas Southcote, Esq., and co-heir of her mother, Grace, daughter and heiress of John Barnhouse, Esq., of Marsh in Devon, and by her had a son and heir—I. Sir Thomas Ridgway, who was employed in Ireland in a military capacity to Elizabeth, and planted the first Protestant colony in Ireland. He was high sheriff of Devon in 1600, and received the knighthood at the accession of King James to the throne of England. He was elected one of the knights of the shire for the county of Devon in the first parliament called by the king, who continued to employ him in some of the highest places of trust and command in Ireland, and had him sworn in the privy council. He was advanced to the dignity of baron, Nov. 23, 1612, created a peer of the kingdom of Ireland, in 1616, as baron of Galen-Ridgway, and advanced, in 1652, to the earldom of Londonderry. He married Cicely, sister and co-heir of Henry Mackwilliam (the lady was maid of honor to Queen Elizabeth), and had issue: Robert, his heir; Edward, Mackwilliam, Maria, died young, and Cassandra, married to Sir

Francis Willoughby, Knight. His lordship was succeeded by his eldest son, Sir Robert Ridgway, second earl of Londonderry, who married Elizabeth, daughter and heir of Sir Simon Weston, Knight, of Lichfield, and was succeeded by his son, III. Sir Weston Ridgway, third earl of Londonderry, who married Martha, daughter of Sir Richard Temple, Bart., and left several daughters and two sons, Robert and Thomas. The eldest son, Sir Thomas Ridgway, fourth earl of Londonderry, married Lucy, daughter of Sir William Jopson, Bart., and had two daughters, his co-heirs, viz.: Lucy, married to Arthur, fourth earl of Donegal, and Frances, married to Thomas Pitt, Esq., M. P. for Wilton, who was created earl of Londonderry. His lordship died March 7, 1713, when all his honors, including the baronetcy, became extinct. Tor Mohun, the old Ridgway estate in Devon, was sold about 1768 by the earl of Donegal to Sir Robert Polk, Baronet. The site of the Abbey of Tor was purchased from the first earl of Londonderry in 1653 by John Stowell, Esq., of Indiano, from whom Sir George Cary, Knight, purchased it in 1662. Arms—Sa. A pair of wings conjoined and elevated. Arg.

Richard Ridgway and his wife, Elizabeth, left Waterford, Berks Co., England, and sailed for America in the ship "Jacob and Mary," of London. They arrived in the Delaware river in July, 1699. Their eldest son, Thomas, was twelve years old when they arrived. Richard settled with his family in Springfield township, Burlington Co., N. J., where he died, leaving two sons, Thomas and Richard. Thomas married Anna Paws, daughter of Joseph Paws, and moved to Little Egg Harbor, N. J., where he died, in 1724, leaving eleven children, named Jacob, Job, Timothy, Thomas, Edward, Richard, John, Robert, Catherine, Elizabeth and Anna. Of these sons, Thomas, John and Robert married and spent their days in Egg Harbor. Jacob, the great-grandfather of the subject of this sketch, went to Springfield township, in Burlington county, on a farm known in later years as the "Michael Earl Farm." Richard (son of Thomas) went to Long Island, where his descendants still reside. John, born in 1705, was quite a celebrated Quaker minister. He married Phœbe Ballinger, and left five children, named John, Phœbe, Jacob, Thomas and Anna. Of these, Jacob became the greatest millionaire of Philadelphia, and was the father of Madam Rush, wife of Dr. Benjamin Rush, of that city. John married Elizabeth Wright, and died in 1845, leaving eight children, named David, born in 1777; Sarah, born in 1779; Caleb, in 1781; John, in 1784; Jacob, in

1787; David W., in 1791; Andrew C., in 1793, and Thomas, in 1797. Richard Ridgway, brother of Thomas and son of the first Richard, married Elizabeth Drews, and settled near Trenton, N. J., where he died, leaving several children. Joseph, the eldest, born in 1701, and wife, Abigail, lived near Burlington, and had four sons and four daughters, named David (born in 1733), Allyn, Joseph, Henry, Mary, Sarah, the names of the others being unknown. Mary married Solomon Thomas, of Springfield, N. J.; Sarah married Joseph Pancoast, father of Dr. Pancoast, of Philadelphia. David married Jane Burr, and moved to Trenton, N. J., and had four sons and four daughters, named David, Richard, Burr, Robert, Abigail, Rachael, Sarah and Hannah. Abigail married John Livzey, of Philadelphia; Rachael, John Evans; Sarah, John Johnson, and Hannah, Aaron Middleton. Richard, born in 1773, was married at Wysox, Bradford Co., Pa., 1808, to Sarah Cowel. This comprises all branches of the descendants of Richard Ridgway that I am able to discover in America. Another branch of Ridgways is found in Massachusetts. They came to this country at an earlier date, as will be seen by the following: 1st. John Ridgway and wife, Mary, admitted to the church in Charleston, Mass., in 1652. Mrs. Ridgway died Dec. 20, 1670. 2d. John, whose wife's name was Hannah, died in Charleston, Dec. 10; 1721. 3d. James Ridgway, son of John and Hannah Ridgway, born in Charleston, Oct. 13, 1698. His wife's name was Mehitable. 4th. Joseph Ridgway, son of James and Mehitable, was born, April 6, 1735, and died in 1815. He married, as his first wife, Abigail Bell, and as his second wife, Mary Ridgway, daughter of James Ridgway and his wife, Mary Braizer, of another line of Ridgways. Frank Ridgway, the subject of this sketch, was born on a farm in Gloucester county, N. J., in 1859, and moved to Baltimore ten years later, where he received a limited education, mostly in private schools. He entered the United States signal corps, in 1879, as a private, and was placed in charge of a military telegraph line in Arizona and New Mexico, where he remained until his term of service expired, in 1884, having been promoted to sergeant in 1880. After this he came east, re-enlisted in the signal corps in 1885, and remained until the service was transferred from the department of war to the department of agriculture, in 1891. He was stationed in Washington, D. C., until the latter part of 1885, and then sent as observer to Cape May Point, N. J. After this he was transferred to Cape Henlopen, Delaware breakwater, as sergeant in the signal corps, having charge of the military telegraph line between Cape Henlopen and Chincoteague island, and was sent thence to Sandy Hook, N. J., and from there to Manchester, N. H., where he remained until September, 1887. He was then ordered to Atlantic City, N. J., where he remained a short time and was transferred to Washington, D. C., being occupied there until May 31, 1888. Mr. Ridgway was then transferred to Harrisburg, Pa., where he remained until June 9, 1896, and then came to Pittsburg, where he has since been stationed, and has given splendid satisfaction. Mr. Ridgway is an enthusiastic Mason, having attained the thirty-second degree, and is a Shriner. He is a member of the First Presbyterian church of Pittsburg, Pa.

THOMAS G. McCLURE, county treasurer of Allegheny county, was born in Pittsburg in 1856, and there reared and educated. Leaving school at the age of fourteen, he entered the employ of a tin plate and metal firm, and continued with this concern until 1891. For four years before this time he had been a member of the firm. In 1891 Mr. McClure started in for himself in the tin plate and metal business, under the name of McClure & Co. This concern has had a most prosperous existence, and now does an extensive and profitable business. Besides this Mr. McClure established, in 1899, a tin plate mill in Washington, Pa. Mr. McClure has been for many years prominent in public life. He was elected a member of the Pittsburg council in 1883, and served six years in the common council and four in the select council. During this period he was one of the most influential councilmen. He served on the finance committee, and was for the last three years of his service chairman of the sub-committee on appropriations. During his last year he was a member of the committee on the Carnegie library, and chairman of the committee on building and grounds for the library. He was elected treasurer of Allegheny county in 1899. He is at present treasurer of the city and county republican executive committee. Mr. McClure is an enthusiastic member of the Masonic fraternity, where he has attained the thirty-second degree, and is a Knight Templar and Shriner. He is a member of the United Presbyterian church.

JOHN A. BLEICHNER, alderman from the twenty-fifth ward, South Side, Pittsburg, is a prominent real estate and insurance man. He was born in the ward which he now represents, in 1870, and there he was reared and given a limited education in the common schools. When twelve years old, he left school and worked for two years in a glass factory. After this he went to Ligonier, Westmoreland county, and spent four years on a farm. Returning to Pittsburg, Mr. Bleichner worked a year for Jones & Laughlin, at the same time attending night school. He accepted a clerkship with his brother, George J. Bleichner, in a real estate office, and was so employed for six years. He was elected alderman, in 1896, his ability and faithful service in this capacity winning him re-election, in February, 1901. Mr. Bleichner belongs to no secret order. He is a member of the Catholic church and the Knights of Columbus.

CHARLES F. McKENNA, a member of the Allegheny county bar and prominent citizen of Pittsburg, and veteran Union soldier in all the great battles of the Army of the Potomac, from Antietam to Appomattox, was born in Pittsburg, Oct. 1, 1845. He is of Irish ancestry, his grandparents and their ten children—six sons and four daughters—coming from County Tyrone and settling in the city of Pittsburg in the year 1830. His father, James McKenna, died in the city of Pittsburg when the subject of this sketch was less than one year old. His mother survived her husband's death until the year 1884, when she died in her eighty-fourth year. A family of six children—all of whom reached mature years—survived the death of James McKenna. The late Hon. Bernard McKenna, for twelve years judge of the second (police) district court of the city of Pittsburg, served as mayor of Pittsburg for the term of three years, from 1893 to 1896, and who died, June 20, 1903, was a brother of Charles F. McKenna. Mr.

McKenna, the subject of this sketch, received his early education in the public day and night schools of Pittsburg. He was apprenticed in his fourteenth year to learn the lithographers' trade and attained great success as an engraver and artist. In his sixteenth year he left this employment in response to President Lincoln's call of July, 1862, for 300,000 more Union soldiers and enlisted as a private soldier in Company E, 155th regiment Pennsylvania volunteers, recruited in the city of Pittsburg. This regiment was assigned to duty with Humphrey's division and became part of the famous 5th corps, Army of the Potomac, and within two weeks after enlisting in Pittsburg, the division reached the battlefield of Antietam, and for three years following, until the close of the war by surrender of Confederate armies under General Lee, Private McKenna carried a musket, participating in the great battles of Fredericksburg, Chancellorsville, Gettysburg, the Wilderness, Cold Harbor, Petersburg, Five Forks and Appomattox. Among the Pittsburgers who served in the same command were Col. E. Jay Allen, the late Gen. A. L. Pearson, Col. Jno. H. Cain, Col. Jno. Ewing, Major Geo. M. Laughlin, Harry M. Curry, Saml. Kilgore, Wm. Shore, John F. Hunter, Col. S. W. Hill and Jno. H. Kerr. After the war, Mr. McKenna returned to Pittsburg and entered upon the study of law with the law firm of Mitchell & Palmer. In 1869 he was admitted to practice at the Allegheny county bar. He has been in constant and successful general practice of his profession in Pittsburg ever since. He possesses an enviable reputation in western Pennsylvania as an able and reliable counsel and advocate. In the many years of legal practice he has been connected with many celebrated cases reported in the United States and State supreme court reports. He has been the counsel for the Catholic diocese of Pittsburg and cemetery and charitable organizations, under the administration of three bishops—the late Rt. Rev. M. Domenec, the late Rt. Rev. John Tuigg and of Rt. Rev. R. Phelan, present bishop—until the year 1892, when he resigned the position because of the increasing demands of general practice. Mr. McKenna has also been the general solicitor of the Western Pennsylvania humane society since its organization, over thirty years. He is also counsel for Ladies of the G. A. R. home at Hawkins Station. During the continuance of existence of the City National and City Savings bank of Pittsburg he was solicitor. Mr. McKenna is a charter member of Post No. 3, G. A. R., and of the Union Veteran legion encampment, No. 1, of Pittsburg, having been elected colonel of the latter organization, composed of veterans of the Civil war who had served not less than two years in the field. At all times Mr. McKenna, on memorial day celebrations and at campfires and reunions, has been active and has responded to invitations as a speaker. In 1872 Mr. McKenna married Miss Virginia White, daughter of the late Dr. N. W. White, of Allegheny city. Although not blessed with children, no happier or more cheerful couple than Mr. and Mrs. McKenna could be found anywhere. Mr. McKenna enjoys remarkably vigorous health, and seems to be still in his prime for intellectual work. No member of the legal profession devotes himself closer or more unremittingly to the duties of his position than does Mr. McKenna. In politics he has acted with the democratic party in national campaigns, but has frequently exhibited independent qualities in bolting unsatisfactory nominations and in actively supporting reform movements in local politics.

HUGH YOUNG, national bank examiner at Pittsburg, was born in County Down, Ireland, Dec. 14, 1832. He came to America alone in 1850, and located in Wellsborough, Pa., where he has since made his home. In 1856 he became special correspondent for the New York Tribune at Lawrence, Kan.; remained in that capacity a year, and then returned to Pennsylvania, where he studied law and was admitted to the bar, but never practiced. In July, 1863, he enlisted as a private in Company F, 35th Pennsylvania volunteer infantry, and two days later was elected first lieutenant. He served until August, 1863, acting as quartermaster. Returning to civil life, Mr. Young became a candidate for the State legislature in 1876 and was elected. The following year he was appointed national bank examiner, and acted as such until February, 1888, when he retired from office and became president of the Wellsborough National bank. He remained in this position until 1891, when he was appointed national bank examiner for Pittsburg, in which capacity he has been, since then, successfully engaged. Mr. Young is a member of the F. and A. M., I. O. O. F., and Cook post, G. A. R., at Wellsborough.

WILLIAM J. ZAHNISER, contractor, Pittsburg, was born on a farm in Clinton county, Ia., in 1857, but has spent most of his life in Allegheny county. He came with his parents to Allegheny city in 1865, and a year later moved to Lawrenceville, now seventeenth ward, Pittsburg, where he was reared and educated. He graduated from the ward school in 1873, and then started in to learn the carpenters' trade, his father, J. W. Zahniser, being at that time a large contractor. In 1883, the father went to try his fortunes in the west, and Mr. Zahniser took up the contracting business, in which he has since been successfully engaged. He has long been a prominent man in his community, and, in 1900, the people of the seventeenth ward elected him to represent them in the select council. Mr. Zahniser is a member of the F. and A. M., Royal Arcanum and A. O. U. W. He belongs to the Seventh United Presbyterian church of Pittsburg.

BENJAMIN W. STOUFFER, alderman from the thirty-third ward since 1860, has been a resident of Pittsburg for about half a century. Coming to Pittsburg in 1854, he went into the drug business, in which he spent some time, and later engaged in the commission business. He was made superintendent of the Clinton iron and steel company, in 1860, and has held that position ever since. In 1860 he was elected member of the school board, and has filled the position most creditably since that time. He has been for the past twenty-one years a member of the central board of education. In politics he has always been an active republican. Mr. Stouffer is a man whose kind heart and generous disposition have won him the respect of the community and the friendship of all with whom he has been associated. He is a member of the F. and A. M., K. of P., Royal Arcanum, Heptasophs and A. O. U. W. In religious belief he is a Presbyterian.

JOHN WOODS NESBIT, United States pension agent at Pittsburg, is a son of James McConnell Nesbit, who was born in Allegheny county, Pa., in 1810, and died in 1877, and a grandson of John Nesbit, a native of the north of Ireland. J. W. Nesbit was born in South Fayette township, Allegheny Co., Pa., May 12, 1840; was raised on a farm, and received his education in the common schools. On Aug. 22, 1862, he enlisted as a private in Company D, 149th Pennsylvania volunteer infantry, and served with the Army of the Potomac under Generals Burnside, Hooker, Meade and Grant, taking part in the battles of Chancellorsville, Gettysburg, Mine Run, the Wilderness, Laurel Hill, Spottsylvania, North Anna, Cold Harbor, Petersburg, Weldon railroad, Hatcher's Run, and other minor actions. He was promoted to the position of corporal, July 7, 1863, and was made sergeant, Sept. 1, 1864. He went through the entire term of service without a scratch. He was struck in the breast in the Wilderness, May 6, 1864, by a sharpshooter's ball, but a needle case in his breast pocket, together with a roll of shelter tent, protected him from serious injury. Sergeant Nesbit was known as a reliable man, and was complimented for bravery on the field of North Anna. He was mustered out of the service at the close of the war, and returned home with his company. On his return from the army, he resumed farming, and later became active in military affairs, politics and business. He organized an independent military company, and was elected captain, June 1, 1868. This company was known as the "Free Rangers," and was mustered out of the service, June 1, 1873. In 1875 he organized Company C, 14th regiment, N. G. P., and was elected captain on August 14th of that year. On July 9, 1893, he was elected major, and assumed command of the second battalion of the regiment. On May 12, 1898, Major Nesbit enlisted for the Spanish-American war, but resigned soon after to resume his duties as United States pension agent, to which position he had been previously appointed. Being an active republican and interested in county politics, he became a candidate for the State assembly, was nominated and elected, and represented the sixth district, Allegheny county, in the sessions of 1881, 1883, 1889, 1891 and 1893. He was appointed superintendent of the State arsenal at Harrisburg, Pa., by Governor Hastings, Feb. 1, 1895, and served until Dec 16, 1897, when he resigned. On June 1, 1896, he was elected president of the sixth assembly district republican league, was appointed United States pension agent at Pittsburg by President McKinley, Dec. 18, 1897, and was reappointed by President Roosevelt, Jan. 31, 1902. Major Nesbit is actively engaged in business, and takes a prominent part in the promotion of local enterprises. He owns and manages a stock and fruit farm at Beechmont, Pa.; is owner of the Oakdale insurance agency; is president of the Oakdale armory association; secretary of the Oakdale cemetery company; president of the Melrose cemetery company at Bridgeville, Pa.; director of the First National bank of Oakdale; director of the Farmers' mutual insurance company, of Oakdale; interested in the Carnegie, McDonald & Cannonsburg street railway company; director of the Chartiers telephone company; member of the board of managers of the Boys' industrial home at Oakdale, and secretary and treasurer of the Oakdale printing and publishing company. Major Nesbit is a member of the First Presbyterian church at Oakdale, is a member of Union Veteran legion, No. 1, Pittsburg, and of Post No. 153, G. A. R., Carnegie. He resides with his family on Hastings avenue, Oakdale.

WILLIAM THOMAS LINDSEY, clerk of the United States district court for the western district of Pennsylvania, was born in the village of West Middletown, Washington Co., Pa., some fifty odd years ago. When a boy he attended Vermillion college at Hayesville, Ohio. Leaving college in 1869, he read law with the late Judge Alex. W. Archeson, of Washington, Pa. He also taught a select school in his native town one session, and later was principal for a short time in the public schools of Pittsburg. In 1871 he resigned his position as principal, and became chief clerk of the said court, which office he filled for twenty years, and was then appointed to his present position. Since 1891 he has been United States commissioner. For several years he was a member of the board of school control of Allegheny city. Mr. Lindsey is president of the Elizabeth bridge company, and a director in the Mercantile trust company, the Central accident insurance company, Jack's Run bridge company and North Side bridge company. He was an aide-de-camp on the staff of former Gov. William A. Stone, with the rank of lieutenant-colonel. Colonel Lindsey is a member of the Sons of the American Revolution. He is a descendant of Capt. Samuel Lindsey, an ensign of the 3d battalion, Pennsylvania provisional regiment, commissioned May 3, 1758, and commanded by Col. Hugh Mercer. He is also descended in a straight line from John Pancoast, a Quaker, who came to America from England prior to 1676, and, with William Penn and others, was one of the signers of the jury concessions, March 3, 1676.

CHARLES F. KIRSCHLER, who represents the fifth ward in the select council of Allegheny city, Pa., is a typical German-American citizen. He was born in Butler county, Pa., in 1864, his parents, Christopher and Christina Kirschler, being well-known residents of that county. When Charles was about eight years of age, the family removed to Allegheny city, where he attended the common schools of the second ward, and, after the death of his father, which occurred in 1876, he took a course in Duff's and in the Iron City business colleges. His first employment was in the Third National bank of Allegheny city, as messenger. He soon rose to the position of discount clerk, then bookkeeper of the discount department, and finally to that of general bookkeeper, where he continued to Jan. 1, 1893. At that time he bought the fancy grocery business of James Lockhart, on Federal street, but after conducting that business for about a year, he sold out to accept the position of secretary and treasurer to the D. Lutz & Son brewing company. This place he held for five years, and continued as treasurer for three years longer. On July 1, 1901, he formed a partnership with F. H. Tooher for the purchase of the Newell Hotel, in the city of Pittsburg, which they still operate. Throughout his career, Mr. Kirschler has been somewhat active in politics. He is a member of both the county and city republican committees, being the treasurer of the latter. In 1901 he was elected to the select council for the term ending in 1905. In the council he is the chairman of the finance committee, as well as a member of several other important committees. In 1892 he was married to Miss Ida, daughter of John McClurg, of Allegheny city, and they have two children, Carl F., Jr., and Elizabeth. Mr. Kirschler is a member of Allegheny lodge, No. 339, B. P. O. Elks. In his business, fraternal and political relations he enjoys the full confidence of his associates, and those who know him best speak of him in terms of high praise.

HENRY EYNON, alderman from the thirteenth ward, Pittsburg, was born in South Wales, in 1852, and there reared and educated. He came to America in 1870, locating in Pittsburg, where he has since resided. He was for twenty years engaged as a contractor and builder, and, in 1895, was elected alderman from his ward. His services during the first term in the council were so appreciated by the people that, in February, 1900, they elected him for a second five-year term. Mr. Eynon is a member of the Heptasophs, and belongs to the Congregational church. He was married, in 1873, to Miss Sarah Lewis, daughter of David Lewis, and is the father of one boy and five girls.

JAMES DUNLAP WALKER, the eldest son of William and Margaret (Dunlap) Walker, an alderman of the twentieth ward, Pittsburg, Pa.; a prominent citizen and Civil war veteran, is one of the best known and most highly-respected old soldiers in Pennsylvania. He was born in Allegheny city, Pa. June 6, 1846, and attended public and private schools there, afterwards completing his education at the Iron City business college, returning his test papers and enlisting for the war on the same day. In August, 1862, he enlisted as a private in Company B, 15th Pennsylvania volunteer infantry, and served about two months, taking part in the battle of Antietam, and also in the pursuit and capture of the daring confederate general, John Morgan, by Shackelford's cavalry. He then enlisted in the famous Knap's Pennsylvania battery for three years, or during the war, and from the date of enlistment participated in all the marches and battles of that celebrated organization until mustered out at the age of nineteen, in Pittsburg, June 14, 1865. In an hour and a half of fierce fighting at Wauhatchie, Tenn., with four guns in action, the battery lost twenty-six men killed and wounded out of forty-six officers and men engaged, and of forty-eight battery horses which went into the engagement, all but two were disabled. At the battle of Pine Mountain, Ga., this battery fired the shot which killed General Polk, known as the "bishop-general" of the confederacy. The organization was with General Sherman in his famous march to the sea and through the Carolinas and is spoken of in his memoirs as the "famous battery." Colonel Walker was taken prisoner near Blackwater, N. C., by General Hampton's confederate cavalry, and confined in the confederate prisons at Raleigh, N. C., and at Danville, and later spent some time in the noted Libby prison at Richmond. After the war Colonel Walker spent two years in the west working at his trade of bricklaying, and then, returning home, engaged in the business of general contracting, in partnership with his father, up to 1879, afterwards continuing the business alone until 1894. In 1886 he removed to the city of Pittsburg, and, in 1898, was appointed an alderman by Governor Stone to fill a vacancy, being elected to the same position at the next general election for a term of five years. Colonel Walker has been a member of the G. A. R. since 1867; is a past commander of Post No. 88, department of Pennsylvania, G. A. R.; served four terms as president of the Allegheny county association of Union ex-prisoners of war, and is a past president of the Allegheny G. A. R. association. He was for three terms chairman of the executive committee of the Union ex-prisoners of war, and was elected national commander of that organization in 1901, and re-elected in 1902 and 1903. At present he is commander of Knap's battery veteran association. He served in the Pennsylvania State legislature from 1876 to 1881, and as an officer of the National guard and chairman of the military committee of the Pennsylvania house of representatives for three sessions, was very active and successful in securing legislation looking to the betterment of the condition of the old soldiers and soldiers' orphans, and the reorganization of the Pennsylvania national guard. A deserved compliment in recognition of his services at that time was his appointment by Gov. Henry M. Hoyt to the position of chief of artillery, with the rank of colonel, in which position he served four years. He is now superintendent of erection of the Andersonville State military commission, which plans to erect a monument to the 1,849 Pennsylvania soldiers who died in Andersonville confederate prison and are buried in the national cemetery at Andersonville, Ga. Colonel Walker is a member of the B. P. O. E., Americus club, and other fraternal societies. He is of Scotch-Irish extraction, and of direct descent from the fighting preacher of the "Walls of Derry."

F. W. MUELLER, president of the Pittsburg brewing company, was born in Germany in 1847, and reared and educated in his native country. Coming to America in 1873, he located, first, at Cincinnati, Ohio, and later at Hamilton, Ohio, where he remained twelve years. He came to Pittsburg in 1887 and engaged in the brewing business, in which he has been unusually successful. Mr. Mueller was made president of the Pittsburg brewing company, Feb. 22, 1900, as a compliment to his ability and industry, and has filled this responsible position most creditably.

JOHN P. OBER, treasurer of the Pittsburg brewing company, was born in Allegheny city, Pa., Aug. 21, 1848. He was reared in Allegheny city, and educated in the common schools, leaving school when fourteen years old. He worked in the brewery of his father, George Ober, remaining in his employ until he reached the age of twenty-two, and then, in partnership with William Eberhardt, started a brewery in Allegheny city in 1870. The company was incorporated, in 1883, as the Eberhardt & Ober brewing company, and continued until 1900, when it was merged into the Pittsburg brewing company, of which Mr. Ober was made treasurer. While a resident of Allegheny city, Mr. Ober took a keen interest in the welfare of his city, and served for sixteen years in the select council, representing the thirteenth ward. Mr. Ober is a director in the German National bank, in the Safe Deposit bank of Allegheny and in the Central accident insurance company. He has a beautiful home in Schinley park, Pittsburg. In speaking of him, a prominent lawyer friend of his makes this statement: "Mr. Ober is one of the representative business men of Pittsburg, and prior to coming to this city filled a large place in city affairs in Allegheny city, in whose highest representative body he served with distinction for many years. In financial circles, both there and in Pittsburg, he is held in high esteem. He contributes to many charitable purposes, and his public spirit was demonstrated in one instance by his donation of a beautiful fountain to the city of Allegheny. No man stands higher in business circles than Mr. Ober." Mr. Ober is a member of the Masonic fraternity, I. O. O. F. and B. P. O. E.

WILLIAM ALLEN MEANS, alderman from the twenty-first ward, Pittsburg, was born in Allegheny city, Pa., in 1863. He is a son of Allen Means, also a native of Allegheny county, now retired. His parents moving to Plum township, Allegheny county, in 1869, William A. Means lived there on a farm until 1874, the family moving at that time to East End, Pittsburg. There he attended the public schools, completing his education in the high school. Leaving school in 1880, he became clerk in the office of A. H. Leslie, at that time alderman from the seventeenth ward, and now director of public safety. He remained in Mr. Leslie's office for thirteen years, and was engaged for several years by his brother, A. J. E. Means, then alderman from the twenty-first ward. In 1897 he became a candidate for the position of alderman on the republican ticket, was elected, and, in February, 1902, was re-elected, this time on the citizens' ticket. Mr. Means is a prominent Presbyterian, and has sung in the choir of his church for the past eighteen years. He was one of the organizers of the East End gymnastic club, now extinct, and was president of that organization for one year. He is at present a director of the Lincoln Avenue building and loan association. Mr. Means is a member of the Junior Order of United American Mechanics, Royal Arcanum and Protected Home Circle.

BENJAMIN L. H. DABBS, photographer, was born in Edgeworth, Allegheny Co., Pa., in 1871, but has resided in Pittsburg since 1879. When a boy, he attended school in Pittsburg, and later completed his education at the Pennsylvania college at Gettysburg. Returning to Pittsburg, he was employed for about five years by the French spring company, and then took up photography as a vocation, his father, also named B. L. H. Dabbs, being a photographer. He was engaged with his father until the death of the latter, which occurred in September, 1899, and has since that time conducted the business most successfully for himself. Mr. Dabbs belongs to no secret orders. He is a member of the United Presbyterian church.

STEPHEN P. STONE, United States marshal for the western district of Pennsylvania, was born in what is now the borough of Bridgewater, Beaver Co., Pa., in September, 1854. He attended school until he reached the age of sixteen, studying in the public schools and at Beaver academy. In 1877 he was appointed deputy prothonotary for Beaver county, Pa., was elected to the same office two years later, and re-elected in 1883. In 1885 he was appointed assistant cashier of Beaver depository, and served as such until 1890, when his ability and attention to duty won him promotion to the position of cashier, in which capacity he is still engaged. Mr. Stone was appointed to his present office by President McKinley in April, 1901, and was reappointed by President Roosevelt, Jan. 1, 1902. He is a stockholder in the Beaver Valley traction company, of which he has been treasurer for the past ten years. Mr. Stone is a Master Mason and Knight Templar, and a member of the I. O. O. F., Jr. Order of United American Mechanics and B. P. O. E. In religious belief he is an Episcopalian.

JOHN DOWNEY, alderman from the fifth ward, Pittsburg, has been prominent in public affairs for many years, and is a man widely and favorably known. He was born in County Down, Ireland, in 1840, and lived in Ireland until 1869, when he came to America, locating in Pittsburg. On coming to this city, he entered the employ of Oliver & Phillips, prominent hardware merchants; remained with them a year, and then spent eighteen months in Leetonia, Ohio. He then returned to Pittsburg, where he has since resided. Since 1879 he has conducted a bakery, which is doing an increasingly extensive business. Mr. Downey has served two terms on the school board and two terms on the central board of education. He was elected alderman from the fifth ward, in 1898, for a five-year term. Mr. Downey is a member of the Roman Catholic church.

JOHN H. ARMSTRONG is an enterprising and ambitious business man, successful alike as a public officer and in his business dealings. He was born in Dublin, Ireland, Sept. 30, 1861, and, in 1877, came to America, locating in the twelfth ward, Pittsburg. On coming to Pittsburg, he became bookkeeper for Frank Armstrong, coal dealer, and was thus employed until 1890. He was elected, in 1896, to represent the twelfth ward in the Pittsburg common council, and re-elected in 1898. He also served as police magistrate by appointment under Recorder J. O. Brown. Mr. Armstrong is an energetic business man, and does a thriving business in real estate, insurance, collections, etc. Besides this, he is president of the North Avenue stair company and the Boon & Hill wall paper company. Mr. Armstrong is a prominent Mason, being a past commander of Ascalon commandery, No. 59, Knights Templars, and a Shriner, and is also a member of the B. P. O. E. He affiliates in religion with the United Presbyterian church, and resides at No. 522 Winebiddle Ave.

FRANCIS X. BARR, clerk of courts of Allegheny county, was born in Pittsburg, Aug. 22, 1864. He is the youngest son of the late Hon. James P. Barr, founder of the Pittsburg Post, the leading democratic newspaper in Pennsylvania. Mr. Barr received his early education in private schools in Pittsburg, and later attended Fordham college, New York. He read law in the office of Willis F. McCook, Esq., practiced his profession for six years, and then retired from active practice to associate himself with the business management of the Pittsburg Post. Mr. Barr comes from an old democratic family, whose members have been influential in democratic politics in Pennsylvania for the past fifty years. He was elected to his present position on the citizens' and democratic ticket. Mr. Barr is a young man who has established himself firmly in the business world, a man of good habits and spotless integrity.

EDWARD C. VIERHELLER, alderman from the thirty-sixth ward, Pittsburg, is a native of that city. He was born in 1866, and attended the public schools until he reached the age of sixteen, when he began keeping books for his father, John P. Vierheller, a drygoods merchant. He remained in the employ of his father ten years, bought out the store, but sold it shortly afterwards to take up the fire insurance business, in which he is still successfully engaged. In August, 1897, he was appointed alderman from the thirty-sixth ward by Governor Stone to fill a vacancy, was elected to the position in 1898 for a five-year term, and again in 1903 for another five years. Alderman Vierheller has long been prominent in republican politics. He was formerly a member of the republican county committee, and is at present a member of the republican city committee. He is secretary of the German building and loan association.

ALBERT YORK SMITH, attorney and register in bankruptcy, Pittsburg, was born in what is now the thirty-second ward, Pittsburg, in 1854. His father, C. B. M. Smith, was a prominent attorney in his time, and, in 1845-6, was city solicitor of Pittsburg. Albert York Smith received his primary education in his native city, mostly in private schools, and then attended Yale university, graduating from that institution in the class of 1875. After graduation he studied law with his father, and afterwards with the late Samuel Harper, who was register in bankruptcy. He was admitted to the bar in 1880, and, in 1889, was appointed to the office which he has filled most creditably since that time. Mr. Smith is a member of Delta Kappa Epsilon fraternity. He is vice-president of the Yale alumni of western Pennsylvania, and belongs to the University club. He is a member of the Heptasophs and Royal Arcanum, and the Presbyterian church. In politics he is a republican, and takes an active interest in party affairs.

DAVID FOULKE COLLINGWOOD, treasurer of Allegheny county, Pa., was born in the "old sixth," now the seventh, ward, Pittsburg, and was reared and educated in the public schools there. Leaving school at the age of sixteen, he went into the wholesale and retail drug house of Joseph Fleming, remaining a year, after which he worked a year at the same business for Harris & Ewing. He spent a short time in laboratory work, but being unable to stand this occupation, he soon gave it up and became weigh-master in the converting mill, and later operated "the screws" on the blooming mill rolls of the Pittsburg Bessemer steel works (now Carnegie Homestead mills). After this he entered the employ of Thos. J. Watson, oil broker, as bookkeeper and confidential clerk, holding this position until about 1884, when he went into the insurance business, in which he has since been successfully engaged.

Mr. Collingwood resides in North Braddock, and served as school director of his borough for ten months in 1896. He is an enthusiastic member of the Masonic fraternity, in which he has attained the thirty-second degree, and is a Shriner. He is also a member of the Pittsburg and the Monongahela clubs. In religious belief he is a Presbyterian.

MILLARD F. LESLIE, funeral director in Pittsburg, and treasurer of the Funeral directors' association of Allegheny county, was born on a farm in Westmoreland county, Pa., Sept. 5, 1850. When ten years old, he moved with his parents to Chartiers, now Edgecliff, a village in Westmoreland county, where the father kept a general store. Here Mr. Leslie attended the public school until he reached the age of fifteen, when he moved with his parents to Freeport, Armstrong Co., Pa., and spent two years at the Freeport academy. His father's death then put an end to his schooling, and the boy went to work as brakeman for the Allegheny Valley railroad, now the river division of the Pennsylvania system. Mr. Leslie continued in the employ of this railroad until 1882, being promoted first to freight conductor, afterwards to passenger conductor. He was employed in the latter position for the last eight years of his service. Coming to Pittsburg, in 1882, he opened an undertaking establishment, in company with his brother, A. H. Leslie, under the firm name of M. F. Leslie & Bro. This firm continued for thirteen years, until 1895, when A. H. Leslie retired, and the livery end of the business was sold. Mr. Leslie has since managed the undertaking branch of the business. He has a handsome new chapel at No. 191 Forty-third St. The new building is a credit to Lawrenceville, and shows the progressive spirit of its owner. This is the first of the kind that has ever been erected in Lawrenceville, and is indeed a beautiful structure. It stands on a plot of ground twenty-one by sixty-five feet, and is two stories high, facing directly on Forty-third street and Eden alley. The first floor consists of an office, assistants' room, bath, packing room and reception room, all of which are beautifully finished in mahogany and onyx wainscoting, tile floor with a handsome marble mantel. The office fixtures are also mahogany. In the basement will be found a laying-out and trimming room done up with cemented floors and walls. The second story is where the new chapel is located, and in the front of the room three beautiful art windows cast a lovely glow of light all over the apartment, giving it a handsome effect. On the second floor is found a reception room, toilet room, bath, etc. The entire building is lighted with electric lights, with telephone connection at his chapel and also at his residence, No. 173 Forty-third St. Mr. Leslie is a member of the I. O. O. F., Jr. O. U. A. M., Maccabees, Royal Arcanum and several other societies. He affiliates with the Methodist Episcopal church, and is a republican in politics.

EDWARD J. FRAUENHEIM, vice-president of the Pittsburg brewing company, was born in Pittsburg, on Feb. 13, 1865. His father, Edward Frauenheim, was formerly, for many years, an important factor in business affairs in Pittsburg. He was president of the Iron City brewing company, and an officer and director in a number of other companies, among them the German National bank and the Epping-Carpenter company. The subject of this sketch was educated at St. Vincent's college, from which institution he graduated with honor. He then entered his father's office, where he remained until the death of the latter. Upon the organization of the Pittsburg brewing company, he was elected vice-president. Beginning his business career equipped with a good education, a splendid physique, and an abundance of energy and perseverance, Mr. Frauenheim has by close application to business, and the practice of fair dealing, earned for himself a most enviable reputation in the business world as a man of business ability and strict probity. He is interested in a financial way in various large institutions in Pittsburg, and is actively engaged in several manufacturing enterprises. Mr. Frauenheim is president of the Iron City sanitary manufacturing company and of the Zelienople extension company; he is vice-president of the Duquesne fireproofing company, and director in the German National bank and the East End savings and trust company. He is likewise a member of the board of directors of Mercy hospital. In June, 1903, he was appointed to the office of city treasurer by Mayor W. B. Hayes.

Mr. Frauenheim is a democrat, and while not actively participating in politics, he was honored by his party with election to the national convention in Chicago, in 1896. He is married, and with a charming wife and seven children resides in a beautiful home on Rebecca street, in the East End, Pittsburg. Mr. Frauenheim is a member of the Duquesne club, of the Monongahela club and the Columbus club.

THOMAS B. MORELAND, SR.

THOMAS B. MORELAND, funeral director, East End, Pittsburg, was born in the twelfth ward, Pittsburg, in 1870, but has been almost all his life a resident of the East End. His father, Thomas B. Moreland, Sr., was for many years engaged in the livery and undertaking business in the East End. He was born in Dromore, County Down, Ireland, in 1828, and came to Pittsburg when twenty-two years old. He went into the livery and undertaking business in 1858, with David L. Mitchell, the firm being known as Moreland & Mitchell. A branch of the business was established in the East End, in 1870, of which Mr. Moreland took charge, but, in 1874, he dissolved partnership with Mr. Mitchell and conducted the business in the East End alone. Mr. Moreland was probably the most widely known business man in the East End, a man who enjoyed a remarkably large circle of acquaintances, and was admired and respected by all who knew him. He was a director of the Liberty National bank, of the Dime savings and loan association, and was prominently identified with every movement to advance the interests of the East End. Thomas B. Moreland, the subject of this sketch, was reared in the East End, and graduated from the public schools in 1884, and from Newell Institute in 1888. He entered the employ of his father, and, on the latter's death, April 15, 1902, succeeded him in the livery and undertaking business. Upon the death of President William McKinley, Mr. Moreland had the honor of being a prominent assistant at his funeral at Canton, Ohio. He is a director of the Liberty National bank and the Dime building and loan association. Mr. Moreland is a thirty-second degree Mason, a Knight Templar and Shriner, and a member of Allegheny lodge. No. 339, B. P. O. E. In politics he is a republican.

I—6

ALEXANDER BLACK, alderman from the thirty-first ward, Pittsburg, is a Scotchman by birth, and has resided in Pittsburg for over thirty years. He was born in Glasgow, in 1847, and reared and educated in Scotland. In 1865 he went to Newport, Monmouthshire, England; resided there several years, and, in 1871, was married to Miss Mary Clapp, daughter of John W. Clapp. Mr. and Mrs. Black have five children, two boys and three girls. In 1872 Mr. Black came to Pittsburg, where he was engaged as a journeyman tailor until 1883, at which time he went into the real estate and insurance business, in which he has since that time been employed. In 1901 he became a candidate for alderman of the thirty-first ward, and was elected for a five-year term. Mr. Black is prominent in business circles, and is treasurer of the Home building and loan association of the thirty-first ward. He is a member of the Independent Order of Odd Fellows and the Knights of the Mystic Chain, and belongs to the United Presbyterian church. He is a republican in politics.

JOHN BRADLEY, clerk in the office of the prothonotary of Allegheny county, was born in Lanarkshire, fourteen miles from Glasgow, Scotland, in 1841. He came to Allegheny county with his widowed mother in 1852, and worked in the coal pits, as he had done in Scotland since his eighth year. He continued at this work in America until 1873, except during the Civil war. In July, 1862, he enlisted to fight for his adopted country, as a private in Company C, 123d regiment, Pennsylvania volunteer infantry, and served until disabled by a wound in the left arm, received at Fredericksburg, Dec. 13, 1862. Coming to Pittsburg in 1873, Mr. Bradley was engaged for a short time as a clerk for his brother-in-law, and, in December of that year, became clerk in the office of the prothonotary, in which office he has been a trusted official for almost thirty years. In 1885 he was elected to the office, and was twice re-elected, after which he became chief clerk and served as such until Jan. 20, 1903. On Jan. 10, 1903, he was appointed oil inspector for Allegheny county by the court of common pleas, No. 1. Mr. Bradley is a Mason, and a member of the I. O. O. F., Royal Arcanum and Post No. 151, G. A. R.

THOMAS A. ROWLEY, deceased, was born in Pittsburg, in 1809, reared and educated there. He held the position of clerk of courts of Allegheny county prior to the Mexican war, and was so employed when the war broke out. Mr. Rowley went into the war as second lieutenant and adjutant in the 2d Pennsylvania infantry; he was afterwards promoted to captain, and assigned to the regiment of Col. George M. Hughes, Maryland and District of Columbia troops, serving in that capacity until the close of the war. Returning to Pittsburg, he became street commissioner, and later clerk of courts. In 1856 Mr. Rowley became captain of the Washington infantry, a militia company. The company was, on the outbreak of the Civil war, raised to a battalion, and later to a regiment, Mr. Rowley becoming first major and then colonel. After its first three months' service, the regiment enlisted, its name being changed at that time from the 13th to the 102d regiment, Pennsylvania volunteer infantry. Mr. Rowley served as colonel of his regiment until Dec. 29, 1862, when he was promoted to the position of brigadier-general, and assigned to the command of the 1st brigade, 3d division, 1st army corps. At the battle of Gettysburg, after the death of Gen. J. F. Reynolds, General Rowley commanded the division, having charge throughout the battle, after the first day's fight. The gallant general was himself wounded on that bloody field, and, being incapacitated for field service, was assigned to the command of the department of Maine, with headquarters at Portland, serving until April, 1864. He was then assigned to the department of western Pennsylvania, with headquarters at Pittsburg, holding this position until the close of the war. In November, 1864, he was brevetted major-general. After the war, General Rowley was appointed deputy United States marshal for western Pennsylvania by President Johnson, and in Grant's first administration he served one term as United States marshal for the same district. After this he devoted his attention to pension claims, and was so engaged up to the time of his death, which occurred in June, 1894. General Rowley was a Royal Arch Mason and Covenanter, and a member of the Presbyterian church. He was a son of George Rowley, a veteran of the War of 1812, and a grandson of William Rowley, who served in both the Revolution and the War of 1812. General Rowley's son, Henry T. Rowley, clerk to the county commissioner of Allegheny county, is also a veteran of the Civil war, making the fourth generation of soldiers in the Rowley family. Henry T. Rowley was born in Pitt township, now the eleventh ward, Pittsburg, in 1847. He was actively engaged in the Civil war, and at its close he returned to Pittsburg, where, for seven years, he was employed in the engineering corps of the P. & C., now the B. & O., railroad company. He worked until 1883 in the book and stationery store of J. R. Welden & Co. He then entered the office of the county commissioners, in which he has been a trusted official for twenty years. He was also for some years borough clerk of Wilkinsburg. Mr. Rowley is a member of the F. and A. M., being a Knight Templar in that fraternity.

URIAH BELLINGHAM, vice-president of District No. 5, United Mine Workers of Pennsylvania, was born in Staffordshire, England, and has been a resident of Banksville, Pa., since 1880. He was born Oct. 17, 1857, and, in 1860, moved with his parents to Lancashire, going two years later to Leeds, Yorkshire. Mr. Bellingham began working in the Yorkshire mines when only nine years old, and continued to do so until he reached his majority. Coming then to America, he was employed in the coal mines at Banksville until 1900, when he was elected vice-president of the United Mine Workers of Pennsylvania. In this capacity his services were rewarded by re-election in 1901, and again in 1902. Prior to this, from 1896 to 1901, he was a member of the district executive board of the same association. Mr. Bellingham is a member of the Knights of Pythias and Sons of St. George, and belongs to the Established Church of England. In politics he is a republican.

CHARLES J. PEDDER, real estate broker, was born in Pittsburg, Pa., in 1869, in the thirty-fifth ward, and there reared and educated in the common schools, graduating at the age of fourteen. After taking a business course in Duff's business college, he went to work with his father, who was at that time managing the Wayne iron and steel works (Brown & Co.). Mr. Pedder served as chemist and superintendent of the steel department of these works for a period of seven years, and then went into the real estate business, in which he has been very successful. In politics Mr. Pedder is a republican, and has taken an active interest in public affairs. He was elected to the select council of Pittsburg in 1895, and also served a term in the State legislature; was president of his local school board for a number of years, and, in 1900, was honored by being requested to represent his district on the central board of education, which office he is still holding. Mr. Pedder belongs to the Trinity Episcopal church, and is a member of the Masonic and the Elk fraternities.

CHARLES C. McGOVERN, alderman from the thirty-fourth ward, East End, Pittsburg, was born in the sixth ward, Pittsburg, March 6, 1874. He was reared in his native city and attended school there, graduating in 1889 from the College of the Holy Ghost. Mr. McGovern's first business venture was an express line, which was conducted for five years under the name of McGovern & Co. Selling out his business, he became special policeman on the Pittsburg force, and after eighteen months' service was made patrolman. He was employed in this capacity until 1898, when he raised a company for the Spanish-American war. The company was not needed, however, so Mr. McGovern enlisted as a private in Company A, 14th Pennsylvania volunteer infantry, and served fourteen months. In February, 1899, he was mustered out a first sergeant. Since the war he has continued to be interested in military matters. He is captain on the staff of Col. W. E. Thompson, of the 14th regiment, Pennsylvania national guard, and is also adjutant of that regiment. After the war, Mr. McGovern returned to his place on the police force, and, a month later, was placed on the detective force, where he served from April, 1899, to November, 1902. In politics he is a stalwart republican, and was elected alderman from his ward in February, 1900. He did not open an office, however, until November, 1902. In religious belief Mr. McGovern is a Catholic.

JAMES M. FULLERTON, one of Pittsburg's leading undertakers, and secretary of the Funeral directors' association of Allegheny county, was born in Pittsburg, in 1850, son of John and Unity (Galaher) Fullerton. John Fullerton, son of William and Elizabeth (Wilson) Fullerton, was born at Omagh, County Tyrone, Ireland, Sept. 7, 1810, and died in Pittsburg, Dec. 20, 1901. He came to Pittsburg with his mother and seven brothers and sisters, in 1823, and resided in that city for over three-fourths of a century. Being bound, when a boy, an apprentice to Samuel Boyce in the tobacco business, he learned all the branches of the trade, and was for fifty-eight years a successful tobacco dealer, retiring, in March, 1895, at the age of eighty-five. He was one of the original stockholders in the Second National bank and in the Pittsburg insurance company, of which he was director and in the organization of which he took an active part; was an active republican, a prominent church worker, and at all times an influential and respected citizen. He married Unity Galaher, May 21, 1839, and had five children, viz.: John T., Susan A., William W., Samuel R. and James M. Mrs. Fullerton died, Sept. 7, 1895, at the age of seventy-six. James M. Fullerton, whose name heads this sketch, attended school until he reached the age of nineteen, and then entered the employ of his father, and engaged in the tobacco business until 1884, having become a member of the firm in 1883. In 1884 he left the firm and established himself in the undertaking business, in which he has since risen to prominence. He is also director of the Pittsburg insurance company, is interested in the Keystone laundry, and has other extensive financial interests. Mr.

Fullerton has long been prominently identified with the interests of the republican party, has served as chairman of the republican ward committee of the fourth ward, and been honored with the office of school director in his ward. He is president of Penn. State funeral directors' association, and secretary of Allegheny county funeral directors' association. He is a member of the Masonic fraternity, the I. O. O. F., K. of P., B. P. O. Elks, Jr. O. U. A. M. and A. O. U. W. Although not a member, he is a regular attendant upon the services of the Methodist Episcopal church.

HARRY W. LOWE, city gauger of oils, Pittsburg, was born in Pittsburg, in the thirtieth ward, in 1866, and, in 1873, moved to the thirty-first ward, where he still lives. Here he attended the public schools, and afterwards Curry university, from which he graduated in 1883. He started in business life as a clerk for the Pittsburg news company, in whose employ he remained for two years, and then spent two years at the trade of making molds. After this he entered the employ of the Oliver iron and steel company, as shipper, and remained with that firm four years. In 1891 Mr. Lowe, with others, organized the McKinley tin plate company, with a capital stock of $10,000 and a plant on Water street, becoming bookkeeper for the concern. In 1892 this company was merged into the Aliquippa tin plate company, capital $45,000, with a plant at Aliquippa, Pa., and Mr. Lowe as superintendent of the mill. The concern, with many others, was wiped out in the panic of 1893, and Mr. Lowe then entered the public service, his first position being in the office of the register of deeds. He remained in this office about a year, and then was transferred to the office of the collector of delinquent taxes, where he was employed as deputy collector until June, 1902, when he was appointed to his present position by Recorder J. O. Brown. During his career in the public service Mr. Lowe has won many friends, who wish for him the success which should be the reward of ability and faithful attention to duty.

MATTHEW A. HANLON, funeral director at No. 110 Frankstown Ave., East End, Pittsburg, was born in the ninth ward of that city, in 1865. In childhood he moved with his parents to the sixteenth ward, where he was reared and educated, attending school until he reached the age of seventeen. He started in the undertaking and livery business in 1888, and has been successfully engaged in this business since then. Besides his business on Frankstown avenue, he owns another establishment at No. 5126 Butler St. He is a member of the Catholic church, and belongs to no political party, being an independent in politics. Mr. Hanlon's father, John Hanlon, is still living, though retired from active life. He was born in Donegal, Ireland, in 1831, and came to America in 1848. During the Civil war he enlisted in the Union army as a private in the Pennsylvania volunteer infantry, and served until 1865.

GEORGE W. THEIS, vice-president and secretary of the Monongahela river coal and coke company, was born in Monroe county, Ohio, Feb. 3, 1857, where his father, George Theis, was engaged in farming, stock-raising, general merchandising, and as a leaf tobacco merchant. Amid those scenes of varied activity, Mr. Theis grew to manhood, attending the country schools near his home. In 1874 he entered Duff's commercial college, of Pittsburg, graduating in 1875. He then returned to his home in Ohio, where he spent two years as manager of his father's leaf tobacco business. In 1877 he returned to Pittsburg, and from that time until 1885, with the exception of one summer spent in Colorado, he held responsible positions as accountant and general office man in various lines of business. However, Mr. Theis' successful business career began in 1885, when he accepted a position as accountant with Capt. C. Jutte & Sons, who were then engaged in the steamboat and coal business. He soon thereafter became interested in various enterprises with the Messrs. Jutte, which were successfully continued until January, 1890, when all the joint interests were merged into a new company, styled C. Jutte & Co., of which Mr. Theis became an active partner. From that time the growth of the company's business was phenomenal, and when the company sold out to the Monongahela river consolidated coal and coke company, in 1899, it was regarded as among the largest and foremost shippers of coal from the Monongahela river. Besides the above-mentioned business, Mr. Theis is largely interested in other enterprises. He is a director in the German-American savings and trust company, and president of several minor corporations. On the whole, he may justly be classed as one of Pittsburg's most successful business men. Mr. Theis united with the Masonic fraternity in 1882, being a member of Lodge No. 45, F. and A. M. and of Zerubbabel chapter, and also Ascalon commandery, K. T. He is a member of the German Protestant Evangelical church.

NICHOLAS H. BRADY, butter dealer in Pittsburg, was born in Baltimore, Md., in 1842. He came to Pittsburg with his parents in infancy, and was reared and educated in that city. Being compelled to leave school at an early age in order to earn his own living, he sold papers and worked at various employments until April, 1861, when he enlisted for a four-months' service in Company D, 12th regiment, Pennsylvania volunteer infantry, under command of Col. David Campbell. At the close of his first term he enlisted in a picked independent company of cavalry, 110 in number, to serve as body-guard to Gen. James Negley. After six or seven months, this company was discharged, and Mr. Brady then joined the telegraph corps, serving until the close of the war. During the war he took part in both engagements at Fredericksburg, in the second battle of Bull Run and in several minor skirmishes. The war over, Mr. Brady returned to Pittsburg, and was for several years engaged with his brother in the flour and feed business. In 1892 Mr. Brady became district agent for Swift & Co., of Chicago, his territory embracing all of western Pennsylvania, and has held this responsible position since that time. He is a member of Post No. 157, G. A. R. In politics he is a republican.

PATRICK C. BYRNE, deceased, was for over twenty-five years a prominent Pittsburg undertaker. He was born in Pittsburg, in 1854, and reared and educated there. When a young man, he engaged in contracting for street improvements, and, in 1876, went into the livery and undertaking business, following this vocation up to the time of his death, which occurred Aug. 13, 1902. He was at first associated with a Mr. McCabe, the firm continuing up to 1898 as Byrne & McCabe, when the partnership was dissolved, and Mr. Byrne established himself in business at No. 5214 Butler St. Mr. Byrne was a Catholic in religious belief. He belonged to the democratic party, and took an active part in politics, although never desirous of political preferment himself. Upon his death his widow inherited the business, and his son, Clem Byrne, assumed the responsibility of managing it. Clem Byrne is a rising young business man. He attended the Pittsburg schools, and, later, the Iron City college, from which he graduated in 1900. He also is a Catholic in religious belief.

THOMAS P. HERSHBERGER, of the firm of Hershberger & Son, funeral directors, thirty-sixth ward, Pittsburg, was born in the thirty-first ward of that city, in 1831, was reared there, and given a rudimentary education. Leaving school at the age of nine years, he went to work in a nail mill located on Penn avenue, where the store of Joseph Horner now stands. Here he was employed four years, and afterwards worked for three years as a feeder at the nail factory of Bailey & Brown. He spent a year in the Lawrence mill, now the Painter rolling mill, then worked for fourteen years in the Woods nail factory, having charge of four machines. In 1862 he opened a livery stable and undertaking establishment, and has been engaged in this business for over forty years. Mr. Hershberger has been for years a leader of the prohibition party; he was one of the organizers of the party in Allegheny county, and for fifteen years its chairman. He has the distinction of being the only prohibitionist who ever held a seat in the common council of Pittsburg. He is known as a man of strong individuality, and of character beyond reproach. He owns some seventy-five houses and other buildings in Pittsburg. Mr. Hershberger is a member of the A. O. U. W. and I. O. O. F. He is a member and officer of the Methodist Episcopal church.

SAMUEL M. DUVALL, in the court of common pleas, No. 1, Pittsburg, is a distinguished veteran of the Civil war and a prominent member of the Grand Army of the Republic. He was born in what is now the ninth ward, Pittsburg, in 1832; was reared there, and received a schooling of only six months' duration. At the age of seventeen he learned to make tacks in the mill of Chess, Cook & Co., and was there employed until the outbreak of the Civil war. On Aug. 15, 1861, he enlisted as a private in Company E, 102d Pennsylvania volunteer infantry, and served until mustered out in Pittsburg, June 29, 1865. In May, 1862, he was made corporal, soon afterwards was promoted to sergeant, then to orderly sergeant, and, on Dec. 13, 1862, to second lieutenant. He served as second lieutenant of Company E until November, 1864, when he was made captain of the company. Captain Duvall fought at Williamsburg, Fair Oaks, Savage Station, Malvern Hill, second Bull Run, White Oak Swamp, Fredericksburg, Chancellorsville, and then took part in the "stick in the mud" campaign under Burnside. In the first day's fight in the Wilderness he was wounded and incapacitated for further duty until the corps was sent to Washington to repel Early's demonstration. After this he fought in front of Fort Stevens, at Charlestown, Winchester, Fisher's Hill, Cedar Creek, the siege of Petersburg, and at Sailor's Creek. His gallant service in the war completed, Mr. Duvall returned to the iron mill, and worked at his trade as a tack maker until 1880, when he was appointed to his present position. In 1867 he joined Post No. 35, now J. W. Patterson post, No. 151, G. A. R., in which he has been commander and has held all the other offices, including that of trustee, in which capacity he served six years. He has also served as deputy inspector of the G. A. R.

for western Pennsylvania, and was, in January, 1902, elected president of the G. A. R. association of Allegheny county. Captain Duvall is a member of the Blue lodge in Lodge No. 269. He belongs to the Eighteenth Street Methodist Protestant church, and has served eighteen years as superintendent of its Sunday-school.

THOMAS G. DAVIS, assistant treasurer of the Pittsburg & Allegheny telephone company, Pittsburg, was born in Tredegar, England, in 1868, and came to America with his parents in infancy, the family locating in Pittsburg. Here Mr. Davis was reared and received a common-school education, leaving school in 1884 to enter the employ of the American rapid telegraph company, now the Postal telegraph-cable company. He began as messenger boy, and rose from this position to bookkeeper, and finally to cashier and chief clerk. He left this company in December, 1902, to accept his present position. Mr. Davis is a chapter Mason, and a member of the I. O. O. F. and the Heptasophs. In politics he is a republican.

WILLIAM DODDS, secretary and treasurer of District No. 5, United Mine Workers of Pennsylvania, was born in Haswell, Durham Co., England, in 1864. He attended the schools of his native county when a boy, and at the age of twelve went to work in the mines. Six months later, his parents persuading him to leave the mines, he spent fourteen months as a teacher. His health began to fail as the result of unsanitary surroundings, and for about fifteen months he was employed by a merchant tailor in Haswell. After the death of his mother, Mr. Dodds and his sister moved to Marston Rocks, Durham county, where he spent several years on his uncle's farm. In 1881 he decided to try his fortunes in America, and located at Banksville, Allegheny Co., Pa., where he has since resided. He worked as a coal miner in the mines of Hartley and Marshall until February, 1898, when he was elected vice-president of District No. 5, United Mine Workers for Pennsylvania. His services in this capacity were so appreciated, that in February, 1899, Mr. Dodds was elected secretary and treasurer of the organization. He has since been three times re-elected. Mr. Dodds is a member of the Elks, Knights of Pythias and Sons of St. George, and belongs to the English Episcopal church. In politics he is a republican.

JACOB SOFFEL, alderman from the thirty-second ward, Pittsburg, and court crier of the court of common pleas, No. 2, was born in Adenbach, Rhenish Bavaria, on June 1, 1843, and came to America in 1858, going to Pittsburg, where his older brother, Peter, had previously located. In 1860 he began working in a shoe store in Pittsburg, and remained there until September, 1864, when he enlisted as a private in Company B, 107th Pennsylvania volunteer infantry. His first battle was at City Point, Va. He then served two months before Petersburg, and after that went with his regiment to tear up the Weldon railroad. On the way back, Mr. Soffel was in the rear guard, and experienced there three days of almost continuous fighting. In the next battle, at Hatcher's Run, the regiment went in 600 strong, and came out with only 113 men. After this Mr. Soffel took part in the engagements at Five Forks, Sailor's Creek, Gordonsville and Amelia Court House, was present at Appomattox, then returned to Pennsylvania and was mustered out at Harrisburg, in July, 1865. Mr. Soffel's war record is a most creditable one. He brought from the conflict the scars from two injuries, one received at Hatcher's Run, and the other in a fight in northern Virginia. After the war he returned to Pittsburg, and engaged in the grocery business from 1867 to 1875, after which he took up 160 acres of land in Kansas, and engaged in farming until 1880, although, as Mr. Soffel facetiously puts it, the principal crop was grasshoppers. Returning then to Pittsburg, he was engaged until 1883 as court interpreter, and then, being thrown out of office by a hostile democratic administration, obtained the position of court crier, which he has since held. Mr. Soffel has been for years a prominent Pittsburg politician, and always an ardent republican. In 1885 he was elected alderman from the thirty-second ward, and has since been re-elected three times to that position, without opposition. He is a director in the South Hills investment company, is a member of the F. and A. M., I. O. O. F. and Knights of Pythias, and belongs to the German Protestant church.

GEORGE B. CHALMERS, United States customs appraiser, Pittsburg, has been in the government employ for over a quarter of a century. He was born in Aloa, Scotland, in 1839, and came with his parents, in 1848, to Pittsburg. In April, 1861, he became a private in the Pittsburg city guards, and at the outbreak of the Civil war, enlisted for three months, the company becoming then Company K, 12th Pennsylvania volunteer infantry. His first term of service over, Mr. Chalmers enlisted, on Aug. 1, 1861, as a private in Company K, 63d Pennsylvania volunteer infantry, under Col. Alex. Hayes, and served as such until May 15, 1862, when he was made first lieutenant of the company. In December of the same year he became captain, and as senior captain, he had charge of the regiment on many occasions during the war. He served throughout the Peninsular campaign, receiving at the battle of Fair Oaks an injury so severe as to disable him for some six weeks. After this he took part in the engagements of second Bull Run, Chantilly, Fredericksburg and Chancellorsville, and was present during all the three days of terrible fighting at Gettysburg. Captain Chalmers was in command of four companies on the skirmish line, and participated in all the battles of the Army of the Potomac. In the Wilderness he was so badly wounded as to incapacitate him for further fighting, so he was honorably discharged from the service at the Annapolis hospital on Aug. 6, 1864. He was then obliged to go on crutches for four months afterwards. On receiving his discharge, Captain Chalmers returned to Pittsburg, and was engaged in business for ten years with his brother, John B. Chalmers, a general contractor. In June, 1874, he was appointed and commissioned United States customs appraiser in the United States custom-house at Pittsburg by President U. S. Grant, and has been in the custom-house ever since, except during the first administration of President Cleveland. Mr. Chalmers is a republican in politics. Although now a resident of the fourteenth ward, he formerly lived in the eighth ward, and represented that ward in the city council for several years. He is a member of the A. O. U. W. and of the Union Veteran legion, and was the first national commander of that organization.

JEREMIAH DANIEL BUCKLEY, of Pittsburg, Pa., a prosperous lawyer, was born in County Kerry, Ireland, June 24, 1848, son of Daniel and Nano Buckley, both natives of Ireland. Mr. Buckley, when a mere infant, accompanied his parents to America, and the greater part of his life has been spent in Allegheny county. The advantages of a thorough and systematic school education were denied him, but he has largely overcome those deficiencies by vigorous application and well-selected readings, which, combined with a mind naturally clear and bright, have placed him on a secure educational basis. The early part of his life was devoted to steel work, and for a number of years he was the manager of a mill. Subsequently Mr. Buckley read law in the offices of C. F. McKenna, and also with former Judge Fetterman, was admitted to the bar of Allegheny county in 1896 and since then has practiced in Pittsburg, where he is a member of all courts and enjoys a lucrative legal business. Mr. Buckley has been prominently identified with municipal affairs, having served eighteen years as a member of the board of education and for almost five years represented the thirty-fourth ward in council. He was married at Pittsburg, in 1870, to Sarah McDavid, and they have five living children, viz.: Daniel J., a member of the bar and in the office with his father, born July 4, 1872; Ellen Nellie, born in September, 1876, and the wife of Peter Fosnight; Sarah Gertrude, born June 21, 1879; Laura Mabel, born April 1, 1883, and Nano Marie, born Dec. 6, 1884. Mrs. Buckley died on June 15, 1885, and Mr. Buckley was married the second time to Minnie H. Ziegler, by whom he has had three children: Minnie E. Z., born May 23, 1894; J. Dewey, born May 18, 1898, and Mary, born Nov. 9, 1903.

FRANK D. SAUPP, president of the Young Men's tariff club of Pittsburg and secretary and treasurer of the Pittsburg Physicians' supply company, is a prominent Pittsburg business man. He was born and reared at Loretto, Pa., and attended school there, afterwards completing his education at St. Francis' college, from which he graduated in 1881. He then went to Braddock, Pa., where he was employed for eight years in the mechanical engineering department of the Carnegie steel company. In 1897 he came to Pittsburg, and became secretary and treasurer of the Physicians' supply company. Besides being president of the Young Men's tariff club, which is a social rather than a political organization, Mr. Saupp is also a member of the Americus club, but belongs to no secret orders. In political belief he is a republican.

GEORGE H. STENGEL, register of wills, Pittsburg, has been for years a prominent member of the Pittsburg bar, and is known as a man of sturdy honesty, of an aggressive, able, and energetic nature. He is about forty-five years of age, and has been a resident of Pittsburg since 1864, with the exception of five years, from 1881 to 1886. After the usual preparatory education, he took a course of study at the Western University of Pennsylvania, going abroad to complete his education at the University of Heidelberg. He began practicing law in 1886, and is a man well equipped to perform those duties of his office which require a legal training. Mr. Stengel served in the Pittsburg common council from 1896 to 1898, and during this time stood openly for clean and honest government. Throughout his career he has always been actively connected with those who oppose dishonesty and extravagance in public office.

GEORGE WILLSON GOSSER, a member and secretary of the board of assessors of Pittsburg, was born in Pittsburg in 1853, attended school there, and, in 1867, graduated from the public schools. He then learned the machinists' trade and entered the employ of Carnegie & Co. He remained with this firm twenty-one years, until 1892, serving in various capacities, and was steadily advanced until, at the last, he was a roller, and had charge of the plate department. In 1892 Mr. Gosser organized the Lawrenceville (Pa.) bronze company, and has been secretary and treasurer of the organization from the first. He was elected a member of the board of assessors in 1897, and was re-elected in 1900. In 1895 he was elected a member of the school board and served four years. In the same year he was elected a member of the central board of education, was re-elected in 1897, and again in 1901. Mr. Gosser is a prominent member of the Masonic fraternity, in which he has attained the thirty-second degree, and is a Knight Templar and a Shriner. He is a member of the Presbyterian church.

CHARLES H. SACHS, of Pittsburg, Pa., a prominent attorney-at-law, with offices at No. 427 Diamond St., was born in Russia, Sept. 29, 1877, son of Hyman D. and Libbie Sachs, both natives of Russia. His father died in Pittsburg, May 7, 1900, and his mother now resides in that city. Charles H. Sachs accompanied his parents to the United States in 1883, located in Pittsburg, and received his literary training in the second ward school and at the academical department of Pittsburg high school. He matriculated at the Pittsburg law school, and there was graduated with the initial class of that institution in 1897. He was admitted to practice in Allegheny county, September, 1898, and now has a comfortable law business, being a member of all Pennsylvania courts and of the United States circuit court. On his admission to the bar, Mr. Sachs became a partner of Alexander Spiro, under the firm name of Spiro & Sachs; in September, 1901, H. C. Levey was admitted, and the name became Levey, Spiro & Sachs; in May, 1902, Mr. Spiro retired, and the firm was changed to Levey & Sachs; in April, 1903, that firm was dissolved, and since that time Mr. Sachs has maintained an independent office. He was the organizer of the Cosmopolitan National bank of Pittsburg, and for over a year was a member of its directorate. Mr. Sachs is a member of the Independent Order of B'nai B'rith, is unmarried, and resides in the seventh ward.

MALCOLM GRIERSON, of Pittsburg, Pa., a successful attorney, with offices in the Methodist Protestant building at No. 422 Fifth Ave., was born in Birmingham, England, Dec. 13, 1878, son of Donald and Celene Grierson. He came to America with his parents when only four years of age, located in Toronto, Canada, and four years later removed to Braddock, Pa. Mr. Grierson was educated in the graded and high schools of North Braddock, graduating from the latter institution in 1896, and then taught school in Allegheny county for several years, during which time he was also reading law in the office of Thomas Lawry. He was admitted to the bar of Allegheny county in September, 1901, and since has practiced in Pittsburg with much success. On March 1, 1903, Mr. Grierson became a partner of his former preceptor, Thomas Lawry, under the firm name of Lawry & Grierson, and they enjoy a splendid law business. Mr. Grierson resides in the borough of North Braddock, and is a prominent member of the First Methodist church of that borough and vice-president of the Epworth league of that church. Thomas Lawry, the senior member of the firm, was born at St. Ives, England, March 28, 1857, son of Henry and Mary Lawry, both natives of England and both deceased. Mr. Lawry came to America with his mother in 1864, his father having preceded them, and they located at Johnstown, Cambria Co., Pa. He was educated in the elementary courses in the public schools of Johnstown, and later attended the high school of Ann Arbor, Mich., where subsequently he was graduated from the law department of the University of Michigan with the degree of bachelor of laws. He was admitted to the bar of Michigan in 1892, soon after his graduation, and in September of that year was admitted to the bar of Allegheny county. He practiced his profession at Pittsburg until 1898, when he removed to Seattle, Wash., and resumed his practice in that city. Failing to become imbued with the "Seattle spirit," after a residence of two years on Puget sound, Mr. Lawry returned to Pittsburg, and has since met with much success in his professional career in the metropolis of western Pennsylvania. He served as solicitor for the borough of Braddock from March, 1896, to March, 1898, was also solicitor for the Braddock school board for two years and for five years was a justice of the peace of Braddock township. During his residence in that borough, Mr. Lawry also published a newspaper called the Braddock Journal, which was well received. He is a member of all courts in Pennsylvania and of the Masonic lodge at Ann Arbor, Mich. Mr. Lawry was married at Pittsburg, Pa., Feb. 19, 1903, to Mrs. Alice Aukerman, and their home life is an ideal one.

A. WALTER RINEHART, manager of the Postal telegraph-cable company, Pittsburg, was born in Pittsburg, in the fourth ward, in 1864. He is a son of Prof. Edward E. Rinehart, and grandson of Wm. Rinehart, one of the pioneers of Pittsburg. He was reared and educated in Pittsburg, graduating from the common schools in 1877. In 1886 he was married to Miss Mary F. Young, daughter of John and Mary Young. Mr. John Young is general superintendent of the Philadelphia heating company. To this union were born three sons, viz.: W. Wallace, A. Walter, Jr., and Jno. C. Mr. Rinehart began to learn telegraphy in 1877, and was employed until 1887 by the Baltimore & Ohio and the Western Union telegraph company. He then entered the office of the Postal telegraph-cable company, where he served six years as assistant chief operator and five years as night manager. His ability and attention to duty won him promotion in January, 1902, to the position of manager. Mr. Rinehart is a republican in political belief, and while never an aspirant for office, has always taken an active interest in the affairs of his party. He is a member of the Presbyterian church.

CHARLES B. McFAIL, manager of the Holmes electric protective company of Pittsburg, was born in Waterville, Me., in 1861, and, in 1873, moved with his parents to Presque Isle, Me. Mr. McFail then entered the employ of the American union telegraph company at Portland, Me., and was engaged by this company and others for several years in the construction of telegraph lines. He first became connected with the Holmes electric protective company in 1884, and has been in the employ of this company since then. Here his faithful services and native ability won him, in 1889, the position of manager, which he has since held. Mr. McFail is an ardent republican in politics, but while taking a great amount of interest in the welfare of his party, has never held office or cared for political preferment for himself. He is a member of the Masonic fraternity and of the Episcopal church.

WILLIAM F. WALSH, alderman from the thirty-fifth ward, Pittsburg, was born on a farm in Bedford county, Pa., in 1867. He is a son of William F. and Margaret (Morrissay) Walsh, and they were the parents of six children: Margaret, Thomas A., John E., Patrick J. and Mary A., all deceased, except Patrick J. and our subject, Wm. F. The father died July 6, 1888. The mother is still living in Pittsburg with her son, P. J. Our subject's parents brought him to Pittsburg in 1869, and there Mr. Walsh was raised and educated in the public schools. He attended school until he reached the age of eighteen, and then spent three years working for his father, William F. Walsh, a general contractor. Mr. Walsh was married, Aug. 15, 1889, to Mary J. Golden, daughter of Patrick and Mary Golden, and to whom was born one child, Richard J. After this he was employed at the Duquesne club, until March, 1900, when he was appointed to his present position by Governor Stone. Although appointed only to fill a vacancy, Mr. Walsh served his ward so well that in February, 1901, the voters elected him to the office for a five-year term. In politics he has long been an active republican. He is a member of the Knights of Maccabees. He and his wife belong to the Catholic church. Mr. Walsh, besides being alderman, is a prominent real estate and insurance man.

ROBERT J. H. MALONE is the eleventh of a family of thirteen children born by the marriage of William and Ruth Ann (Bevington) Malone, both of whom were natives of Washington county, Pa., in which they passed their entire lives, the father finally passing away at the age of seventy-four years and the mother in her seventy-ninth year. Of their large family, five were sons and eight were daughters, all of whom grew to maturity, though two of the sons and three of the daughters are now deceased. The subject of this sketch was born, Dec. 2, 1853, on a farm near the present village of Bulger, on the Pittsburg, Cincinnati, Chicago & St. Louis railroad, in Washington county. In youth he manifested a strong inclination for an education, and applied himself diligently at the public school near his home. He finally entered Sewickley academy, then being conducted by Prof. and Mrs. James Dickson, took a full course and was duly graduated therefrom; but during this period ceased his attendance long enough to teach a term of school at his old home. Succeeding his graduation, he was elected assistant principal of the Sewickley public schools, and the following year was chosen principal of the public schools of Tarentum, in which capacity he officiated for the period of three years. He then resigned in order to accept higher duties and responsibilities as principal of the public schools of Etna, Pa., and as such served acceptably for five years, adding much to the efficiency of the educational system of that town. He finally resigned his school duties in order to take up the study of law, in 1884, in the office of H. T. Watson, on Diamond street, Pittsburg, and there he remained hard at work until April, 1887, when he was duly admitted to the bar. On April 1, 1888, he and William J. Barton took offices together in the Yoder law building, at the corner of Fifth and Wylie avenues, and there they have remained associated ever since, receiving a fair patronage from the public. During his active career as a lawyer he has served as school director in the borough of Etna for twelve years, and was at one time borough solicitor. In 1902, when the First National bank of Etna was organized, he became a stockholder therein, and was elected its president, which important position he continues to fill. Soon after his admission to the bar, he married Miss Jennie L. Meyer, of Sharpsburg, Pa., and took up his residence in Etna, and there they have continued to reside. To their marriage the following children have been born: Elsie M., Robert W. (deceased), Stanley H., Roy E., Bernice K. and Lillian Hope. Mr. Malone is a member of the Heptasophs and of Etna Borough council, R. A. He is identified with the United Presbyterian church of Etna.

JOHN J. McALINNEY, of Pittsburg, Pa., a successful young attorney, with offices at No. 1105 Frick building, was born in County Tyrone, Ulster province, Ireland, Oct. 11, 1878, son of Bernard and Mary Ann (O'Brien) McAlinney, both natives of County Tyrone, Ireland, and residents of Pittsburg since 1880. His parents had ten children, three of whom died in infancy, and the surviving ones, exclusive of himself, are: Joseph M., Isabel T., Margaret, Rose E., Bernard E. and Bessie. John J. McAlinney, when but two years of age, accompanied his parents to the United States, settled in Pittsburg, and since has made that city his home. He acquired his rudimentary education in the public schools, later attended the central high school, and was there graduated in 1899. He then read law in the office of L. M. Plumer, a well-known attorney of Pittsburg, and subsequently attended the Pittsburg law school, where he was graduated with the class of 1902 and received the degree of bachelor of laws. He was admitted to the bar on June 21, 1902, began the practice in July of that year and is now regarded as one of the most successful and best-equipped of the younger members of the Pittsburg bar. Mr. McAlinney is well versed in the principles of law, and this knowledge, combined with the native wit and ability so characteristic of the Irish race, makes him a worthy opponent in the forensic field and assures him much success in his chosen profession.

JOHN PIERCE, assistant to Theodore J. Shaffer, president of the Amalgamated association of iron, steel and tin workers of the United States and Canada, was born in County Wexford, Ireland, in 1845. He came with his parents to America in 1848, the family locating first at Chartiers, Allegheny Co., Pa., and then moving, in 1854, to Grand Rapids, Mich. Here both parents of Mr. Pierce died, the mother in 1858 and the father in 1862. The boy came to Pittsburg, beginning work on Oct. 10, 1862, in the nail department of Jones & Laughlin's iron mill. Mr. Pierce remained in the employ of Jones & Laughlin until Aug. 6, 1897, beginning as a nail feeder, and ending as roller in the plate mill. After this he spent a year in Birmingham, Ala., and then gave up active work to devote his attention to the association of which Mr. Shaffer is president. Mr. Pierce first joined the Amalgamated association of steel, iron and tin workers of the United States and Canada in 1877, was elected trustee in 1899, and assumed his present position as assistant to President Shaffer in June, 1900. In religious belief he is a Catholic, and in politics a democrat. He served as school director from the twenty-fourth ward, Pittsburg, for three years, from 1884 to 1887.

JOHN CARNEY, funeral director in Pittsburg, was born at St. Johns, N. B., in 1845, and came to Boston, Mass., with his parents, when six months old. Here he lived until his eighth year, moving then to Brady's Bend, Armstrong county, where he attended school, and resided until 1865. At the age of fifteen he went to work in the rolling mill of the Brady's Bend iron company, remaining with this firm five years, and being employed at the last as a rougher. In 1865 he came to Pittsburg, became a heater for Jones & Laughlin, and remained with this firm until 1898, when he went into the undertaking business, at which he has since been engaged. He is a Catholic in religious belief, and a democrat in politics.

Mr. Carney's son, John J. Carney, who is nominally the head of the undertaking establishment now located at No. 2526 Carson St., South Side, Pittsburg, was born in the twenty-fifth ward, Pittsburg, in 1872. He was reared and educated in Pittsburg, attending the public schools, and afterwards the Holy Ghost college, from which he graduated. Having completed his education, he became timekeeper in the Bessemer department of the Jones & Laughlin iron mill; was employed there about two years, and then, in September, 1895, embarked in the undertaking business, which has been his occupation since then. Mr. Carney passed the required examination in January, 1896.

CLARENCE LEMOYNE PHILLIS, of Pittsburg, Pa., a successful architect, was born in upper St. Clair township, Allegheny Co., Pa., April 6, 1852, son of William T. and Hannah Little (Arneel) Phillis. His paternal ancestors were German, and the great-grandfather of the subject of this sketch, Joseph Phillis, was the first member of the family to settle in that part of Pennsylvania. Joseph was a window glass blower, and located at what is now the South Side of Pittsburg, where he reared his family, consisting of two sons and a daughter, viz.: Jacob Joseph, Lewis, and Susan, who married a man by the name of Ryan. Jacob Joseph Phillis, grandfather of Clarence L., married a Miss Verner, and their only child was William T., the father of the subject. William T. Phillis was born in the vicinity of Temperanceville, Allegheny Co., Pa., and when quite young lost both of his parents through death, his father having been drowned in the Ohio river, at the confluence of Saw Mill run, about 1826. William T. Phillis was adopted by his mother's family, where he remained until about eighteen years of age, when he became a soldier in the Mexican war. After that war he returned to the vicinity of Pittsburg and engaged in steamboating on the lower river until 1861. He then enlisted for a three-year service in the Union army, and, at the expiration of his term of service, re-enlisted and served throughout the remaining days of that sanguinary struggle. Later he returned to South Side, Pittsburg, was employed by Jones & Laughlin for some time, and died on Sept. 27, 1872. His wife died on July 13, 1879. Their children were: Margaret Ellen, Clarence L., William H., Mary A. and Franklin S. (deceased). The following genealogical table is taken from the family Bible of Mr. Phillis' maternal grandmother, Margaret E. Holmes, who was born in County Tyrone, Ireland, in 1779, viz.: William Holmes married Jane Neal, in 1673, and they had two children: Katie, born Oct. 8, 1674; James, born in 1676. William Holmes died in 1695, at the age of forty-seven years, and Jane Neal Holmes died in 1707, aged fifty-four years. Katie Holmes married Robert Carnahan, in 1693, but no children to this union are recorded. James Holmes married Ellen Graham, in 1706, and to them were born: Twin boys, in 1707, both of whom died in infancy; John, on July 13, 1709; Margaret, in 1712; Thomas, in 1714. James Holmes and his son, John, were lost at sea in 1727; Margaret died in 1718, and Ellen Graham Holmes died in 1739, at the age of sixty-two years. Thomas Holmes married Hannah Little, in 1740, and their children were: James, born 1742, date of death missing; Ellen, born 1745; Margaret, born 1748; William H., born 1750; John, born 1753. Thomas Holmes died in 1786, Hannah Little Holmes in 1772, and Ellen married Hugh Marshall, in 1766, but left no children. Margaret Holmes married David Gray, in 1771, and died, in 1793, without recorded issue. John Holmes married Mary Kincaid, in 1776, and their children were: John, born in 1778; James, born in 1781. Mary (Kincaid) Holmes died in 1789, and her husband married Catherine Wallace, in 1793, she being a widow with one son, Harry Wallace, and they had the following children: William M., born 1795; Thomas H., born 1797; Margaret E., born 1799, and John and James, with no record of date of birth. Catherine (Wallace) Holmes died in 1822, but the date of the death of her husband is not shown. William M. Holmes died in 1878, aged eighty-three years, and was buried in Iowa. No record of marriage or death of Thomas Holmes. Margaret E. Holmes married John Arneel, in 1821, and their children were: Mary, born 1824; Hannah, born 1826; Margaret J., born 1828. John Arneel died on the voyage from Ireland to America, and was buried in Canada, about 1830, and his widow married James Stewart, in 1847, by whom she had no children. Margaret E. (Arneel) Stewart died on April 14, 1869, at the age of seventy years, and her husband, James Stewart, died Oct. 19, 1871. Hannah L. Arneel married William T. Phillis, in 1849, and their children were: Margaret E., born May 30, 1850, married a Mr. W. T. Powell, and died on May 28, 1891; Clarence L., subject of this sketch, born April 6, 1852; William H., born Oct. 29, 1854; Mary A., born June 5, 1857; Franklin S., born Oct. 24, 1859, and died Sept. 16, 1877. Clarence L. Phillis received a common-school education, and began his business career in a rolling mill, where he remained for four years. Later he learned the trade of carpentering and followed that line of work for a number of years. Subsequently he returned to the rolling mill, where for a time he was in charge of the mechanical operations of the mill. For the past twelve years he has followed his present vocation of architecture, and has met with success in that profession. Mr. Phillis has been married three times. He was first married to Rachael Hermany, and they had three children: John Franklin, an architect, born Dec. 26, 1876, and married, on Oct. 9, 1902, Estella M., daughter of Alexander W. and Caroline Douds, of Turtle Creek, Pa.; Alice Leah, born in March, 1878, and Hugh, who died in infancy. Mr. Phillis was married on the second occasion to Mary S. Shoemaker, by whom he had one son, Clarence M., born June 24, 1889. His third marriage was with Mrs. Caroline (Brehm) Keitz, a widow with one son, William, and their wedded life is an ideal one.

CHRISTOPHER MAGEE, Jr., of Pittsburg, Pa., a prominent attorney, was born in that city, Oct. 3, 1863, son of Christopher and Elizabeth Louise (McLeod) Magee. Christopher Magee, Sr., was born in Pittsburg, Dec. 5, 1829, and is the son of Christopher and Jane (Watson) Magee. He is a graduate of the Western university, and also of the University of Pennsylvania at Philadelphia, from which institution he was graduated in the classics in 1849, and from the law department in 1851. He entered on a successful practice in Allegheny county, secured and maintained high rank as an advocate and counselor, and, in 1886, was appointed judge of the court of common pleas by Governor Patterson. In the fall of that year he was elected to succeed himself in that position for a term of ten years. He also served in the State legislature and in the common council, and is still in the active practice of law, being one of the oldest and most respected members of the Allegheny county bar association. Christopher

Magee, Jr., received his classical education at the University of Pennsylvania, graduating in the class of 1887. He then read law in the office of Judge Dallas, of Philadelphia, and was graduated from the law department of the University of Pennsylvania, in 1889, with the degree of bachelor of laws, the degree of bachelor of arts having been previously awarded him by his alma mater. Since then Mr. Magee has devoted his entire attention to his profession, and stands high at the bar. He was married at Bridgeton, N. J., on June 1, 1892, to Julia Vodges, daughter of Rev. Edward P. and Carrie (Titus) Heberton, and the following children have been born to them: Christopher, on March 28, 1893; Margaret Mitchell, on Jan. 4, 1895; Helen Heberton, on April 27, 1897; Norman Heberton, on Dec. 31, 1900, and Julia Heberton, in September, 1902. Mr. Magee is a member of the Presbyterian church, and is identified with its efforts toward the elevation and betterment of the human family.

EDSON KIMMEY, superintendent of the Postal telegraph-cable company at Pittsburg, was born in Albany, N. Y., in 1868, and resided there until 1885, when he graduated from the Albany high school. He then went to work for the Baltimore & Ohio telegraph company, entered the employ of the Commercial Union telegraph company in 1886, and was engaged for a time in establishing various offices in the northern part of New York. In 1887 he became operator for the Baltimore & Ohio at Long Branch, N. J., and, in the same year, was sent to New York city, where he was employed as operator to the superintendent of the metropolitan district of the company. In 1888 he entered the employ of the Postal telegraph-cable company, as operator in New York. His rise since that time has been deservedly rapid. In 1893 he became manager at Albany, N. Y.; was sent to Pittsburg in the same capacity in 1900, and, in March, 1902, became superintendent of the Pittsburg district. This district includes West Virginia, and extends on the north to the New York State line, and on the east to Altoona, Pa., and Hancock, Md. Mr. Kimmey is a member of the Blue lodge, F. and A. M.

CHARLES F. ANDERSON, alderman from the fourth ward, Pittsburg, was born in the ward which he now represents, Aug. 12, 1849. His father, Robert Anderson, a prominent man in his time, was appointed postmaster of Pittsburg, in 1852, and served six years. The subject of this sketch was reared and educated in Pittsburg, and left school at seventeen years of age to learn the moulder's trade, at which he worked until 1874. He first entered the employ of the city in 1878, and has since that time held many responsible public positions. From 1878 to 1880 he was clerk in the office of the city treasurer; from 1880 to 1887 clerk in the office of the county commissioners. He was appointed clerk in the office of William H. Barclay, United States pension agent, where he remained four years, and then went into the office of Bernard McKenna, who was at that time alderman from the fourth ward. In 1893 Mr. Anderson was appointed alderman to succeed Mr. McKenna, who had resigned to become mayor of the city. In February, 1894, he was elected to the same office for a five-year term, and, in 1899, was re-elected. Mr. Anderson is a democrat in political belief. He is a member of the Catholic church.

CORNELIUS F. FORD, captain of Station No. 5, Pittsburg police force, is a native of the eleventh ward, Pittsburg, and has been on the police force of that city since 1889. Captain Ford was born in March, 1854; received a common-school education, and at sixteen years of age went to work for a wholesale liquor firm. He was employed by this firm about two years, and then, for several years, held a position in a rolling mill. In 1889 he resigned to accept an appointment as patrolman, serving in this capacity until 1901, when he was promoted to the position of captain. Captain Ford is a republican in politics. He is a member of the Roman Catholic church.

THEODORE RAYBERT McLAIN, chief clerk to the collector of delinquent taxes, city of Pittsburg, was born at Johnstown, Pa., in 1874. Moving in infancy to Punxsutawney, Pa., with his parents, he lived there the first seven years of his life, the family moving then to Greensborough, N. C., where they remained until 1884. Coming with his parents to Pittsburg, Mr. McLain attended the public schools, and, in 1891, graduated from the high school. He then entered the office of collector of delinquent taxes as clerk, and was, in 1899, promoted to the position of chief clerk in that office, the position which he now holds. In politics he is a republican. He is a member of the Sixth Presbyterian church. Mr. McLain became a private in Company E, 14th regiment, Pennsylvania national guard, in 1889, and served ten years, passing through all the grades until he attained the position of first lieutenant. In the Spanish-American war he accompanied his regiment as second lieutenant of Company B, and was mustered out at Summerville, S. C., Feb. 28, 1899, with the rank of regimental adjutant.

JOHN K. DORRINGTON, a retired coal man, of Pittsburg, was born, Jan. 10, 1828, on a farm near Carnegie, Allegheny Co., Pa.; came to Pittsburg in infancy, and was there reared and given a primary education in the ward school. Afterwards he spent two years at Frankfort academy. In 1849 he took the overland route to California, where he worked for three years in the gold mines. In the fall of 1852 he returned to Pittsburg by the Nicaragua route. In 1855 he was married to Miss Elizabeth M. Hezlep, of Allegheny city; went to Minnesota, and settled on a farm near St. Peter, on the Minnesota river. In 1862 a fierce rebellion broke out among the Sioux Indians at Fort Ridgely, near New Ulm. He shouldered his gun, and with some of his neighbors started for New Ulm, where the frontier settlers were concentrating to give battle to the Indians. The next day after the arrival at New Ulm, the Indians surrounded the town, and the battle commenced, lasting forty hours. The Indians were defeated, the town saved from devastation, and the women and children from massacre. In 1864 he sold his property in Minnesota, returned to Pittsburg, and went into the river coal business, continuing in the same for thirty-two years. In 1896 he retired from active business.

EDWARD STANLEY CORLETT, superintendent of East Liberty station, Pittsburg postoffice, was born on the Isle of Man in 1870, and in infancy came to America with his parents. The family located first at Elizabeth, Allegheny county, then moved to a farm near Homestead, and afterwards to Homestead. The subject of this sketch received a common-school education in the Homestead schools, and when ten years old, went to work in a glass factory. He spent two years in the glass factory, two years on a farm, and then became timekeeper and weigh-master in the open hearth department of the Carnegie steel company's plant at Homestead. He gave up this position in 1890, and, coming to Pittsburg, spent a year in the night school of the Iron City business college. He took the civil service examination, and was appointed as messenger in the registry department of the Pittsburg postoffice. Mr. Corlett has been employed in the postal service ever since, and has risen rapidly to his present important position. In 1892 he was made special delivery clerk, and as such had charge of all the city special delivery service. In 1898 he became weighmaster, and about a year later, when the present postmaster, George L. Holliday, came into office, Mr. Corlett was made superintendent of Station C, on the South Side. Here he remained until July, 1902, when he was transferred to his present place, which, in point of business, ranks above all other stations in the city. Mr. Corlett is a Mason, and belongs to the Blue lodge. He is a member of the East End board of trade.

PATRICK DOLAN, president of District No. 5, United Mine Workers of Pennsylvania, was born of Scotch-Irish parents, at Court Bridge, Lanarkshire, Scotland, in 1858, and came to America in 1886, locating at McDonald, Pa. Mr. Dolan began working in the mines in Scotland when only eight years old, and, on coming to McDonald, continued to work as a miner until 1896, when he was elected president of District No. 5. In this capacity he has served so faithfully and shown such a fitness for the position, that he has been re-elected each year—in 1901 and 1902—without opposition. On Dec. 12, 1901, at a convention of the American Federation of Labor held at Scranton, Pa., Mr. Dolan was elected, without opposition, as one of the two delegates from America to the meeting of the British trades congress, which was held in England in September, 1902. Mr. Dolan is a member of Lodge No. 11, B. P. O. E., of Pittsburg; Fort Pitt conclave, Independent Order of Heptasophs, Old Glory chapter, American Insurance Union, Knights of Maccabees and Ancient Order of Hibernians. He belongs to the Roman Catholic church, and in political belief he is a republican.

JEREMIAH CARNEY, of Pittsburg, Pa., a successful lawyer, with offices on Diamond street, was born in Allegheny city, Pa., Dec. 12, 1870, son of John J. and Jane (Evans) Carney, both residing at South Side, Pittsburg. Mr. Carney was educated in the thorough public schools of Pittsburg and at Curry university. Then he read law in the offices of Walter Lyon, a prominent lawyer and former lieutenant-governor of Pennsylvania, and was admitted to the bar on Sept. 17, 1892. Since then Mr. Carney has practiced in Pittsburg with much success, is a member of all courts, and holds a position of honor and respectability among the attorneys of Allegheny county. He was married in Allegheny city, Feb. 25, 1896, to Emma Whitney, and their home life is a pleasant one. Mr. Carney is a member of the Junior Order of United American Mechanics and of the Knights of Pythias. He is a resident of Knoxville, Pa., and is serving his second term as a councilman of that borough.

WILLIAM MONROE BENHAM, an attorney of Pittsburg, Pa., was born on April 8, 1866, in Auburn, N. Y., a son of De Witt C. and Cynthia A. Benham. His forefathers were early settlers on this continent, his ancestor, John Benham, coming to America from England in 1630 on the ship "Mary and John," and making his home in New England. Mr. Benham received his preliminary education in the public schools of New Brighton, Beaver Co., Pa., and was graduated from Geneva college, Pa., in the class of 1887, being awarded the general excellency prize for the highest grade of any student in the institution during that year. Having pursued the classical course, the degree of bachelor of arts was conferred upon him. In the autumn of 1889 he entered the law department of Columbia university, New York city, where he remained during the prescribed time of three years, being graduated therefrom in June, 1892, with the degree of bachelor of laws *cum laude*. At the commencement exercises the committee on awards presented him with the first prize of $250 for greatest knowledge and highest attainments in his law studies. While at Columbia, Mr. Benham read law in the office of Carter, Hughes & Kellogg, of New York city, and at a general term of the supreme court of the State of New York, held in the city of New York on Dec. 7, 1891, was admitted to practice in the several courts of that State. During his first year at Columbia, he was elected president of his class, consisting of 250 members, and upon the resignation of Dr. Theodore Dwight as warden of the law department, in June, 1891, he was selected by his classmates to present to Dr. Dwight a handsomely embossed memorial. Mr. Benham, after receiving his diploma from Columbia, in June, 1892, returned to Pittsburg, where, in September of that year, he took the prescribed examination and was admitted to the Allegheny county bar. He at once commenced the practice of his profession in Pittsburg, and in due time was admitted to practice in the supreme and superior courts of Pennsylvania and in the United States circuit and district courts. He has met with success in his profession, having a large clientage both in the civil and criminal courts, besides representing a number of corporations. Mr. Benham enjoys the trial of cases, and before a jury is a forcible and effective speaker. Mr. Benham belongs to several organizations. He is a member of the Knights of the Ancient Essenic Order, and in the year of 1901 was elected supreme senator of the order, the highest office in the country. He belongs to the Masonic fraternity, being a member of Crescent lodge, No. 576, of Pittsburg, and also of Pennsylvania consistory, which gives him the thirty-second degree in Masonry. He is also a member of Pittsburg lodge, No. 11, B. P. O. Elks, the Allegheny county bar association and the University club. Politically, Mr. Benham is a republican, and has for years performed effective work on the stump for his party. He has held several offices in his party, having been president of his district organization, member of the county committee, and is at present on the twentieth ward committee and one of the three committeemen from that ward. He has been a delegate to various republican conventions, and has presided over a number of them and upon several occasions has placed in nomination certain candidates for office. Mr. Benham is called upon very frequently to deliver public addresses of various kinds, as he is a fluent and eloquent speaker.

JOHN WILLOCK BROWN, of Pittsburg, Pa., a rising young attorney, was born on the South Side, Pittsburg, Oct. 4, 1879, a son of James and Mary Elizabeth (Willock) Brown. His father is a native of Allegheny county, and was for several years prominent as a business man of the South Side. In October, 1897, he, with his father and family, removed to Wilkinsburg, Pa., where he and his father engaged in the real estate business and became well known as successful real estate brokers. His mother is a native of Allegheny county and a member of the Willock family, which is very prominent and influential in the county. John Willock Brown was educated in the schools of Pittsburg, having attended the twenty-eighth ward and the Pittsburg high school, graduating from the latter institution in 1897. During the following year his attention was devoted to post-graduate study. In September, 1899, he began the study of the law in the office of Brown & Stewart, prominent attorneys of Pittsburg, and also attended the Pittsburg law school, where he was graduated with the class of 1902. Subsequently he was admitted to the bar of his native county and State, and since has devoted his talents and energies to his profession, in which he has met with considerable encouragement and achieved a splendid standing among the younger attorneys of Allegheny county.

WILLIAM KAUFMAN, of Pittsburg, Pa., a successful practitioner of law, with offices at No. 413 Fourth Ave., was born at No. 16 Cedar Ave., Allegheny city, Pa., Nov. 9, 1871, son of Simon and Sibilla (Marks) Kaufman, the former a native of Germany, who settled in Pittsburg in 1849, and for many years was successfully engaged in the manufacture of clothing. He died in Allegheny city, May 10, 1900, and is survived by his wife, who is also a native of Germany, and now resides in Allegheny city. William Kaufman was educated in the elementary branches in the schools of Allegheny city, graduating from the high school in 1887, and subsequently spent two years at the Western University of Pennsylvania. He then matriculated in the law department of the University of Michigan, at Ann Arbor, and was graduated from that sterling institution in 1891. He took a special course at Harvard law school, was admitted to the bar of Allegheny county, September, 1892, and since has continuously practiced in Pittsburg, where he is a member of all courts and of the Allegheny county bar association. Mr. Kaufman has rapidly established himself in the practice of his profession, and now stands well among the attorneys of Pittsburg. He is recognized as an able and careful counselor and an active and aggressive advocate, and enjoys a fine practice. He is a member of Allegheny lodge, No. 223, F. and A. M.; Park lodge, No. 973, I. O. O. F., and Hope lodge, No. 243, K. of P. Mr. Kaufman served as president of the Concordia club of Allegheny city for two years, and is now a member of the governing council of that organization.

ANDREW WATSON FORSYTH, of Pittsburg, Pa., a well-known attorney-at-law, was born in St. Louis, Mo., Oct. 14, 1874, son of William R. and Jeannette (Black) Forsyth. His father was born about 1849, and died at Pittsburg in 1885, and his mother was born in Allegheny county, and died at Pittsburg in 1897. Andrew W. Forsyth accompanied his parents to Pittsburg when a mere infant, and was reared and educated in that city, attending the graded and high schools and the Western university. He is a graduate of both the classical and law departments of the Western university—from the former in 1897 and from the latter in 1900. Since then Mr. Forsyth has practiced his profession at Pittsburg, where he is a member of all courts and enjoys a lucrative practice.

ALBERT P. MEYER, one of the younger attorneys of the Allegheny county bar, is certainly one who is worthy of mention in these volumes. Shakespeare has said that "Some men are born great, some achieve greatness and some have greatness thrust upon them." Whatever degree of greatness Albert P. Meyer may have reached, has been achieved by untiring industry and the exercise of superior judgment. He is the son of William C. and Sophia Meyer, and was born at Sharpsburg, Pa., Oct. 26, 1876. His early education was obtained in the public schools of his native town, and after a brief term in the preparatory school of the city of Pittsburg, he began the study of law in the office of ex-Governor Stone. On June 8, 1901, he was admitted to practice at the bar of Allegheny county, and since that time he has been engaged in the active practice of his chosen profession. He was married, June 21, 1902, at Lisbon, Ohio, to Miss Ella G. Miller, a resident of the city of Cleveland. His offices are at No. 202 Bakewell building.

GEORGE L. ROBERTS, of Pittsburg, Pa., a distinguished attorney, with offices in the Park building, was born in Rushford, Allegany Co., N. Y., Jan. 7, 1852, son of Benjamin Titus and Ellen (Stow) Roberts. He acquired his early education in the schools of Buffalo, and later graduated at the University of Rochester, New York. Then he removed to South America, where for five years he was in the employ of the Argentine government. Subsequently he returned to the United States and read law in the offices of Wallace Brown and M. F. Elliott, of Bradford, McKean Co., Pa., where he was admitted to the bar in 1880. He practiced in that county with much success until 1895, when he removed to Pittsburg, was admitted to the Allegheny county bar, and since has been continuously in the practice at Pittsburg and in West Virginia. He was admitted to the bar of West Virginia in 1895, and

GEORGE L. ROBERTS.   CHARLES G. CARTER.   DAVID E MITCHELL.

devotes a considerable part of his time to practice in that State. He is a member of all courts, the Allegheny county and the Pennsylvania State bar associations, and is senior member of the prominent law firm of Roberts & Carter. He is president of the Bradford, Bordell & Kinzua railway company, and is a member of the chamber of commerce and of the Pittsburg country club. Mr. Roberts was married at Wilcox, Pa., Jan. 8, 1888, to Winnifred, daughter of John L. and Mary Murphy, and their home life is happy and halcyon. Charles Gibbs Carter, member of the law firm of Roberts & Carter, was born at Titusville, Pa., April 14, 1867, son of Col. John J. and Emma (Gibbs) Carter. He was educated in the public schools of Titusville and at Phillips academy, of Andover, Mass., where he was graduated in 1887. Subsequently he matriculated at Yale university and was graduated from that famous college in 1891, with the degree of bachelor of arts. He then studied law in the office of Mortimer F. Elliott, of Wellsboro, Tioga Co., Pa., and at the University of Virginia, and was admitted to the bar of Tioga county in 1893, to the bar of Allegheny county in 1894, and also to the bar of West Virginia the same year. He is a member of all courts in Pennsylvania and West Virginia and practices in both States. Mr. Carter is a member of the Duquesne, Union, Pittsburg law, Yale and Automobile clubs, and is also a member of the Pittsburg chamber of commerce. He was married in Pittsburg, Jan. 6, 1900, to Elizabeth, daughter of George P. and Hannah B. (Fahnestock) McBride, and they have had two daughters, Emma and Mary, the former dying in infancy. Mr. Carter is one of Pittsburg's prominent citizens and resides in the twentieth ward. David E. Mitchell, an associate member of the law firm of Roberts & Carter, was born in Titusville, Pa., Jan. 15, 1876, son of Claude and Dora (Eaton) Mitchell, the former being cashier of the Bradford National bank, of Bradford, Pa., and the latter dying on Aug. 15, 1895. Mr. Mitchell was educated in the rudimentary branches in the graded and high schools of Bradford and completed his classical training at Harvard university, where he was graduated in 1897 with the degree of bachelor of arts. He then entered Harvard law school, was there graduated in 1899 with the degree of bachelor of laws, and was admitted to the bar of Allegheny county in 1900. Since that time Mr. Mitchell has been continuously in the practice at Pittsburg, where he is a member of several courts and enjoys a fine law business.

ARTHUR D. RODGERS, of Pittsburg, Pa., a well-known young attorney, with offices at No. 222 Bakewell building, was born in that city, May 8, 1875, son of Hugh H. and Martha (MacGinnis) Rodgers, both now residing at McKee's Rocks, Pa. His father has retired from active life, but during his business career was prominent as a mechanical engineer, and is well known in McKee's Rocks and that section of the county. His parents had six children, viz.: John H. (deceased), George G., Robert G., Hugh H., Isabel and Arthur D. Mr. Rodgers' ancestors, both paternal and maternal, were members of the colonial families of America, and both of his grandfathers were soldiers in the patriot army during the American Revolution. Arthur D. Rodgers acquired his classical education in the schools of Pittsburg and under the tuition of Rev. Charles Hogue, an Episcopal clergyman. Then he read law in the office of Thomas Patterson, a leading attorney of Pittsburg, and attended the Pittsburg law school, where he was graduated, in 1901, with the degree of bachelor of laws. Mr. Rodgers entered upon the practice of his profession shortly after graduating, and has met with much success in the law. He is a bright and energetic young man, and is destined to succeed well in his vocation.

JOHN MORRISON HUNTER, of Pittsburg, Pa., a distinguished attorney-at-law, was born in Cowanshannock township, Armstrong Co., Pa., Sept. 19, 1850, son of James and Susan (Kinley) Hunter, both natives of Westmoreland county, Pa. James Hunter, father of the subject, was a son of James Hunter, a native of Ireland, and was born on Dec. 18, 1818. He spent his entire life in the Keystone State, and was prosperously engaged in farming and blacksmithing. Susan Kinley was descended from the Cunninghams on the maternal side, her mother having been Mary Cunningham and a member of a prominent family. John M. Hunter acquired his education in the common schools of Indiana county, and at the academies at Covode, Indiana and Elder's Ridge, Pa. He then read law in the office of Edward S. Golden, of Kittanning, Pa., and was admitted to the bar of Armstrong county, Nov. 23, 1873, where he practiced with much success for a number of years. In October, 1888, Mr. Hunter was admitted to the Allegheny county bar, and since has practiced continuously in Pittsburg, where he has achieved high standing as an attorney and is regarded as one of the ablest members of the Allegheny county bar. Mr. Hunter is a member of all courts and controls a magnificent practice. He was married in Armstrong county, Pa., July 4, 1892, to Belle, daughter of Frank and Mary Powell, of Armstrong county, Pa., and they have had four children, James B., Mary G., A. Marion and Grace V. Mr. Hunter and his family are members of the First Presbyterian church of Oakmont, of which organization he has been a trustee for fifteen years.

CHRISTIAN F. OYER, alderman from the eleventh ward, Pittsburg, was born, Sept. 16, 1850, within a block of where he now has his office. His parents were both natives of Prussia, who came to America early in the past century. His father, Christian Oyer, was for many years engaged in the manufacture of cigars and chewing tobacco. Christian F. Oyer, the subject of this sketch, attended school until he reached the age of fifteen, when his father's death made it necessary for him to go to work. He worked at his father's trade as a journeyman until 1875, and then went into business for himself. In 1895 he was elected alderman, in which capacity he so pleased his constituents that they re-elected him in 1900. Since giving up the tobacco business, Alderman Oyer has devoted his attention to real estate and insurance. From 1893 to 1899 he served on the school board, representing the eleventh ward, his father having also been a school director for nine years. Alderman Oyer is a member of the Heptasophs, Jr. O. U. A. M., Knights of Pythias and Improved Order of Red Men. In religious belief he is a Lutheran, and in politics an ardent republican.

STEPHEN J. TOOLE, alderman from the first ward, Pittsburg, was born in New Orleans, La., in 1859, but came to Pittsburg in infancy, and was there reared and educated. He attended school until he reached the age of thirteen, selling papers on the streets after school hours, and later was employed for five years, folding papers in the office of the Pittsburg Daily Chronicle. After this he went into a boiler factory, and there learned the sheet iron workers' trade, being engaged at this vocation until 1885, when he became a professional baseball player. Mr. Toole was a well-known baseball player for five years, was a member of the American association, and played on the clubs of Brooklyn, Kansas City and Rochester. Giving up baseball, he entered the public service as wharfmaster of Pittsburg, and held this position until February, 1893. In February, 1892, he was appointed alderman by Governor Pattison, and was elected to the office a year afterwards. His well-deserved popularity next won him re-election in 1898. Mr. Toole is worthy past president junior of the Pittsburg Aerie, No. 76, Fraternal Order of Eagles. He is a member of the Catholic church.

ANDREW S. MILLER, of Pittsburg, Pa., a distinguished attorney-at-law, with offices at No. 409 Grant St., was born in Chartiers township, Washington Co., Pa., April 8, 1844, son of Thomas and Annie (Reed) Miller. Mr. Miller received his early education in the common schools of Washington county, later attended the academy at Hickory, Pa., and was graduated from Washington and Jefferson college in 1869. Then he attended the Columbia law school of New York city, subsequently read law in the office of Maj. A. M. Brown, of Pittsburg, and was admitted to the bar of Allegheny county in 1873. He has been in continuous practice in Pittsburg since that time, and is now one of the oldest and ablest practitioners of the county. He controls a splendid practice and is a member of all courts. Mr. Miller has been a member of the Bellevue school board for four years, two years of which time he served as its president. He was also a member of Bellevue council for three years, and held the position of director of the poor for Allegheny county for two years. In 1862 Mr. Miller enlisted in the 123d Pennsylvania volunteers, participated in the battles of Fredericksburg, Antietam, Chancellorsville and other important engagements, and was mustered out in August, 1863. He is now a member of the John B. Clark post, No. 162, of the Grand Army of the Republic, and takes an active interest in its affairs. He was married in Allegheny city, April 15, 1873, to Elizabeth A. Reed, and they have three sons: Thomas A., a prominent physician of Bellevue; Harry A., clerk in the Union National bank of Pittsburg, and Frank B., a student of Washington and Jefferson college. Mr. Miller and his family are members of the United Presbyterian church, in which organization Mr. Miller holds the position of an elder.

WALTER R. BLACK, chief clerk to the Hon. J. O. Brown, recorder of Pittsburg, was born in Saltsburg, Indiana Co., Pa., Nov. 15, 1867. In 1872 his parents moved to Tarentum, Allegheny county, and there the subject of this sketch was reared and educated. He graduated from the Tarentum schools in 1882, tutored two years, and then taught five years in the public schools at Tarentum and other places in Allegheny county. Mr. Black came to Pittsburg in 1890, obtaining the position of registration clerk in the office of the bureau of health. Here he remained three years, and, in 1893, was made chief clerk in the bureau of fire. He held this position until February, 1900, when he returned to the bureau of health as chief clerk, and, on Dec. 1, 1901, was appointed to the responsible position which he has since held. Mr. Black is a member of the Blue lodge in Masonry. In religious belief he is a Methodist, and is a prominent member of the Methodist Episcopal church of Tarentum, in which he has served as trustee, and, since 1898, as Sunday-school superintendent. He is also assistant superintendent of the Sunday-schools of the Asbury Methodist Episcopal church in Pittsburg.

DANIEL J. McCARTHY, who, at the time of his death, was jury commissioner of Allegheny county, was born in England in 1861, but spent almost all his life in America. Coming to Braddock, Allegheny county, in 1863, he was reared in that city, and attended school until he reached the age of fourteen, when he started to learn the printers' trade. From a printer he became a journalist, and, in 1881, started in Braddock a weekly paper, which he called the Tribune, continuing the publication of this paper until 1891. In 1890 Mr. McCarthy bought the News, a Braddock daily paper, and ran this paper until 1900. He had long been interested in politics, and was, in 1887, appointed by President Cleveland to be postmaster of Braddock, and had at that time the distinction of being the youngest postmaster in the United States. He was elected jury commissioner in 1897, and re-elected in 1900. Mr. McCarthy was a member of St. Brendan's church. Among his business interests he was secretary of the Sadie Belle gold mining company at St. Joseph's, Utah. Mr. McCarthy was married, June 27, 1889, to Sarah E. Churchill, daughter of Michael and Sarah (Beach) Churchill. Two children were born to them, Madeleine and Ursula. Mr. McCarthy died, May 6, 1903.

GEORGE B. PARKER, of Pittsburg, Pa., a well-known attorney-at-law with offices at No. 426 Diamond St., was born in West Finley township, Washington Co., Pa., Oct. 2, 1862, son of the late Warren and Margaret (Sutherland) Parker. His father was born in Washington county, Pa., Oct. 19, 1826, and was a son of Hiram and Nancy (Heaton) Parker. Warren Parker spent his entire life in his native county, where he was extensively engaged in agriculture until his death, Dec. 24, 1892. Margaret Sutherland Parker was born in West Finley township, Washington Co., Pa., in February, 1830, daughter of Daniel Sutherland and his wife, who, prior to marriage, was a Barnes. Mrs. Parker now resides in her native township and is the mother of three children, viz.: George B., Addie M., and C. W. Parker, bookkeeper in the Second National bank of Pittsburg, who married Gertrude McCullough, and has a son, Theodore. George B. Parker was reared on his father's farm and acquired his early educational training in the common schools of his native township. Later he attended the State normal school of California, Pa., where he was graduated in 1888, and then for several years taught school with much success in Washington and Allegheny counties. Subsequently he read law in the office of Thomas D. Chantler, of Pittsburg, Pa.; was graduated from the law department of Dickinson college, of Carlisle, Pa., in 1896, and has since continuously practiced in Pittsburg. Mr. Parker is a member of all courts, has a splendid practice, and stands high among the attorneys of Allegheny county.

JOHN S. WELLER, of Pittsburg, Pa., a successful attorney-at-law, with offices in the Park building, was born in Somerset county, Pa., Nov. 1, 1867, son of the late Dr. Fred S. and Mary A. (Hammer) Weller. His elementary education was acquired in the public schools of Bedford county, by private tuition, and later attended the Pennsylvania State college, where he was graduated as a civil engineer in the class of 1889. Subsequently he was employed on the surveying staff of the United States geodetic survey, where he made a fine record. Then Mr. Weller read law in the offices of Russell & Longenecker, prominent attorneys of Bedford county, and he was there admitted to the bar in September, 1891. He prosecuted his practice in Bedford county with success, served as district attorney for that county from 1894 to 1897 and, in 1898, was elected to the State senate from the thirty-sixth district for a four-year term. Mr. Weller removed to Pittsburg in the fall of 1901, where he is a member of all courts and enjoys a large and lucrative practice. He is a member of Hyndman lodge, A. F. and A. M., and of Bedford chapter of Royal Arch Masons. His political affiliations are with the republican party.

JOSEPH HAYS, attorney at No. 429 Diamond St., Pittsburg, is a native of Washington county, Pa., where he was born Jan. 9, 1832. His father was Alexander Hays, also a native of Washington county, where he resided from the date of his birth, in 1795, until his death, in 1845. His mother was Ann V. (Stevenson) Hays, also born in Washington county, in 1802, and died in 1881. Joseph Hays attended a private school at Cross Creek, Pa., and later attended Washington college, graduating in 1857. He read law in the office of Montgomery & Gibson, of Washington, and was admitted to the bar of Washington county in 1865, and to the Allegheny county bar the same year. He has been in continuous practice in Pittsburg since that date, and is one of the oldest practitioners in Allegheny county. He has served five terms as a member of the select council for the thirty-sixth ward, Pittsburg, and represented the fourth legislative district in the legislature during 1875-1876. Mr. Hays has always affiliated with the democratic party. He is a member of Franklin lodge, No. 221, F. and A. M., of Pittsburg, and his religious views are Presbyterian. In 1859 he was married to Elizabeth A. Crawford. They have three children: Edgar V., cashier of the Union savings bank; Frank C, bookkeeper in the Allegheny National bank, and Anna M., wife of Rev. S. J. S. Moore, residing in Minnesota. Mr. Hays is regarded as one of Pittsburg's prominent and respected citizens.

CHARLES A. LOCKE, of Pittsburg, Pa., a successful practitioner of law, with offices in the St. Nicholas building, was born in Philadelphia, Pa., Dec. 8, 1875. His father was John Jacob Locke, of Philadelphia, who died in 1879, and who, at the age of sixteen, enlisted as drummer boy in Company E, 20th Ohio heavy artillery, and later served as a lieutenant of mounted infantry in a Tennessee regiment of the Union army in the Civil war. His mother was Emma (Wiese) Locke, daughter of Adam Wiese, who was the first president of the German National bank of Allegheny, Pa. Mr. Locke graduated from the Allegheny high school in 1893 and from the law department of Western University of Pennsylvania in 1897. He read law with George Elphinstone, city solicitor of Allegheny city, and also with John Scott Ferguson. He was admitted to the bar of Allegheny county in September, 1897, to the supreme court of Pennsylvania in October, 1902, and to the superior court of Pennsylvania in April, 1903. He is also a member of the United States district and circuit courts and of the Allegheny county bar association. Mr. Locke is a member and a steward of Calvary Methodist Episcopal church of Allegheny city, and is a director of the central branch of the Y. M. C. A. of Pittsburg. He is a young man of ability, integrity and energy, and is sure to achieve permanent success in the great and exacting profession which he has chosen as his life's work and in which he has already made rapid strides.

LUCIUS L. HILL, superintendent of Station D of the Pittsburg postoffice, at Wilkinsburg, has been in the postal service since he was sixteen years old. He was born in Pittsburg in 1874, and educated in the public schools. His first position in the public service was that of messenger at Station B, at Lawrenceville, under his father, Robert A. Hill. He remained at the Lawrenceville station six years, attaining the grade of mailing clerk, and was then transferred to Station A, in the East End, where he remained nearly two years as a distributor. Mr. Hill was then appointed chief clerk on the mail car running between Stations A and B, held this position some three and a half years, and, in February, 1901, became superintendent of Station D. Mr. Hill is a republican in political belief. He is a member of the Jr. O. U. A. M. and belongs to the Presbyterian church.

GEORGE J. KAMBACH, of Pittsburg, Pa., a well-known lawyer, with offices in the Bakewell building, was born in Pittsburg, Sept. 5, 1876, son of George A. and Lillie E. (Nolte) Kambach. His ancestors on both sides were of German extraction, and his grandparents settled in Allegheny county about 1835. His paternal grandfather was Frederick Kambach, a successful stone-mason and contractor, and his maternal grandfather was Jacob Nolte, a prominent citizen of his day. George A. Kambach, father of the subject, was born in Pittsburg, May 3, 1850; is a successful glass-worker, and has spent his entire life in that city. He has served as a member of the school board of the twenty-sixth ward, and is prominently identified with the trade organizations, in which he has held a number of important offices. George J. Kambach was educated in the splendid public schools of his native city, attending the graded and high schools, and is well equipped by natural and acquired qualifications for a professional career. He read law in the office of Henry Meyer, a prominent attorney of

Pittsburg, and subsequently attended the Pittsburg law school, where he was graduated, in 1900, with the degree of bachelor of laws. He was admitted to practice in September, 1899, and is meeting with much success in his professional career.

MARION H. MURPHY, of Pittsburg, Pa., a leading attorney, with offices in the Bakewell building, was born in Allegheny city, Jan. 27, 1875, and is a son of William and Elizabeth (Hayleigh) Murphy, both now residing in Pittsburg. His father was born in Pittsburg, and for many years was engaged in the wholesale commission business in that city, but is now retired from active affairs and is quietly spending his declining years in his native city, where he is highly esteemed and respected. The mother of the subject was born in Tennessee, where her father was a prominent ante-bellum planter and a distinguished citizen. His parents had the following children: Agnes, wife of John M. L'Amour, of Pittsburg; Aida V., wife of W. C. Weckerle, of Pittsburg; William H., Francis W., Marion H., and Horace Dorsey (deceased). Marion H. Murphy was educated in the schools of Pittsburg, attending the graded and high schools, and later read law in the office of Watterson & Reid, prominent attorneys of Pittsburg. Mr. Murphy was admitted to the bar in September, 1896, and has since been in continuous and successful practice, being a member of all State courts and of the United States supreme court. He is the legal representative of the London guaranty and accident company (limited), of Chicago, and also of the Standard life and accident association of Detroit. Mr. Murphy is prominently identified with the democratic party, was secretary of the county democratic committee for three years, and has also occupied the same position on the city committee of his party. He has been closely connected with the political affairs of the city and county for a number of years, and has performed herculean tasks for his friends. He is also president of Duquesne council, No. 264, Knights of Columbus, resides in the twentieth ward, and is widely and favorably known throughout the county.

OLIN G. A. BARKER, M. D., of Pittsburg, Pa., specialist on the disease of the eye, was born in Ebensburg, Cambria Co., Pa., Jan. 14, 1872, son of Florentine H. and Margaret (Zahm) Barker, his father being a native of Lovell, Me., who came to Cambria county in 1857, and is engaged in the mercantile business at Ebensburg. He was educated in the graded and high schools of his native town, graduating from the latter institution in 1890, and one year later entered Lafayette college, where he was graduated in 1895, with the degree of bachelor of philosophy, and in 1899 his alma mater bestowed on him the degree of master of science. He matriculated in the medical department of the University of Pennsylvania in 1895, and was graduated from that famous institution in 1898. He was resident physician in the State hospital at Ashland, Pa., for one year, when he went to Europe and took special courses on the diseases of the eye. He attended lectures at Berlin, Vienna and London, and devoted two years to the study of his specialty. In 1901 he returned to Pittsburg, and since has practiced with much success, his entire time being given to diseases of the eye, his office being at Nos. 1114-1117 Westinghouse building; hours, 9 a. m. to 2 p. m. He is a member of the dispensary staff of Mercy hospital and of the staff of Pittsburg free dispensary. He is also a member of the Allegheny county, the Pennsylvania State and the American medical associations, the American academy of medicine, and of the Monongahela club. He is prominently identified with the Masonic fraternity, being a thirty-second degree Mason, and a member of the Mystic Shrine. Dr. Barker is a member of the East Liberty Presbyterian church. The great-great-grandfather of Dr. Barker was John Barker, born in 1742, who, with a brother, served in the Revolutionary war, and was specially mentioned for gallant conduct at the battle of Bunker Hill. Dr. Barker's father served two years in the Civil war as a member of the 209th Pennsylvania volunteers, and upheld the record of his ancestors for gallant and meritorious services. Richard Barker, who was one of the original settlers of Andover, Mass., and who received the first land-title issued by that town (1643), was the head of the Barker family in America, and from him Dr. Barker is descended.

WILLIAM FISHER.

MRS. MARY FISHER.

WILLIAM FISHER and MARY (DUNLOP) FISHER, his wife, both now deceased, were natives of Paisley, Scotland. Mr. Fisher was born Dec. 22, 1822; attended school, and learned the trade of a broadcloth weaver in Paisley, and came to America in 1845. He first located at Canton, Ohio, to which place his brother, James, had come some years before. There he worked for awhile at his trade, when he removed to Pennsylvania, locating at Pittsburg. Finding no opportunity open to him as a weaver, he found employment in various occupations for a time, and then entered the iron works of James Rees as an apprentice. By close attention to his duties, he learned rapidly and was promoted accordingly until he became the foreman of the works. A little later he purchased an interest in an iron mill at Sixteenth street and Penn avenue, and finally bought out the other five partners, becoming the sole owner of the works. About the year 1881 he removed to Twenty-fourth and Smallman streets, where he continued the business until his death, which occurred May 5, 1895. During his residence in Pennsylvania he lived in Allegheny city, Glenfield and Pittsburg. In all these places he was affiliated with the Presbyterian church, to which he was a liberal contributor. He was also a prominent Mason, being a member of St. John's lodge, No. 219, F. and A. M.; Zerubbabel chapter, No. 162, R. A. M.; charter member of Ascalon commandery, No. 59, K. T., and Ancient Accepted Scottish Rite, thirty-second degree, S. P. R. S. Mary Dunlop was the daughter of William Ritchie and Martha (Lang) Dunlop. Her father was a shawl manufacturer of Paisley, and she learned the business of shawl-making in her father's factory. At the time of her marriage to William Fisher, she was the widow of Mr. Mackie, but had no children. Her father was a native of Kilwinning, Ayrshire, Scotland; he was twice married, and by his first wife he had several children, all of whom, except William and Mary, died young. After the death of his first wife, he married Isabella Marshall. One son, David, was born to this second marriage. When he was about five years old he removed with his parents to Glasgow, where he learned the business of designing, engraving and lithographing, and since 1890 he has been a resident of Pittsburg. William Fisher and Mary Dunlop were married at Allegheny city, July 3, 1850. To them were born eleven children, viz.: Janet, born April 7, 1851, now the wife of Thomas McNeill, of Homewood, Pa.; Martha, born Feb. 5, 1853, married William Phillips, and died May 3, 1899; David, born Feb. 27, 1855, and died Nov. 26, 1897; William, born Feb. 26, 1857, and died July 22, 1868; James, born Oct. 30, 1858, and died Nov. 21, 1872; Mary, born Nov. 7, 1860, and now the wife of George Gray; Andrew, born April 11, 1863; Elizabeth, born July 24, 1865, and now the wife of A. F. Leggate, a real estate dealer on Fourth avenue, Pittsburg, Pa.; Isabella, born July 24, 1865, now the wife of Albert N. Eames; Margaret, born Dec. 4, 1867, and died Oct. 11, 1888, and Lilly, born March 13, 1870. Mrs. William Fisher died Feb. 2, 1900. Andrew Fisher was born in the third ward, Allegheny city, Pa. He was educated in the public schools of Allegheny city and Glenfield, a private school in Allegheny city, and two years in the Western University of Pennsylvania. He then read law in the office of John Barton & Sons, one of the leading law firms of Pittsburg, and was admitted to the bar of Allegheny county, Dec. 22, 1888, since which time he has been in continuous practice. He practices in all of the local, State and federal courts, though he confines his practice entirely to civil cases. He was married in Allegheny city, Feb. 27, 1890, to Miss Evalina L., a daughter of August and Henrietta Hartje. They have three children: Eleanor Marie, born May 16, 1892; Harold Edward, born Jan. 31, 1895, and Henrietta, born Oct. 21, 1899. The family lives in the twenty-second ward, and both Mr. and Mrs. Fisher belong to the Presbyterian church.

ROBERT J. CUNNINGHAM, controller of Allegheny county, Pa., was born at Elizabeth, Pa., in 1860, and came to the second ward, Pittsburg, with his parents when three years old. From there the family moved to Sewickley, Allegheny county, which Mr. Cunningham has since made his home. When a boy, he attended school in Pittsburg, graduating from the Pittsburg schools in 1872, and then finished his schooling at Dickson's academy in Sewickley, from which he graduated in 1878. Mr. Cunningham became a pilot on the river, under his father, Capt. William Cunningham, and was so engaged for three years. After this he spent a year as circulation man for the Pittsburg Times, and for two years was special editor of the Sunday edition of the Pittsburg Leader. In 1892 he took up the life insurance business, in which he was engaged for several years, until he was elected to his present responsible position. Before this he was for seven years a member of the Sewickley council. Mr. Cunningham is a member of the Masonic fraternity and of the Methodist Episcopal church. In politics he is a prominent republican, and is actively interested in local party affairs.

WILLIAM WASHINGTON CAMPBELL, of Pittsburg, Pa., a prominent attorney, with offices at No. 413 Grant St., was born at Paisley, Scotland, May 26, 1842, son of Hugh and Agnes (Johns) Campbell. His family is of Scotch ancestry, and his father, Hugh Campbell, was a son of William and Jane Campbell, and a shawl manufacturer in his native land. He came to America in 1847 with a company which intended to manufacture shawls in California, but owing to the constant harassing of the Indians, this project was abandoned, and Hugh Campbell became a trooper in the United States cavalry. He saw distinguished service in the Mexican war, participated in a number of bloody fights, and was so severely wounded at Pueblo that he died from the effects of his wounds.

He had three children: William W.; Hugh, who died in Aberdeen, Miss., in May, 1901, and John P., who resides at Marietta, Ohio. Mrs. Campbell, mother of the subject, died in Fairmont, W. Va. William W. Campbell accompanied his parents to America when only five years of age, and after a short stay in St. Louis, removed to West Virginia. He was educated in the Marietta academy and college of Marietta, Ohio, and at the beginning of the Civil war entered the government service as a telegraph operator, and at the same time also acted in that capacity for the Baltimore & Ohio railroad. He was stationed at Oakland, Md.; then at Rowlesburg, W. Va., and, in 1864, at Fairmont, W. Va., where he received and published the bulletin pertaining to Lee's surrender. At the close of the war he was placed in charge of a station for the Baltimore & Ohio railroad at Fairmont, where he remained for a number of years, and subsequently held the same position with that company for many years at Farmington, W. Va. In the meantime he was devoting his leisure to the study of law, and was admitted to the bar in 1880, after passing a splendid examination conducted by John J. Hoag, Altheus Heymond and Judge A. Brooks Fleming. He practiced in West Virginia with much success until 1889, when he removed to Pittsburg, was admitted to the bar of Allegheny county, and since has continuously practiced in that city. Mr. Campbell is a democrat, and while living in West Virginia took an active part in politics, holding the office of commissioner of deeds and being defeated for the office of county clerk by the narrow margin of eleven votes. He has been twice married—first, to Elmina, daughter of Jacob and Jane Straight, of Fairmont, W. Va., and they had ten children: Jane Agnes, who died at the age of six years and six months; Mary Martha, wife of Robert T. Walsh, of McKeesport; William H., who married Jessie Griffith and resides in Pittsburg; Guy Edgar, who married Edith Phillips and is a broker in Pittsburg; Betsey Blanch, wife of Harry T. Foley, of Philadelphia; Clyde S., a resident of Texas; Maud Ella, wife of Elmer Schrock, of McKeesport; Lula Margaret, wife of W. R. Worthington, of Greensburg; Otto C., resident of Pittsburg, and Ruhamie Belva, wife of Malcolm B. Brady, of Philadelphia. Mrs. Campbell died in Crafton, Pa., Oct. 19, 1897, and is buried in the Phillips burial ground near Crafton. Mr. Campbell was married the second time, on Feb. 28, 1899, to Catherine, daughter of Matthew and Jessie Howard, of Allegheny city, and they have one daughter, Aurelia Alta, and one son, Robert Burns, born Sept. 19, 1903. He is a member and past noble grand of Henry Lambert lodge,

No. 475, I. O. O. F., of Pittsburg and is past grand of Electic lodge of Farmington, W. Va., of which lodge he is a charter member, and also of Campbell lodge of Spencer, W. Va. He is a past chief patriarch and representative to the grand encampment. Mr. Campbell is a member of the First Presbyterian church of Crafton, and resides at Wilkinsburg, Pa.

THOMAS J. WILSON, whose offices are located at No. 422 Fifth Ave., Pittsburg, Pa., is one of the prominent and successful attorneys of the Allegheny county bar. He was born, June 9, 1864, in North Sewickley township, Beaver Co., Pa., and is the son of Jefferson and Lizzie (Couch) Wilson. His father was a native of North Sewickley township, Beaver county, and his mother was born at New Castle, Pa. Both are still living and now reside in Chippewa township, Beaver county, where Mr. Wilson is an extensive fruit-grower as well as an inventor of considerable merit. Thomas Jefferson Wilson was educated in the common schools of his native county, after which he took a course in Geneva college, at Beaver Falls, Pa. While attending this institution he read law at home, and after leaving the college, he entered the University of Michigan, at Ann Arbor, graduating with the class of 1891. He located at Roanoke, Va., where he was admitted to the bar and where he practiced for about a year, when he contracted malarial fever which compelled him to seek a change. For the next two years he traveled through the south for the purpose of eradicating the malarial fever from his system. In this he was successful, and, in 1894, located at Pittsburg, was admitted to the Allegheny county bar, and has since that time been engaged in practicing in the local and State courts, his attention being given almost exclusively to civil cases. He has a large clientage, which is constantly increasing. He has been solicitor for the borough of Pitcairn ever since its incorporation, and is one of the most popular residents of that borough, in the affairs of which he takes a deep interest, not because he is the solicitor, but because he feels it to be his duty as a citizen. In this matter his example is worthy of emulation, for the highest duty of citizenship is to know what to do, and then to have the courage to do it.

CHARLES EDWARD THEOBALD, of Pittsburg, Pa., a leading member of the Pittsburg bar, with offices in the Bakewell building, was born on Oct. 23, 1872, in Shaler Township, Allegheny Co., Pa., a son of Charles and Caroline (Oliger) Theobald, both natives of Germany, and residents of Allegheny county since 1850. The mother now resides at Millvale, Pa., the father having died on Oct. 5, 1899. C. E. Theobald acquired his literary education in the public schools, and was graduated from the Allegheny high school in June, 1890. He then took up the profession of teaching, having been identified with the Millvale public schools for a number of years with marked success. He later abandoned the school room and matriculated in the law department of the University of Michigan, at Ann Arbor, graduating from that famous seat of learning in June, 1898, with the degree of bachelor of laws. He was admitted to the Allegheny county bar the same year, and has since continuously pursued the practice of law at Pittsburg as a member of all the State and federal courts, enjoying a splendid practice. Politically, he has always been a republican and an aggressive worker in the ranks of that party.

EDWARD H. FLOOD is one of a group of talented and ambitious young attorneys upon whose shoulders will some day fall the burden of conducting the extensive legal interests of the wealthiest and most progressive business center of the United States—the city of Pittsburg and Allegheny county. Mr. Flood was born in Pittsburg, Dec. 6, 1877. His father, James Flood, has been connected with the firm of Arbuckle & Co., in that city, for upwards of thirty years, and at the present time holds the position of manager. His mother is a native of Allegheny county, her parents, Edward and Mary A. Houston, being one of Pittsburg's pioneer families. Mr. Flood received his education in the schools of his native city, and, in 1898, graduated with honors from the

Pittsburg central high school. He then entered the law department of the Western University of Pennsylvania and graduated with the class of 1901. While in attendance at the university, he became associated with the management of the Western University Courant, holding the position of editor until his graduation. Conscientious and careful in his profession, Mr. Flood has already acquired a responsible and important practice at the Allegheny county bar.

GEORGE W. FLOWERS, an attorney-at-law, with offices at No. 1214 Frick building, Pittsburg, Pa., is a descendant of some of the oldest families in western Pennsylvania. His father, John H. Flowers, was a native of Allegheny county, and his mother, Sarah A. (Lenhart) Flowers, was born in Westmoreland county, and is still living in the little town of Irwin in that county. George W. Flowers was born in Allegheny county, May 15, 1860. His primary education was acquired in the schools of Irwin. He then attended Washington and Jefferson college at Washington, Pa., for one year, and graduated from Yale college with the class of 1884, receiving the degree of bachelor of arts. Soon after graduating, he entered the law office of Judge Alexander D. McConnell, of Greensburg, Pa., and began the study of law. While thus employed he was appointed by Governor Beaver to the office of prothonotary of Westmoreland county, to fill a vacancy caused by the death of John Chamberlain. Although a young man, he filled the office for the remainder of the term, acquitting himself with credit and demonstrating the wisdom of the governor in making the appointment. He finished his legal studies in 1889, and was admitted to the bar of Westmoreland county. The following spring he removed to Pittsburg, and shortly after taking up his residence in that city, he was admitted to the Allegheny county bar. His practice extends to all the courts of the two counties of Allegheny and Westmoreland, as well as the State and federal courts. At the present time he is the solicitor for the borough of Irwin, a position he has held for a number of years, which shows the confidence reposed in him by those who know him best and whose interests have never been neglected when intrusted to his care. He is also interested in a number of important enterprises, being a director and solicitor of the Parkersburg iron and steel company and the Cannonsburg iron and steel company, president of the Central foundry and car company, and a director in several national banks. On June 14, 1894, he was married to Miss Sara E. Gregg, of Irwin, Pa. Mr. Flowers is a member of the county bar associations, and a member of Westmoreland lodge, No. 518, Free and Accepted Masons, and has been honored by his lodge by being elected to the office of worshipful master, the highest in the lodge, where he fully sustained the good opinion of his brethren who conferred upon him this distinction. Besides his membership in the Masonic fraternity, he belongs to the University and Union clubs and the Reformed church.

HUSTON QUAIL WALKER, of Pittsburg, Pa., a prominent attorney, with offices in the Bakewell building, was born in Clinton township, Butler Co., Pa., on Tuesday, Nov. 4, 1862, son of William H. and Caroline (McCafferty) Walker, the former born in Butler county, Pa., and the latter at Lewistown, Pa., and both now residing in Butler county. Mr. Walker was educated at Washington and Jefferson college and by private tutors, and for a time taught in the public schools of Butler. He studied law in the offices of Judge McJunckin and Judge Galbraith, was admitted to the bar of Butler county, May 25, 1891, and there practiced with much success until January, 1895, when he removed to Pittsburg, having been previously admitted to the bar of Allegheny county in December, 1894. Since then Mr. Walker has continuously practiced at Pittsburg, where he is a member of all Pennsylvania and the United States district and circuit courts. He has held the position of a school director of Wilkinsburg, where he resides, and is well known throughout that section of the county. He was married in Butler county, Pa., Sept. 5, 1888, to Margaret E. Bovard, and, while they have no children, yet their home life is a rarely happy one. Mr. Walker and his wife are members of the First Presbyterian church and are prominently identified with its works of charity and benevolence.

MAJOR ROBERT M. EWING, a Pittsburg attorney, with offices in the People's savings bank building, was born in Bell township, Westmoreland Co., Pa., Jan. 31, 1868. His parents, James H. and Eleanor J. (Rhea) Ewing, were natives of Armstrong county, where the Ewing family were among the pioneer settlers. Both parents of our subject are still living, residing at Saltsburg, Indiana Co., Pa. The maternal great-grandfather of Major Ewing was Hon. William Findlay, a member of every session of congress from 1790 to 1820, save two, the sixth and seventh. At the convention of the western counties of Pennsylvania, held in 1794 at Parkinson's Ferry, which was called in connection with the whiskey insurrection, Hon. William Findlay was one of the two special deputies appointed to wait upon President Washington at Carlisle, to assure him of their willingness to submit, and to dissuade him from sending an armed force west of the Allegheny mountains. Their mission was successful. Robert M. Ewing was educated in the common schools of Westmoreland county, the Saltsburg academy, and Washington and Jefferson college, Washington, Pa. While taking his collegiate course, he taught in the public schools, and was for a time an instructor in the preparatory department of Kiskiminetas college. Upon leaving college he entered the law offices of Watson & Keener, Indiana, Pa., and, in June, 1892, was admitted to the Indiana county bar. Soon afterwards he removed to Allegheny county, where he was admitted to the bar in June, 1893, and since that time has been in continuous practice in that county. In 1889, while reading law at Indiana, he enlisted in Company F, 5th regiment, Pennsylvania national guard, and during the Homestead riots was clerk of the company. When he left Indiana county he severed his connection with the military organization, but in 1896 he was appointed regimental sergeant-major of the 14th regiment, Pennsylvania national guard, and, in February, 1898, was elected second lieutenant. In July, 1898, he recruited a company, which was afterwards attached to the 17th regiment, Pennsylvania national guard, and in August of the same year he was elected junior major of the regiment. When the 17th regiment was mustered out and the 14th was reorganized, he was made the senior major of the regiment, a position which he still holds. Major Ewing was married, June 14, 1894, to Miss Anna S. Davis, a daughter of McLain and Caroline Davis, of Indiana, Pa. One daughter, Caroline Isabel, has been born to this marriage, on March 13, 1897. In politics Major Ewing is a republican. He takes an active interest in political matters, particularly in those affecting the welfare of Wilkinsburg borough, where he lives, and which he has ably represented as a school director. He and his wife both affiliate with the Presbyterian church. His father is the son of John and Martha (Hart) Ewing and his mother the daughter of Isaac and Elizabeth (Carruthers) Rhea, all belonging to the oldest families of Armstrong county.

JOHN L. PRESTLEY, of Pittsburg, Pa., a prominent attorney, with offices in the St. Nicholas building, was born in Upper St. Clair township, Allegheny Co., Pa., Nov. 4, 1870, son of James Prestley, D. D., who died on April 1, 1885, and his wife, Martha Lindsay, who is now living. The Prestley family is of Scotch-Irish ancestry, and the name was originally spelled Priestley. James Prestley, father of the subject, was a son of Nathan and Elizabeth (Betty) Prestley, and was born in County Down, Ireland, June 23, 1815, and accompanied his parents to America in 1819. He was a graduate of the Western university, and was a minister of the United Presbyterian church, with charges in Cincinnati, New York and Pittsburg, and died at Carnegie, Pa. John L. Prestley was educated at the University of Wooster, Ohio, where he was graduated in 1891. Subsequently he read law in the office of Hon. J. J. Miller, a prominent and able attorney (now judge of the orphans' court, Allegheny county), and was admitted to the bar in December, 1893. Mr. Prestley is a member of all courts and of the Allegheny county bar association, and enjoys a lucrative practice. He resides at Carnegie, Pa., and at present is burgess of that borough. He is a member of Centennial lodge, No. 444, of the Ancient Free and Accepted Masons, and is closely identified with that great fraternity. On May 12, 1898, he was mustered into the United States service as second lieutenant of Company K, 14th Pennsylvania volunteers, for duty in the Spanish-American war, and served until mustered out on Dec. 20, 1898.

JAMES F. KANE, of Pittsburg, Pa., a well-known attorney, with offices at No. 503 Wylie Ave., was born in Pittsburg, Aug. 28, 1868, son of William and Ellen (McKeever) Kane, the former a native of Ireland, who came to America, first settled in New York and subsequently resided in Pittsburg for fifty years. His mother was a native of Allegheny county, resided there all her life and died on Feb. 5, 1898. James F. Kane was educated in the public schools of Pittsburg, and was graduated from the St. Charles college of Maryland and later from the St. Vincent's college of Westmoreland county, Pa. Mr. Kane read law in the office of W. J. Brennan, a prominent lawyer, and was admitted to the bar in September, 1896. Since then he has been continuously in the practice, is a member of all courts and has a splendid standing among the attorneys of the county. Mr. Kane was appointed a police magistrate by Mayor Hayes, on April 1, 1903, and is making a fine record in that capacity. He was married in Pittsburg, July 20, 1898, to Ella A., daughter of Thomas F. and Catherine Breen, and they have one son, Joseph, who was born on May 23, 1899. Mr. Kane is well known in Pittsburg as an able lawyer, an upright judge and a good citizen.

ALFRED CAHEN, of Pittsburg, Pa., a well-known attorney, with offices at No. 412 Grant St., was born at Zanesville, Ohio, Nov. 16, 1870, son of Marx and Johanna (Berg) Cahen, the former a native of France, who died in 1887, and the latter born in Germany, and now residing at Columbus, Ohio. Mr. Cahen was well educated in the literary branches in the public schools of Columbus, Ohio, and then studied law at the Ohio State university, where he was graduated on June 12, 1894, with the degree of bachelor of laws. He was admitted to the supreme court of Ohio on Dec. 7, 1893, and subsequently read law in the offices of Joseph Stadtfeld, and was admitted to the bar of Allegheny county in September,

1894. Mr. Cahen is a member of all courts, including the supreme court of the United States, and has a splendid practice. In 1898 Mr. Cahen enlisted in Company D, 18th regiment, Pennsylvania volunteers, as a private for service in the Spanish-American war; was mustered into the United States service at Camp Daniel H. Hastings, at Mt. Gretna, Pa., May 12, 1898, and served in the capacity of a private soldier until the command was mustered out of service at Pittsburg, April 19, 1899, when he was commissioned by Governor Stone as captain of Company D. Mr. Cahen was married at Pittsburg, Pa., Dec. 17, 1902, to Edith, daughter of Emanuel and Pauline Weiler, and their married life has been a happy one.

WILLIAM E. NEWLIN, attorney-at-law, with offices located at No. 404 Frick building, is probably one of the busiest lawyers in the city of Pittsburg. Besides his large clientage, he is interested in various manufacturing and mercantile enterprises, being the president of the Heilman-James company, the secretary and treasurer of the Farmers' manufacturing company, and within the last year he has organized the Pittsburg casket company, of which he is treasurer and one of the directors. Much of the success of all these undertakings is due to his intelligent and well-directed efforts. He was born in West Newton, Westmoreland Co., Pa., May 30, 1861. His parents were Benson H. and Ann H. (Van Kirk) Newlin, the latter still living. As a boy, he attended the public schools of Elizabeth and the McKeesport academy. Later he attended the Indiana State normal school, and, in 1889, graduated from the law department of the Michigan university, Ann Arbor, with the degree of bachelor of laws. In September of the same year he was admitted to the bar of Allegheny county, and began his professional career. His course has been steadily onward and upward. Besides his private practice and the business enterprises with which he is so intimately associated, he is the city solicitor for the city of McKeesport. In his domestic affairs he is as fortunate as he is in his business matters. He was married to Miss Elizabeth M. Harrison, of McKeesport, and one son has been born to them.

GEORGE AUSTIN JOHNSON, attorney-at-law, No. 422 Fifth Ave., Pittsburg, Pa., was born in Washington county, the same State, and is the son of George Wolfe and Eunice (Smith) Johnson, the former a native of Green county, and the latter of Washington county, both of Pennsylvania. George A. Johnson was educated in Waynesburg college, from which institution he was graduated in the class of 1885 with the degree of bachelor of science. Soon afterwards he entered the law department of the University of Michigan and completed a full course of studies therein, graduating in the class of 1890. Previous to his attendance at this famous school, he read law in the office of Wyly, Buchanan & Walton, Waynesburg, Pa. In December, 1890, he was duly admitted to the bar of Green county, and continued to practice at Waynesburg for the space of three years as the junior member of the firm of Teagarden & Johnson. In 1893 he secured admission to the bar of Allegheny county, and the same year formed a partnership with J. F. Calhoun, Esq., under the business name of Calhoun & Johnson. He has since continued to practice his profession at Pittsburg with steadily increasing success, until at the present time he has a large and profitable clientage. His success has been most gratifying, and is due solely to his fitness for the higher duties and responsibilities of the greatest of all professions. His power at the bar is shown by his splendid success both as a pleader and as a counselor. He practices in all the county, State and United States courts, and has won many notable cases by sheer force of intellect and knowledge of the law. At the present time he is the solicitor for Versailles borough, for the city of McKeesport school district, for North Versailles township and school district, and for Versailles township and school district. For a time Mr. Johnson held the office of burgess of Waynesburg borough. The confidence reposed in him by his fellow-citizens is due to his high ability in his profession. He takes an active and successful part in the public affairs of McKeesport, in which town he resides. He has found time amid the arduous duties of his profession to polish his mind and manners by reading good books and joining good company. He is a member of Versailles council, Royal Arcanum. He was married, on May 18, 1889, to Miss

Debbie Thomas, of Waynesburg, Pa., she dying on May 14, 1895. On Nov. 2, 1898, he was united in marriage with Miss Ella Nira Wilson, of Beaver Falls, Beaver Co., Pa.

ROBERT GIBSON MATTERN, delinquent tax collector for Allegheny county, for county, road, poor, dog and State taxes, was born in Hollidaysburg, Blair Co., Pa., March 29, 1859. George Mattern emigrated from the valley of the Rhine in 1750, and settled in Maryland. He came from near the Swiss mountain, the Matterhorn, from which it is thought the family name was derived. He was the father of nine children, one of whom, Jacob, the grandfather of the subject of this sketch, settled in the Spruce creek valley, Huntingdon Co, Pa., about the year 1779. It is worthy of note that some member of the family has ever since resided in the house that he at that time erected. It was there that Jacob Mattern, Robert's father, was born in 1806. Upon arriving at manhood, he followed farming for several years, when he removed to Pittsburg and engaged in merchandising. He retired from business, was married to Margaret Gibson, a native of Bedford, Pa., and removed to Blair county, where he lived retired at Hollidaysburg until the death of his wife, in 1873, when he again took up his residence in the city of Pittsburg, and died there in May, 1893. Three children were born to Jacob and Margaret (Gibson) Mattern, viz.: Robert G., Frank H., and Margaret, who died in her early childhood. Robert G. Mattern was educated in the public school of Hollidaysburg and at a private school in the city of Pittsburg. He began life as a clerk in the glass works of Bakewell, Pears & Co. Since that time his clerical ability has been recognized by some of the leading banking and commercial concerns of Pittsburg. On leaving the glass works he became the corresponding clerk for the Penn bank. He was next in the employ of the Pittsburg oil exchange, then with the Pittsburg steel works for a number of years, and later with A. M. Byers & Co., wrought iron pipe manufacturers. He left this firm to become the secretary and treasurer of the Standard boot and shoe company, where he remained until appointed to his present position. He received the appointment of tax collector in February, 1903, but did not assume active duty until the following September. In all the positions held by Mr. Mattern, his conduct has been marked by the fidelity, integrity and ability with which he discharged his duties. Few men have ever served their employers more faithfully or have been more honored in the service than he, and to his splendid ability and sterling integrity is chiefly due his appointment to his present honorable and responsible position. In this place he has the entire confidence of his superior officers, as well as the people of the community, and it is safe to predict that he will retire from it with a clean record and greater laurels. Mr. Mattern is a member of Pittsburg conclave, Order of Heptasophs, and resides in the twenty-second ward of that city. He was married, Feb. 16, 1893, to Miss Minnetta Ihmsen, of Pittsburg. Mrs. Mattern is a daughter of William and Jane (McCloskey) Ihmsen, and a granddaughter of Christian Ihmsen, the founder of the glass bottle industry in Pittsburg.

CLARENCE ELMORE WALLACE, attorney-at-law, whose offices are located at No. 1214 Frick building, Pittsburg, Pa., is a descendant of the Wallaces of Westmoreland county. His father, William M., and his mother, Ellen M. (Smith) Wallace, were both born of Scotch-Irish parentage in the county of Westmoreland. Mrs. Wallace died in 1877, but the father is still living in the county where he was born and where he is now engaged in agricultural pursuits. Clarence E. Wallace was born in Fairfield township, Westmoreland Co., Pa., Sept. 1, 1873. Like all farmer boys, he attended the district schools until he was old enough and far enough advanced in his studies to attend the academy, after which he entered the higher institutions of learning, and graduated from the California State normal school with the class of 1894. For the next three years he was employed as a teacher, one year of which he was principal of the Glenfield public schools, and two years vice-principal of the Derry schools. He then attended the law department of the Michigan university for one year and the law department of the Western University of Pennsylvania for two years, graduating with honors from the latter institution in 1900. While attending the Western university, he read law in the offices of G. C. Lewis and George W. Flowers, two eminent Pittsburg attorneys. In June, 1900, he was admitted to the bar, and since that time has practiced his profession in all the courts of Allegheny county. He is solicitor for the school board of Homewood sub-school district of Pittsburg, Pa. On Sept. 28, 1900, he was married to Miss Sara E. Zahniser, of Fredonia, Mercer Co., Pa. They have one child, Margaret J. R., who was born on Dec. 26, 1901. Mr. Wallace is a member of the Hamilton Avenue United Presbyterian church, and lives in the twenty-first ward of the city of Pittsburg.

CURTIS M. WILLOCK, of Pittsburg, Pa., one of the younger members of the bar, was born in Allegheny city, Pa., Dec. 17, 1875, son of Samuel M. and Linda (Haines) Willock, both surviving and residing in Allegheny city, Pa. The great-grandfather of Curtis M. Willock, Alexander Willock, and his brother, Noble Willock, were two of the original 107 voters on the first registry list of the county, compiled in 1804. The ancestry of the Willock family is of Scotch descent. Alexander Willock settled in Pittsburg in 1792, and kept the first inn opened in that city. In 1815 he and his family removed to what is now known as Willock Station, on the Baltimore & Ohio railroad, where he spent the remainder of his life. The grandfather of the subject of this sketch was born at Willock Station, and engaged in agricultural pursuits until his death in 1892. The father of Curtis M. was born on the old homestead farm at Willock Station in 1841, and is now proprietor of the Waverly oil works of Pittsburg. Curtis M. Willock was graduated at Princeton university in 1896, and from Harvard law school in 1899, and was admitted to the bar at Pittsburg, March 24, 1900. He is a member of all courts, stands well with his fellow members of the bar, and controls a good practice. He was married in Pittsburg, May 3, 1900, to Mary C., daughter of John Stevenson, Jr., of Sharon, Pa., and their home life is an ideal one. Mr. Willock is secretary of the Voters' civic league, member of the Third Presbyterian church, and resides in the twentieth ward.

WILLIAM SHERMAN MAXEY, attorney-at-law, with offices at No. 1409 Keystone building, Pittsburg, Pa., is the son of Thomas and Ann (Price) Maxey, both of whom were natives of Wales. Thomas Maxey came to America about the time he reached his majority. For a number of years he worked as a coal-miner in the vicinity of Carbondale and in Carbon county, Pa., but for the last forty-eight years he has been a resident of Susquehanna county, where he now lives retired. Ann Price came with her parents to America when she was seven years old, and lived in Pennsylvania until her death, which occurred in April, 1895. She was the mother of seven children, as follows: John, Annie, widow of Z. D. Jenkins; Margaret, wife of C. P. Chamberlain; Jennie, wife of W. G. Morgan; Thomas J., of Homestead, Pa.; William S., and Edwin M. Maxey. William S. Maxey was born in Clifford township, Susquehanna Co., Pa., Nov. 26, 1868. His education was obtained in the common schools, the Keystone academy, of Factoryville, Pa., and, in 1890, he was one of a large class that graduated from the State normal school at Mansfield. Soon after this he was duly registered and read law in the office of F. I. Lott, of Montrose, Pa. At the August term of court, in 1893, he was admitted to the bar of Susquehanna county. He immediately formed a partnership with his old preceptor, and practiced in Montrose, as the junior member of the firm of Lott & Maxey, until 1899. During this time the firm were the solicitors for Susquehanna county for five years. In 1899 Mr. Maxey retired from active practice. In 1901 he graduated from the Southern normal university, Huntingdon, Tenn., with the degree of bachelor of laws, and in September of that year he was admitted to the bar of Allegheny county. Since that time he has been practicing his profession in the city of Pittsburg with gratifying results. Among his clients is the Gilkinson American detective bureau, for which he is the general counsel. He is a past chancellor of Montrose lodge, No. 473, Knights of Pythias; a member now of South Side lodge, No. 158, of Pittsburg, and a member of Æneas conclave, Independent Order of Heptasophs, of Montrose, Pa. Mr. Maxey takes an active interest in political matters, and in both State and national campaigns has rendered service as one of the political orators in behalf of the republican party and its principles. He was married, March 15, 1902, in New York city, to Miss Anna M. Huson, and both he and his wife affiliate with the Baptist church. He lives in the fourteenth ward of the city of Pittsburg. His brother, Edwin Maxey, the youngest of the family, is an educator, lawyer and author of note. He is a member of the bar of Missouri, Illinois, Dakota and Pennsylvania; has been dean of the Southern normal university, Huntingdon, Tenn.; was assistant dean of the law department of Wisconsin university in 1903, and has held the position of lecturer in the Columbia law school at Washington, D. C. By his own efforts he has won every educational title which can be obtained in this country, has been a contributor to a number of the leading periodicals, and is the author of a book entitled "Some Questions of Larger Politics," which has had a large sale. He was recently elected as one of the instructors on corporation and international law in the University of West Virginia, at Morgantown, W. Va.

LAWRENCE P. MONAHAN, attorney, at No. 433 Fifth Ave., Pittsburg, is a native of Greensburg, Westmoreland county, where he was born July 2, 1876. His parents were Daniel and Gertrude (Brandt) Monahan, the latter having died Feb. 18, 1882. Mr. Monahan's primary education was obtained in private schools and at Fordham college, New York city, from which institution he graduated in 1897, receiving the degree of A. B., and, in 1900, the degree of A. M. Fordham college had a military department under the supervision of the United States government. Mr. Monahan was major in command in his senior year, and in competitive examination received a certificate that entitled him to a commission in time of war. At the outbreak of the late Spanish war, Mr. Monahan was, in accordance with the certificate, tendered an appointment as lieutenant in the regular service. He decided to take up the study of law, and to that end he entered the Pittsburg law school, graduating with the class of 1900, and receiving the degree of LL. B. He at once associated himself with the law firm of A. M. Brown & Sons, and having been admitted to practice in all the courts of the State, he entered upon what has proven to be a very successful professional career. He is a member of both the Allegheny county and Westmoreland county associations, and represents several large corporations as their solicitor. Mr. Monahan's practice is not confined to any particular court, and this affords him an extensive acquaintance, which has resulted in a large clientage. Mr. Monahan is a resident of the twentieth ward, where he is regarded as one of the most promising young professional men in the city.

THOMAS M. BENNER, of Pittsburg, Pa., a leading attorney-at-law, with offices at No. 427 Fifth Ave., was born in Allegheny city, Pa., May 7, 1873, son of Thomas M. and Mary (Armstrong) Benner, the former a native of Tioga county, Pa., who spent his entire life in Allegheny county and for many years was connected with the iron industry of Pittsburg. During the Civil war the elder Benner served in the 110th Pennsylvania volunteers, and later was prominently identified with the Grand Army of the Republic, being a member of Post No. 88, of Allegheny city, until his death, May 28, 1898. The mother of the subject of this sketch was born in Ireland, but came to the United States when an infant, and now resides in New York. Thomas M. Benner acquired his literary training in the thorough public schools of Allegheny city, attending the graded and high schools; then matriculated at the law department of the University of Michigan, at Ann Arbor, from which he was graduated with the class of 1896, receiving the degree of bachelor of laws. Subsequently he completed his studies in the offices of R. B. Scandrett, a prominent lawyer. He was admitted to the bar of Allegheny county in September, 1897, and since has practiced successfully in Pittsburg, where he is a member of all courts and has high rank as an attorney. He is a member of the Methodist Episcopal church, the Duquesne, the University and the Belleview clubs, and is a resident of the fourteenth ward. Mr. Benner is a director of the Duquesne printing company and a number of other corporations, and is well known in the financial world.

WALTER MORRIS, fire insurance underwriter, located in the German fire insurance company building, No. 218 Fourth Ave., Pittsburg, Pa., is the son of Robert and Maria (Thrower) Morris, both of whom were members of old English families, some of the Morris antecedents being lords of the manor in Surrey county, where Robert was born, in the town of Guilford, Oct. 31, 1805. In 1826 he emigrated to America, located at Pittsburg, and engaged in the grocery business—first, as a retail, and later as a wholesale dealer. His business prospered from the start, and in a few years he was at the head of the largest wholesale grocery house in the city of Pittsburg. For some time he conducted the business in his own name, and later under the firm name of Morris & Haworth. In 1855 he retired from business and lived a retired life until his death, which occurred at Norwich, England, June 21, 1866. During the time he was in business in Pittsburg, he lived in Allegheny city, where he was well and favorably known and where he took an active interest in all public affairs, never consenting to hold a public office. He was a director in several important banking institutions. Maria Thrower was born in Saxlingham, Norfolk Co., England, Sept. 17, 1810, and died at Norwich, Jan. 10, 1881. Her remains rest by the side of those of her husband in the Norwich cemetery. Robert and Maria Morris were the parents of five children: Frances, born in Halesworth, now the wife of William Symonds, of Ampleforth, Yorkshire, England; Maria, born in Allegheny city, now the wife of Robert George Bagshaw, sheriff of Norwich, England; Walter, the subject of this sketch; Georgiana, wife of Sydney W. Cook, a lace manufacturer of London, and a son of the mayor of Southampton, England; and Robert Riches, born in Allegheny city, who was traveling auditor for the Pennsylvania railroad company for many years, holding this position until he died, at the age of forty-six, at his home in Crafton, Pa., Sept. 3, 1889. Walter Morris was born in London, England, May 6, 1846. He was instructed by a private tutor at Norfolk, England, and, in 1862, came to America. In November of that year he enlisted in Walling's battery, light artillery, and served through the Civil war, participating in all the principal engagements of the southwest. He was mustered out at

Washington, D. C., Nov. 17, 1865. Upon leaving the army, he returned to Pittsburg and accepted a position with the Pittsburg, Fort Wayne & Chicago railroad company. He remained with this company until 1874, when he went into the offices of the Allemania insurance company as bookkeeper. In 1876 he was elected secretary of the Citizens' insurance company of Pittsburg, and retained this position until 1887, when he resigned, much to the regret of the directors of the company, to go into business for himself. He is now engaged in a general fire insurance business, representing the Westchester, Williamsburg City and Greenwich companies of New York; the Dutchess insurance company of Poughkeepsie, N. Y., and the Ben Franklin company of Allegheny, Pa. On May 9, 1867, he was married to Miss Mary E. Cowling, a daughter of James and Emily Cowling, of Allegheny city. Five children have been born to them, four of whom are now living: Robert James, born April 3, 1869, and died Aug. 17, 1898; Jessie Emily, born Dec. 30, 1871; Walter C., born Nov. 24, 1873, and is now employed in his father's office; Mary Elizabeth, born June 2, 1878, now the wife of C. C. Gray, of Ingram, Pa., and Charles Weaver, born April 20, 1885. He and his wife are both members of the Episcopal Church of the Nativity, at Crafton, Pa. He is a past commander of General Hays post, No. 3, G. A. R., of Pittsburg, and belongs to Allegheny lodge, No. 223, Free and Accepted Masons. He is an unassuming, but at the same time a very popular citizen, taking an active interest in everything that tends to promote the welfare of the borough of Ingram, where he resides.

GEORGE W. HEPLINE, superintendent of Arsenal station, Pittsburg postoffice, was born in Pittsburg, in the twenty-seventh ward, in 1874. He is a son of John and Cordelia Hepline, both natives of Pennsylvania, his father being a ship carpenter. He attended the ward schools when a boy, left school at the age of twelve, but afterwards studied for a time at the Pittsburg business college. In 1893 he passed the civil service examination, and the following year received an appointment in the Pittsburg postoffice as clerk in the D. P. O. department. Here he remained about eighteen months, then was transferred to Station A, now known as East Liberty station, and was employed as clerk at this station about seven months. After this he was for five years clerk at Station C, or Carson station, and then, in December, 1902, was appointed to his present position as a deserved reward for his long and faithful service. He was married, on Nov. 10, 1898, to Miss Olive E. Seibert, daughter of Geo. D. and Mary Seibert, of Pittsburg, Pa. They have had only one child, G. Millard, who died, Jan. 20, 1901, at two years of age. Mr. Hepline is a member of several fraternal orders, and he and his wife both belong to the First Methodist Protestant church, South Side, Pittsburg. In politics he is a republican.

THOMAS DAVID MacCLOSKEY, of Pittsburg, Pa., a prominent attorney and counselor-at-law, with offices in the Bank for Savings building, was born in Somerville, Mass., Jan. 7, 1873, son of Thomas and Abigail (Warnock) MacCloskey, both natives of the Bay State and now residing at Somerville. Thomas D. MacCloskey was educated in the elementary branches in the grammar and high schools of Somerville, and later attended Geneva college, where he was graduated, in 1893, with the degree of bachelor of arts. He then matriculated at the Harvard law school and was graduated from that famous institution, in 1899, with the degree of bachelor of laws. He was admitted to the bar of the supreme court of Massachusetts in the fall of 1899, and after a practice of a few months in Boston and Somerville, removed to Pittsburg, where he was admitted to the bar of Allegheny county in September, 1900. Since that time Mr. MacCloskey has practiced with much success in Pittsburg, where he is a member of all courts and of the Allegheny county bar association. He is a member of the McKinley lodge, No. 318, of Allegheny, of the A. F. and A M., and of Ethel lodge, No. 314, of the Independent Order of Heptasophs. Mr. MacCloskey is a leading member of the North Presbyterian church of Allegheny city and is assistant superintendent of the afternoon Sunday-school of that church. He resides in the second ward of Allegheny city and is well known in both cities.

JAMES WILSON DICKSON, M. D., one of the distinguished physicians of Allegheny city, Pa., was born in Sewickley, Allegheny Co., Pa., Aug. 10, 1852. His father, Stephen Dickson, was a prominent contractor and builder of Sewickley, who died in 1855. Dr. Dickson's mother was a Miss Annie Porter, who is still living in the town of Sewickley. James Wilson Dickson received a good education in the Sewickley academy, and Jefferson college, Cannonsburg, Pa., after which he read medicine in the office of his uncle, Dr. John Dickson, for two years, and graduated from the Jefferson medical college, Philadelphia, with the class of 1875. Since that time he has been engaged in the practice of his profession in Allegheny city. Ever since the days of Hippocrates there have been in every country and every age unselfish persons who stood ready to make sacrifices for suffering humanity. Such a man is Dr. James W. Dickson. Thoroughly in love with his calling and imbued with the knowledge of the nobility of his chosen profession, he has never turned a deaf ear to the appeals of the afflicted. Nor has he allowed himself to fall behind in the march of progress. Although more than a quarter of a century has elapsed since he received his diploma as a physician, from one of the greatest medical colleges in the country, he has kept himself fully informed with regard to the new discoveries in the science of medicine and is considered one of the most progressive physicians of western Pennsylvania. He is a member of both the county and State medical associations and the Physicians' protective association. He served with distinction as the city bacteriologist of Allegheny city, and while in that position made many valuable suggestions for the promotion of the public health. Dr. Dickson was married, in June, 1898, to Miss Sarah Callahan, an estimable young lady of Allegheny city. He takes an active interest in all matters pertaining to the public welfare, particularly those affecting the fifth ward of Allegheny city, where he resides. He has served his ward ably in the common council, and, in 1903, was the republican candidate for sheriff of the county, being elected, Nov. 3, 1903, by 1,768 majority.

ULYSSES GRANT MARKS, of Pittsburg, Pa., a successful attorney, with offices in the Bank for Savings building, was born in Beaver county, Pa., son of the late James and Margaret J. Marks. Mr. Marks acquired his elementary educational training in the public schools of his native county and the academy of Bridgewater, Pa., and after teaching for two years in his native county, entered the Western University of Pennsylvania, which he attended for three years. Subsequently he matriculated at Westminster college and was graduated from that institution in the class of 1891. The following year he entered the law department of Columbia university, New York city, where he took a three years' course. He removed to Chicago, and, in December, 1895, entered the law office of Judson F. Goehing, a prominent attorney of that city, and, in May, 1896, was admitted to the bar of Illinois. Mr. Marks at once began the practice in Chicago, and there met with much success for three years, when he removed to Pittsburg, in 1899, and entered the law firm of Brown & Stewart. In June, 1900, Mr. Marks was admitted to the bar of Allegheny county, and has since practiced in Pittsburg, where he now has a fine clientage and stands well among the prominent attorneys of the city.

CHARLES W. HAMILTON, of Pittsburg, Pa., a successful attorney-at-law, with offices in the Bakewell building, was born at McKeesport, Pa., March 11, 1873, son of James B. and Jennie A. Hamilton, both natives of Allegheny county, the former now residing in Elizabeth, where he was elected to the office of prothonotary for a three-year term, beginning Jan. 1, 1904. Charles W. Hamilton was educated in the graded and high schools of Elizabeth, and later attended the Pittsburg academy. On leaving school he began as an accountant in the office of the recorder, and subsequently matriculated at the Dickinson law school, where he was graduated on June 7, 1897, with the degree of bachelor of laws. In September, 1897, Mr. Hamilton was admitted to the bar of Allegheny county, and has since been in continuous practice in Pittsburg, where he is a member of all courts and enjoys a splendid clientele. He is a member of the Junior Order of United American Mechanics and the Royal Arcanum, and served for six years as a member of Company I, 14th regiment, Pennsylvania national guard, and when the call for volunteers was made, he enlisted, on April 27, 1898, as a member of Company I, 14th regiment, Pennsylvania volunteer infantry, serving with the regiment until Sept. 27, 1898, when he was discharged.

EDWARD JAMES SMAIL, of Pittsburg, Pa., a distinguished attorney, with offices in the Bakewell building, was born in the borough of Greensburg, Westmoreland Co., Pa., Dec. 24, 1859, son of Samuel and Catherine (Mainhart) Smail, both born and reared in Hempfield township, Westmoreland Co., Pa., but now residing at Braddock, Allegheny Co., Pa. Mr. Smail acquired his rudimentary educational training in the public schools of Johnstown, at the Greensburg academy and under private tutors. In 1880 he was graduated from the State normal school at California, Pa., and began to read law in the offices of ex-Governor Stone, of Pittsburg. He was admitted to the bar on Jan. 6, 1883; has practiced continuously since in Pittsburg, where he is a member of all courts and of the Allegheny county bar association. Mr. Smail is prominently identified with some of the leading fraternal orders, being a member and past master of Braddock's Field lodge, No. 510, A. F. and A. M.; member of Shiloh chapter, No. 257, Royal Arch Masons; Tancred commandery, No. 48, of Knights Templars; Pennsylvania consistory, and Syria temple of the Mystic Shrine. Mr. Smail is also exalted ruler of Pittsburg lodge, No. 11, B. P. O. Elks; member of the Monongahela council, No. 122, of the Junior Order of American Mechanics; the Edgar Thompson council of the Royal Arcanum; the Braddock lodge, No. 180, of the Ancient Order of United Workmen; the Pittsburg chamber of commerce; the Americus republican club; the Young Men's tariff club, and the Masonic country club. He is president of the board of education of the borough of Braddock, where he resides; has served as solicitor of the boroughs of Braddock and Rankin, and of various school districts. He is president and solicitor of the Pittsburg & Indiana gas company; a stockholder in the Union National bank of Braddock, and one-fourth owner of the Braddock land company. Mr. Smail was married to Ella Dyer, daughter of F. D. and Eliza A Eshelman, of the second ward of Allegheny city, descendants of the pioneer Pennsylvania Dutch, and they have had four children, viz.: Blanch Ella, born June 24, 1884, and died Aug. 22, 1897, at the age of thirteen years; Hazel Inez, born Jan. 14, 1886, and a graduate of Linden Hall seminary; Edward James, born Dec. 22, 1888, now at Nazareth Hall, preparing for college, and Nellus Urilda, born June 20, 1900. Mr. Smail is an active worker in the ranks of the republican party, and he and his family are members of the First Christian church of Braddock.

JAMES H. THOMPSON, M. D., of Pittsburg, Pa, a prominent specialist on gynecology, was born in Emsworth, Allegheny county, July 30, 1859, son of Henry Van Thompson, a millwright of Emsworth, and of his wife, Jane (Moore) Thompson. Dr. Thompson attended the public schools of his native county and the Allegheny college, at Meadville, where he was graduated in a classical course in 1884, receiving the degree of bachelor of arts, and one year later the degree of A. M. was given him by his alma mater. Then he matriculated at the Hahnemann medical college, of Chicago, and was graduated from that institution in 1886. Dr. Thompson was resident surgeon of the Homœopathic hospital, of Pittsburg, Pa., for two years, and, in 1888, began to practice medicine in Pittsburg. He was engaged with his large general practice until 1894, when he went to Europe to take postgraduate courses in gynecology. He studied under Professor Martin at Berlin for six months, spent eight months in Vienna, studied six months in Paris under Professors Pean and Pozzi, and at Heidelberg under Professor Koenig. After two years spent in study on the continent, Dr. Thompson returned to Pittsburg, and has devoted his entire time to gynecology, in which specialty he has been very successful, and stands among the leading physicians of the county. He maintains offices at Nos. 313 and 314 Smith block, and resides at the corner of South Negley and Walnut streets, East End, Pittsburg. Dr. Thompson is a member of the Allegheny county and the Pennsylvania State homœopathic medical societies, the American institute of homœopathy, of which he is chairman of the department of gynecology, and of the East End homœopathic doctors' club. He is also a member of the Pittsburg country club, the republican party and the First Presbyterian church. He has served on the surgical staff of the Homœopathic hospital since 1888, and is one of the best-known physicians of the city. The grandfather of Dr. Thompson was a surgeon in the Revolutionary war, and seven of his brothers were surgeons in the eastern part of the United States.

JOHN M. WILSON, M. D., of Pittsburg, Pa., a prominent physician, was born in Dennison, Ohio, Aug. 14, 1872, son of Thomas H. and Harriet (McCulloch) Wilson, his father being a prominent physician of Ohio, who has practiced in that State for thirty-five years with much success. His mother was a native of Harrison county, Ohio, and died in 1897. Dr. Wilson's maternal ancestors came to America prior to the Revolutionary war, and were members of the patriot army during the struggle for independence. His father served in Company H, 8oth Ohio volunteers, during the Civil war, and is said to be the youngest veteran now living that served through the entire war, he having enlisted when only fifteen years of age. Dr. Wilson was educated in the rudimentary branches in the graded and high schools of Dennison, graduating from the last-named school in 1889. He spent two years at Scio college, later matriculated at the medical department of the Western University of Pennsylvania, of Pittsburg, and was graduated in 1896, with the degree of doctor of medicine. He was resident physician in the Pittsburg city hospital for two years, in 1898 began a general practice, and has met with much success in his professional work. Dr. Wilson is a member of the Allegheny county, the Pennsylvania State and the American medical associations, the West Pennsylvania medical society and the Pi Beta Phi medical fraternity. He is also a Knight Templar, thirty-second degree Mason, and member of the Mystic Shrine and I. O. O. F. He is city physician of Pittsburg, assistant to chair of orthopedic surgery in West Pennsylvania college, and medical examiner for the Metropolitan, the New England mutual and the State life insurance companies. Dr. Wilson is also a member of the republican party. A brother of his, Dr. R. A. Wilson, was appointed assistant surgeon in the United States army in 1898, and has made a fine record in that capacity.

WILLIAM H. LOGAN, grocer at No. 221 Fifth Ave., Carnegie, was born in Shirland, Allegheny Co., Pa., Feb. 16, 1846. His father, David Logan, was born in Pennsylvania in 1800, and died in 1862, and his mother, Elizabeth (McDonnell) Logan, born in 1812, died in 1895. David Logan was a farmer by vocation, but was also an itinerant minister of the gospel and an authority on scriptural subjects, often taking part in debates on religion. He owned a farm in North Fayette township, on which he and all his children were born. This farm, which has been in the family for three-fourths of a century, is now owned by his son, David M. Logan. William H. Logan, the subject of this sketch, is the eldest of five children. Of these, John A., a twin brother of William H., died Aug. 29, 1886, and Hugh L., a general merchant, born in 1852, died on Aug. 18, 1886; George is a farmer in Allegheny county and also interested in oil, and David M. resides on the old home farm. William H. Logan attended the public schools and supplemented his education at Clinton academy. He also attended lectures in the Physio-Eclectic medical college in Cincinnati, Ohio, and received his diploma in 1878, but never practiced medicine, preferring to devote himself to mercantile pursuits. He came to Carnegie from Shirland in 1884, and has since then been successfully engaged in the grocery business. On May 5, 1869, Mr. Logan was married to Miss Harriet L. Williams, daughter of Ashley and Elizabeth (West) Williams, of Henry county, Ky. Her father, a carriage-maker by trade, was an ardent republican, a loyal Union man, and though not enlisted in the army, volunteered to fight in the battle of Perryville, which occurred near his home. After the war he was employed as inspector of materials used in the construction of government wagons. In 1888 Mr. and Mrs. Williams celebrated their golden wedding, at which all the living children were present. Mr. Williams was born April 3, 1815, and died May 20, 1890; his wife, born April 8, 1817, died June 10, 1898. Of eleven children born to Mr. and Mrs. Williams, Mrs. Logan and two others, Mrs. E. S. DeHoff and Frank W., both of Indianapolis, survive. The deceased are: Allen, Thomas, Alexander, James, Webster, George, Martha and John. Mr. and Mrs. Logan have had three children: Elizabeth, a graduate of the music department of the Pittsburg female college of the class of 1894, has been for several years engaged most successfully in teaching music. She is now pursuing her studies in music under the tutelage of Prof. A. M. Foerster, an instructor and composer, of Pittsburg. Ashley, born Feb. 21, 1875, died on Aug. 3, 1879, and Joseph J. is a mechanical engineer in the employ of the Pan Handle railroad. Mr. Logan and family are members of the Christian church. He has passed through all the chairs of the Masonic fraternity, the Odd Fellows and American Mechanics, and is a member of the Knights of Malta. In politics he has ever been an ardent republican. Mr. Logan and his family are respected people, and stand well in the community of which they form an important part.

ELMER ARMSTRONG, of McKee's Rocks, Pa., a prominent dealer in real estate, was born in Hibbardsville, Athens Co., Ohio, on Dec. 21, 1878. He is a son of Elza B. and Elizabeth (Hibbard) Armstrong, and is the eldest of three children, all of whom are now living and, besides himself, are: Charles Crawford and Ruth, who live at the old homestead in Athens county, Ohio. His father conducts a stock farm of 640 acres, which has been in the family since 1798, his great-grandfather having settled there at that time. His paternal grandfather was Elmer Armstrong, and his paternal great-grandfather was Thomas Armstrong, who settled the homestead in Athens county. His father is now actively in charge of his farm, but his mother died on Feb. 17, 1896. Elmer Armstrong was educated in the elementary courses in the public schools of his native county, and completed his classical training at the Ohio university. While still a student at college, he became interested with his father in the management of their stock farm, remained in business with him for a number of years, and, later, went into the milling business at Columbus, Ohio. In the spring of 1899, Mr. Armstrong came to McKee's Rocks, where he engaged in the grocery business with his brother-in-law, Frank E. Coe, remaining with that concern until 1901, when he disposed of his interest in the store and began the real estate business with his present partner, C A. Carter. He was married, on Oct. 2, 1900, to Mary Elsie Coe, of Hibbardsville, Ohio, and their wedded life has been a halcyon one. Mr. Armstrong is independent in his political beliefs, and is a member of the Cumberland Presbyterian church of his old home in Ohio. Mr. Armstrong is a gentleman of recognized ability, and stands high in the business and social circles of the home of his adoption.

FRANK J. SEIFRIED, a prominent wholesale liquor dealer at Carnegie, was born in Austria, Sept. 3, 1867. His parents, Frank and Amelia (Gaidost) Seifried, came to America in 1882, and settled near Beach Cliff, Allegheny county, where they still reside. Mr. Seifried keeps the general store at Cliff Mine. Mr. Seifried and wife are members of the German Roman Catholic church at Carnegie. Of their three living children, F. J., the subject of this sketch, is the oldest; Steven K. is interested in mining machinery, and Mary is postmistress. F. J. Seifried was educated in Austria, and on coming to America attended night school, working during the day in his father's store. In 1890 he began mercantile pursuits for himself, opening a small store in Carnegie. Afterwards he also ran a store for a short time at Bower Hill, and another at Glendale, and still owns the store buildings he occupied in those places. The store in Bower Hill he sold to his brother, Steven K. Seifried, and, in 1891, engaged with John Roach in the wholesale liquor business. He has since bought out his partner, and is now sole proprietor of a large and flourishing liquor house. Mr. Seifried was postmaster at Cliff Mine from 1889 to 1895, and, on his moving away, his sister has filled the position most satisfactorily since. In 1893 he was treasurer of a building and loan association at Bower Hill, which was dissolved after a short time. June 6, 1895, Mr. Seifried married Miss Rosa Kawasky, a native of Allegheny county, daughter of Frank and Katherine (Holeman)

Kawasky, both natives of Germany, and both now deceased. Mr. and Mrs. Seifried have had four children. Herbert died when seven months old, Nov. 19, 1899. The others are: Lawrence F., Eugene M. and Margaret Rose. Mr. Seifried and his wife are members of the German Roman Catholic church at Carnegie. In politics Mr. Seifried has always been an ardent republican, as is his father also. He is a progressive, industrious business man, and his dealings are all as honorable as they are profitable.

WILLIAM M. SCOTT, hardware merchant at No. 214 Main St., Carnegie, was born in Allegheny county, June 17, 1853. His parents, Thomas and Lucinda (Snodgrass) Scott, are both dead. Mrs. Scott, who was the daughter of John Snodgrass, died July 4, 1861. Her husband died Aug. 11, 1902, at the advanced age of ninety years. Thomas Scott came to this country from Ireland when about sixteen years old, and settled in Allegheny county, where he was for many years a well-known farmer and prominent old settler. Of ten children of Thomas and Lucinda Scott, five died when young, and those living are: John, a shipper in a wholesale grocery house in Pittsburg; Sarah, widow of S. B. McGarvy, and living with her daughter, Mrs. F. V. Blair, at Camden, Pa.; Alexander M., a wholesale grocer, living in Braddock; William M., the subject of this sketch, and Elizabeth, who married Charles C. Robinson and resides at No. 215 Lehigh Ave., Pittsburg. William M. Scott received a common-school education and began his business career, at first as a member of the firm of Robinson, Scott & Co., dealers in general merchandise, continuing at this for three years. His next venture was in the same business in a company store at Coal Bluff, Washington county, under the firm name of W. M. Scott & Co. After seven years in the store at Coal Bluff, Mr. Scott did not embark in business for a few years, and, later started, at Federal, Allegheny county, a general store under the name of the Federal store company, and remained as sole owner and manager of this business for four years. In February, 1900, he came to Carnegie and opened his present store, where he carries a full line of hardware, stoves, pumps, paints and oils, and general household furnishings, and is doing a steadily increasing business.

On Oct. 14, 1885, Mr. Scott married Miss Hattie Morrison, of Washington, Pa., daughter of James and Sarah Jane Morrison, both of whom are now living in Nottingham township, Washington county. Mrs. Scott had one sister, Anna Lois, now at home, and another, Henrietta, who married C. A. Fry, a dry-goods merchant of Brownsville, Pa. Three children were born to William M. Scott and wife: Sarah B., James M. and Lois G. Mrs. Scott died July 25, 1895. She was born June 14, 1863. Mr. Scott was married to Mary E. Cowen, of Fort Scott, Kan., Jan. 20, 1903, and now resides at No. 61 Lincoln Ave., Carnegie, Pa. Mr. Scott is an active worker in the Presbyterian church and an elder of that church.

JOHN HENRY (deceased), iron and steel manufacturer, was born at Port Talbot, Glamorganshire, Wales, in 1842. His parents, Evan and Elizabeth Henry, were well and favorably known throughout the community. The father, a copper roller by trade, filled the position of precentor at the Dyffryn church for thirty years, with constant faithfulness and great credit. The late John Henry was the eldest of six children. Of his brothers and sisters, David, Thomas and Elizabeth are dead, and Llewellyn and William are living in Wales. From early youth, John Henry was remarkable for his good habits, straightforwardness and earnest ambition. He loved his home and native land, but America offered him a broader field and more advantageous surroundings, and in 1866, accompanied by his life-long friend, William Hughes, he came to Pittsburg. In America he met many ups and downs, but profited by his reverses, and in the end succeeded better than he had hoped. At the Frankstown rolling mill, owned by the late Grey Brothers, of Soho, he went through the lower grades of his trade patiently, but persistently, and in 1869 he was given charge of a sheet mill at Apollo, Armstrong county, where he worked four years, giving the best satisfaction as a roller and mechanic, and laying the foundation of an extensive fortune and a brilliant future. In 1873 he received the appointment of manager of the Ironton steel works, Ironton, Ohio, and in 1877 was engaged by the Chisolms, of Cleveland, Ohio, to manufacture sheet steel, being one of the first in this country to make the production of that article a success. In 1879 he returned to Apollo and took up the superintendence of the mill where he had made his first start as a roller, and soon the concern was in a flourishing condition, turning out superior brands of iron and steel sheet, which commanded an enviable market. In 1883, with Messrs. Kirkpatrick and Carter as partners, he erected the Chartiers iron and steel works, and was its general manager from the start. The success of this undertaking was phenomenal from the first; the iron and steel sheet turned out was as near in quality to the Russian iron sheet as any brand in the American market, and readily commanded the highest price. In 1899 the mill was sold to the steel trust, and later on, with other mills of the trust, was absorbed by the United States steel corporation; but with both companies Mr. Henry was retained as manager. In 1901, during the iron workers' strike, when the combine ordered the Chartiers mill to be dismantled, he strained every effort to prevent it, but in vain, and after the dismantling he tendered his resignation. The higher officials refused to accept it, and up to the time of his death, he filled the position of inspector, making trips occasionally to the various mills of the company, in an advisory capacity. Mr. Henry was killed, Aug. 16, 1902, by falling between the train and the platform at the Fourth avenue depot, Pittsburg, while en route for Alma, Mich., to spend a month at the sanitarium at that place. Mr. Henry was a man of sterling worth, intensely active, prompted by lofty ambitions, and endowed with unconquerable courage. Besides being a successful manufacturer, he was a gifted man of affairs, and endowed with the business instinct of a financier. He was a heavy stockholder in various enterprises, among them the First National bank of Carnegie, and the Carnegie trust company, holding the office of director in both institutions. In 1892 Mr. Henry was married to Jennie Pettigrew, whose parents, John and Jane (Hines) Pettigrew, natives respectively of Scotland and England, were married in Scotland, and on coming to the United States, in 1862, settled at Cambridge, Ohio. Here, on Feb. 15, 1872, the father, when about sixty years old, was instantly killed by the falling of earth in an embankment. His wife, now seventy-five years old, makes her home with Mrs. Henry. Mrs. Henry was the youngest of nine children. Only one other survives, Mrs. William Noble, now a widow, who resides in Cambridge, Ohio, in the old home-place where her family settled in 1852. Besides the widow, Mrs. Henry, four children mourn the loss of an affectionate father: Gwendoline, John, William and Elizabeth.

JOHN JOSEPH BULLION, pastor of St. Mary Magdalene Catholic church at Homestead, was born in Sharpsburg, Allegheny Co., Pa., in 1856, son of John and Catherine (Ruttinger) Bullion, natives of Bavaria, who came to America in 1852 and located in Sharpsburg. Mr. and Mrs. John Bullion had eight children, Agnes, John J., Mary, Michael, Joseph, Mina (Mrs. Joseph Jacobs), Charles and Annie (deceased). Father Bullion was educated at St. Michael's seminary at Glenwood, Pa., and at the Seminary of St. Sulpice at Montreal, Canada. In 1878 he was ordained to the priesthood by Bishop Fabre, of Montreal. His first mission was at Dudley, Huntingdon Co., Pa., where he went in January, 1879, and remained a year and a half as pastor of the Church of the Immaculate Conception. He was transferred as assistant at St. Peter's church, Allegheny, serving in that capacity nearly a year, and, in the spring of 1881, was assigned to Homestead as pastor of St. Mary Magdalene parish. At that time church services were held in a hall on Sixth avenue, there being no church building, but in a short time a church was erected on Tenth avenue at a cost of about $4,000. At this time the congregation numbered about fifty families, but the membership increased so rapidly that better accommodations were needed, and, in 1888, a two-story church and parochial school building was erected, which cost $10,000. This building was destroyed by fire, Dec. 5, 1890, and, in 1891, a fine, four-story brick building for school purposes was erected on its site at a cost of $25,000. The corner-stone of the present church was laid Oct. 20, 1895, the ceremonies being under the direction of Bishop Phelan, bishop of the diocese, and the church was dedicated on December 13th of the next year. This church, which stands at the corner of Tenth avenue and Amity street, was erected at a cost of $80,000, and is the finest church, outside of Pittsburg, in the diocese. It has a seating capacity of 1,200. Its erection was mainly due to the efforts of Father Bullion, who has built up the church until it now has a membership of 2,500, comprising some 500 families. The parochial school in connection has an enrollment of about 500. Father Bullion is a member and director of the C. M. B. A. and a member of several other societies. He is one of the directors of the Carnegie library at Homestead.

NATHANIEL MONTGOMERY, a prominent farmer of Wilkins township, and for nineteen years elder in the Beulah Presbyterian church, was born in Wilkins township, Allegheny Co., Pa., June 23, 1843. His father, Nathaniel Montgomery, born Feb. 8, 1816, was by vocation a farmer, and a member of Beulah church. His wife was Mary (McCully) Montgomery. The subject of this sketch was educated in the public schools, and has been a farmer all his life. He has long been a prominent man in his community, where he has served as school director. In 1884 he married Mary F. Pitt, now deceased. On May 22, 1895, Mr. Montgomery took as his second wife, Marion, daughter of James and Elizabeth Peterson, residents of Allegheny county, though of Scotch descent. Mr. Peterson, who was born in Scotland, March 15, 1826, was for many years superintendent in the Newtown coal mines, and opened up mines Nos. 2, 3 and 4. Mrs. Montgomery is the third of a family of seven children. She is also a member of the Beulah church, which is the oldest church in the county.

LOUIS ZINSSER, of Millvale, Pa., manager of the American baking company, was born in Germany, Sept. 13, 1859, son of Christian and Eliza (Michael) Zinsser, his father now living in Germany and a prosperous baker. Mr. Zinsser attended the public schools of his native land until fourteen years of age, and then spent two years at a soldiers' school. On leaving, he learned the baking business under his father, and for two years was thus engaged. The next three years of his life were spent in the German army, and at the expiration of his term of service came to America, settled in Pittsburg, and for two years was in the bakery of Adolph Zinsser. He went with Marvin & Co., of Pittsburg, and was with them for six years; in 1891 he started a bakery on his own account on Troy Hill, where he prospered until 1900, when he removed to Millvale, and there incorporated a business under the name of the American baking company, with himself as president and manager. This venture has been a decided success, and they have a large and profitable patronage. He was married, in 1885, to Emma Dotzenroth, and they have two children, Matilda A. and Gezena E. Mr. Zinsser is a member of the German Lutheran church, the German military shrine and the republican party. He has made three trips to Europe since coming to America, and is well posted on European affairs. Mr. Zinsser is a safe and conservative business man, and possesses the confidence of the entire community.

DAVID L. DAVIS, roller at the Zug & Co. (limited), rolling mill, Pittsburg, is one of the most prominent men of Scott township, and secretary of the school board. He was born in Allegheny county, Pa., Nov. 5, 1865, a son of David and Tamar (Parry) Davis, natives of Monmouthshire, Wales. The father was a mill worker in Wales, and on coming to America, in 1857, continued at the same work in this country, being employed most of the time in Pittsburg. He was a heater, and worked for twenty-four years for Dilworth, Porter & Co. He retired from active life at the age of sixty, and died sixteen years later, Feb. 4, 1900, and his wife at the age of seventy, May 9, 1899. Mr. and Mrs. Davis were residents of Scott township for thirty-six years, were widely respected people, and influential members of the Baptist church. They had eleven children, as follows: William, a heater, residing in Carnegie; Margaret, afterwards Mrs. John C. McGrew, who died in 1893 when forty years old; John, who died when four years old; Emma, now Mrs. Frank Richards, of Crafton, Pa.; Mary, now the wife of George Bradley, of Pittsburg; Martha, now Mrs. William Lee, of Sutton, W. Va.; Lizzie; David L., the subject of this sketch; Jennie, a teacher in Pittsburg; Birdie, who died when two years old, and Harry, a grocer, of Scott township. D. L. Davis was educated in the public schools of Pittsburg, and after completing his education began to work in the mills, continuing to be a sheet iron worker ever since. He was first employed as a doubler, then as a rougher, and has for the past eleven years been engaged as a boss roller. He has always been a faithful and efficient workman, and enjoys the confidence of his employers. On March 25, 1899, Mr. Davis was married at Marietta, Ohio, to Miss Jean Chadwick, daughter of James and Permelia (Saunders) Chadwick, of Washington county, where James Chadwick was a prominent farmer and an elder in the Prosperity Presbyterian church. He died when sixty-seven years old, Dec. 24, 1896, and his wife died Jan. 28, 1888, in her fifty-eighth year. Mrs. Davis is the youngest of eight living children. The others are: Steven S., a hotel keeper of Culver, Ind.; Mrs. Orlando Baglin, of East Liverpool, Ohio; W. W., of Sunset, Pa.; John H., state's attorney at Tuscola, Ill.; A. Lincoln, a gardener, of Washington, Pa.; Isaac N., a farmer, of Prosperity, Pa., and Mrs. R. B. Gilson, of New Matamoras, Ohio. One child, James M., died in infancy. Mr. Davis is vice-president of the Domestic land company. He is now serving his third term as member of the school board, to which he was elected in 1894. He is an enthusiastic member of the Masonic fraternity, being a member of Centennial lodge, No. 544; Cyrus chapter, No. 280, of Carnegie, and Chartiers commandery, No. 78, Knights Templars. He is also a prominent member of the Knights of the Golden Eagle and the J. O. U. A. M. In politics he is an ardent republican.

STEWARD LE ROY McCURDY, M. D., of Pittsburg, Pa., a leading physician and specialist in orthopedy, was born in Bowenstown, Ohio, July 15, 1859, son of Peter and Mary A. (Bowen) McCurdy. He was educated in the common schools of Dennison, Ohio, and has taken a number of special courses. He was graduated from the Columbus medical college in 1881; attended a full course at the New York post-graduate college and hospital, and received the degree of master of arts from Scio college in 1894. He was a trustee of the Ohio medical university during 1887-93, and was professor of orthopedic surgery at that institution from 1887 to 1891, inclusive. He is now professor of anatomy and surgery, trustee and secretary of the dental department of the Western University of Pennsylvania at Pittsburg, and professor of orthopedy in the medical department of that college. Dr. McCurdy is surgeon for the P. C. C. & St. L. and the Pennsylvania railroads, and is president and member of the association of surgeons of the Pennsylvania system of railroads. He is a member of the American orthopedic association, member of the Pennsylvania State, the Ohio State and the American medical associations. Dr. McCurdy has frequently contributed articles on orthopedy to the medical journals, is the author of a manual on orthopedic surgery and a text-book on "Oral Surgery," the latter being a treatise on the application of general medicine and surgery to dentistry. Dr. McCurdy was married, in 1887, to Susan Riggs, of Dennison, Ohio. Dr. McCurdy keeps thoroughly abreast of the latest advancements of his specialty, and has spent several winters in New York city attending post-graduate courses in orthopedic surgery.

HARRY J. SEIBEL, contractor and builder at Carnegie, was born in Allegheny county, Pa., Feb. 18, 1872. His parents, Andrew and Mary A. (Seibel) Seibel, were born in Germany, married in Germany in 1869, and came to America in 1872, locating at first in Pittsburg. Mr. Seibel had been a gardener in Germany, and has followed this vocation since coming to America. In 1873 he came to East Carnegie, and lived there twelve years, and then bought a farm of his own of fifty-four acres, on which he has since resided. He is now sixty-three years old, and his wife fifty-four. They are members of St. Joseph's Catholic church, Carnegie. Harry J. Seibel, the subject of this sketch, is the eldest of thirteen children, all born in Allegheny county. Of these, six died in early life, and Charles A., born Feb. 19, 1885, died March 12, 1894. Of those now living, Rosa is the wife of Peter Britner, of Glendale, and has four children, Tony, Florence A., Tillie M. and Matilda; Mary A. married Fred Barthon, and lives on Hill street, Glendale; Anna J. is a saleswoman; August and Andres H. are assisting their father on the farm. Harry J. Seibel attended the public schools of Carnegie when a boy, and worked for his father. Being naturally handy with tools, he determined to learn the carpenters' trade, and has been unusually successful in his chosen vocation. After learning his trade, he also spent one year as a dealer in all kinds of live-stock. On Aug. 24, 1898, he was wedded to Miss Carrie Weber, and after marriage worked two years at his trade, and then spent over two years as a hotel keeper. It was while in that business that his wife died, June 12, 1901. She was born Sept. 9, 1873. Mrs. Seibel was the daughter of Phias and Mary (Cutner) Weber, natives of Germany, who came to this country and were married in Pittsburg. Mrs. Seibel was a member of St. Joseph's Catholic church, was a woman of many friends, and her death was a severe blow to all who knew her. Mr. Seibel has one child living, Mary Anna. His son, Joseph H., born March 3, 1901, died on June 7th of that year. Mr. Seibel has been unusually successful in his business, and has amassed a considerable fortune. He is at present building fifteen houses of his own on Bower hill, and fourteen for other people. He owns building lots in Idaville, Carnegie, Chartiers township, Scott township, Collier township, and Upper St. Clair and Lower St. Clair townships. He has been quite active in public life, and has served as a member of the board of electors of Scott township one year. He holds stock in the Domestic land company, of Carnegie, and the Chartiers valley building company. He is a member of St. Joseph's Catholic church.

J. K. M. PERRINE, M. D., of Pittsburg, Pa., a well-known physician and specialist on the diseases of the eye, ear, nose and throat, was born in Idlewood, Allegheny Co., Pa., Nov. 20, 1870, son of T. C. and Sarah Josephine (Morange) Perrine, his father having been a member of the firm of Eli Edmundson & Son, dealers in hardwood furniture and upholstering, and is now a member of the firm of Edmundson & Perrine, engaged in the same business. The elder Perrine is a native of Allegheny county, and his ancestors were among the first settlers of the county. Dr. Perrine's maternal great-grandfather, John Morange, was the first steel nail manufacturer west of the Allegheny mountains, and the grandfather of Dr. Perrine, James K. Morange, was a prominent oil-broker of Pittsburg. Dr. Perrine attended the public schools of Pittsburg, the Willard preparatory school and the Western University of Pennsylvania. He entered the Hahnemann medical college, of Philadelphia, and was graduated in 1893 He came to Pittsburg as resident physician of the Homœopathic hospital for a short time, and then went to Philadelphia and attended a special course in the Polyclinic college for graduates of medicine. On leaving this school, Dr. Perrine went to Germany, where he took special courses in the diseases of the eye, ear, nose and throat, at Göttingen, Heidelberg and Berlin, and spent two years on the continent in studying this specialty. In 1895 he returned to Pittsburg, and since has devoted his attention to practicing his specialty, in which he has met with much success, and stands well among the physicians of Pittsburg. He is a member and ex-president of the Allegheny county homœopathic medical society, member of the Pennsylvania State medical association, the American institute of homœopathy, the East End homœopathic doctors' club, and is a member of ophthalmological and dispensary staffs of the Homœopathic hospital.

WILLIAM THOMAS TREDWAY, of Coraopolis, Pa., one of the leading lawyers of Pittsburg, Pa., was born in Warsaw, Coshocton Co., Ohio, on Feb. 12, 1862, and is the son of Crispen and Melvina (James) Tredway. His parents had six children, viz.: Clara Victoria Sharples, William Thomas, Joseph Fleming, Sarah Olive Elder, Garrett Emmett and Cora Iva Barrett. His father was a successful farmer, and his paternal ancestors came originally from England. There were three brothers that came to America; one went to Maryland, another to New York, and the third to some point in the west. The grandfather of William Thomas descended from the branch that settled in Hartford county, Md., and his great-grandfather, Crispen Tredway, settled in Coshocton county, Ohio, in 1770. His maternal ancestors were of German descent, his great-grandfather, Elias James, taking up a tract of land, under the congressional act, in Bedford township, Coshocton Co., Ohio. Mr. Tredway secured his elementary education in the Donley school, of Bedford township, Coshocton Co., Ohio, which he attended until his seventeenth year, and then went for two terms to the West Bedford public school. There he received a certificate to teach in the Ohio public schools, and taught for one year at Brush college, near what is now the postoffice of Tunnel Hill, Ohio. At the close of his school, in the spring of 1881, he attended a preparatory course at the Ohio Wesleyan university, and later matriculated at the Jefferson academy, of Cannonsburg, Pa. In the fall of 1883 Mr. Tredway entered Washington and Jefferson college, going into the sophomore class, and was graduated from that famous institution on June 24, 1886. During his preparatory course he was a member of the Philo society, and at college of the Philo and Union societies. He was business manager of the Washington-Jeffersonian, the college paper, for two years, and during that time the paper was cleared of debt for the first time in fifteen years. He was also business manager of the Pandora, the college annual, the first number of which was published by his class in 1884, while a sophomore. He was also elected poet of his class, and delivered an honorary oration at the graduating exercises. On leaving school, he became a law student with the firm of Weir & Garrison, of Pittsburg, Pa., and was admitted to the bar Dec. 22, 1888. He remained with that firm until 1892, when he became associated with Stone & Potter, and remained with them until the partnership was dissolved, William A. Stone becoming governor of the State, and W. P. Potter being appointed to a seat on the supreme bench of Pennsylvania. He is still associated with the firm of Stone & Stone. During this entire time Mr. Tredway's offices have been in the Bakewell building, of Pittsburg. Mr. Tredway makes a specialty of corporation and municipal corporation law, and stands high at the bar of Pittsburg. He was married, on March 14, 1894, to Cora Alice, daughter of Thomas Fawcett Watson, a highly respected citizen and one of the oldest residents of Coraopolis borough, and they have two children, Jean Watson and William Thomas, Jr. Mr. Tredway has been solicitor for the borough of Coraopolis since 1891, with the exception of three years, and is now discharging the duties of that position. He organized the Pittsburg, Neville Island & Coraopolis railroad, and represented it until it was completed and merged into the West End company. He also organized the Coraopolis National bank, the Ohio Valley trust company and the Valley trust company of the East End, Pittsburg, now the East End savings and trust company, all of which corporations he represents. While at college he was a member of the Phi Delta Theta fraternity, was one of the charter members of the Pennsylvania Alpha Alumni chapter of that fraternity, and in 1902 represented that body at the biennial convention, which met at the Majestic hotel, in New York city. He is a charter member and was first secretary of the Pittsburg circle, No. 48, of the Protected Home circle, and is a member of the Odd Fellows, the Knights of the Maccabees, the Royal Arcanum, Woodmen of the World, and the Americus republican club of Pittsburg. He is also a member of the Blue lodge, Royal Arch and Chapter Masons, the American Institute of Civics, and the Methodist church, of which body he is a trustee. Mr. Tredway is a republican by birth, conviction and practice, and has taken an active part in political matters of both the county and State. He is the republican county committeeman from Coraopolis, has been for the past three years a delegate to the State conventions, and has made political speeches throughout the county during many campaigns. He was a member of the campaign committee in 1903. Mr. Tredway has never sought political office, and his efforts have been for the furtherance of good government and the selection of the right men to serve the public in official capacities.

MANSFIELD A. ROSS, of Coraopolis, Pa., member of the firm of Ross, Shannon & Staving, manufacturers of confectionery, in Pittsburg, Pa., was born in Addison township, Somerset Co., Pa., March 15, 1853, son of Moses A. and Cynthia A. (Mitchell) Ross. His parents had ten children, seven of whom are now living. His father was a merchant of the Keystone State for many years, and his paternal ancestors came from Masontown, Pa., his great-grandfather having been a color-bearer in the patriot army during the American revolution, under Mad Anthony Wayne. The Ross family is of Scottish origin, having come from the highlands of that country, and removed to Ireland to escape religious persecutions. Robert Ross, the great-great-grandfather of M. A. Ross, was born in 1709; married, in Ireland, Jane Latta, and came to America, where his son Robert was born in 1753. At the commencement of the Revolutionary war, Robert Ross the second entered the Continental army in the company which was commanded by Capt. James Taylor, and which was a part of 4th Pennsylvania battalion, commanded by Col. Anthony Wayne. Robert Ross served in the battalion during the second year of the war in Canada, was mustered out at the expiration of his term of service, and re-enlisted under General Wayne, with whom he served until the close of the war. According to family records, he was regimental color-bearer, and participated in the battles of Stony Point, Brandywine, and others in which his command was engaged. At the close of the war, he removed to Fayette county, Pa., where he was captain of a militia company which served in the Indian wars in Ohio and Indiana, and was severely wounded during Crawford's Sandusky expedition. He had a family of eight children, one of his sons, Robert, having been born in 1786, and at the age of twenty-three married Elizabeth Virginia Le Maire. Her father was a native of France, and her mother, Elizabeth Monshi, was also a native of that country, having been born in Paris. They were Catholics, loyal to King Louis XVI., and in 1791 took passage for the United States, during which voyage Elizabeth Virginia was born. Robert Ross the third served as a private soldier in the War of 1812, was taken prisoner at Detroit, and paroled. He again enlisted, participated in the fights at Lundy Lane and Fort Erie, being severely wounded at the latter engagement. Subsequently he enlisted in the regular army and died at Baton Rouge, La., in 1822. His son, General M. A. Ross, the father of Mansfield A. Ross, was born in Masontown, Fayette Co., Pa., in 1810, and was twice married—first, to Diana Mitchell, and the second time to Cynthia A. Mitchell, a sister of his former wife and the mother of Mansfield A. Ross. General Ross was very prominent in military matters, having been captain of the Addison infantry, and rose through the various grades to brigade commander. He was also at different times a member of the Grand and National divisions of the Sons of Temperance, was first school director of Addison, and a member of the Methodist Episcopal church, of which he served as a member of the general conference in 1869 and four terms as a member of the lay electoral conference. For seventeen years he was clerk of the township, was a man of superior mental attainments, and possessed a fine library. Two of Mr. Ross' maternal great uncles, James and Thomas Mitchell, were soldiers of the patriot army during the American revolution, and his great-grandfather, Captain Andrew Friend, was known far and near as a scout and Indian fighter of the early days. Mr. Ross obtained his early education in the public schools of Somerset county, and, when eighteen years of age, left his books to engage in the general merchandise business with one of his brothers, opening a store in Addison township. He remained there for five years, and then went to Coraopolis to follow the same business. He prospered in the general mercantile line in that borough for ten years, and was engaged in the real estate business in that town for three years. Mr. Ross then formed a partnership with Messrs. Shannon & Staving, who for the past three years have been conducting a large wholesale and manufacturing confectionery business in Pittsburg. Mr. Ross was married to Carrie A. Frey, of Brandonville, W. Va., and their home-life is indeed a happy one. Mr. Ross is a republican, a thirty-second degree Mason, a member of the Odd Fellows, the B. P. O. Elks, the Americus club of Pittsburg, and the Sons of the American Revolution. He is also a director in the Coraopolis National bank and the Ohio Valley trust company, and is well known in financial circles. Mr. Ross is a man that combines good business qualifications with unusual geniality of manner, and he and his wife are noted for their hospitality, which they dispense with a lavish hand in their beautiful home in Coraopolis.

JAMES A. SUTER, a prominent commission merchant of Braddock, was born in Bedford county, Pa., March 11, 1858. His parents, Solomon and Elizabeth (Heiner) Suter, were both of German descent. Mr. Suter attended school in his native county, where he lived on a farm, and when eighteen years old started to learn the carpenter trade. For eight years he worked as a carpenter and joiner, and was able, from the savings of his labor, to open a small grocery near his present location at No. 849 Braddock Ave. After another eight years, which were years of prosperity, he started in the commission business, where he soon built up an extensive trade and secured a competency. His upright dealings marked Mr. Suter as a man to be trusted with larger things, and in May, 1901, he was chosen director of the First National bank of Braddock, and also as director in the Braddock trust company, which was organized in May, 1901, with a capital stock of $125,000, and a surplus of the same amount. Mr. Suter was married, June 28, 1887, to Emma, daughter of John D. and Phœbe (Slick) Boyce. The Boyce family came from Michigan, and the Slicks are natives of Bedford county, Pa. Mr. and Mrs. Suter have three daughters, all in school, Gertrude, Corene and Evlyn. The family lives in a beautiful home at No. 227 Holland Ave., which was erected in 1900. Mr. Suter is a member of Bessemer tent, No. 92, Knights of Maccabees; Braddock Field lodge, No. 510, F. and A. M., and Braddock lodge, No. 78, Independent Order of Heptasophs. He and his family are members of the First Methodist Episcopal church of Braddock. In politics Mr. Suter is a republican.

CHRISTIAN D. STEEL, undertaker and embalmer, Carnegie, Pa., was born in Franklin county, Pa., Feb. 6, 1839, son of Samuel and Nancy (Dietrich) Steel, and comes from an old and respected Pennsylvania family. His grandfather, Rev. John Steel, who was a Presbyterian minister at Carlisle, Pa., was a captain in the colonial army during the Revolutionary war, and commander of Fort Steel, which was named for him. His father, Samuel Steel, born Jan. 2, 1802, was a woodworker and afterwards a farmer, and a man of decided political views. He moved to Baltimore in 1849, and in 1857 left Baltimore and took up his residence in Union township, Allegheny county. He was an old-line whig, with abolition tendencies, and later an ardent republican. He and his son, while in Baltimore, cast the only two votes cast in Baltimore county in favor of Fremont for president. He died in 1863. Mr. Steel is descended on his mother's side from an old Pennsylvania family. His grandparents were Christian and Susan Dietrich. His mother, Nancy Dietrich, died in 1883, at the age of seventy-one. She was reared as a member of the German Reformed church, and died a devout Presbyterian. Christian D. Steel is one of ten children. The others are: Mary M., who married James Smith, and died when about forty years old; Andrew B., born in 1835, who fought in the 46th Pennsylvania volunteer infantry, in the armies of the Potomac and Cumberland, and was killed in battle when twenty-nine years old; Samuel, ex-senator, who resides at Greentree, Allegheny county, a veteran of the Civil war; Susan S., wife of Christian Lampe, a retired Civil war veteran, living near Pittsburg; David S., who lives in Pittsburg; John R., a farmer in Allegheny county; William, who died when five years old, in 1852; Catherine D., who resides at the home of her brother, Samuel, and Ella, now Mrs. John Holmes. Christian D. Steel attended school when a boy and worked on his father's farm. In 1862 he enlisted in Company H, 78th Pennsylvania volunteer infantry, and served three years, being honorably discharged in August, 1865. He fought under General Thomas at Franklin and Nashville, and in several minor engagements. After the war Mr. Steel engaged in the dairy business in company with three brothers, and afterwards the brothers embarked in the livery business, discontinuing this in 1883. Since that time Mr. Steel has been in the undertaking and embalming business with his brothers, and has met with encouraging success. He learned embalming when a young man. Mr. Steel has amassed a considerable fortune, and is a stockholder in both of the Carnegie banks. On Nov. 1, 1874, he was married to Miss Amelia Bradwell, a native of Allegheny county, daughter of Jacob and Frances Bradwell, both of whom are now deceased. A son of Mr. Steel, Jacob Steel, is in the undertaking business. He married Miss Mary Beadling, and has one child, Christian D. Christian D. Steel, the subject of this sketch, is a member of the G. A. R. In politics he has always been an ardent republican.

FRANK J. KLUMPP, chairman of the department of assessors, Pittsburg, was born in Pittsburg in 1867, and there attended the common schools. Afterwards he also attended Duff's commercial college, and graduated from that institution in 1895. When fourteen years old, Mr. Klumpp learned to make lamp chimneys, and was engaged in this work for about fifteen years. In 1899 he gave up this vocation, and, in September of that year, was elected to his present office to fill an unexpired term, and re-elected in 1901. In the shake-up which the Ripper bill caused, Mr. Klumpp fell with the rest, but was reappointed by Recorder J. O. Brown. Mr. Klumpp has long been prominent in various branches of public activities. In 1893 he was elected to the school board from the twenty-eighth ward, and served in this capacity until 1897. He also served two terms in the common council of Pittsburg as the representative of his ward, being elected in February, 1896, and re-elected, without opposition, in 1898. In the fall of 1898 he was elected to the legislature from the fifth district, and in this contest received a handsome plurality of votes over four experienced political opponents. Mr. Klumpp belongs to the Masons and the Junior Order of United American Mechanics. He is a member of the German Evangelical church.

LABANNA H. WALTER, real estate, insurance and loan agent, and notary public, of Carnegie, was born in Westmoreland county, Pa., April 18, 1844. His parents were David and Dorcas (Carnahan) Walter. Mrs. Walter was the youngest daughter, by his second marriage, of David Carnahan, a pioneer settler of Pennsylvania, and famous Indian fighter. David Walter was a farmer and blacksmith, and also kept a country store on his farm. He was born in 1814, and died in 1877, in Coffee county, Tenn., where he had moved in 1870. He and his wife were members of the Presbyterian church. He took an active interest in educational affairs, and was a trustee of an academy at his death. In politics he was an ardent abolitionist, and believed in a vigorous prosecution of the war against slavery. His wife, Dorcas (Carnahan) Walter, died in 1885, when seventy-seven years old. Mr. and Mrs. David Walter had nine children. Of these, Mary died when eight years old, and three others died in childhood; Philip was killed in Tennessee by a falling limb from a tree, while trying to stop a forest fire, having previously served three years in the Civil war as a private in Company G, 4th Pennsylvania cavalry, Army of the Potomac; Nancy J. married William Alcorn, and lives near Saltsburg, Westmoreland county; David C. is a farmer, residing in Westmoreland county; Malvina is now Mrs. Williamson, and lives near Murrysville, Pa., and L. H. Walter, the subject of this sketch, who was educated in the schools of his native county and afterwards farmed for a time. In August, 1864, he enlisted in the Civil war, and was discharged from the service in May, 1865. In September, 1882, he embarked in the insurance business, and has been successfully engaged in this business ever since. He was at first in the employ of R. H. Brown, but has been for the past ten years conducting an agency in his own name. He has also for the past eight years been a notary public. Mr. Walter was married, March

16, 1870, to Miss Anna M. Thorn, a native of Pennsylvania and daughter of Robert and Elizabeth (Calhoun) Thorn. Mr. Thorn is now dead, but his wife is still living, an honored resident of Butler, Pa. Mr. and Mrs. Walter have two children, John T. and David J. The latter is associated in business with his father. Mr. Walter is collector for the Royal Arcanum, treasurer of the Anchor building and loan association, and a member of the board of trade. He and his wife are prominent members of the First Presbyterian church of Carnegie.

WILLIAM F. ENGLEHART, of Coraopolis, Pa., superintendent of the shipping department of the Consolidated lamp and glass company, was born in Washington county, Ohio, July 7, 1858, son of Peter and Anna Maria (Rien) Englehart. His parents had six children, five of whom are now living. His father was a successful farmer, and his ancestors on both sides came from Germany. Mr. Englehart obtained his early education in the Matamoras district school of Washington county, and when fourteen years of age went to work on his father's farm. He followed that vocation until he was eighteen years of age, when he secured employment in the glass works of Hobbs, Brorunier & Co., of Wheeling, W. Va. He continued with that concern for twelve years, and then went to Fostoria, Ohio, to work in the shipping department of the Butler art glass works. That plant was destroyed by fire, and he went with the Fostoria lamp and shade company, of which he was a stockholder, and when the lamp and shade company was consolidated, he continued his relation as stockholder and superintendent of the same department. During his residence in Fostoria, Mr. Englehart went into the oil business, under the firm name of Landis, Kopp & Englehart. They operated oil wells for a time with indifferent success, but later bought forty acres of woodland that proved exceedingly remunerative. When the Fostoria company removed to Coraopolis and became part of the Consolidated lamp and shade company, Mr. Englehart came with them as superintendent of the shipping department, and has since filled that position with signal ability. He was married, on June 2, 1896, to Ida Elizabeth, daughter of F. W. Harmon, of Hicksville,

Ohio, and they have one son, Wallace Harmon, who was born on July 4, 1902. Mr. Englehart is a republican in politics, and is now serving his second term as councilman of the borough. He is a member of the Methodist Episcopal church, and a stockholder in the Coraopolis National bank and the Ohio Valley trust company. Mr. Englehart is a quiet, unassuming gentleman, has many friends, and is the true type of the good citizen.

CHARLES A. COOPER, of Coraopolis, Pa., a member of the civil engineering firm of Edeburn, Cooper & Co., of Pittsburg, Pa., was born in Moon township, Allegheny Co., Pa., Nov. 25, 1845, son of William and Nancy (Gilchrist) Cooper. His father was a prosperous bookbinder, and died at the age of seventy-five, and his mother survived to her eighty-third year. He is of Scotch-Irish descent; his paternal great-grandfather was a soldier in the Continental army during the struggles of the colonies for independence, serving under Anthony Wayne, in Captain Macey's company, was wounded at Three Rivers, and for some time was confined on the British prison ships. Nearly the whole of Charles A. Cooper's life has been spent in Pittsburg. He obtained a thorough training in his profession of civil engineering in the special schools of Pittsburg, and, when twenty-one years of age, secured a position with the United States government on the survey of the Ohio river, remaining on that work for two years, and then went with the Pan Handle railroad. Later he engaged in surveying for the water-works in Pittsburg, and in 1871 became a member of the present firm of Edeburn, Cooper & Co. Since then he has been instrumental in completing many large contracts, among them being the first survey for the Pittsburg & Lake Erie railroad, the new water-works at Sewickley, Pa., Wellsville, Ohio, and Coraopolis, Pa. He also built the first general sewerage plant in Pennsylvania at Wilkinsburg, where he constructed twenty-one miles of sewer. He located and built the Montour railroad, opened the mines of the Imperial coal company, and has planned and executed a great deal of paving for the boroughs of that section of the State. He made his residence at Coraopolis in 1887, and was one of the incorporators of the Coraopolis National bank, of which institution he is now vice-president. He is also a director in the Ohio Valley trust company, and was one of its incorporators. He was married, in 1870, to Margaret J. Meek, of Moon township, and they have three children: F. M., member of his father's firm; Mrs. Mary Cooper Davidson, and Ethel. Mr. Cooper is a republican and a member of the Presbyterian church.

DR. WILLIAM CONNER SHAW, a general medical practitioner, with offices located at No. 1009 Wylie Ave. and No. 213 Frick building, Pittsburg, Pa., is a descendant of one of the oldest Scotch-Irish families in Pennsylvania. His great-grandparents, Samuel and Elizabeth (Lowry) Shaw, came to America about the year 1771, and settled in the Juniata valley, where they lived until 1785, when they removed to Allegheny county and purchased a farm near the town of Wilmerding. His grandfather, David Shaw, was born in County Down, Ireland, May 21, 1761, and came with his parents to America while still in his boyhood. At his death the farm near Wilmerding, which he had inherited from his father, became the property of his two sons, William A. and John Shaw, the former of whom was Dr. Shaw's father. Dr. Shaw's paternal grandmother, Jane Ekin, was born in York county, Pa., Aug. 2, 1764, and died Aug. 4, 1866. She was the daughter of Robert and Margaret (Jamison) Ekin, who came from County Derry, Ireland, about the middle of the eighteenth century and settled in York county, but afterward removed to Versailles township, Allegheny Co., Pa. On the maternal side his mother was Sarah Theresa Conner, the eldest daughter of Rev. William Conner, a United Presbyterian minister, whose last charge was at Blairsville, Indiana Co., Pa. He was a son of Cornelius Conner, Jr., who, with his two brothers, John and William, and his father, Cornelius Conner, Sr., served in the American army in the war for independence. Cornelius Conner, Sr., was a sergeant in Capt. Benjamin Harrison's company, in the 13th Virginia regiment, during the Revolution, under Col. William Russell. The Conners were also noted Indian fighters. After the Revolution the family settled in Allegheny county at the same time and in the same neighborhood with the Dents, Craigs and Nevilles, who were among the first settlers of the city of Pittsburg. Dr. Shaw's maternal grandmother, Margaret (Murdoch) Conner, was a native of County Antrim, Ireland, near Belfast. The paternal grandparents were members of the Old Brush Creek A. R. Presbyterian church, near what is now Larimer station. This church was presided over by the celebrated Hendersons (Matthew, Sr., and his son, Matthew, Jr., and Ebenezer, father of Matthew, Sr.) as pastors. The latter Henderson also at that time supplied the First United Presbyterian church of Pittsburg. Dr. William C. Shaw was born on the farm in Versailles township, where his father before him was also born, Feb. 7, 1846. During his boyhood he worked on the farm and attended the common schools of the township, where he received his primary education. In February, 1864, he entered Newell's institute at Pittsburg, where he spent two years preparing himself to enter college, and was graduated from Washington and Jefferson college, at Washington, Pa., in 1869. He read medicine for one year in the office of Dr. W. R. Hamilton, of Pittsburg, after which he matriculated in the Bellevue hospital medical college, of New York, from which institution he graduated with honors on the last day of February, 1872. For the next six months he studied with Prof. Joseph W. Howe, of New York, and then took the competitive examination for admission to the Bellevue hospital as resident surgeon for a term of two years. He passed the examination over all competitors and served as resident surgeon from 1872 to 1874. During the last eighteen months of his term he was on the second surgical division, serving under such eminent surgeons as Frank H. Hamilton, Louis A. Sayre, H. B. Sands, Stephen Smith and Alexander B. Mott. At the expiration of his hospital service he came to Pittsburg and began the general practice of medicine and surgery on Wylie avenue, not far from his present location. Dr. Shaw was married, Nov. 1, 1877, to Miss Martha M. Lewis, daughter of J. C. and Sarah (Sargent) Lewis. His wife's father was the senior member of the firm of Lewis, Bailey, Dalzell & Co., iron manufacturers, of Sharpsburg, Allegheny county. Dr. and Mrs. Shaw have two daughters: Sarah Louise, who graduated from Wilson college in 1902, and Jennie Ekin, who is now attending that institution. From 1876 to 1878 Dr. Shaw was on the medical staff of the Mercy hospital, of Pittsburg, and from 1878 to 1887 he was on the surgical staff of the same institution. Since 1889 he has occupied the position of physician and obstetrician to the Bethesda home, and until recently was alternate surgeon for the Pennsylvania and Pan

Handle railroad companies. Since 1881 he has been the medical examiner for the Equitable life assurance society of New York, and for the National life insurance of Vermont since 1882. He is also examiner for the Home, Manhattan and Mutual life insurance companies of New York, the Michigan Mutual, the New England, and the Bankers', of Des Moines, Ia., and surgeon for the Employes' liability and accident company, of London, and the Fidelity and Casualty company of New York. He is a member of the Allegheny county and the Pennsylvania State medical societies, the American medical association, the American academy of medicine, the Alumni society of Bellevue hospital, the Pittsburg chapter of the Sigma Chi fraternity, and is a life member of the Pittsburg free dispensary, and the Western Pennsylvania exposition society. He is also a member and one of the elders in the United Presbyterian church of Bellevue; a life member of the Scotch-Irish society of America, of which he is secretary for western Pennsylvania, and the Scotch-Irish society of Pennsylvania. In political matters he always acts with the republican party, though he seldom plays an active part in political campaigns. He resides at No. 300 Lincoln Ave., Bellevue, at the corner of Thomas Ave., and besides his office at No. 213 Frick building, he maintains another main office at No. 1009 Wylie Ave. Dr. Shaw has a large practice, and in the treatment of diseases is eminently successful, owing to the thorough training he received while in college and in Bellevue hospital, and the progressive spirit of the man who keeps fully up with the new remedies and discoveries concerning his profession.

DR. ALVIN ST. CLAIR DAGGETTE, whose offices are located at No. 400 South Craig St., is one of the best-known and most popular physicians in the city of Pittsburg. His ancestors were among the first settlers of western Pennsylvania. His paternal great-grandfather, John Daggette, served from 1775 to 1782 in the American army during the war of the Revolution, being several times discharged, but each time re-enlisting. During his last enlistment, from June to December, 1782, he was a sergeant under Captain Sexton and Colonel Walbridge. After the war he settled in Erie county, Pa., having formerly been a citizen of Vermont.

His son, George Daggette, married Rachel Morton, whose great-uncle, Thomas Morton, settled upon a tract of land, in 1767, near what is now the town of Buena Vista, in Allegheny county, and received a patent for it in 1771. Upon his death, this farm passed to his nephew, Allen Morton, the father of Rachel, who was the grandmother of Dr. Daggette, and who inherited the farm upon the death of her father. It was upon this farm that Dr. Alvin S. Daggette was born, March 17, 1856. His parents were John Morton and Mary McColly (Kelly) Daggette, who had inherited the old Morton homestead. Dr. Daggette is the second of a family of six children. The others, in the order of their ages, were: Mary Ra Laura; Olive T., who died in 1883; Kate Emma, wife of Noah Rhodes, the cashier of the Smithton bank, at Smithton, Pa.; Bertie Wallace, who, with the eldest daughter, still lives upon the homestead, and Frank Summerfield, a member of the W. W. McBride paper company, of Pittsburg. Dr. Daggette received his early education in the common schools of Allegheny county. This was supplemented by a course in the State normal school located at Indiana, Pa., after which he taught in the public schools of his native township for several years. Deciding to enter the medical profession, he attended the Western Reserve university of Cleveland, Ohio, and graduated from the medical department of that institution on March 2, 1881. After graduating, he first located at Shaner Station, Westmoreland Co., Pa., where he was engaged in general practice until November, 1886, when he removed to Pittsburg. In his new location he soon succeeded in establishing a large practice, and is one of the most popular family physicians in the city. His work is of a general character, including all branches of medicine and surgery. He is a member of the Allegheny county and Pennsylvania State medical societies; the Academy of sciences and art, and art society, of Pittsburg, the American association for the advancement of science, and is president of the Western Reserve alumni association, of western Pennsylvania. He is also a member and deacon of the Bellefield Presbyterian church, of Pittsburg. Dr. Daggette was married, May 7, 1885, to Miss Fannie Flotilla Prescott, of Youghiogheny, Westmoreland county, and they have one child, William Morton Clair. While living at Shaner Station, in Westmoreland county, Dr. Daggette served on the school board of Sewickley, and was also treasurer of the school funds. He was also surgeon for the Baltimore & Ohio railroad relief association. In all these positions he won the confidence of his employers, because he was always attentive to their interests and prompt in the discharge of his duties. The same is true of his private patients. They know that he can always be trusted to come to their relief on short notice, and his popularity is due as much to his readiness to respond to the call of the suffering as to his thorough knowledge of the science of medicine.

HORACE S. RITTER, M. D., of Pittsburg, Pa., a well-known physician, was born in Tioga, Tioga Co., Pa., June 17, 1865, son of Frederick D. and Albina (Vermelyea) Ritter, his father having served through the Civil war as surgeon and major in the 4th Pennsylvania reserves; later was a successful physician of Tioga, Pa.; then removed to Gaines, Pa., where he practiced until his death on March 12, 1897. Dr. Ritter's paternal ancestors came to America in 1760, located in Otsego county, N. Y., where Andrew Ritter, his grandfather, gained fame as a soldier in the Revolutionary war, being a member of the famous Mohawk guards of that State. His mother was the daughter of Horace C. Vermelyea, well known as a true disciple of Izaak Walton, and who was prominently identified with the fishing clubs of New York until his death, in 1878. His ancestors came from Holland, settled in the Amsterdam colony in New York, and were prominently identified with that body. Dr. Ritter was educated in the rudimentary branches in the public schools of Tioga, was graduated from the Wellsboro high school in 1878, and then entered Alfred university, of Allegany county, N. Y. He attended that school for three years, later matriculated at St. Joseph college at Buffalo, N. Y., where he was graduated in 1883, with the degree of bachelor of arts. In 1886 he secured the degree of master of arts from that institution. The next year was spent at the Buffalo college of pharmacy, and in 1884 he entered Jefferson medical college, and there was graduated in 1888, with the degree of doctor of medicine. He was in the hospitals of Philadelphia for two years, when he removed to Elmira, N. Y.; there made a specialty of the eye, meeting with much success until 1901, when he came to Pittsburg, and has since prospered as a general practitioner of medicine and surgery. In 1897 the honorary degree of doctor of laws was conferred on him by the University of Montreal. Dr. Ritter has been eye surgeon to the Ogden Memorial and other hospitals in Elmira, from 1892 to 1901, and is a member of the Chemung county, the Tioga county, the New York State and the American medical associations, the Elmira academy of medicine and the Military surgeons' association of the United States. He is a member of the Masonic fraternity, having obtained the consistory and Knights Templars degrees; of the Mystic Shrine; of the B. P. O. E.; of the Sons of Veterans, of which he is first lieutenant in New York State, and is a member of the first class of the Loyal Legion since the death of his father. He was married, in 1888, to Clara Alys, daughter of Charles Scheffel, of Williamsport, formerly a prominent lumber dealer, but now retired from active life. Dr. Ritter is a member of the Episcopal church, and is identified with religious and philanthropic work in the city.

JAMES HARVEY McCABE, deceased, late of Coraopolis, Pa., for many years a successful farmer, was born in Moon township, Allegheny Co., Pa., May 3, 1814, and was the son of James E. McCabe. His father was descended from Owen McCabe, who came to America in the early days from County Tyrone, Ireland, and founded the McCabe family in America. Our subject's ancestors have been prominent in the affairs of the country, a number of them serving in the patriot army during the struggles of the colonies for independence, and otherwise known in the council chamber and on the field of battle. James Harvey McCabe had eight children, three of whom are now living, William Reed, John M. and Junius D. He was a successful and prosperous farmer during his business career, with the exception of a short period in early manhood when he was on the river. He was a member and strong supporter of the old whig party, and at the birth of the republican party cast his allegiance with it and promulgated its tenets the rest of his life. His religious affiliation was with the Presbyterian church, and for many years was an elder in different churches of that denomination; first, in the old Sharon church in Moon township; later, in Forest Grove church in Robinson township, and at the time of his death, in the church at Coraopolis. Mr. McCabe was married to Dorcas, daughter of

James Reed, of Findley township, Allegheny county, and they had eight children. Mr. McCabe's life was a long and useful one, and his passing through the world was of distinct benefit to the section in which he lived. He died on April 10, 1891, having exceeded the biblical limit of a man's life, and his death was sincerely regretted by the entire community.

WILLIAM H. H. LEA, postmaster of Carnegie and one of the leading men of Allegheny county, was born in Allegheny county, Pa., Jan. 18, 1846, son of William Lea and Mary Verner Lea. William Lea was a contractor and carpenter, and a well-known man of his time. He was born on a farm owned by his father, also named William Lea, who owned an extensive farm near Carnegie and gave his name to Leasdale Station. He was the son of Maj. William Lea, an officer in the English army, who came to America some time between 1770 and 1780, and took up the farm which remained in possession of the Lea family until 1896. Major Lea's eldest child was the first white child born in the vicinity. He had also three other children, Robert, William and Samuel. The major lived to be almost ninety years old, and his wife also lived to a good old age. William H. H. Lea, the subject of this sketch, is the eldest of four children. The others are: Mansfield B., a resident of Etna borough; Cassius M., who lives in Carnegie, and Margaret E., who married E. H. Leasure, and also lives in Allegheny county. William H. H. Lea received his education in the schools of Scott township, Allegheny county, and then, Dec. 7, 1861, when less than sixteen years old, he joined the 112th Pennsylvania veteran volunteers, and fought valiantly throughout the war, being mustered out as a lieutenant some four years after his enlistment. During the war he was never wounded and never taken prisoner, and came out in much better physical condition than when he enlisted. He had the honor of being first assistant provost marshal under Capt. John B. Kreps, of Petersburg, Va., and also agent of the Freedmen's bureau in Prince Edward and Amelia counties, Va., and at Berksville Junction after Lee's surrender. After the war Mr. Lea spent several years as a miller at the Woodville flour mills, and in 1870 came to Mansfield, which is now Carnegie, and was employed for some time as a clerk. On Aug. 3, 1889, he was appointed postmaster of Mansfield Valley, Pa., under President Harrison, and served five years. He was also for four years clerk in the prothonotary's office in Pittsburg, and then resigned to become postmaster at Carnegie, Pa., appointed by President McKinley, and is still acting as postmaster, having proved a capable and efficient official. Mr. Lea has held a number of positions of trust and responsibility, has served a year as justice of the peace, been connected with the building association of Carnegie, and is now a member of the board of trade. He was married, May 30, 1872, to Miss Kate E. McQuitty, daughter of Andrew McQuitty. The children born of this union are: A. Blanchard, engineer; Robert W., electrician; Mary E., a graduate of Westminster college, now teaching in Carnegie high school; Sylva B., money order clerk and cashier of the Carnegie postoffice, and Ben H., student in the Carnegie high school. Mr. Lea and family are members of the United Presbyterian church. He is a member of the G. A. R., and has been adjutant for the past eleven years.

WILLIAM JORDAN, pastor of St. Francis' German Catholic church, at Homestead, was born in the province of Baden, Germany, Sept. 13, 1861, son of Sebastian and Tecla Jordan. He was reared in his native country, and attended the University of Freiburg, from which he graduated in 1886. In 1887 he came to America and entered the theological department of St. Vincent's college, Latrobe, Pa. After completing his religious education, he was ordained to the priesthood in 1888 by Bishop Phelan, and assigned to his first charge as assistant pastor of St. Mary's church, Altoona, Pa., where he remained four years. In 1892 Father Jordan was assigned to St. Cecilia parish, Rochester, Pa., where he remained two years, and then went to Wexford, Allegheny county, as pastor of St. Alphonsus' church. In 1897 Father Jordan was assigned to Homestead, where he has since remained and distinguished himself as a faithful and conscientious worker for the church. When he came to Homestead the church had a membership of 120 families, but now contains only seventy families, because the Polish element of the congregation broke off and formed a church of its own. The seating capacity of St. Francis' church is about 450, and the parochial school in connection has an attendance of seventy pupils.

ORANGE SCOTT COLE, locomotive engineer, residing at 110 Railroad Ave., Carnegie, was born in Lawrence county, Pa., Oct. 4, 1849. His father, Encer Cole, born Nov. 27, 1827, is still living, though long since retired from active life, but his mother, Anna P. (Houlette) Cole, died Aug. 17, 1898, when seventy-seven years old. The father was for many years a prominent farmer and dealer in live-stock, and furnished horses for the army during the Civil war. He was married, Nov. 23, 1848, to Mrs. Anna P. Brown, formerly the wife of Caleb Brown, of Newcastle, who had one son by this marriage, Lafayette Brown. Lafayette Brown served three years as a private in Battery M, 1st United States light artillery, during the Civil war. He was employed as a railroad conductor after the war and lost his life in an accident while making a coupling By her marriage to Mr. Cole, Mrs. Cole had five children, of whom the subject of this sketch, Orange S., is the eldest. Of the others, Mary E. is now Mrs. William Henry, of Youngstown, Ohio; William M., a resident of Carnegie, is a roundhouse foreman; Edwin W. is in the hotel business at Darlington, Beaver Co., Pa., and Lizzie J. is married to Henry J. Polock, a resident of Carnegie, and foreman of the carpenters of the Pan Handle railway. O. S. Cole, the subject of this sketch, was educated in the common schools and the high school at Mount Jackson, Lawrence county. During the Civil war he assisted his father in buying and shipping horses, and later, in 1870, began his life-work as a railroad man. He was first employed for ten months as a wiper, then promoted to fireman, and two years later, Jan. 27, 1873, was given charge of an engine. Mr. Cole has been for thirty years an engineer on the Pan Handle railroad, and his long service in the employ of the same company tells of ability and faithful attention to duty. He came to Carnegie Aug. 9, 1870, and has ever since been one of her honored residents. He was for six years a member of the school board, and while he was secretary of the board, an addition to the first ward schoolhouse was erected and numerous minor building improvements were made. On Dec. 11, 1872, Mr. Cole was married to Miss Mary E. Young, of Carnegie, daughter of Joseph and Margaret Young, both now deceased. Mrs. Cole's brother William is now dead, and six other brothers and sisters are living: Ellen K., now Mrs. N. J. Knolten, of Philadelphia; Robert, baggage master on the P. C. & Y. railroad; Eliza J.; Elizabeth, now Mrs. W. W. Connor; Joseph, an engineer, residing in Carnegie, and John, also an engineer. Mr. O. S. Cole and wife had seven children: Cora B., now Mrs. Frank Mercer, a resident of Carnegie; Edwin J., also a resident of Carnegie, who married Anna Mary Burgan; William J., now employed as a passenger brakeman; Burtie, who died in 1882, when two years old; Nettie O., at home, housekeeper for her father; George H., fireman on the Pan Handle railroad; Ella M., attending Carnegie high school. Mrs. Cole died July 16, 1900. She was born Nov. 26, 1855. She was a devout Christian, an active member of the United Presbyterian church, and a woman whose life was an inspiration to her many acquaintances. Mr. Cole is a member of the Masonic fraternity, Royal Arcanum, Knights of Pythias, Knights of the Golden Eagle and Junior Order of United American Mechanics. He has been for years a prominent and influential citizen of Carnegie. In politics he is an ardent republican.

DR. JAMES FRANCIS PHILIPS, whose family name is derived from the word "Philip," meaning a lover of horses, located at No. 2139 Wylie Ave., Pittsburg, Pa., was born in the little village of Library, Allegheny county, May 17, 1859. The town of Library was so called because it contained the first circulating library established west of the Allegheny mountains, and has grown but little since it was first founded. Dr. Philips is the son of David L. and Nancy (Allison) Philips, his father being a contractor and builder, who died in 1893. His ancestors were among the early settlers of Pennsylvania. Dr. Philips' great-grandfather, David Philips, came with his parents, Joseph and Mary Philips, to America in 1755, from Pembrokeshire, Wales, and settled near the town of West Chester, Pa. During the Revolutionary war, General Washington's army was located for a while near the Philips homestead, and David and his three brothers rendered the American general valuable service in the way of giving information concerning the people inhabiting that section of the State. In a personal interview with General Washington, they obtained permission to form a company, and each of the four boys received a commission: David as captain, two as lieutenants, and the fourth as ensign, which was then a commissioned office. After the war, Capt. David Philips settled at Library, Pa., where he organized the Peters Creek Baptist church, of which he was pastor from 1783 to 1829, being the first Baptist minister west of the Allegheny mountains. He died in 1829, and lies buried in the graveyard at Library, his grave being marked by a Revolutionary marker. Dr. Philips' mother was a lineal descendant of one of the old Holland families that settled in the colony of New Amsterdam at a very early date. Dr. Philips was educated in the public schools of Allegheny county and at Piersol's academy, at Bridgewater, Beaver Co., Pa., from which some of the greatest men in the country received their education. After leaving the academy, he taught for nine years in the public schools of Allegheny and Beaver counties. He entered the College of Physicians and Surgeons, at Baltimore, Md., and graduated in 1889, after a three-year course. The same year he received the degree of M. D. from the Medico-Chirurgical college, of Philadelphia. On May 8, 1889, he located at his present address and began the general practice of medicine. He is a member of the Allegheny county medical society, the American medical association, Dallas lodge, No. 508, Free and Accepted Masons; Beaver lodge, No. 248, Independent Order of Odd Fellows, located in West Bridgewater, Beaver county; member of Beulah conclave, No. 296, Order of Heptasophs, and Center Avenue lodge, No. 124, A. O. U. W., and the Masonic country club. From 1890 to 1895 he was vaccine physician for the city of Pittsburg. During the year 1901 he was surgeon to the police force and fire department of the city of Pittsburg, and for the same period was physician to the bureau of health. From 1894 to 1898 he was examiner for the Manhattan life insurance company, of New York, and from 1896 to 1900 he was examiner for the Illinois life association. He is now the examiner for the Order of Heptasophs and for the Ancient Order of United Workmen. Politically, Dr. Philips is a republican, but was one of the instigators and promoters of the citizens' party in Pittsburg, having been chairman of the party organization in the eleventh ward from the beginning of the movement. He is a member of Christ Methodist Episcopal church. Dr. Philips is in the highest sense of the term a self-made man. His genial disposition makes friends, but he holds those friends through the sterling qualities that he has developed by careful study and training. His patients know him for a conscientious physician and humane man. They know, too, that they can rely fully upon his word, and have faith in his skill and his promises.

WILLIAM U. SMITH, wagon-maker at Carnegie, was born in Pennsylvania, July 13, 1841, son of W. D. and Martha (Uffington) Smith, natives, respectively, of England and New Jersey. W. D. Smith was a music dealer in Pittsburg, and afterwards taught music. He came to Carnegie in 1867 and died there in 1872. Martha (Uffington) Smith is still living in Carnegie at the advanced age of eighty-eight. Mr. Smith was a deacon of the Baptist church, of which his wife is also a member. William U. Smith, the subject of this sketch, is the only one living of three children born to Mr. and Mrs. W. D. Smith. The first-born son, Thomas, died in infancy, and the youngest, Frank, was killed in the battle of Auldey's Gap, Va., in July, 1863. He enlisted with a Pittsburg company and fought with the army of the Potomac in the battle of Gettysburg about a week before his death. William U. Smith also fought in the Civil war, and was wounded in the left arm when fighting at Antietam. He enlisted in 1862, in Company A, 9th Pennsylvania reserves, army of the Potomac. His first battle was at South Mountain; then came the battle of Antietam, in which he received the wound that disabled him for further service. He was honorably discharged from the service, after several months spent in a hospital, in May, 1863. Mr. Smith was educated in the common schools of his native county and, in 1858-59, was second clerk on a steamboat. In 1860 he began clerking in a flour mill in Nashville, Tenn., and was there when the Civil war broke out. In 1862 he returned to the north to join the army and fight for his country. After completing his service in the war, Mr. Smith went to England, where he remained two years, returning in 1866 to begin his business as a wagon-maker.

For two years he worked for another firm, and then started in for himself. Mr. Smith is a good workman, naturally skilful with tools, and his products are well known and find ready sale. He takes an active interest in the welfare of that community, and has held several offices of trust. In politics he is a republican. He was burgess of Carnegie two years, school director thirteen years, and has been assessor, with the exception of two terms, continuously since 1872. He is a member of the board of trade, and has been for the past ten years secretary of the Anchor building and iron association. On Jan. 24, 1872, Mr. Smith married Harriet Maria Lewis, daughter of Alfred and Harriet Lewis, of England. Mr. and Mrs. Smith have five children, as follows: Frank B., chemist at Iola, Kan., who married Miss Bessie Lawton; Joseph A. L., a printer by vocation, captain of Company K, 14th regiment, Pennsylvania volunteer infantry; Lillian V., a graduate of the Pittsburg school of designs and teacher of painting; Gertrude V., who married Percy Davis, and lives in the thirty-sixth ward, Pittsburg, and William U., Jr., attending the Carnegie schools. Mr. Smith is a prominent member of several secret societies, is secretary of the I. O. O. F., and keeper of the records and seal of the K. of P. He is a member of the Union Veteran legion, of Pittsburg.

DANIEL WEBSTER WYLIE, of Pittsburg, Pa., a prominent contractor, was born in Hancock county, Pa., Oct. 31, 1854, son of John M. and Jane (Henderson) Wylie. His parents had six children, two of whom are now living, his brother being George O. Wylie, of Pittsburg. His father was a successful farmer, and both his maternal and paternal ancestors were from Scotland and strict adherents to the Presbyterian faith. Mr. Wylie secured his early education in the public schools of Hancock county, later attended a preparatory course at the Frankfort Springs academy, of Beaver county, and then matriculated at the Waynesburg college. He was graduated from that institution in 1880, and later studied law with James P. Sayer, of Washington, Pa., but never practiced that profession. Mr. Wylie was married, in 1882, to Ida, daughter of Jesse Hunnell, of Waynesburg, Pa., and then came to Pittsburg, where he was prominent in the insurance business as general agent for the Dwelling House insurance company of Boston and the Phœnix life of Hartford. He prospered in that business for eight years, then engaged in his present line of real estate and contracting, and now controls large interests. He is secretary of the City realty trust, of Pittsburg, and is also a director of the Standard trust company, of Butler, Pa., which he organized. His political affiliations are with the republican party, and he is a member of the Presbyterian church.

PAUL B. DOYLE, M. D., a prominent physician of Allegheny, located at No 2006 Beaver Ave., was born in Leechburg, Armstrong Co., Pa , on April 14, 1864. His parents were Moses and Ellen B. Doyle. Dr. Doyle received his early education in the public schools, after which he took a medical course at the Western University of Pennsylvania, graduating in the class of 1897. He at once entered actively into the practice of his profession, locating in Allegheny. His efforts have been rewarded by a constantly increasing patronage and also by his selection as the consulting physician and surgeon of several large manufacturing concerns and insurance companies, among them being the American locomotive company, the Pennsylvania wheel company and the Pennsylvania casting machine company. He is examiner for the Fidelity mutual insurance company, Philadelphia, also for the Bankers' life, Des Moines, Ia., and of three fraternal orders, viz.: the I. O. of Heptasophs, the Maccabees and the National Union. Dr. Doyle is a prominent Mason, holding membership in Davage lodge, No. 374, F. and A. M.; in Allegheny chapter, No. 217; in Allegheny commandery, K. T., No. 35, and consistory of the valley of Pittsburg. He is also a member of Lodge No. 339, B. P. O. Elks; of Zion lodge, No. 1057, I. O. O. F, and of the Maccabees, the Heptasophs and the National Union. He is a member of the alumni of Western university, a member of the Western Pennsylvania medical club, also of the Brighton country club, the Scilorl club and the Humboldt club. Politically, he is a republican. He is a member of the Union M. E. church of Allegheny.

WILLIAM WESLEY WOLFE, M.D., No. 24 North Diamond St., Allegheny, was born in what was, at that time, Allegheny township, but now known as Bethel township, Armstrong Co., Pa., on Jan. 16, 1851. His parents were Noah C. and Mary (Patterson) Wolfe, the former being a native of Armstrong county, where he was born, Nov. 14, 1818, reared and engaged in agricultural pursuits all his life, dying at Kittanning, Nov. 7, 1896, after a long and useful career. The mother of the doctor was born in Wilmington, Del., May 25, 1818, and came west of the mountains with her parents when she was two years old. They settled near Cannonsburg, Pa., but her parents subsequently removed to Armstrong county, where she met and married Noah C. Wolfe, the marriage taking place on March 9, 1843, attended with the usual festivities so popular in those days. She survived her husband until June 6, 1902, when she, too, passed to her reward in the great beyond. Their children are: Sarah Jane, born Sept. 29, 1844, married William R. Huston, Oct. 16, 1872, and resides in Homestead, Pa.; Findley Patterson, born Feb. 23, 1846, practicing law in Kittanning, married Maggie E. Mateer, Nov. 24, 1881; Perry Fleming, born Jan. 15, 1848, married Cornelia Beissinger, March 13, 1872, and died March 5, 1874; Joseph Alcortis, born June 22, 1849, died in February, 1850; William Wesley, the subject of this sketch, and Dorcas Catharine, born Dec. 1, 1853. The grandparents of Dr. Wolfe were Mathias G. and Sarah (Wagle) Wolfe. The former was born May 5, 1788; married Sarah Wagle, April 13, 1813, and died in September, 1867. Sarah Wagle was born Sept. 24, 1791, and died in September, 1838. Their children were as follows: Catharine, who died in 1895; Christina, born May 22, 1816, died Aug. 29, 1899; Noah Calhoun, father of our subject; Elizabeth, born June 21, 1821, died Aug. 19, 1889; Adnam Robert, born March 21, 1824, died in October, 1900; Obadiah L., born May 23, 1827, died in 1892; Sarah N., born Sept. 8, 1831, and residing in Wilkinsburg, Pa., and the youngest child of this marriage is Permanda A., born April 27, 1834, now Mrs. Fry, who resides in Clinton, Pa. By a second marriage with Maria (Murphy) Keesey, there were the following children: Elmira M., born Feb. 24, 1844, now Mrs. Cornman, residing in Kittanning; Louis J., born May 13, 1845; Solomon P., born July 2, 1846; Squire D., born March 8, 1849; Nancy J., born Feb. 9, 1850, now Mrs. David Walters, residing at Ford City, Pa.; Anna M., born Dec. 20, 1851, now Mrs. John Beatty, residing in Pittsburg. W. W. Wolfe acquired his primary education in the common schools of Armstrong county, after which he taught school for ten years in Armstrong and Clarion counties. During his last years in the school-room, he devoted a part of his time to the study of medicine, and, in 1878, entered the Cleveland homœopathic hospital college, Cleveland, Ohio, and graduated in February, 1880, receiving the degrees of M. D. and F. H. S. He at once began the practice of his chosen profession at Freeport, Pa., where he soon acquired an extensive practice, but decided to locate in Allegheny, and, since 1884, he has been in continuous practice there. He is a member of both the State and county homœopathic societies, and is a member of Ionic lodge, No. 525, F. and A. M., of Allegheny; of Allegheny chapter, No. 217, and of Pittsburg consistory and Allegheny council. He is a Shriner; a member of Darling council, No. 888, Royal Arcanum; Triumph circle, No. 101, Protected Home Circle; Guiding Star conclave, No. 273, Improved Order of Heptasophs; Guiosuta lodge, Order of Iroquois; Allegheny lodge, Order of Americus; Allegheny lodge, No. 339, B. P. O. Elks; Allegheny senate; Knights of Ancient Essenic Order; Order of the Golden Rod, and council of Jr. O. U. A. M. Dr. Wolfe is examining physician for all of the above-named orders except the F. and A. M., the Elks and the Essenics. He is now serving as school director for the tenth ward. On June 14, 1899, he was united in marriage with Miss Ada Byron Swindell, of Allegheny, the daughter of the late William Swindell. The following children bless this union: William E., born May 22, 1900, and Harold S., born Sept. 8, 1903. Dr. Wolfe's great-grandfather, Jacob Wolfe, was a native of Berks county, Pa., and a Revolutionary patriot, having served under Washington at Brandywine and Valley Forge, and fought in many of the principal battles of the Revolution. He married Christina Kepple, and their children were: George, Michael, Mathias G., Jacob, John, Christina, Elizabeth, Joseph, David and Solomon. Jacob Wolfe was a noted violinist, and had the honor of playing many times for General Washington. A reunion of the Wolfe family was held on Sept. 14, 1888, at which all the living members of the family were present, and an address was delivered by Findley P. Wolfe, a prominent attorney of Kittanning, Pa. This reunion was held at the old homestead in Allegheny township, amid the scenes so dear to the hearts of those who were reared there or in that vicinity, and recalled to the succeeding generations present many traditions of hardship and toil, and of perseverance and pleasures, which attended the lives there of those illustrious ancestors, who persistently braved the trials of pioneer life, that they and their posterity might enjoy the fruits of their toil.

REV. JOHN SZABO, a Greek Catholic priest, was born, April 15, 1861, at Vulsinka, Ung Co, Hungary. He is a son of the late Michael and Cecilia (Ferencsik) Szabo. His father was a priest before him, and his mother was the daughter of Michael Ferencsik, late bishop's consultor in north Turicza, Hungary. Father Szabo received his elementary education partly from his father and in the schools of his native town. His higher education was acquired in different schools. The first four classes were taken in the Ungvar gymnasium, or college, the fifth in Iglo, the sixth in Szigeth, the seventh in Kesmark, and the eighth in Rozsnyo, where he received the "testimonium maturitatis," or college diploma. For the next four years he attended the theological seminary of Ungvar, and while in this institution he distinguished himself by being awarded the highest honors in oratory. While in the seminary he was assigned as "cantus praefectus" for one year to teach the church singing. On Sept 7, 1886, he was married to Amalia Danilovics, a member of the celebrated priest's family. On the 26th of the same month he was ordained to the priesthood by the late Greek Catholic bishop, John Kovacs de Pasztely, and soon after his ordination he was appointed military chaplain, with the rank of lieutenant, by Emperor Francis Joseph. His first parish, which he held for about eighteen months, was in Ignecz, Hungary. After that he was assistant priest in north Mihaly for three months, when he was appointed to take charge of the parish of Hribocz (Gombas), near the city of Munkacs, Hungary. He remained in charge of this parish for three and one-half years, when he came to America, through the effort of a lifelong friend, Rev. Eugene Volkay, of Pleasant City, Ohio, landing in the United States on July 16, 1892. At that time there were only twelve

Greek Catholic missionaries in the United States. Now there are sixty pastors and many fine churches in all parts of the country. His first work after arriving in this country was at Trenton, N. J., where he settled and where he organized a Greek Catholic congregation and erected a fine brick church. While stationed at Trenton he also organized the first Greek Catholic congregation of Philadelphia, Pa. After about fourteen months at Trenton, he removed to Punxsutawney, Pa., and took charge of the Greek Catholics of seven counties. About this time he became the principal mover in the organization of societies in different parts of the country, known as the "Greek Catholic Union," which has a membership now of over 12,000. In this work and other missionary work, he visited all the eastern States as far as Salem, Mass. He traveled as far south as Birmingham, Ala.; west to Denver and Pueblo, Col.; to Whiting and Diamond, Ind., and to St. Louis, Mo., and also through West Virginia. Reports of his work at these points were published in the Hungarian papers, such as the Gorog Katholikus Szemle, the Listok, and the Karpati Lapok, the same being edited in his native country. He remained at Punxsutawney for seven and a half years, building a church and parish house during his stay. It was while here that he took out his naturalization papers in the Brookville court-house, and became an American citizen. On July 7, 1901, he took up his residence in Pittsburg, where he has charge of a Greek Catholic church on the South Side, located on Carson street, between Sixth and Seventh streets. This congregation numbers about 500 families with a total membership of nearly 5,000 people, most of whom are from the mother country of Hungary. In 1902 the church had a jubilee celebration, on the occasion of the tenth anniversary of Father Szabo's arrival in this country. Father Szabo and his wife have seven children—four boys and three girls. The boys are: Nicholas, Alexius, Dionisius and John. The girls are named Yolande, Irene and Magdalena. Nicholas is attending St. Vincent's college, Latrobe, Pa., and the others are students in the Pittsburg schools. Of the seven children, three—Nicholas, Yolande and Alexius—were born in Hungary, the others being born in this country. A brother of Father Szabo, the Very Rev. Orestes Szabo, is the rural dean of district Szt. Miklosiensis, in Seleszto, Hungary, where he also has a sister, Mrs. Maria Petricska. Father Szabo is a member of the Royal Arcanum, and speaks several European languages. Through his influence his brothers-in-law—Rev. Basilius Volosin, pastor of the Greek Catholic church at Passaic, N. J.; Rev. John Hrabar, a

Greek Catholic priest of Philadelphia, and Rev. John Danilovics, theologian of the Dunwoodie seminary, of New York, and some others—have been induced to come to this country. He is very enthusiastic over his newly-adopted country, for Puritan customs and humane institutions, for freedom of religion, and from the pulpit he often advises his people to become Americanized and to bless the Almighty that He gave to mankind the glorious "land of the free and the home of the brave."

PROF. FRED F. WILCOX, No. 19 Montgomery Ave., East, in the city of Allegheny, is attracting considerable attention on account of the success he is having in the treatment of diseases through magnetic healing. He was born and reared in Geneva, Ashtabula Co., Ohio, on July 9, 1855. Calvin C. and Emily A. Wilcox, old and respected residents of Ashtabula county, were his parents. Professor Wilcox acquired his earlier education in Geneva's excellent public schools. After arriving at the age when all young men are usually anxious to get out into the world and make their mark, Mr. Wilcox decided to try his fortunes at railroading in the west, and although successful, he finally concluded that the transient nature of his work would never permit him to permanently locate in any one place; therefore, he resigned his position and turned his attention to mercantile pursuits, in which he was successfully engaged at Ashtabula, Ohio, for twelve years. As he had discovered, some time prior to disposing of his business in Ashtabula, that he possessed unusual magnetic power in curing disease, he decided to thenceforth devote his whole time to the practice of magnetic healing, and, until 1899, among his friends and acquaintances of a lifetime in Ashtabula, he demonstrated beyond the shadow of a doubt his remarkable power to cure the afflicted, as numerous testimonials will prove. Desiring a larger field, he determined to locate in Allegheny, and, since 1901, he has successfully practiced his profession there. He is a member of Geneva lodge, No. 334, F. and A. M., of Geneva, Ohio. Professor Wilcox might be termed a socialist, from a political standpoint, but he rarely takes any especial interest in politics.

GEORGE L. SUTTER, of Pittsburg, Pa., a leading attorney-at-law, with offices at No. 409 Grant St., is a native of Pittsburg, born Dec. 15, 1874, son of Louis and Amelia (Zeigler) Sutter, both born in Pittsburg, and now residing at Beaver Falls, Beaver Co., Pa. George L. Sutter acquired his rudimentary education in the graded and high schools of Beaver Falls, Pa., and later matriculated at Geneva college, where he was graduated in 1894, with the degree of bachelor of science. He studied law at the University of Michigan, at Ann Arbor, and was graduated from that excellent institution in 1898. Mr. Sutter was admitted to the Allegheny county bar in December, 1898, and since has been continuously in the practice at Pittsburg, where he is a member of all courts and has a remunerative practice. He was married in Pittsburg, June 11, 1902, to Emma C., daughter of William and Elizabeth Ruske, and their wedded life has been one of ideal felicity. Mr. Sutter is a member of Beaver Valley lodge, No. 478, of the Ancient Free and Accepted Masons, and is closely identified with that great order.

REV. STANLEY JASTRZEMBSKI, pastor of the Immaculate Conception Roman Catholic church of Carnegie, Pa., was born in Lomza city, Russian Poland, Nov. 17, 1872, and is the son of Anthony and Joanna (Kowalska) Jastrzembski. After attending the primary schools of his own town, he spent eight years at the classic gymnasium, or high school, and then entered the theological and philosophical seminary of Sejny, Poland, where he remained until he completed the five-year course. In 1896 he was ordained to the priesthood by the Rt. Rev. Bishop Casimir Ruszkiewicz, the ceremony taking place in the city of Warsaw. His first charge was as assistant priest in Turoil, Poland, where he remained for three years, and for the next two years he occupied a similar position at Biatszewo. By permission of Bishop Anthony Baranowski, of the diocese of Sejny, Father Jastrzembski came to the United States, landing in this country on June 25, 1902. For the first three months after his arrival here he was assistant priest at St. Josaphat's Roman Catholic church, on the South Side of the city of Pittsburg. From there he was transferred to St. Francis de Paul's rectory, at Ford City, Pa., as an assistant priest. Five months afterwards he came to Carnegie to take charge of the Immaculate Conception church, where he is now stationed and where his labors are being crowned with success.

THOMAS B. SCANDRETT, director of the department of public safety of Allegheny city, Pa., was born in that city, in 1859, and for a number of years has been identified with some of its leading mercantile institutions. He is a son of William A. and Mary A. Scandrett, both of whom were born in Allegheny city. In 1868, while Thomas was in attendance at the third ward public school, his father was appointed warden of the Allegheny county jail for four years, and the family removed to Pittsburg. In 1871 the boy finished his education in the second ward school of Pittsburg, and soon afterwards went to work for Joseph D. Weeks. Later he entered the employ of W. C. Armor, a prominent merchant, with whom he remained until 1880, when he went to the Goodwin Bros., of East Liverpool, Ohio, as boss warehouseman and shipper in their crockery establishment. He stayed with the Goodwins until 1884, when he came back to Pittsburg as general manager for D. P. Collins, of the Pioneer five and ten-cent store. This position he held a number of years, but finally left it to accept a place with the Star Union Line railroad as clerk. On April 6, 1903, he was appointed to his present position of director of public safety. In 1886 he was married to Miss Lydia K. Moore, of Alliance, Ohio, and one daughter, Mary K., has been born to them. Mr. Scandrett is a member of Riddle lodge, No. 315, Free and Accepted Masons, of East Liverpool, Ohio, and is also a member of the Methodist church. In politics he is a republican, and takes an active interest in the movements of his party. He resides in the third ward of Allegheny city, at No. 1308 Esplanade St.

REV. AUG. A. VOGT, associate priest at St. Joseph's Roman Catholic church, Mt. Olivet, Pa., is a native of Dahm, Westphalia, Germany, where he was born Jan. 26, 1875. His parents were Frank and Elizabeth Vogt, both of whom were Westphalians. Father Vogt began his education by an attendance of seven years in the parish schools of Helden, Westphalia, after which he spent three years in the gymnasium at Attendoen, and, in 1893, he came to America. He finished his collegiate education by a two-and-one-half-year course at Herman, Butler Co., Pa. He then took a two-year course in philosophy and a three-year course in theology at St. Mary's seminary, Baltimore, Md., and, on July 7, 1900, was ordained in the priesthood at St. Vincent's college, Pittsburg, Pa. Since that time he has been associate priest at St. Joseph's church, where he has made many friends

JOHN E. KUHN, whose office is at No. 435 Diamond St., is a member of the Allegheny county bar and a native of the county. He was born in Versailles township, Aug. 6, 1845, where his father, the late David Kuhn, then resided. His mother was Jane (Cavan) Kuhn. Mr. Kuhn acquired a good common-school education, and afterwards attended the Wooster university, Wooster, Ohio, from which he graduated in the class of 1871. He studied law in the office of James J. Kuhn, of Pittsburg, and, on Jan. 6, 1874, was duly admitted to practice at the Allegheny county bar, and has since continued in active practice in Pittsburg. He is a member of all the courts and the county bar association. He was married in Pittsburg, on June 12, 1879, to Miss Bella Arthurs. They have but one child, James J. Mr. Kuhn is a member of Shady Side Presbyterian church. He resides in the twentieth ward, and is a republican in politics.

JAMES DICKSON.

JAMES DICKSON, gardener on Neville island, was born April 30, 1822, on Prince Edward island, and is a son of William and Jane Dickson. He came to America with his parents in infancy, the family landing at Philadelphia and going thence by wagon to Pittsburg. The father, William Dickson, a Scotchman by birth, married Jane Patterson, and had by this union six children: David, William, Peter, Margaret J., Mary Anne and James. Of these, only two are living, Margaret J. and the subject of this sketch. William Dickson was a carpenter by trade, an excellent mechanic, and helped erect many buildings in Pittsburg. He died in Allegheny at the age of eighty-four. His wife, also a native of Scotland, died in Pittsburg. James Dickson began to work at gardening on Neville island at an early age, and afterwards went into business for himself. The firm of James Dickson & Sons, gardeners, does now the most extensive business of the kind in Allegheny county, making large shipments to New York, Philadelphia and Pittsburg. They grow the finest asparagus in the market, and had the honor of supplying the asparagus for Prince Henry's banquet in Chicago in 1902. Their other principal products are rhubarb, lettuce and cucumbers. James Dickson was married, Oct. 13, 1842, to Miss Mary Hamilton, daughter of David and Mary Hamilton, and to them have been born eleven children, all of whom are living, viz.: William, Mary Anne, Jane P., Lizzie, David, John, Emma J., Maggie L., Algernon B., Finley S. and Wilson C. They have forty-two grandchildren and twenty-eight great-grandchildren. There have been only three deaths in the Dickson family in the past sixty years. Mrs. Dickson was born on Neville island, Oct. 15, 1822. Mr. Dickson is one of the oldest and most respected citizens of the county, and has always been a prominent man in his community, having held all the offices in his township. He was formerly an ardent whig, a supporter of Henry

A. B. DICKSON.

Clay and William H. Harrison, and since the death of the whig party has been a loyal republican. He is a Presbyterian in religious belief, and, with his wife, was a charter member of the Neville Island Presbyterian church. He is a prominent and enthusiastic member of the Masonic fraternity, in which he has attained the thirty-second degree, and is a Knight Templar and Shriner. He and his wife, both now eighty-two years old, are still hale and hearty. They have lived happily together for over sixty years.

Algernon B. Dickson, who is manager of the firm of James Dickson & Sons, is a son of James Dickson, and one of the prominent young men of Allegheny county. He was born on Neville island, Nov. 12, 1863, and was educated in the township schools. Like his father, he is actively interested in the welfare of Neville township, in which he has held various public offices. He is an active member of the Presbyterian church of Neville island, in which he is a trustee. He is a stockholder of the North American bank of Pittsburg, and in the Frank H. Hieber wagon manufacturing company of McKee's Rocks, the Coraopolis industrial supply company and the Masonic hall association of Allegheny city, Pa. He is a thirty-second degree Mason, member of McKinley lodge, No. 318, of Allegheny; Duquesne chapter, No. 193, of Pittsburg, and Pittsburg commandery, No. 1, K. T.; of Pennsylvania sovereign grand consistory, S. P. R. S., valley of Pittsburg, thirty-second degree; of Syria temple, A. A. N. O. M. S. Mr. Dickson was married, on June 28, 1893, to Miss Lida S. Means, daughter of Robert and Eliza Means, of Allegheny city. Robert Means was for thirty-five years an employe of the Wayne iron and steel works, was an ardent temperance worker, a man of excellent character, and in politics an influential democrat. He died June 2, 1900. He was married, June 12, 1845, to Miss Eliza S. Wood, of Pittsburg, daughter of Samuel and Margaret Wood. Samuel Wood was in his day a well-known Pittsburg business man. To Mr. and Mrs Robert Means were born eleven children, of whom four, besides Mrs. Algernon B. Dickson, are living, viz.: Minerva, Edward, Samuel and Sarah. Mrs. Means was born in Pittsburg, April 29, 1822, and was educated in the third ward school of Pittsburg, under Mrs. Adeline Whitter, principal of the girls' department. Mrs. Means died April 28, 1898.

FRED W. PATTERSON, chief road engineer of Allegheny county, is the son of John W. and Almina (Wendt) Patterson, and was born in what is known as South Side, or Birmingham, Pittsburg, Jan. 29, 1860. Among the first pioneers in Allegheny county was his great-great-grandfather, Nathaniel Patterson, born in Culpepper county, Va., in 1729, who accompanied General Washington to this point when he made his first perilous trip across the mountains with a surveying party. He was an assistant surveyor to Washington in that expedition, and aided in establishing the original survey in this vicinity. The French and Indian war coming on, the party was compelled to return to Virginia and get ready for the conflict which was to decide the ownership of this disputed territory. After the close of the war, or about 1760, he returned to this locality with his family and settled near Dravosburg, in Mifflin township, where he died, Aug. 9, 1795. The farm on which he settled is still in the possession of his descendants. His son, Andrew Patterson, the great-grandfather of our subject, was born in Culpeper county, Va., in 1755, and came to Mifflin township with his father. He became a surveyor of note, and died in 1808. His son, Nathaniel Patterson, the grandfather of the subject of this sketch, was born in Mifflin township in 1795. He served in the War of 1812 as corporal in a regiment known as the "Pittsburg Blues," was a surveyor by profession, and was elected recorder of Allegheny county in 1859. As stated in the beginning of this sketch, John W. Patterson and Almina (Wendt) Patterson were the parents of Fred W. Patterson, the former, John W., being born in Chartiers township, Allegheny county, on May 4, 1835, where he was reared to manhood. On the breaking out of the great Civil war, he offered his services in defense of the Union, and was made colonel of the 102d regiment, Pennsylvania volunteer infantry. He participated with his command in many hotly-contested engagements, but was killed at the battle of the Wilderness, on May 5, 1864. The G. A. R. post, No. 151, of Pittsburg, was named in honor of him. Fred W. Patterson received his earlier education in the public schools of Pittsburg; later he completed a course in civil engineering at the Western University of Pennsylvania, after which he accepted a

position with the Pennsylvania railroad company, and remained with them until 1887, when he accepted the position of chief engineer with the Pittsburg & Lake Erie railroad, which he filled until 1889. He then engaged with the Baltimore & Ohio railroad as engineer of maintenance of way for its Pittsburg division, which position he held until elected city engineer of McKeesport, in 1891, where for six years, or until appointed to his present position, he faithfully served his constituency. Since 1897, when he became chief road engineer of Allegheny county, he has accomplished wonderful improvements in the development of the public highways, and the wisdom of his selection for that important position has been fully demonstrated. In New Brighton, on June 11, 1885, occurred his marriage with Miss Mary Searight, an estimable young lady of that place. They have had four children, two of whom are living: John W., who is at present a cadet at the New York military academy, and David F. Mr. Patterson joined the Masonic order in 1881, and became a member of Tancred commandery in 1887, and a Shriner in the same year. We have briefly compiled in this sketch a few facts pertaining to the life and ancestry of one of Allegheny county's native sons, who, reared here, is devoting the best efforts of his life in behalf of her people and the generations to follow.

REV. THEOFAN A. OBUSHKEVICH, a Greek Catholic priest, who has been located at Carnegie, Pa., since April, 1903, was born in Zydnia, Galicia, Austria, Sept. 12, 1841. His parents were Alexander and Euphrosina (Pryslopski) Obushkevich. Twelve years of his life were spent in school—four years in the public schools, four years in the college at Eperies, Hungary, and four years in the theological colleges of Lemberg and Przemysl. He was ordained a priest on April 6, 1867. Shortly after his ordination he was given the charge of a parish at Radocyna, Galicia, Austria, and remained there for three years. His second parish was at Rostoki, where his charge lasted three years. Next he was for twelve years in charge of the parish of Hanczowa, Galicia, Austria. After this he was for four years at Uscicruskie, Galicia, Austria, at the end of which time he came to the United

States, landing in this country on July 1, 1889. Since coming to this country his work has been divided among the following parishes: one year at Shamokin, Pa.; six years at Olyphant, Pa.; five years at Mayfield, Pa.; six months at Mahanoy City, Pa , and since April 10, 1903, he has been in charge of the Greek Catholic congregation at Carnegie, Pa , where he has already taken the preliminary steps toward the building of a large church. Father Obushkevich has inherited to a great degree his love for his chosen calling, as his father was a prominent priest in Galicia, Austria.

WILLIAM F. ZOELLER, member and chairman of the Knoxville council, and a prominent wholesale liquor dealer of Pittsburg, was born, in 1859, in East Birmingham, now the twenty-sixth ward of the city of Pittsburg. His parents, John and Fredericka Zoeller, were both natives of Germany. The former died in 1887, and the latter, at the age of seventy-six, is now living with her son. Mr. Zoeller's paternal grandfather came to this country from Würtemberg, Germany, in 1832, and located in Allegheny county, on a farm which is now partly owned by the subject of this sketch. William F. Zoeller received his primary education in the public schools of his native ward, after which he attended the Western University of Pennsylvania for two years. He then learned the bakers' trade, which he followed for five years in the city of Pittsburg. About the time he reached his majority he became associated with Jacob Gommel in the wholesale liquor business. The firm handled several specialities, the foremost among them being Swiss stomach bitters (first prepared by Dr. Arnold Koch in 1870) and black gin. In 1886 Mr. Gommel died, and since that time the business has been carried on by Mr. Zoeller. The trade of the house has increased from year to year, until its goods are distributed all over the United States by jobbers, and a number of traveling men are employed. Mr. Zoeller also makes a wild-cherry tonic and a cough cure that meet with popular favor wherever they are introduced. In the midst of all his business cares, Mr. Zoeller finds some time to devote to the general good of the community. Politically, he is a republican, as were his father and grandfather before him. His election to the council attests his popularity with his neighbors, and his elevation to the chairmanship of that body shows that his fellow councilmen have full confidence in his integrity and executive ability. Besides his duties as councilman and the demands of his wholesale liquor trade, he is a director and first vice-president of the St. Clair savings and trust company. Mr. Zoeller's wife was Miss Carrie Dowden, a daughter of B. A. Dowden, of Pittsburg. They have four children: Karl W., aged twenty-two years, and traveling for his father's firm; Joseph Roy, aged seventeen; Carrie F., aged sixteen, and Robert F., aged nine. Mr. Zoeller and family are members of the Evangelical Lutheran church. In all his business transactions he has been punctual in the performance of his promises, and his standing in business and political circles to-day is due to his square dealing and to the fact that he never betrayed a friend.

JOHN FITE, the proprietor of the Elgin butter, cheese and egg house, at Nos. 537 to 545 Liberty Ave., Pittsburg, is well known in mercantile circles. His father, George Fite, was a native of Germany, but came to America in 1843 and settled in what is now the city of McKeesport, where the subject of this sketch was born, Sept. 9, 1846. In the schools of McKeesport he received the major part of his education, and at the age of fourteen years went into a general store at McKeesport as a clerk. During the eight years he remained in this position he learned many things concerning the business of buying and selling goods. When he was about twenty-two years old he came to Pittsburg as a salesman in the dry-goods store of Love Bros., at the corner of Fourth and Market streets. He remained with this firm for about twelve years, when he decided to go into business for himself. Starting with a small capital, he began selling Elgin creamery butter and cheese to dealers. From this humble beginning he has managed, by indefatigable industry and the application of modern business methods, to build up one of the largest wholesale houses in his line in the city of Pittsburg, doing a volume of business of more than $1,000,000 annually. While living at McKeesport he was married to Miss Elizabeth Gorthardt, and to the marriage seven children were born, of whom three sons and two daughters are still living. The sons all occupy responsible positions in their father's business. W. G. Fite is the credit man of the house, Charles J. is the principal buyer, and Frank S. is the floor manager. One daughter, Luella M., is married, and the other, Clara M., is living with her parents at home. Mr. Fite is also the owner of considerable real estate in the city of Pittsburg. Most of his property is located in the East End, in the vicinity of Highland Park and Jeannette. Notwithstanding the demands of his constantly growing business, he still finds time to attend to church duties and indulge in social intercourse. His entire family are members of the Bethany Lutheran church of Pittsburg. He is a thirty-second degree Mason, being a member of Pittsburg lodge, No. 508, Pittsburg consistory of the Scottish Rite, and Syria temple of the Mystic Shrine. Politically, he is a loyal republican, though he rarely takes an active part in the contests of the political arena, preferring to give his attention to his business, and the visitor to the Elgin butter, cheese and egg house never fails to come away with the impression that it is one of the best conducted mercantile concerns in the great and busy city of Pittsburg.

HENRY M. DAVIDSON, attorney-at-law, with offices at Nos. 618 and 619 Bakewell building, Pittsburg, Pa., is a native of West Deer township, Allegheny Co., Pa., where he was born in 1870 He is a son of Henry and Mary Davidson, well-known residents of West Deer township. His mother died in 1877. Mr. Davidson was educated in the common schools, spent two years in the Pennsylvania State college, and graduated from the Western University of Pennsylvania in 1891. While attending college and the university, he worked as a civil engineer during vacations. In June, 1891, he took the preliminary examinations to read law with the Allegheny law association, and was at once appointed clerk of the association. During the two years that he served as clerk he prosecuted his legal studies, and, in 1893, was admitted to the bar. He began the practice of law in Pittsburg, locating at No. 435 Diamond St., where he remained until his removal to his present location. Politically, Mr. Davidson is a republican, and, in 1899, he was elected to the common council of Allegheny city, representing the second ward of that municipality, in which he resides. Two years later he was triumphantly re-elected, and before the expiration of his second term he was made secretary of the citizens' organization of Allegheny city. On May 6, 1903, he was appointed collector of delinquent taxes for Allegheny city, which position he still holds. He was married, in 1900, to Miss Amelia Shaffer, of Allegheny city, and they have one child, an infant son. Mr. Davidson has a good law practice, and in his private business he enjoys the entire confidence of his clients, as in his official capacity he enjoys the full support and trust of his constituents.

CHARLES A. ANDERSON, a prominent banker and manufacturer of Braddock, was born in what is now the fourth ward, Pittsburg, Nov. 7, 1862. His father, Joseph N. Anderson, was a son of Renix and Sarah (Nelson) Anderson, and a grandson of James Anderson, an Irishman who emigrated to America. Joseph N. Anderson was a prominent hotel keeper of Pittsburg, giving up the business in 1872, and at the time of his death, Aug. 9, 1890, was a director in the Braddock National bank and Pittsburg National Commercial bank. Ann Eliza Anderson, the mother of the subject of this sketch, was the daughter of George H. Bell, sister of Mrs. Allen Kirkpatrick and Mrs. George H. Chalfant, and a descendant of James Bell, the great-grandfather of our subject. He is now buried in the Presbyterian graveyard at Hunterstown, Adams Co., Pa., about three miles from the town of Gettysburg, having this inscription on his tombstone: "Here lies James Bell, a soldier of the Revolution, aged ninety years." James Bell came from Ireland to this country at the early age of twelve years, and settled in Chester county, Pa. His father and brothers were tories, or King George men. When the Revolutionary war started, James ran away from home at the age of eighteen years, and enlisted in the Colonial army. Mr. Bell, being a first-class penman, was appointed clerk at General Knox's headquarters, General Knox being chief of artillery He fought in the battle of Monmouth, and was very well acquainted with Mollie Pitcher, of Revolutionary fame. He married Rebecca Horner, of Hunterstown, immediately after the Revolutionary war. Mr. Bell lost all trace of his family during the war; some years after he heard indirectly that they were living in Washington county, Pa. Starting on horseback, he rode all the way out there, only to find that several months before they had started on a flatboat down the Ohio river to settle at some place in Kentucky. He never heard of them again. Charles A. Anderson received an education in the Pittsburg schools, and when nineteen years old, started in the hotel business. In May, 1890, he became a partner and treasurer of the Shook-Anderson manufacturing company, of Pittsburg. On Nov. 1, 1900, this company consolidated with Atwood & McCaffery, Pittsburg valve and machine company, pipe-fitting department of the Wilson-Snyder manufacturing company, and A. Spear & Sons' foundry, under the name of the Pittsburg valve, foundry and construction company. The new company employs over 600 men in the manufacture of valves and general fittings, rolling mill and blast furnace supplies, the output going to every State in the Union and many foreign countries. Mr. Anderson is treasurer of the consolidated company, and is also director in the Braddock National bank, which is rated as one of the strongest banks in the country. Mr. Anderson was a school director in Braddock township before the organization of North Braddock as a borough, and has been since that time an active member of the school board. He was married, Nov 12, 1885, to Miss Katherine McKinney, daughter of Robert and Katherine (Laman) McKinney, old settlers in what is now the first ward of North Braddock. Bessemer station of the Pennsylvania railroad was formerly called McKinney's station, after Mr. McKinney. The children of Mr. and Mrs. Charles A. Anderson are: William John McKinney, who died in infancy; Charles A., Jr., born Sept. 11, 1888; Margaret Virginia, born Jan. 5, 1891; Katherine, born Oct. 26, 1892; Robert Nelson, a twin brother of Katherine, and Martha, born March 16, 1895. Mr. Anderson erected, in 1890, a handsome stone and brick mansion on Bell avenue, and there resided until August, 1903, when he removed to his new home, on the corner of Jackson and Farragut streets, nineteenth ward, Pittsburg. Mr. Anderson and wife, also Virginia and Charles A., Jr., are members of the Braddock United Presbyterian church. Mr. Anderson is a republican in national politics, but votes without regard to party lines in municipal elections.

EDWARD J. McILVAIN, director of the department of public works of Allegheny city, was born in the city of Pittsburg in the year 1858, in what was known as Bayard's Town. His education was chiefly obtained in what was then the old fifth ward school. Leaving school, he learned the trade of bricklaying; after serving his apprenticeship and working at the trade, he started, in 1878, in business for himself as general contractor, later becoming a partner in the firm of Sloan & McIlvain, the firm doing a large amount of municipal work for the cities of Pittsburg and Allegheny and the surrounding boroughs. About the time he began the contracting business he was married. Mr. and Mrs. McIlvain have two children living: Anna Loretta, who is the wife of Norman McFerron, and a son, Edward Taylor McIlvain. Mr. McIlvain has been connected with various other industries besides the contracting business. He resigned all his contracting interests in April, 1903, to accept the position as director of the department of public works of Allegheny city. He is a member of the Masonic bodies of Allegheny city and Pittsburg.

JAMES W. GRAY, superintendent of the bureau of water assessment of Allegheny city, Pa., is a native of the city where he now holds his official position. He was born in the year 1863, and is a son of the late Alexander, who died in 1881, and Anna Gray, old residents of the second ward. It was in the public school of this ward that James received the greater part of his education, for at the age of seventeen years he went to work for the firm of Oliver Bros. & Phillips as city bookkeeper. While with this firm he worked his way upward until he had charge of the shipping department in the mill. In 1887 he was appointed to the city engineer's office and continued in that position until 1891, when he was appointed to his present position of superintendent of the bureau of water assessment, in which his work has been universally approved, as may be seen by his long continuance in the office. In 1892 he was married to Miss Beatrice Harrington, of Allegheny city, Pa., and is now a resident of the fifteenth ward. Mr. Gray is a member of Pittsburg lodge, No. 219, Free and Accepted Masons, and is also a member of the Pittsburg consistory, and Allegheny lodge, No. 339, B. P. O. Elks. In both private and official life, Mr. Gray is a modest, unassuming gentleman, who treats every one with courtesy and consideration. It is chiefly to this trait of character that he owes his popularity and his success, though, in addition to it, he is a man of high executive ability and full of resources that enable him to meet and overcome difficulties that to men of inferior endowments would seem well-nigh insurmountable.

REV. JOHN SUTKAITIS, pastor of St. Casimir's church, South Side, Pittsburg, Pa., was born in Lithuania province, Russia, May 1, 1870. His father, Anthony Sutkaitis, was also a native of Lithuania. Mr. Sutkaitis was educated in various institutions. His early training was in the State college at Suvalki, finishing the course at this school when he was but eighteen years of age. He spent four years in the Catholic seminary, and at the age of twenty-two he came to America, landing at New York, Jan. 22, 1892. From New York he came to Pittsburg, where he attended St. Vincent's college for one year, and, on June 16, 1893, he was ordained to the priesthood. Soon after his ordination he was placed in charge of St. Casimir's parish, and was given the duty of organizing it. He began his work in the basement of St. Paul's cathedral, and remained there until Jan. 6, 1894, when the congregation bought the Methodist Episcopal building on Carson street, between Sixth and Seventh streets. At that time the congregation numbered about seventy-five families. It soon grew to such proportions that the church on Carson street had to be abandoned, and a new location was found on the corner of Sarah and Twenty-second streets. The property was purchased from the South Side passenger railway company, and work upon the new buildings was begun in 1901. Within a year a new church, school and parish house were erected, at a cost of $150,000, and the congregation moved into its new quarters, which are among the finest on the South Side. The congregation numbers at the present time about 5,000 souls, and in the work of organizing and building up this parish, Father Sutkaitis has demonstrated his executive ability and fitness for his divine calling. He has worked hard, but he has seen his labors crowned with success, and he feels a just pride in the results that he has accomplished.

ALEXANDER GRAY, superintendent of the bureau of electric lighting of Allegheny city, Pa., is a resident of the second ward of the city, where he was born in 1856. His parents, Alexander and Anna Gray, were of Scotch-Irish stock, coming from Ireland in 1849, and settling in Allegheny city, where his father died in 1881. As a boy, Alexander attended the old second ward school, in which he received most of his education. On leaving school, he started to learn the plumbers' trade with John Patton, one of the leading plumbers of Allegheny city, but after two years he gave up the undertaking, and for the next year he was employed in a furniture store. Railroading had a peculiar fascination for him, and he left the furniture store to become a fireman on a locomotive on the Pittsburg, Fort Wayne & Chicago railroad. At the expiration of nearly four years in this employment he had mastered all the intricacies of the railway locomotive and was promoted to the position of an engineer. Three years later he quit the throttle to become a steam-fitter with the well-known firm of Kelly & Jones, of Pittsburg, with whom he continued a number of years, leaving their employ to become the chief engineer for the Standard manufacturing company, where he remained for twelve years. In April, 1903, he was appointed by Mayor Wyman to his present position for a three-year term, his long experience and thorough knowledge of steam engines and appliances being his best recommendation for the place. Mr. Gray was married, in 1883, to Miss Emma Fisher, of Lawrence county, Pa. To their union three children have been born, viz.: Charles A., Henry and Dorothy Fisher Gray. In politics he is a republican, but has never been an aspirant for public office. He is a member of the Methodist church and several benevolent orders, belonging to R. Biddle Roberts lodge, No. 530,

I. O. O. F.; National Union, and various Masonic bodies, as Stuckrath lodge, No. 430; Allegheny chapter, No. 217; Allegheny commandery, No. 35, and Pittsburg consistory, Ancient and Accepted Scottish Rite, in which he has reached the thirty-second degree.

CHARLES W. LIGHTHILL, alderman of the fifth ward of Allegheny city, Pa., was born in the ward in 1835. His father, John Lighthill, died in 1880, and his mother, Nancy Lighthill, died in 1897. Charles was educated in the John Kelley and first ward schools, and upon leaving school was apprenticed to a coach-builder. After learning his trade, he worked two years at it in New Haven, Conn., but at the end of that time came back to Allegheny city, where he obtained a position on the river as a ship carpenter. He followed this occupation for four years, and then for about the same length of time was engaged on the Pittsburg wharf. After leaving this place, he followed the river for ten or twelve years, floating coal to the south. This coal trade was divided into two periods, before and after the Civil war. During the war he worked for the United States at Bridgeport, Ala., building boats for the use of the government. Since the war he has worked at various occupations, but the greater part of his time for several years was spent on the river, being made a master in 1880. For ten or twelve years he was in the employ of the Lindsey & McCutcheon iron works. His first election to the office of alderman was in 1872, serving five years. He was again elected alderman in 1899, and continues in that position, his offices being at No. 1237 Ridge Ave. In the meantime he served four years as a member of the common council of Allegheny city. When he was about twenty-four years of age he was married to Miss Caroline Fergeson, of Washington county, Pa., and they have two children, Sarah and Sidney C. Lighthill. Mr. Lighthill is one of the leading republicans of the fifth ward, taking an active interest in all questions affecting the public welfare. His wide experience has made him a good judge of human nature, and he is rarely mistaken in his estimates of men.

EDWIN B. JENKINS, a prominent and successful broker of Pittsburg, Pa., was born in Kingwood, W. Va., Sept. 16, 1868, and is the son of William M. and Elizabeth (Gibson) Jenkins. His education was acquired in the common schools of his native town. When he was twenty years of age he came to Pittsburg and went into business with his uncle, Marshall L. Jenkins, in the oil trade. Edwin Jenkins was elected a member of the oil exchange in the fall of 1889, and continued a member until the exchange went out of existence. He then engaged in business as a broker in stocks and grain in Pittsburg, under the firm name of E. B. Jenkins & Co., in which he is at present. In November, 1892, the firm was incorporated with a capital stock of $100,000. On Feb. 12, 1893, Mr. Jenkins was married to Miss A. Lora Crumrine, a daughter of Valentine Crumrine, of Beallsville, Pa. To this marriage two daughters—Helen and Gertrude—have been born, both girls still in school. Mr. Jenkins is a member of the Methodist Episcopal church of the East End, Pittsburg.

ADAM STORK, alderman of the seventh ward of Allegheny city, Pa., is a native of Germany, where he was born in the year 1847. His parents, Leonard and Katherine Stork, came to this country about 1852 and settled in Allegheny city, where his mother died in 1868, and his father in 1885. Mr. Stork attended the third ward school, in which he received his education, and from the time of his leaving school until the Civil war, he was employed in the Banner, Hope and Eagle cotton mills. In 1864 he enlisted as a private in Company G, 212th Pennsylvania infantry, and served until June 13, 1865, when he was mustered out in Virginia and returned to Allegheny city. He was then employed as engineer in the works of G. Wettach & Sons and Lappe & Sons until the election of Thomas Megraw as mayor, in 1878, when he went on the police force. Mayor Megraw's successor, Lewis Peterson, Jr., appointed Mr. Stork a lieutenant of police, and, in 1885, he was elected alderman of the seventh ward, with his office at No. 165 Chestnut St. He continued in both positions—alderman and police lieutenant—until Sept. 18, 1886, having charge of police work at night. Mr. Stork during this period frequently acted as mayor in the absence of Mayor Wyman, and discharged the duties with ability and fidelity. Under Mayor R. T. Pearson he served as lieutenant of police and also as alderman of the seventh ward. In 1890 he dropped the police part, and since that time he has continued as alderman only, except for serving as police magistrate under Mayor Wm. M. Kennedy. Mr. Stork has always been a republican in politics, and for fifteen years has represented his ward upon the republican county committee. Although a partisan, he has a large number of personal friends among his political opponents, having won their regard by his straightforward course in the performance of his duties.

SAMUEL ABERNATHEY, alderman from the first ward, Allegheny city, Pa., is one of the representative men in the city where he was born in 1854, and where he has passed the greater part of his life. His father, John Abernathey, died in 1894, though his mother, Katherine, is still living. Samuel obtained his education in the public schools of the first, second and third wards of Allegheny city, and began his business career in a tobacco store as a clerk. In the course of time he abandoned this occupation, and for several years followed the river, holding various positions on the steamers plying in and out of Pittsburg. Upon leaving the river, he engaged in the restaurant business in Pittsburg, returning later to Allegheny city, where he took up his residence. Soon after his return he was elected constable for the first ward, and at the expiration of his term was re-elected, serving altogether seven years, when he was elected alderman from the first ward, which position he still holds. He was married to Miss Mary Maple, of West Virginia, who died in 1893, leaving two sons, George and Albert, both of whom are now married. Mr. Abernathey is a member of Lorena lodge, No. 198, Knights of Pythias, which is the only secret or fraternal organization to claim him as a brother. In

April, 1903, he was appointed police magistrate under Mayor Wyman. In this position he has shown the genuine judicial temperament, his decisions being based on justice and generally meeting with popular approval.

JOHN A. FAIRMAN, a prominent retired funeral director and livery keeper, of Allegheny city, Pa., has been identified with the business interests of Allegheny city for almost half a century. He was born in what is now the fourth ward of the city, in 1845, and is a son of Robert and Agnes Fairman, both of whom are well remembered by the older inhabitants of the city. Robert Fairman died Oct. 5, 1878, and his wife on June 20, 1895. John A. Fairman's early education was acquired in the fourth ward public school, after which he took a course at Duff's college, Pittsburg, and entered upon his business career as an assistant in William Rorah's photograph gallery, which was the first west of the mountains in Pennsylvania. While thus employed, the Civil war broke out and young Fairman, fired by the patriotic impulses which at that time found lodgment in the hearts of so many American citizens, left his peaceful occupation to take up arms in defense of his country. He first enlisted as a private in the 1st battalion, Pennsylvania cavalry, but later became a member of Knapp's Pennsylvania battery. He served until February, 1864, being captured at Averasboro, N. C., and was for some time an inmate of the famous Libby prison. At the close of the war he returned to Allegheny city and became associated with his father in the undertaking business. In 1869 he went to Cleveland, Ohio, as secretary and treasurer of the Forest City pipe works, manufacturers of steam and gas pipes. In 1873 he sold out his interest in the company, returned to Allegheny city, and opened an undertaking and livery establishment on Beaver avenue. Afterwards he removed to Sandusky street, where he conducted the business successfully until 1879, when he sold out, and for the next two years was not actively engaged in any business. In 1881 he became connected with the Pittsburg oil company, in sinking wells, etc., in which he continued until 1884, and since that time he has been looking after his interests in that vicinity. Mr. Fairman is a prominent figure in the lodge and club life of Allegheny city. As early as 1867 he joined Franklin lodge of Free and Accepted Masons, but later transferred his membership to Allegheny lodge, No. 223. He is also a member of Allegheny chapter, No. 217, Royal Arch Masons, and Lorena Orr chapter, No. 18, Order of the Eastern Star. As a member of Abe Patterson post, No. 88, Grand Army of the Republic, he has held the office of commander, an honor that any man might covet. He belongs to Allegheny lodge, No. 339, B. P. O. Elks, of which he is a past exalted ruler, and in which he now holds the important office of trustee. He was also the chairman of the building committee, having in charge the work of remodeling the Elks' home on Cedar avenue. Mr. Fairman has always been a consistent republican, but the only office he has ever held was that of member of the common council of Allegheny city. He was prominently mentioned in connection with the office of sheriff of Allegheny county, but positively refused to become a candidate. Throughout his entire business career he has been distinguished by his uprightness and integrity. As a member of the council he considered it his duty to guard the interests of the people, and that duty was always well performed. As a young man, a member of Knapp's battery, the same devotion to duty marked his military conduct. Had he been willing to desert his post at a critical moment, he might have avoided capture and imprisonment, but he preferred capture, or even death, to dishonor.

ADDISON J. BRINKER, alderman of the twelfth ward of Allegheny city, was born in Butler county, Pa., April 23, 1840. In 1847 his parents removed to Allegheny city, where he received the greater part of his education in the public schools. After a residence of seven years in Allegheny city, the family returned to Butler county, where his father, Jacob Brinker, died in 1855. The death of his father threw a good part of the burden of the family support upon Addison, and he went to work in the mines, digging coal. In the spring of 1856 he obtained a position on the old Pennsylvania canal, where he continued for some time, and later, in 1857, went to Meadville to learn the trade of an iron-molder. About a year later he went to Pittsburg and found employment on the river.

During the Mormon troubles of 1858 he was in the United States service under Gens. Percy S. Smith and W. S Harney. After a four-month campaign against the Mormons, he returned to Pittsburg and worked in the oil fields until 1861. Upon the breaking out of the Civil war, Mr. Brinker returned to Butler county and enlisted as a private in Company I, 12th Pennsylvania volunteers, for the three-month service, under Capt. Biddle Roberts. At the expiration of his term of enlistment he again entered the service, this time as first sergeant in Company H, 102d Pennsylvania volunteer infantry. In February, 1862, he was promoted to second lieutenant, and went through the Peninsular campaign to Harrison's Landing, when he resigned and returned home. He recruited a company and a third time entered the army, his company becoming Company G, 137th Pennsylvania infantry, in which he started as a private, but was soon promoted to orderly sergeant, then sergeant-major and acting adjutant under Col. J B. Kiddoo. On the last day of the battle of Chancellorsville, at the request of the officers of the line, Mr. Brinker took command of the regiment. After nine months' service with this regiment, he returned home, and from that time until December, 1863, he acted as United States detective for Pennsylvania. From December, 1863, to the close of the war he was stationed at Brady's Bend, Pa., at work upon the rolls. After peace was restored, he went to Meadville and secured a position on the police force, serving until 1869, when he resigned to become the chief of police at Franklin, Pa. Two years later he resigned this position to become chief at Butler, Pa., where he remained until 1875, when he came to Allegheny city. For a little while he was connected with the street railway company, but was soon appointed detective, under Chief Robert Hague, at the first exposition. After the exposition he went on the police force as lieutenant in charge of the day division, under Mayor Peterson, and continued in this place until 1884. After serving as constable for a short time in the fall of 1884, he was appointed alderman for the twelfth ward, and held the position for five years. For about nine months he was on the police force, when he was again appointed alderman for a term of five years, and at the expiration of this term he served as alderman for about eight months in the tenth ward. He then moved back to the twelfth ward and was again appointed alderman, this time by Governor Hastings. After the term of his appointment expired, he was with the Bell telephone company, as an inspector, for four years, when he was a fourth time chosen alderman, this time by popular election. His present office is located at No. 1517 East St. He has been appointed police magistrate two terms, and is at the present time holding that office. Throughout his entire career Mr. Brinker has been a close adherent to the principles and tenets of the republican party. He was married, in 1873, to Miss Jane McCleary, of Allegheny city. His wife died in 1901, leaving one son named Blaine. Mr. Brinker is a member of the English Lutheran church, and Lodge No. 128, United Workmen. His long official career has rendered him one of the best-known men in Allegheny city, and in his whole course of life, whether as a soldier, a policeman or an alderman, he has never shrunk from a responsibility nor swerved from a duty.

WILLIAM A. FORD, secretary and treasurer of the Ben Franklin fire insurance company, with headquarters in the Berry building, on Ohio street, Allegheny city, Pa., has been with that company over twenty-five years, and has worked his way up from the ranks. His parents were William W. and Mary A. Ford, both of whom are deceased. The subject of this sketch was born in 1854, in the second ward of Allegheny. Until he was fourteen, he attended school in his native city. Then the family removed to Newport, Ky., where they lived for several years, the father following the occupation of a steamboat captain on the Ohio river. Here William attended the business college of Bryant, Stratton & De Hand, and after graduating from the institution, he became a clerk on his father's boat. In 1877 he was married to Miss Lydie E. McCune, of Allegheny city, Pa., and the next year gave up the river to accept a position with the Ben Franklin fire insurance company. In this business he rose rapidly, filling successively all the places in the offices until he reached his present position. He and his wife have three children, William A., Jr., Fanny L. and Howe R. The family reside in the second ward, where for twelve years Mr. Ford has been a member of the school board. Since taking up his residence in Allegheny city he has taken an active part in political campaigns, in which he has always identified himself with the republican party. He has served on both the city and county committees, and was for six years a member of the common council. He is a thirty-second degree Mason, holding membership in Stuckrath lodge, No. 430; Allegheny chapter, No. 217; Allegheny commandery, No. 235; Pittsburg consistory; and Syria temple, Nobles of the Mystic Shrine. He is also a member of the Royal Arcanum and the Heptasophs. Mr. Ford and family attend the North Avenue Methodist Episcopal church.

HENRY HAUSER, wharfmaster of Allegheny city, Pa., is a lifelong resident of Allegheny county. He was born in the fourth ward of Allegheny city in 1860, received his entire education in the public school of that ward, and at the age of eleven years began his life-work as an employe of the malleable iron works. After learning his trade, he was employed for some years by the Crawford malleable iron works of Allegheny city, and later by the Pittsburg locomotive works. Next he was connected with the Speers manufacturing company, and still later with the James Hunter River avenue lime company, as collector. Mayor John R. Murphy appointed Mr. Hauser to the city fire department, and for some time he was captain of hose company No. 10. From that company he was transferred to engine company No. 14, and as captain of that company he opened the new house on Perrysville avenue, but afterwards returned to his old quarters with the "Tens." Altogether, he was a member of the department for eleven years, and until he was appointed to his present position, in April, 1903, by Mayor Wyman. His father, Pius Hauser, died in 1895, his mother, Caroline Hauser, having died the previous year. Mr. Hauser is a consistent republican in all things political, having been a member of the county committee for the last ten years. He served nine years on the tenth ward school board, and for six years of that time he was chairman of the board. He is one of the charter members of the Republican progressive association of the tenth ward, and one of the original organizers of the celebrated Duquesne drum corps. In the matter of secret and fraternal societies, Mr. Hauser is a member of Fidelia lodge, No. 415, Independent Order of Odd Fellows, which he joined in 1882; Hope lodge, No. 243, Knights of Pythias; Ricka lodge, No. 5, Junior Order of United American Mechanics, and the Perrysville conclave of Heptasophs. His church connection is with the Second Christian congregation, whose place of worship is on Observatory hill. He was married, in 1882, to Miss Elizabeth Arnold, of Allegheny city, and they have one daughter, Lyda May.

JOHN LINWOOD BROWN, superintendent of the bureau of water supply of Allegheny city, Pa., and son of William and Margarette Brown, was born in England in 1848, but came with his parents to America in his boyhood. The family settled in Philadelphia, where John graduated from the city high school, and afterwards entered the Baldwin locomotive works as an apprentice, taking in the various departments of machinist, pattern and boiler-making and draughting, in the meantime taking two courses in mechanical engineering. After serving his apprenticeship, he entered the railway service as a locomotive engineer, but in a little while returned to the Baldwin works, and for some time was employed in delivering engines in different parts of the United States, Mexico, Cuba, Brazil, Peru, Chili, and other South American countries, Russia and Canada. Later he was employed in the same capacity by the Pittsburg locomotive works. He then again entered the railroad service as master mechanic and superintendent of the Southern Wisconsin railroad, and later with the I. B. & W. and the Mexican Central lines, finally becoming master mechanic of the Pittsburg & Western. On July 5, 1871, he was married to Miss Elizabeth G. Hunt, of Belle Center, Ohio. They have one daughter, Marguerite, who is now the wife of Louis B. Hawkins. Mr. Brown is prominent in Masonic circles, holding membership in all the different bodies of that order, from the Blue lodge to the Mystic Shrine. He is a past exalted ruler of Allegheny lodge, No. 339, B. P. O. Elks; past grand chancellor of the Knights of Pythias for the State of Indiana, and past grand officer for several other bodies. He is also a member of the American society of mechanical engineers and of the Franklin institute, and is an ex-member of the National association of master mechanics. He resides in the third ward of Allegheny city, where he usually acts with the republican party in political contests.

REV. BOSILJKO BEKAVAC, pastor of St. Nicholas' Roman Catholic church, of Allegheny city, Pa., was born in Obrenovac, Hercegovina, Aug. 5, 1870. He was educated in the schools of his native country and in Italy, and, in 1895, was ordained to the priesthood. Father Bekavac is fitted by nature for the work and offices of the priest, and from the time of his ordination until 1900 he served as a rector in his home country with a marked degree of success. In 1900 he came to the United States of America, settling at Allegheny city, Pa., and taking charge of his present parish, where his labors have been crowned with the same favorable results as his work in the Fatherland. The parish of St. Nicholas is one of the most populous in the diocese, having a congregation of several hundred families and representing about 4,000 workingmen. Soon after taking charge of the parish, Father Bekavac went to work to improve the church property, and since that time he has erected the present buildings on Ohio street at a cost of about $82,000, the church edifice being one of the best in the city, and one of which both pastor and parishioners are justly proud.

FRANK B. HARKINS, the genial and popular real estate agent and police magistrate of Allegheny city, is one of the best-known men in the city. He was born in Allegheny county, March 14, 1853, and is of Irish extraction, as the names of his parents, Dennis and Bridget, would plainly indicate. His father died in 1890, and his mother in 1895. When Frank was still in his early boyhood, the family moved to Pittsburg, and there he received his first schooling under the private tutorage of Jeremiah Donovan. After this he attended the Brothers' school, and later the ward schools, until he was about ten years of age, when he went to work in the Phillips & Bess glass house. When he was twelve years of age the family went west, locating at Chilton, Calumet Co., Wis., where he spent four years in school, thus completing his education. His parents then returned to Pittsburg, and Frank found employment in the McKee glass house, on Nineteenth street, where he worked until he was eighteen years old, when the family moved to Allegheny city, taking him along. His next position was in the iron works of Oliver Bros. as a puddler, at which he continued until 1884. From 1884 to 1887 he served as an officer of the western penitentiary of Pennsylvania. In 1892 he was elected alderman of the eleventh ward, and, in 1897, was re-elected for another term of five years. He served six years as police magistrate under Mayors Kennedy and Wyman, and was re-appointed by Recorder Murphy. In 1903 Mayor Wyman appointed him police magistrate of the third district for three years, with offices at No. 3 police station, on Preble avenue. Mr. Harkins was married, April 23, 1876, to Miss Annie Boyle, of Pittsburg. They have seven children, viz.: Annie, John A., Frank J., Dennis B., James A., Mary K. and Edward B.

REV. JOHN B. DUFFNER, pastor of the Most Holy Name parish, Troy Hill, Allegheny city, Pa., was born at Schoenenbach, Amt Villingen, Baden, Germany, June 19, 1843. His parents were James and Walburga Duffner, both now deceased. Father Duffner began his collegiate studies at Maria Stein, Basel, Switzerland, a Benedictine abbey, now for some years abolished. His later studies were at the Benedictine abbey of Engelberg, Obwalden, Switzerland, and at Sarenen, near Luzerne. His philosophical studies were completed at the quondam Jesuit college, Brieg, Canton Wallis, Switzerland, and his theological studies at the seminary at Chur, Switzerland. While on a trip through the United States, he stopped for a few days, in the fall of 1867, at Pittsburg, Pa., and in November of that year, without previous intention, he entered the then existing St. Michael's seminary, of the diocese of Pittsburg, where he was also ordained priest by the Rt. Rev. Bishop Domenec, on Jan. 25, 1868. Since his ordination, Father Duffner has been laboring as a priest in the diocese of Pittsburg and Allegheny, Pa. His first station was that of assistant priest to Rev. Father Tomchina, pastor of St. Augustine's, at

Lawrenceville, Pa. After a few months at Lawrenceville, he was appointed rector of St. Agnes' congregation, near McKeesport, Pa., where he remained about two years. Next he founded St. Peter's parish, South Side, Pittsburg, and was the pastor of the parish from November, 1871, to September, 1892. During seventeen years of this time he was president of the German St. Joseph's orphan asylum. In September, 1892, he was appointed pastor of the Most Holy Name parish, Troy Hill, Allegheny city, Pa., and has been there ever since. His parish numbers about 700 families, and in every one of them the genial, kind-hearted priest is a welcome visitor.

REV. FRANCIS J. McCABE, pastor of the Church of the Annunciation, Allegheny city, Pa., and son of Andrew and Mary Ann McCabe, was born in the township of Gallin, parish of Killinkere, County Cavan, Ireland, Sept. 4, 1865. At the age of sixteen years he had completed the course of study in the national schools, and then entered the seminary at Ballyjamesduff, where he studied rhetoric and the classics. After a four-year course in this institution, he passed the examination for admission to All Hallows' college, Drumcondra, Dublin. In that college his studies were logic and philosophy, which he prosecuted for two years, when he came to the United States. In July, 1887, shortly after arriving in this country, he began his theological studies in St. Vincent's seminary, at Beatty, Pa. He completed his studies here, and was ordained priest on May 28, 1890. After a few weeks' vacation, he was appointed by Rt. Rev. R. Phelan, bishop of the diocese of Pittsburg, to the office of assistant priest to the Rev. Matthew Carroll, at St. Andrew's church, Beaver avenue, Allegheny city, Pa. About July 1, 1892, he was ordered to leave St. Andrew's and take charge of St. Mary's church at Kittanning, Armstrong Co., Pa., where he remained a little more than six months, leaving there about the middle of January, 1893, and the same month organizing, under direction of his bishop, and taking charge of the new parish of the Annunciation in Allegheny city. Father McCabe applied himself with zeal to his task of building up a church in the new parish, and measured by results, he has certainly succeeded. At the time of his taking charge there were only sixty-five Catholic families in the parish; now there are about 300 families, and the property of the church, on Norwood avenue, is worth more than $50,000.

WILLIAM G. MANNING, city assessor of Allegheny city, Pa., is a man of varied attainments. He was born in the city of Pittsburg, in 1851, his parents being Richard and Elizabeth Manning, both of whom are now deceased, the former departing this life in 1856, and the latter in 1898. Owing to the death of his father, William's opportunities to secure an education were somewhat curtailed, and while still in his boyhood, he started out to fight the battle of life for himself. His first employment was with the Fort Pitt glass company, of Pittsburg, where he stayed for two years. He then entered the employ of the Armstrong & Abby machine company, and in the four years that he was with them he became an accomplished machinist. A life in the machine shop was not to his liking, however, and he went into the rolling mill of Anderson & Woods, where he remained for eleven years. Next he was in the employ of Sloan & McIlvain, contractors and builders, for about eight years. For a little more than a year he was in charge of the lights and machinery of the Allegheny county jail, and, in April, 1903, he was appointed to his present position for a term of three years. Mr. Manning has always taken a lively interest in political affairs, acting invariably with the republican party. In 1884 he was elected to the common council of Allegheny city, and was re-elected in 1885, and again in 1886. He was then out for several years, but in 1898 he was again elected to the council, serving until 1901. In 1878 he was married to Miss Gertrude Schulte, of Allegheny city. Three daughters—Mary, Marguerite and Martha—have been born to them. Mr. Manning is a member of Lodge No. 128, of the National Union; the Allegheny Turnverein and the Troy Hill singing society. In the various business positions he has held he has been trusted by his employers, in his political relations he has been respected, and in his lodge and club membership he is universally popular.

LAFAYETTE WILLS, city clerk of Allegheny city, Pa., is a man whose ability and popularity are attested by the successes he has achieved both in business and politics. He was born in Allegheny city in 1868, his parents, Henry and Henrietta Wills, being well-known residents of the city. After a few years' attendance at the fourth ward school, Lafayette went to work in the Chambers glass house, in the South Side of Pittsburg, where he remained for five years. For the next seven years he was connected with the Armstrong cork company, of Pittsburg. He then learned the machinists' trade with James Reese & Son, of Pittsburg, serving an apprenticeship of four years. In 1892 he was appointed clerk to the city comptroller of Allegheny city, holding that position until November, 1901, when he was elected city clerk for the unexpired term of one year. Mr. Wills is an enthusiastic republican, and is recognized as one of the most faithful and efficient of the party workers in Allegheny county. He is a member of both the city and county republican committees, and his elevation to the office of city clerk is but a fitting reward for his long continued party services. He belongs to Allegheny lodge, No. 339, B. P. O. Elks, and is one of its most popular members.

REV. FRANCIS GLOJNARIC, pastor of the Croatian Roman Catholic Church of St. Nicholas, Millvale, Allegheny city, Pa., is a native of Cresnjevec, Croatia, Austria-Hungary, where he was born in 1864. In early life he decided to enter the priesthood, educated himself for that purpose in the schools of his native land, and was ordained at Zagreb in 1887. Until 1894 he had charge of a church in Croatia. Then, knowing that a large number of his countrymen were in America without the services of a priest who could speak their mother tongue, he sailed for this country. Upon arriving in the United States, he went directly to Allegheny city, where he was at once placed in charge of the old St. Nicholas'

church on Ohio street. In 1900 he took charge of the present parish at Millvale, a parish representing nearly 2,000 members. Since becoming the pastor of this congregation, he has built a church and a school building at a cost of about $54,000. Father Glojnaric is a tireless worker, and his work is a labor of love rather than one of ambition. Although he takes pleasure in the thought that his people are well provided for in the way of a house of worship and a school building, he derives far more real pleasure from the knowledge that they are comfortable in their homes and spiritually happy.

JOHN GRAEBING, Jr., assessor of Allegheny city, Pa., was born in what is now the third ward of that city, in 1845. His parents were John and Frederika Graebing, both of whom are now deceased. He attended the public school in the third ward, and afterwards a private institution, studying both English and German. His first position was with the Pittsburg, Fort Wayne & Chicago railway, as a clerk in the offices of the company. About 1859 he went with his father to Beaver county, Pa., where he was engaged in the hotel business until 1869, when his father was elected sheriff of Beaver county, and he became a deputy in the office for a term of four years. Upon leaving the sheriff's office he acted as bookkeeper and secretary of several institutions, and continued in this position until 1879, when he went to Pittsburg and took up the business of real estate dealer and mortgage broker. This business he conducted successfully until April, 1903, when he was appointed assessor of the city. Mr. Graebing is a solid republican in all matters pertaining to politics, and for the last ten years has been a member of the Allegheny county and city republican committees. In 1899 he was elected to the common council from the fifth ward, and was re-elected in 1903. In 1866 he was married to Miss Lucinda McKnight, of Beaver county. Six children were born to this union: John C., Harry, Emma, Grace, Samuel W. and Frank. All except Frank are still living. Mrs. Graebing died in 1901. Mr. Graebing is a member of St. James' lodge, No. 459, Free and Accepted Masons, of Beaver county; Eureka chapter, No. 167, and Allegheny commandery, No. 35, Knights Templars.

He is also a member of the Odd Fellows, Elks, Heptasophs, Home Circle, and several other orders. Mr. Graebing and family are members of the Third United Presbyterian church of Allegheny city.

ROBERT K. COCHRANE, the sixth-ward member of the common council of Allegheny city, Pa., and a well-known contractor and builder, has passed his entire life in Allegheny county, having been born in the sixth ward of Allegheny city in 1872. His first schooling was obtained in that ward, and afterwards he took a course in Curry university, Pittsburg, graduating in 1889. During the three years immediately following his graduation, he was the bookkeeper for the Western Pennsylvania phonograph company, of Pittsburg, and for the next five years he was with the Sherriff machinery company, also of Pittsburg. He was then with Fried & Rieneman, pork packers, of Pittsburg, until April 1, 1901. His mother, Katherine Cochrane, died in 1893, and the death of his father, George A. Cochrane, occurring on Oct. 25, 1900, he and his brother, George A., Jr., formed a partnership to carry on their father's business, which was well established. This partnership took effect on April 1, 1901, and still continues. Robert Cochrane is a steadfast republican in all things pertaining to partisan politics, and was elected on that ticket, in February, 1903, to represent his ward in the common council, where he is on the committees on library, corporations and public works. Mr. Cochrane is a member of Allegheny lodge, No. 223, Free and Accepted Masons; Allegheny chapter, No. 217, Royal Arch Masons; Allegheny commandery, No. 35, Knights Templars; Syria temple, of Pittsburg, Nobles of the Mystic Shrine; Allegheny lodge, No. 339, B. P. O. Elks, and Manchester council, No. 124, Independent Order of United American Mechanics. He is also a member and one of the trustees of the Sixth United Presbyterian church of Allegheny city. He belongs to the Brighton country club and is an influential member of the Americus republican club. In 1891 he was married to Miss Pearl Cassilly, of Allegheny city, and to this union have been born three children, George A., Robert K. and Helen V., all of whom are now attending school. In all the different lines of business in which Mr. Cochrane has been engaged he has been successful. Quick to grasp a situation, he soon masters the intricacies of whatever he undertakes. Although less than three years have elapsed since he and his brother succeeded to their father's business, they have managed it with such skill and judgment that the firm is well and favorably known, and is on the highroad to prosperity.

THOMAS W. HARVEY, banker and member of the common council of Allegheny city, representing the sixth ward, was born in the city of Pittsburg, Pa., in 1864. His parents were Richard and Elizabeth Harvey, the former of whom passed away in 1897, but the latter is still living. When Mr. Harvey was about three years of age the family removed to Allegheny city, locating in the sixth ward. There he received his first instruction in the public school of the ward, completing the course of study when he was eighteen. He then graduated from Duff's commercial college, Pittsburg, and took a position in the financial department of the Cleveland & Pittsburg railroad, where he rose to be chief clerk of the department. After leaving the railroad offices, he spent one year as traveling salesman for a wholesale glass house, and then went into the cashier's department of the Pennsylvania railroad, in the offices at Pittsburg. He remained in this position until 1888, when he went into the Enterprise National bank, at No. 1601 Beaver Ave., Allegheny city, as teller, and is still connected with this bank, holding the position of teller and assistant cashier. Politically, Mr. Harvey is a steadfast republican. For four years he was a member of the sixth ward school board, and, in February, 1903, he was one of three straight republicans elected from that ward to the common council. His appointment to the council committees on finance and corporations was a fitting recognition of his qualifications for such a position—qualifications acquired and developed by years of training and experience in the railroad offices and the bank. Mr. Harvey is a familiar figure at all Masonic gatherings in Allegheny city and Pittsburg. He is a member of Stuckrath lodge, No. 430; Allegheny chapter, No. 217; Allegheny commandery, No. 35, Knights Templars, and Syria temple, Nobles of the Mystic Shrine. He is also a member of Humboldt association, No. 445, Royal Arcanum; Pittsburg conclave, No. 89, Independent Order of Heptasophs; Zion lodge, No. 1057, Independent Order of Odd Fellows, and the Fourth United Presbyterian church of Allegheny city. In October, 1885, he was married to Miss Jessie McElwee, and to them have been born five children, Thomas E., Laura V., George B., Grace E. and Arthur W. Mrs. Harvey, like her husband, is a native of Allegheny county, where her family is well known.

PETER BOLSTER, alderman of the thirteenth ward of Allegheny city, Pa., is a native of Bavaria. In 1847, when he was but seventeen years of age, his parents came to America and settled at Gettysburg, Pa., and later at Reading, Pa. His father and mother, Frederick and Mary Bolster, both lived to a good old age, the former dying in 1886, and the latter in 1887. Peter received his education in the Reading public schools, after which he was apprenticed to a mason to learn the trade. He served his time and worked at his trade in Reading until 1860, when he removed to Allegheny city, located in the third ward, and went to work as a bricklayer. In 1863 he was elected constable of the third ward and served for two years, when he was appointed to a place on the police force by Mayor John Morrison. He was soon promoted to lieutenant of police, and later to a captaincy, serving in that capacity until 1869, when he was elected alderman of his ward. He was re-elected at each succeeding election until 1879, when he became deputy sheriff, holding the position for three years. He was then appointed United States storekeeper at the Guckenheimer distillery for a term of four years. At the expiration of that time he removed to the seventh ward, and was soon afterwards appointed health officer, serving several years. In 1890 he changed his residence to the thirteenth ward, where he was elected alderman under Governor McGarie, was re-elected under Governor Hastings, and again under Governor Stone. During this time Mr. Bolster was a school director for twelve years, a good portion of the time being president of the third ward school board. In September, 1851, he was married to Miss Nancy Amsly, who died in September, 1858, leaving four children. About a year after the death of his first wife he was married to Miss Eva E. Kleihn, and to this marriage there were born nine children, three of whom —Retina E., Louis and Emilie—are still living. His second wife passed away on March 14, 1903, leaving him for the second time a widower. Mr. Bolster is a member of Jefferson lodge, No. 288, F. and A. M.; Independent Order of Odd Fellows; Granite lodge, No. 664, and Kurner lodge, No. 45, Knights of Pythias. He is also a member of the German Lutheran church. For some time he was president of the church organization, and is now a member of the board of trustees. Politically, he has always been a republican, and as such he has held his various official positions.

JOHN HOCK, the thirteenth-ward member of the select council of Allegheny city, Pa., was born in the second ward of that city in 1863. His parents were Adam and Katherine Hock, both of whom are now deceased, the latter dying in 1880 and the former in 1892. As a boy, John attended the Name of Jesus parochial school, in which he acquired his education. Upon leaving school, he started in to learn the cabinet-makers' trade. Circumstances, however, constrained him to change his occupation, and during the next few years he was successively employed in a grocery, a shoe store and a machine shop. He then spent four years in learning the cabinet-makers' trade, and later learned the business of paper-hanging. In 1889 he opened a wall-paper store at No. 63 Lourie St., which he conducted until 1894, when he started his hotel and place of entertainment at No. 225 Lourie St., in which he has ever since continued. Although Mr. Hock has thus been engaged in different lines of business, it must not be inferred that he is a "Jack of all trades and good at none," for in all his ventures he has been measurably successful, and has accumulated enough of this world's goods to render him, if not independent, at least comfortable. On all questions of a political nature he acts with the democratic party, and his political standing may be seen in the fact that in 1899 he was elected to the common council, and in 1901 to the select council, from the thirteenth ward. In the select council he was appointed on the committees of public works, public safety and grade crossings, three of the most important of the standing committees. He was married, Aug. 1, 1893, to Miss Mary Walsh, of Allegheny city, Pa., and four children have been born to the union, Mary, John, Anna and Joseph. Mr. Hock is a member of the Holy Name Roman Catholic church. In both church and political circles he has a large number of acquaintances, who esteem him for his real worth, and who, knowing his merits, are ready to entrust him with the management of their affairs.

JOHN H. KEANE, a plumber of Allegheny city, Pa., is one of the representative young business men of that city. He was born there in 1870, and received his education in the Sacred Heart and the St. Andrew's schools. His first work was in a steel mill, where he was employed for about three years, after which he was for a few months in the sheet-iron department of the Righter & Connelly works. In 1888 he started in to learn the plumbing trade with Henry Fishering, one of the leading plumbers of Allegheny city, but a year later changed to the shop of Weldon & Kelly, of Pittsburg. He remained with this firm for five years, during which time he learned the trade thoroughly, and, in 1894, went into the business for himself, locating at No. 696 Preble Ave., Allegheny city. At the close of a year he sold out to George Davis and went to Frankfort, Ky., opening a plumbing establishment there. He soon returned to Allegheny city, however, and bought a partnership interest in the old house with Mr. Davis, where he still continues. In 1902 the firm removed to their present commodious quarters at No. 655 Preble Ave. Mr. Keane is a democrat, and is recognized as one of the leaders of that party in the ninth ward, where he resides. In February, 1901, he was elected to the common council, and, in 1903, he was re-elected by a decisive majority, the general opinion being that he was an able and trustworthy representative of the ward. In the council he was appointed on the committees on corporations, grade crossings and public works. On Christmas day, in 1893, he was married to Miss Rose G. Hannan, of Allegheny city, and one son, William H. Keane, has been born to them. Mr. Keane is a member of Allegheny lodge,

No. 339, B. P. O. Elks, and Lodge No. 285, Knights of Columbus. He is also a member of St. Andrew's Catholic church, at which he and his family are regular attendants.

RICHARD McCORMICK, a prominent democratic politician of the first ward of Allegheny city, Pa., was born at Richmond, Va., June 1, 1862, and is the son of Dillian J. and Bridget McCormick. When Richard was about three years old the family removed to Wheeling, W. Va., where he attended the parochial schools, securing a fair education, after which he went to work in the Riverside iron works, while still in his boyhood. At the age of seventeen he had learned the trade of a puddler and had charge of a furnace. He remained with the Riverside iron works until he was nearly twenty-two years old, when he went to Pittsburg, where for the next four years he was in the employ of Chess, Cook & Co. and Jones & Laughlin. Returning to Wheeling, he was for some time with the Whitaker iron company, when he was appointed keeper at the West Virginia State prison, and was shortly afterwards promoted to the position of deputy warden. He surrendered the place after a few months and worked at his trade for Lindsley & McCutcheon, of Allegheny, until 1889. In the meantime he represented Royal lodge, No. 34, Amalgamated Association of Iron and Steel Workers, at the national conventions of 1887 and 1888. In 1889 he took a position with the National tube company, in the furnace department of the McKeesport works. In 1892 he left the tube works to become a fireman on the Baltimore & Ohio railroad. Two years later he became associated with the banking house of N. Holmes & Son, of Pittsburg, remaining with them until 1895, when he was granted a license to conduct a hotel in East Pittsburg. His establishment there, which he conducted until 1900, was fitted up at an outlay of about $40,000, being one of the best appointed in that section of the city. In 1900 he was a candidate for the legislature, and on account of political considerations a renewal of his license was refused. Mr. McCormick then bought his present place of business, at No. 105 Ohio St., Allegheny city, which he has ever since conducted. For ten years he has been a member of the democratic county committee, and takes an active part in all political movements, especially those bearing on city and county government. In 1903 he represented the first district in the democratic State convention at Harrisburg. On March 25, 1882, he was married to Miss Mary Campbell, of Wheeling, W. Va. They have one son, Dillian J. McCormick, who was graduated in 1902 from Mt. St. Mary's college, located at Emmetsburg, Md., and who is now a member of the Allegheny county engineering corps. The young man bids fair to follow in his father's footsteps. Mr. McCormick is an influential member of the Allegheny county liquor league, representing that organization in the legislature of 1901. He is also a prominent life member of Allegheny lodge, No. 339, B. P. O. Elks. Both father and son are well known in Allegheny city, where those who know them best will testify to their worth and popularity as citizens.

DR. FRANK H. FREDERICK, one of the leading young physicians of Allegheny city, and councilman of the fifth ward, was born in Richmond, Ohio, in 1870. He attended the district school in his boyhood days, and at the age of sixteen became the teacher of the same school. When he was seventeen years old he entered Richmond college, took the full four-year course, and graduated in 1891. He spent one term in the college at Delaware, Ohio, and began his medical education in the Western University of Pennsylvania. In 1897 he received his degree of M. D. from the university, and for the next year was interne in the Allegheny general hospital. In 1898 he opened an office for the general practice of medicine at No. 1335 Rebecca St., Allegheny city, where he is still located, and where he has built up a large practice. Although his first consideration is for his patients and in keeping up with the march of medical progress, Dr. Frederick still finds time to take an interest in matters relating to public policy. He is particularly interested in having a good local government, and his activity along this line led to his election to the common council, in February, 1903. He was elected on the straight republican ticket, having affiliated with that party ever since he reached his majority. As a member of the council, he was appointed to places on the committees on corporations and finance, two of the leading committees of the municipal legislature. Dr. Frederick is well known in fraternal orders, being a member of Stuckrath lodge, No. 430, Free and Accepted Masons, and of the Pittsburg consistory, in which he holds the rank of a thirty-second degree Mason; Allegheny lodge, No. 339, B. P. O. Elks, and Ethel conclave, No. 314, Order of Heptasophs. He was married, in 1899, to Miss Mary Patterson, of Allegheny city, an estimable lady, who shares with him his triumphs and sympathizes with him in his troubles.

MICHAEL J. BROWN, the proprietor of the Hotel Brown, at No. 615 Preble Ave., Allegheny city, Pa., was born in Westmoreland county, Pa., in 1854. His parents, John and Josephine Brown, are both deceased. When Michael was a small boy the family removed to Allegheny city, where he has resided ever since. He received his education in the public schools of the ninth ward, after which he began his business life as an employe of the Oliver & Lewis manufacturing company, in their hinge factory. From that time until about fourteen years ago he worked in the various mills of the county. He then assumed the management of the Hotel Brown, which he conducted for his mother until 1891, when he took full control, and has continued in that business until the present time. Under his management the Hotel Brown has become one of the popular hostelries of the city, as he has a kind word for every one and is attentive to the wants of his guests. He was married, in 1901, to Mary (Woods) Murphy, of Allegheny city, who is as popular with the patrons of the hotel as her genial husband. Mr. Brown is one of the best-known democrats of the ninth ward, and has been twice elected to represent the ward in the select council, the first time in 1897, and the second in 1901. As a member of the select council, he was honored by a place on some of the most important committees, being one of the committee on public works, the committee on public safety and the committee on public corporations. His record as a councilman is characteristic of the man. It is an open book, in which one may read of his sterling integrity, his ready grasp of public questions, and his devotion to public duty.

JOHN McNALLY, member of the common council of Allegheny city, Pa., from the ninth ward, is a native of the ward he so ably represents in the municipal legislature. His father, Thomas McNally, represented the ward for twelve years in both the common and select councils, and the son seems to have inherited his faculty for readily grasping municipal problems and dealing with them. John McNally was born in 1876. His elementary education was obtained in the public schools of Allegheny city, after which he attended, for a short time, the Holy Ghost college, and finished his education at St. Vincent's college, located at Latrobe, Pa. Upon leaving school, he became associated with his father in the liquor business in Allegheny city, and continued in that vocation until the death of his father, in 1902, when he succeeded to the business. His mother, Mary McNally, passed to her final rest in 1891. In February, 1903, Mr. McNally was chosen by a handsome majority to represent the ward in the common council, and is now serving in that capacity. He is regarded as one of the solid business men of the city, and is an influential member of St. Andrew's Catholic church.

WILLIAM E. KIMBERLIN, who represents the second ward of Allegheny city, Pa., in the common council, was born in Allegheny city, in 1861, and at the age of three months became a resident of the second ward, where he has lived ever since. His entire education was acquired in the public schools of the ward, for at the age of fifteen years he went into business for himself, starting a meat market on Beaver avenue. Five years later he went into partnership with his father in the same line of business. This partnership lasted until 1898, when he sold out his interest to his father and associated himself with the Pittsburg provision and packing company, located on Hare's island, as a buyer of small stock, assuming charge of that department, for which his long experience gave him the essential qualifications. Mr. Kimberlin was married in 1882 to Miss Ella Bourne, of Allegheny city, and three sons have been born to the marriage. The eldest son, Oliver J., is now a page of the Allegheny city common council; the second son, Frank B., is connected with the Pittsburg packing company as weighmaster, and the third son, Howard S., is in the high school. Politically, Mr. Kimberlin is a republican, and takes an active interest in political affairs, particularly those affecting the local interests. In 1895 he was elected to the common council, and has been re-elected at each succeeding election, now serving his fourth term. He is chairman of the council committee on public safety, and a member of the committees on corporations, public works and finance. He is a thirty-second degree Mason, holding membership in the following Masonic bodies: Allegheny lodge, No. 223; Allegheny chapter, No. 217; Allegheny commandery, No. 35; the Pittsburg consistory, Ancient and Accepted Scottish Rite, and Syria temple, Nobles of the Mystic Shrine. He is also a member of Allegheny lodge, No. 339, B. P. O. Elks. He and his family are members of the Emanuel Episcopal church.

JOSIAH S. DUFF, one of the leading physicians of Allegheny city, Pa., and representative of the first ward in the common council, was born in Belmont county, Ohio, in 1855. His parents, Thomas and Margaret Duff, have both joined the silent majority, the former passing away in 1875, and the latter in 1888. As a boy, Dr. Duff attended the public schools of his native township, and later the high school in the town of Saint Clairsville. After graduating from this high school, he entered Franklin college, at New Athens, Ohio, but did not complete the course, changing off to the medical college there. He then prosecuted his medical studies under Dr. Coleman, a prominent physician of Columbus, Ohio, and graduated from the Columbus medical college in 1881. Soon after receiving his degree, he located in the town of Cadiz, Harrison Co., Ohio, and began the general practice of medicine. He remained at Cadiz about eight years, during which time he took the medical course in the University of New York, graduating from that institution in 1888. In 1886 he was elected coroner of

Harrison county, Ohio, for a term of four years, and at the expiration of that time, he removed to Allegheny city, Pa., settling in the first ward, where he soon built up a lucrative practice. He formed the acquaintance of the leading local politicians, and being an active republican, was admitted to the councils of that party's leaders. In February, 1903, he was elected to represent the first ward in the common council, where he has been honored by appointment on the finance, library and public safety committees. But Dr. Duff's activity in political matters has never been permitted to interfere with his professional duties. He is, first of all, a physician, and the wants of his patients receive his first consideration. He is a member of Allegheny county medical society, American medical association and of Allegheny lodge, No. 339, B. P. O. Elks. He is also a member of the United Presbyterian church. In his church, his lodges, the city council and his private practice, Dr. Duff is held in high regard because of his scholarly attainments, his gentlemanly bearing, and above all, his sterling character.

JOSEPH WEIS, third-ward member of the common council of Allegheny city, Pa., was born in Baden, Germany, in 1850. His parents were Joseph and Akoda Weis, the former of whom died in 1878. Joseph was educated in the schools of Baden, after which he learned the trade of brewer, and at the age of eighteen came to America. Locating in Allegheny city, he obtained employment with the Heckelman brewery, in the third ward, until 1873, when he started in business for himself, opening what was called the Hoffman brewery. He continued in the business until 1877, when he converted his brewery into a malt house. In 1890 he started the hotel and café at No. 717 Chestnut St., of which he is still the proprietor and manager. The malt house was remodeled into a flat in 1894, and since that time he has devoted himself exclusively to his hotel and his official duties as councilman. Mr. Weis is a democrat in politics, and it was as a representative of that party he was elected to the council in February, 1903. In the council he is a member of the committees on public works, library and water supply. Mr. Weis is a member of the Turnverein, several German clubs, the Catholic mutual benefit association, No. 79, and the Catholic church. He was married, in 1871, to Miss Josephine Hoffman, of Allegheny, Pa. She died in 1880, and the following year he was married to Theresa Grapp, of Allegheny city. By this second marriage he has three children, named Joseph, Jr., Mary and Helen. Mrs. Weis died in 1891. Mr. Weis is regarded as one of the substantial business men and representative citizens of the third ward, and his place of entertainment is one of the popular resorts of the city.

HERMAN KAPPELER, member of the Allegheny city common council from the fourth ward, was born in Germany in 1860. Until he was about fourteen years of age he attended the schools of his native town. The family then emigrated to America and settled in Butler county, Pa., where Herman found employment in Stehle's furnishing store. His parents, Gregory and Ottilea Kappeler, both died in the year 1896. About 1878 Herman went to Braddock, Pa., and entered the metal department of the Carnegie steel works, remaining there for two years. He then went to Pittsburg, and for the next two years was employed in a grocery. In 1883 he went to the Lake Chautauqua company, of Pittsburg, as a helper, but gradually rose to the position of assistant superintendent, in which he continued for several years. In 1898 he started the Anti-trust ice company, of Allegheny city, with offices at No. 919 Ohio St. For some time Mr. Kappeler had a hard fight to establish his business, as all the large ice dealers combined against him. He finally overcame all the difficulties, putting his company on a sure footing, where it still continues, with himself as manager and principal owner. Politically, Mr. Kappeler is a republican, and, in February, 1903, he was elected to the common council from the fourth ward. He is a member of the council committees on water supply, library and corporations. In 1884 he was married to Miss Mary R. Dietz, of Allegheny city. He and his wife are regular attendants at St. Mary's Catholic church, and he is a member of Allegheny lodge, No. 339, B. P. O. Elks. Mr. Kappeler deserves great credit for the victory he achieved over the opposition of the combined ice interests of the city, and in a way he is a benefactor to the people of Allegheny city, in that he made it possible for them to secure their ice supply at reasonable prices, thus deserving all the success that has come to him.

ELLIOT McCALL, senior partner of the firm of McCall, Rowlan & Newburn, live-stock brokers, is a native of Franklin county, Pa., having been born in the city of Chambersburg, Dec. 13, 1842. While he was still in his early boyhood, his parents removed to Mt. Carroll, Ill. Here Mr. McCall attended a private school and afterwards graduated from the Mt. Carroll academy. For several years he assisted his father, Henry McCall, in the management of his farms, and in buying and shipping cattle. In 1864 he enlisted as a private in Company A, 145th Illinois infantry. The regiment was assigned to detail duty until the following summer, when the men were honorably discharged at Springfield, Ill. While serving with his regiment, Mr. McCall was one of the 100 men detailed to guard the remains of President Lincoln in the Springfield cemetery. After the war he returned to Mt. Carroll, where he again became associated with his father in farming and live-stock operations. About this time he also taught school a few terms. At Fairhaven, Ill., was a school that had trouble to retain a teacher on account of unruly boys. Mr. McCall held a high-grade certificate and was given the principalship at Fairhaven. He soon discovered that heroic treatment was the only thing that would be of any avail in the management of the school, so he called up three of the ringleaders in mischief and gave them a severe drubbing. His determined methods won the respect of the young ruffians, and the school afterwards became one of the best in the county. In 1868 Mr. McCall came to Pittsburg with a carload of horses. After disposing of them he decided to remain in Pittsburg, and became associated with the firm of Saddly, Havens & Co., at the central stockyards. Later the firm was known as Saddly & McCall, and still later as McCall & Co. For the last twelve years he has been at the head of the firm of McCall, Rowlan & Newburn, doing a general live-stock brokerage business, and is one of the best-known houses of its kind in the east. Mr. McCall is a republican, and although he takes a lively interest in political contests, he could never be persuaded to become a candidate for public office, preferring to devote his time and talents to his live-stock business, for which he is peculiarly adapted. His brother, Samuel W. McCall, has for many years represented the eighth Massachusetts district in congress.

COURSIN L. MOHNEY, who represents the tenth ward of Allegheny city, Pa., in the common council, is a native of Clarion county, Pa., where he was born in 1860, his parents being Samuel and Elizabeth Mohney. Until he was sixteen years of age, Mr. Mohney attended the public schools. After leaving school, he taught for about three years in Jefferson county, Pa., and then came to Pittsburg, where he took a commercial course in Duff's college. Shortly after finishing his education, he began contracting and building, operating throughout the country. He followed this business until 1901, when he became one of the firm of Langenheim, Cochran & Co., with offices and works located at Nos. 1221 to 1225 Penn Ave., Allegheny city. Mr. Mohney is a member of Allegheny lodge, No. 1057, Independent Order of Odd Fellows; Lodge No. 157, Junior Order of United American Mechanics, and Allegheny lodge, No. 214, Ancient Order of United Workmen. Politically, he is a stanch democrat, and has always taken a keen interest in questions of public policy. In February, 1903, he was elected to the common council from the tenth ward, and upon the organization of the new council, he was appointed on the committees on surveys and public works—committees for which his long experience as a contractor and builder gave him a peculiar fitness, as his colleagues have learned. In 1883 Miss Annie Degroff, an estimable young lady of Verona, Pa., became Mrs. Mohney, and four children were born to this union. Two of these children, Eva and Clyde, are still living, Clare and Paul being deceased. Although not an old man, Mr. Mohney's life has been one of unusual activity, and he has accomplished as much as many men who are his senior by several years. Some of the largest and finest buildings in Pittsburg, Allegheny city and the surrounding country have been erected under his personal supervision, and few contractors are better known or sustain a higher reputation.

SIMON O'DONNELL, general manager of the Pittsburg union stockyards, and one of the principal stockholders in the Pittsburg packing company, is a notable example of a self-made man. He was born in Ireland in 1847, but at an early age came with his parents to America. Circumstances prevented his receiving more than a common-school education, and even while attending the New York public schools, he drove cattle at the markets, on Saturdays and during vacation time, to assist his parents. There was something about the cattle business that had an irresistible attraction for the little Irish lad, and at the age of twelve years he went to Champaign county, Ill., with a large stock-dealer, named B. F. Harris. This was the beginning of Mr. O'Donnell's career as a stockman. Five years later he was at the Fort Wayne yards in Chicago, superintending the shipment of cattle bought by the United States government for army supplies. Shortly after the war, in 1867, he went to Jersey City and took charge of the stockyards which had just been established there. While in charge of the Jersey City yards, Mr. O'Donnell formed the acquaintance of Samuel W. Allerton, of Chicago, who is said to be the largest cattle-raiser in the world. Mr. Allerton saw in the young Irishman a stockman of more than ordinary ability and judgment, and took him to Chicago, where he was placed in charge of the buying and selling departments of Mr. Allerton's immense business. For more than thirty years Mr. O'Donnell was associated with Mr. Allerton, and the acquaintance thus formed ripened into a friendship that remains unbroken. It was largely through Mr. Allerton's influence that the Pennsylvania railroad company selected Mr. O'Donnell as manager of the central stockyards at Pittsburg, and, on Jan. 1, 1898, placed him in full control of the yards. Although the yards were finely equipped, they had never done a satisfactory business until after Mr. O'Donnell was placed in charge. As an advertising measure, he inaugurated the "annual fat-stock show." The first exhibition of this kind was given in 1899, and the experiment has been repeated every year since with increasing interest in the undertaking. According to one of the Pittsburg papers, over 60,000 visitors attended the fat-stock show on one day, during the exhibition of 1901, and at the close of the show some of the prize winners sold at auction for more than twenty-one cents per pound, gross, the highest price ever paid for cattle in this country. Mr. O'Donnell received hundreds of congratulatory telegrams from stockmen and railroad magnates all over the country, on his successful conduct of the enterprise. It is said that Mr. O'Donnell knows more men in the live-stock trade than any other man in the United States. Besides being manager of the new union stockyards, he is a director in the Pittsburg packing company, and a member of the firm of Smith, Carey & Co., at the Chicago union stockyards. On Nov. 7, 1867, he was married to Miss Margaret Pearson, of New Jersey, who died April 23, 1903, and to this union two daughters and one son have been born. One of the daughters recently died. Mr. O'Donnell is a member of Pittsburg lodge, No. 11, B. P. O. Elks; the Order of Foresters, and other fraternal and benevolent organizations, but generally prefers the society of his own family circle. Starting in life with no capital except intelligence, strict honesty, steadfast devotion to duty, a high order of executive ability, and, above all, a determination to succeed, he has risen, step by step, to be one of the leading stockmen of the country. Known and trusted by millionaires and railroad presidents, he has never become unduly impressed with his own importance, but to his friends he is always the same genial, great-hearted Simon O'Donnell.

JESSE H. SHEASLEY, first-ward member of the common council of Allegheny city, Pa., and one of the principal stockholders in the Specialty paint company, was born in Armstrong county, in 1868, and is the son of William T. and Sarah Jane (Williams) Sheasley, highly respected citizens of Kittanning. The father is now living a quiet, retired life after years in the lumber business. Mr. Sheasley received the major part of his education in the district schools of Armstrong county, and started in at an early age to learn the ship-building trade, in the yards at Brown's station. At the age of nineteen he went to Pittsburg, where he obtained employment with the Pittsburg & Western railroad company as a depot carpenter. After one year with the railroad company, he went to the Manchester steamboat docks, where he remained for three years, when he formed a partnership with W. S. Lyons in the grocery business, at No. 728 Rebecca St., Allegheny city. This partnership lasted for seven years, when Mr. Sheasley bought his partner's interest and continued the business by himself until 1900, when he sold out, and took an active part in the organizing of the Penn oil and paint company, and a little later became the treasurer of the Specialty paint company, of Pittsburg. Mr. Sheasley takes an active interest in political matters and is one of the republican leaders in the first ward. In February, 1903, he was elected to represent the ward in the common council, and his record there has shown that the people of the ward made no mistake in entrusting their interests to his keeping.

JOHN G. ALLMAN, junior member of the firm of Hilldorfer & Allman, is a native of Allegheny city, Pa., where he was born in 1872. He is a son of George and Amelia Allman, the latter of whom passed away in 1873, leaving him without the tender care of a mother when he was but one year old. Until he was eleven years of age he attended the Etna public school, and from that time until he was fourteen he was in attendance at the third ward public schools in Allegheny city. He then started to work in the rope store of Gerwig & Sons, on Penn avenue, but after three years with this firm, he went with Zoller & Co. to learn the trade of a butcher. For three years he remained with this firm at their establishment in Spring Garden borough, and then entered the employ of John S. Wilson & Co. at the Diamond market. Since 1899 he has been in partnership with Joseph P. Hilldorfer at the same market where both members of the firm served several years as journeymen. From the first, the business of the firm has been eminently satisfactory. The two young and active butchers, filled with a desire to please, and handling nothing but the best the market afforded, drew to their counters some of the best patrons of the market. Having once secured them, it was not difficult to hold their trade, for the motto of Hilldorfer & Allman is: "Good goods and full weight." No difference of political opinion is ever likely to disrupt the harmony of the partnership, for Mr. Allman, like his partner, is an unswerving republican, and a resident of the tenth ward. He is a member of Etna Borough council, No. 961, Royal Arcanum; Allegheny lodge, No. 339, B. P. O. Elks; Pittsburg lodge, No. 50, Knights of Pythias, and Iron City lodge, No. 182, Independent Order of Odd Fellows. In 1897 he was united in marriage with Miss Mary Brinker, of Etna borough, and two little sons, Roy and William, have come to brighten their home.

SIMON SCHLEICH, member of the common council from the fourth ward of Allegheny city, Pa., is a native of the eighth ward of the same city, where he was born in 1854, his parents being John and Agnes Schleich. Both parents have passed away, the father dying in 1879, and the mother in 1892. Simon attended the St. Mary's Catholic school until he was fourteen years of age, when he went to work with the Crawford manufacturing company, of Allegheny city, to learn the trade of brass and iron molder. He stayed with the Crawford company for eight years, and since that time he has been connected with some of the leading firms in that line of work in both Allegheny city and Pittsburg, being at present with the McKenna Bros. Mr. Schleich and family are members of St. Mary's Catholic church, where he attended school as a boy. He is also a member of Lodge No. 79, Catholic Mutual Benefit Association; Bailey & Farrell manufacturing company's beneficial association, of Pittsburg, and Pittsburg lodge, No. 184, Iron and Brass Molders' association. In the last-named organization he has been both recording and corresponding secretary, treasurer, trustee and delegate to several of the national conventions of the Iron and Brass Molders' union. In political matters he is a democrat, and is generally an active participant in political movements. In February, 1903, he was elected to represent the fourth ward in the common council, where he is a member of the committees on water and public safety. In 1880 he was married to Miss Katherine Scheigg, of Allegheny city, and nine children have been born to them. Of these, Agnes and Bertha are married; Katherine, Flora and Simon are deceased, and Laura, Stella, Hilda and Edna are living at home with their parents. Through hard work and economy, Mr. Schleich has succeeded in obtaining a comfortable home for himself and family.

SAMUEL J. GRENET, one of the youngest and most prominent and respected citizens of Allegheny city, whose efficient services as deputy sheriff form a part of the history of Allegheny county, Pa., was born in the sixth ward, in 1869. His parents, Capt. James H. and Matilda (Faulkner) Grenet, have both passed away. When a boy, Samuel attended the public schools of the fifth and sixth wards for a short time only. At the age of twelve, he secured employment with a milk dealer. From here he entered the brickyards of his maternal grandfather, Henry Faulkner, where he remained until his sixteenth year. About this time he entered the iron mills of the Oliver iron and steel company, in the lower part of Allegheny, and continued in their employ until 1896, when the firm closed down its plant. He then accepted a position in the department of highways and sewers of Allegheny city under Robert McAffee, banking commissioner of Pennsylvania, who was at this time the director of the department of public works. In January, 1899, William C. McKinley was elected sheriff of Allegheny county, and upon assuming the duties of his elective office, he appointed Mr. Grenet one of his deputies, which position he held until September, 1902, when he resigned. In February, 1902, he was elected alderman in the eleventh ward, and remained in this office until April 10, 1903, when he resigned as alderman and re-entered the sheriff's office. On Jan. 4, 1904, James W. Dickson, sheriff of Allegheny county, appointed Mr. Grenet his chief deputy for a term of three years, which position he now holds. Mr. Grenet has been for many years an active participant in political affairs, being a close adherent to the platform of the republican party. He is now chairman of the eleventh ward republican executive committee, and is a recognized party leader of this city. He is a member and one of the organizers of the Union League club of Allegheny city, where he is held in high esteem. He is also identified with the Young Men's republican tariff club of Pittsburg, and a member of Allegheny lodge, No. 339, B. P. O. Elks, and the Knights of Maccabees. In 1897, Mr. Grenet married Miss Bessie D. Workman, of Allegheny city, and they have one son, Oliver J. Mr. Grenet rarely forgets an acquaintance, and usually greets every one with a smile and a kind word. To these qualities he doubtless owes his success as a politician, and it is quite probable that still further honors await him. The parents of James H. Grenet were Henry J. Grenet and Lettia Grenet. The father of James H. Grenet was killed in the war at the battle of Cedar mountain, Aug. 9, 1862. His mother, Lettia Grenet, died Nov. 25, 1897, at Pittsburg. His parents came to Allegheny city from Philadelphia, Pa., in 1847. His father was born on the coast of Brazil, South America, in the year 1819. The parents of Matilda (Faulkner) Grenet were Henry Faulkner and Sarah Faulkner. They were both born in Allegheny city. Henry Faulkner was a well-known brick manufacturer of Allegheny city, his parents being among the first settlers in Allegheny county. They settled in what was afterwards known as Manchester. The name of the Faulkners often appears in the history of Allegheny county. The war record of Capt. James H. Grenet: Enlisted with Capt. H. K. Tyler, of Company E, 7th Pennsylvania volunteers; first three months' service from April 16, 1861, as a corporal. On April 24th, he was promoted to sergeant; discharged Aug. 5, 1861. Re-enlisted Sept. 6, 1861, Company B, 4th Pennsylvania cavalry, with Capt. Samuel B. Young, now United States general. Promoted from first sergeant to second lieutenant, Nov. 4, 1864; to first lieutenant, Dec. 13, 1864; to captain, March 8, 1865; mustered out with the company, July 1, 1865, a veteran.

SAMUEL F. BOYD, who represents the fourteenth ward in the common council of Allegheny city, Pa., is a native of the second ward of that city, having been born there in 1868. His parents are Thomas M., Sr., and Mary Boyd, old and highly respected citizens of Allegheny city. While Samuel was still in his early childhood, the family removed to Shoustown, where he received his first intellectual training in the Shoustown public schools. It was while living here that he earned his first money (fifteen cents) by working on the Pittsburg & Lake Erie railroad bridge. When he was about sixteen years of age his parents changed their residence to the second ward of Allegheny city, and there he finished his education in the public schools of the ward, leaving school at the age of nineteen. He then went into the bakery of James McClurg to learn the trade, and remained there for four years. Upon leaving Mr. McClurg he accepted a position as assistant shipper in the house of James B. Scott & Co., No. 328 Second Ave., now Follansbee Bros., at Second, Third, Short and Liberty streets, where he still continues. Mr. Boyd has for many years been a consistent republican and has never refused to give his aid to any honorable movement to advance the interests of his party. In February, 1903, he was elected to the common council from the fourteenth ward, and is now serving on the committees on public works, water and surveys. He is a member of the German Lutheran church; Monument Castle lodge, No. 157, Knights of the Mystic Chain, and Allegheny conclave, No. 212, Independent Order of Heptasophs. On Oct. 9, 1891, he was married to Miss Louise Becker, a handsome and accomplished young lady of Reserve township, Allegheny county, Pa., and one daughter, Naomi, has been born to them. Mrs. Boyd is the daughter of Charles and Louisa (King) Becker, the father being justice of the peace for twenty four consecutive years in his township, and is also ex-captain of the 9th Pennsylvania reserve corps. Mr. Boyd is a modest, unassuming gentleman in his intercourse with his fellowmen, but, nevertheless, he is one with the courage to do the right as his judgment leads him to see it.

ABNER B. PRUETT, president of the Specialty paint company, incorporated, located at No. 3209 Liberty Ave., Pittsburg, Pa., is a native of Parke county, Ind., where he was born Jan. 7, 1871. He is a son of Cyrenius and Elizabeth Pruett, members of one of the oldest and most highly respected families in western Indiana. Mr. Pruett received his first schooling in the little village of Mansfield, in his native county, and later attended the Neosho Falls college, taking the full course. Until he was about eighteen years of age, he stayed with his father on the farm. In 1890 he came to Allegheny city, where he found employment with the Allegheny gas company, in the manufacture of artificial gas. He remained with the gas company for two years and then entered the employ of a paint manufacturing company, of Allegheny city. For eight years he continued with this firm, learning every detail of the business. In 1900 he formed the Penn oil and paint company, though the company was not really incorporated until two years later, with Mr. Pruett as president. The company later purchased the interests of the Specialty paint company, being now known by that name. Politically, Mr. Pruett is a republican, and although he takes an active interest in the political affairs of Avalon, where he resides, he has never aspired to public office, preferring the more certain returns from his business, to which he devotes his attention. He was married to Miss Etta McClain, of Allegheny city, in 1890, and they have three children, Jessie, Ethel and Abner. Mr. Pruett is a member of the Baptist church, and consistently practices the tenets of his religion in his dealings with his fellow-men.

CHARLES A. SPICER, second-ward member of the common council of Allegheny city, Pa., is one of the leading photographers of Allegheny county. He was born in Jefferson county, N. Y., in 1854, and is the son of Charles A., who died in 1895, and Achsa L. Spicer, who died in 1901. While Charles was still in his early childhood, the family removed to Wellington, Ohio, where he received his elementary education in the public schools. He afterwards attended Oberlin college, at Oberlin, Ohio, and then went into a photograph gallery at Wellington, to learn the business. In this line of work he soon developed a skill that was almost phenomenal and as a result his advancement was so rapid that at the age of twenty he went into business for himself. Three years later he went to Pittsburg, Pa., where for about two years he was associated with the veteran photographer, B. L. H. Dabbs. In 1890 he removed to Allegheny city, locating at No. 410 Federal St., where he still conducts the business, having one of the best-appointed studios in the city. Upon coming to Allegheny city he soon became identified with all political movements, being an enthusiastic republican. In February, 1903, he was elected to represent the second ward in the common council. In that body he is chairman of one of the sub-committees on public safety, and a member of the committees on water and charities. The committee on public safety is one of the most important committees of the council, and to be selected for the chairmanship of any of its sub-committees is indeed an honor, but the manner in which Mr. Spicer has conducted the affairs that have come before his committee shows him to be a man of fine executive power, and that the work is in good hands. He was married, in 1894, to Miss Ida Fisher, of Allegheny city, who shares her husband's popularity in Allegheny city society.

JOSEPH JOHNSON GILCHRIST, a prominent member of the legislature of the State of Pennsylvania, was born on a farm near Darlington, Beaver county, on Oct. 13, 1872. He was the fifth child of Jeremiah Murry and Mary Ann (Arthur) Gilchrist, the father a native of Westmoreland county, and the mother of Ireland, coming to America when a child. Jeremiah Murry Gilchrist, a highly respected citizen and business man of Allegheny, was descended from Squire Murry, of Murrysville, an old and respected resident of the city which bears his name. Mr. Gilchrist was engaged in the river coal business during his active years, and upon his death, the business was continued by his three sons, Joseph J., James O'C. and Harry. Mr. Joseph J. Gilchrist received his education in the fourth ward public schools of Allegheny city, whither the father had moved on his taking up the coal business. In 1900 Mr. Gilchrist was elected to the office of school director of the fourth ward, and in this position attended to the needs and looked after the welfare of the schools of that ward so well that his ability was soon recognized, and that, together with his popularity, made it evident that he was cut out for a public career. He served his ward two years as school director, and then became a candidate on the citizens' ticket for a seat in the State legislature. After a hotly contested campaign, he was declared elected, and the very fact that he was on the citizens' ticket is evidence of the high regard in which he is held by all who know him. Mr. Gilchrist is unmarried. He is a member of the Junior Order of United American Mechanics, and of the Ancient Free and Accepted Masons, in Allegheny lodge, No. 223; Allegheny chapter, No. 217; Allegheny commandery, No. 35, and Syria Temple, A. A. O. N. M. S.

HARRY W. MILLER, of Homestead, Pa., the popular and efficient teller of the Homestead National bank, was born in Mifflin township, Allegheny county, Sept. 11, 1878, and his family history is recited in the sketch of J. Clyde Miller in this work. Harry Miller was educated in the public schools, and completed his classical training at the Ada college, Ada, Ohio. On leaving college, Mr. Miller secured a position as bookkeeper with the Homestead National bank, and shortly afterwards was appointed to his present position of teller, in which capacity he has made a record which is a credit to himself and highly satisfactory to the stockholders of the bank. Mr. Miller is financially interested in a number of home enterprises, and is treasurer of the Elber land improvement company. He is a prominent member of the Homestead troop, charter member of the local lodge of Elks, and a member of the Knights of Malta, the Junior Order of United American Mechanics, the Knights of the Maccabees, and the Bankers' and Bank Clerks' mutual benefit association.

OLIVER A. GAILEY, the chief assessor of Allegheny city, was born in Indiana, Indiana Co., Pa., in 1862, and is a son of Andrew and Margaret Gailey. Andrew Gailey was one of the best-known builders in Indiana county. After a common-school education in the ward schools of his native town, Oliver learned the carpenters' trade with his father. At the age of seventeen he came to Allegheny city, where he worked as a journeyman carpenter for some years, and then became a contractor on his own account. Some of the best buildings in Allegheny were erected by him while in this business. In 1890 he became interested in real estate operations, and being a man of cool judgment and inclined to look at all propositions in a dispassionate way, he has made a success of this line of business, because he has avoided everything that looked like wild speculation. He is eminently well qualified

as chief assessor of the city, because of his intimate acquaintance with the property and his thorough knowledge of its value. In political matters he is an uncompromising republican, and is recognized as one of the party leaders in the fifteenth ward, where he resides. He was married, in 1883, to Miss Addie L. Mead, of Indiana, Pa., and his wife is one of the most estimable ladies of Allegheny city, where she has made many friends.

WILLIAM SHALER ROSS, burgess of Homestead, was born in Allegheny city, Pa., Aug. 12, 1859. He is the son of John and Sarah (McGeehan) Ross, both natives of Pennsylvania. His grandfather, Sample Ross, was one of the pioneer farmers of Fayette county. His maternal grandfather was Bryce McGeehan, a native of Lawrence county and a veteran of the War of 1812. His great-grandfather, also named Bryce McGeehan, was one of the first missionaries to go among the Indians of the west. He was a Scotch Presbyterian. John Ross, the father of our subject, was reared in Fayette county; was a carpenter by trade, and started the first planing and saw mill, in connection with building steamboats, on the "Point," in the city of Pittsburg. He was the father of eleven children, viz.: Bryce, Sample, John T., John, Henry, Walter, William S., James, Samantha, Jennie and Effie. Of these children, William S., Samantha and Jennie are the only ones now living. John Ross was an elder and one of the founders of the United Presbyterian church of Emsworth, where he died in 1895. William S. Ross has spent his entire life in Allegheny county. He was educated in the common schools there; was for seven years an official of the Dixmont hospital for the insane, Allegheny city, and later was for two years an assistant of Dr. Samuel Ayers in the management of the insane department of the city farm, Homestead. In 1894 he embarked in the wholesale and retail oil business at Homestead, and continued in that line for about three years, in connection with the grocery business. In 1896 he was elected tax collector of Homestead, and served two terms of three years each, retiring from the office in 1903. He was elected burgess by a large majority, and is now filling that office. He was married, in 1885, to Sadie G., daughter of Jacob Carnes, of

Westmoreland county, Pa. They have six children, Malcolm, Effie L., Dale, Florence, Kenney and Gertrude. Mr. Ross is a member of several fraternal and benevolent societies and the United Presbyterian church. In politics he is a solid republican, and as a member of that party he was elected to the offices he has held, though while in office he discharged his duties with rare impartiality.

JOHN M. DUFF, M. D., of Pittsburg, Pa., a distinguished physician and surgeon and specialist in abdominal diseases, was born in Westmoreland county, Pa., Oct. 10, 1849, son of James H. and Susan (Miller) Duff. His father was a physician in Westmoreland county, died there in 1885, and is survived by his wife, who now resides in Wilkinsburg at the age of eighty-five years. Dr. Duff attended the public schools of Westmoreland county until eleven years of age, then entered the Laird institute and was graduated from there in 1868. The next year was spent in teaching in the public schools, after which he matriculated at the Western University of Pennsylvania, and was graduated from the classical course with the class of 1872, receiving the bachelor of arts degree. Three years later he received the master of arts degree from that institution, and, in 1888, the degree of doctor of philosophy was bestowed on him by his alma mater. On graduating from the university, in 1872, he entered Jefferson medical college, at Philadelphia, and was graduated from that noted school in 1874, with the doctor of medicine degree. The same year, Dr. Duff began the practice of medicine in Westmoreland county and a short time afterwards removed to Pittsburg, where he did a general practice until 1896, when he decided to confine his practice to gynecology and surgery. Dr. Duff is one of the leading physicians of Pittsburg, and is closely identified with many organizations relating to his profession, being a member and ex-president of the Allegheny county medical society, ex-president and one of the founders of the South Side medical society, ex-president of the Pittsburg obstetrical society, member of the Westmoreland county, the Pennsylvania State and the Tri-State medical societies, honorary member of the Lehigh Valley medical society, member of the

American associations of obstetricians and gynecologists, the American academy of medicine, president of the section of obstetrics of the American medical association and is professor of obstetrics and gynecology in the West Pennsylvania medical hospital. Dr. Duff is also a member of the surgical staff of the West Pennsylvania, Passavant, South Side and Rynaman hospitals. When a lad of fourteen years and ten months of age, he entered the United States army, participated in most of the great battles and served until the close of the Civil war. He was slightly wounded in the fights before Petersburg, and also served some time in prison. He was married, in 1878, to Jennie E., daughter of Rev. James Kirk, D. D., LL. D., and of his wife, Abbie (Morrell) Kirk, of Pittsburg, and to them has been born five children. Dr. Duff is a member of the Bellefield Presbyterian church. He served as a school director of Pittsburg for twenty-eight years and has made many political speeches.

THOMAS C. WAITE, assessor of Allegheny city, Pa., is a native of the village of Bethel, Clermont Co., Ohio, where he was born in 1846. His mother, Sarah Waite, died when he was only one month old, and his father, William C. Waite, was killed at the second battle of Bull Run, in August, 1862, and was buried in the trenches on the field. After the death of his mother, Mr. Waite removed to Allegheny city, and was adopted by his aunt, Mrs. Thomas Charles. It was in the public school of the third ward that he received his first instruction. In 1857 another removal was made, this time to Emsworth borough, where a four-year course completed his education. He then learned the drug business, and was engaged in that line for about twenty-five years in the city of Pittsburg, being twelve years at the corner of Fifth avenue and Smithfield street. Subsequently he was nine years in the treasurer's office of Allegheny county, serving under three different treasurers—Witherow, McCandless and Bell. In April, 1891, he retired from the treasurer's office, but was immediately employed in the assessor's office of Allegheny city, and, in April, 1903, he was appointed to his present position by Mayor Wyman for a term of three years. He resides in the eleventh ward of Allegheny city, has always been a republican, and for ten years was a member of the board of school directors. In 1869 he was married to Miss Mary F. Crawford, of Emsworth, Pa., and to this marriage there have been born five children, Jennie F., Sarah E., Gertrude I., Thomas C., Jr., and Jessie May. Mr. Waite is a member of Allegheny lodge, No. 339, B. P. O. Elks, and of the Central Presbyterian church, in which for twelve years he has held the office of ruling elder.

MILTON BEDELL, of Duquesne, Pa., a prosperous wholesale liquor dealer and member of the council from the second ward, was born in Jefferson township, Allegheny Co., Pa., March 4, 1862, son of William and Lidia A. (Large) Bedell, both natives of Jefferson township. His paternal grandfather, Andrew Bedell, was a native Pennsylvanian and a pioneer farmer and distiller of Jefferson township, where he married Rebecca, daughter of Isaac Ferree, one of the first settlers of that township, and a prosperous blacksmith and gunsmith and manufacturer of powder. Isaac Ferree was a noted craftsman of his day, skilled in the different branches of industry that he essayed, and his mechanical ingenuity and ability have descended to his posterity in an unusual degree, especially to the Bedell branch of the family. The paternal great-grandfather, Joel Ferree, was a colonel in the War of 1812, taking a regiment from Pittsburg at that time. The maternal grandfather of Milton Bedell was Thomas Large, who spent the major portion of his life in Allegheny county, where he was a successful farmer. Jonathan Large, father of Thomas and great-grandfather of our subject, was one of the founders of the Large distilling company, at Mount Washington, Pa., in 1796, which concern produced the celebrated Large whiskey. This was the first distillery in the Monongahela valley, and the original still was on exhibition at the Pittsburg exposition in the early nineties. William Bedell, father of Milton, was for many years an active and progressive farmer of Jefferson township, where he is now quietly living, retired from the cares and anxieties of business. He had a family of thirteen children, viz.: Andrew (deceased), Isaac, Milton, Maggie J., Mary H., Sarah E. (deceased), William

S., Anna R. (deceased), Arminda V., John H. (deceased), Leroy, Charles H. and Fanny L. Milton Bedell was reared on the old homestead, and completed his educational training at the high school of West Elizabeth. In 1889 he located at Duquesne, embarked in the grocery business, and followed that line with much success until 1894, when he founded his present prosperous wholesale liquor establishment. Mr. Bedell was married, July 6, 1892, to Margaret C., daughter of John and Anna M. (Vogel) Werner, of West Elizabeth, and has one daughter, Annie L. Mr. Bedell is a member of William Youdan lodge, No. 647, Independent Order of Odd Fellows. He is a leading republican, was a member of the first council of the borough of Duquesne, and has since served almost continuously in that body.

FRANK J. SCHELLMAN, alderman of the sixth ward of Allegheny city, Pa., was born in 1853, and reared in the ward he now represents. He is a son of Frank M. Schellman, who was killed some years ago by a runaway team at Jack's Run station. Alderman Schellman was educated in the public schools of the sixth ward, where he has grown up with the population, and is one of the best-known citizens of the North Side. He has always been noted for his energy, and at the age of nineteen years he began his business career by starting a tobacco store, and after building up a good trade, sold the business to good advantage. In 1882 he again embarked in the tobacco business and continued in it until 1891, when he was appointed alderman by Governor Pattison to succeed the late George Shepherd. Up to the campaign of 1896, Mr. Schellman had always been a democrat, but that year, like a great many other members of the party, when the national convention declared in favor of the free and unlimited coinage of silver, he renounced his allegiance to the party and came out squarely for McKinley. Mr. Schellman is unmarried and lives with his mother on Market street. He is a member of the Independent Order of Odd Fellows, the Knights of Pythias, the Knights of the Golden Eagle, the Junior Order of United American Mechanics, the Heptasophs, and Pittsburg lodge, No. 11, B. P. O. Elks. He is also a member of the Lutheran church, and in his church and lodge relations, as well as in the community where he has passed his life, he has a high standing. Mr. Schellman can well be called a self-made man, and his success in business and in political channels is due to his sterling integrity and that indomitable energy for which he has always been distinguished.

C. C. RINEHART, of Pittsburg, Pa., a distinguished homœopathic physician, was born in the city where he now lives, on Jan. 6, 1844, son of William and Mary Ann (Ing) Rinehart. His father was a wholesale tobacco merchant and a member of the firm of W. & D. Rinehart, of Liberty avenue, Pittsburg. William Rinehart was a son of David Rinehart, who was a native of Chester county, Pa., a farmer, and came to Allegheny county in 1805, where, three years later, Dr. Rinehart's father was born. A paternal great-uncle served in the War of 1812. Dr. Rinehart attended the graded schools and the high school of Pittsburg, was with his father in the tobacco business for three years and for three years was a clerk in the First National bank of Pittsburg. He was with his father for eight years, reading medicine in the meantime with Dr. Cote, and later under Dr. McClelland. He entered the Hahnemann medical college, Philadelphia, and was graduated from that famous homœopathic school in 1878. The same year he began the practice of his profession in Hazlewood, a part of Pittsburg, and there practiced successfully for fourteen years, when he moved to the East End, and there has maintained his offices since. He devotes his time to general practice, and now has offices in the Empire building. Dr. Rinehart is among the leading homœopathic physicians of western Pennsylvania, enjoys a large and lucrative practice, and is closely identified with a number of associations pertaining to his profession, being a member of the American institute of homœopathy, member and ex-president of the Pennsylvania State homœopathic medical society, member of the Allegheny county homœopathic medical society, the East End homœopathic doctors' club, of which he is vice-president, and a member of the staff of the Homœopathic hospital of Pittsburg. He was married, in 1870, to Laura V., daughter of John and Hannah (Broadhead) Robson, of Pittsburg, and they have two children:

Frank Atwood, in the insurance business in Pittsburg, and Laura B., residing with her father. The father of Mrs. Rinehart was a native of New Castle, England, as was his wife, and he was a member of the firm of John Robson & Son, of Pittsburg, dealers in coke and lime. Dr. Rinehart served two short terms during the Civil war with the 15th and the 193d Pennsylvania volunteers.

GUSTAVE A. MUELLER, M. D., of Pittsburg, Pa., a prominent physician and specialist on diseases of the ear, nose and throat, was born in Crestline, Ohio, Nov. 10, 1863, son of August C. E. Mueller, a native of Pomerania, Germany, who came to America in 1855 and located in Ohio, and of his wife, Elizabeth (Von Dorschlag) Mueller, also a native of the Fatherland. Dr. Mueller attended the third ward school of Allegheny city, and was graduated from the Sharpsburg academy. Later he attended the University of Michigan, and then matriculated at the Hahnemann medical college of Chicago, and was graduated from that well-known homœopathic institution in 1885. Dr. Mueller began the general practice of medicine in Allegheny city soon after graduating, and was there city physician from 1885 to 1894. During the latter year he sailed for Europe to study the nose, ear and throat, attended post-graduate courses in Berlin, Heidelberg, Munich, Vienna, Paris and London, and spent two years abroad perfecting himself in his specialty. Since that time he has practiced in Pittsburg, confining his practice to the nose, ear and throat, and for a time had offices at No. 400 Penn Ave., but in 1900 removed to the Empire building, where he now enjoys one of the best practices in Pittsburg. He is a member of the staff of surgeons of the homœopathic hospital, and has charge of the ear, nose and throat work in that institution. He has been three times appointed a member of the State board of medical examiners, is a member of the faculty of the Pittsburg training school for nurses, member and ex-president of the Allegheny county homœopathic medical society, member of the East End doctors' club, the Pennsylvania State homœopathic medical society, the American institute of homœopathy, and the American homœopathic, ophthalmological, otological and laryngological society. Dr. Mueller is also a member of the Masonic fraternity and the Odd Fellows, having held all offices in the local lodge of the latter order, served as representative to the grand lodge, and medical director of the Odd Fellows' endowment association. He was one of the incorporators of the Bank of secured savings of Allegheny city, and is a member of the University, Duquesne, Monongahela, Pittsburg country, Highland golf and other clubs; the Sportsmen's association of Cheat mountain, and of the alumni of Hahnemann medical college. Dr. Mueller was married, in 1891, to Grace Swan, daughter of Wm. B. and Grace (Swan) Miller, her mother having been the daughter of Robert Swan, one of the oldest citizens of Allegheny city, and an uncle of Mrs. Mueller's was postmaster of Allegheny city for several years. They had one child, Robert Swan Mueller, born in 1893, and now a pupil of the public schools of Pittsburg. Dr. Mueller was again married, in 1900, and on this occasion to Nell W., daughter of H. C. and Louise (Worthington) Anderson, of Steubenville, Ohio, and their wedded life has been an ideal one.

WILLIAM GEYER, eleventh-ward member of the Allegheny city common council, and retired capitalist, was born in Allegheny city, Pa., July 28, 1850. His parents, David and Salomona Geyer, are both deceased. His father was a large garden farmer and William was associated with him in raising and marketing the produce of the farm until his thirtieth year. As a boy he attended the public schools and the St. John's Lutheran school, where he obtained a good practical education. In 1883 he became associated with his brother Frederick, and Frederick Herman, in the establishment of a brickyard on Woodlawn avenue, Allegheny city, which they successfully conducted for fifteen years. Since that time he has been engaged in building and selling, or renting, houses, though he has practically retired from all active business. Mr. Geyer has always been an active republican, and at the municipal election, in February, 1903, he was chosen to represent the eleventh ward in the common council. When the council was organized, he was placed on the library, water and survey committees, where he has won the regard of his constituents by his faithful attention to, and the intelligent discharge of, his duties.

In 1880, he was married to Miss Sarah Falck, of Allegheny city, and the union has been blessed by the birth of the following children: Edward, Elmer, now deceased; Stella, William, Ralph, Carl and Thelma. For years he has been a consistent member of the Lutheran church, carrying into his daily life the precepts inculcated by the teachings of his religion.

DR. OTTO CARL GAUB, a promising young surgeon of the city of Pittsburg, is a native of the city where he is now engaged in the practice of his profession. He is the son of Jacob and Katharine (Erbe) Gaub, and was born on Oct. 2, 1873. Both his parents are natives of Germany—his father of Wurtemburg, and his mother of Hesse. His father came to America in 1853, and was for many years in the grocery business in Pittsburg, but is now living a retired life. Katharine Erbe came to this country with her parents in 1858. Dr. Gaub received his early education in the public schools of Pittsburg, graduating from the high school in 1891. He then entered the medical department of the University of Pennsylvania and graduated in 1894. For one year following his graduation he was resident physician in the Mercy hospital of Pittsburg, after which he engaged in general practice until 1900, when he spent about a year in the hospitals of New York and Philadelphia, and took a post-graduate course in the Philadelphia polyclinic institute. Later he went abroad, visiting the leading hospitals of Germany, France, Austria and Italy, and took a special course in the University of Berne, Switzerland. Returning to this country, he became associated with Dr. R. W. Stewart in the practice of general surgery, with offices at No. 4715 Fifth Ave., where Dr. Gaub also resides. From 1895 to 1900 Dr. Gaub was gynecologist at the Pittsburg free dispensary, and from 1895 to 1901 was on the staff of the Roslia maternity hospital and foundling asylum. He is now on the surgical staff of the Mercy hospital, and associate to the chair of theory and practice of surgery and clinical surgery in the Western University of Pennsylvania. He is a member of the Allegheny county, Pennsylvania State and the Fort Pitt medical societies; the American medical association, and the Phi Kappa Psi fraternity. He is also a member and past master of Crescent lodge, No. 576, Free and Accepted Masons, of Pittsburg. Dr. Gaub is considered by the profession as being one of the foremost of the younger surgeons of the city. His standing, however, is due to his thorough preparation, as well as to a natural talent for his chosen profession.

DR. WILLMER A. LATIMORE, one of the popular young Pittsburg physicians of the eclectic school, was born at West Newton, Westmoreland Co., Pa., Oct. 5, 1869. His father, Robert H. Latimore, is a native of Ireland. He came to this country while still a young man and located in Pittsburg, where for about twenty years he was associated with Charles Armstrong in the coal-mining business in Allegheny county. He then went to Westmoreland county and developed the Yough Slope mines. His wife was a Miss Emily Greenawalt, and they are both now living in the East End, Pittsburg. Dr. Latimore was educated in the schools of West Newton, and took a two-year course in the classical department of Westminster college. Until 1890 he was associated with his father in the coal business. He then read medicine in the office of Dr. Greenawalt until 1892, when he entered the Eclectic medical institute of Cincinnati, Ohio, and graduated from that institution in 1896. Soon after his graduation he returned to Pittsburg and began general practice with Dr. Greenawalt, with whom he is still connected, though Dr. Greenawalt has almost retired from active practice. Dr. Latimore is a member of the alumni association of the Eclectic medical institute, Alpha chapter of the Tau Alpha Epsilon fraternity, the Monongahela club, and the Shady Side United Presbyterian church of Pittsburg. He is prominent in Masonic circles, being a member of Lodge No. 45; Zerubbabel chapter, No. 162; Pittsburg commandery, K. T., No. 1; Pennsylvania consistory, No. 320, A. and A. Scottish Rite, and Syria temple, Nobles of the Mystic Shrine. He was married, in 1902, to Miss Nellie T. James, of Pittsburg, and resides in the Delaware apartments on North Highland avenue, with offices at No. 517 Wylie Ave. Dr. Latimore has a large and lucrative practice which is constantly on the increase, enjoying the confidence of his patrons, and the respect of his brother physicians.

JAMES HARVEY IRWIN, Sr., deceased, was, in his day, one of the representative business men of Allegheny county. He was born in Mifflin township on Sept. 16, 1825, and was a lineal descendant of one of the oldest families in that section of the State. His paternal grandfather, Joseph Irwin, was born in the southern part of Ireland in 1710. In 1732, more than forty years before the Declaration of Independence, he came to America, taking up a tract of land and obtaining the patent, calling it the "Wormwood Farm," and located in what is now Mifflin township. There he followed the vocation of a farmer until his death, which occurred in 1790. There his son, James Irwin, grew to manhood; married Miss Margaret Whittaker, the daughter of a neighboring farmer, and one of the children born to this union was James H. Irwin, the subject of this sketch. On June 10, 1860, he was married to Miss Eliza West, the daughter of Matthew and Mary West, who were among the early settlers of the county. To this marriage there were born three children, James Kennedy, Ettie M. and Dessie, who is now the wife of R. L. Thompson, of Ben Avon. After his marriage, Mr. Irwin located at East Bethlehem, Washington Co., Pa. In 1870 he came to Pittsburg, and soon afterwards began dealing in real estate and investing in various enterprises, in which, owing to his sound business judgment, he was usually successful. He continued in this business all his life, and from the very nature of his occupation he formed many acquaintances, a large majority of whom became his steadfast friends. Politically, Mr. Irwin was a whig in his earlier years. Upon the organization of the republican party, he became one of its stanchest adherents, and remained so until 1876, when he voted for Tilden, and from that time to his death he was a supporter of democratic principles. He was a member of the United Presbyterian church, and died firm in that faith on Feb. 9, 1901. His widow is still living, and is a resident of Ben Avon, a beautiful suburb of Pittsburg. The son, J. Kennedy Irwin, M. D., who is well known in Pittsburg as a physician and specialist on diseases of the eye, was born in Washington county, Pa., Sept. 18, 1862, but shortly afterwards removed to Allegheny county, and has since resided there. Dr Irwin attended the common schools of Allegheny county, and later St.

Vincent's college, at Latrobe, Pa., where he was graduated in a classical course in 1882, receiving the degree of master of arts. He then entered the Illinois State pharmaceutical college, and was graduated in pharmacy in 1884. Then he attended Jefferson medical college of Philadelphia, and graduated from that institution in 1888 with the degree of M. D. For four years after graduating he practiced in Philadelphia with Prof. L. Webster Fox, a prominent lecturer on ophthalmology. At the end of that time he came to Pittsburg, where he has taken an eminent position among the leading physicians of the city. He resides at Ben Avon, has offices in the Smith building, and devotes the major portion of his time to diseases of the eye. Dr. Irwin is a member of the Philadelphia county medical society, the American medical association, the alumni of Jefferson medical college, is medical examiner for the New York life insurance company, and chief medical director of the Order of Unity. He was married, in 1891, to Margaret, daughter of Richard M. and Pauline (Miller) Webb, her father having been a prominent leather manufacturer of Jersey City, N. J. They had two children, James H., Jr., and Richard Webb. Mrs. Irwin died on July 4, 1896, and is sincerely mourned by a large circle of friends.

DR. GEORGE L. HAYS, one of the leading young surgeons of Pittsburg, Pa., is of Scotch-Irish stock. His ancestors came originally from the north of Ireland, in 1732, and settled in the Scotch-Irish settlements in Northumberland county, Pa. His great-grandfather, Capt. John Hays, was a soldier in the American army during the Revolutionary war, serving with distinction at the battles of Princeton, Germantown, Brandywine, and in several other important engagements. Dr. Hays was born near the town of Kahoka, Clark Co., Mo., July 15, 1869, and is the son of Alfred and Elizabeth (Moran) Hays. He was educated in the public schools of his native county, the Bellefonte academy, Bellefonte, Pa., and graduated from the medical department of the University of Pennsylvania, Philadelphia, in 1895. For one year immediately following his graduation, he served as resident physician in the Mercy hospital, Pittsburg, after which he began general practice of medicine and surgery. Since 1899 he has devoted his entire time and attention to surgery, serving as assistant on the surgical staff of the Mercy hospital. He has been surgeon to the 14th regiment, Pennsylvania national guard, since August, 1900; is a member of the Allegheny county medical society, the Pennsylvania State medical society, the American medical association, the Pittsburg academy of medicine, the Fort Pitt medical society, and is associate to the chair of theory and practice of surgery and clinical surgery in the Western Pennsylvania medical college. He is also a member of the University club; Bellefonte lodge, No. 268, Free and Accepted Masons, and the Sons of the Revolution. His offices, at No. 4704 Fifth Ave., where he also resides, are superbly equipped with every modern appliance known to surgery, but above all mechanical devices stands the skillful surgeon in the person of Dr. Hays, who has successfully performed some very delicate operations, and who has a pardonable ambition to stand at the head of his chosen profession.

DR. NICHOLAS ALBRECHT, genito-urinary specialist, with offices at No. 1121 Carson St., Pittsburg, Pa., was born in the South Side of that city, July 27, 1879. His father, Henry Albrecht, was born in Baden, Germany, in 1847; came to America in 1873, and located at Pittsburg, where he has ever since been engaged in the wholesale cigar and confectionery business. The maiden name of Dr. Albrecht's mother was Katharine Steiner, of Betch Lorraine, a province of Germany. Dr. Albrecht was educated in the schools of his native city, graduating from the Pittsburg high school in 1896. He then entered the medical department of the Western University of Pennsylvania and graduated in 1901. After receiving his degree from the University of Pennsylvania, he spent a year in the hospital of Johns Hopkins university at Baltimore, Md., studying genito-urinary diseases and surgery, and then began the practice of his chosen specialty in the South Side, with his office in its present location. Although one of the youngest specialists in the city, he has been able to secure a generous share of the business in his line, and has a flattering prospect for the future. His study did not stop when he received his diploma from the university, but he keeps in close touch with the progressive thinkers and writers in his specialty, realizing that only by such a course can he hope to succeed, or to rise above the physician of mediocre ability. Dr. Albrecht comes of a family of physicians, having seventeen cousins engaged in the practice of medicine in different parts of the United States.

JOHN MURRAY MOLAMPHY, of Munhall, Pa., a prominent and progressive citizen and burgess of that borough, was born in Ottawa, Canada, June 16, 1842, son of John and Julia (Keough) Molamphy, natives of County Tipperary, Ireland. His paternal grandfather, Morgan Molamphy, came to America about 1838, locating in Ottawa, Canada, where he engaged in farming until his death. His wife was Catherine Ryan. Mr. Molamphy's maternal grandparents were James and Catherine (Cummings) Keough, also early settlers of Ottawa, Canada. John Molamphy, father of the subject, was a farmer of Canada nearly all of his life and had a family of eleven children, five of whom survive, viz.: John M.; Catherine, wife of Patrick Sullivan; Julia, wife of James McKnight; James; Mary, wife of John Brastow. John M. Molamphy was educated in the public schools of his native city and there served a three-year apprenticeship as a general blacksmith. In the fall of 1860 he came to the United States, located at Cohoes, N. Y., where he was employed in an axe factory for eighteen months, and in November, 1862, enlisted as a private in Company F, 4th New York volunteers, participating in the fights of Chapin's farm, Drury's Bluff, Petersburg and Fort Fisher, and was honorably discharged with the rank of sergeant in August, 1865. Then he located in Pittsburg, entered the employ of Kloman, Carnegie & Co. as a blacksmith, and since that time has been with the Carnegie interests. After a service of eight years at Pittsburg, he was made a foreman and later became superintendent of the Pittsburg mill. In 1892 he was sent to Homestead as superintendent of the transportation and labor departments of the Homestead steel works, which position he held until April, 1902, when he was retired on full pay for life. During this period he held various other positions of importance with the Carnegie interests, and in 1891 was presented by the company with a fine block of steel stock for efficient services rendered. Mr. Molamphy is a member of the firm of Alman & Molamphy, furniture and hardware dealers, of Munhall, and is a stockholder in the Monongahela trust company and the Homestead hardware company, both of Homestead, Pa. He was married, in 1866, to Margaret, daughter of James Robinson, of Ontario, Canada, and they have five children: Mary, wife of Redmond Dougherty; William, John, Julia and Joseph E. Mr. Molamphy and family are members of the Catholic church and he is also a member of the Knights of Columbus, the C. M. B. A. and the Elks. He is a stanch republican in his political affiliations and is the present burgess of Munhall.

ROBERT BRIERLEY, of Mifflin township, Allegheny county, a successful farmer, was born on the old Brierley homestead in Mifflin township, Sept. 28, 1840, son of Thomas and Mary (Lynch) Brierley. The Brierley family had its initiation in America with the advent of John Brierley, a native of the Emerald Isle, who married Ann Jackman, Dec. 13, 1743, and landed in America, July 28, 1750, settling in Harford county, Md., about twelve miles from Bellaire, where as late as 1885 his stone house was standing and occupied. His descendants are many in Maryland, Virginia, Pennsylvania and the western states and bear the reputation of honorable and upright people. His children were: Margaret, born March 23, 1745; Elizabeth, born March 12, 1747; Robert, born April 12, 1749; Henry, born Jan. 21, 1750; Jane, born May 16, 1753; George, born Feb. 22, 1755; Isabella, born Dec. 2, 1759; John, born Jan. 16, 1762; Richard, born April 22, 1764, and Thomas, born April 22, 1770. Robert Brierley, the eldest son, was born in Ireland, April 12, 1749, and accompanied his parents to Harford county, Md., where he was reared. In 1777 he came to Allegheny county, Pa., where he secured a deed for a large tract of land in Mifflin township, part of which is now occupied by his grandson. He was married to Elizabeth Bell, of Harford county, Md., and their children were: Anne, who married Isaac Harris; Elizabeth, who became the wife of Harry Neel; Jane, who married Archibald Job; Thomas, who espoused Mary Lynch; Ellen, who married Samuel Wilson. Jane Brierley, of the third generation in America, was born on the old Brierley homestead in Mifflin township, Aug. 23, 1796, and on Oct. 8, 1816, married Archibald Job, who was born in Baltimore, Md., March 10, 1784. They left Pittsburg in an "ark," or house built on a flatboat, in 1820, and floated down the Ohio river to Cairo and from that point up the Mississippi river to St. Louis, where they spent the winter. The following spring they advanced to the mouth of the Illinois river, proceeded up that stream to where Beardstown was later founded, and there Mr. Job entered a large tract of land and became one of the foremost men of that part of the country, having filled a number of county offices and served several terms in the legislature. Mr. Job reared a large family, the sons being well-to-do and honorable citizens and the daughters noted for their beauty, intelligence and force of character. Mrs. Job was living at Ashland, Ill., as late as 1876, then being eighty years of age and remembering perfectly the most minute incidents of her early life, often speaking of Abraham Lincoln, whom she had boarded and befriended in the early days of his career. Thomas Brierley, only son of Robert and Elizabeth (Bell) Brierley, was born on the old homestead in Mifflin township, Sept. 10, 1800, and there died on March 17, 1881. He spent his entire life on the old homestead, following the even tenor of his way, and was an honorable and prosperous citizen. He was married to Mary A., daughter of Thomas and Mary (Kirtland) Lynch, natives of Ireland, and reared a family of six children, viz.: Elizabeth; Robert; Mary (deceased) who was the wife of John Lyon; Adelaide, wife of William Cox; Emeline (deceased) and Thomas. Robert Brierley, of the fourth generation in America and the subject of this sketch, was also born on the old homestead in Mifflin township, where he now resides and is successfully engaged in agricultural pursuits. He was educated in the common schools, and on June 5, 1884, married Cordelia Irene, daughter of John and Caroline (Arner) Fink, of Poland, Mahoning Co., Ohio, and they have had five children, viz.: Cornelius, Charles W., Robert E., Jesse A. and Mabel Roberta. Mr. Brierley is one of the most prominent and substantial farmers of Mifflin township, and he and his family are members of the Lebanon Presbyterian church. He is a large stockholder in the Homestead national bank, of which he is vice-president, and his political affiliations are with the republican party. Thomas Lynch Brierley, the youngest child and second son of Thomas and Mary A. (Lynch) Brierley, was born on the Brierley homestead, in Mifflin township,

Oct. 21, 1851, and on Dec. 28, 1876, was married to Ella S., daughter of Robert and Mary (McFadden) Rath and a member of one of the oldest families of Mifflin township. They have four living children: Thomas B., Clara E., Robert R. and Ella S. Mr. Brierley is a prominent farmer and, in connection with his brother Robert, is now cultivating the old farm in Mifflin township. His religious connections are with the United Presbyterian church, and in his political convictions and affiliations he is a stanch republican.

DR. SAMUEL HODGENS RALSTON, whose residence and offices are located at No. 402 Penn Ave., Pittsburg, is one of the prominent physicians of the city. As a boy, Dr. Ralston attended the public schools of Beaver county and the Beaver academy, and, preparatory to the study of medicine, graduated from the Vermillion institute, of Hayesville, Ohio. Next he entered the Western Pennsylvania medical college, and, in 1896, was graduated with the degree of M. D. For one year he was the resident physician at the Allegheny county poor farm, after which he began the general practice of medicine in the city of Pittsburg, in which he still continues. Dr. Ralston is a member of the alumni association of the Western Pennsylvania medical college; a member of the Americus club, a political organization, and one of its principal officers; and is the medical examiner for the Travelers' insurance company of Hartford, Conn. He is a loyal republican, and has become prominent in city politics. In February, 1903, he was elected school director for the fourth ward. He is unmarried. He is a brother of Dr. B. Stewart Ralston, of Neville street and Center avenue, East End, and of W. W. Ralston, the real estate broker. They belong to a family of early settlers of Pennsylvania. His father, W. W. Ralston, was a distinguished Presbyterian clergyman. He died in December, 1895, aged sixty years. For some time he was pastor of the Presbyterian church at Bridgewater, Beaver county; from 1868 to 1876 at Uniontown, Fayette county; for several years at Xenia, Ohio, and, at the time of his death, was pastor at Pitcairn, Pa. Dr. Ralston's mother was Martha (Hodgens) Ralston, a daughter of Thomas Hodgens, who, about the beginning of the nineteenth century, was engaged in the business of calico-printing and tanning morocco leather in Philadelphia. In 1804 he removed to Washington county, settled at Cannonsburg, and started the first tannery west of the Alleghany mountains. Here Martha Hodgens and W. W. Ralston were married, and here Dr. Ralston, the subject of this sketch, was born, May 1, 1867, on the farm where his maternal grandfather first settled, and where his maternal grandmother, Mary (Graham) Hodgens, is still living, in comparatively good health, in her 100th year.

CHARLES SCHMITT, manager of the Homestead brewing company, is one of the progressive and successful business men of the city. He is the son of Frederick and Frances Schmitt, and was born in Mifflin township, Allegheny Co., Pa., Jan. 15, 1859. His father came to the United States about the year 1850, and located in Mifflin township, where he followed for many years the vocation of a coal miner. He died at Homestead, in 1889, after rearing a family of seven children: John, Joseph, Charles, Frank, Ferdinand, Peter and Mary, of whom John, Frank and Peter are deceased, the others still living. Charles Schmitt obtained his education mainly in the common schools of Mifflin township. After leaving school, he worked for a time as a miner, then in the Homestead steel works until 1885, when he started in the grocery business, which he followed for fourteen years. In 1899 he assisted in organizing the Homestead brewing company, being one of its principal promoters, and has been the manager of the company ever since it began business. On May 17, 1888, he was married to Miss Sophia, daughter of Barney and Frances (Mahler) Schmid, of Pittsburg, and to them have been born six children: Elmer, Madeline, Marie, Paul, Frances and Jerome. Mr. and Mrs. Schmitt are members of St. Mary Magdalene's Roman Catholic church of Homestead. He is also a member of the German Eintracht singing society, the Knights of St. George, the C. M. B. A., and Lodge No. 650, B. P. O. Elks. In politics, he is a stanch democrat. He was appointed postmaster of Homestead by President Cleveland in 1885, and served four years, receiving three different commissions on account of the growth of the office. When President

Cleveland was elected a second time, in 1892, Mr. Schmitt was the unanimous choice of his party for the postmastership, and he was accordingly again appointed and again served four years. The executive ability displayed in the management of the post-office, he has brought to the Homestead brewing company, which has placed it upon a sound business basis and the high-road to success. The product of the Homestead brewery is second in quality to none in the country, and its popularity is largely due to the genial and efficient manager.

DR. BENEDICT STEWART RALSTON, one of the leading physicians of the East End, Pittsburg, Pa., was born at Havre de Grace, Harford Co., Md., April 15, 1866. He is the son of Rev. Walter W. and Martha (Hodgens) Ralston. (For account of parents and ancestors see the sketch of Dr. S. H. Ralston.) Few men have a better general education than Dr. B. S. Ralston. After attending the common schools of Fayette and Beaver counties, Pa., he graduated from the Beaver high school; attended the Piersoll academy at Bridgewater for two years; graduated from the Vermillion institute, and from the Western Pennsylvania medical college in 1889. During the year immediately following his graduation, he was the resident physician of the Western Pennsylvania hospital. In 1890 he began the general practice of medicine at the corner of Penn avenue and Main street, Pittsburg. Four years later he established a second office at the corner of Neville street and Center avenue. He maintained both these offices until 1903, when he disposed of his Main-street office, and since then has conducted all his business from the other office, where he is at present located. Dr. Ralston is a member of the Allegheny county and Pennsylvania State medical societies, the American medical association, the Association of military surgeons of the United States, the Pittsburg hunt club, the Pittsburg country club, the Duquesne club, the Bellefield Presbyterian church of Pittsburg, and is a life member of the alumni association of the Western Pennsylvania college. From 1895 to 1896 he was on the staff at the Home for incurables in the city of Pittsburg. Since 1894 he has been city physician for the fifteenth and sixteenth wards, and since 1897 he has been surgeon to the 18th regiment, Pennsylvania national guard. He is also surgeon for the Pittsburg railway company and the veteran corps of "Duquesne Grays." He was married, in 1894, to Estelle, the only daughter of Edward Groetzinger, one of the leading carpet merchants of the city of Pittsburg.

JOHN MONTGOMERY, a carpenter of Whitaker, and a veteran of the Civil war, was born at Bridgeport, Fayette Co., Pa., Aug. 19, 1842. He is a son of Hugh, a native of Columbus, Ohio, and Anna (Johnston) Montgomery, a native of Connellsville, Pa., and a great-grandson of Gen. Richard Montgomery, who fell at the battle of Quebec in 1775. Hugh Montgomery spent most of his life in western Pennsylvania, a paper-maker by trade, following that business when it was customary to finish and rule writing-paper by hand. He died at Smithton, Westmoreland county, Oct. 2, 1877, at the age of seventy-seven. John Montgomery received his education in the common schools. On Sept. 24, 1862, he enlisted as a private in Company F, 18th Pennsylvania cavalry. His regiment was in active service until July 11, 1865, when it was mustered out at Cumberland Gap, Md., under general orders from the war department. It participated in a number of engagements, in which the subject of this sketch, like his illustrious ancestor, did his part. He was with the regiment at the battles of Hanover, Hunterstown and Gettysburg, Pa.; at South Mountain, Smithsburg, Hagerstown, Boonsboro, Fredericktown, Falling Waters, Snicker's Gap, Culpeper Court House, Raccoon Ford, Brandy Station, Buckland Mills, Gainesville, New Baltimore, Stevensburg, Gorman's Ford, Kilpatrick's raid to Richmond, Mine Run, Spottsylvania Court House, North Anna river, Yellow Tavern, in front of Richmond, Hanover Court House, Ashley Station, Cold Harbor, White Oak Swamp, Weldon railroad, Charlestown, Shepherdstown, Limestone bridge, Winchester, Front Royal, Milford, Waynesboro, Bridgewater, Brock's Gap, Mount Olive, Round Top Mountain, Cedar Creek and Mount Jackson. He received a saber wound at Hanover, Pa., June 30, 1863, and was promoted to corporal for gallant conduct during the fight. Later he was promoted to the rank of sergeant. After being discharged, he went to Washington county, Pa., where he finished learning the carpenters' trade, and in 1873 he removed to Allegheny county, where he has lived ever since. He has been a resident of Whitaker since 1894. He was married, July 3, 1873, to Rosanna, daughter of Thomas and Sarah S. (Wilkes) Granger, of Williamsburg, Pa. They have had seven children: William James and Samuel George (deceased); Lillian, wife of Arnold V. Smith; Hugh H., Rosanna (deceased), Louisa M. and Ruth M. Mr. Montgomery and his wife are members of the Methodist Episcopal church. He is a member of Griffin post, Grand Army of the Republic, at Homestead, and Encampment No. 1, Union Veteran legion, of Pittsburg. In politics he is a republican and takes a lively interest in all questions of a political nature. It is fitting that men like Mr. Montgomery should occupy places in these pages. His record as a soldier in time of war should be preserved, and his usefulness as a mechanic in time of peace is worthy of emulation by coming generations.

GILBERT PALEN, the genial and gentlemanly proprietor of the hotel at Brighton road and Palen way, was born at Detroit, Mich., in 1862, and is the son of George and Lucy Palen, the former of whom is now deceased. When Gilbert was about eight years old, the family removed to Pleasantville, Venango Co., Pa., and it was at this place that he received his first education. Two years later they removed to Allegheny city, settling in the third ward, where he attended school for three years, when his parents again changed their residence, this time locating in the eleventh ward. Like all boys, Gilbert did a little of everything until he was twenty years old. Then he went into the retail ice business, having his office at his present place of business. He continued in this line until 1892, when he opened a hotel, in connection with the vocation of a liquor dealer, his place being one of the best on the Brighton road. In 1882, he was married to Miss Laura Anderson, of Perrysville, Pa., and they have two children living, Sarah and Bertie, and three deceased, Myrtle, Gustavus and Charlie. In politics, Mr. Palen is an uncompromising republican. He was elected to the common council in 1897, and was twice re-elected, serving three terms in all. He is a member of the Chubby fishing club, of Allegheny city, and is a great lover of the sport for which the club was organized.

MILO GIBSON CONLIN, of Duquesne, Pa., president of the Home title and trust company, was born at Coal Bluff, Washington Co., Pa., June 8, 1857, son of Joseph and Sarah (Gibson) Conlin, both natives of Washington county, Pa. His paternal grandfather, John Conlin, was a pioneer farmer of Washington county and both he and his wife lived to be 100 years of age, there being but two weeks' difference in their deaths, and, as he was just two weeks older than his wife, their lives were almost exactly of the same length. His maternal grandfather was also a pioneer of Washington county and a well-known citizen of that section of the Keystone State. Joseph Conlin, father of the subject, was a prosperous merchant of Coal Bluff, Washington county, and of West Elizabeth, Allegheny county, at which place he died on April 14, 1901. He was the father of seven children, six of whom grew to maturity, viz.: William (deceased); Annie; Deliah, wife of William Campbell; Mary; Milo G.; Erdin, wife of Dr. A. H. Aber, and John (deceased). Mr. Conlin was reared at Coal Bluff, attended the common schools of his native town, the public schools of West Elizabeth and the McKeesport academy. His first work was that of a coal-weigher at Jones' Station, on the Monongahela river, and in 1888 he began general merchandising at that place. He continued at Jones' Station with much success for a time, and then removed to Duquesne, where he established a large department store. In 1897 he disposed of that business and became tax collector, to which office he had been elected the previous spring. Mr. Conlin filled that important position with skill and ability for three years, and at the same time devoted a part of his energies to the real estate business, which he now continues. When the Home title and trust company was chartered, in December, 1902, he was elected president of that corporation and since has directed its affairs in that official capacity. He was one of the organizers of the Duquesne electric light company, of which he became treasurer and held that position until the company sold out to the

McKeesport electric light company, in 1897. Mr. Conlin was married, in 1878, to Jennie, daughter of George and Rachel (Galbraith) Jones, of Pittsburg, and they have four living children, viz : Joseph, George, John and Earl. Mr. Conlin is a member of the Odd Fellows, the Elks and the Maccabees, and his political affiliations are with the democratic party. Mr. Conlin has been prominently identified with the growth and advancement of Duquesne and is ever ready to lend his might to any movement that is for the permanent improvement and betterment of the borough.

WILLIAM CHARLES ECKBRETH, of Hays Borough, Pa , proprietor of the Hotel Eckbreth, was born in Baldwin township, Allegheny county, Nov. 5, 1863, son of Henry and Elizabeth (Miller) Eckbreth, his father a native of the Fatherland and his mother born under the stars and stripes. His father was born at Hanover, Germany, June 11, 1832, son of Henry and Mary Eckbreth; came to America in 1847, located at McKeesport, and worked as a coal-miner there and in Westmoreland county until 1902, when he retired from active life and is now quietly residing at Hays Borough. The elder Eckbreth was the father of twelve children, viz: Henry; Mary E. P., wife of Otto E. Wolf; Elizabeth E. C., wife of Thomas Swaney; Charles W., J. Theodore, S. Melinda, wife of George B. Eckman; W. Henrietta, wife of William H. Myers; Anna M., John S.; Sarah C., wife of John Lutz; Sulibell and Walter W. William C. Eckbreth was reared in Allegheny county, educated in the public schools and began his business career as a coal-miner, which occupation he successfully followed for twenty years. In November, 1902, Mr. Eckbreth embarked in his present business of conducting the hotel which bears his name, and has met with much success in that line of endeavor, having the leading hotel of the borough and enjoying a good patronage. He was married, in May, 1892, to Mary, daughter of Charles Flidow, of Homestead, and they have one living daughter, Sarah M. Mr. Eckbreth and his wife are members of the English Lutheran church. Mr. Eckbreth is a member of the Knights of Pythias, and is a republican in politics.

LOUIS ROTT, of Homestead, Pa., a prominent financier and president of the First National bank, was born in the duchy of Brunswick, near the Hartz mountains, Germany, Oct. 22, 1844, son of Christian and Louisa (Heiseker) Rott, both natives of the duchy of Brunswick, where his father was an industrious and successful blacksmith until he came to America, in 1850. His father located at Pittsburg on coming to the United States, and continued his trade of blacksmithing until his death. He and his wife were consistent members of the High Street Lutheran church, and were the parents of the following children: Frederick, a resident of Pittsburg; C. Z. F., manager of a glass factory at Jeannette, Pa., and Louis. Louis Rott accompanied his parents to America when only six years of age, was educated in the splendid schools of Pittsburg, and when fourteen years of age commenced an apprenticeship in the retail drug business. He learned that profession in five years, and then entered into a partnership with his former employer, which lasted until the business was closed out twelve months later. He then entered the employ of the wholesale drug firm of B. L. Fahnestock & Co., and for sixteen years served them in various capacities. In 1882 Mr. Rott embarked in the drug business at Homestead, and conducted the same with much success for six years. In 1888 he assisted in the organization of the First National bank of Homestead, was elected its first cashier, later was elected vice-president, and was recently made president of that splendid institution. Mr. Rott is also connected with the Homestead brick company, the Mifflin land and improvement company and the Homestead baking company, and for the past twenty years has been secretary of the Homestead building and loan association, which he assisted in organizing. Mr. Rott is a member of Lodge No. 991, Odd Fellows; Boaz council, Royal Arcanum; Amity conclave, Heptasophs; Lincoln castle, Knights of Mystic Circle; the Knights of Pythias, and the Blue lodge and chapter Masons. Mr. Rott has been treasurer of the borough for the past ten years, served on the school board for two years, and represented his ward in the council for three years. He was married, on July 19, 1876, to Arabella J., daughter of Robert McCandless, and they had three children: L. Edwin, cashier of the First National bank of Homestead; R. George, with the Homestead steel company, and Albert John, an invalid. Mrs. Rott died on Nov. 29, 1889, and, on May 17, 1891, Mr. Rott was married to Margaret Virginia McCandless, a sister of his former wife, and their wedded life has been a rarely happy one. Mr. Rott is senior warden of St. Matthew's Episcopal church of Homestead, and in his political opinions and affiliations is a stanch republican.

HUBERT PAXTON WIGGINS, of Homestead, Pa., one of the owners of the Messenger publishing company, publishers of the News-Messenger, a leading daily paper, was born at Redwood Falls, Minn., July 16, 1870, son of Coulter and Adelaide M. (Craigen) Wiggins. Mr. Wiggins is descended, on his father's side, from John Kinter, and traces his ancestry as follows: Coulter Wiggins, born in White township, Indiana Co., Pa., Jan. 23, 1840; Robert Wiggins, born on Ackerson's farm, White township, Indiana Co., Pa., March 26, 1810, and died June 25, 1890; Eliza Coulter, born in Indiana county, Pa., April 11, 1817, married Robert Wiggins, Nov. 2, 1836, and died June 20, 1855; Thomas Wiggins, born on Ackerson's farm, White township, Indiana Co., Pa.; Elizabeth Lytle, born near Princeton, N. J., and married Thomas Wiggins; Samuel Wiggins, native of Ireland, of Scotch descent, came to the United States in the latter part of the eighteenth century; Margaret Wiggins, his wife, native of Ireland, of Scotch descent; James Coulter, father of Eliza Coulter, born in Georgia, Sept. 30, 1791, and died March 6, 1863; Catherine Kinter, native of Indiana county, Pa., born on Dec. 27, 1791, married James Coulter, and died on March 15, 1852; John Kinter, native of Huntingdon county, Pa., served three terms of three months each in the patriot army during the American Revolution, and died in his eighty-second year; Isabella Findley, native of Huntingdon county, Pa., married John Kinter, and died in her ninetieth year; Philip Kinter, emigrant from Holland; Barbara King, wife of Philip Kinter, emigrant from Holland. Mr. Wiggins is descended, on his mother's side, from the Craigens of Scotland, one of whom, Robert Craigen, fought in the battle of Culloden, March 16, 1746, and the ancestral line is as follows: Adelaide M. Craigen, born in Hampshire county,

W. Va., Dec. 23, 1843, married Coulter Wiggins, Aug. 15, 1868; Jacob I. Craigen, born in Hardy county, W. Va., May 10, 1807, was a slave owner at the opening of the Civil war, but espoused the federal side, experienced many thrilling adventures, and now resides on the old farm, at the age of ninety-seven; Eliza Sein Parsons, born at Washington, D. C., in 1811, married Jacob Craigen, April 3, 1833, and died Oct. 13, 1872; John Craigen, born in Winchester county, Va., and died at the age of fifty-seven years; Mary Lee, native of Hardy county, W. Va., married John Craigen, and died in her eightieth year; Robert Craigen, born in Scotland, emigrated to Maryland, and finally located in Winchester county, Va.; Susanna Perrin, native of Maryland, married Robert Craigen; George Lee and Keziah Borgart, parents of Mary Lee, resided in Hardy county, W. Va.; Joseph Parsons, father of Eliza Sein Parsons, born at Rye Beach, Mass., moved to Washington, D. C., and was a trader and merchant; Elizabeth Betsy Monroe, a native of Washington, D. C., and the wife of Joseph Parsons. Coulter Wiggins, father of H. P. Wiggins, removed from Redwood Falls, Minn., where he had gone in search of health, to his former house at Indiana, Pa., and, in 1890, located at Blairsville, Pa., where he now resides and practices law with much ability and unusual success, and is one of the leading citizens of that community. At Indiana his son was reared and educated, being a graduate of the State normal school at that place, and later he located in Homestead, Pa., where he secured employment as a printer, which trade he had learned at Indiana, in the establishment of M. P. & J. R. Schooley, then the proprietors of the Homestead News. Subsequently, Mr. Wiggins purchased the plant of the Homestead Messenger, a daily paper, and associated with him Miss Sarah Parry. The News was then bought, and the two papers consolidated as the News-Messenger. Later Miss Parry disposed of her interest to A. D. Slocum, and Messrs. Wiggins and Slocum have continued the newspaper and jobbing business under the name of the Messenger publishing company, and have one of the best equipped plants in the Monongahela valley, while the News-Messenger is a splendid daily paper, which carries great weight and exerts an immense influence in the community. The young men have also acquired considerable property about Homestead. Mr. Wiggins was married, in 1896, to Miriam E., daughter of Thomas L. Parry, a retired mill roller of Homestead, and they have one child, Hubert Parry.

JAMES LAWRY, of West Homestead, Pa., real estate, insurance and news agent, and collector for the Farmers' saving fund and loan association, of Pittsburg, was born at St. Ives, Cornwall, England, March 24, 1861, son of Henry and Mary (Lory) Lawry. His paternal grandparents were Henry and Nannie (Martin) Lawry and his maternal grandparents were John and Alice Lory. His parents came to America in 1863, located in Johnstown, Pa., where his father was employed in the iron ore mines, and later became a soldier in the Civil war. Prior to coming to America, he followed the tin and copper mining industry in England, and after the Civil war in America, returned to Johnstown and resumed his vocation of mining until the strike of 1873. Then he went to Latrobe, Pa., where, with others, he opened and enlarged the Loyalhanna shaft, and subsequently removed to Houtzdale, Pa., where he resided until 1875, after which he was employed in Bedford county by the Wigton coal company until 1877, when he entered the service of the Edgar Thompson steel works, at Braddock, where he remained until 1880, when he left that concern and went to England to inspect some mines. He was there killed, in 1881, by the breaking of the wire rope on the elevator in a shaft, which precipitated him and nine others to the bottom of the same, killing the entire number. He was the father of twelve children, viz.: Mary A., wife of William H. Phoebe; Richard, Henry, William, John; Hannah, wife of John Tresise; Elizabeth J., wife of Alexander F. Redpath; Thomas; Annie, wife of Cornelius Dickinson; James; Sarah, wife of Robert E. Nelson, and Priscilla. James Lawry was reared in Pennsylvania, educated in the public schools, and when eight years of age began doing odd jobs about the coal mines, where he was employed for eight years. In 1877 he located at Braddock, and for five years was in the employ of the Edgar Thompson steel works. In 1882 Mr. Lawry went to Pueblo, Col., and helped to start the new steel works at that place. He then removed to Homestead, where he was employed in the mills until the strike of 1892, then for about two years he was employed by Mr. Charles Schmitt as clerk and solicitor for him in the grocery business. In May, 1894, Mr. Charles Schmitt, having been appointed postmaster at Homestead, sold out his grocery business,

Mr. Lawry then embarking in the same business for himself, and for six years prospered. Since 1901 he has successfully followed his present business of a real estate, insurance and newspaper agent, owning a very valuable newspaper route in West Homestead. He was married, on June 14, 1883, to Julia A., daughter of Dr. Thomas W. and Bertha G. (McCabe) Blackburn, of Covington, Ky., and they have five children, viz.: Olive M., Thomas L., James D., Richard H. and George C. Mr. Lawry is a member of the Independent Order of Heptasophs and the Modern Woodmen of America, and his political affiliations are with the republican party.

WILLIAM BOST, a well-known carpenter of Whitaker, where he has lived since 1892, is of German parentage. He is a son of Henry and Catherine (Renn) Bost. His father came to America about the year 1851 and located in Allegheny county, where he resided until his death. For about twenty years he followed the occupation of a coal-miner, and afterwards lived practically a retired life in the village of Whitaker, where he died in 1886 at the age of fifty-seven. Matthew Renn, his maternal grandfather, came to America in 1852, settled in Mifflin township and spent the remainder of his life there. William Bost was born in Mifflin township, Jan. 1, 1857. He is one of a family of seven children—all boys—viz.: John, Jacob, William, Valentine, Frank, Henry and Lewis. He received a common-school education and began life as a miner, which occupation he followed for about ten years, when he went to work as a heater in the Homestead steel works. In 1892 he made another change in his occupation and since that time he has worked continuously at carpenter work, assisting in the erection of some of the finest buildings in the county. He owns his home at Whitaker and is looked upon as one of the substantial citizens of that thriving village. On March 14, 1881, he was married to Miss Gertrude Rushe, a daughter of Nicholas and Mary Rushe, of Mifflin township. His wife's parents are both natives of Germany, though of French extraction. They have nine children living: Henry N., John G., Peter A., Gertrude M., William L., M. Florence, J. Oliver, L. Pearl and an infant daughter,

Roberta M. Mr. Bost and his family are members of St. Francis' Roman Catholic church, of Homestead. He is a charter member of Whitaker tent, No. 425, Knights of the Maccabees; the Carpenters' and Joiners' union, and the Turnverein. In politics he is independent. Believing in the saying of the late President Hayes, that "He serves his party best who serves his country best," he carefully weighs every proposition touching the public weal and casts his vote on the side which he conscientiously believes will secure the greatest good to the greatest number.

CHARLES ADOLPH SCHULZ, postmaster and merchant at Hays Park, Pa., was born in Mifflin township, Allegheny county, Aug. 19, 1857. His parents, Carl and Amelia (Sewald) Schulz, were natives of Germany, born near Saarbrücken-on-the-Rhine. His father came to America about 1845, and was for several years employed in a brewery at Birmingham, later locating in Mifflin township, where he continued in the brewery business. During the Civil war he conducted the first licensed hotel at Braddock, Pa. The greater part of his life was spent in Allegheny county, and he died at Whitaker, in April, 1900, at the age of seventy-three years. (See sketch of Rudolph Schulz for account of paternal grandfather, John Schulz.) The maternal grandfather, Peter Sewald, was born in Germany, but came to America about 1850, settling in Mifflin township, where he conducted a flour-mill. It was there that Carl Schulz married his daughter, Amelia, and to them were born nine children, seven of whom are still living. They were: Charles A.; Emma; Herman; Wilhelmina, married to Henry Bost, but now deceased; Amelia, wife of Lawrence Schopp; Frederick (deceased); William; Catherine M., wife of Otto Barthol, and George. Charles A. Schulz, the subject of this sketch, received his education in the public schools. Since arriving at manhood he has been engaged in various occupations, including building, managing a brewery at Homestead, and operating a stone-quarry. He spent seven years in the west, principally in Kansas and Missouri, the greater part of which time he was engaged in merchandising. He was appointed postmaster at Brandsville, Mo., by President McKinley. Returning to Pennsylvania in 1898, he located at Whitaker, where he has since operated a general store, and has served as postmaster of Hays Park since 1902. Mr. Schulz was married, April 15, 1890, to Anna, daughter of Frederick and Wilhelmina (Dasler) Barthol, of Germany. They have two children living, Hans and Amanda. Mr. Schulz takes an active interest in political matters, in which he is identified with the republican party.

LINDLEY SPENCER LAWSON, of Homestead, Pa., president and general manager of the Lawson manufacturing company, was born near Perrysville, Allegheny Co., Pa., Jan. 24, 1870, son of James N. and Frances (Osborn) Lawson, both natives of Pennsylvania. His paternal grandfather, James Lawson, was a native of Ireland, a carpenter by trade, and among the early settlers of Allegheny county, where he was engaged in farming. He was married to Mary Nixon and they had a family of three children, of whom James N. was the eldest. James N. Lawson was also a carpenter by trade, and for a number of years successfully followed that occupation, but in 1880 located at Homestead, being among the first settlers of that borough, and there engaged in the plumbing business until 1898. He met with much success in that venture, retired from business in 1898 and died on Oct. 27, 1899. His children were: Mary J., wife of O. C. Waters; Oliver O., James A.; Lizzie, wife of Dr. F. F. Sumney; Oscar P., Lindley S., William E.; Harriet J., wife of J. N. Hoffer, and Howard L. Lindley S. Lawson was reared and educated at Homestead, where he attended the public schools and learned the trade of gas-fitting, which he followed for ten years, four years of which time he was a partner of his father. In 1896 he invented what is known as the Lawson gas water-heater and gas-burners for cook-stoves, which he manufactured until 1901 on his own account, and then organized the Lawson manufacturing company, with a capital of $25,000, with himself as president and general manager. This business is in splendid condition, almost doubling itself each year and paying handsome dividends to the stockholders under his splendid management. Mr. Lawson was married, on June 3, 1891, to Harriet M., daughter of John and Mary (Chew) Mailey, of Homestead, Pa., formerly of California, Pa., and they have had three children: Lindley F. M., Harold B. and Lynn. Mr. Lawson is financially interested in the Enterprise land improvement company (limited) and is one of the prominent and progressive citizens of Homestead.

THOMAS S. GRANGER, of Whitaker, Pa., a successful grocery merchant, was born in Liverpool, England, July 4, 1844, son of Thomas and Sarah (Frazzackly) Granger. His father came to America in 1849, located on the South Side of Pittsburg, where he was joined by his family in 1851, and engaged in mining until his death, in St. Clair township, in 1871, at the age of seventy-one years. His family consisted of five children that grew to maturity, viz.: Thomas S.; Henry (deceased); Rosanna, wife of John Montgomery; Richard, and William (deceased). Thomas S. Granger was reared in St. Clair township, educated in the common schools, and began life as a miner. At the outbreak of the Civil war, he enlisted in Company B, 62d Pennsylvania infantry, July 12, 1861, as a private, and participated in the battles of Fredericksburg, second Bull Run, Yorktown, Hanover Court House, seven days' fights in front of Richmond, Antietam, Spottsylvania Court House, Chancellorsville, Mine Run, Cold Harbor, Laurel Hill, and many lesser engagements. He was wounded at Laurel Hill and Cold Harbor and was honorably discharged on July 13, 1864. On leaving the army, he returned to his home in Pennsylvania, engaged in mining in Baldwin township, and later followed the carpenters' trade with much success. He has been a resident of Mifflin township since 1886, and, in March, 1899, embarked in the grocery business at Whitaker, in which he has since prospered. He has been twice married—first, to Mary, daughter of George and Elizabeth (Davis) Upperman, of Lower St. Clair township, by whom he had two children, viz.: Charles H. and Alma B., wife of Burt Layton. He was married on the second occasion to Margaret, daughter of Christian and Margaret Horn, of Homestead, and they have two children, viz.: Christ H. and Margaret S. Mr. Granger is a prominent republican of Mifflin township, and one of the leading citizens of that part of the county.

ALEX. HOLOZSNYAY, of Homestead, Pa., pastor of the St. John's Greek Catholic church, was born in County Ung, Hungary, March 28, 1867, and was educated in the diocese of Munkacs, graduating from the Munkacs university in 1891. The following year he was ordained a priest at Repede, and was pastor of Bukovinka church until 1899, when he came to the United States and was assigned to the pastorship of St. John's Greek Catholic church, of Homestead. At that time the church had a membership of 200 families, and under his charge they have increased the membership to 300 families and now are constantly gaining in numbers. This parish was organized in 1895; the present church was erected the same year, but owing to the rapid increase in the size of the congregation, it has been necessary to let a contract for a much larger edifice, which is to be a handsome structure of brick and stone with a seating capacity of 500. The parochial school, connected with the church, is a splendid institution and now has eighty pupils. Father Holozsnyay is a prominent member of the Sojedinenia Greek Catholic society, which has a membership of 11,000, and formerly served as secretary of that organization.

RUDOLPH SCHULZ, mine host of the popular Hotel Whitaker, at Whitaker, Allegheny Co., Pa., was born in Mifflin township, of the same county where he now resides, Oct. 8, 1867. His parents were Albrecht and Raghena (Reis) Schulz, both of whom were born near Saarbrücken-on-the-Rhine, Germany. About the year 1847 his father came to America, and soon afterwards located in Mifflin township. He was a man of varied attainments, being a cabinet-maker by trade, a violinist of considerable ability, a veterinary surgeon, and for twenty-one years operator of a stand on the Pittsburg market for the sale of vegetables raised upon his farm in Mifflin township. John Schulz, the grandfather of Rudolph, was a teacher for several years in the German schools.

He came to America about 1849, purchased a farm in Mifflin township, upon which part of the village of Whitaker is now located, and died there in 1879. Rudolph is one of a family of nine children, viz.: Mary, wife of Charles Eichler; Gustave, Dora, Sophia, Rudolph; Catherine, wife of Henry Lawrence; Peter; Margaret, wife of Wm. Rhome, and Caroline. Seven of the children are still living, Dora and Sophia being deceased. The father died in 1887. Rudolph was educated in the common schools of Mifflin township. After farming for about eight years, he engaged in the real estate and produce business, in which he continued until 1901, when he became the proprietor of the Hotel Whitaker. He has been twice married, his first wife being Miss Lydia Wilding, and his present wife was Miss Nellie M. Price, a daughter of John and Helen (McKelvey) Price, of Mifflin township. By his second wife he has one son, Albrecht Stewart Schulz. Mr. Schulz is a supporter of the Lutheran church, and in politics is an unswerving republican, often being called on to serve as a delegate in the county and State conventions of his party. In business he is energetic, the popularity of his hotel being due to his enterprise and genial disposition.

FREDERICK DIERSTEIN, of Hays Park, Pa., a prominent merchant and justice of the peace, was born near Saarbrücken, Germany, Nov. 30, 1864, son of Louis and Elizabeth (Ries) Dierstein, who came to America in 1881, locating in Mifflin township, where his father was employed as a miner for many years. His parents had four children, viz.: Sophie, wife of Frank J. Ackerman; Frederick; Bertha, wife of Jesse Lantz, and Clara, wife of Fred Gotsheck. Frederick Dierstein remained in Germany until his sixteenth year, when he accompanied his parents to Mifflin township, where he received a common-school education, and began life as a clerk in the Pittsburg Bessemer steel works in 1881. He remained in that position for five years, and then went with Jones & Laughlin as assistant shipping clerk, in which department he remained for seven years. Later he became shearer and recorder for the last-named firm, and ably filled those positions for nearly nine years. In 1901 he located at Whitaker and began his present business. He was married, in 1888, to Sophia, daughter of Christian Miller, of Germany, and they have had six children, viz.: Clara E., Jesse P., Lillie B., Elsie K., Louisa and Ester. He is a member of the German Reformed church, the Red Men, the German soldiers' association, the D. O. H. and the Whitaker fire company. While a resident of St. Clair township, Mr. Dierstein held the office of register and assessor of the third district for six years; in October, 1902, was appointed justice of the peace of Mifflin township, and in the spring of 1903 was elected for a term of five years. He is identified with the republican party in politics, and is an active worker for its advancement and success. In 1903 Mr. Dierstein organized the Whitaker volunteer fire company's band, of which he is president and director.

JOHN LEADBEATER, of Munhall, Pa., a prosperous and successful carpenter, was born in North Versailles township, Allegheny county, Pa., Nov. 29, 1874, son of John J. and Jane (Davis) Leadbeater, natives of England and Wales, respectively. His paternal grandfather, John Leadbeater, came to America in 1855, locating in Mifflin township, where he followed his trade of blacksmithing until his death, which occurred at Dravosburg. His maternal grandfather, John Davis, came to the United States about 1850, first located at Pittsburg and later removed to McKeesport and subsequently to Munhall, where he died. He was employed in the various mines of the Monongahela valley for many years and was prominent in the different communities in which he made his home. John J. Leadbeater, father of the subject, was a successful blacksmith and for many years was employed by W. H. Brown & Co. He died in 1891, at the age of fifty years, and was the father of twelve children, viz.: William (deceased); Hannah, wife of William Sellers; Nellie; Sarah, wife of George Wilson; Laura, wife of James A. Porter; Mary, wife of William Drake; Margaret, wife of Wilson Sheasley; John, Alice, Thomas, Edwin and Joshua. John Leadbeater was reared in Mifflin township from ten years of age, educated in the public schools and worked with his father at blacksmithing until the death of the latter. Then he began in the mines, and for the last five years has devoted his attention to the carpenters' trade, at which he has been quite successful and has accumulated a good competency. Mr. Leadbeater is a member of the Odd Fellows and the Carpenters' union of Homestead, and is a member of the republican party, in which organization he is an active and able worker.

JOHN MARSHALL ORRIS, of Whitaker, Pa., a well-known contractor and builder, was born in Union township, Allegheny county, March 22, 1864, son of Abraham and Annie (Marshall) Orris, natives of Allegheny county, Pa., and England, respectively. His paternal grandfather, John Orris, was a native of Pennsylvania, a coal-miner by occupation, and for many years a resident of Allegheny county, but in later life a resident of Irwin, Pa., where he died at an advanced age. His maternal grandfather, John Marshall, a native of England, came to America about 1853, and located in Union township, Allegheny county, where he engaged in his trade of carpentering until his death. Abraham Orris, father of the subject, was reared in Union township, where he still resides and there follows his vocation of mining. He had a family of six children, viz.: John M.; Lizzie, wife of William Porter; Joseph; Ada M., wife of John Snyder; George, and Annie, wife of John Durst. John M. Orris was reared in his native township, educated in the public schools, and was engaged in mining at different times for several years. In the meantime, Mr. Orris had become proficient at the carpenters' trade, and since 1887 has devoted his attention to that line of industrial effort. Since 1899 he has been engaged in building and contracting as a member of the well-known firm of Strang & Orris, and they are now doing an extensive business, and stand well in the industrial and financial world. He was married, on May 28, 1885, to Annie, daughter of Frank and Georgiana (Johnson) Taylor, of Union township, and they have had seven children born to them, viz.: Charlotte, Georgiana, Chester W., Francis A., Lizzie, Anna and John M., Jr. Mr. Orris is a member of Progressive lodge, No. 492, Knights of Pythias, and Whitaker tent, No. 425, Knights of the Maccabees, and his political affiliations are with the republican party.

WALTER EDSON STEFFY, M. D., of Duquesne, Pa., a leading physician and surgeon, was born at Rural Valley, Armstrong Co., Pa., Jan. 29, 1870; son of Rev. John T. and Margaret (Logan) Steffy, both natives of Armstrong county and of Scotch-Irish and German descent, respectively. His paternal grandfather, John T. Steffy, was a native of Pennsylvania, a pioneer farmer of Armstrong county, though a tanner by trade, and later was employed in the mills at Sharpsburg, which were the first rolling mills of that section. He was also engaged in other occupations, but the major portion of his life was devoted to tanning in Armstrong county, whence he removed to Duquesne in 1890, where he lived quietly until his death in 1901, at the age of seventy-nine years. His wife was Mary Earhart, and she was a woman known for force of character and many virtues. The maternal grandfather of Dr. Steffy, Samuel Logan, a native of Allegheny county, Pa., was a prosperous blacksmith and followed that line of industry during his entire business career. Rev. John T. Steffy, father of the subject, was reared in the Keystone State, educated at Mount Union college and for thirty years has been a minister of the Methodist Episcopal church, at present being stationed at the Washington church, South Side, Pittsburg. He had a family of eight children, viz.: Walter E.; Vernetta, widow of Enos Register; Mary B.; Estella, wife of Frank McGill; Blanch, James, John T. and Priscilla. Dr. Steffy was reared in his native State, educated in the normal school at California and at the Western university, of Pittsburg, and for two years attended a pharmaceutical school at Pittsburg, subsequently matriculated at the medical department of the Western Pennsylvania university, where he was graduated in 1894, with the degree of doctor of medicine. Dr. Steffy initiated his professional career at Allegheny city, where he practiced for one year, and in 1895 removed to Duquesne, where he has since met with much success and ranks high among the leading physicians of that part of the county. He was married, on May 29, 1889, to Anne A., daughter of Dr. John T. and Margaret (Hazlett) Black, of Duquesne, and their home life is one of rare happiness. Dr. Steffy is a member of the Methodist Episcopal church, also member of United States pension examining board, and is a thirty-second degree Mason and an Elk. Dr. Steffy was a member of the medical staff of McKeesport hospital for five years, physician to the board of health for three years and in many ways prominently identified with the medical profession. Dr. Steffy has also been called on to serve the borough in other capacities than professional, and was a member of the council from the first ward for three years, in which position he made a fine record. He was one of the promoters, and is now a director, of the Home title and trust company and in many ways is one of the prominent figures of that community.

JAMES BICKERTON, the efficient postmaster of Duquesne, Pa., was born in Wheeling, W. Va., Jan. 9, 1844, and is the son of William and Dorothy (Breminger) Bickerton, natives of England and Petersburg, Huntingdon Co., Pa., respectively, and is of English and German ancestry. His father, now a resident of Kansas, at the age of ninety years, came to America in 1831, and located at Wheeling, W. Va., where he operated a coal mine for about fifteen years and was also married, about 1845. Later he removed to Elizabeth, Pa., where he was superintendent of a mine for thirty-five years, and subsequently removed to his present home in Kansas. He reared a family of five children, viz.: Eliza, wife of Robert Cardurll; Ann, wife of George Grant; Clara, wife of George Young; Josephine, wife of Patrick Herron, and James. James Bickerton was reared in Allegheny county from one year of age, was educated in the common schools and then was employed about the mines under his father for a number of years. He was a soldier of the Civil war, serving in Company D, 123d regiment of Pennsylvania volunteers, and participated in the battles of Antietam, Fredericksburg, Chancellorsville and others. In August, 1863, he again enlisted, this time in Company C, 14th Pennsylvania cavalry, spent fourteen months doing scouting duty with that command and at the close of the war was honorably discharged. He then went to Kansas, where he remained for six years, and later engaged in the coal business in Illinois and Ohio. In 1889 Mr. Bickerton located at Duquesne, Pa., and was there engaged in the grocery business until 1897, when he was appointed postmaster by President McKinley, re-appointed in 1898, and in April, 1902, was nominated as his own successor by President Roosevelt. He was married, on July 24, 1866, to Mary, daughter of John R. and Lucretia A. (Wilson) Mickey, of West Elizabeth, Pa., and they have eight living children, viz.: Mildred D., wife of Albert N Smith; Mattie E., Charles C.; Nellie, wife of John W. Elliott; George W., James W., Wilbur L. and Hazel M. Mr. Bickerton and his wife are members of the Methodist Episcopal church, and he is a member of Samuel Black post, Grand Army of the Republic, of McKeesport; West Elizabeth lodge, No. 442, Knights of Pythias, and of the republican party. Mrs. Bickerton's maternal great-grandfather Wilson, was a soldier in the Revolutionary war and her grandfather, John, was a participant in the War of 1812, in which contest his wife, Mary, also lent her aid by molding bullets for the new republic.

JOHN A. FISHER, the leading photographer of Homestead, Pa., was born at Oil City, Pa., May 9, 1869. Several generations of the Fisher family have lived in Pennsylvania. Christian Fisher, the great-grandfather of the subject of this sketch, was for many years a farmer of Snyder county. He came, in his boyhood, with his parents from Germany, being among the early Pennsylvania Dutch settlers, while John Fisher, the grandfather, was a soldier in the War of 1812. John A. Fisher is a son of John P. and Eldretta (Thompson) Fisher, his mother being a native of Kentucky. Her father, William N. Thompson, came of Revolutionary stock. The parents of John A. Fisher are still living in Pittsburg, where his father is engaged in the photograph business, though for many years he was an operator in the oil fields of western Pennsylvania. John A. Fisher was educated in the public schools of Oil City, graduating from the high school in 1885. In 1889 he began the study of photography in Pittsburg, and after mastering all the intricacies of the art, he started in business for himself, locating at Homestead. His reputation as a photographer was soon established, his work being excelled by none in the county. On March 27, 1901, he was married to Miss Charlotte, the daughter of Edward and Charlotte Ensell, of Pittsburg, and they have one little daughter, Margaret. Mr. Fisher is a modest, unassuming man; one of the kind that devotes his time to his business and his family, though he keeps himself informed on questions relating to the general welfare, and intelligently discharges his duties as a citizen.

JOSEPH ALEXANDER DOYLE, M. D., of Homestead, Pa., a prominent physician, was born in Birmingham, now the South Side of Pittsburg, Pa., Oct. 15, 1861, son of Joseph A. and Elizabeth (Jones) Doyle, and is of Irish-Hessian and Welsh descent. His paternal grandfather, Charles Doyle, was a native of eastern Pennsylvania, a carpenter by trade and one of the early settlers of Street's Run, or what is now Hays Borough, Allegheny county, where he was engaged in the manufacturing of barrels and kegs. He was also a millwright, and built water-wheels, mill machinery, cider presses and other articles needed by the pioneers. His father, the great-grandfather of the subject, was for many years a resident of Allegany county, N. Y., and was the first postmaster of Painted Post, N. Y. The maternal grandfather of Dr. Doyle was John Jones, a native of Wales, who settled in Allegheny county in 1819, making the journey on foot from Baltimore. He was a stone-mason by trade, one of the early contractors of Pittsburg, and erected the original stone wall around Lebanon church in Mifflin township, which is one of the old landmarks of that vicinity. Charles Doyle was a soldier in the War of 1812, and had a family of eight children, among whom were: William, Joseph A., Henry; Sallie, who married a Mr. Dobson; Maria, who married Seth Wilmont. Joseph A. Doyle, father of the subject, was born at what is now Hays Borough, Allegheny county, in 1824; was reared in Pittsburg, where he served an apprenticeship at the glass-workers' trade, and for over fifty years was engaged in the manufacture of glass in Pittsburg and vicinity. He has been a resident of Homestead since 1873, and reared a family of five children: Mary, wife of William Stimely; Emma, wife of Charles Bryce; William H., Joseph A., and Elizabeth, wife of William H. Byrnes. Dr. Doyle was reared in Allegheny county, educated at the Thiel college, Greenville, Pa., and for two years was engaged in the glass business at Phillipsburg, now Monaca, Pa. He later learned the glass-blowers' trade with Bryce, Higher & Co., which he completed in 1882, and followed that vocation until 1889, when he began the study of medicine at Bellevue hospital medical college, New York city, where he remained for one year. Then he entered the medical department of the Western Reserve college, Cleveland, Ohio, where he was graduated in 1893, and at once commenced the practice of his profession at Homestead, where he has since met with much success in that vocation. He was married, on April 26, 1888, to Sarah E., daughter of Dr. H. DeLa and Elizabeth Cossitt, of Greenville, Pa., and they have two children, Joseph A. and Sarah E. Dr. Doyle and his wife are members of the United Presbyterian church, and he is a member of the Allegheny county medical society and the Masonic fraternity. His political associations are with the republican party.

JOHN C. KIMBERLIN, assistant water assessor of Allegheny city, Pa., was born in that city in 1859, his parents, Thomas and Mary Kimberlin, being well-known residents of the second ward, where John C. received his primary education. After completing the course in the public school of the second ward, he attended for a time the Beaver college, Beaver, Pa., and then served an apprenticeship at the plumbing trade. From 1889 to 1893 he conducted a plumbing establishment of his own on Washington avenue. In 1893 he was appointed to his present position, under Director of Public Works MacFee, and has been continued in it through all the subsequent administrations, which is certainly good evidence that he is both capable and faithful in discharging his duties. In 1884 he was married to Miss Ida B. Miller, of Allegheny city, and one daughter, Norma B., has come to bless this union. Mr. and Mrs. Kimberlin are members of the Episcopalian church. Mr. Kimberlin is a member of Twin City council, No. 601, of the National Union, and Pride of the West lodge, No. 37, United Workmen. In politics he is a republican, and always takes an active part in the political affairs of both city and county. His political views, however, do not interfere with the impartial exercise of his official powers, all being treated alike.

JAMES A. RUSSELL.

JAMES A. RUSSELL, president of the Braddock First National bank, was born in Scotland, July 8, 1840, son of William and Helen (Lindsay) Russell. William Russell was a blacksmith, a son of Alexander and Jane (Forester) Russell. In 1852 he came to America with his family, locating first in McKeesport, and later in Washington county, where he died. James A. Russell, the subject of this sketch, was apprenticed to a cabinet-maker, and, on Nov. 28, 1861, he opened a business of his own in Elizabeth. Four years later he moved to Braddock, and in April, 1866, started a cabinet and undertaking establishment. The business prospering, he erected, in 1884, the three-story brick building, opposite his present stand at No. 836 Braddock Ave., which he still owns. He also owns a number of other properties in Braddock, North Braddock, Rankin and Homestead, and has extensive interests in mines and other property in Colorado, New Mexico and the State of Washington. In 1897 Mr. Russell erected the handsome and commodious undertaking rooms at No. 836 Braddock Ave., and in January, 1901, turned the business over to his son, Robert. Robert Russell was born in 1876, attended Washington and Jefferson college, and is now studying in the medical department of the Western University of Pennsylvania. James A. Russell married Miss Mary Melissa Wilson, Sept. 2, 1862. Mrs. Russell is a daughter of Abram and Jane (Kennedy) Wilson, both descendants of pioneer families of Butler county. Of the five children born to Mr. and Mrs. Russell, only two are living. They are: Robert, mentioned above, and Helen, a graduate of the State normal school at Indiana, Pa., who lives with her father at No. 310 Holland Ave. Mr. Russell was one of the founders of the First Presbyterian church, of which he is now an elder. He is a member of Braddock Field lodge, No. 510, F. and A. M., and several other fraternal orders. He has been prominent in the municipal life of the borough, serving two terms on the board of education, two terms as justice of the peace, and also as burgess and auditor of the borough. About twelve years ago he was elected director of the First National bank, soon promoted to vice-president, and upon the death of W. H. Watt, Aug. 12, 1901, was elected president of the bank. The First National bank was organized in 1882, has a paid-up capital of $100,000, undivided profits of $75,000, and total assets amounting to $800,000, and is recognized as one of the strongest and most substantial institutions of its kind in America.

HARRY ERNEST JOHNS, the successful editor of the Homestead Press, was born near Honesdale, Wayne Co., Pa., June 13, 1874, son of Benjamin and Eliza (Parkyn) Johns, natives of Pembrokeshire, Wales, and Cornwall, England, respectively. His paternal grandfather, Thomas Johns, was a farmer of Wales, and his maternal grandfather, Joseph Parkyn, was from Cornwall, England, and a prominent farmer of Wayne county, Pa. The father of the subject of this review came to America in 1851, located near Honesdale, Wayne Co., Pa., where he embarked in the lumber business, being a sawyer by trade, and in later life purchased a large farm near Honesdale, which was known as the Parkyn homestead and on which he resided until his death. He reared a family of nine children, viz.: Esther, wife of Edwin Kabelin; Mary, wife of E. L. Gleason; Naomi, wife of George Kabelin; Orange J., Warren, Chiliom B., Harry E.; Elsie, wife of Eugene Kabelin, and Archer R. Harry E. Johns was reared in Wayne county, Pa., educated in the public schools of Honesdale and was for some time engaged in teaching school in his native county. The next four years were devoted to the insurance business at Braddock and Homestead, three years of which time Mr. Johns was superintendent of agencies for the Prudential insurance company, of Newark, N. J. In 1897 he became a reporter on the Homestead News, later established the Homestead Bulletin, a weekly paper which was later merged with the Homestead Press, when he became secretary and one of the directors of the Homestead Press printing company and was selected as editor of the journal, which position he has since ably filled. He is also a director and member of the Kilgore & Atkinson sporting goods company, one of the largest wholesale concerns of that kind in western Pennsylvania. He was married, on Feb. 16, 1895, to Ida E. McGuire, of Homestead, and they have one daughter, Mildred. Mr. Johns is a prominent member of the Baptist church and has been superintendent of its Sunday-school at Homestead, for four years. He is a past commander of the Knights of Malta and a member of the Odd Fellows, in both of which orders he is an active figure. Mr. Johns is a stanch republican in his political faith and adherence and takes a great deal of interest in politics, believing it to be the duty of all good citizens to contribute to the proper government of the community, and for the past five years has served as a member of the school board from the first ward of Homestead, which position he resigned in the spring of 1903 to take his seat in the borough council, to which he was elected for a term of three years.

JAMES K. P. SHOEMAKER, of Homestead, Pa., a prominent real estate dealer and a well-known citizen, was born at Berlin, Somerset Co., Pa., Oct. 4, 1845, son of Levi and Maria (Fair) Shoemaker, natives of Berlin and Allegheny townships, of Somerset county, respectively. His paternal grandfather was John Henry Shoemaker, a native of Berks county, Pa., and among the pioneers of Somerset county, was a tailor by trade and a son of Henry Shoemaker, who was a native of Germany and one of the early settlers of Berks county, Pa., where he reared a family of five sons: Anthony, Abraham, John Henry, Frederick and Peter. John Henry Shoemaker had two sons, Levi and Henry, the eldest of whom is the father of subject and now resides at Berlin, Pa., where he was born in 1812, and has lived his entire life, now being ninety-two years of age. Levi Shoemaker was a tailor in early life, later engaged in farming, but since 1890 has lived quietly, retired from the cares of an active career. He had a family of six children: Lucinda (deceased), James K. P., Mary E., wife of Cyrus Musser; Clara (deceased), Rebecca, and Agnes, wife of John R. Turner. James K. P. Shoemaker was reared and educated in his native village, and in 1862 enlisted in Company F, 142nd Pennsylvania volunteer infantry, as a private and saw distinguished service in the Civil war, participating in the battles of Chancellorsville, Gettysburg, Wilderness, Spottsylvania, North Anna river, Tolopotomy creek, Bethesda church, Cold Harbor, Petersburg, Weldon railroad, Peebles farm, Chapel house, Hatcher's run, raid to Bellfield, Boydton plank road, Five Forks, and was present at Lee's surrender. He was honorably discharged at Washington, D. C., May 29, 1865, and on his return home engaged in farming, later taught school and has also been identified with mercantile pursuits. He spent several years in West Virginia, where he was engaged in farming and stock-raising, and in April, 1888, came to Homestead, where he has since resided. Mr. Shoemaker is extensively engaged in real estate operations and has made an unqualified success of that line of commercial endeavor. He was married, on Dec. 27, 1866, to Mary E., daughter of Daniel and Jane (Keltz) Carns, of Somerset county, Pa., and they have had eight children, viz.: Cora J., wife of H. A. Robson; Daniel W.; Oden H. and Benjamin L., twins; Nida I., wife of Andrew W. Soderberg; Levi C.; Darlie O. V. and Mamie B. V., twins. Mr. Shoemaker is a member of Gen. Charles Griffin post, No. 207, Grand Army of the Republic, and of the Union Veteran legion, Encampment No. 1, of Allegheny county, Pa. His political affiliations are with the democratic party.

CHARLES VON MOSS, alderman of the eighth ward of Allegheny city, Pa., was born Jan. 28, 1860, and educated in the ward he now represents as alderman. His parents were John and Elizabeth Von Moss. The mother is still living, but the father died in 1868. When only fourteen years of age, Charles left school and went to work for the Bindley hardware company, of Pittsburg. He continued in the employ of this firm for eleven years, leaving it in 1885 to become one of the stockholders in the Star Lake ice company of Allegheny city. In the winter of that year he was so seriously injured by an explosion of natural gas that he was unable to engage in any business actively for four years. Then he again embarked in the ice business, but was soon afterwards appointed clerk in the office of the city treasurer of Allegheny for two terms. He was then appointed, and two years later was elected, constable of the eighth ward, serving until 1901, when he was elected alderman for the five-year term expiring in 1906. Mr. Von Moss was married, in 1879, to Miss Susan Stuver, of Allegheny city, and they have had eighteen children. In politics he is a republican. He believes in good government and the enforcement of the laws, and in the exercise of his official powers has always tried to carry that idea into practice. As a result, he is a popular official, and retains the confidence and support of his constituents.

WILLIAM JAMES DORSEY, of Duquesne, Pa., proprietor of the Hotel Dorsey, was born at Newport, County Tipperary, Ireland, Sept. 14, 1843, son of William and Mary (Carmoody) Dorsey, who came to America about 1850, locating in Cambria county, Pa., where for a number of years his father was employed by the Pennsylvania railroad. The elder Dorsey died at Bennington station, and was the father of the following children: Mary (deceased), wife of John Larkin; Annie (deceased); William J., John, (deceased); Minnie (deceased); Michael (deceased), and Nicholas (deceased). William J. Dorsey was reared in Cambria county from his seventh year, and was educated in the public schools and at St. Francis college, Loretto. In 1857 he went to Philadelphia, where he was employed in a bakery up to the Civil war. On Jan. 7, 1862, Mr. Dorsey enlisted in Company E, 91st regiment, Pennsylvania volunteer infantry, and remained with that command until mustered out at City Point, Va., Jan. 7, 1865. This regiment was organized at Philadelphia from Sept. 9 to Dec. 4, 1861, with Edgar M. Gregory as colonel; Edward E. Wallace, lieutenant-colonel; George W. Todd, major, and was part of the Army of the Potomac, in the district of Washington, from January, 1862; 1st brigade, 3d division, 5th army corps, Army of the Potomac, from Sept. 3, 1862; 3d brigade, 2d division, 5th army corps, Army of the Potomac, from May, 1863; 2d brigade, 2d division, 5th army corps, Army of the Potomac, from January, 1864; 1st brigade, 1st division, 5th army corps, Army of the Potomac, from April, 1864; 1st brigade, 2d division, 5th army corps, from June 6, 1864; 2d brigade, 1st division, 5th army corps, Army of the Potomac, from June 14, 1864; 3d brigade, 1st division, 5th army corps, Army of the Potomac, up to the close of the war. Mr. Dorsey participated in the many battles and engagements in which his regiment took part, to give an account of which would be necessary to write the history of the Army of the Potomac, and during his entire military career bore himself well. At the close of the war he returned to Pittsburg, where he clerked in a store for two years, and then for the next two years was engaged in the liquor business at Shaner station. In 1869 he located in Mifflin township and engaged in the hotel business at Coal Valley until 1873, when he began general merchandising at Rock Run and prospered at that venture until 1884. Then he again went in the hotel business at Coal Valley, and there remained until 1889, when he removed to Duquesne, there engaged in various businesses until 1898, when he began his present hotel business in that city. He was first married, on March 3, 1870, to Mary E., daughter of James and Rosanna (Fowler) Hamilton, of Pittsburg, and they have three living children, viz.: John H., Rosanna and Lizzie. Mrs. Dorsey died in 1884, and he was again married, in 1891, to Julia Brossman, of Pittsburg, by whom he has had five children, viz.: Annie, Minnie, Charlie, Julia and Essie. Mr. Dorsey is a prominent member of Samuel Black post, No. 59, Grand Army of the Republic; is a Knight Templar Mason, and is independent in his political affiliations.

ELIJAH PENELTON FAIDLEY, of Duquesne, Pa., a prominent real estate dealer and insurance agent, was born in Somerset county, Pa., Aug. 1, 1841, son of Peter and Elizabeth (Meyers) Faidley, both natives of Somerset county, Pa. His paternal grandfather, John Faidley, was a farmer by occupation and a soldier in the War of 1812, married Barbara Kriter, and was a solid and upright citizen. His maternal grandfather, John Meyers, a native of Germany and a weaver by trade, spent the last thirty years of his life in Somerset county, Pa., where he died when about sixty-nine years of age. Peter Faidley, father of the subject, was born in 1812, and was by occupation a contractor and builder. He died in 1873, was married three times, and the father of twenty-four children, seventeen of whom grew to maturity. Elijah P. Faidley was reared near Meyersdale, Somerset Co., Pa.; educated in the common schools, and, on April 18, 1861, enlisted as a private in Company A, 10th reserve volunteer corps, for duty in the Civil war, and served three years and three months in that sanguinary conflict, being wounded on three different occasions and taking part in many of the noted battles of the war. He was mustered out at Pittsburg, June 11, 1864, and for the next twenty-two years was employed in the mills of Pittsburg and vicinity. In 1893 Mr. Faidley embarked in the real estate business at Duquesne, and has since met with much success in that vocation, now being the leader in that line of business in the borough and enjoying a splendid clientage. He was happily married, in 1865, to Mary, daughter of William and Anna (Waring) Mercer, of Loudoun county, Va., and they have two living children: John W. and Gertrude, wife of William L. Granger. Mrs. Faidley died in 1891, and he was again married, in 1893, this time to Mrs. Grace (Forsyth) Ferguson, daughter of Adam Forsyth, of McKeesport, Pa., and they have one child, Edna May. He is a member of the Methodist Episcopal church, the Grand Army of the Republic and the republican party, and has served on the school board and in the council of Duquesne.

HARRY PRUNO HUGO QUECK, of Homestead, Pa., the popular proprietor of the Hotel Queck, on Eighth avenue, was born in Zwickau, Saxony, Germany, Sept. 26, 1863, son of Anton Ludwig and Caroline (Kahlart) Queck, natives of Germany and Austria, respectively. His parents came to America in 1865, located at Saltsburg, Allegheny county, where his father worked as a pit carpenter for two years, and then removed to Penny's, on the Youghiogheny river, where he was employed in the mines of that vicinity until the early seventies. Then he went to Turtle Creek and there followed mining until 1881, when he removed to Homestead and embarked in the wholesale liquor business. In 1881 he commenced the hotel business at Homestead and continued in that line with much success until his death in 1895, at the age of sixty-six years. He had four children that grew to maturity, viz.: Harry P. H.; Anna M., widow of Paul Barthol; Albert H., and Oscar A. Harry P. H. Queck was reared in Allegheny county and educated in the public schools and at Duff's business college, Pittsburg, and since 1881 has been a resident of Homestead, where he was employed in the steel mills until 1892, when he entered the hotel business under his father. On the death of the latter, in 1895, Mr. Queck succeeded to the business, which he has since conducted with much success. In 1902 he erected his present fine hotel, which is a splendid brick structure of three stories and equipped with all modern improvements. He was married, on

Aug. 25, 1889, to Emma Amelia, daughter of Henry and Sophie (Ackerman) Meyer, of Mount Washington, Allegheny Co., Pa., but formerly of Germany, and they have had four children, viz.: Edna C., Myrtle E., Florence M. and Hazel P. Mr. Queck and wife are members of St. Mark's Evangelical Protestant church, and he is prominently identified with the Odd Fellows, the German Turner Singverein and the D. O. H.

GEORGE HENRY METCALFE, whose business is that of sanitary plumber and gas-fitter, is one of the promising young business men of Homestead, Pa. He is a son of Matthew S. and Catherine E. (Siemon) Metcalfe, the father having been born in Yorkshire, England, and the mother near Berlin, Germany. John Metcalfe, the paternal grandfather of George, came to this country in 1841, locating in the anthracite coal regions, where for several years he followed the occupation of a coal-miner. He then came to Pittsburg and settled in the little village of Minersville, which is now a part of the city, where he spent the remainder of his life. His wife was a Margaret Schlender. The maternal grandfather, Henry Siemon, came to America in 1848 and located in Pittsburg, where for many years he followed his trade of blacksmith. Matthew S. Metcalfe, George's father, has been a resident of Pittsburg ever since 1853. At the age of twelve years he began work in the coal mines and followed the vocation of a miner until 1881. At that time he formed a partnership with two others, under the firm name of Berry, Metcalfe & Watson, as coal operators. The firm did a successful business for several years, when Mr. Metcalfe withdrew and engaged in the business of merchandising. He is now retired. George H. Metcalfe is one of a family of six children, his brothers and sisters being Ida M. and Matthew (deceased); Anna, now wife of Thomas Pritchard; Eva and Henrietta. He was born in Pittsburg, Sept. 16, 1876, and was educated in the public schools of his native city. He began life as a bookkeeper for the firm of F. C. Kohne & Co., in 1892, and continued to discharge the duties of bookkeeper and estimator for that firm until 1899. That year he went to Neu & Harmeier as bookkeeper and superintendent. At the expiration of eighteen months, he purchased Mr. Harmeier's interest and the business was continued as E. W. Neu & Co. to March, 1903, when Mr. Metcalfe sold out and embarked in business for himself. On Aug. 21, 1900, he was married to Fannie E., daughter of Robert Painter, of Elizabeth, Pa. Mr. Metcalfe is a member of the Royal Arcanum and Order of Americus societies and the Presbyterian church. Politically, he is a republican, and although interested in public questions, he devotes the greater part of his time to his business, in which he has been quite successful.

WILLIAM GEORGE FORRESTER, of Whitaker, Pa., a prosperous mill worker in the employ of the Homestead steel works, was born in West Elizabeth, Allegheny Co., Pa., Jan. 19, 1873, son of James and Mary E. (Penn) Forrester, natives of Illinois and Pennsylvania, respectively. His maternal grandfather, Lemuel Penn, resided in Allegheny county for many years, was a coal-miner by occupation, served in the Civil war, and died at West Elizabeth in 1896, at the age of eighty-five years. James Forrester, father of the subject, has been a resident of West Elizabeth for upwards of thirty years, and for the past seventeen years has been an employe of John A. Snee, a prominent gas and oil operator. James Forrester is the father of the following children that grew to maturity, viz.: James L.; Hettie J. (deceased), wife of Charles C. Dunlap; William G.; Jeannette, wife of Henry Wilson; Gilberta, wife of Hengist Briggs; Margaret, wife of William Spence; Alice J., wife of Harry Longdusky; Mary, and Robert. William G. Forrester was reared in West Elizabeth, and there educated in the public schools. He began his business career as a coal-miner, following that occupation at different times in the vicinity of West Elizabeth until 1898; resided at Homestead until 1901, then removed to his present home at Whitaker, where he has erected a comfortable dwelling. He was married, on Aug. 10, 1892, to Lucy, daughter of John and Jane (Gration) Wilson, of Mifflin township, and they have three living children, viz.: Mary Jennie, Iva B. and James E. Mr. Forrester is a member of Gray Eagle tribe of the Improved Order of Red Men, and in his political associations and convictions is a republican.

LOUIS F. HOLTZMAN.

LOUIS F. HOLTZMAN, one of the most prominent and progressive business men of Braddock, was born in that borough, Oct. 4, 1856. His parents were Louis and Teresa Holtzman, natives of Alsace, who came to America in the early fifties. Mr. Holtzman received his education in the public schools, worked seven years as a coal-miner, and three years in the rail department of the Edgar Thompson mill. In March, 1886, Gov. Robert E. Pattison appointed him justice of the peace, and since then Mr. Holtzman has been four times elected for five-year terms in this office, the last time without opposition, although he belongs to the minority party in Braddock. For twenty years he has been a prominent member of the Braddock council, and has been for several years past, president of that body. During this time he has upheld many measures for municipal improvements, and has been the recognized champion of good government. Mr. Holtzman has held many positions of trust, the most important of which is that of personal representative of Mr. Charles M. Schwab in the erection of the new St. Thomas' Roman Catholic church, which Mr. and Mrs. Schwab have given the city. He is trustee of the $100,000 fund which has been donated for that purpose, and has exclusive authority to select the architect, decide upon the plans, and let the contracts. Mr. Holtzman owns, at No. 918 Braddock Ave., one of the best-appointed fire insurance offices in Braddock, controlling the agency for ten strong companies, and is doing a thriving real estate business, which requires the services of several assistants. On Aug 26, 1880, he was married to Mary, daughter of Patrick and Rose (McKeown) McMonigle, early settlers of Port Perry. The children of Mr. and Mrs. Holtzman are: Alice and Rose, who are students at the Seton Hall academy, of Greensburg, and Robert, who is attending the Braddock public schools. Mr. Holtzman and family are members of the Roman Catholic church.

DAVID SHANAHAN, of Duquesne, Pa., pastor of the Holy Name Catholic church, was born in County Waterford, Ireland, Sept. 15, 1866, son of David and Margaret (Phelan) Shanahan, both natives of Ireland. Father Shanahan was reared to manhood in his native country, educated at St. John's college, of Waterford, and at St. Patrick's college, County Carlow, where he was ordained to the priesthood in 1891. The same year he came to America, was appointed assistant priest to St. Peter's church, of Allegheny city, and eighteen months later was transferred to St. John's church, at Altoona, as assistant pastor, and there remained for two years. Then he was assigned to St. John's church, at Coylesville, Pa., as pastor, and for two years and nine months was in charge of that pastorate, where he was largely instrumental in remodeling the church building at a cost of $10,000. In November, 1897, Father Shanahan was sent to Duquesne as pastor of the Church of the Holy Name, which at that time was quite small, with a membership of only about 120 families and an inadequate church building. Father Shanahan has caused to be erected, at the cost of $60,000, a handsome structure of buff vitrified brick, richly trimmed with Cleveland sandstone, with a seating capacity of 900, and in every way adapted for the sacred purposes for which it is used. The church, which is of Gothic style of architecture, is 135 feet long, and 56 feet wide (66 at the transepts), and has two towers, one 165 feet and the other 92 feet high. The corner-stone of the church was laid July 30, 1899, by the Right Reverend Bishop Phelan, and the church dedicated by that dignitary in 1901. Father Shanahan also had a fine brick dwelling-house erected at a cost of $8,000, which was begun at the same time as the church edifice, but completed in 1899. He is an able and earnest worker in the field of religious endeavor, and under his charge the church has had a splendid growth, now having a membership of more than 200 families, and is in every way blessed with success and prosperity.

FRANK J. McPARTLAND, proprietor of the Junction hotel, on the River road, near Braddock bridge, was born in Connellsville, Pa., July 23, 1874. He is a son of Charles and Mary (Collins) McPartland, both of whom are natives of Ireland, but came to this country in 1867. They settled at Connellsville, where the father worked in the mines until 1893, when he retired and removed to Mifflin township, where he still resides. They had eleven children, seven of whom grew to maturity, as follows: Anna, wife of William Collins; Margaret, wife of James H. White; Mary, wife of J. G. Guffey; Frank J.; John, who died in the Philippine islands while in the service of the United States during the Spanish-American war, Thomas and Charles. Frank J. McPartland was reared in Connellsville, where he attended the parochial schools, securing a good, practical education. He began life on his own account as a miner, but worked at that occupation only a short time, changing it for the more congenial one of bookkeeper in a grocery store at Homestead, where he remained for seven years. In 1901 he entered into his present business, which he has ever since successfully conducted, his hotel being one of the most popular places of entertainment in Allegheny county. Mr. McPartland is a member of St. Mary Magdalene's Catholic church, of Homestead. He takes a great interest and an active part in political matters, being one of the most energetic republicans in Mifflin township. He is frequently called upon to serve as judge of the election, is now a member of the county central committee, and has repeatedly represented his district in political conventions.

JESSE S. LANTZ, who for nearly twenty years has been a steel melter in the Homestead steel works, was born in Wheeling, W. Va., Aug. 29, 1865, and is the son of Jesse and Mary (Heppert) Lantz. When he was about one year old, his parents came to Allegheny county, Pa., where he has lived ever since. Up to the age of fourteen years he attended the common schools, and then went to work in the coal mines, following this occupation for about five years, when he entered the Homestead steel works and learned the trade at which he is now employed. On Sept. 29, 1885, he was married to Miss Bertha, the daughter of Louis and Elizabeth (Ries) Dierstein, of Mifflin township, and they have four children living: Bertha, Elmer, Earl and Mabel. In 1889 Mr. Lantz became a resident of Whitaker, where he has ever since resided and where he owns valuable property which he has accumulated by his industry and frugal habits. He is a member of Whitaker tent, No. 425, Knights of the Maccabees, and in politics is independent. Young men can learn a useful lesson from the life of Jesse S. Lantz. Born of humble parentage and forced by circumstances to begin life for himself at an early age, he has overcome all obstacles, until now, while still less than forty years of age, he is in a measure independent. While others have complained of ill luck or hard times, he has boldly faced the situation and successfully solved the problem of human life. Among his neighbors, he is honored and respected, because he has demonstrated by his example the value of industry and self-reliance. By a faithful discharge of his duties, he has won the regard of his employers, as is shown by his long service in the employ of one of the greatest concerns of its kind in the country.

CHARLES FREDERICK GOLDSTROHM, of Duquesne, Pa., a prominent and progressive citizen, was born within what is now the limits of that borough, Nov. 14, 1854, son of Konrad and Rosina (Pfaff) Goldstrohm, natives of Hesse Darmstadt, Germany, who came to America in 1849, married in New York city, and settled in Mifflin township, Allegheny Co., Pa., in 1852. There the elder Goldstrohm followed the occupation of a farmer for three years, and then embarked in the butchers' business at Deutschtown, where he continued with much success until 1891, when he retired from business and removed to a farm, where he died in 1894, at the age of sixty-eight years. He was a son of Youst and Barbara Goldstrohm, the latter dying in 1859, and one year later the former came to America, located at Elizabeth, Pa., where he resided until his death, in 1881, at the age of eighty-six years. The maternal grandfather of our subject was John Pfaff, who came to America in 1872, and died in New York city three months after his arrival. Konrad Goldstrohm reared a family of ten children, viz.: August, Charles F., Konrad, Frederick; Louisa, wife of William McKelravey; Heinrich, William S.; Rosina, wife of Washington Daff; Emma and Katherina, deceased. Charles F. Goldstrohm was reared in Mifflin township, educated in the common schools, and began his business career as a farmer, driving a milk wagon and later driving a meat wagon for his father. In 1874 he embarked in the meat business on his own account, in which he continued until 1892; then for four years was in the real estate and loan business; from 1896 to 1898 operated a coal works in Jefferson township, formerly owned by Thomas Foster, his father-in-law, and has since devoted his attention to the real estate and loan business at Duquesne, in which he has met with unusual success. He was happily married, on Aug. 31, 1877, to Christiana B., daughter of Thomas and Ellen (Bayne) Foster, of

Coal Valley, and they have nine living children, viz.: Pressley R., Thomas F., Nellie, Charles F., Jr., Grover C., Vila G., Zila G., Christiana B. and Karl J. A. Mr. Goldstrohm was reared in the Lutheran church, but his family are members of the United Presbyterian church. Mr. Goldstrohm is a prominent democrat, served as postmaster of Dravosburg under Cleveland's first administration, had the Duquesne postoffice established, and for four years he was president of the board of health of that borough, and is treasurer of the National beneficial association of Pennsylvania. He is closely connected with the advancement and progress of that part of the county, and is a man upon whom the community relies to take a leading part in any movement for the good of the borough that promises to be of a solid and substantial character.

JOSEPH KENNEDY, of Duquesne, Pa., a retired gardener and one of the oldest and most prominent citizens of that borough, was born in Indiana county, Pa., Oct. 9, 1831, son of David and Catherine (Snyder) Kennedy. When twelve years of age, Mr. Kennedy came to Allegheny county, and for several years was employed in the mills in various capacities, and later began mining coal for W. H. Brown & Co., miners, with whom he remained for seventeen years. About 1866 he located in Mifflin township, there engaged in farming on an extensive scale, and about 1873 purchased a farm of seventy acres, on which is now located the borough of Duquesne. Mr. Kennedy sold his farm for manufacturing sites, and nearly thirty acres of the original place is now occupied by the Carnegie steel works. He has been prominently identified with the growth and progress of the borough, having erected nineteen houses, and otherwise been instrumental in its advancement and prosperity. Mr. Kennedy was married, on Oct. 14, 1852, to Priscilla, daughter of Joseph and Jane (McFarland) Burchfield, of Pittsburg, and they have had the following children, viz.: Joseph B.; David; Anna, wife of Howard L. Black; Katie (deceased), wife of Samuel Kelly; William; Charles; Lillian, wife of James O. Reneker; John; Fannie (deceased), Frank (deceased) and Auriles. Mr. Kennedy and his wife are consistent members of the First Methodist Episcopal church of Duquesne, and were among the founders of that organization, which now has a large membership and of which Mr. Kennedy was an officer for many years. His political affiliations are with the republican party, and for three years he was a member of the school board of Mifflin township. Mr. Kennedy is one of the substantial citizens of that part of the county, and commands the respect and esteem of all who know him.

EMIL W. NEU, of Homestead, Pa., senior member of the firm of Neu & Weber, sanitary plumbers, was born at Winona, Minn., Aug. 15, 1866, son of Christian Neu, who was born on July 4, 1843, at Kreishunfeldt, Kuhrhessen, Germany. He emigrated to America, landing in New York on July 4, 1857, and immediately proceeded to Pittsburg, where he learned the bakers' trade. Christian Neu served three years and three months in the Union army during the Civil war, being a member of Company G, 74th Pennsylvania volunteer infantry, and was so severely wounded while doing scout duty at Freeman's Ford, that he was left on the field for dead. Subsequently he partially revived, was sent to the hospital and completely cured of his wounds, and at the end of his service received an honorable discharge. He returned to Pittsburg, resumed his trade, and, in 1865, married Maria Bieber, a native of the same place in Germany as was her husband, but who came to America on Sept. 9, 1863, and located in Pittsburg. Christian Neu was in business for himself on the South Side, Pittsburg, for eight months and then moved to Winona, Minn., where he conducted a baking establishment for fifteen years. In 1881 he returned to Pittsburg, re-established himself in the baking business on the South Side, and there prospered until his death, April 2, 1891. His family consisted of eight children, viz.: Emil W., Adolph G.; Fredericka, wife of Louis Will; Louisa, wife of Charles Kessler; Alexander, William, Alfred and Harry. Emil W. Neu was reared in Winona and Pittsburg, attended the public schools of both cities, and received his commercial training at Duff's business college, Pittsburg. In 1884 he began his business career as clerk and bookkeeper in a Pittsburg plumbing shop, acted in that capacity for five years, and then served an apprenticeship at the plumbing trade, which he completed in three years. In April, 1892, Mr. Neu came to Homestead, where he managed the plumbing establishment of Louis Heilig for two years, and then, with Henry W. Harmeier, purchased the business of Mr. Heilig, which they conducted under the firm name of Neu & Harmeier. They prospered in that venture, and the firm was continued until Jan. 1, 1902, when Mr. Harmeier disposed of his interests to George H. Metcalfe and Joseph A. Weber, and the business was run under the name of E. W. Neu & Co. until March 16, 1903, when the style of the firm became Neu & Weber. Mr. Neu was happily married, Nov. 25, 1891, to Annie, daughter of Bernard Krebs, of Pittsburg, and they have one living daughter, Irene. Mr. Neu is prominently identified with the Royal Arcanum, the Order of Americus, the Independent fire company, No. 1, and the Turn and Gesang-Verein Eintracht. Mr. Neu is a prosperous and progressive business man, a good citizen, and a provident husband and father.

MICHAEL FRANCIS MUELLER, of Duquesne, Pa., pastor of St. Agnes' Roman Catholic church at Thompson's Run, Mifflin township, Allegheny Co., Pa., was born at Luxemburg, Germany, June 27, 1864, son of John and Anna (Steinmetz) Mueller, who came to America in 1870, locating at Kirby, Wyandot Co., Ohio, where Father Mueller was reared to manhood. He attended the parochial schools of that section, then the college conducted by the Jesuits at Detroit, Mich., where he completed his classical and philosophical training. He received his theological education at St. Vincent's, near Latrobe, Pa., and was ordained to the priesthood in 1893, in St. Paul's cathedral, by Bishop Phelan. His first charge was as assistant to Rev. J. B. Duffner, at the Holy Name church, Troy Hill, Allegheny city; then was assistant to Rev. Joseph Suhr, at SS. Peter and Paul's church of Pittsburg, where he was for one and a half years; next was sent as pastor, *pro tempore*, to St. Joseph's church at Verona, where he remained for fifteen months. The next two years were spent in charge of St. Alphonsus' church at Wexford, Allegheny county, and, in 1900, Father Mueller was assigned to his present charge. St. Agnes'

church was organized about 1867, with a membership of forty families, and now has about 120 families, although the membership was much larger prior to the erection of churches at Duquesne and Homestead, both of which have drawn from St. Agnes' membership. The present church edifice was erected in 1866 at a cost of $12,000, and has a seating capacity of 400. The parochial school is in fine condition, with an attendance of 120 pupils, and in every way is a high class institution. There is also a splendid parochial residence and a home for the sisters. Father Mueller organized the Ladies' Christian mutual benevolent association in 1902, which has forty-eight members, and gives promise of much usefulness in the future.

FREDERICK WILLIAM PIRL, of Duquesne, Pa., senior member of the firm of Pirl & Kroeger, general blacksmiths, and burgess of that borough, was born in Mifflin township, Allegheny county, June 22, 1867, son of Frederick and Catherine (Goldstrom) Pirl, natives of Germany, where they were married, and about 1850 came to the United States and settled in Mifflin township. There the elder Pirl worked as a coal-miner for several years, later purchased a farm and resided on the same until his death, Feb. 15, 1891, at the age of sixty-nine years. He reared a family of seven children, viz.: Margaret, wife of Henry Habermann; Mary, wife of Charles Fletcher; Rosie, wife of Fred J. Koler; Catherine, wife of Henry Doney; William; Louisa, wife of William Auberle, and Frederick W. The last five children were born in the same house, which now stands in the second ward of Duquesne. Frederick W. Pirl was reared on the old farm homestead, which he now owns, and attended the Germantown public school, and also spent three years in the public schools of Pittsburg. In 1885 he began his apprenticeship at the blacksmiths' trade in McKeesport, and served three years, after which he worked as a journeyman until 1890, when he went to the oil fields of Venango county, Pa., where he remained for two years. In 1892 he located in Duquesne and embarked in the blacksmith business as a member of the firm of Pirl & Evans, which partnership continued for one year, when he purchased Mr. Evans' interests and conducted the business under his own name. He prospered in that venture, and, in 1899, sold an interest in his concern to William Kroeger, and they have since met with much success under the firm name of Pirl & Kroeger. Mr. Pirl was married, Sept. 25, 1893, to Jean, daughter of William and Jean (Frazer) Minford, of Wood Run, Washington Co., Pa., and they have five children, viz.: Catherine, Carl, Louisa, Jean and Thomas. Mr. and Mrs. Pirl are members of the Presbyterian church, and he is a member of the Elks, Odd Fellows and Masons. He is also a director of the First National bank of Duquesne, served ten years in the council, and is now burgess of the borough.

JOSEPH SUBASIC, of Allegheny city, Pa., director of the American baking company, of Millvale, was born in Croatia, Austria, May 11, 1854, son of Marquis and Mary (Dokman) Subasic. He was educated in the public schools of his native land, and when fourteen years of age went to Germany and there was in business for fifteen years. He came to the United States in 1885, and was employed in Bennett's rolling mill for six years; then was stationary engineer for Banerlein brewing company for six years, and, in 1900, became a director of the American baking company, of Millvale. Mr. Subasic has served as treasurer, for the last four years, of the National Croasian society, which has 16,000 members, and during 1902 above $150,000 passed through his hands. He is also president of St. Nickolas Croasian church of Allegheny city, and of the St. Cirilus and Matod societies of that city. He was married, in 1879, to Mary Bestig, of Austria, and they have had twelve children, of whom the following are living, viz.: Barbara, wife of Joseph Liebig; Mary; Joseph, a student of St. Mary's parochial school; John, attending the same institution; Emma, student at the eighth ward school; William and Anna, at home. He is a member of St. Nickolas Catholic church of Allegheny city, the Croasian German Military Shrine, the National Union, and of the republican party. Mr. Subasic is regarded as a successful business man and is a citizen of high standing, as evidenced by the numerous positions of honor and trust which he has held.

HENRY H. BUENTE was born at No. 847 Main St., in the fourth ward, Allegheny city, March 1, 1848. He is a son of John H. and Rosina C. (Speilmyer) Buente, daughter of John H. Speilmyer. John H. Buente was born in Osenbruck, Hanover, Germany, Jan. 31, 1822; came to the United States in July, 1840, and learned the trade of plasterer, which occupation he followed for the remainder of his life. Rosina C. (Speilmyer) Buente was born in Fenna, Hanover, Germany, Jan. 8, 1827, and came to America at a very early age with her parents, who settled in Pittsburg on Dec. 20, 1836. John H. Buente and Rosina C. Speilmyer were married, July 3, 1845, in Pittsburg, and moved to the fourth ward, Allegheny city, the same year. To them were born six children: William H., who died in infancy; Henry H., Edward A.; Rosina H., now Mrs. George Riddle; John F. and William A., all of Allegheny. John H. Buente enlisted in Company F, 61st regiment, Pennsylvania volunteer infantry, Aug. 1, 1861, and was killed in the battle of Malvern Hill, July 1, 1862. Henry H. Buente's paternal grandfather was a native of Hanover, Germany, and was a farmer by occupation. His maternal grandfather came to America in 1836, was a carpenter by occupation, and died of yellow fever while on a steamboat trip down the Mississippi, and was buried upon its shores, in 1837. Henry H. Buente, the subject of this sketch, was educated in the fourth ward public school of Allegheny, where he graduated. He afterwards attended night school, but was obliged to discontinue at the age of thirteen, when his father went to the war. He went to work in the tobacco factory of W. & D. Rinehart, on Wood street, Pittsburg, where he remained one and one-half years. From there he found employment in the Samuel Reynolds malleable iron works, Allegheny city, and remained in that position for the same length of time. He was next employed in Shoenberg's horseshoe mill, Pittsburg, operating a steam-hammer for nearly four years. Mr. Buente then decided to enter business for himself, and, accordingly, took up the wholesale and retail tobacco business in Allegheny city, where, two years later, he became interested in real estate. This occupation he followed for seven years. In company with his brother, Edward A. Buente, he engaged in the retail grocery business in

1877 under the firm name of Buente & Bro., in Allegheny city, in which he was very successful. He retired, however, in 1888 on account of impaired health. In 1889 Mr. Buente was first elected to the Allegheny city common council from the second ward for a term of two years, and was re-elected in 1891 and 1893, retiring from politics in 1895. He was appointed superintendent of the Carnegie library buildings on Oct. 1, 1895, which position he continues to hold. As such he has charge of the entire building, with a staff of ten assistants. Mr. Buente was married to Wilhelmina G. Myers, daughter of Henry Myers, of North Huntingdon township, Westmoreland county, on Oct. 1, 1874. To them have been born two children: Ida H., born Jan. 20, 1877, married to Charles E. McKenry, and lives in the East End, Pittsburg; and Frank H., born May 5, 1881, educated at Williams' business college, and is now bookkeeper for R. J. Steenson & Co., of Allegheny city. Mr. Buente is a republican in politics, and has held many honorable positions in the councils of his party. In religious belief Mr. Buente and his family are Lutherans, and are members of the Bethel church of that denomination. Mr. Buente is also a member of the Jr. O. U. A. M., Wm. Thaw council, No. 396; Improved Order of Heptasophs, Beaver avenue conclave, No. 83, and of Citizens' auxiliary, Post No. 88, G. A. R. Mr. Buente is a very affable gentleman, and highly esteemed by all who know him.

NICK ACKERMAN, of Whitaker, Pa., a successful contractor and builder, was born in Mifflin township, Allegheny county, March 11, 1863, son of Adam and Annie (Cramer) Ackerman, both natives of Germany. His paternal grandfather, John N. Ackerman, came to America about 1850; settled in Mifflin township, where he engaged in farming and reared a large family. His maternal grandfather was John Cramer, also a native of Germany and an early settler in Allegheny county, where he died at an advanced age. The father of Nick Ackerman was a farmer and is now quietly living at Whitaker. He is the father of thirteen children, eight of whom grew to maturity, viz.: Mary, wife of John Rushey; Minnie (deceased), wife of Jacob Bosh; Frank J.; Nick; George; Teresa, wife of Nicholas Weasion; Kate (deceased), wife of

John Plank; Annie (deceased), wife of George Steiner. Nick Ackerman was reared in Mifflin township, educated in the graded and high schools of Pittsburg, served his apprenticeship at the carpenters' trade with John Bosh, and for the past sixteen years has been successfully engaged in building and contracting. He was married, on Jan. 1, 1887, to Mary, daughter of August and Aurelia (Scheren) Schindler, of Mifflin township, and they have five children, viz.: Harry, Amelia, Elmer, Sylvester and Cecelia. Mr. Ackerman is a member of St. Joseph's Catholic church of Homestead and of the Maccabees, and his political affiliations are with the democratic party.

WILLIAM JOSEPH FILCER, of Duquesne, Pa., senior member of Filcer & Blair, editors and proprietors of the Observer, was born in West Newton, Pa., Feb. 8, 1871, son of George P. and Anna (Strebig) Filcer, natives of Center and Fayette counties, respectively, and of German descent. His paternal grandfather, Peter Filcer, was a native of Germany, and his maternal grandfather, William Strebig, was born in eastern Pennsylvania, a miller by trade, and for over sixty years a resident of West Newton, Pa. William Strebig married Mary Vance, of Brownsville, Pa., a member of a prominent Keystone family and a woman of many fine traits of character. George P. Filcer, father of William J., was a boiler-maker by trade, and spent the major portion of his life at Connellsville, Pa., where he was married. He was a soldier in the Civil war, served throughout that sanguinary conflict as a private, and subsequently was for many years foreman in the Baltimore & Ohio railroad shops at Connellsville, where he died in 1886. His children were: William J., George E., Margaret M., wife of William Reese, and John M. William J. Filcer was reared in Connellsville, educated in the public schools of that borough, and there learned the printers' trade in the Courier office. Subsequently he worked for six years as a journeyman in Connellsville and McKeesport, and, in 1894, located at Duquesne, where he purchased an interest in the Observer, and has since been connected with that journal as one of the editors and proprietors. Mr. Filcer was happily married, June 29, 1893, to

Myrtle, daughter of Harmon and Missouri (Ringler) Hay, of New Haven, Pa., and they have one daughter, Myrtle Margaret. He is a member of the Holy Name Catholic church, and his political affiliations are with the democratic party.

JONAS MECHLING KISTLER, of Homestead, Pa., assistant superintendent of the Prudential insurance company of America, was born in Franklin township, Westmoreland Co., Pa., Aug. 29, 1858; son of Samuel and Eva S. (Loughner) Kistler, both natives of Westmoreland county, Pa., his father having been born in Franklin township and his mother at Greensburg. His father lived for nearly seventy years on one farm in Franklin township, where he died in 1883, at the mature age of eighty-five years. Samuel Kistler was twice married, first to Miss Fink, who bore him eighteen children, thirteen of whom grew to maturity, viz.: Mary A., wife of Jacob Mann; Jacob, Josiah, Michael F.; Catherine (deceased), wife of Josiah Wagaman; Henry J., Paul F.; Aggie M., wife of Levi Glunt; Annie, wife of John Carroll; Lizzie, wife of Henry Oburn; Sarah (deceased), wife of Calvin McCormick; Lydia, wife of Peter Frissell, and John (deceased). His second marriage was with Eva S. Klingensmith, widow of Lewis Klingensmith and daughter of John Loughner, who, by her former marriage, had two children, Cyrus and Lewis, and who bore Mr. Kistler five children, viz.: Jonas M.; Phœbe R., wife of James P. Heckman; Fannie R., wife of J. S. Stotler; Emma S., wife of Jesse B. Klingensmith, and Eli L. Jonas M. Kistler was reared on the home farm in Westmoreland county, there educated in the common schools, and when seventeen years old left home for Iowa and Nebraska, in which states he worked as a farm hand for two years. In the fall of 1879, Mr. Kistler returned to Pennsylvania and in the following spring became a locomotive fireman on the Pennsylvania railroad, being promoted to an engineer in the fall of 1885, and for ten years continued with that company as engineman. In 1895 Mr. Kistler engaged in the butcher and dairy business at Derry Station, near Latrobe, Pa., where he remained for eighteen months; then for two years was manager of a grocery business at Irwin, Pa.; in March, 1899, located at Homestead, where he conducted a variety store for nine months, then entered the employ of the Prudential insurance company as a solicitor and six months later was appointed to his present position of assistant superintendent, with headquarters at Homestead, and since has ably discharged the complex duties of that important office. Mr. Kistler was married, on Sept. 19, 1883, to Flora E., daughter of John C. and Matilda J. (McGuire) Spear, of Derry Station, Pa., and they have three children, viz.: Robert L., Harry A. and Mildred M. Mr. Kistler and his wife are members of the Methodist Episcopal church and he is a member of Hiram lodge, No. 69, Ancient Order of United Workmen, of Irwin Station; Shidle lodge, No. 601, Ancient Free and Accepted Masons, and of the republican party.

WILLIAM MacBROOM, a retired business man of Homestead, is a native of Ayrshire, Scotland, where he was born Dec. 29, 1840. He is a son of Archibald and Ellen (Robertson) MacBroom. He was educated in the common schools of Ayrshire, and then served an apprenticeship of four years at the boiler-makers' trade in the city of Glasgow. On New Year's day, in 1864, he was married to Margaret, daughter of John and Mary (Barr) Chalmers, of Glasgow, and in the following spring came with his young wife to America, locating at Pittsburg. For three years he worked as a miner at Saw Mill Run. He then went to Mansfield (now Carnegie), and worked several years in the mines there. His father died in Scotland, and in 1866 his mother came to America and joined her son at Carnegie, where she lived until her death, which occurred in 1879. In 1873 William MacBroom was elected constable of Mansfield and held the office until April, 1882, when he removed to Homestead, where he found employment at his trade in the Carnegie mill until 1884, when he was elected constable and chief of police, holding both offices until 1888. He resigned at that time to become the chief of the coal and iron police of the Carnegie steel company, and held that position until he resigned, in 1892. Mr. MacBroom then entered the hotel business as the proprietor of the Garfield house, where he continued until 1899, when he sold out to his son with the intention of retiring from active business. The following year he erected the

Liberty hotel, at the corner of Eighth avenue and McClure street, which has since been conducted by his son, Gilbert, and which is one of the leading hotels of Homestead. He still owns this hotel building, as well as valuable residence property on Fourth avenue. William MacBroom and his wife are the parents of eight children, viz.: John; Mary B., wife of Andrew Helles; Margaret, wife of Daniel W. Williams; Ellen, wife of Harry H. Layman; William, Gilbert, Walter (now deceased), and Jane G., wife of August Meister. Both Mr. MacBroom and his wife are members of the United Presbyterian church. He has been a member of the Independent Order of Odd Fellows for thirty-nine years, and a member of the Knights of Pythias for twenty years. He is also a member of the B. P. O. Elks, which order he joined in 1902, and of the Heptasophs. In politics he affiliates with the republican party, and, like all canny Scots, is never backward in standing up for his convictions.

SAMUEL McELHINEY, a citizen of Mifflin township, was born on a farm in Jefferson township, on June 4, 1868. He is a son of David and Zeruiah (McGowan) McElhiney, both natives of Allegheny county. The McElhiney and the McGowan families are old residents of Pennsylvania and well known in this section of the State, the paternal grandfather having long served his county as commissioner, and John McGowan, the maternal grandfather, being as prominently associated with the history of Allegheny county. The father, David McElhiney, was a farmer by occupation, having removed to Mifflin township in 1891, where he died in 1898 at the age of seventy-one years. He was the father of the following children: Sarah J., wife of William McKee; James, John, Charles, Thomas, Julia (deceased), William (deceased), Samuel, Perry and Joseph. Samuel McElhiney, the subject of this sketch, was reared in his native county and educated in the public schools there, and upon reaching manhood, turned his attention to agriculture and kindred pursuits. On Nov. 19, 1901, he led to the altar Philomena Schweitzer, a daughter of Frank and Annie (Hackler) Schweitzer, of Mifflin township. One son, John B., has come to bless their union. Mr. McElhiney and wife are members of St. Agnes' Catholic church of Thompson's Run, and are prominent in the religious and social circles of the township in which they reside. Mr. McElhiney was elected township treasurer in the spring of 1903 on the democratic and citizens' ticket, for a term of three years.

DAVID BLAIR DUBLIN, of Homestead, Pa., the popular proprietor of the Hotel Dublin, was born in Frankstown, Blair Co., Pa., May 1, 1858, son of Daniel and Susan (Henry) Dublin, both natives of Blair county. His paternal grandfather was also a native of Blair county, of German descent and by occupation a farmer. His maternal grandfather, John Henry, was a native of Yellow Springs, a pioneer farmer of Blair county, where all of his mature life was spent, and was also of German extraction. Daniel Dublin, father of David B., was born and reared in Blair county, for many years was captain of a boat which ran on the canal from Hollidaysburg to Havre de Grace, served three years and nine months in the Union army during the Civil war and died at Williamsburg, Pa., in 1867. He left a family of four children, viz.: Clarence (deceased), David B., James, of Altoona, Pa., and Alfred, of Pittsburg, Pa. David B. Dublin was reared in Blair and Fayette counties, Pa., having resided at Connellsville from his thirteenth to his twenty-second year, and was educated in the common schools, which he left to become a coke-burner. He followed that occupation from 1873 to 1879, and then for three years worked in the rolling mills of Scottdale and Pittsburg. Subsequently he worked at the carpenters' trade in Pittsburg and Connellsville until 1891, when he began the hotel business at Scottdale, and there prospered for two years and eight months. In 1894 Mr. Dublin purchased the Rattigan House, at Homestead, which he conducted for three and one-half years, and, in 1898, purchased his present place on Fifth avenue, which he rebuilt as the Hotel Dublin and has since successfully run. He was happily married, on Sept. 23, 1884, to Bridget, daughter of Edward and Margaret Kelley, of Connellsville, but formerly of Ireland, and has one son, Charles B. Mr. Dublin is a member of St. Mary Magdalene's Roman Catholic church, the Knights of Pythias, the Elks, the republican party, and was one of the promoters of the Homestead trust company, which was organized in 1903. Mr. Dublin has a splendid hotel, with all modern improvements, and conducts a strictly first-class hostelry.

ROBERT HENRY HEATH, of Dravosburg, Pa., the popular and efficient counter clerk in the county recorder's office, was born in Lincoln township, Allegheny Co., Pa., Feb. 22, 1869; son of Henry G. and Rebecca (Davis) Heath, both natives of Lincoln township. His paternal grandfather was Henry Heath, descendant from one of the colonial families of America, members of which have been prominent in the wars of America; William, an uncle of subject, having been killed at the battle of Pea Ridge, and Winfield, a cousin, wounded in the Modoc and Sioux troubles. The Heath family first settled in America at Heathtown, Va. The maternal grandfather of this subject was Enoch Davis, a native of Wales, who resided at West Elizabeth for many years and there was employed in the coal mines of O'Neal brothers until his death. Henry G. Heath, father of Robert Henry, is a resident of West Elizabeth, where for many years he has been engaged in mining, and at present is foreman for the Ella coal company in their mines. Robert Henry Heath was reared in Lincoln township, educated in the primary courses in the public schools and later attended the Grove City academy, the Independent normal school at Lebanon, Ohio, and the Northern Indiana normal school at Valparaiso, Ind. Then he taught school for three years in Mifflin township, Allegheny Co., Pa.; two years in Lincoln township, one year at Port Vue, and at these various places made a distinct success of that arduous calling. Mr. Heath has been more or less connected with the mines from the ninth year of his life until 1903, held the position of mine foreman for four years and also occupied a very responsible position in the mills of McKeesport. At the commencement of the Spanish-American war, he was selected by the mill men as orator on the occasion of the raising of the United States flag over the mills, and acquitted himself with credit and distinction. Prior to this he had made a fine record as a speaker and orator, winning unusual honors in that line at Valparaiso, Ind. In March, 1903, he was appointed index clerk in the recorder's office, and on June 10, 1903, promoted to his present position of counter clerk, which place he fills with skill and ability. Mr. Heath was married, on Oct. 18, 1901, to Sarah, daughter of John and Hannah Lynn, of Mifflin township, and they have one daughter, Rebecca. He is prominently identified with a number of fraternal orders, holding membership in the Junior Order of United American Mechanics, the Ancient Free and Accepted Masons, the United mine workers of America, and the Knights of Labor. Mr. Heath served as a justice of the peace of Mifflin township for five years, and in the fall of 1902 was a prominent candidate for the legislature on the citizens' ticket and, though defeated, received a most flattering vote, running ahead of his ticket by 1,600 votes.

VICTOR HUGO SCHULZ, of Homestead, Pa., a successful and prosperous dairyman, was born in Pittsburg, Pa., Dec. 27, 1879, son of Edward and Mary (Worth) Schulz, both natives of Germany. His paternal grandfather, John Schulz, of Saarbrücken, Prussia, came to America about 1849, and for many years was a resident of Mifflin township, where he was successfully engaged in his profession of teaching, and owned a part of the site of the present village of Whitaker, and there engaged in farming during the latter years of his life. His wife was Rachael Reis, also a native of the Fatherland and a woman of many fine traits of character. The maternal grandparents of Mr. Schulz were Peter and Elizabeth (Stoft) Worth, of Germany. Edward Schulz, father of the subject, is a retired puddler, and for many years a resident of Pittsburg, where he was employed in the different mills of that city, and in 1893 located at Homestead, where he is now quietly spending the declining years of an active and worthy life. Edward Schulz reared a family of five children, viz.: Rudolph E., rector of Coraopolis Episcopal church; Victor H., Otto, Eleanor and Herman. Victor H. Schulz was reared at Homestead from his twelfth year, attended the public schools of that borough, and when fourteen years of age, embarked in the dairy business with a capital of one cow, unlimited energy and a full stock of hope. His business has prospered and grown like the scriptural bay-tree, and at times has expanded to such extent that it has been necessary for him to sell a part of his route. He is now doing a business of $9,000 annually and is one of the progressive and substantial young men of Homestead. Mr. Schulz is a member of the Episcopal church and the Odd Fellows, and his political affiliations are with the democratic party.

ARTHUR PITTS, of Duquesne, Pa., a prominent real estate and fire insurance agent, was born at Johnstown, Pa., May 6, 1864. He is the son of James and Mary (Flint) Pitts, natives of England, who came to America in a sailing vessel about 1853, and located at Johnstown. Here James Pitts engaged in the coal business and as general contractor until 1873, when he removed to McKeesport, where he now resides. Mary (Flint) Pitts died Feb. 22, 1901, at the age of seventy-two years. To Mr. and Mrs. Pitts there were born eight children, viz.: George F.; Enoch W., who is cashier and vice-president of the People's bank of McKeesport; Mary A., Arthur B., Lillian E.; James H., a successful real estate agent of Glassport, Pa.; Charles A. and Frank, the two latter deceased. Arthur B. Pitts was reared at McKeesport, educated in the public schools of that city, and for thirteen years was there employed in the National tube works. In 1890 he located at Duquesne, and there was employed as a clerk in the real estate office of his brother, George F. Pitts, until Feb. 25, 1899, when he engaged in the real estate business on his own account, handling his own property as well as that of others, and has since met with much success in that venture. On Sept. 21, 1901, he purchased the entire business of his brother, Geo. F. (now located in Pittsburg), the confidence of whose former patrons he enjoys. On its organization, he was elected a director of the Home title and trust company of Duquesne, one of the most successful institutions in the borough. He is also a notary public and secretary of the Duquesne board of health. Mr. Pitts was happily married, Nov. 10, 1891, to Anna B., daughter of Philip and Christiana (Mohn) Rissler, of McKeesport, and their home life is an ideal one. He is a member of the First Methodist Episcopal church of Duquesne; Eclipse lodge, No. 892, Independent Order of Odd Fellows; Vesta lodge, No. 352, Knights of Pythias, and major of 3d battalion, 1st regiment,

U. R. K. P.; also member of Vesta company, No. 64, Uniform rank, Knights of Pythias; McKeesport lodge, No. 136, B. P. O. Elks; Aliquippa tent, No. 70, Knights of the Maccabees; White Rose council, No. 1932, Royal Arcanum, of which he is past regent. He is also a member and treasurer of Duquesne commandery, No. 331, Knights of Malta. His political associations are with the republican party, having served from 1894 to 1897 as tax collector of Duquesne, and is prominent in political affairs.

LESTER HAVEN BOTKIN, M. D., of Duquesne, Pa., a prominent physician, was born at Claysville, Washington Co., Pa., Dec. 13, 1859, son of George W. and Nancy (McCracken) Botkin, natives of Fayette and Washington counties, respectively, and is of Scotch-Irish descent. His father was a resident of Claysville for many years, in early life was a stage driver on the National pike, dealt in livestock to some extent, and held the position of a justice of the peace for a number of years. He was also a commissioner of the National pike, and had a family of seven children, four of whom grew to maturity, viz.: George W., now deceased; Emma, wife of David Frazier; Lewis C., a practicing physician of Burgettstown, Pa., and Lester H. Mr. Botkin was reared in Claysville, educated in the public schools of that place, and there began the study of medicine under Dr. J. M. Sprowls, a capable and successful physician. In 1887 he matriculated at the medical department of the West Pennsylvania college, Pittsburg, where he was graduated in 1888, with the degree of doctor of medicine. Then he located at Duquesne, there initiated his medical career, and has since met with much success in his profession, being regarded and esteemed as one of the leading practitioners of that section of the county. Dr. Botkin was married, March 21, 1883, to Jennie, daughter of James and Catherine (Miller) McKee, of Claysville, Pa., and they have four children, viz.: George McKee (deceased), Mabel, Bessie and Robert L. Dr. Botkin and his wife are members of the Presbyterian church. He has been surgeon of the Carnegie steel works, Duquesne, since 1889, and also has served the Pennsylvania railroad in a similar capacity during the same period. He is one of the progressive and public-spirited citizens of Duquesne, and despite the exactions of a busy professional career, has found time to devote to municipal affairs, having been a member of the school board for eight years, and is now serving his second term as councilman from the first ward.

JOSEPH H. McKEE, physician and surgeon, of Carnegie, is one of an old and honored family. His great-grandfather, John McKee, fought all during the Revolutionary war, and was personally acquainted with Lafayette. On the occasion of Lafayette's visit to America, in 1824, Mr. McKee went to Brownsville, Pa., to see him and brought home a silk handkerchief which the famous Frenchman had given him. John McKee was also a soldier in the War of 1812. His son, Henry, an early settler, had a son, Finley, father of the subject of this sketch. Finley McKee was a school teacher by profession, teaching school in the winter and farming during the summer months. He was one of the pioneer teachers of Pennsylvania, was noted for his success as a teacher, and rendered a great service to his State at a time when learning was not plentiful. He married Eliza A. Harper, whose ancestors came to Pennsylvania at an early day from Scotland. Finley McKee was born in 1828, and died in 1895. His wife died four years later, at the age of sixty-seven. Of the nine children born to Mr. and Mrs. Finley McKee, Daniel, a State normal graduate, is a Methodist minister at Columbia, Pa.; Anna married C. Blair, a farmer in Fayette county; Henry died at the age of fourteen; Joseph H. is the subject of this sketch; Clement L., a graduate of Washington and Jefferson college, is pastor of the Second Presbyterian church at Wellsville, Ohio; William F., a graduate of Ada college, Ohio, is a Presbyterian minister at Turtle Creek, Pa.; Margery H., who graduated from the California State normal school and taught school for several years, is married to James P. Hagen and lives on a farm in Fayette county; Mary E. is teaching school in Perryopolis, Pa., and Joel S., a graduate of Ada college, taught school several years and is now a bank clerk in Connellsville, Pa. Joseph H. McKee was born in Fayette county, Pa., Feb. 26, 1862. After attending the public schools he became a student at the Southwestern State normal school, graduating in 1884, and later a member of the class of 1891 of the Western Pennsylvania medical college, of Pittsburg. He earned his way through college by teaching school, and studied medicine in the office of Dr. Ellis Phillips, of New Haven, Pa. Immediately after completing his preparation for a medical career, Dr. McKee began to practice medicine at Woodville, Allegheny county, and six years later moved to Carnegie, where, since 1898, he has devoted his time to a steadily increasing practice. He holds the position of medical examiner for several societies and for the Prudential life insurance company. He is a member of the Carnegie board of health and belongs to several secret orders, among them the National Union, Order of Scottish Clans and Protected Home Circle, and is a past president of the latter organization. He is also a member of the Presbyterian church, of which he has for several years been a ruling elder. Mr. McKee was married, in 1893, to Miss Lottie L. Keller, of Woodville, daughter of D. P. Keller, an officer in the Allegheny county workhouse, and granddaughter of David Nelson Lea, a member of the Clarke expedition and one of the first settlers of western Pennsylvania. Dr. McKee and wife have had two children. Joseph H. is living, but Wilbur F. died when three months old.

JOSEPH ALOYSIUS WEBER, of Homestead, Pa., a member of the firm of Neu & Weber, sanitary plumbers, was born in Mifflin township, Allegheny Co., Pa., April 10, 1880, son of Joseph and Theresa (Goldbach) Weber, natives of Germany and Baldwin township, Allegheny county, Pa., respectively. His maternal grandfather was Bernard Goldbach, who came to America about 1854, settled in Baldwin township and there engaged in farming. His wife was Sophia Bott and a most estimable woman. Joseph Weber, father of our subject, came to America about 1876, engaged in farming in Mifflin township, and is now interested in a plumbing business at Duquesne. His living children are: Henry W., Joseph A., Louis, Cecelia, Emma, Frederick, Mary, Veronica, William, Phyllis and Jennie. Joseph A. Weber was reared in Mifflin township, educated at St. Agnes' parochial school, of Thompson's Run, and after serving a five-year apprenticeship at the plumbers' trade, became a member of the firm of E. W. Neu & Co., sanitary plumbers, of Homestead. This firm met with much success from Dec. 31, 1901, to March 16, 1903, when the firm was changed to Neu & Weber, under which name they have since enjoyed a splendid business. Mr. Weber was happily married, on April 13, 1901, to Emma, daughter of Charles Leisegang, of Baldwin township, and they have one daughter, Margaret. Mr. Weber and his wife are members of the St. Francis Catholic church, of Homestead, and he is a member of the Armour Plate council, Order of Americus. Mr. Weber is a young man of exceptional ability and unusual energy and is making a great success of his industrial career.

OSCAR PATTERSON LAWSON, of the Lawson plumbing company, of Homestead, Pa., was born near Perrysville, Allegheny county, Feb. 9, 1868. He is a son of James N. and Frances P. (Osborne) Lawson. (For family history, see the sketch of L. S. Lawson). His entire life has been passed in Allegheny county, where he attended the public schools, served his apprenticeship at the plumbers' trade in his father's establishment, and where he worked for several years as a journeyman plumber. His father began business in 1875. After his death, in 1900, the business was continued under the name of James N. Lawson's Sons, until 1901, when it was incorporated as the Lawson plumbing company, Oscar P. Lawson and William L. Davis being the proprietors and incorporators. It is one of the leading plumbing concerns in Homestead. Mr. Lawson has been twice married. His first wife was Elizabeth, daughter of John and Margaret (Peterson) Gibbs, of Homestead. By this marriage he has one child, James A. His second wife is Grace E., daughter of Matthew and Margaret E. (Wood) Thomson, of Jefferson, Ohio. To this second marriage there have been born three children: Grace E., Hilda F. and M. Percival. In politics he is independent, voting as his judgment dictates, for the men and measures that he thinks will best subserve the public interests. He is a member of Homestead lodge, No. 1049, Independent Order of Odd Fellows, the Order of Americus, and the Methodist Episcopal church.

CHARLES C. REEL, one of the leading funeral directors of Allegheny city, was born in the fourth ward of that city, Oct. 2, 1859. He is the son of John A. Reel (deceased), and a great-grandson of Casper Reel, Sr., who was the first white man to settle in Ross township, Allegheny county. Conrad Reel, the eldest son of Casper Reel, Sr., was the first postmaster in Ross township. He and his sons established the first woolen mills west of the Allegheny mountains, at Perrysville, in 1824, the mills being removed to Allegheny city in 1841, and were in operation until 1890. John A. Reel, the second son of Conrad Reel, was born at Perrysville, in March, 1830, and died in 1892. Margaret Reel, his widow, is still living and resides on Sherman avenue, in Allegheny city. The other children of Conrad Reel were: Jacob G., the eldest, who is living at the old homestead on Church avenue; Mrs. Annie E. McGuire, widow of the late Hugh McGuire, of New Brighton, Pa., and William H. Reel, who died in 1901. John A. Reel was the father of eleven children, of whom the following are living: Charles C., the subject of this sketch; Francis M., who is foreman for the Mackenzie-Davis lithographing company, of Pittsburg; John A., Jr., senior member of the firm of Reel & Michels, plumbers, of Allegheny city; Harry G., who is associated with Geo. B. Henderson in the butter and egg business in Pittsburg; Homer I. J., a plumber; Cecilia M., wife of George B. Henderson; and Anna K., who resides at home with her mother. Charles C. Reel was educated in the parochial and public schools of his native city, after which he served an apprenticeship at the machinists' trade with the firm of James Rees & Son, of Pittsburg, remaining in the employ of this firm for six years, when he accepted a position with the Westinghouse air brake company, remaining for about ten years. He then took a course of embalming in the Oriental college of embalming, graduating in 1892. His first place of business was on Federal street, in Allegheny city, but later he removed to his present location at No. 215 West Ohio St., where he has one of the best appointed undertaking establishments in the county and has the confidence of the best people in the two cities. Besides this business he is interested in various other enterprises, being executor, administrator and trustee of several different estates, a stockholder in the Mount Royal cemetery company, the Pennsylvania college of embalming, and various other interests. Mr. Reel is a member of several fraternal organizations, being treasurer of Ethel conclave, No. 314, of the Improved Order of Heptasophs; trustee of Branch No. 43, of the Catholic mutual benefit association; deputy grand knight of the Knights of Columbus; a member of Lafayette council, No. 447, Young Men's Institute, and of Allegheny lodge, No. 339, of the B. P. O. Elks. He is also one of the executive committee of the Allegheny county funeral directors' association. In 1883 he was married to Miss Lizzie D. O'Neil, of Mason City, W. Va. She is a descendant of one of the early settlers of southern Ohio and West Virginia.

AUGUST ABBOTT, ice dealer of Carnegie, was born in Allegheny county, Pa., May 10, 1853. His parents, Christian and Helena (Schmeltz) Abbott, were both born in Germany. Christian Abbott, born June 16, 1825, came to America when ten years old. He followed, for several years, the vocation of a glass-worker, then took up farming, and later bought in Scott township, Allegheny county, the farm which is now owned by his heirs. Later he purchased from the Rev. Mr. Cloakey another farm, which is also owned by his heirs. The last years of his life he spent in retirement at Carnegie. He died June 22, 1897. During his life he was a prominent member of the Lutheran church, in which he held several offices. At different times he held several minor public offices, among them being the positions of assessor and school director. His wife died Aug. 12, 1896, at the age of sixty-six. Christian Abbott and wife had nine children, of whom the subject of this sketch was the second. The others are: Carolina, now Mrs. Charles Schmeltz, who lives in Scott township; Amelia, wife of John Wise, a resident of Baldwin township; Edward, a farmer at Mount Lebanon; Kate, who married Charles Gettle, of Homestead; Lizzie, now Mrs. George Kuhlman, of Coraopolis; Anna, now Mrs. Adolph Doer, of Homestead; Rosa, who is also a resident of Allegheny county, and William, who lives at Bellevue. August Abbott, the subject of this sketch, received a common-school education, and learned the trade of a butcher, working at his trade for four years in Pittsburg. He came to Carnegie, where he followed his vocation as a butcher for twenty years. In 1895 he embarked in the ice business, and has since been engaged in this line, meeting with marked success. He employs twelve men, and his plant has a capacity of twenty-five tons a day, producing ice for Bridgeville, Oakdale and the surrounding towns. In 1880 Mr. Abbott married Miss Helena Stauffer, a native of Germany, who came to America with two brothers and a sister, when eighteen years old. Mr. and Mrs. Abbott have seven children. Florence is a student at Pittsburg academy, Sylvia C. is a graduate of Carnegie high school, and the others, Hallie, Nellie, Jennie, Frederick and Christian, are younger children at home. Mr. Abbott and wife are members of the Lutheran church, in which Mr. Abbott is president of the congregation, and several of the children are United Presbyterians. Mr. Abbott is a member of the American Mechanics. He has found his time too much occupied with business duties to take an active interest in politics.

ROBERT C. CRAIG, A. M., M. D., of Pittsburg, Pa., a successful physician, was born in Staunton, Va., Aug. 6, 1875, son of William E. and Annie E. (Ayres) Craig, the former a prominent lawyer and United States attorney. Dr. Craig was educated in the Staunton academy and at the Roanoke college, graduating from the latter institution in 1893, with the degree of master of arts. He matriculated at the medical department of the University of Virginia and was graduated from that historic institution in 1896, with the degree of doctor of medicine. On graduating, he entered the United States marine hospital service and was stationed at St. Louis for one year, at New York city for two years, and had charge of the service at Pittsburg for three years, until April, 1902, when he resigned from the service and since has been engaged in practice in Pittsburg. Dr. Craig resides in the East End, has offices at No. 414 Smith block, and has met with much success in his practice. He attended a post-graduate in general surgery at the New York polyclinic in 1899-1900 and keeps well posted on the advances of his profession. Dr. Craig was partly instrumental in getting an appropriation of $125,000 for a marine hospital, which is now being constructed on the United States arsenal grounds. He had charge of the marine staff of Mercy hospital for some time, is medical examiner for a number of life insurance companies, and for the United States marine corps, U. S. N., is a member of the Allegheny county medical society, the Phi Delta Gamma fraternity and the alumni of the University of Virginia.

JOHN T. BROWN, vice-president and general manager of the Damascus bronze company, of Pittsburg, Pa., has been connected with the railroad and manufacturing interests of the country ever since he was ten years of age. He was born in the city of Philadelphia, on April 17, 1845. His parents were John and Mary Jane Brown, both descendants of Revolutionary heroes. His father died in 1882 in his eighty-eighth year, and his mother in 1868. John T. Brown attended the Philadelphia public schools until he was about ten years old, when he obtained a position as core boy in the Richards & Norris locomotive works. He remained in the works until 1863, when he enlisted as a private in Company H, 196th regiment, Pennsylvania volunteer infantry, but after serving six months was discharged on account of ill health. For the next nine years he was with the Hook smelting company, and six years after with the Baltimore locomotive works, being foreman in the latter concern. He was then with the Paul S. Reese tubal smelting company for eight years as superintendent. In 1886 he started the Crown smelting company, of which he was general manager and which had at that time one of the largest and handsomest works of its kind in the United States. In 1893 Mr. Brown came to Pittsburg and assumed the management of the Damascus bronze company as vice-president, general manager and part owner. This concern does the largest business of any in the country, its leading products being phosphorized copper and the celebrated Damascus nickel bronze, which was invented by Mr. Brown in 1897 and which is now widely used by railroad companies on their locomotives. In 1867 he was married to Miss Almira L. Weaver, of Philadelphia, and five children have come to bless their union: Loretta, Linda, Raymond, Deborah and John, Jr. Mrs. Brown is a highly estimable lady, a graduate of the Philadelphia girls' high school, and her parents, like those of her husband, were descended from Revolutionary stock. Mr. Brown is a member of Duquesne post, No. 259, Grand Army of the Republic, of Pittsburg, and of the various mechanical organizations. In politics he is a republican and takes an active and intelligent part in the political affairs of the ward where he resides.

PROF. SYLVESTER STOTLER was born on the farm, twelve miles east of Fort Pitt, in what is now Penn township, on the land first settled by his grandfather, Rudolph Stotler, who came from Lancaster county at a very early age. Rudolph Stotler, a Revolutionary war veteran, was of Holland Dutch descent, born in 1750 in Lancaster county, and was twice married, being the father of five children by his first wife, and eleven by Frances Stotler, his second. He died at the age of seventy-five years, in 1825, and is buried in Mt. Hope cemetery, Penn township, where his wife, Frances, is also buried, having lived thirty-one years after her husband's death. Professor Stotler is the son of Emanuel Stotler, who was born in 1815 on the Stotler farm. Mr. Stotler remained at home, clearing land on the old farm, built a log house, and, in 1843, married Barbara Stoner, daughter of Christian Stoner, who had also come from Lancaster county to Allegheny county. Barbara was one of six children who married and settled in the county. She still lives on the old farm, at the age of eighty-two, active and in excellent health. The parents lived on this farm, which they had reclaimed from the forest, and raised a family of nine children, five of whom are living: Sylvester, Nancy A., Elizabeth, Leah and Frances (twins), Perry, Rudolph, John and Alice. John lives in California; Frances Gillooly, in Kansas; Elizabeth, wife of David Shepard, died in 1885; Leah resides at the old homestead; Perry, married, and living in Kansas, died suddenly; Rudolph died on the farm, and Alice when a child. Sylvester Stotler was educated in the common schools of his township, and while yet in school, was elected to teach in the Adams district, which he did for five years. The sixth year he was elected superintendent of schools of Reserve township, where he remained sixteen years, resigning to accept the position of principal of the thirteenth ward school of Allegheny city, a position he has held for eighteen years. Under his management the school has built up from a corps of three teachers to seventeen, and in standard of work is as high as any in the city. Professor Stotler has the enviable record of having taught school for forty years consecutively, taking his vacations only in summer, ready for work again each fall. He has had many opportunities of bettering his position and receiving higher salary, but has steadfastly declined all inducements, preferring to remain where his work has been appreciated and so remarkably successful. This school is his pride, many of the pupils now in attendance being the children of former pupils. Mr. Stotler's success is due to his keen knowledge of human nature, to his deep sympathy and sincere interest in the lives of parent, teacher and pupil, to his kindly nature, endearing him to all. The facilities Mr. Stotler found for his education were very poor, while those of his parents were still poorer. He often tells of the experience he has heard his father relate of the log schoolhouse with no floor, oiled paper for windows, smooth blocks placed on the lap in place of desks, and the open fire at one side of the room, the smoke escaping through the mud and stick chimney built on the outside of the house. Even in Mr. Stotler's day, quills were used for pens, and indigo used for ink. Professor Stotler's parents belonged to the Baptist church of their township, that being the only church near, though they were doubtless of Lutheran stock. Professor Stotler's love for children caused him to choose teaching as his life-work. He is opposed to corporal punishment as a rule, but believes in appealing to the reason and honor of the children, who come to him unhesitatingly with their troubles, knowing that their grievances will be righted. The thirteenth ward school stands unique in one particular, in that no corporal punishment is inflicted by teachers or principal, though the rules of the board do not prohibit it, and yet no school is better governed, or under better control. Professor Stotler's influence is great, and his example is a very powerful factor in the life of the ward. His long service in this school and his strong hold on the people are sufficient proof of the respect and esteem in which he is held. The thirteenth ward public school is his greatest monument, and the record of his work there constitutes the noblest lesson of his life. Professor Stotler is a Presbyterian; he joined the Millvale church in 1875, and the Pittsburg church in 1879. He is a member of the celebrated physical and health club known as the Ralston club, with extensive headquarters in Washington,

D. C. He is an ardent advocate of careful attention to health as affected by diet, habits and the like, and uses no tobacco, intoxicants or other injurious things, thus doing as so few in this world do—practices as he preaches.

JAMES W. SHIELDS, president of the Osceola coal company, at Emblem, Pa., is one of the best-known and most successful coal operators in what is known as the Pittsburg district. He is a son of Thomas and Margaret (Walker) Shields, both of whom were born in Lanarkshire, near Coatbridge, Scotland, and came to this country in 1848, settling in Pottsville, Luzerne county. Within a year they moved to Elizabeth, on the Monongahela river, where James W. was born on Dec. 25, 1851. Before he was a year old, the family moved to Greenock, on the Youghiogheny river, where they lived until the death of the father and mother, the former in 1884, the latter in 1897. The father followed the occupation of a coal-miner until ten years prior to his death, when he became interested as an operator. He was a man of sterling integrity, and much respected by all who knew him. James W. was the fourth of a family of ten children—five boys and five girls—of whom four sisters and one brother are still living. James W. attended the village school until the age of eleven, when it became necessary for him to go to the mines to earn something toward the support of the family. He studied as opportunity offered, but, as he aptly puts it, "the best part of my education was acquired in the hard school of experience," and, therefore, he has not forgotten what he learned. He tended trap-door at fifty cents a day, drove a mule and mined coal until he was twenty-one, when he went to Kansas and tried the life of a farmer for a time. This not coming up to his expectations, Mr. Shields went to Iowa and engaged in mining coal, and then tried the same occupation in Missouri. His next move was railroading, then mining again in Maryland, Indiana and Kentucky, and after fourteen years' absence, took charge of the Osceola mines as superintendent and manager, in which capacity he acted for three years. Mr. Shields then made his first venture as an operator by purchasing, in 1885, a half interest in what was known as the Republic coal company, at Sewickley. In

1889 he purchased the present mines at Osceola, where his first day's work was performed. These mines were opened in 1840, and were the first in the Youghiogheny region. Mr. Shields' thorough knowledge of mining has been gained by actual experience, for he has filled every position about the mines from trap-door boy to general manager. These pioneer mines are still operated, and, as they are managed by progressive men, are supplied with the latest and most approved electric and mechanical devices for mining and handling coal. The mines are located on the Baltimore & Ohio railroad, at Emblem station, on the Youghiogheny river, where more than 200 miners are employed, and the daily output is about 1,200 tons of coal. This coal is shipped to New York, Philadelphia and Baltimore, east, and to all points reached by the Baltimore & Ohio railroad system in the west. A great deal of the success of the company is due to the energy and ability of the president, Mr. Shields, who knows the mining business so well that he is quick to grasp situations as they arise, and to take advantage of opportunities in many ways that a less experienced man would be unable to see. He was the first operator in the Pittsburg district to concede the semi-monthly pay. He also served five years as a member of the old board of arbitration and conciliation, and he has always been among the foremost in the State in movements designed for the betterment of the miners in particular, and the working classes in general. In movements of this kind he has been a tireless worker for fifteen years. Besides his interests in the coal mines, Mr. Shields is also interested in several other lines, such as gas companies and banking institutions. He is a director in the United States banking concern, and has a high standing in financial circles of Pittsburg and vicinity. On Dec. 17, 1875, Mr. Shields led to the altar Mary A. Wray, a native of Indiana, and a daughter of James M. and Mahala C. (Sherrill) Wray. Four children came to brighten their home: Ida B., now the wife of Irwin M. Fickeison, of the Whitney & Stephenson company; Lillian B., Thomas G. (deceased), and Marguerite. The family have been republican in their politics, and Methodist in their religion. Mr. Shields became a member of the Unity lodge, No. 344, A. F. and A. M., of Perrysville, Ind., in 1875, and retained his membership there until June 27, 1892, when he became a charter member of Blyth lodge, No. 593, of West Newton, Pa.

WILLIAM F. SHROYER, insurance agent and dealer in real estate and mortgage loans, at Wilkinsburg, Pa., was born in Garrett county, Md., in 1866. In 1894 he came to Wilkinsburg and established his present business, in which he has a large patronage, due to his business enterprise, his genial disposition, square dealing and his thorough knowledge of the different lines in which he is engaged. In connection with his business he has traveled extensively, though never in the capacity of a salesman. He was married, in 1890, to Redena A. Anderson, a daughter of John and Mary Anderson, of Ursina, Pa., and they have one son, named Wilber R. F. Shroyer. His wife's father is the leading blacksmith of Ursina. Mr. Shroyer is a member of the Methodist Episcopal church and several fraternal orders. He is a member of Wilkinsburg lodge, No. 384, Knights of Pythias; W. H. Devore lodge, No. 676, Independent Order of Odd Fellows, and Encampment No. 280, of the same order. His residence and office are in the second ward of the city, and he takes an active interest in everything that has a tendency to promote the general welfare or the prosperity of the community. In political matters he affiliates with the republican party, but he has neither held public office nor been a candidate for it.

JOHN YULE STRANG, of Whitaker, Pa., a successful contractor and builder, was born at Town Hill, Fifeshire, Scotland, Jan. 15, 1874, and is a son of James and Janet (Yule) Strang, who came to America in 1879. They located at Elizabeth, Allegheny county, where the father was employed in the mines, and, in 1886, removed to Mifflin township, where he has since been employed in the Munhall mines. He is the father of nine children, viz.: Janet, wife of Charles Eckels; Christiana, wife of Francis A. Taylor; John Y., William G., Robert, Maggie, Bessie, James and Alexander. John Y. Strang was reared in Allegheny county from his sixth year, educated in the common schools, and when twelve years of age began his business career as a coal-miner, which occupation he successfully followed for thirteen years. At odd times Mr. Strang had learned the carpenters' trade, and since 1899 has been engaged in building and contracting, residing in Mifflin township since 1886, and at Whitaker since 1901. Mr. Strang was married, on Dec. 24, 1896, to Lizzie, daughter of John and Sarah (Jackson) McGough, of St. Clair township, and they have three children, viz.: William R., John Raymond and Sadie Leona. Mr. Strang is a prominent member of the Maccabees, Knights of Malta and the Odd Fellows. His political affiliations are with the republican party.

GUSTAVUS J. LIGHTENHELD, of Pittsburg, Pa., a prominent and well-known lawyer, with offices at No. 510 Fourth Ave., was born in Buffalo, N. Y., Aug. 26, 1852, son of George N. and Anna (Mueller) Lightenheld, both natives of Germany, and his mother now residing in Allegheny city. Mr. Lightenheld attended the fourth ward public school of Allegheny city, and, in 1869, became a private in Company C, the "Duquesne Grays," a prominent military organization. In 1870 he matriculated at the Western University of Pennsylvania, in 1873 visited Washington, D. C., with his command, and on his return was appointed assistant regimental instructor of the college cadets, which commission he held until his graduation in 1874. Mr. Lightenheld then entered the office of A. B. Hay, a prominent practitioner of law, and there prosecuted his studies until 1876, when he was admitted to the bar on May 13th, and for twenty-seven years has been continuously in the practice at Pittsburg. He has made a magnificent record in both the criminal and the civil courts, controls a fine business, and is a member of courts in Pennsylvania and in the District of Columbia. Mr. Lightenheld is prominently identified with a number of leading organizations, being a past officer of the "Duquesne Grays" veteran corps, member and past officer of the Junior Order of United American Mechanics, past officer of the Knights of the Golden Eagle, past officer of the Knights of Pythias, past officer of the Red Men, and a member of the Germania Liederkranze. He was married in Allegheny city by the Reverend Hay to Henrietta, daughter of Jacob Pack, and they have had five children, one of whom is now living, Ida, wife of Philip J. Reitmeyer. Mr. Lightenheld resides in the thirty-sixth ward of Pittsburg, and is prominent throughout the city.

GEORGE B. FORSYTHE, a retired farmer living on a ninety-acre farm near Carnegie, was born in Washington county, Nov. 24, 1836. His mother, Margaret (Henry) Forsythe, was of Irish birth, her father coming to Pennsylvania in 1760, while his father, George Forsythe, was for many years a prominent farmer in Washington county, and later in Knox county, Ohio, near Mt. Vernon, where he bought a farm of 250 acres, and resided there until his death, which occurred about 1852. His paternal grandfather was a Scotchman, who settled in Mifflin township in 1755, where many of his descendants yet live. Mr. and Mrs. George Forsythe were members of the United Presbyterian church. Mrs. Forsythe lived with her son, George B., the subject of this sketch, for many years, and later went to live with another son, Calvin, in Kansas, where she died at the age of eighty-six. Mr. and Mrs. Forsythe had ten children, viz.: Harriet, afterwards Mrs. Millinger; Henry, who served four years in the Civil war; James, a Presbyterian minister; Margaret, who married Joseph Ryburn; Joseph, a doctor who practiced and died in Salem, N. Y., in 1855; George B.; Susan, who married Judge Glenn, of Colorado; Robert, a twin brother of George B.; Sarah and Calvin, the latter also serving in the Civil war. Of these, Henry, George B., Margaret and Sarah are living. George B. Forsythe attended the public schools, and had started advanced studies at Wilmington, when the outbreak of the Civil war called him from his books to fight for his country. Enlisting on Aug. 27, 1861, in Company B, 100th Pennsylvania volunteer infantry, he served first in Sherman's army, then in the Army of the Potomac, then in Grant's army, and then again in the Army of the Potomac. During the war he fought with distinction in many engagements: at the second battle of Bull Run, at Chantilly, South Mountain, Md.; Antietam, Fredericksburg, the siege of Vicksburg, Jackson, Blue Springs, Tenn.; Campbell Station, Tenn.; the siege of Knoxville, Tenn.; in the

Wilderness (two days), and at Spottsylvania, Va. At Spottsylvania, on May 7, 1864, a rebel bullet struck him in the hip, inflicting an injury from which he has never fully recovered. This injury incapacitated him for further fighting, and after many months in hospitals at Fredericksburg, Washington city and Staten island, he was given a furlough, and went to visit his brothers in New York. Returning to his regiment, he was honorably discharged, after a service of almost four years. His war service over, Mr. Forsythe took up farming in Allegheny county, Pa. Since 1884 he has resided on a valuable farm of ninety acres, lying near Carnegie. On Sept. 26, 1866, Mr. Forsythe married Miss Margaret Henry, daughter of William Henry, and has by this marriage two children living. Cora is now the wife of Harry Walk, a farmer of Allegheny county, and has seven children, and George H., who resides near Newbern, N. C., married Ettie Young, of Bloomington, Ill, and has two children. The first wife died in December, 1897, and Mr. Forsythe married Miss Lettie Weller, a native of Montgomery, Orange Co., N. Y. One child, Joseph W., has been born of this second union. Mr. Forsythe and wife are members of the Presbyterian church, in which Mr. Forsythe has been for many years an elder. He is a member of the Loyal Legion post, No. 1, of Pittsburg, Pa.

WM. VALLANDINGHAM NOBLE, of Homestead, Pa., a prominent citizen of Mifflin township, was born near Steubenville, Ohio, Dec. 5, 1866, son of Tarleton W. and Sarah (Lewis) Noble, the father a native of Ohio and now residing in Ritchie county, W. Va., and the mother a native of Virginia and a member of a distinguished family of the Old Dominion. William V. Noble was reared in Ohio and West Virginia, and was educated in the public schools, the West Liberty State normal school of West Virginia, and the Illinois normal school, near Bloomington. Since his twentieth year, Mr. Noble has taken a deep interest in politics, voting on national issues with the democratic party, but in local matters believes in casting his ballot for the best man regardless of creed or political associations. He has been closely identified with the democratic citizens' party of Allegheny county since 1902.

Mr. Noble was engaged in various occupations in Illinois, Ohio, West Virginia and Pennsylvania, and since 1897 has been permanently located in Mifflin township, where he follows farming, gardening, contracting, buying and selling produce, and coal-mining. He is thoroughly identified with the business interests of the township, and ranks high in financial, political and social circles. He was married to Mary Alice, daughter of William and Frances (Hague) Bowden, formerly of England, but now of Mifflin township, and the home life of Mr. Noble is a happy one. He is a member of the Odd Fellows, the Ancient Order of United Workmen, the Modern Woodmen and the Order of Americus.

J. B. MARTIN, an esteemed and well-to-do citizen of Tarentum, is living a retired life in a comfortable home after a strenuous and successful career as a mechanic. He is of Scottish blood on both sides of the house, and can boast of a sturdy and patriotic ancestry who fulfilled all the duties of good citizenship during their quiet, but useful lives. His grandparents were John and Barbara (Forester) Martin, who came from Scotland many years ago and located in Allegheny county when its population was comparatively sparse. They spent the remainder of their lives in the cultivation of the soil, and passed peacefully away after reaching more than the allotted years of three score and ten. Peter Martin, one of their sons, accompanied his parents from the old country when a young man, and subsequently became a farmer in Fawn township. He married Jenette, daughter of James Blackstock, who came from Scotland to Butler county, Pa., at an early day, and spent his last days in that part of the State. Peter Martin died in 1859, and his wife in 1888. They were the parents of eight children, of whom seven are living. The Martins were republicans in politics, and the father, who was well-to-do, contributed liberally of his money to assist the soldiers during the Civil war, and did all he could to aid the country in its great struggle for existence. J. B. Martin, one of the seven surviving children was born in Fawn township, Allegheny Co., Pa., July 27, 1851. He was brought up on his father's farm, and attended the common schools at intervals as he grew to man's estate. When sixteen years old, he entered a blacksmith's shop with a view of perfecting himself in that line of business, and eventually became a journeyman blacksmith of superior qualifications. He worked for wages at various places in Allegheny county, but finally went into business for himself in Fawn township. In 1888 he came to Tarentum and continued in his chosen occupation at that point until 1901, when he sold his business, and has since lived in retirement, in his handsome and commodious residence on East Ninth avenue. His political affiliations have always been with the republican party, and he served in the council three years. In 1879 Mr. Martin married Miss Lida A. Smith, of Fawn township, who died May 18, 1892, leaving three children, Grace, Roy and Verna. In 1896 Mr. Martin married Miss Cora, daughter of James S. Christa, a prominent farmer of East Deer township. The second wife died Aug. 26, 1896. Mr. Martin has been a stockholder in the People's National bank since its organization, is a member of the Methodist Episcopal church, and stands high in the community as an exemplary citizen.

WILLIAM G. FAWCETT, of McKeesport, Pa., prominently identified with the brick-making industry of that city, was born on Aug. 24, 1851, in South Side, Pittsburg, Pa., son of William and Margaret (Robinson) Fawcett, his father having been street commissioner of Pittsburg for many years, and later a prominent coal merchant. The elder Fawcett brought the first tow-boat up the Monongahela river, and was closely identified with the business interests of the county until his death in 1884. Mr. Fawcett was educated in the common schools of Allegheny county, his first work being that of a farmer on the land owned by his father in Versailles township. In 1893 he and his brothers began making brick at McKeesport, and since that time have successfully continued that business, now being among the leading manufacturers in that line in that part of the county. He was also associated with his brother in the drug business for a number of years, and has been interested in the commercial and financial growth of the town in several ways. He was married, in 1885, to Alice, daughter of William and Eliza Sittman, of Westmoreland county, Pa., and they have five children, viz.: Wilbert, Eliza, John, Margaret and Glenn, all except the eldest attending the local schools. Mr. Fawcett is a prominent and influential member of the republican party, and has served in the council of McKeesport, and as secretary of the board of school controllers of Versailles township. He is a member of the Methodist church, and is identified with its works of charity and benevolence.

PROF. JOHN MORROW, superintendent of schools of Allegheny city, was born at Midway, Washington Co., Pa., and is a son of Alexander and Eleanor Morrow, late of North Fayette township. He attended the common schools, Paris academy of Washington county, later the academy at Mansfield (now Carnegie), and the State normal school at Millersville, where he graduated in 1865. After graduation he took charge of the Fallston graded schools, in Beaver county, and then of the Shady Side school, in the East End, Pittsburg. Later he succeeded Josiah (later Judge) Cohen in charge of the Hebrew school on Hancock street, then became principal of the South Pittsburg school until 1868. Professor Morrow was next chosen principal of the fourth ward schools of Allegheny city, where he remained fourteen years, until elected to succeed the well-known educator, Prof. L. H. Durling, as superintendent of the Allegheny schools, a position he has acceptably filled to the present time. He has filled many positions in educational circles, among them that of president of the Pennsylvania educational association, of which body he has also been treasurer for many years. Professor Morrow took an active part in the Civil war, enlisting from Lancaster, Pa., and is now a member of G. A. R. Post No. 162, of Allegheny. He was married, in 1898, to Mrs. S. R. Morrow, daughter of William and Allatha Gilchrist, late of Keene, Coshocton Co., Ohio. Professor Morrow is a man of easy and natural manners, not difficult to approach, and possesses a keen appreciation of the humorous. His principal characteristic is his hard-headed, common-sense view of practical questions. Professor Morrow is a splendid example of the Scotch-Irish character, combining the sensitiveness and tenderness of the Irish with the cold, practical, hard-headed intellect of the Scotch.

As an instructor, he is inimitable; as a superintendent, he stands unexcelled. He is the embodiment of moral power, intellectual force, and keen insight into men and events, and into the motives and principles which govern them. The teachers, in whom he takes a fatherly interest, and, in fact, all who know him, admire him as a man and a citizen.

JOSEPH STEWART, of the Ulrich-Stewart manufacturing company, of Allegheny, Pa., was born in Coleraine, County Derry, Ireland, March 21, 1851, and is the son of William and Mary Ann (Wray) Stewart, both of whom were natives of that county. The father was born in 1823, and died in 1891. His whole life was passed as a farmer, and he was a fine specimen of the better class of the Irish peasantry. The mother was born May 2, 1824, and is still living on the old homestead near Coleraine. She is a niece of Dr. Robert Wray, who came to Pittsburg at an early date, and who in his day was a very prominent physician. Joseph Stewart is the eldest of a family of ten children, all of whom reached the age of maturity, the others being Mary, who married Abraham Bodys; Jane W., who became the wife of Thomas Likin; Hugh R., now practicing law in the city of Chicago; Thomas C., connected for a number of years with the Westinghouse air brake company; Matilda M., now the wife of Samuel J. Keith; John W., living on the old homestead in Ireland; Samuel M., of Cincinnati, connected with a large manufacturing company; Robert W., a prominent physician and surgeon of Pittsburg, and Annie K., still at home. The two eldest daughters are deceased, but the others are now living. During his boyhood, Joseph attended the public schools in his native town, and in 1868 came to America. He located at Pittsburg, where he learned the trade of machinist, and in 1871 took up his residence in the first ward of Allegheny city, becoming at that time connected with the Pittsburg locomotive works. He remained with this concern until January, 1903, when he resigned to attend the session of the State legislature, to which he had been elected at the preceding election. On June 1, 1903, he became a member of his present firm, which manufactures a full line of gas and steam engines, all sorts of pulleys, hangers, etc., does high-pressure steam-fitting, and makes all kinds of heating and ventilating appliances. Mr. Stewart has always taken a lively interest in questions of a public nature, and is a firm believer in the principles of the republican party. In 1895 he was elected to the common council from the first ward of Allegheny city. His record there was approved by a re-election in 1897, and two years later he was chosen to represent the ward in the select council. This position he resigned in November, 1902, when he was elected to the legislature, as already stated. He is a member of the Ninth United Presbyterian church of Allegheny, and is one of the trustees. He is also a member of the F. and A. M., B. P. O. Elks and the Ancient Order of United Workmen.

JOHN OMSLAER, member of the select council from the eighth ward of Allegheny city, Pa., was born in the fourth ward of that city in 1856. His parents were Henry and Sarah Omslaer, both of whom died in the year 1894. When John was about six years old, the family removed to Duquesne borough, which later became the eighth ward of the city. There he attended the public schools, then he took a course at Newell's institute in the city of Pittsburg, and finished his education at the Iron City college. After spending about a year in the pine regions of Pennsylvania, he came back to Allegheny city and went to work in the river lumber trade. He followed this business until 1882, when he went into the city treasurer's office and served three years. At the expiration of that time he went back to the river, and for some time was connected in various capacities with steamboat navigation. In 1880 he was married to Miss Katherine Stenker, of Allegheny city, and they have four daughters: Susan, May, Katherine and Sarah. Mr. Omslaer is a solid republican, and never hesitates to declare his political opinions. In 1900 he was elected as the eighth ward member of the school board, serving two years. He was then chosen to represent the ward in the select council for a term of four years. In the council he is the chairman of the water committee, and a member of the finance and survey committees. He is a member of the United Presbyterian church; Allegheny lodge, No. 145, Independent Order of

American Mechanics, and the Pride of the West council. As a member of the city council, and in his dealings with men, he is distinguished for his sturdy character and strict adherence to principle.

ANDREW J. MALARKEY, a long-time resident of Tarentum, has had a varied and successful career as a Union soldier, driller for oil railroads, and brick manufacturer. His ancestry, both on the side of father and mother, has been identified with Pennsylvania from the days when that State was the frontier and the scene of those bloody border wars which figure so largely in history. His father, Henry Malarkey, was born in Butler county in 1791, and his mother, Elizabeth (Wolf) Malarkey, at Allegheny city in 1801. Daniel Malarkey, the grandfather, was a native of Scotland, born in 1765, and married a Miss Margaret Hines, of Germany, born in 1764, and died July 8, 1848. He came to Butler county in boyhood, and later engaged in farming, which occupation he pursued until his death, Oct. 10, 1846. His son, Henry, father of our subject, went to Swissvale in 1864, afterwards to Tarentum, and, in 1872, removed to Missouri. A year later he returned to Pennsylvania, and died at St. Petersburg, Nov. 11, 1873, his wife surviving until 1900. The latter's parents were natives of Ireland, and became early settlers of Armstrong and Westmoreland counties. Henry and Elizabeth Malarkey had nine children—six sons and three daughters—but of these, only three are now living, John, David A. and Andrew J. Five of the sons were in the Civil war on the Union side, and two of these, George and Henry F., were killed in battle while serving as members of Company F, 100th Pennsylvania regiment, known as the "Round Heads." John also belonged to this command, while David A. was a member of the 137th regiment, Pennsylvania volunteer infantry. Daniel, the eldest son, being exempt from military duty, enlisted and served as a member of the home guard. Andrew J. Malarkey, youngest of the children of this patriotic family, was born at Saxonburg, Butler Co., Pa., Aug. 3, 1846. He grew up on his father's farm, attended the neighborhood schools, and led the usual uneventful life of a country boy until his sixteenth year, after which, to use the expressive phrase of this age, "there was something doing." Not to be behind his brothers in patriotism, young Andrew enlisted, in June, 1862, as a member of Company F, of the 56th regiment, Pennsylvania militia, with which he served three months. Desiring more active service, he re-enlisted, Feb. 3, 1863, in Company L, 14th Pennsylvania cavalry, commanded by Col. J. M. Schoonmaker. With this regiment he enjoyed enough excitement during the ensuing two years to satisfy the most ambitious boy. He took part in the severe fighting at Winchester, Fisher's Hill and Woodstock, and was in many skirmishes during and after the famous Lynchburg raid. On Oct. 3, 1864, he was taken prisoner at Mt. Jackson, in the valley of the Shenandoah, Va., but after a detention of ten days, succeeded in obtaining a parole. With this brief exception, he lost no time with his regiment, to which he returned after leaving prison, and was discharged in September, 1865, at Leavenworth, Kan. After the war, Mr. Malarkey worked in the railroad service for seven years, and then engaged in the oil business. He drilled for oil from New York to Tennessee, and during his long connection with that business, a period of twenty-eight years, he met with the usual discouragements and disappointments, but on the whole was quite successful. Eventually he retired from the oil business, and for several years has been engaged in the manufacture of brick at Bartley's station, on the Bessemer road. He is also interested in the coal business and in gold-mining in Colorado. Since his retirement from the army, he has made his home at Tarentum, where he owns the finest residence in the town, built by himself on East Tenth street in 1892. Mr. Malarkey is a charter member of Eli Hemphill post, Grand Army of the Republic, which was organized in 1878. His other fraternal connections are with Pollock lodge, No. 502, F. and A. M.; Wellsville, N. Y., chapter, No. 143, R. A. M.; St. John's commandery, No. 24, Olean, N. Y., Knights Templars, and B. P. O. E., No. 644, at Tarentum. Though a democrat originally, he supported Lincoln, also Grant at his first election, and McKinley in 1896 and 1900. In November, 1864, Mr. Malarkey married Mary C., daughter of Samuel Wolf, who is mentioned in another part of this work. He and his wife are members of the Methodist Episcopal church at Tarentum. Of their three children, Harry E. died at the age of nineteen years, Samuel H. is with his father in the brick business, and John L. is a lawyer by profession.

JOSEPH CAMPBELL, retired miller, residing at Woodville, was born in County Down, Ireland, on New Year's day, 1840. His parents were James and Margaret (Alberthnot) Campbell. James Campbell was a farmer in Ireland. He died in 1882, when seventy-five years old, and his wife in 1883, at about the same age. Joseph Campbell is one of twelve children, of whom five, besides himself, are living: Mrs. Charles Pierce, Mrs. Samuel McVey, Miss Eliza, Miss Margaret and Mrs. William Frew. Mr. Campbell was educated in Ireland, and learned there the trade of milling, at which he spent four years before coming to the United States. He landed in America on June 11, 1871, and came to Allegheny county two months later, locating at Woodville, where he has since resided. He at once took charge of the Woodville flouring mill and ran it for eleven years, then bought the property, and has been owner and manager for over thirty years. In 1901 the mill was remodeled and fitted out with the most modern milling machinery, so that it is now the best equipped mill in western Pennsylvania. The mill grinds wheat, corn, buckwheat and rye, and has a capacity of fifty barrels a day. It is excellently located on Chartiers creek, and can be run either by water power or steam. For the past four years natural gas has been used as fuel, the mill being provided with a gas well near by. A side-track on Mr. Campbell's property connects it with the Chartiers branch of the Pennsylvania railroad, and, in all, the mill has facilities of three railroads, which carry the products in every direction. The mill is a structure forty by sixty feet in size, with four stories, with a slate roof, and the sheds and side toward the railroad track protected against sparks by a sheet-iron covering. As a further safeguard against fire, there is a stand-pipe running up through the center of the mill, and each floor is provided with twenty-five feet of rubber hose. In all his long experience, Mr. Campbell has never suffered loss by fire. The fifty-horse-power engine with which the mill is equipped has never suffered a breakdown, because Mr. Campbell is, besides being a practical miller, an engineer and mechanic as well. On Dec. 8, 1860, Mr. Campbell was married to Miss Agnes Rogers, a native of County Down, Ireland, and has had thirteen children. Of these, Elizabeth died when twenty-one years old, Robert died when twenty-three years old, Agnes died at the age of twenty-one, and three others died young, two being twins. Those living are: James, a clerk at his father's mill; William W., a miller; Maggie, who married John Wilson, who is employed in a railroad office in Pittsburg, and lives in Woodville; David R., an assistant in the mill, who married Alice Gudbub; Lottie C., Joseph L. and Clara J. W. He has also eight grandchildren. His daughter, Mrs. Wilson, has three children, Joseph L., Howard R. and Agnes M., and lost one child, James, who died when three years old; and his son, David R., has four children, Jacob R., Joseph A., David R. and Mary E., and had another child, Harry, who died when two years old. Mr. and Mrs. Joseph Campbell are members of the United Presbyterian church of Woodville, of which Mr. Campbell is treasurer and trustee. Mr. Campbell is treasurer of the building and loan association and a member of the grain exchange. In politics he has always been a republican. Mr. Campbell is a man whose life has been as honorable as it has been prosperous. He is a man of spotless integrity, and the products of his mill are noted for their honest value, which gives them a ready sale. He has won for himself in the community an enviable standing as a miller, a citizen and a friend.

JOHN A. KEYS, attorney-at-law, with offices at No. 604 Bakewell building, Pittsburg, Pa., is one of those men who have come up from the ranks by sheer force of will and indomitable energy. He was born in Washington township, Greene Co., Pa., Jan. 16, 1856. His parents, both of whom are now deceased, were John and Hannah (McLelland) Keys. As a boy, John A. Keys attended the common schools of his native county. Later he took a preparatory course in Monongahela college, at Jefferson, Pa., and, in 1877, graduated from Washington and Jefferson college, located at Washington, Pa., The following year he began the study of law in the offices of Wyly, Buchanan & Walton, of Waynesburg, Pa., but before completing his studies he went to St. Louis, Mo., where he took a full course in the law department of Washington university, graduating in 1881. He was at once admitted to the St. Louis bar, and for three years practiced his profession in that city. In 1884 he returned to Pennsylvania, and from that time until 1898 he was engaged in school work. While thus employed he became acquainted with Miss Lucy R. Bayard, a daughter of Samuel and Rebecca A. Bayard, of Greene county, and, on Sept. 6, 1888, they were married. To this union one daughter, Florence Rebecca, has been born. In 1898 Mr. Keys was admitted to the Allegheny county bar, and since that time has been engaged in practice in Pittsburg. He is the solicitor for several corporations, and in February, 1903, was elected burgess for the borough of Wilkinsburg, which office he now holds. He is a member of Wilkinsburg council, Royal Arcanum, and a member and elder of the Presbyterian church of Wilkinsburg.

W. J. CAMPBELL, a prosperous farmer of West Deer township, comes of Irish ancestry, who, for generations back, were successful tillers of the soil. His grandfather came from Ireland during the early years of the last century, settled in Allegheny county, married a native of Pennsylvania, and died an honored citizen, after devoting his life to the cultivation of the soil. His son, Thomas A. Campbell, married Jane, daughter of James Ross, who came from Ireland and married a Miss Anderson, of Pennsylvania, and died near Kirksville, Mo. His widow ended her days in West Deer township at an advanced age. Thomas A. Campbell owns ninety-five acres of land, and has farmed with success in his native township. He is an adherent of the republican party, and has held the office of road commissioner for two terms. He is a member of the Methodist Episcopal church, while his wife was connected with the United Presbyterian church until her death, which occurred Dec 11, 1890. Their family consisted of seven daughters and one son, all living except one of the former. W. J. Campbell, the only son, was born in West Deer township, Allegheny Co., Pa., Feb 23, 1859. He grew up on his father's farm, enjoyed the usual school routine, and obtained a thorough mastery of the details of farm work by the time he had attained to manhood's estate. For some time he has had charge of the homestead, and has managed the affairs with discretion and good judgment. Politically, he affiliates with the republican party, and, with his wife, renders allegiance to the United Presbyterian church. On Sept. 26, 1889, Mr. Campbell was united in marriage with Miss Rachael, daughter of George Hoffman, a prominent farmer of West Deer township. They have five children, Loyd Webster, Norman Ray, Bertha Ione, Clifford Anderson and William Kenneth.

GEORGE MAURER, of Clairton, Pa., is a native of Lawrence county, Ohio, where he was born in 1862. He is a son of Christopher and Mary Ann (Rhodes) Maurer. Christopher Maurer was born in Baden, Germany, in 1832, and came to this country at the age of eighteen years, settling in Lawrence county, Ohio, where, with the exception of one year spent in La Grange, Tenn., he remained until 1877, when he removed with his parents to Athens county, Ohio, locating in the Hocking valley, where he still resides and follows the occupation of a stationary engineer. Mary Ann Rhodes, the mother of our subject, was born in Nassau, Germany, in 1831. When she was thirteen years of age her family, consisting of father, mother and five children, came to America and located on a farm near Galveston, Tex. Shortly after their arrival, they were all stricken with a plague, and in three weeks the entire family, with the exception of Mary Ann and one brother, John, succumbed to the disease. After this calamity, the two survivors remained in Texas but a few months, when they removed to Lawrence county, Ohio, where Mary Ann first met and afterwards married Christopher Maurer. Seven children have been born to this union, viz.: John, Adam, George, Katy, Christian, Joseph and Frank, the two latter deceased. George, the third son, attended the Lawrence county schools during his boyhood, and upon leaving school, he began working in the mines of that county. He followed the occupation of a coal-miner in the Ohio and Hocking valleys until 1884, when he came to the Monongahela valley, where he continued his work as a miner. On the last day of the year 1888 he was married to Charlotte J., the eldest daughter of Evan and Sarah A. Beedle, of Jones' Station, Pa. Five children have been born to them: Evan B., born Nov. 22, 1889; Mary A., born July 28, 1891; John C., born Aug. 5, 1893; Edna M., born

Feb. 21, 1896, and George E., born Jan. 28, 1898. At the time of her marriage to Mr. Maurer, Charlotte J. Beedle owned a half interest in the grocery store of Beedle & Co., at Elben Station, Pa., S. D. Beedle, her brother, being her partner in the business. In 1897 she and her husband, Mr. Maurer, who had continued his work in the mines since his marriage, purchased the interest of S. D. Beedle, and continued the business under the name of C. J. Maurer. From that date Mr. Maurer devoted most of his attention to the interests of the store. In April, 1902, he removed to Clairton, Pa., but did not close out the business at Elben Station until the following March. In the spring of 1903 he started in the livery business at Clairton, and later added to this, contract hauling, dealing in grain, hay and vehicles. He is also a prominent dealer in real estate, in which business he has been very successful, especially in property at Blair postoffice and Elben Station, Pa. Mr. Maurer is a member of the St. Clair Roman Catholic church of Clairton, and in politics is an enthusiastic republican. While living in Washington county he served one term as school director of Union township. In this position he demonstrated his ability to grapple with public affairs, which he conducted with the same diligence and fidelity that has made him so justly successful in his personal concerns.

ROBERT BECK, city assessor of Allegheny city, Pa., was born in Allegheny city in 1863. He is a son of the late Peter Beck, who died in 1887, and Magdalena Beck, who is still living. Mr. Beck's first education was obtained in the public school of the third ward of his native city. Next he took a course at Duff's college, in the city of Pittsburg, and then served a five-year apprenticeship at the tailors' trade. For sixteen years he was employed as a cutter by the well-known and popular tailoring firm of Lehman & Kingsbeher, of Pittsburg, and left his position with them in April, 1903, to accept the one he at present occupies. Mr. Beck was appointed by Mayor Wyman for a term of three years. Politically, he is a democrat without guile. For four years he has been secretary of the democratic city committee; scarcely a convention has been held in recent years in which he has not been present as a delegate, and in the city he is looked upon as a leader of his party. His appointment as a democrat gave general satisfaction to his party associates. In 1889 he was married to Miss Philamea Auth, of Allegheny city, and they have three interesting children, Irene, Colleta and Robert. Mr. Beck is a member of St. Mary's Catholic church, where for twelve years he has been one of the choir. He is also a member of the Heptasophs, the C. M. B. A. and the Knights of St. George, in all of which he has a high standing.

GEORGE W. SNAMAN, a leading merchant on Federal street, was born Oct. 12, 1839, in Baltimore, Md., and is a son of George and Katherine (Spangler) Snaman. He came with his parents to Allegheny city in 1840, and remained with them until his eleventh year, when he left home to look after himself. He began his career as an errand boy for the merchants of Federal street, later entered the employ of Dunlap, Luker & Co. as clerk, and then formed a partnership with Mr. Dunlap, whom he afterwards bought out. Mr. Snaman has been in business on Federal street for twenty-five years, engaging in the carpet and wall-paper business, and is kept busy looking after his increasing interests. In politics he is a republican, and is proud of the fact that he cast his first vote for Abraham Lincoln, in 1860. He takes great interest in the welfare of his ward, has been a member of the common council, and chairman of the same for three years, and is now chairman of the finance committee of the select council, having been in the council for twenty years. In 1862 Mr. Snaman enlisted in Company E, 123d Pennsylvania volunteers, in the signal corps, and served nine months. He was married, Oct. 3, 1865, to Ellen J. Dunlap, daughter of his former partner, Capt. H. M. Dunlap, and to them have been born eight children: Carrie D., married to A. M. Irwin; E. E., living in Pittsburg; Harry B. and Walter H., in business with their father; George S., living in Allegheny city; Bessie G., at home; Frank B., married and lives in Allegheny city, and Charles, a high school student. Mr. Snaman's father died in 1886 and his mother in 1865, both being buried in Uniondale cemetery. The father was a cabinet-maker by trade and was the father of nine children, seven of whom are living. Of these, Lewis clerks in his brother's store, but the rest are scattered. Mr. Snaman is practically a self-made man, both in education and business. Eleven years is a very tender age to begin fighting life's battles, but Mr. Snaman has done it nobly, and has come out stronger in character for having so nobly striven.

EDWARD P. JOHNSTON, principal of the seventh ward school, Allegheny, was born in Brownsville, Fayette Co., Pa. His parents were William H. and Eliza (Brown) Johnston, who descended from pioneer settlers of that historic town, coming from the north of Ireland. W. H. Johnston was a successful building contractor, and erected many prominent buildings in Washington and Fayette counties. He was an ardent supporter of all educational movements, and from the labor of his own hands provided the means that graduated from higher institutions of learning five sons and two daughters. He was a man six feet, three inches tall, and of robust physical and mental strength. He was prominent for many years in the politics of his town and county, and was president of the council and a director of the Monongahela bank at the time of his death. He believed in the gospel of hard work, and in times like these, when so many think of work only to avoid it, it is a credit to his family that they have inherited this virtue as well as the educational tendencies of their father. He was an Episcopalian and a Mason. The subject of this sketch received his education in the public school of Brownsville and the Indiana State normal school, graduating from the latter in 1879. Since graduating, Mr. Johnston has been principal of the schools at Freeport, Brownsville, Pittsburg and Allegheny. He is a man of positive and mathematical mind, forms his own opinion of men and things, and advocates them with a sincerity that no one doubts. His school work is marked by an energy and enthusiasm that always succeeds. He leads his school, and has stimulated the educational sentiment of his district to a wonderful degree. The seventh ward school employs twenty-three teachers and has enrolled 1,100 pupils. Mr. Johnston married Miss Mary E. Fullerton, a successful teacher in the Freeport schools, and to them has been born one child, Eliza Brown Johnston, a third-year student in the Allegheny high school. Mr. Johnston is an Episcopalian and a Mason.

WILLIAM TUNSTALL, secretary and treasurer of the Homestead valve manufacturing company, was born on Squirrel Hill, Pittsburg, Pa., Aug. 23, 1849. His father, Joshua Tunstall, was a son of William Tunstall, a native of England, who came to America about 1827, locating the next year in Pittsburg, where he spent the remainder of his life as a pattern-maker. He married Alice Lord, and had three children, Ruth, Elizabeth, and Joshua, who for many years conducted a dairy farm on Squirrel Hill, and died at the age of seventy-six. Joshua Tunstall married Nanny Winders, and his children were: Alice, wife of Frederick Hazely; Elizabeth, wife of John B. Goodworth; Rachel, wife of Bruce Augustine; Lois, who married J. S. Seimon; William Miles, and James. William Tunstall's maternal grandfather was Joseph Winders, also a native of England, for many years in the coal business in Allegheny county. William Tunstall, the subject of this sketch, was reared in Pittsburg, and educated in the public schools of that city. When a young man, he served a three-year apprenticeship as a carpenter, and, in 1871, moved to McKeesport, where he learned the pattern-makers' trade, and followed his vocation there until 1876, when he moved to Port Perry and entered the employ of the Carnegie steel company. He was also employed by the Homestead steel works, in which for seven years he had charge of the pattern department. When the Homestead valve manufacturing company was organized, in 1894, Mr. Tunstall was one of the organizers, and has been since that time a member of the board of directors, and since 1898 has been secretary and treasurer of the company. In 1870 Mr. Tunstall married Elizabeth, daughter of George W. and Julia A. (Cornelius) Bail, of Allegheny county, and has five children: Lois, now Mrs. T. F. Vankirk; Miss Leal, Clifford E., William, Jr., and Claire. Mr. Tunstall is a member of Homestead lodge, No. 650, Benevolent and Protective Order of Elks. In politics he is a republican, and has served for twelve years as a member of the borough council of Homestead.

ROBERT C. YOUNG.

ROBERT C. YOUNG, baggage-master and mail agent on the P. C. & Y. R. R., at Carnegie, was born near Bridgeville, Allegheny county, July 8, 1846. His parents, Joseph and Margaret (Roach) Young, were respectively of Beaver and Allegheny counties. The father was a farmer and carpenter, noted for his vigor of body and mind, and was born March 14, 1818, near New Castle, Pa., and died March 8, 1869, at Mt. Lebanon; the mother, born Feb. 4, 1820, and died April 10, 1881. There were ten children: William, born Nov. 18, 1841; Ellen Jane, born May 21, 1843; R. C., born July 8, 1846; Annalyza, born March 22, 1848; Margaret E., born Jan. 2, 1850; Mary, born Sept 9, 1853; Mary E., born Nov. 26, 1855; infant son, born March 7, 1859; Joseph H., born May 27, 1860; Thomas John, born April 2, 1862. Mary died July 31, 1855, infant son died March 7; 1859, and William died Oct. 13, 1868. On the night of Jan. 16, 1857, the home in which Joseph Young and family lived was burned, and the family suffered great hardship, both on that night and during the rest of the winter. It was the coldest night for many years, and the nearest neighbor living over a mile away, all the members of the family were badly frozen. Mr. and Mrs. Joseph Young were hardy pioneers of that early day, and even now are remembered by many with most tender recollections. Robert C. Young, the subject of this sketch, received a very limited education, but worked at home on the farm and at making brooms. When twenty-three years old he came to Mansfield (now Carnegie), and started at the railroad business, being at first employed on a construction train and helping to lay the Chartiers branch of the Pan Handle. Later he became the assistant station agent at Carnegie, holding that position for nine years. In 1881 he went to McKeesport, where he was employed for a time in the National tube works; then returned to Carnegie, beginning as a brakeman on the P. C. & Y. R. R., and

MRS. ANNIE L. YOUNG.

then taking charge of the baggage and mail car. He has held that position continuously since that time, and has proved himself a capable and efficient employe. Mr. Young was married, Oct. 29, 1874, to Annie L. Clark, a resident of Carnegie, and daughter of George and Eliza (Walker) Clark. Her father was a painter by trade, and was for many years a school director. He was a prominent worker in the Presbyterian church, an elder and a member of the choir. He died in 1887 at the age of sixty-two; his wife still survives him, and is in her seventy-seventh year. Mr. Clark was a son of George and Abigail (Caldwell) Clark, the father a blacksmith near Carnegie, while Mrs. Clark's parents were James and Matilda (Buining) Walker. Of the seven children born to Mr. and Mrs. George Clark, Jr., Mrs. Young, wife of the subject of this sketch, was the first-born, and of the others, Matilda died at the age of thirty-eight; James W., George H., William J. and Robert B. are all painters residing in Carnegie, and Abigail C. is now the wife of George Hay, of Tarentum. Mr. and Mrs. Robert C. Young have three children living: George A., a graduate of Duff's business college, and now individual bookkeeper in the Colonial trust company, at Fourth avenue, Pittsburg; Joseph H., educated at Carnegie and Pittsburg academy, now receiving teller at Holmes & Sons' bank, and William H., attending high school. One child, Robert Dickson, born July 18, 1883, died Jan. 7, 1886. Mr. and Mrs. Young are members of the United Presbyterian church, and Mr. Young has been a teacher and worker in the Sabbath-school for many years. In politics he is a republican.

ROBERT L. HENDERSON, a prominent republican, and member of the common council of Allegheny city, Pa., from the third ward, was born in the ward in 1857, and is the son of Robert, who died in 1879, and Mary Henderson, well-known and honored residents of the city. Robert, Jr., attended the third ward school until he completed the course of study and then entered the Western University of Pennsylvania. At the age of twenty he left the university and went to work for the McClure coal company as superintendent of their works at Painter, Pa. His success in this position soon led to his promotion to that of general superintendent of all the company's works throughout the coke region. He is at present associated with Gilbert T. Rafferty, with offices in the Lewis building, Pittsburg, Pa., though he resides at No. 1317 Boyle St., Allegheny city. In February, 1903, he was elected to represent the third ward in the common council, where he is now serving on the committees on finance and charities. Mr. Henderson is a member of Allegheny lodge, No. 339, Benevolent and Protective Order of Elks, and is always one of the foremost men in the charitable acts of his lodge. Throughout his entire business and political career, his course has been distinguished by careful attention to the details of his duties and a strict integrity. As a result, he has the confidence and esteem of all who know him.

JOSIAH PAINTER, of Natrona, Pa., a successful and highly prosperous farmer, was born in Butler county, Pa., April 22, 1830, son of Joseph and Christina Painter, the former a native of Westmoreland county, and the latter of Armstrong county. They were the parents of six children, five of whom are living, and the subject of this sketch was the only son. Joseph Painter was a successful farmer, owning 100 acres of land, a republican in politics, and he and his wife were members of the Lutheran church. Josiah Painter was reared on a farm in Fawn township, Allegheny county, was educated in the common schools, and has devoted his entire business life to farming. He was also engaged in the market business for twenty years, and in both of these lines he has been unusually successful, and now has 300 acres of land in Fawn township, 152 acres in Harrison township, and 85 acres in Buffalo township, Butler county. In 1900 he located on the Freeport road, in Harrison township, near Birdville, and has since resided there. Mr. Painter is a republican, and he and his wife attend the Presbyterian church. He was married, in 1853, to Mary J. J. McKee, a native of Washington county, Pa., and the following ten children have been born to them, viz.: Salinda, Robert (deceased), Joseph (deceased), Annie, Gilbert E., Jennie, William, Maud, Charles (deceased) and Harry (deceased). Mr. Painter has enjoyed a long and highly successful life, and is well and favorably known in the community in which he lives.

GEN. JOHN NEVILLE.
(*Silhouette.*)

JOHN HUNTINGDON CHAPLIN.

LIEUT. WILLIAM CRAIG CHAPLIN.

NEVILLE FAMILY CREST.

LIEUT. COM. JAMES CROSSAN CHAPLIN

JOHN M. CHAPLIN.

JAMES CROSSAN CHAPLIN.

GEN. JOHN NEVILLE.
A Distinguished Soldier and Citizen.

Gen. John Neville was a son of Richard Neville and Ann Burroughs, who was a cousin of Lord Fairfax. He was born in Virginia, July 26, 1731, and was an early acquaintance of Washington, and served with him in Braddock's expedition. He was in Lord Dunmore's expedition in 1774, the last war in which Americans were engaged as the subjects of the king of Great Britain. The earl of Dunmore at that time was the governor and commander-in-chief of the colony and dominion of Virginia. General Neville made large entries and purchases of land on Chartiers creek, and built a house there, into which he was about to move when the Revolutionary troubles began. He was elected a delegate to the provincial convention of Virginia, which appointed George Washington, Peyton Randolph and others to the first continental congress, but was prevented by sickness from attending. On Aug. 7, 1775, the provincial convention of Virginia ordered him to march with his company and take possession of Fort Pitt. He was colonel of the 4th Virginia regiment in the Revolution, subsequently he was a member of the supreme executive council of Pennsylvania, and of the Pennsylvania convention which ratified the federal constitution. He was also a member of the convention which formed the constitution of Pennsylvania. General Neville was a descendant of the earl of Warwick (Neville), the king-maker of England. In 1791, at the urgent solicitation of President Washington and Secretary Hamilton, he accepted the appointment of inspector of the revenue in the fourth survey of the district of Pennsylvania, which he held until the fiery ordeal of the whiskey insurrection had passed. In May, 1793, congress passed material modification to the law, but all to no purpose. The excitement increased; not only were collectors visited with violence, but those who complied with the law. The adversaries of the law went so far as to burn the barns and tear down the houses of the collectors and others, and threaten with death those who should disclose their names. So strong was the public feeling that one word in favor of the law was enough to ruin any man. It was considered as a badge of toryism. No clergyman, physician, lawyer or merchant was sustained by the people unless his sentiments were in opposition. On July 16, 1794, a band of about forty individuals attacked the mansion of Gen. John Neville, chief inspector of western Pennsylvania, situated eleven miles southwest of Pittsburg.

It was defended by Major Kirkpatrick, a brother-in-law, with eleven men from the garrison at Pittsburg. The attack was previously made with small arms, and the house having been set on fire, the garrison was obliged to surrender. One of the insurgents was killed.

General Neville was one of the most zealous patriots of the Revolution, and a man of great wealth and unbounded benevolence. During "starving years" of the early settlement in that region, he contributed largely to the necessities of the suffering pioneers, and, when necessary, he divided his last loaf with the needy. In accepting the office of inspector of the revenue, he was governed by a sense of public duty, doing so at the hazard of his life and the loss of all his property. All his Revolutionary services and his great popularity were insufficient to shield him from public indignation, and his hospitable mansion was consumed to ashes in the presence of hundreds who had shared his bounty or enjoyed his benevolence. The story of this insurrection has in it more of thrilling interest than the best of the historical novels, for the greatest men in the land, from President Washington down, were concerned in it. Among these were Albert Gallatin, Senator Ross and Gen. John Neville; in fact, all the men of note in the State. General Neville was appointed agent at Pittsburg for the sale of lands, under act of congress, of May 18, 1796, entitled: "An act for the sale of the lands of the United States in the territory northwest of the Ohio," etc. General Neville built, at his own expense, the first Protestant Episcopal church west of the Allegheny mountains, in 1790. At that time there was no parish, or, in fact, Episcopal diocese in this county, the country hereabout being included in the territory under the New York diocese. With the founding of the St. Luke's, as it was called from the first, of Chartiers, Allegheny county, a parish was carved out, and Rev. Francis Reno was brought on from the east and ordained by Bishop White. General Neville paid the bills for his preparation for the ministry. John Neville was a man of considerable wealth for those times, and was, beyond doubt, the ablest and most prominent man in this end of the State. He married Winifred Oldham, a daughter of Colonel Oldham, of a noted Virginian family. He died on July 29, 1803, in what is now known as Neville township, and was buried in the Trinity churchyard of Pittsburg.

Gen. Pressley Neville was his only son, and Amelia his only daughter. Pressley was born Sept. 6, 1755, at Winchester, Va., and died Dec. 1, 1818. Gen. Pressley Neville married Nancy

Morgan, the accomplished daughter of the celebrated General Morgan, leader of the rifle corps of the Revolution, and she, Breckenridge says, "blessed him with an offspring as numerous and as beautiful as the children of Niobe." Gen. Pressley Neville was an aide-de-camp on General Lafayette's staff, and an accomplished man of fine education. His declination to become a candidate for congress, Aug. 4, 1798, was a very great disappointment, the district at that time being composed of Greene, Washington and Allegheny counties. He entertained on different occasions two of the most distinguished characters in the history of France—the duke of Orleans, afterwards King Louis Philippe, and that other uncrowned king, the Marquis Lafayette. When the revolution, which broke out in 1789, upturned the monarchy of France, the exiled heir to the throne, with his two brothers, Montpensier and Beaujolais, took refuge in America. In 1794 the future king of France, accompanied by his two brothers, reached Pittsburg. Gen. Pressley Neville then lived at the corner of Water and Ferry streets, and being the friend of the outcast and the oppressed, he was importuned by a French resident to entertain the strangers. To this he at first demurred, saying that while he was "the friend of Rochambeau and Lafayette and the friend of the unfortunate Louis—not as a monarch, but as a man," he hesitated as an American to receive the representatives of the fallen monarchy. But his humanity and hospitality overcame all other scruples, and he received the noted Frenchmen into his home and entertained them during their stay in Pittsburg. Louis and his kinsmen never forgot the kindness of General Neville. Afterwards, when a son of the latter, Capt. Frederick Neville, of the United States navy, happened to be in Marseilles, Louis, then king, sent for the young officer and lavished upon him every attention. At the ceremonies in Pittsburg over Washington's death, a famous oration was delivered by Gen. Pressley Neville, Jan. 11, 1800.

Amelia Neville married, Feb. 1, 1785, Maj. Isaac Craig.

MAJ. ISAAC CRAIG.

A Renowned Citizen and Soldier of the Early Days.

Maj. Isaac Craig was born near Hillsborough, County Down, northeastern coast of Ireland, in the year 1741, and emigrated to America in 1765. At the beginning of the Revolutionary war he took up arms in defense of his adopted country's rights, determined not to lay them down until with his life or the establishment of freedom. In November, 1775, he was appointed a first lieutenant of marines in the navy, and served ten months in that capacity, on board the "Andrew Doria," commanding marines. This vessel formed one of the squadron of Commodore Hopkins, which captured Fort Nassau and Montague, on the island of New Providence, in the West Indies. The governor himself was captured, together with many valuable stores, then much needed by the Americans, and subsequently used in Rhode Island and on the Delaware. Of these, a minute inventory was made by Lieutenant Craig. Upon return to harbor, in October, 1776, he was commissioned captain. In the November following, the marines were ordered into the army as infantry, and performed artillery duty. He was commissioned in March, 1777, a captain of artillery, under command of Colonel Proctor. Upon the promotion of Major Ford to the lieutenant-colonelcy, Captain Craig was entitled to the majority, but through misunderstanding, caused by his absence at sea, the supreme executive council appointed Capt. Andrew Porter to the vacancy. This led to a strong letter of protest on the part of Captain Craig, dated at Philadelphia, Feb. 21, 1782. The council reconsidered and revoked the order, and conferred priority of commission as major on Captain Craig, in the 4th regiment or artillery, annexed by resolution of congress to the Pennsylvania line. He participated in a number of battles, among them Trenton, Princeton, Monmouth and Brandywine. Major Craig was ordered to Fort Pitt to join General Clark in an intended expedition against Detroit, which, however, failed to take place. At Fort Pitt he performed various services to the satisfaction of the government, and became noted for his energy, activity and integrity. During his service at Fort Pitt he availed himself of the land laws of the State by taking up some valuable tracts of land. The first land sales were made by the Penns to Maj. Isaac Craig and Stephen Bayard in the "Manor of Pittsburg," in 1784. In 1797 he and Gen. James O'Hara built the first glass-works erected in western Pennsylvania, preceding those of Albert Gallatin at Brownsville a few months.

On Feb. 1, 1785, he was married to Amelia, only daughter of Gen. John Neville, then living at Bower Hill, on the Chartiers creek, and became the father of a numerous family, some of whom followed the military instinct of their father: Percy Craig was senior surgeon of the United States army, and medical director under Gen. Zachary Taylor in Mexico; Henry Knox Craig was general and chief of ordnance, United States army, and Isaac

Eugene Craig was lieutenant in the engineer corps of the United States. Some lived until a very recent period.

Oldham Craig, a well-known Pittsburger, died Oct. 4, 1874, on his way to Florence, Italy, to visit a son.

Amelia Neville Craig died Oct. 27, 1879.

Maj. Isaac Craig died on Montour's (now Neville) island, May 4, 1825, and was buried in Trinity churchyard, Pittsburg.

Maj. Isaac Craig's eldest son was Neville B. Craig, who was prominent in the early trials of the country, and was born in the Colonel Bouquet redoubt on March 29, 1787. He studied at the Pittsburg academy, graduated at Princeton college, and was admitted to the Allegheny county bar on Aug. 13, 1810. He was a successful lawyer, but in 1829 became the owner and editor of the Pittsburg Gazette, which he converted into the first daily in Pittsburg, continuing until 1841, when he disposed of his interest. As an editor he was bold and successful, devoting his vigorous powers to the best interests of the city of his birth and his country. He was the author of several historical works, one of them a history of Pittsburg. He was solicitor of the city of Pittsburg from 1821 until 1829. In 1822 he formed a partnership with Hon. Walter Forward, lasting several years.

JOHN HUNTINGDON CHAPLIN.

From an Address to the Allegheny County Bar Association, Dec. 1, 1888, by Chief Justice Daniel Agnew.

This time the Green Mountain State contributed her gift to Pittsburg's noted lawyers. John Huntingdon Chaplin, of Royalton, Vt., was born there in 1782. His parents were William Chaplin and Judith (Huntingdon) Chaplin. Mrs. Chaplin's brother, Samuel Huntingdon, was a signer of the Declaration of Independence. John H. Chaplin was graduated at Yale college, Connecticut, and came to Pittsburg in 1805, where he studied law with Henry Baldwin, and was admitted to practice Nov. 15, 1808. On June 28, 1809, he was married to Harriet Craig, eldest daughter of Maj. Isaac Craig, of the United States army, and Amelia (Neville) Craig, only daughter of Gen. John Neville, then of Bower Hill, on Chartiers creek, near Pittsburg. By this marriage Mr. Chaplin became connected with two of the most distinguished families in western Pennsylvania. On July 25, 1809, William Chaplin, his father, wrote to Mr. and Mrs. Craig a very kind and flattering letter of congratulation, dated at Bethel, near Royalton,

Windsor Co., Vt., and bore testimony to the high character of his son. His only regret was the great distance intervening, which made strangers of both families. The date of this letter and that of the marriage show that letters must have taken a month to go and a month to come. This fact reminds us of the advance in our time of all that relates to convenience in travel, and to the unity and greatness of our country. The news by telegraph would have taken less than an hour to find its way over this widespread land, and by mail only a few days. A portrait of John Huntingdon Chaplin, painted in Boston, is said to have been on exhibition recently in Gillespie's art room, on Wood street, Pittsburg, the queue and powdered hair denoting the fashion of the early time. Mr. Chaplin was at one time worshipful master of Lodge No. 45, of Pittsburg, an order of Masons chartered by the provincial grand lodge of England, Dec. 27, 1785. This lodge (No. 45) celebrated its centennial in Pittsburg, Dec. 27, 1885.

The purchase of Florida was made of Spain in 1819. That country was supposed by many to be—as it was called by Ponce de Leon when in search of the fountain of health and beauty—the "land of flowers," and many Americans, on its cession to the United States, emigrated thither, hoping to find wealth and fortune, as well as health and pleasure, within its orange groves and ever-blooming plants. Among these aspirants of hope was John H. Chaplin, who moved to Pensacola in the year 1820. He there practiced his profession successfully, and was in a fair way to redeem the promises of his aspirations, when cut off by yellow fever, Aug. 24, 1822, just as he was about to bring his long exile from home to an end and to return to his loved ones, whose separation from him had been a constant sorrow. Mr. Chaplin left a wife and two children—one a son, William Craig Chaplin, who became a lieutenant in the United States navy, and married Sarah J., a daughter of James Crossan; the other a daughter, Amelia Neville Chaplin (now a widow), who married Thomas S. Shields, Esq., attorney-at-law and a large landholder, of Sewickley, Pa., Oct. 8, 1832.

LIEUT. WILLIAM CRAIG CHAPLIN.

The only son of Harriet Craig and John Huntingdon Chaplin was born in Pittsburg, April 11, 1810. He was a lieutenant in the United States navy, in sea, shore or special service, from 1826 to 1851, and died in the officers' quarters, at the Charlestown navy yard,

Boston, Mass., April 25, 1856. The following is an order to Lieut. William Craig Chaplin to take charge of a boat expedition on the River Sambas, west coast of Borneo, March 18, 1845:

[Copy]
U. S. FRIGATE CONSTITUTION,
Off the Island of Borneo,
March 18th, 1845.

Sir:—I have to direct that you proceed with the boats placed under your charge and command, into and up the Sambas River. On entering, should you find a Dutch establishment there, you will stop at the same and make enquiry of the officer or person in charge thereof, whether such establishment is of the Government of Holland or belongs to a private or incorporated company of Merchants.

In either case it is desirable to ascertain if they have authority to prevent Americans from trading with the Rajahs and Natives on the Coast or in the River. This enquiry is one to which I respectfully call your attention, as involving great delicacy, propriety and prudence on your part.

You will endeavor to ascertain how far up the River the Rajah resides, and where the first Native village is situated. You will proceed thither with great caution and prudence, ever bearing in mind the treachery attributed to the Malay character, and more particularly to the inhabitants of the Island of Borneo.

The object of this visit is to ascertain as far as practicable, the disposition of the Rajah and his subjects to have Commerce with the people of the United States, and the cause heretofore of its interruption,—the articles they have to dispose of, and those they are desirous of obtaining in exchange.

You will be furnished with three boats—one, the gig, in which you will hold your communication with the Natives:—the others will take a position by your direction to cover your retreat, should treachery or murder be attempted. Let no offence be offered to the Natives by any under your command, and should wrong be committed on their part do not attempt to correct it by letting a greater wrong be done by those under you.

The First Lieutenant, Mr. Paine, will furnish every thing necessary for the expedition. As I am entirely ignorant of the geography of the place ("Sambas"), or even its location on the River, your own mind will point out the prudence of not passing by villages of such importance, that bodies of men collected therein might cut off your retreat.

If you can induce the Rajahs or any of the chief men to visit the ship, you are authorized by me to assure them of a kind reception, and a guarantee to them of a safe return to their own village unharmed. If they ask for presents they will receive them from the ship on making their visits.

To give minute directions for every step proper for you to take is impossible. Much is therefore left to your judgment and prudence, in which I have entire confidence, and am

Very Respectfully,
Your obedient Servant,

Lt. William C. Chaplin, }
U. S. Frigate Constitution. }   Percival,
                                                              Captain.

From imperfect information obtained since the above was written, I infer that this River is in possession of the Dutch and that there is a Dutch establishment thereon. If you find such to be the case it will not be necessary to proceed higher up the River than such establishment, where you will get all the information that can probably be obtained. You will therefore return as soon as convenient. It is not my wish to have the crews of your boats exposed more than the circumstances make necessary.

Percival.

[Copy]

U. S. Ship Constitution,
Coast of Borneo,
March 21, 1845.

Sir:—In compliance with your orders of the 18th inst., I proceeded with the boats under my charge to the entrance of the "Sambas" River, where I found a small native village called Ramon-Kat and a guard boat of the Dutch Government. To the officer in charge I reported the name and character of the ship and my wish to ascend the River to the town of "Sambas"; to this no objections being offered, we entered the main branch of the Sambas at noon of the 19th. This river we found to be a trifle over a mile in width and preserving a uniformity, not only in its dimensions, but in its soundings and the character of its borders; the latter are formed by a thick undergrowth of Mangroves, through which the water penetrates to some distance, affording no landing except upon the thickly interwoven roots of this tree, and those of the Yzer wood. (We had occasion to cook two meals for the boats' crews upon these remarkable banks.)

In consequence of the great disparity between the ebb and flood tides (the former running eight hours and the other but four and a half), we did not reach the mouth of the South branch until midnight of the 19th; this branch of the Sambas is 22 or 23 miles from the sea, and varies in width from 30 to 45 yards, and its borders are similar to those of the main stream, affording no foundation for towns or villages. Being detained at the entrance of this branch by the ebb tide, I despatched Dr. Reinhardt to a village situated on a narrow stream a few miles from our anchorage; he was fortunate in obtaining a few specimens of plants,—a small Sampan which had accompanied us from the guard boat gave him a better opportunity to examine the banks of this shallow stream, than one of our own boats could have done.

At daylight on the 20th, after a night of incessant rain, we arrived at the town of "Sambas," twenty miles from the main stream. I called at once upon the Governor and made the report usual in such cases; with unlooked for hospitality he offered me a house and cooking establishment for the men, and invited the officers to domesticate themselves in his own house; this kindness on his part was further increased in the course of the day by accompanying me to the Chinese and Malay Towns, and the frankness of his replies to all my enquiries.

From the information which follows, obtained from Governor Baumgardt, I felt satisfied that your order of the 18th did not require me to proceed any higher up the River.

This part of Borneo embracing the Sambas and all its branches, extending from 32' of South latitude to 2° 40' of North and from 108° 40' East to 110° 57' of East longitude, comprising an area of 26,304 square miles, contains a population of 50,000 Malays, 50,000 Dyaks and 50,000 Chinese, and is entirely under the control of the Dutch Government to whom it was ceded in 1817, and has been held by it without interruption since that period.

Its commerce though limited is entirely unrestricted, excepting the articles of Salt and Gunpowder; these are monopolies of the Dutch Government and are contraband in vessels of other nations. There is also a small duty upon Tobacco, which is brought from China and the island of Java, but with the exception of these articles, all the Dutch possessions in the Island of Borneo are free to the traders of all nations. There is however an inconsiderable Port duty of one rupee per ton levied upon all vessels that ascend the River.

It is matter of surprise that this large territory affords *no articles* of commerce,—completely inundated at high water, communication with the few mountains observable from the coast is only to be had by means of boats, and two of these mountains afford to the Dutch Government its only source of revenue and to the natives their only article of trade. (I should except however a close grained wood called the Yzer, principally used by the Chinese for furniture.)

The trade of the Sambas, consisting chiefly of plain bleached, unbleached and printed cottons and calicoes, has been monopolized by the English for many years—the Dutch do not even attempt to compete with them; the natives pay in gold; this metal is brought from the mountains before spoken of and becomes their only article of commerce, as soon as freed from the earth in which it is found, by the simple process of washing, and is worth eight hundred rupees or three hundred and twenty dollars to the pound. It is to be regretted that the demand on the part of the Natives for cotton fabrics should be so inconsiderable, as the navigation of the River and the access to it is extremely simple and uniform, and the character of the Natives, if not naturally docile, are rendered incapable of aggression by the close surveillance of the Dutch authorities, and vessels drawing 12 or 13 feet may ascend with perfect ease and safety to the town of Sambas.

I transmit herewith a chart of the River, which the Governor offered to allow us to copy, and in closing my report I cannot avoid

again referring to the kindness of Governor Baumgardt, the frankness of his communications, his cordially expressed desire that our commerce with this colony should again be renewed, and his regret that business and the preparations he is making to leave for Batavia prevented him from visiting you on board the "Constitution."
I am very respectfully,
Your obedient Servant,
(S) W. C. CHAPLIN,
Lieut.

CAPTAIN JOHN PERCIVAL,
Commander U. S. Ship Constitution.

J. CROSSAN CHAPLIN,

Lieutenant-Commander United States Navy,

Eldest son of

Sarah J. Crossan,   William Craig Chaplin,
                    Lieutenant U. S. Navy,
                    1826 to 1851.

Born in Pittsburg May 14, 1836.   Died at sea Sept. 23, 1866; buried in Saint Leonard's church-yard, Sept. 24, 1866, Bridgetown, Barbadoes, West Indies.

Entered the United States navy Oct. 4, 1850.

Lieutenant-Commander Chaplin was among the first to distinguish himself at the beginning of the Rebellion, having an enviable reputation for ability and pluck. At the time of his decease he was the executive officer of the steam-sloop "Monocacy," ten guns and 1,030 tons. Commander Carter pays a tribute to the character of the deceased, "whose record," he says, "for daring and cool courage in the performance of his duty is not surpassed by that of any other in the service." His whole naval service covered sixteen years, of which twelve were spent at sea.

NAVY DEPARTMENT,
June 29, 1861.

Lieut. J. Crossan Chaplin, United States Steamer Pawnee.

Sir:—Annexed is an extract from Commander S. C. Rowan, in relation to your gallant conduct at Mathias Point, on the 27th inst., when you had command of a detachment from the U. S. Steamer Pawnee. The Department highly appreciate your brave and heroic bearing on the trying occasion, and is happy to communicate to you the complimentary extract from the report of your commanding officer.   I am respectfully, etc.,
GIDEON WELLES,
Sec'y of the Navy.

EXTRACT.

I beg leave to call the attention of the Department to the gallantry, coolness and presence of mind of Lieut. Chaplin, of the

Pawnee, commanding the party on shore. He remained steady and cool amongst a perfect hail of musketry from hundreds of men, while he collected his own people and made good his retreat without leaving the enemy a trophy beyond a few sand bags and some axes, and, so far as I can ascertain, the muskets of the wounded men. The last man left the shore with him, and not being able to swim to the boat with his musket, Lieut. Chaplin took on his shoulders musket and all and safely reached the boat without a scratch, save a musket-hole through the top of his cap. Four days later he was tendered the command of the privateer Savannah. In October, 1864, while in command of the United States Steamer Commodore McDonough, he was highly complimented by Rear-Admiral Dahlgreen for the efficient condition of his ship and the good order of his crew. In the hour of danger his presence of mind never forsook him. Cool, calm and courageous, he was of such stuff as heroes are made. In the social side his many virtues shone to equal advantage. He was one of nature's noblemen, and not one of the large circle who shared his friendship will ever forget his genial ways and warm heart.

IN MEMORY OF THE GALLANT CHAPLIN.

By the Hon. Jonas R. McClintock.

LATROBE, PA., Oct. 26, 1866.

To the Editors Pittsburg Chronicle:

The announcement of the death of your lamented young townsman, Lieut.-Commander J. Crossan Chaplin, of the United States Navy, at the Island of Barbadoes, W. I., has not failed to fill with deepest sorrow the hearts of more than one fireside in this beautiful valley. His lamented father, who was an ornament to the profession of the sailor—springing from the best blood of the Revolution—was known and cherished in private life as one of nature's noblemen. The gallant son did not fail to catch the inspiration that distinguished the father in less perilous times, preparing himself on the first blast of the bugle of insurrection, to assume a glorious prominence, and do honor to the arm of the service to which he was so closely wedded. His daring and chivalry were the first to shed lustre on our little navy after the breaking out of rebellion. Off Mathias Point he served with gallant conduct. A shell entered the Valley City, and, passing through the magazine, exploded on the berth-deck, setting it on fire. James Crossan Chaplin, the commander, jumped down into the magazine himself, and, while giving directions to the men who were dashing water on the fire, passed up loose cylinders of powder. The fireworks on board ignited, and rockets whizzed and shot off, blue lights blazed up amid the ammunition, while the vessel reeled to the heavy broadsides that never slackened. The shell room caught fire, and for a few moments it seemed as if the vessel must be blown out of the water. But Lieut.-Commander Chaplin kept the men steady, working himself like a common sailor to extinguish the fire. John Davis, the gunner's mate, seeing the flames breaking up on every side, jumped on an open barrel of powder, and sat down on the head to cover it with his person. Lieut.-Commander Chaplin seeing him quietly seated there, ordered him in a peremptory tone to get down and help put out the fire. The brave fellow replied: "Don't you see, sir, I can't, for if I do, the sparks will fall on the powder. If I get down, Captain, we shall all go up." Though the danger was imminent and the scene terrific, Lieut.-Commander Chaplin could not refrain from smiling at the imperturbable coolness of the man. A more daring act cannot be conceived, and he was promoted for it, as he ought to have been. The fight was so quickly over, that Rear-Admiral S. C. Rowan did not fire even his twenty-four rounds. When the master's mate planted the stars and stripes on the fort, one long, loud cheer went up from the whole flotilla. The Daiching in the meantime grounded in the Combahee, right under the guns of a rebel battery. Lieut.-Commander Chaplin fought her bravely to the last, and, when he found her a wreck, set her on fire, and escaped with his crew.

NOTE.—From the Hon. J. T. Headley's "Farragut and Our Naval Commanders," pages 410, 411 and 490; printed 1867.

JOHN MONTOUR CHAPLIN.

John Montour Chaplin was born Jan. 5, 1849, at officers' quarters, navy yard, Memphis, Tenn., the fourth son of Sarah J. Crossan and Lieut. William Craig Chaplin, of the United States navy. He received his education under private tutors in Pittsburg and at the academy at Tuscarora, Academia, Pa., graduating in 1866. He then became confidential clerk to his uncle, Col. James M. Cooper, and, resigning his position, became discount and bills of exchange clerk in the Bank of Pittsburg. After ten years of successful work there, he became manager of the Pittsburg clearing-house, where he remained for twenty-one years and retired as assistant manager. He was treasurer of the Bankers' and Bank Clerks' mutual benefit association in 1891, and became president in 1894. He was an active participant in the organization of both the Duquesne and the Pittsburg clubs. He was secretary and treasurer and a member of the board of governors of the latter in 1879-80. Mr. Chaplin is an Episcopalian, and in politics a republican.

The most beautiful place on Neville island is that owned by John M. Chaplin. He lives in a beautiful colonial house, surrounded by spacious grounds, winding drives and walks, and many beautiful floral beds, resembling a park. There are 160 trees, standard and ornamental, some of which are very rare, the entire grounds being snugly inclosed by a well-trimmed hedge. Mr. Chaplin is a great dog fancier; he is the possessor of a splendid "Great Dane" and numerous fox terriers, and, withal, an historic homestead. Mr. Chaplin is a member of the Pennsylvania Society of Sons of the American Revolution, and also a member of the Pittsburg chapter of the Society of the Sons of the American Revolution.

ANCESTRY OF JOHN MONTOUR CHAPLIN.

Sarah J. Crossan.   M. William Craig Chaplin, Feb. 8, 1833.
B. Pittsburg, Jan. 14, 1813.
D. Jan. 24, 1901. Buried in Allegheny Cemetery.
―――――――――――――Son of―――――――
    Harriet Craig. M. John Huntingdon Chaplin, July 5, 1809.
    B. Fort Pitt, Dec. 25, 1785.
    D. on Neville Island, Allegheny Co., Pa., May 6, 1867.
―――――――――――Daughter of―――――――
Major Isaac Craig.   M. Feb. 1, 1785.   Amelia Neville.
B. 1741 in Ireland.   B. Winchester, Va., 1763.
Came 1765 to Philadelphia.   D. Pittsburg.
Lieut. in U. S. Navy, Capt. & Maj. in U. S. A.
Commander Fort Pitt in 1785.
D. Pittsburg, May 14, 1826.
Buried in Trinity Churchyard.
―――――――――――Daughter of―――――――
General John Neville.   M. Aug. 24, 1754,
B. Occoquan, Va.,   at Winchester, Va.
    July 24, 1731.
Colonel 4th Virginia Rgt. during Revolution.
Member Penna. "Board of Property."
Member Penna. "Supreme Executive Council."
Member convention to ratify Federal constitution.
Revenue Officer U. S. during Whiskey Insurrection.
Built at his cost the first Episcopal Church
                west of the Allegheny Mountains.
Prominent in Business.
D. Pittsburg, July 29, 1803.
Buried in Trinity Churchyard.
―――――――――――Son of―――――――
Richard Neville of Va. and Anna Burroughs,
                     Cousin to Lord Fairfax.
See Pages 478-9 of "Egle's Penna. Genealogy."

ANCESTRY OF
JOHN MONTOUR CHAPLIN.

———————————Fourth Son of———————————
Lieut. Wm. Craig Chaplin, U. S. Navy, in sea, shore or special.
B. Pittsburg, April 11, 1810.
D. April 25, 1856, at the Charlestown Navy Yard, Boston, Mass.

    John Huntingdon Chaplin, atty. at Law.
    B.
    D. at Pensacola, Fla., 18—.
    ———————————Son of———————————
    Benjamin Chaplin.   M.
    B.
    D. Royalton, Vermont.

Winifred Oldham.
B. Winchester, 1736.
D. Pittsburg, 1787.
Buried in Trinity Churchyard.
———————Daughter of———————
Anna Conway   and John Oldham.
of Virginia.   B. in Virginia, 1705.
    ——————— Son of ———————
Colonel Samuel Oldham.   M. Elizabeth Newton.
B. Westmoreland Co., 1680.   B. Wilmington, Va , 1687.
D. Westmoreland Co., 1762.   D.   1759.
                          ———————Daughter of———————
————Son of————   John Newton.
Thomas Oldham of Va.   Son of Willoughby Newton.

————Son of John Oldham————
who came to Virginia in March, 1635.
See Penna. Genealogy, page 479.

    ——————— Son of ———————
    Christopher Huntingdon.
    B. in England.
    Came to Rockberry, Mass., 163–.
    Came to Norwich, Conn., 1660.
    D. Norwich, Conn., June 28, 1706.

    ———————Son of———————
Simon Huntingdon.   M. Margt. Baret
B. in England.   of Norwich,
D. in ship off coast   England.
of Massachusetts, 1633.

Service from 1826 to 1851.

Amanda Sarah Huntingdon.
B Windham, Conn., June 26, 1761.
D. Allegheny, Pa.
———————Daughter of———————
Colonel Jabez Huntingdon.   M. Aug. 6, 1760
B. Windham, Conn., 1738.
Graduated at Yale, 1758.
Member Conn. Council, 1764-81.
High Sheriff, 1782.
D. Nov. 24, 1782.
———————Son of———————
General Jabez Huntingdon.
B. Norwich, Conn., Jan. 26, 1691.
D. Norwich, Sept. 25, 1752.
Very prominent in civil and military life.
Married May 21, 1725.
Mrs. Sarah Wetmore.
B. 1700.
D. Norwich, Conn., March 21, 1783.

General Jabez Huntingdon.
———————Son of———————
Christopher Huntingdon.   M. May 26, 1681,   Sarah Adgate,
B. Nov. 1, 1660.   B. Jan., 1663.
D. April 24, 1735,   D. Feb., 1706,
at Norwich, Conn.   at Norwich.
Deacon, 1695-1735.
First Townsman, 1695-1709.
Large landholder.
———————————————————————————Daughter of———
M. 1652.   Ruth Rockwell,
of Windsor, Conn.
B. England, Aug. 1, 1633.
———————Daughter of———————
Wm. Rockwell.   M. April 14, 1624,   Sussanan Chapin.
Came over in the   in England.   B. Dorchester,
"Mary and John."   England.

William Rockwell was a Puritan, who, in 1630, with 140 families, organized into a church and left England for America. His family is of Norman origin, running back to Sir Ralph de Rockville, a knight of the 10th century. The widow of William Rockwell afterwards married a member of this colony, Matthew Grant, the ancestor of General and President U. S. Grant. See "Savage's Genealogical Dictionary," Vol. 3, page 558, also "Rockwell Family in America, from 1630 till 1873."

Judith Elderkin.
B. Norwich, Conn., 1743.
D. Sept. 24, 1786.
——————————Daughter of——————————
Colonel Jedediah Elderkin, of Norwich, Conn. Attorney of Colony of Connecticut, member of "Committee of Safety" under Governor Trumbull during Revolution; very prominent in civil and military affairs. Died at Windham, Conn. He descended from
John Elderkin, of England, who came to Massachusetts in 1637, and Norwich, Conn., 1664. Married 1660 Elizabeth, widow of William Gaylord, of Windsor, Conn.
He died at Norwich, June 23, 1687, aged 71.
See "Savage's Genealogical Dictionary."

| Deacon Thomas Adgate of Saybrook, Con. one of the original proprietors of Norwich, Con. D. July, 1707. | M. 1660 | Mrs. Mary Bushnell, widow of Richard Bushnell. Born Mary Marvin, in England, 1629. |

——————————Daughter of——————————
Matthew Marvin. M.—— Elizabeth——
Born in England.
Came to America, 1635.
Mem. Genl. Council of Connecticut, 1654.
Died 1687.
See "Marvin Genealogy," Boston, 1848, pages 3, 4, 37, 38.

JAMES CROSSAN CHAPLIN.

Among the successful young business men of whom Sewickley is justly proud, Mr. James Crossan Chaplin holds a prominent place. He has been a business man since his fifteenth year, and has made a record that boys ought to know. Mr. Chaplin was born in Pittsburg, Sept. 7, 1863, his parents being James Crossan Chaplin, lieutenant-commander United States navy, and Martha (Harris) Chaplin. When Mr. Chaplin was three years old, his father died, leaving three children, whose early years were spent in Missouri. In 1879 Mrs. Chaplin removed to Sewickley, and James accepted a position in the Citizens' National bank, where he occupied several positions. He resigned in order to accept a better position in the Fidelity title and trust company, remaining there for about ten years—first as teller, then as treasurer—and upon the formation of the Colonial trust company, he was appointed its vice-president. In Sewickley Mr. Chaplin has always been interested in local politics; he filled two terms in the council, and is now its president. He is a vestryman and the treasurer of St. Stephen's Protestant Episcopal church, and is connected with a number of business enterprises and director of several financial institutions. In society, Mr. Chaplin and his wife, formerly Miss Fanny Campbell, daughter of the late Col. David Campbell, are as prominent as Mr. Chaplin is in business circles.

Mr. Chaplin's grandfather was William Craig Chaplin, a lieutenant in the United States navy, 1826 to 1851. His grandmother was Sarah J. Crossan, daughter of James Crossan. Mr. Chaplin comes of one of the oldest families in Pittsburg, a descendant from officers prominent in Revolutionary times. He is a member of the Pittsburg chapter of the Society of the Sons of the American Revolution.

JULIUS GOTTFRIED, wholesale liquor dealer in Carnegie, was born in the province of the Rhine, Germany, Aug. 6, 1857. His parents were Frederick and Amelia (Wuesthoff) Gottfried, both natives of Germany, where Mr. Gottfried was a postmaster and afterwards a silk-weaver and served for a time in the German army. He came to the United States in 1863, arriving in July of that year, while his family landed in New York on September 9th of the same year. After a short residence in Yonkers, N. Y., and Springfield, Ill., Mr. Gottfried came to Pittsburg in 1865, arriving on the day that President Lincoln was shot. He was ever afterwards a resident of Allegheny county, and was engaged in the hotel business from July, 1873, up to the time of his death, which occurred March 3, 1884. He was born Jan. 6, 1829. His wife was born April 30, 1829, and died Jan. 29, 1886. Both were members of the German Evangelical Lutheran church. Julius Gottfried, the subject of this sketch, is the only surviving child of Mr. and Mrs. Frederick Gottfried. Ferdinand, who was born in 1848, died Nov. 9, 1871, in Cincinnati, Ohio, of black smallpox, and Arnoldina died when three and a half years old. Julius

Gottfried attended the schools of the sixth ward, Pittsburg, and at an early age went to work as messenger boy for the old Pacific & Atlantic telegraph company, remaining at this position from October, 1869, until the spring of 1871. He then went to work for a branch office of the firm of Virtue & Yarston, New York publishers, where he remained a short time, and then entered the employ of G. J. Young & Sons, show-case manufacturers, remaining in the employ of this firm until 1874. The next year he spent as a cigarmaker, and then worked as a bar-tender for several years, and on July 3, 1877, started for himself in the saloon business in Pittsburg. In April, 1878, Mr. Gottfried took charge of Uncle Sam's hotel at New Castle, Pa., and a few months later returned to Pittsburg, where he had charge of the Manning house until Jan. 1, 1881. At this time, in company with his father, he opened a hotel at No. 364 Fifth Ave., Pittsburg, but discontinued it a short time afterwards, and, on March 25, 1881, took charge of the White house at Perrysville, Allegheny county, and remained there until Sept. 9, 1884, when he moved to the sixth ward, Pittsburg, and continued in the hotel business until March 10, 1886, and then became Pittsburg collector for the Crescent brewing company, of Aurora, Ind. From June, 1887, to July 5, 1889, Mr. Gottfried was employed as a hotel clerk, and then opened, in his own name, a wholesale liquor business in Carnegie, and continued the business until April 30, 1891. He then started a restaurant, which he ran until May 1, 1892, when he returned to the hotel business, and was manager of the Commercial house, at Carnegie, until Oct. 2, 1894. He then became a traveling salesman for the Rockford chair and furniture company, of Rockford, Ill., and later was salesman on the road for A. Wolf & Co., wholesale liquor dealers of Pittsburg. On Aug. 21, 1897, Mr. Gottfried embarked in his present business as a wholesale liquor dealer in Carnegie, and has been successful. On Jan. 6, 1881, Mr. Gottfried married Miss Catherine Schmidt, daughter of J. Wolfgang and Margaret (Thoma) Schmidt. Mr. Schmidt died Nov. 7, 1900, at the age of eighty-one. His wife died in 1864. Mrs. Gottfried has six brothers and sisters living—George, John, Elizabeth, Anna, Lucy and Andrew. Five children have been born to Mr. and Mrs. Gottfried as follows: Amelia A., stenographer and typewriter for the United States cast-iron pipe and foundry company, of Scottdale; Selma L., a student in bookkeeping; Laura L. E., stenographer and typewriter; Julius E. and Herbert E. Mr. Gottfried and family are members of the Lutheran church. Mr. Gottfried is prominent in several select societies, being a member of Centennial lodge, No. 544, F. and A. M., and Cyrus chapter, No 280, R. A. M.; past chief of Mount Moriah lodge, No. 360, I. O. O. F., and past chief of Marshfield castle, No. 476, K. of G. E.

DR. J. A. BURGOON, the eminent Pittsburg specialist and president of the Burgoon medicine company, located at No. 126 Sheridan St., East End, Pittsburg, was born March 12, 1842, in Clarion county. He is the eldest son of Dennis Burgoon, the name formerly spelled Burgoyne, of French extraction, and Susanna (Short) Burgoon. He attended the common schools of Clarion county, later taking up the study of medicine, and graduating from the Pennsylvania medical college in 1870. Dr. Burgoon was married, Sept. 11, 1866, to Sybilla Aaron, daughter of a highly respected citizen of Clarion county, by whom he had two sons, Peter A. and George A., both of whom are now in business for themselves in Pittsburg. Dr. Burgoon came to Allegheny city in 1888, locating on the spot where the postoffice now stands, and remaining there for four years, after which he removed to a more central position, No. 907 Penn Ave., and still later to No. 126 Sheridan St., East End. Dr. Burgoon is one of Pittsburg's self-made men. When he came to Allegheny city, in 1888, he had little beside his rugged energy, his knowledge of his profession and an indomitable will. After prospering some years, he sold half interest in his Allegheny laboratory for a big sum, being in the end dragged down by a bank failure. Dr. Burgoon's never-give-up spirit exerted itself, and he started a second time in Pittsburg, where he soon began to build up the fortune and success which have followed. The Chicago Trade Review says of him: "A few years ago Dr. Burgoon started in business penniless, with no stock in trade but an honorable and untarnished name—a reputation for sterling honesty and unlimited ambition and energy—to-day his position is a proud one indeed—his name an honored one wherever known—a loved and a revered name wherever the merits of his remedies have penetrated—a blessed name in thousands of homes where loved ones have been brought up from the dark valley of the shadow of death, once more to take their place at the family fireside, thanks to the marvelous power of those remedies which he alone prepares. A few years ago, an unknown physician—to-day, the peer of the highest in the land. A few years ago, the compounder of medicine in a small way—to-day, with facilities increased a thousand fold, unable to meet the demand. A few years ago, in an obscure position—to-day, in a commanding one. He owns and operates the Hutchison cancer hospital at Sewickley, a very noted and modern one in every way, and is the discoverer and owner of the only positive and sure cure for cancer, and has hundreds of cures of malignant cancers to attest to this statement. Not by idleness and wishing for success, not by looking back to count the milestones or looking forward with fear to the vista of the future, has Dr. Burgoon attained the pinnacle of a noble ambition, but by unceasing work has he earned name, fame, emolument and glory. It was such men and such careers as Dr. Burgoon's that the poet had in mind when he said:

" 'The heights of great men, gained and kept,
  Were not attained by sudden flight,
  But they, while their companions slept,
  Were toiling upward in the night.' "

JUDGE JACOB JAY MILLER, a native of Somerset county, where he was born in 1857, came to Pittsburg many years ago, and has become thoroughly imbued with the Pittsburg spirit. He is the son of the late Jacob D. Miller, a resident of Somerset county and a minister in the German Baptist church. He received his early education in the public schools, later attending the Indiana State normal school at Indiana, Pa., from which institution he was graduated in 1879, at twenty-two years of age. He began teaching in the public school at the age of twenty-four, closing his teaching career as principal of the sixteenth ward schools of Pittsburg. He read law in the offices of ex-Judge W. J. Baer, of Somerset, and, in 1881, decided to cast his lot in Pittsburg. In 1884 Mr. Miller was admitted to the Allegheny county bar, and two years later took a course in the law department of the University of Virginia. He had become acquainted with the city during his three years' experience in teaching (from 1881 to 1884), and on returning to

Pittsburg to open his office, he was already prepared to cope with the conditions as they existed. Clients were few in the early history of his career, but while he waited he studied, and it was not long before he had more than he could do. In 1901 he formed a partnership, which was known as Miller, Prestley & Nesbit, both of his partners studying law under him. In 1902 Mr. Miller was elevated to the bench as judge of the Orphans' court for a term of ten years. In politics he is a stanch democrat, and it is not a little significant that he was chosen from a strong republican section. Judge Miller takes an active interest in public affairs, and his voice has been heard in the service of his party during many campaigns. The Duquesne club, the Pittsburg club and the Junta club are places where Judge Miller is well known, being a member of all three. He is also a prominent Mason, being a member of the Duquesne lodge, the Pittsburg chapter and Tancred commandery. He is also active in church work, being a vestryman in Calvary Episcopal church, a member of the board of trustees of the diocese of Pittsburg, and also a member of the board of directors of Kingsley house. In 1894 he was married to Annie M. Clark, a daughter of the late Judge Silas M. Clark, of Indiana, who, from 1882 to 1891, was a supreme court justice. His family consists of himself, his wife and one son, Clark Miller.

EDWIN COLLINS HASLETT is a prominent real estate dealer of Allegheny county, and is the son of George M. and Marion W. Haslett, the former a native of Pittsburg, Pa., and the latter of St. Louis, Mo. His father was for many years connected with river navigation, beginning as a cabin boy and filling nearly every position on a steamboat up to that of captain. He died in 1892. Edwin Collins Haslett was born in the city of Pittsburg, Aug. 11, 1865. His education was obtained in the common schools of that city and at Curry institute. Upon finishing his education, he learned the business of photographer, followed it for a number of years, and, in 1899, turned his attention to real estate, his greatest undertaking along the new line being the founding of Lincoln Place. Securing possession of 106 acres of land lying eight miles from Pittsburg, two and one-half miles from Homestead and three miles from McKeesport, he platted it and placed it on the market as a residence suburb. With that energy which has always characterized his undertakings, he has made Lincoln Place one of the most popular residence districts in Allegheny county. More than half of the lots have been sold, several fine residences have been built, streets have been improved, churches and schools established, and a postoffice secured, all of which has been chiefly through his influence or by his efforts. In November, 1892, Mr. Haslett was married to Lulu, the daughter of William and Louisa Platts, of Pittsburg. They have five children, Grace, Margaret, Edwin C., Lulu and George. Mr. Haslett is a member of the Pentecostal church. He affiliates with the republican party politically, though he is an ardent advocate of the principles of prohibition. In this regard he teaches by example as well as precept, for he is a man of temperate habits, and is considered one of the most enterprising and public-spirited men in the beautiful suburb he established.

ROBERT BRINTON KENNEDY, of Whitaker, Pa., a valued employe of the Pressed Steel car company, Carnegie office of Homestead, was born at Fayette City, Pa., July 23, 1867, son of John and Sarah (Stockdale) Kennedy, natives of Washington county, Pa., and of Scotch-Irish descent. His paternal grandfather, Isaac Kennedy, a miller by trade and for many years a resident of Fayette county, Pa., married Lydia Short, and was one of the prominent figures of his day. His maternal grandfather, Allen Stockdale, was a native of Washington, Pa., a stonemason by trade, and married Letitia Allen. John Kennedy, father of the subject, "followed the river" for years, beginning at the very bottom and rising to the rank of captain, from which position he retired in 1883, and since 1901 has resided at Whitaker. Captain Kennedy had a family of eleven children, nine of whom grew to maturity, viz.: Joseph, William, Isaac, John, Lewis (deceased), Albert, Robert B.; Mary, wife of Joseph Hite; Azadell, wife of C. L. Wilson. Robert B. Kennedy was reared in western Pennsylvania and educated in the public schools and at the Iron City business college of Pittsburg, where he was graduated in 1888. He began his business career as a clerk, and has filled his present position with the Pressed Steel car company since 1900. Mr. Kennedy has been a resident of Whitaker since 1901, and is a charter member of Whitaker tent, No. 425, Knights of the Maccabees, of which tent he was the first record keeper. Mr. Kennedy is a prominent member of the democratic party, and in the spring of 1903 was appointed clerk of Mifflin township to fill an unexpired term, showing the regard in which he is held in the community.

CHRISTIAN F. VONDERA, of Homestead, Pa., a retired shoe merchant and a prominent citizen, was born in Baldwin township, Allegheny Co., Pa., March 27, 1852, son of Henry and Christiana Wilhelmina (Heisterberg) Vondera, both natives of Germany. His paternal grandfather, Frederick Vondera, came to America about 1861, and resided in the South Side, Pittsburg, until his death. His maternal grandfather, Christian Heisterberg, came to the United States in 1849, locating in Blossomville, Baldwin township, Allegheny county, where he followed his trade of shoemaking. The father of the subject was also a shoemaker, and came to Pennsylvania from the Fatherland in 1847, settled in Baldwin township, and was there engaged in business for some time. In the fall of 1863 Henry Vondera purchased a tract of land in Mifflin township, now known as the Vondera place, and there resided until his death, in 1897, at the mature age of seventy-four years. He was the father of the following children: Christian F.; Frank H.; Lena, wife of Frank Bost; Mary, wife of Peter Sorg; Charles H., and Louise, wife of William Hall. Christian F. Vondera was reared in Allegheny county, educated in the common schools, and began his business career on his father's farm. In 1880 he began the shoe business at Homestead, in which he was successfully engaged until 1897, when he retired, and since has resided at the old Vondera place. He was married, on Oct. 3, 1878, to Caroline, daughter of Conrad and Mary (Muth) Keitzer, of Baldwin township, Allegheny county, and they have four living children, viz.: Henry C., William E., Annie C. and Margaret M. Mrs. Vondera's paternal grandparents were Henry and Margaret Keitzer, of Hesse Darmstadt, Germany, who settled in Baldwin township, Allegheny county, about 1845, and there Henry Keitzer and his son, Conrad, engaged in their trade of wagon-making with much success. Mr. Vondera and his wife are members of the Evangelical Lutheran church, and he is a stanch republican in his political convictions and associations.

JOHN McGROGAN, locomotive engineer, residing at No. 323 Second Ave., Carnegie, was born in Beaver county, Pa., Feb. 4, 1860. His parents, John and Joanna McGrogan, natives of Ireland, came to America on a sailing vessel in 1845, and after landing in New York, proceeded directly to Allegheny county, where they spent the remainder of their days, Mr. McGrogan following the vocation of a miner. Both are now dead; the father died when sixty-five years old, March 14, 1895, and his wife in 1862, at the age of thirty. They were earnest, hard-working people, and devoted members of the Roman Catholic church. Besides John McGrogan, the subject of this sketch, they reared three other children: James, who lives at Walker's Mills; William, a resident of West Newton, Westmoreland county, and Margaret, now Mrs. Constantine Gallager, of West End, Pittsburg. John McGrogan received his education in the schools of Allegheny county, and, after school days, worked for a time with his father in the mines. On Feb. 4, 1884, he became a railroad fireman, and on Nov. 16, 1888, was given charge of an engine. He has been a locomotive engineer ever since, always in the employ of the Pennsylvania railroad company, and is widely known as a man of unusual skill and ability in his profession. He is employed on the Carnegie wreck train, and has associated with him in the wreck crew, Messrs. C. C. Elwarner and E. M. Meyers, whose biographies appear elsewhere in this book. Mr. McGrogan was married, June 16, 1886, to Miss Anna McCaffrey, a native of Carnegie, and a daughter of Peter and Catherine McCaffrey, both now deceased. They were members of the Roman Catholic church. Besides Mrs. McGrogan, Mr. and Mrs. McCaffrey were the parents of four other children, all living: Charles, a resident of West Newton, foreman for the Pittsburg coal company; Simon P., foreman for the Pittsburg coal company at Bridgeville, Pa.; James, a railway conductor, and William, a roller at McKeesport. Mr. and Mrs. McGrogan have seven children: Frances, Joseph V., Kitty, Madaline, Irene, George and John. Mr. McGrogan is interested in local politics, and is a prominent and popular man in the community. He and his wife are members of the Roman Catholic church.

CHRISTIAN REUKAUF, a prominent merchant of the twelfth ward, Allegheny city, was born in Saxony, in the southern part of Germany, on July 15, 1833. He is a son of Valentine Reukauf, an old warrior who fought under Napoleon, and was born in the village of Christus. His occupation was farming, which he did on a large scale, raising many horses and cattle in connection with his agriculture. He became wealthy in his vocation, leaving a considerable share to each of eleven children. Valentine Reukauf was educated in the village school, which was unusually thorough at that time, leaving at the age of eighteen years for the life of a soldier, which he followed for eighteen years. He was married at the age of thirty-eight to Rossina Miller, born in 1805, daughter of John Miller, the burgomeister of Christus and a well-known and respected citizen. Christian Reukauf's paternal grandfather was Michael Reukauf, a native of Christus. Christian Reukauf came to this country in 1850, landed in New York but settled in Philadelphia, where he was married and resided fourteen years. He had learned the tailor trade in Germany, but after coming to Philadelphia learned the whip-making trade, working for the Bader & Adamson whip company for seven years. He then learned to boil glue, working at that another seven years. After this they moved to Pittsburg, and thence to Allegheny city, where he has since resided. Mr. Reukauf also learned the tanners' trade, being in the employ of Lappe & Haz, tanners, remaining with them for sixteen years. He then went into the grain business and has prospered sufficiently to warrant his continuance in that line. Mr. Reukauf was married in 1850 to Mary Steinbacher, a native of Philadelphia, daughter of Michael Steinbacher, who came from near Wittenburg, Germany. To them were born eight children, four of whom are deceased. Those living are: William, the eldest, a member of the fire department in Allegheny, married and has three children; Harry, foreman in McKinney's hinge factory, also married and has two children; Mary, now Mrs. Riefer, of Allegheny, has three children; and Clara, now Mrs. Fred Streiner, living with her father, and the mother of four children. Those who are deceased were four sons: John, Eddie, Charlie and Augustus. Mrs. Reukauf died in 1902, mourned by all who knew her. She was a woman who was admired for her noble Christian character, her acts of kindness and charity, and for her intelligence. She reared her children in the German Evangelical faith. Mr. Reukauf is a man of fine physique and robust health, having never been sick in his life. In politics, he has been a republican since coming to this country, having cast his first vote for Abraham Lincoln. All his sons are also republicans. Mr. Reukauf has been elected member of the board of control in the twelfth ward and was selected as president of the board of control of the twelfth ward public schools in March, 1902. The K. of P. is the only secret organization which claims him as a member. Mr. Reukauf is one of the substantial and reliable citizens of the city and is known as a man of honor and integrity.

JACOB TRESSEL, the genial and popular proprietor of the Seventh Avenue hotel, Homestead, Pa., is an ideal landlord. Courteous and attentive to the wants of his guests, he has made many friends by his good-natured disposition and the skill displayed in caring for his patrons. His chief ambition seems to be the desire to please, and to see that none go away from his house dissatisfied. As a result, his table is surpassed by none in the city, and his café is patronized by the best people of Homestead and vicinity. He was born at Canton, Ohio, Oct. 8, 1869. His parents were Jacob and Mary (Siebert) Tressel, the former a native of Germany, and the latter of Lancaster, Pa., though of German ancestry. Jacob was educated in the public schools of his native town, and at an early age he manifested an inclination to engage in the hotel business. His first experience in this line was as an employe of the Hotel Anderson, at Pittsburg. Later he was at the Palmer house, Chicago, and the Herald Square hotel, New York city. In these celebrated hostelries he learned all the details of the business, and, in 1900, assumed the management of the Altamonte house, Altoona, Pa. A year later he became the proprietor of the Seventh Avenue hotel at Homestead, which he has since successfully conducted, the popularity of the house increasing almost daily. Mr. Tressel was married, Feb. 8, 1894, to Miss Mary Burgin, a daughter of Rudolph L. and Mary (Hoffer) Burgin, of Allegheny county, Pa. He is a stanch republican in politics, but has never been a candidate for any office, finding more pleasure and profit in catering to the wants of the traveling public. He belongs to Cap Sheaf lodge, No. 159, Order of Heptasophs, Pittsburg, where he is always welcomed as one of its most popular members.

JOSEPH MacMATH, the genial proprietor of the Hotel MacMath, was born in County Durham, England, Feb. 18, 1864, and is a son of James and Margaret (Blackley) MacMath. His father was a full-blooded Scotchman, and his mother was an Englishwoman. An accident in the mines in England caused the death of James MacMath, and his wife, with three children, came to America and settled at Lock No. 3, on the Monongahela river, in Jefferson township, Allegheny Co., Pa. There the children grew to manhood and womanhood. Elizabeth is now the wife of John Keennist; Maggie is the wife of John Wilson, and Joseph, the subject of this sketch, is a resident of Homestead. During his first years in America, Joseph attended the public schools of Jefferson township, but in order to assist his mother in providing for her family, he went to work when he was but eleven years old. In 1886 he located at Homestead, and for three years was employed in the Homestead steel works. He next engaged in the occupation of bartender, which he followed until 1897, when he embarked in business for himself, and since that time he has successfully conducted the Hotel MacMath, one of the leading hostelries of the city of Homestead. He was married, June 4, 1891, to Miss Jennie E., the daughter of Alexander and Mary Keltz, of Derry, Pa. They have three children, Mearna, Walter and Harry. Mr. MacMath is prominent in secret and benevolent society work, being a member of Homestead lodge, No. 479, and Uniform rank, No. 37, of the Knights of Pythias; Homestead lodge, No. 650, B. P. O. Elks;

Gray Eagle tribe, No. 393, Improved Order of Red Men; Monongahela council, No. 123, degree of Pocahontas, I. O. R. M.; Homestead lodge, No. 253, F. of A.; Mizpah lodge, No. 2324, Knights and Ladies of Honor, and Clan MacKenzie. In all these orders and societies he is an honorable and honored member. He also takes an active interest in political affairs, in which he is always identified with the republican party.

B. O. FAIR, a merchant in Glenfield borough, Allegheny county, son of Philip and Nancy J. Fair, of Armstrong county, was born Nov. 10, 1875, and educated in the public schools of Washington township. He spent his first fourteen years on the farm, and then became a clerk in his brother's store in Irondale, Ohio. After seven years as clerk, he and his brother, Ross, bought the stock of goods of the brother George, forming a partnership under the firm name of Fair Bros. After a short time the firm sold the stock again to the brother, George Fair, B. O. Fair accepting a clerkship with the People's company store, of New Cumberland, W. Va., where he remained one year. He again formed a partnership with his brother, under the old firm name of Fair Bros., in a general store, and after two years again dissolved partnership to go into business for himself in the grocery and fresh meat lines, in Verona, Pa. In 1900 he bought the stock of goods of T. Philips & Bros., engaged in general merchandising, and has an up-to-date store with a first-class trade. Mr. Fair was married, in 1897, to Lue Wolfe, daughter of Joseph and Rosanna Wolfe, of East Liverpool, Ohio, and to them has been born one son, Clarence S., born Nov. 4, 1901. Philip Fair, father of B. O. Fair, was born in Armstrong county in 1832; married, in 1860, to Nancy J. Gregg, only daughter of George and Mary Gregg, and to them were born nine children, all of whom are living—Harvey, George, Anna, Samuel, Charles, Ross, Barney, Otto and Claude. Mr. Fair was a stone-cutter by trade, was a man of good character, and was prominent officially, having held most of the offices in his own township. He was a member of St. Mark's Lutheran church of Limestone, and was connected in its official relations, having been a deacon for many years. He died May 3, 1898. His wife,

Nancy J. Fair, is living with her son in Glenfield. George Gregg, her father, was a raftsman, and was drowned in the Allegheny river. His wife, Mary Gregg, afterwards married Alexander Roofner, and to them were born ten children. She died in 1878. Philip Fair was the son of John and Mary Fair, and John Fair was the son of Michael and Mary Fair, and a native of Armstrong county. He was the father of four children: William, Philip, Susanna and Chambers. William died at the homestead, in Armstrong county, and Chambers was a soldier in the Civil war, and died in the hospital at Hagerstown, Md. Mary Fair, wife of John Fair, was the daughter of Henry Christman. Michael Fair, father of John Fair, was born near Philadelphia in 1775, and died in 1860. He was a great hunter, and lived at a time when population was sparse and wild game plenty. He crossed the Allegheny mountains by wagon in company with Jacob Steelsmith, they being the first settlers in Armstrong county. Michael Fair married Mary Steelsmith, the daughter of Jacob Steelsmith. Michael Fair was the son of John Fair, of Saxony, Germany. John Fair came to America in 1776 and settled near Philadelphia, arriving just in time to enlist as a soldier in the Revolutionary war.

DR. S. CAMERON BOWES, whose residence and offices are located at No. 815 Wylie Ave., Pittsburg, Pa., has been engaged in the general practice of medicine in that city since 1893. He was born in Toledo, Ohio, April 18, 1864, and is the son of Robert U. and Elizabeth B. (Robinson) Bowes. For many years his father was the general agent of the New York life insurance company, but he is now retired and lives in the city of Pittsburg. His mother is a native of Blair county, Pa., and lived there until her marriage. Dr. Bowes was graduated from the Toledo high school, and until 1887 was employed in the wholesale drug house of Benton, Myers & Co., of Cleveland, Ohio. In 1889 he began the study of medicine, and, as a preparatory measure, he attended the medical department of Wooster university, Cleveland, for one year. He entered the Western Pennsylvania college, Pittsburg, and graduated from that celebrated school in 1893. The same year he commenced the practice of his profession, locating at

No. 1222 Penn Ave., where he remained two years, removing to his present location. He is a member of the alumni association of the Western Pennsylvania medical college and the Order of Heptasophs, being the medical examiner for the insurance department of that order. Dr. Bowes is unmarried. In politics he is a steadfast republican and takes an acute interest in public affairs, but never to the disadvantage of his patients, whom he always regards as being entitled to his first consideration. By this devotion to his duty he has rendered himself deservedly popular, not only with his patrons, but in the profession.

JOHN PHILLIPS.

MRS. ROBERT PHILLIPS, of Glenfield, Pa., a cultured and highly-esteemed woman, was born in Pittsburg, Pa., April 1, 1852, daughter of Mr. and Mrs. Thomas W. Johnson, her father having been born in Pittsburg in 1816, and her mother, whose maiden name was Caroline Stutton, in England on July 10, 1832. Her parents were married in Pittsburg, in 1849, and had two children: the oldest, Margaret E., who married Jerome Frisby, on Jan. 17, 1866, and is now a widow, residing in Allegheny city, and the mother of three children: Kate Rolfe, wife of U. S. Jones, of Aliquippa Park; Roswell Benton and William F., both sons being successful carpenters. The younger, Rachel W., is the subject of this résumé. Thomas W. Johnson, the father of Mrs. Phillips, was a successful merchant of Pittsburg, and for many years was associated with his brother, Samuel, in a business venture at Smithfield and Liberty streets, where they did a large business and enjoyed a full measure of prosperity. Rachel W. was married, on April 4, 1878, to Robert Phillips, and they have had ten children born to them, viz.: Lillie and Buela (deceased), Charles Clyde, an employe of the Southern Pacific railroad and a trustee in the Glenfield Presbyterian church; Joseph Larmour, with the United States steel company; Edgar Laird, an employe of the Westinghouse air brake company and a member of the 18th regiment of the national guard of Pennsylvania; Victor Wilson, also with the United States steel company; Adala Sherwood, Dudley Alexander, Ralph Eustace and Robert Austin. All of her sons are young men of ability and industry, and are, without exception, fine examples of morality and integrity. Robert Phillips, her husband, was born on Nov. 28, 1848, in Stony Ford, County Antrim, Ireland, son of John and Eliza Belle Phillips, the former a son of Thomas Phillips, who spent his entire life near Belfast, Ireland. John Phillips brought his family to America in 1852, and became a successful farmer on Neville island, where he resided until his death, March 6, 1896. He was survived by his wife for several years, and she died on Nov. 1, 1901. Robert Phillips received a common-school education, then became a carpenter and contractor, and for several years was associated with the firm of T. Phillips & Bros., of Glenfield. That concern did an immense business until the death of T. Phillips, Jan. 26, 1899, when the firm was dissolved, and since that time Robert Phillips has devoted his attention to the lumber trade. Mr. and Mrs. Phillips have a family of which they may be justly proud, and Mrs. Phillips is a woman who has the respect and esteem of the entire borough in which she resides.

FRANK BOST, of Homestead, Pa., a prosperous blacksmith, was born at McKeesport, Pa., Feb. 25, 1861, son of Henry and Catherine (Renn) Bost, natives of Saarbrücken-on-the-Rhine, Germany, who came to the United States in 1842, and settled in Allegheny county, Pa., where his father followed the occupation of mining, and later ran a hotel at what is now Duquesne. The elder Bost was also on the county detective force for four years, died in Mifflin township, and was the father of the following children: John (deceased), Jacob, William, Valentine, Frank, Henry and Lewis. Frank Bost was reared in Allegheny county, educated in the public schools, and when fifteen years of age commenced his apprenticeship at the blacksmiths' trade and served four years. Then for one year he worked as a journeyman at McKeesport, and, in 1881, embarked in business on his own account at Homestead, where he has since continued with much success. Mr. Bost is the pioneer blacksmith of that borough, and has long been known for the high class and character of his work, as well as for his splendid standing as a man and as a citizen. He was married, on Nov. 30, 1883, to Lena, daughter of Henry and Christiana Wilhelmina

(Heisterberg) Vondera, of Mifflin township, Allegheny county, but formerly of Germany, and five children have been born to Mr. and Mrs. Bost, viz.: Charles H., Edna, Alma, Relda and Frank, Jr. Mr. Bost enjoys the confidence and esteem of all who know him; he has been entrusted with a number of public offices in Mifflin township, and his public record, like his private one, is of splendid character.

GEORGE H. ZIMMERMAN, of Glenfield, Pa., a prominent and successful contractor, was born on July 24, 1868, and is a son of Charles and Catharine Zimmerman. His father was born in Germany, and about 1840 came to America and settled in Pittsburg, and there worked at his trade of tanning. The elder Zimmerman was a soldier in the Civil war, enlisting in the 5th West Virginia mounted infantry, and served through the entire war, participating in a number of important battles, and at the second battle of Bull Run received a gun-shot wound in the leg which confined him to the hospital for a short time. On his recovery, he rejoined his command and served until the close of the war, when he was honorably discharged. The mother of the subject was a native of Butler county, Pa., of German descent, having been born in 1830, and died on March 17, 1900, leaving the following children: Louisa and Frank (deceased), George H., Philip E., Clara M. and Emma M. The paternal grandfather of our subject was a participant in the wars between the Catholics and the Huguenots of France, and, being a Protestant, left the land of his birth and sought an asylum in the country that assures liberty in thought and action, settling in America, and there passed the remaining years of his life in peace and contentment. His wife was a Miss Ohl, and was a daughter of parents who were among the earliest settlers of Butler county. George H. Zimmerman was educated in the splendid public schools of Sewickley, worked as a laborer for a short time, and then began his present business as a contractor for sinking oil wells, in which occupation he has met with much success in that line. He has been a member of the council of Glenfield, and is a member of the Knights of the Maccabees. He was married, on Dec. 24, 1891, to Ida M. Luster, and to them have been born the following children: Charles S., born July 20, 1893; Woren C., born July 30, 1895, and Ada May, born July 15, 1899. Mrs. Zimmerman is the daughter of Samuel and Marie Luster, her father having been born in 1830, and died in 1895, and her mother being born in Allegheny county, April 6, 1826, and now resides at Glenfield. Mrs. Zimmerman's father was a prominent farmer and a soldier in the Civil war, serving in Company H, 1st Pennsylvania regiment of light artillery, until wounded, about a year after his enlistment, when he was honorably discharged for physical disability. Her maternal grandfather, Charles Brooks, was of English descent and a soldier of the American Revolution, having enlisted as a volunteer under General Washington in Loudoun county, Va.; participated in many of the important battles, and served throughout the entire war. On one occasion his leg was slightly grazed by a cannon ball, and though not dangerously hurt, this wound never healed, but continued to be a source of much annoyance until his death. Charles Brooks was married three times, was the father of eighteen children, and lived to the ripe old age of ninety-five years.

FREDERICK HERING, a prominent contractor of Allegheny city, Pa., and member of the common council from the twelfth ward, was born in the third ward of that city on March 7, 1866. His parents are Michael and Christine Hering. Until he was about twenty-six years of age, he continued to reside in the ward where he was born, attending school up to his fourteenth year. He then became associated with his father in the house-moving and raising business, continuing in that occupation until 1886, when he was taken into full partnership. At present the business is conducted under the firm name of A. Hering & Bro., with offices at No. 1010 Middle St., Allegheny city, and is well known throughout the county. Mr. Hering is a stanch republican, and, in February, 1901, was elected to represent his ward in the common council. His services were so entirely satisfactory to his constituents that two years later he was re-elected, and is now in his second term. He is a member of the committees on surveys, public works and water, and is chairman of the sub-committee of surveys. In 1891 he was married to Miss Wilhelmina Bapst, of Allegheny city, and they have three children, viz.: Lillian, Elma and Frederick. Mr. Hering is an influential member of the National Union and of the Knights and Ladies of Honor.

ROBERT B. PAGAN, of Haysville, Pa , prominently identified with the oil industry of that part of the county, was born on Sept. 12, 1855. He is a son of Robert Pagan, a native of Dumfries, Scotland, who came to America in the spring of 1836, at the age of twenty-one years, and here followed his trade of stone-cutting for a number of years, assisting in the stone work on the old Williamsport bridge, and also doing that kind of work for a railroad company. The dust from the stone later began to affect his lungs, and consequently he gave up that trade and engaged in farming in Ohio township, where he died on March 27, 1893, at the age of seventy-eight years. Robert B. Pagan was educated in the splendid schools of Ohio township, and when seventeen years of age, began to learn the trade of a flour-miller, and after accomplishing that object, was in charge of a mill for eleven years. He was compelled to seek another occupation on account of impaired health, and for three years conducted a blacksmith and repair shop at the old N. W. Mitchell mill, on the Little Sewickley creek. Subsequently he began drilling artesian wells, and later oil and gas wells for C. J. Hammel; then for one year was a contractor on his own account, but was compelled to quit that business on account of losing his tools while engaged in sinking a well. He then became field foreman for the Fisher oil company for thirteen years, and since that time has been in charge of an oil lease for the Haysville company. He was married, on Dec. 30, 1886, to Sarah E. Merriman, and they have three children, viz.: Bessie Annie, born Aug. 4, 1888; Sarah Ellen, born March 1, 1890, and Elmer Robert, born July 27, 1897. Mrs. Pagan was born on Nov. 27, 1870, and is the granddaughter of one of the first settlers of Allegheny county, who owned a large tract of land in Aleppo township and was a prominent citizen of his day. Mr. Pagan's mother, whose maiden name was Brant, was born in Berlin, Germany, Jan. 29, 1828, and settled in Pittsburg at the age of eighteen years. She was married when twenty, is the mother of seven children, and is now seventy-six years of age, and a hale and hearty old lady.

HENRY B. LATSHAW, of Glenfield, Pa., an important figure in the oil industry of that section, was born in Butler county, Pa., Jan. 24, 1848, and is a son of John and Fannie Latshaw. The father was born in Berks county, Pa., May 25, 1819; died at his home in Barkeyville, Venango Co., Pa., April 29, 1901, and is buried in the Barkeyville cemetery. He was a thrifty and successful farmer, and one of the prosperous business men of that part of the county. Henry B. Latshaw spent his early life on the farm, and when he attained his majority, began as a laborer in the lumber industry, which he followed for four years. Then he became connected with the oil business, working for the Bradfoot oil company, the Union oil company, and for more than ten years has been foreman of the Midland division of the Forest oil company, which was formerly known as the South Pennsylvania company, of Oil City, Pa. John Latshaw, his father, married Fannie, daughter of Adam Tinsman, she having been born in Butler county, Pa., and died on May 19, 1875, and is buried by the side of her husband in the Barkeyville cemetery. The Latshaws are of German ancestry, his grandfather, John Latshaw, having come to America with his four brothers and settled in Berks county, Pa., where they became a numerous and prominent family. John Latshaw, father of our subject, was the father of thirteen children, eight of whom are now living, viz.: Jacob I., Henry B., Nancy J., Mary Anne, Manuel L., Josiah H., Bertha and Rosa; the deceased ones being David, Levi, Aaron, Sadie and William J. David and Levi Latshaw were both soldiers in the Civil war, the former enlisting as a volunteer in Company K, 4th Pennsylvania cavalry, at the beginning of the war, and was in the following important engagements: Antietam, Blue Ridge, Fredericksburg, Bull Run, Petersburg and a number of others. He saw distinguished service, and after three years' arduous campaigning, re-enlisted for the rest of the war. Shortly afterwards he was captured, confined for three months in Libby prison, and then transferred to Andersonville, where he died after a ten-month imprisonment, and was buried in the soldiers' cemetery of that place. Levi Latshaw enlisted in Company I, 6th Pennsylvania heavy artillery, and during the war was on picket duty until honorably discharged, returning then to his home in the Keystone State. Henry B. Latshaw was married, on Feb. 1, 1877, to Elizabeth, daughter of John and Sarah Young, of Irwin township, Venango Co., Pa., the former a prosperous farmer, who was born in Ireland, Sept. 1, 1826, and died on June 6, 1886, and her mother was born in Pennsylvania, April 4, 1834, and now resides in North Liberty, Pa. Mr. and Mrs. Young had seven children, four of whom are now living, and are among the prominent people of the various communities in which they reside. Henry B. Latshaw has been quite successful in business affairs, and now owns two fine farms—one of eighty acres in Mercer county, Pa., and another of 164 acres in Venango county—both of which are fine pieces of property and fully adapted for the best agricultural results. Mr. Latshaw is a member of the Ancient Order of United Workmen, and his political affiliations are with the republican party. Miss Sadie Young, a niece of Mrs. Latshaw, has been a member of their household for more than fourteen years, and is a bright and accomplished young woman.

EDWARD J. WILLIAMS, of Whitaker, Pa., a prominent citizen and a skilled employe of the Homestead steel works, was born at Irwin, Westmoreland Co., Pa., May 1, 1872, son of William and Jane (Evans) Williams, natives of Wales. His father came to the United States about 1867, located in Westmoreland county, and there engaged in coal mining until 1885, when he removed to Homestead, where he has since been employed in the steel works. The elder Williams is the father of five children, viz.: Edward J., Thomas, John, Albert and Hannah. Edward J. Williams was reared in Westmoreland and Allegheny counties, educated in the public schools, and, with the exception of two years, 1892-93, when he was with the Illinois steel company, has been an employe of the Homestead steel works since 1885. He was married, on June 19, 1898, to Maggie, daughter of James and Ellen (Calnan) Barrett, residents of Homestead, and to Mr. Williams and his wife have been born two children, viz.: William and Mildred May. Mr. Williams is a member of the Odd Fellows, the Knights of the Maccabees and of the republican party. He is prominently identified with the affairs of the township, and, in 1903, was elected one of its auditors, evidence of the esteem and respect with which he is regarded by those who know him best—his neighbors and associates.

JOHN W. MOORE, of Glenfield, Pa., a highly-respected citizen and a prosperous farmer, was born in Allegheny county, Pa., Feb. 3, 1836, son of James and Letitia Moore. The father was born in Northumberland county, Pa., Feb. 3, 1791; married Letitia Young, in 1818, and had fourteen children, eleven of whom grew to maturity, viz.: Harvey, a prominent United Brethren minister, who for twenty years was in charge of a church of that denomination at Clearfield, Pa.; Sarah, Elisha, Thomas M., Eliza A., Margaret, Martha, Emily, John W., Amanda R. and Henry W., a soldier of the Civil war. Two of this large family still survive, namely, John W. and Henry. Their father died on Dec. 2, 1858, and is buried in the Blackburn cemetery, of Ohio township, and their mother, who was born in 1797, died on April 7, 1870. The grandfather of John W. Moore was one of the early settlers of Allegheny county, where he owned a large tract of land which was granted him by the government for his services as a member of the continental army during the American Revolution. John W. Moore was married to Mary A., daughter of James H. and Julia (Kittinger) Parsons, on Dec. 6, 1856, and to them have been born twelve children, viz.: two pairs of twins that died shortly after birth: James Milton, born Aug. 8, 1857; Emma Elizabeth, born Aug. 25, 1859; Ida Ella, born Jan. 2, 1862; George Washington, born April 17, 1864; Cora Dell, born Nov. 19, 1866; Mary Frances, born March 21, 1869; John Wesley, born July 8, 1874, and Robert Parsons, born March 29, 1877. James H. Parsons, who was born in Mifflin county, Pa., May 16, 1809, and died on Feb. 17, 1885, and his wife, who was born in Bellefonte, Centre Co., Pa., May 26, 1811, and died in 1896, were the parents of the following twelve children: John, Theodore, William, James F., Mary Amanda,

Lucinda Elizabeth, Catharine Nancy, Edward, Jacob, George W., Samuel Erastus and Allen Cross. Mr. and Mrs. Moore have twenty-three grandchildren, and are members of the Methodist Episcopal church, with which Mr. Moore has been connected in official capacities for nearly fifty years.

PHILIP C. BURKERT, of Glenfield, Pa., a valued employe of the Pittsburg forge and iron company, was born in Pittsburg, May 3, 1862, son of Christ and Christina Burkert. Mr. Burkert was educated in the public schools of Glenfield, spent his early life on a farm near there, and, in 1884, became an employe of the Pittsburg forge and iron company, with which concern he has since continued, and now occupies the responsible position of bolt-maker. He was married, in 1883, to Cathorina, daughter of John and Lottie Luntz, and to them have been born five children, viz.: Lottie and Christina, twins (deceased); Fred W., Cathorina M. and Anna Gertrude C. The father of Mrs. Burkert, John Luntz, was born in Bavaria, Germany, Oct. 23, 1827; came to America in 1853, and settled in Allegheny county, where he successfully followed agricultural pursuits. John Luntz was married to Charlotte Rothhaar, and to them were born six children, viz.: Magdalena (deceased), Caroline, Margaret, Cathorina, John S. and Adam H. Mrs. Luntz was born in Bavaria, Germany, April 20, 1837; came to America when quite young, and died at Glenfield, Pa., Jan. 30, 1896. John A. Luntz, grandfather of Mrs. Burkert, was born at Neustadt, Bavaria, Germany, in 1780, died in 1835, and is buried in the Schornweisach cemetery. John Rothhaar, the maternal grandfather of Mrs. Burkert, was also born in Bavaria, Aug. 30, 1802, where he married Katherine Miller, and came to America with his family, settling in Mifflin township. To them were born the following nine children: Christ, John, Catharine, Adam, Charlotte, Elizabeth, Margaret, Carolina and Jacob. Mr. Rothhaar died in Jefferson township, Aug. 10, 1868, and his wife, born May 19, 1805, died on the home farm on Feb. 22, 1866. Christ Burkert, father of the subject, was born in Würtemburg, Germany, in 1833; came to America when a young man, and settled in Allegheny county, where he pursued his trade of iron-working.

In 1871 he purchased a farm in Aleppo township, and died in Glenfield, Jan. 1, 1903. Christ Burkert married Christina, daughter of Josa and Christina Sinzinger, of Würtemburg, and to them have been born nine children, all but Philip C., Edward G. and William G. being deceased. Mrs. Christina Burkert died on July 19, 1894, in the sixty-fourth year of her life. His grandfather Burkert was killed while plying his vocation of a teamster by being accidentally thrown from his wagon, and his wife died at Temperanceville, Pa., in her eighty-fourth year.

MRS. AMELIA HAMILTON, daughter of James and Catharine Scott, was born on Neville island, Dec. 13, 1818. Her father, James Scott, of Scotch lineage, was born in Brownsville, Pa., and died in Marietta, Ohio, in his eighty-seventh year. He was the father of eighteen children, twelve of whom lived to rear families of their own. The twelve were: Sarah, Nancy, Alexander, James, Mary, Adam and Maxwell (twins), Amelia, Elsie, Ellen, Catharine and Margaret, all living to be more than fifty years old. James and Catharine Scott had over 100 grandchildren. Mrs. Catharine Scott was the daughter of William and Mary Hughey, of Irish descent. They came from Ireland in the early history of the United States, and settled first in New Jersey, removing later to Robinson township, Allegheny county, where he purchased a large farm. Mr. and Mrs. Hughey were among the thrifty and energetic people of their time, and both lived to see more than three-score years. In religious belief they were Presbyterians. Mrs. Amelia Hamilton was married, Sept. 6, 1843, to James H. Hamilton, of Neville township, and to them were born six children, James A., David D., Mary C. and Hutchinson (all now deceased), Mrs. Nancy A. Kirk, of Allegheny city, and Miss Lydia J. Hamilton, of Neville island. James H. Hamilton, son of David and Mary Hamilton, was born Dec. 20, 1813, and died Dec. 13, 1869, and was a lifelong resident of Neville island. He was a Presbyterian and very active in church work, having held the office of elder for many years. Nancy A., daughter of Amelia and James H. Hamilton, was married, on Sept. 14, 1865, to John M. Kirk, of Allegheny city, a widely-known carriage manufacturer, on

Arch street. He died Jan. 2, 1899 Mrs. Amelia Hamilton has six grandchildren and ten great-grandchildren, of whom the former are: Mrs. Amelia Erwin, of Baden, Pa.; James R. Kirk, of Neville island; Mrs. Geitz, of Allegheny city; Miss Bessie Kirk, Richard D. and W. H. Kirk, all of Allegheny city. The great-grandchildren are: Amelia Hamilton Erwin and James Andrew Erwin, of Baden; Hazel Amelia, Anna, Elizabeth and Thomas S. Kirk, of Neville island; Charles M., George R., Frederick and Richard A. Geitz, all of Allegheny.

JOHN E. SCHELL, of Coraopolis, Pa., a prosperous oil producer, was born in Perry township, Clarion Co., Pa., Sept. 6, 1859, and is the son of James A. and Rachel E. (Bell) Schell. He is the second in order of birth of ten children, eight of whom are living, and, besides himself, are: Lloyd M., William A., James N., Penola M., Florence and Alice (who are twins), and Ida E. Both parents were natives of Pennsylvania, as were his ancestors for many years. His father was a pioneer in the oil business, living until April 20, 1902, when he died at the age of seventy-two years. He was a republican and a Presbyterian, and is survived by his widow, who is now in her seventy-third year. John E. Schell attended the schools of his native township until his eighteenth year, when he went to work in the oil fields of Clarion county, and there remained until he was twenty years of age. Then he went to McKean county, where he was engaged in the same occupation for nine years; later spent a year in the oil fields of Washington county; then came to Coraopolis, where he was a partner of E. A. Culbertson until 1898. In the spring of 1899 he organized the Schell oil and gas company, and since has managed its affairs with skill and ability. This company owns, among its holdings, leases on several hundred acres of land in Monroe county, Ohio. Mr. Schell was married, in 1886, to Ella F. Culbertson, of Rimersburg, Pa., and their wedded life has been an unusually happy one. Mr. Schell is a member of the democratic party, and is a Knight Templar Mason and belongs to the Mystic Shrine. He is a stockholder in the Ohio Valley trust company, a director in the Coraopolis savings and trust company, president of the Coraopolis industrial company, and is prominent in financial circles. Mr. Schell has passed through many trying ordeals in a business way, coming to Coraopolis with a comparatively small sum of money and losing his home by fire shortly afterwards. Nothing daunted by these disasters, he set to work to restore his broken fortunes, and succeeded so admirably that to-day he is reckoned as one of the substantial men of the borough.

JAMES H. GREEN, a prominent photographer and dealer in photograph supplies, of Braddock, Pa., was born in Staffordshire, England, on Feb. 14, 1854. He is a son of John and Louisa (Howells) Green, both natives of Staffordshire. The father was born in 1821, and was a roller by trade, being the manager of a mill there. He came to America in 1879, the family soon following, and settled in Scottdale, Westmoreland Co., Pa., where he engaged in the same business. The mother was a daughter of Elisha Howells, born in 1824, and was the mother of eleven children, five of whom are living. Mr. Green was a man beloved by every one in his neighborhood, and was familiarly called "Father Green," on account of his genial disposition. James H. Green was educated in the public schools until he reached the age of fourteen years, and was then bound out as an apprentice to John W. Bates, where he remained three years, working at the photograph business. He then went into the iron mills with his father, and in the five years that he was there, learned the trade of his father, that of a roller. Mr. Green returned to his former occupation, and finished learning the trade, and, in 1886, formed a partnership with Mr. Joseph Johnson, under the firm name of Green & Johnson, conducting a flourishing business in Scottdale for a number of years. In 1891 Mr. Green opened a fine studio in Pittsburg, but lost everything by fire in less than a year. This was most discouraging and sufficient cause to make many men give up entirely, but having the true English grit in his make-up, he started anew, opening a gallery in Wilkinsburg, one in Braddock, and later one in Homestead, all three thriving from the first. Mr. Green now operates the galleries at Braddock and Homestead, with a fine patronage, having sold the Wilkinsburg gallery to his son-in-law, F. E.

Bingaman. Mr. Green was married, in 1873, to Sophia Parfitt, a daughter of Abraham and Mary Parfitt, of Pensnett, England, and twelve children came to bless their union, only three of whom are living: Mary, wife of F. E. Bingaman; John W., of Edgewood, and Miss Violet. Mr. Green is a member of Marion lodge, No. 526, F. and A. M.; the Tribe of Ben-Hur, and the Woodmen of the World. Mr. and Mrs. Green and family belong to the Baptist church at Wilkinsburg. He has a fine residence in Edgewood, where he and his family enjoy home comforts.

JOHN WACHTER, of Glenfield, Pa., a prominent citizen and a prosperous farmer of Ohio township, was born in that township, Aug. 8, 1851, son of John P. and Frances Wachter. Mr. Wachter was educated in the public schools of Allegheny county, and has devoted his entire attention to farming, of which occupation he has made a complete success, and is one of the leading and best-informed farmers of that section of the county. John P. Wachter, father of the subject of this sketch, was born in Baden, Germany, in 1801, and came to America in 1847, settling on the place where his son now resides. He was a miller by trade, but after coming to America, followed farming until his death, in 1873, at the age of seventy-two years. His remains are buried in the Catholic cemetery at Glenfield. His mother's maiden name was Hout, and she was born on Feb. 14, 1807, and died in 1883. The paternal great-grandfather of the subject was a noted soldier, and served under the great Napoleon on his invasion of Russia, when the flower of the chivalry of "La Belle France," which had conquered most of the armies of the civilized world, was withered by the rigors of the northern climate. John Wachter was married, Jan. 9, 1877, to Minnie, daughter of Amon Lutz, and they have had four children born to them, viz.: George, born April 5, 1878; Charlie, born April 3, 1879; Joseph, born April 17, 1881, and Rosa, born Sept. 6, 1884. Mr. Wachter is widely known in Ohio township, and is very popular with all classes, having been honored with election to all the important positions within the gift of the township, and at the present writing is treasurer of the board of education and tax collector of Ohio township. He is a member of

St. Mary's Catholic church, which he has served in official capacities, and is highly regarded by his neighbors and friends as a man of fine judgment and undoubted business ability.

GEORGE H. HARVEY, resident of Glenfield, son of William M. and Charlotte V. Harvey, was born in Washington, D. C., Nov. 15, 1863, and educated in the public schools of Washington and of New York city. His vocation is that of patent attorney and draftsman. He was married to Anna P. Schulte, and to them were born two children, Aurela C. and James M. Mr. Harvey is a resident of the borough of Glenfield, and has been prominently identified in its official relations, having been a member of the council, board of education, and burgess. Perhaps Mr. Harvey is best known as a genius, having come before the public as the inventor of four patents—the first, a thread protector, used exclusively by the United States steel company, of New York; second, the Harvey system of burning oil, used principally by manufacturers; third, the process of manufacturing gas, and fourth, the Harvey system of making window glass. William M. Harvey, father of the subject of this sketch, son of George Harvey, was born in Washington, D. C. He was a contractor by occupation, leaving it long enough to render his country signal service in the Civil war. He was married to Charlotte May, eleven children being born to this union. Charlotte (May) Harvey, a Virginian by birth, was the daughter of Francis Russell May, a descendant of Lord Russell, and a veteran in the War of 1812. Mr. May was connected for fifty years with the sergeant-general's department of the United States army. He died in 1881 in his eighty-seventh year. The Harveys were among the first settlers of Maryland, being in Lord Baltimore's fleet, which landed first in Virginia in 1632. The Mays, the ancestry on the mother's side, were also early pioneers of the United States. Their first appearance was as traders, about the year 1607.

DAVIDSON DUFF (deceased), son of William and Margaret (Boggs) Duff, was born Sept. 14, 1814, in Ohio township, on what is known as the Duff farm, or "Deer Park." He was educated in the schools of his own township and in the city of Pittsburg, but spent his entire life on the farm, his attention being exclusively given to that occupation. He was married to Mary Mitchell, July 18, 1837, and to them were born eight children: James H., Margaret A., Sarah, William, Caroline, Isabella B., David and Wilton R. Mr. Duff was for thirty years justice of the peace of Ohio township. He was one of its most popular and esteemed residents, being never defeated for office, and elected to all the important ones in his township. For many years he was a member of the board of education. He and his wife were charter members of the United Presbyterian church of Mt. Nebo, of which he was also a trustee. He died Feb. 29, 1896. His wife, Mary (Mitchell) Duff, was the daughter of Harry and Margaret Mitchell, and was born in Ireland, May 8, 1814. She came to this country with her parents in 1835; she was also a very enthusiastic church worker and the embodiment of a noble Christian character. She died May 2, 1902, in her eighty-ninth year. William Duff, father of the subject of this sketch, was born in Ireland, May 6, 1783, coming to this country at three years of age. His father, James Duff, settled first in Westmoreland county, removed to Allegheny county about the year 1800, and bought a farm of 150 acres, joining Dixmont. He died in 1863 on the Duff farm. He came to America in 1786, and from that date the history of this family begins in America. William Duff was one of the first settlers in Allegheny county. On a journey on foot to Ohio in search of a farm, he spent the night at an Indian camp, where he met with many thrilling experiences which the family has often heard him relate. For a long time he lived on the Duff farm in a log cabin, a structure considered in pioneer days a great luxury. He was a very generous-hearted man, and was a Presbyterian in religious views, attending church at Robinson's Run. At the time the church at Mt. Nebo was built, he became a member there, and remained so until his death, which occurred Jan. 18, 1863. He was the father of three children, James, Jane and Davidson. James Duff was a soldier in the

Civil war, enlisting Aug. 31, 1861, in Company B, 4th Pennsylvania cavalry. He was engaged in a number of important battles, as the Seven Days' battle and Antietam, was taken prisoner at White Sulphur Springs, Oct. 12, 1863, and died in Andersonville prison Sept. 12, 1864. Mrs. Margaret (Duff) Graff, the only surviving member of the Duff family, was born Jan. 21, 1842, and resides on the old homestead. She was educated in the schools of her own township, and was married, June 15, 1882, to David Graff, of Tarentum. He was a farmer in his early manhood, but later became engaged in the oil business as driller. He was of German-Irish extraction, and died March 19, 1892. Mrs. Graff is a member of the United Presbyterian church at Mt. Nebo, and is one of its faithful and earnest workers. The Duff family is one of the substantial and trusty families, being known for their honesty and fair dealings in business, and their unquestionable character. Sarah Duff was married, May 30, 1867, to George W. Crawford, and to them was born one child, Harry D. Mrs. Crawford was also a Presbyterian, and died Nov. 12, 1872. David Duff was married to Mary Hamilton, Jan. 13, 1873, and to them were born six children, James S., Olive B., Harry L., Pearl A., Margaret E. and Elmer I. David Duff succeeded his father as justice of the peace in Ohio township, which office he held at the time of his death, Aug. 14, 1897.

FREDERICK TSCHUME, a prominent wholesale liquor merchant of Allegheny city, Pa., and member of the select council from the fourteenth ward, was born in the city of Pittsburg in 1854. When he was about six years of age his parents, the late Samuel and Mary Tschume, removed to Allegheny city, where Frederick acquired his education in the public schools and a private German school. After leaving school, he learned the drug business, in which he continued for six years, when he became associated with J. J. Staud as a salesman. He followed this business for about ten years, when he withdrew and started a grocery on East street. In September, 1902, he retired from the grocery, but continued the wholesale liquor business, in which he had previously become interested. His place of business is at No. 2316

East St. Politically, Mr. Tschume is a republican. He served for three terms as school director, and, in 1897, he was elected to the select council. At the expiration of his term he was re-elected, and is now serving his third term. In the council he is a member of the committees on public works, public safety and grade crossings. He was married to Miss Elizabeth Kanz, of Allegheny city, and to this marriage four children have been born, viz.: Flora, Elizabeth, Stella and Fred, Jr. Mr. Tschume is a member of the Pittsburg court, Independent Order of Foresters, and of St. Peter's Lutheran church. His record as a councilman has been indorsed by the people, as can be seen by his re-election, and in his private business he is regarded as one of the substantial men of the city.

GEORGE THEIN, of Glenfield, Pa., a prosperous and successful farmer of Aleppo township, was born there, Nov. 16, 1848, son of George and Margaret Thein, both natives of Bavaria, Germany, who came to America in 1847, and settled on the farm where their son now resides. His paternal grandfather was a farmer of Germany, who accompanied his son to the United States, and died in Allegheny county at the advanced age of eighty-two years. George Thein, the elder, was the father of four children, viz.: George, Charlie, Anton and Maggie. He died on Nov. 2, 1887, his wife having previously died, the date of her death being May 16, 1882. George Thein, the son, has devoted his entire business career to farming, and has made a great success of his vocation, now owning a splendid farm, equipped with all modern appliances and in every way thoroughly high-class. He was married, on June 5, 1873, to Mary M., daughter of Armond Lutz, her father having died on May 16, 1897, and her mother in 1892. To them have been born seven children, viz.: Margaret, born March 4, 1874; Mary A., born Nov. 20, 1876; John H. and Rosa, twins, born Feb. 12, 1880; Anna L., born Dec. 14, 1881; Elizabeth R., born Feb. 14, 1887, and Frank J., born Oct. 27, 1888. Mrs. Thein is one of a family of eleven children, she having had seven sisters and three brothers, and is in every way a most estimable woman. Mr. Thein served several years as a member of the board of education of Aleppo township, and also held the position of trustee in St.

Mary's church, of Glenfield. He is a successful business man, a courteous gentleman, and a prominent and influential citizen, and in many ways has contributed to the advancement and prosperity of that section of Allegheny county.

DR. JAMES E. MORROW, principal of the Allegheny high school, was born in Brooke county, Va. (now Hancock county, W. Va.), March 28, 1837, and is the son of Alexander Morrow. He was graduated from Jefferson college in 1856, A. B., with an A. M. in 1875, and a Ph. D. in 1889. He began teaching in 1856, studied law and was licensed in December, 1859, and practiced until the beginning of the Civil war, when he enlisted as private, serving as such and as a sergeant until Feb. 20, 1862, when he was promoted to second lieutenant, a little later first lieutenant, and in 1863 was promoted to the rank of captain of Company F, 1st Virginia volunteer infantry, and was on staff duty until his discharge, Dec. 10, 1864. After the war, he resumed his teaching, being principal of the fifth ward schools in Allegheny from 1879 to 1889. He then became principal of the Pennsylvania State normal school at Slippery Rock, which he organized in March, 1889; and in 1891 was elected teacher, and in 1892 principal, of the Allegheny high school. Mr. Morrow was married, in 1867, to Clara J. Johnson, a daughter of John J. and Rebecca M. Johnson, of Cumberland, Md., the latter now living, at the age of eighty-nine years, with Dr. and Mrs. Morrow, in Allegheny city. To this union were born eight children, three of whom, Fred, Earle and Ralph, are deceased; Agnes, the wife of Richard B. Scandrett, Esq.; Jay J., who is captain of United States engineers; Alice, a teacher in the third ward schools, and Dwight W., a graduate of Amherst, Mass., now of Englewood, N. J., a member of the New York city bar and connected with the firm of Simpson, Barnum, Thatcher & Bartlett, Broad Exchange building, New York city; and Hilda, wife of Rev. Edwin Linton McElwaine, Presbyterian minister, of Emlenton, Pa.

PROF. JOHN A. JOHNSTON, principal of the fourth ward school, No. 2, Allegheny, Pa., was born at Brownsville, Pa., and is a son of William H. Johnston, a well-known contractor of building operations in that section of the country. He attended the public schools of his native town and the Millersville State normal, of which institution he is a graduate. After teaching two years in the soldiers' orphans' school at Uniontown, he became principal of schools at Belle Vernon, then at West Newton, Westmoreland county, leaving the latter place to become principal of the Johnstown high school. In January, 1888, he resigned to accept his present position. Professor Johnston is a brother of Prof. Edward P. Johnston, of the seventh ward schools. Professor Johnston stands as one of the leading educators of the city, and his long experience and faithful devotion to the cause of good schools, have made him an influence and a factor in educational circles second to none. On April 5, 1900, he was married to Miss Isabelle Hunter Robertson, a daughter of Rev. William and Agnes (Haddow) Robertson, a United Presbyterian minister living a retired life at East End, Pittsburg. Mr. and Mrs. Johnston have two children, John Adelbert and Janet Margretta. He and his family are members of the Episcopal church.

JOHN FAIRFIELD, of Hites, Pa., a prosperous farmer, was born in Pittsburg, Pa., May 8, 1835, son of Richard and Prudence (Griffin) Fairfield, both natives of Ireland, who came to Pittsburg in 1832 and there remained until 1851, when they removed to a farm of 127 acres which they had purchased in East Deer township. In 1863 they returned to Pittsburg and lived in that city until their deaths. They had a family of seven children, four of whom survive their parents. Richard Fairfield was a whig, later a republican, and owned property in Pittsburg, Hatfield and elsewhere. He and his wife were prominently identified with the Methodist church, of which they were leading members. John Fairfield was reared in Pittsburg, educated in the public schools of that city, and began his business career hauling coal in that city. In 1851-2 he came on the farm where he now resides, has followed general farming, and makes a specialty of breeding Chester white hogs. Mr. Fairfield is a republican, served one term as assessor, and for thirteen years he has been school director. He was married, in 1862, to Eliza J., daughter of John C. and Catherine (Jones) Stephens, both reared and educated in their native country of England, and came to the United States in 1837. John C. Stephens purchased a farm in West Deer township in 1845; there his wife died in 1852, and the same year he removed to Ohio, where he resided until his death in 1857. Mr. and Mrs. Fairfield are the parents of nine children, three deceased. The living are: Robert H., George R., John C., Florence, Alma M. and Olive A. Mr. Fairfield was one of the first grand jurymen that sat in the new court-house at Pittsburg, the year of the centennial of the settlement of Allegheny county.

DAVID REEL, Jr., a prominent citizen of Ross township, is a descendant of Casper Reel, one of the pioneers of Allegheny county. It is worthy of remark that the first settlers of Ross township were generally men of sterling worth. They were just the men best fitted to hew their way through the forests of the new country, and were morally, physically and intellectually endowed to successfully lay the solid foundations for the future generations to permanently rest upon, as well as for the greatness of our country. Physically, they were stalwarts, capable of enduring the hardships that confronted them in the gigantic labors that lay before them. Being energetic, they persevered, and the giant oaks fell before them, to be replaced by beautiful green fields of grain and vegetation. Orchards and vineyards were planted, and thus was agriculture and horticulture firmly established. Morally, they were Christians, and the same energetic spirit was manifested by them in the establishment of churches or places of worship, as well as in worldly affairs. Intellectually, the needs of education were not lost sight of, and school-houses were built of such rude material as the forests furnished for their construction. Yet, rude as they were, the principles taught in those log-cabin school-houses, were the good seeds sown that were destined to crop out in the present and future greatness of our country. Such were the toils and labors of our ancestors. What of the generations that have descended from these nobilities of the young republic? Have they taken up the work where the fathers laid it down? Has the same sterling and progressive spirit animated the children along the lines of demarkations? Have the moral and the intellectual qualifications established by the patriot fathers been fostered and cultured? the answer most emphatically is "Yes." The children have taken it up where the fathers laid it down, and have placed it upon a higher plane. The succeeding generations, upon their advent, have taken it up, and are pressing firmly forward and upward, bearing aloft the standard of this mighty republic, until it is honored and feared by all the nations of the earth. All honor and love is due these dear, brave, old patriot fathers. Peaceful be their silent slumber. Memory of them will ever be cherished and honored by succeeding generations, who will live and flourish upon the fruits of their labor.

Casper Reel (great-grandsire), the first settler of Ross township, was born in Frankfort, Germany, May 11, 1742. He first located in Lancaster county, Pa., where he became a soldier in the Revolutionary war, and served under the command of General Washington. He participated in many of the varied engagements of the war, among which was the battle of Brandywine. A few of his old relics are still in the possession of some of his grandchildren, among which is his old watch, now in the possession of his granddaughter, Almatia L. Reel, and his Bible—which he carried through the war, and which was not only a saviour of the soul, but of the body as well, for it warded off a bullet that otherwise would have killed him—is still in the possession of his grandson, Jacob G. Reel. He came to Allegheny county in 1783, and when the assembly (legislature) passed the land grant act, giving to settlers large tracts of land upon which to settle, he took up a large square tract of land, containing about 1,000 acres, which afterwards proved to be the choicest land in Ross township. It is authoritatively stated that he measured it with a grape vine. In making a selection of land he had the choice of the site upon which Allegheny city is built, but deeming the land unfit for agricultural purposes on account of its low, swampy nature, he proceeded northward about eight miles from Fort Pitt and located the present Reel farm, which has become famous as the choicest farm in the township. Recently a large portion of this farm was sold to a wealthy land company, who intended laying it out in large town lots, the object being to establish a wealthy suburban town and to connect it by electric railway with the city. In the spring of 1792 he built a log cabin upon his tract and planted some peach and apple seeds, but the Indians became troublesome, having come in large numbers from the Ohio territory, so he was compelled to abandon his cabin and return to Fort Pitt. About this time General Wayne, with 3,000 troops, was sent out against the Indians, and so completely routed and defeated them that they never gave the settlers any further trouble. In the year 1795 Mr. Reel returned to his land and was delighted to find his fruit seeds had produced fine young trees. Some of the peach trees were producing fruit. He at once built a log house and moved his family into it, and this became his permanent abode. The road cut through the forest to reach his land was continued by other settlers, and afterwards became the Franklin road. Previous to his location here he had been an extensive trapper, and was an expert fur-dresser, from which occupation he had made a considerable sum of money. Fur-bearing animals were plentiful, especially along the Beaver river, where he had many traps set. He frequently visited these traps by a canoe down the Ohio river. Once, upon returning from his traps in company with his brother-in-law, John Wise, he was hailed by a white man, who, in a pleading manner, wanted to be taken on board; but instead of heeding the appeals of the white man, he gradually headed his canoe to the opposite shore, and at the same time kept up an evasive conversation about the Indians. His brother-in-law insisted that they should go to his relief, but was ordered to lie down in the canoe. Scarcely had he done so, when the Indians rose from their ambush and fired upon the canoe. Fortunately for the occupants, they escaped unharmed, although the canoe was hit in several places. This man with whom he had the conversation was Simon Girty, the Indian renegade.

Previous to 1795 it was the custom of the settlers to assist each other in the raising of their log houses, and for this purpose there was a gathering of the settlers at the Winebiddle farm. Among the number was an Indian, who professed to be friendly with the whites, but when he finally came under the influence of the firewater, drunk on such occasions, his Indian propensities became obvious. His bragging about the number of white scalps he had taken so enraged Casper Reel that he sprang upon the Indian, and with one slash of his knife cut off his ear so quickly that the Indian scarcely knew who did it.

Casper Reel was the first collector north of the Allegheny river, his territory extending to the lakes. He was married, March 2, 1784, to Elizabeth Wise, who was born Oct. 2, 1760, in Lancaster, Pa., and died Aug. 20, 1843. They had ten children, namely: Mary, Jacob, John, Daniel, Conrad, David and Casper, Jr. (twins), William and a twin sister, who died in infancy, and Elizabeth (Mrs. George Quaill). In giving the order of births of this family to a former historian of the county, Casper, Jr., was mentioned before David, when, in fact, David was born several hours before Casper. This correction places David, instead of Casper, as the first white child born north of the Allegheny river. The order of their deaths is as follows: In their younger ages, Daniel, Jacob and John—the latter, while serving as a soldier in the War of 1812, died at Fort Maumee Rapids, April 6, 1813, aged twenty-three years— and William, who was thrown from a fractious horse. The more recent deaths have been those of David, in his seventieth year; Conrad, in his seventy-sixth year; Mary (Mrs. Johnson), in her ninety-sixth year, and Casper, Jr., in his eighty-ninth year.

After Casper Reel had moved his family to his new home, he turned his attention to clearing off the land. Gradually he became thoroughly established upon the farm, though not without the privations and inconveniences that are always connected with the settlement of new portions of the country. Happily, they were not of long duration. Fur animals becoming scarce, trapping was abandoned, and consequently the settlement of the country became more rapid. Isaac Ritche came next, taking up a large tract of land upon the west side of Casper Reel's farm. Others followed in rapid succession, among whom were the Morrows, the Goods, the Hilands, the McKnights and many others. The town (Pittsburg) was much more rapidly settled; in fact, the settlement of the town was so rapid that it actually became a market for much of the surplus products of the land that had now become cultivated by these early settlers. Thus were they all brought into the channels of successful progression. Casper Reel was considered the wealthiest settler in Ross township, and was a man of great influence among the early settlers, to whom he often loaned money. He was a most successful farmer and fruit culturist. Through his influence and foresight the Highland Presbyterian church was established and located upon its present site. In after years the location of this church proved to be a most central one, and by the continuous accessions of settlers it became a numerous body, although it passed through many of the vicissitudes that follow in the wake of religious institutions, and it is still a stanch old church, and at present bids fair to be a church for generations to come. The large burial ground attached to the church was the free, common burial ground for all, and in it lie the bodies of many of the former worshipers, but of late years the ground has been greatly improved and a better system adopted. The oldest person buried here is John McKnight, aged 101 years. In 1795, at the farm residence of Casper Reel, occurred the first marriage in Ross township. It was the union of Christopher Rineman and Charlotte Zimmerman. The ceremony was performed by Squire Robinson, father of the late Gen. William Robinson, of Allegheny city, and the wedding present was a pailful of cherries. The death of Casper Reel occurred Oct. 10, 1824. He was buried in a selected plot of ground upon the farm where, in after years, his wife and sister-in-law and a part of the family were also buried. His grave is still pointed out to succeeding generations.

David Reel, Sr., was born Jan. 22, 1795, upon the first farm that was settled in Ross township, north of Fort Pitt. Notwithstanding the very meager facilities and the limited means for education, Casper Reel provided his children with an education sufficient for the transaction of business in the times in which they lived. When David had grown to manhood, he engaged in the shipping of merchandise from Philadelphia by wagon. He became one of the most successful men in the business, being entrusted with large sums of money to pay for goods bought in Philadelphia. The business of shipping goods to and from Philadelphia by wagons became immense, but when the canal was built it ceased altogether. The next business to engage his attention was delivering mail between Pittsburg and Butler by stage-coach After continuing the business successfully for some years, he married Isabella Wiley, the daughter of sterling parents, and after the death of his father he returned to the old homestead, to improve and cultivate that portion of it received from his father, nearly all of which was heavily timbered. He built a log house in the midst of the forest, and, like his father, began life in the woods. As charcoal was in great demand at that time in Pittsburg, he manufactured much of his timber into it. By this he was enabled not only to clear off the ground for cultivation, but to make some money besides.

Four children were born in this forest home. They were:

George Washington, David, Jr., Mary (who died in infancy), and Wiley. The oldest son, William, was born previous to the return to the farm. It is worthy of note here that in the latter years in which he lived in this log house it became famous for the establishment of Methodism in that part of the county. About the first Methodist camp-meetings held in western Pennsylvania were on a portion of this and the adjoining farm, belonging to George Quaill. As a result of these camp-meetings, there was established a society of worshipers upon a more secure foundation, the outgrowth of which is the Methodist Episcopal church of Bellevue. The society formerly worshiped in the little old school-house in Jack's Run. Ministers were annually sent by the conference of the Methodist Episcopal church to take charge of the circuit, which included Jack's Run. Usually two were sent, one being a single man, who sought his home among the membership. Among the number of single men who were sent to this circuit, who made their home principally at David Reel's, were John J. Jackson, Hiram Miller and Joseph Horner, D. D. The latter remained two years, and made his home entirely with David Reel. He became as one of the family circle, and was loved as a son and brother. At present he is still living, and with pleasure refers back to those days as being the most pleasant and happiest years in his life.

David Reel, being successful in his labors upon the farm, built a more modern house upon another part of it. This house is noted for the superior quality of lumber from which it is built, it having been selected from the choicest lumber of the yards, which, in those days, contained lumber of a better quality than that of the present day. In July, 1852, he moved into the new house, accompanied by Joseph Horner, who remained with them the balance of his second conference year. After having lived in the new house for a few years, he purchased a house and lot in the town of Perrysville. This he greatly improved and moved into, having retired from actual labor upon the farm. After spending some years of peaceful rest from toil and care, he died, and was buried in the old Highland church cemetery. His wife, who survived him some six years, was buried by his side.

William Valentine, the oldest son, was a soldier in the 136th regiment, commanded by Col. Thomas M. Bayne, and participated in the battles of Fredericksburg, Antietam and Chancellorsville. At the expiration of the term of service, which was nine months, he returned, and was afterwards married to Elizabeth Spence, to whom was born a son, Wiley Graham. After the death of David

Reel, Sr., William moved to the farm upon which the new house was built. Shortly after moving to the farm, his wife died. His second marriage to Elizabeth Jackman, daughter of Andrew Jackman, a highly-respected farmer of Ohio township, occurred a few years later, and by this second marriage there were born five children, namely, John J., Mary E., Isabella E., Myrtle E. and Matilda Jane. Mary, the oldest daughter, was married to Marion Taylor, of Ohio, on Jan. 1, 1902, and to them a daughter was born. William Reel is still living upon the farm, and is highly respected as being one of the oldest settlers in Ross township. Religiously, he is a Methodist, being for many years a worthy trustee in the Methodist Episcopal church of Bellevue. Politically, he is a republican. George W., the second son, and Wiley, the youngest son, enlisted in Company E, 101st regiment, and participated in the various engagements about Newbern. They were finally captured and sent to Andersonville prison, where George died. Wiley, who survived the inhuman treatment of the prison, was accidentally drowned near Fortress Monroe, on his way home. David, Jr., was born Jan. 1, 1837, and was educated in the public schools, after which he took a commercial course in the Iron City college, of Pittsburg. When the Civil war broke out, and the first call for troops was made, he enlisted in a company commanded by Thomas M. Bayne. They were sent to camp at Wheeling, but the quota being filled, the company was ordered to return to Pittsburg, where it disbanded. Returning home, he lived with his parents, who were then residing in Perrysville. On Sept. 13, 1866, he married Annie Redpath, the oldest daughter of John Redpath, one of the most successful and influential farmers of McCandless township. After his marriage he moved to Allegheny city. His stay there was of short duration. According to the urgent request of his parents, that he should live with or near them, he returned to Perrysville. After the birth of his oldest son, Ellis, which occurred on Aug. 29, 1867, he moved into the old log house in which he was born, and lived there until the new house, which was then being erected, was finished. At the death of his father, David, Sr., this portion of the estate fell to him, and here he has since resided. There were subsequently born to him two sons, Watson, on Dec. 7, 1869, and Casper, in October, 1875. David Reel, Jr., became one of the most extensive and successful fruit culturists in the township. Many articles were written by him and published in the various publications of the county. Among the most noted articles written by him is one entitled "The Cause, the Effect and the Suggested Remedy for the Pear Blight," published in the National Stockman and Farmer, of Pittsburg. It attracted the attention of many of the principal agricultural writers of the country, who spoke very highly of the article.

Religiously, David Reel, Jr., is a Methodist. He was the principal leader in the removal of the society from Jack's Run to the school hall in Bellevue. In a meeting shortly after the society was located in the school hall, he, in company with six other trustees, decided to build a church, and, to make a beginning at once, they entered into a joint note of $1,000. A building committee was appointed, among whom was David Reel, Jr., and upon him devolved the entire charge and superintendence of the work. How far the enterprise was successful from beginning to finish may be seen by the church of to-day, which is among the most substantial appointments of the Pittsburg conference. He declares the building up of this church to be the best work of his life

Ellis, the first son of David, Jr., was married to Margaret Kercher, a most influential member of the Presbyterian church of Avalon. The wedding took place Feb. 29, 1899. Watson A., the second son, was married to Elizabeth Preston, daughter of D. I. Preston, of Bellevue. This marriage occurred Nov. 15, 1899. To him was born a son, Charles Preston, on April 21, 1902. Ellis Reel is at present a house-painter and resides at Bellevue. Watson A. is a florist and fruit culturist on the farm. Casper is an artistic house-painter, and resides with his parents.

In politics, David Reel, Jr., was formerly a republican. He takes great pride in stating that Abraham Lincoln was the first president for whom he voted. Later he became a prohibitionist, and has been nominated by the party for the legislature in the seventh district.

The old log house which was built seventy-five years ago, the only log house in existence in that section of the country, has been substantially repaired, and with a little attention will stand the passage of time for another generation, as a relic of old times.

There is one notable feature of this family extending from Casper Reel, the great-grandfather, down to the fourth generation, including many of its branches, and that is the temperate and sober habits of which all are possessed.

To these grand old patriot fathers and settlers we owe much gratitude for the benefits, the blessings and the comforts we enjoy from the outgrowth of their toils and tribulations, in laying the foundation of this mighty republic.

JOSEPH P. HILLDORFER, who represents the tenth ward of Allegheny city, Pa., in the common council, is a fine example of a self-made man. He was born in the eighth ward of Allegheny city in 1871, and is the son of P. J. and Burga Hilldorfer, the former of whom died in 1881, and the latter in 1900. Eight months in the common schools comprises all the schooling of Joseph P. Hilldorfer, for upon the death of his father he took up the work of selling papers and blacking boots about the Allegheny and Pittsburg markets to assist his mother. He followed this business until he was twelve years old, when the butchers about the market began to employ him as errand boy. Here is where the inherent strength of character of Mr. Hilldorfer first began to be made manifest. When he was sent upon an errand he did not tarry by the wayside, and upon his return he always made a truthful report. After two years of this kind of service he found employment in the slaughter-house of one of the leading butchers, where he worked for three years. At the age of seventeen he was placed in charge of the killing and dressing of meats at the Western Pennsylvania hospital, being the youngest man who ever held that responsible position. In 1890 he left the hospital and went to the Pittsburg market as an employe, and three years later formed a partnership with John S. Wilson and went into business for himself. The firm of Wilson & Hilldorfer dissolved in 1899, and was succeeded by that of Hilldorfer & Allman, which still continues. Mr. Hilldorfer was elected, in February, 1903, as one of the republican candidates to represent the tenth ward in the common council, and upon the organization of that body, he was appointed upon the committees of public safety, charities, surveys and police, and was made chairman of the health committee. He is a life member of Allegheny lodge, B. P. O. Elks, and a member of Pittsburg Aerie, No. 76, Fraternal Order of Eagles. In 1890 Mr. Hilldorfer was married to Miss Alice Simpson, of Latrobe, Pa., and they have two children, Marie and Bennie. There is an example in the life of Mr. Hilldorfer that is worthy of the emulation of every young man. From the humble newsboy and bootblack he has risen to be one of the substantial business men of his native city, his only talisman being an untiring energy and a spotless integrity.

J. O. BROWN,
Recorder,
PITTSBURG, PA.

D. M. PITCOCK,
McKEESPORT, PA.

E. A. LAWRENCE,
Attorney,
SHARPSBURG, PA.

WILLIAM J. PARKER, a prominent citizen and the leading contractor and builder of the town of Avalon, Pa., was born in Findlay township, Allegheny Co., Pa., Jan. 5, 1855. His parents, Robert and Margaret (Ferguson) Parker, were natives of County Down, Ireland, but came to America in 1845, settling in Pittsburg, Pa. William is one of a family of seven children. His father, Robert Parker, was born in Ireland, and came to America the same year as his parents. He died while on his way back to Ireland on a visit, and his remains rest in the cemetery of Hillsboro, Ireland. Robert Parker was a shoemaker by trade, but owing to his failing health, he was advised to engage in farm work for the benefit from the outdoor air and exercise. Following this advice, he removed to Moon township, where he became a successful farmer, and afterwards achieved considerable reputation as a stock dealer. Much of the farm work and the responsibilities of the management fell upon William, thus restricting his opportunities to acquire an education, though he managed to attend, for a time, the schools of his native township. The lessons he learned in contact with the actual duties and demands of his father's business were perhaps more valuable to him in his life-work than mere book-learning would have been. At the age of twenty-one years he began learning the trade of carpenter, and being of a mechanical turn of mind, he soon became one of the best workmen in the county. In 1878 he formed a partnership with Herman Knoppf for the purpose of carrying on the business of contracting and building. This partnership lasted about four years, since which time Mr. Parker has conducted the business alone. His work has been confined mainly to the suburban towns about Pittsburg and Allegheny city. Avalon, the town in which he resides, has a population of over 4,000, yet a majority of the residences have been erected under his personal supervision. Honesty and punctuality have been his distinguishing characteristics throughout his entire business career, and his highest aim has been to bring to the town of Avalon a good class of citizens. His unselfish devotion to the public weal won for him the regard of his fellow-townsmen, and he has been called upon to serve as burgess and in the council, and has for several years been a member of the board of education.

In all matters pertaining to state or national politics, he is an unswerving republican, and he is an influential factor in determining the local policies of his party. Besides his large business as a contractor, Mr. Parker is interested in a number of other enterprises. He is a stockholder in the Bellevue realty, savings and trust company; the Allegheny fire insurance company, of Allegheny city; the Trilby mining company, of Idaho; the Ohio Valley building and loan association, of Avalon; the Frank Vogel company, manufacturers of pickles and preserves, in which he is also a director; the Masonic Hall association, of Allegheny city, and the Crawford County electric railroad company, of which he was one of the chief organizers. Mr. Parker is prominent in Masonic circles, being a member and past master of Allegheny lodge, No. 223, Free and Accepted Masons; a past high priest of Allegheny chapter, No. 217, Royal Arch Masons; member of Allegheny commandery, No. 35, Knights Templars, in which he is also one of the drill corps; Allegheny council; Pittsburg consistory, in which he holds the thirty-second degree, and Syria temple, Ancient and Accepted Nobles of the Mystic Shrine, in which he holds a life membership. He is also a life member, as well as a charter member, of Allegheny lodge, No. 339, B. P. O. Elks; West Bellevue council, No. 240, Junior Order of United American Mechanics, and Clifton lodge, No. 1066, Independent Order of Odd Fellows. On Dec. 30, 1886, he was married to Miss Emma J. Dickson, daughter of James Dickson, of Neville island. To this marriage there have been born seven children, viz.: Xenia B., William Jerome, Jr., Margaretta F., James Dickson, David La Verne, Samuel Hugh and Algernon Bell, the two last named being twins. Mrs. Parker has a natural talent in music, and was for a number of years instructor and organist in the Presbyterian church of Neville island.

THEO. TONNELE, son of J. L. and Katherine N. Tonnele, and for twenty years chemist for the W. Deweese-Wood company, now the American sheet steel company, was born in New York city in 1858. As a boy, he attended private schools, and completed his education at the Columbia school of mines, from which he was graduated in 1880. Upon graduation he worked as chemist for Professor Richets, of New York; two years for W. P. Shinn, at Wampum, Pa., and in 1882 came to McKeesport to enter the employ of the W. Deweese-Wood company in the same capacity. He has been in the employ of this company ever since, and during his long service has won the confidence of his employers by his ability and faithful attention to duty. Mr. Tonnele was married, in 1883, to Miss Isabella P. Mills, of Hastings-upon-Hudson, N. Y., and has one son, Theo. M. He is a member of McKeesport lodge, No. 136, B. P. O. Elks, of which he has served two terms as exalted ruler, and is also a member of the Knights of Malta. He also belongs to various clubs and societies, viz.: the Duquesne club, University club, Americus club, all of Pittsburg; the Pittsburg country club, the American society of mining engineers, the American association for the advancement of science, the Engineers' society of western Pennsylvania, and others. Mr. Tonnele is a republican in politics. He resides in the twentieth ward, Pittsburg. He is a Presbyterian in religious belief, and is a trustee of the church.

GEORGE H. CALVERT, of Etna, Pa., a well-known lawyer of Pittsburg, was born at Etna, Feb. 2, 1873, and is the son of Alexander H. and Jennie (Scott) Calvert. His father was a native of New Sheffield, Beaver Co., Pa., came to Etna in 1868, and for thirty-three years was pastor of the First United Presbyterian church of that city. George H. Calvert received his elementary education in the public schools of his native city, and was graduated in civil engineering from the Western university, of Pittsburg, in 1893. For one year he was engaged with the engineering department of the Pennsylvania & Lake Erie railroad, at Pittsburg; later matriculated at the Pittsburg law school, and was graduated from that well-known institution in 1897. During the time he was a student at the law school he devoted his leisure to reading in the office of Samuel McClay, a distinguished lawyer of Pittsburg, and on his admission to the bar, in 1898, began the practice of his profession in the office of Mr. McClay. In 1902 he removed to his present suite of offices at Nos. 601 and 603 Frick building, and is now enjoying a rapidly-increasing general practice. Mr. Calvert has two brothers: Henry S., political editor of the Pittsburg Leader, and J. Edward, a chemist of Pittsburg. Mr. Calvert is a member of the United Presbyterian church of Etna, the Royal Arcanum, the alumni association of the Western university, of Pittsburg, and is president of the alumni association of the Pittsburg law school. He is a member of the State bar association, is a republican, and at present is president of the school board of Etna. His maternal grandfather was John Scott, a distinguished jurist of Beaver county and a lawyer of exceptional ability. Mr. Calvert is well equipped for the arduous work of a legal career and is highly regarded as an advocate by the older attorneys of the Pittsburg bar.

JUSTUS SCHROEDEL, member of the common council of Allegheny city, Pa., from the thirteenth ward, was born in that city in 1871, and is therefore one of the youngest members of either branch of the council. His parents, John and Katherine Schroedel, are both deceased, the former dying in 1877 and the latter in 1889. Justus was educated in the public schools of the fourth ward, which he attended until he was ten years of age, and then arranged with the school board to take the instruction in German while he was engaged in selling papers. He was one of the boys that sold papers on the funeral train of President Garfield as it passed through Allegheny city. In 1890, in company with his two brothers, Philip and Jacob, he started the Schroedel & Seibel news agency in the East End, Pittsburg, devoting his entire attention to the building up of the concern. Mr. Schroedel takes an active interest in political matters, in which he is one of the republican leaders of the thirteenth ward. For several years he has represented his ward as a delegate in city and county republican conventions, and for the last six years he has been a member of the county committee. In February, 1903, he was chosen to represent the ward in the common council, where he has been honored by appointment on the committees on public safety, surveys and city digest. He is well known in the club life and fraternal organizations of the city, being a member of Lodge No. 319, Junior Order of United American Mechanics; Allegheny council, No. 229, National Union; the German mutual aid association; the German beneficial association, of Allegheny; Troy Hill Mannerchor; the Mount Troy hunting and fishing club, and the American social club of Allegheny. He is also a member of St. Peter's Lutheran church of Allegheny city. In 1892 Mr. Schroedel was married to Miss Katherine Dahla, of Allegheny city, and two children— Roy H. and Esther S.—have been born to this marriage. Mr. Schroedel is regarded as one of the wide-awake young business men of Allegheny, as well as one of the public-spirited citizens. When the reform movement was started in Allegheny county, he was made vice-chairman, a position he filled to the entire satisfaction of those engaged in the work, and he is now one of the committee of thirty-two to manage the county campaign in favor of good government. In this work he enjoys the full confidence of the people, and his name is frequently mentioned in connection with various offices as a possible and available candidate. These matters, however, do not disturb him in the least. The business of the news agency has grown to such proportions that it is on a well-paying basis, and requires the greater part of his time. Should the will of his fellow-citizens elevate him to a place of greater trust and responsibility than the one he now occupies, he will not be found wanting in either ability or sterling worth to meet the requirements of the situation.

WALTER ASTON, of Munhall, Pa., a skilled hammerman for the Homestead steel works, was born in Wolverhampton, Staffordshire, England, Dec. 16, 1860, son of Charles and Mary Aston. Mr. Aston was reared in Birmingham, England, educated in the public schools, and then served an apprenticeship of seven years at the silver-plating trade. In 1883 he came to the United States and located in Mifflin township, where he entered the employ of the Carnegie steel company as a blacksmith's helper, which position he filled for a short time, and was then transferred to the forging department, and has occupied his present position of hammerman for sixteen years. He was married, on April 6, 1886, to Annie C., daughter of Richard and Mary E. (Carnahan) Straney, of Elizabeth, Pa., her father a native of Ireland and her mother born at Elizabeth, Allegheny Co., Pa. Mr. Aston and his wife are the parents of the following six children: Ada M., William, Flora B., Walter, Earl F., and Cecelia. Mr. Aston is one of the substantial and progressive citizens of Mifflin township, and by industry and frugality has accumulated a fine competency. He is a member of the Episcopal church, the Odd Fellows and the Sons of St. George, and is assistant chief of the local fire company. His political affiliations are with the republican party, and, like all citizens interested in the proper government of the community, he is an active figure in public matters.

GEORGE A. GRABE, a well-known contractor and builder, and resident of the first ward, Wilkinsburg, Pa., was born in Butler county, of the same state, in 1854. He is a son of George G. and Elizabeth (Frieze) Grabe, both deceased, the father dying in April, 1903, and the mother in 1899. After attending the common schools of Butler county, where he obtained a good, practical education, he removed to Allegheny county and began his business career. In 1879 he went west, and from that time until 1887 followed the business of a contractor in Arizona and New Mexico. While a resident of Silver City, N. M., he was elected to represent one district in the city council. In 1890 he returned to Allegheny county, locating at Wilkinsburg. In 1882 he was married to Emma D. Rosenfelder, a daughter of Henry Rosenfelder, a prominent farmer of Allegheny county and a native of Germany. Mr. Grabe and his wife are the parents of eight children, seven of whom—four sons and three daughters—are still living, all single and at home. For twenty-eight years he has been a member of the Ancient Order of United Workmen, and for ten years has belonged to the Order of Heptasophs. He is also a member of St. Paul's Lutheran church. In politics he is an unswerving democrat, and is now serving as councilman from the first ward in the Wilkinsburg city council, being recently elected for a second term.

JAMES L. KELLY, one of the leading young business men of Allegheny city, Pa., and the popular representative of the eighth ward in the common council, was born in the first ward of Allegheny city in 1872, and is a son of James W. and Maria Kelly. When he was about a year old his parents removed to the second ward, where he received his primary education in the public school, after which he attended the Park institute. Upon leaving school he decided to learn his father's old trade—that of a slate-roofer—and he started in at fifty cents per week. The readiness with which he learned the business soon took him out of the fifty-cent class, however, and it was not long until he was receiving the regular wages of a journeyman. In 1901 he became a partner in the Schmidt roofing company, located at Nos. 1018 and 1020 Ohio St., and doing a general roofing business. Ever since reaching his majority, Mr. Kelly has taken an active part in political contests, co-operating with the republican party. He has been a persistent advocate of clean politics and an honest municipal government. In 1902 he was elected to the office of constable in the eighth ward, an office he still holds, but in which he is represented by George Wolf. In February, 1903, he was elected to represent the ward in the common council, where he is a member of the water, library and charity committees. He is a member of St. Peter's Catholic church and of Allegheny lodge, No. 19, Knights of St. George. He has been an active and influential member of the Slate and Tile Roofers' lodge, No. 2704, of Pittsburg, but has not affiliated with the order since he became a member of the firm, and is one of the youngest mechanics in his line of work in the two cities. At the time of his admission to this lodge he was one of the youngest members of the roofers' organization in the United States. For five years he filled the position of financial secretary of the lodge, and was for two years president. In 1899 he was married to Miss Annie Wildman, of Allegheny city, and both Mr. and Mrs. Kelly are universally respected by the best element of society in Allegheny city.

MILLARD FILMORE BAKER, of Glenfield, Pa., a prosperous ferryman on the Ohio river, was born at McKeesport, March 19, 1856, educated in the common schools, and began business life as a deck hand on a steamboat on the Ohio river. He followed that occupation for a number of years, and subsequently became a watchman, in which capacity he served on the steamers, "R. J. Grace," "N. J. Bigby," "Coal Valley" and "George Lyle," all four of which plied the Ohio river. Mr. Baker then began business on his own account as a gardener on Neville island, which he followed for three years; then for a year was in the employ of the Chartiers valley gas company, and since that time has been profitably engaged in his present business of ferryman. Mr. Baker has been married three times—first, to Anna Josephine Daily, in 1876, who died Sept. 2, 1885, by whom he had four children: Rhoda, Charley (deceased July 15, 1883), George and Clara; on the second occasion he was married to Alice Sarah Soult (deceased Oct. 5,

1896), who bore him one child, Alice, and his third marriage was with Alice Whiteman, by whom he had a daughter, Ella May. Mr. Baker is a member of the Junior Order of United American Mechanics, of which order he has served as warden, and is also a member of the Royal Arcanum. He has been successful in a business way, accumulated a competency, and is one of the substantial citizens of the community in which he resides.

CHARLES W. SIMON, one of the firm of M. Simon's Sons, planing-mill operators and lumber dealers, was born in Allegheny city, Pa., in 1862. He is a son of Michael and Marie Simon. For many years his father conducted the planing mill and lumber yard at the corner of Anderson and Robinson streets, in Allegheny city, Pa. He died in 1898, and his wife followed him in 1902. Charles Simon was educated in the public schools of the third ward, and at the age of fifteen went into the planing mill with his father. Upon the death of his father he formed a partnership with his three brothers—Harry, William and John—to continue the business, which they have done successfully, holding all the old customers and bringing to their support a number of new ones. All four of the brothers are skilled in the business, and punctuality in the execution of orders is one of the firm's distinguishing characteristics. Charles W. Simon is, in the highest sense of the term, a public-spirited citizen. He is deeply interested in all movements tending to promote the general prosperity of the city, and is always willing to lend his aid toward insuring their success. He is a republican in politics, and is usually found in the campaign working in behalf of his party candidates, but never at the expense of his private business. From 1889 to 1893 he was a member of the Allegheny city common council, and from 1897 to 1901 he represented the first district in the Pennsylvania legislature. In both these positions his public duties were discharged with the same zeal and fidelity that has marked his course in his personal affairs. He was married, in 1882, to Miss Elizabeth R. Bolster, of Allegheny city, Pa., and seven children have been born to their union. They are: Ada E., Elsa A., Clara M. (deceased), Elmer H., Herbert R., Charles W., Jr., and Leslie F. Mr. Simon holds membership in but one fraternal organization. He belongs to Allegheny lodge, No. 339, Benevolent and Protective Order of Elks, in which he is one of the influential members.

EDWARD WEAVER BOLLMAN, a shearman in the Homestead steel works, is a son of Andrew J. and Lizzie W. (Weaver) Bollman, both natives of Pennsylvania, but of German descent. Andrew Bollman is a wagon-maker by trade, and followed that occupation for many years. He is now residing at Freeport, Pa. Edward W. Bollman was born in Armstrong county, Pa., Jan. 26, 1861. He was reared in Armstrong and Butler counties, where he received the greater part of his education in the public schools. After leaving school, he served a three-year apprenticeship in his father's wagon shop, learning the trade of wagon-maker. In 1881 he went to Homestead and entered the employ of the Homestead steel works as a common laborer. Two months later he was transferred to the machine shops, and from there to the rail mill. From 1885 to 1888 he was employed in the steel mills near Wheeling, W. Va. He returned to the Homestead works, however, and since 1893 he has held the position of shearman in what is known as the twenty-eight-inch mill. Upon his return from Wheeling, in April, 1888, he located at Whitaker, where he has ever since lived. On Christmas day, 1899, he was married to Miss Sylvia M., daughter of William H. and Mary J. (Venaman) Marple, of McMechen, W. Va. Mr. Bollman is a democrat in politics, and is a member of Tent No. 425, Knights of the Maccabees.

CHARLES O. DEVERTS, select councilman for the fifteenth ward of Allegheny city, Pa., was born in Allegheny city in the year 1864, and is the son of Frederick and Sophia Deverts. His early education was obtained in the public schools of the third ward, after which he attended a German private school for almost two years, there completing his education. On leaving school he entered the service of the wholesale millinery establishment of J. D. Bernd & Co. as an errand boy. He remained with this firm for twenty-four years, filling every position in the store. For a number of years Mr. Deverts has taken an active interest in political affairs, always acting with the republican party. He was for several years a member of the school board from his ward, and in June, 1902, he was elected by a unanimous vote to represent the ward in the select council, where he is the chairman of the committee on public works and a member of the committees on finance and charities. Mr. Deverts is a prominent member of the Masonic and club life of Allegheny county, being a member of the Monongahela club of Pittsburg and the Union and Humboldt clubs of Allegheny city. He is a member and past master of Stuckrath lodge, No. 430, Free and Accepted Masons; Allegheny chapter, No. 217, Royal Arch Masons; Allegheny commandery, No. 35, Knights Templars; Pittsburg consistory, in which he holds the thirty-second degree, and Syria temple, Ancient and Accepted Nobles of the Mystic Shrine. He is also a member of the Royal Arcanum and of the Watson Presbyterian church. In 1890 Mr. Deverts and Miss Annie Gant, of Allegheny city, were made husband and wife, and one son, Carl, has been born to their marriage. In his long and successful career in business and politics, Mr. Deverts has made many friends, who speak of him in terms of high praise.

JAMES R. CONNOR, alderman from the seventh ward, Pittsburg, was born on a farm in Pine township, Allegheny county, Pa., Oct. 27, 1869, and lived there until 1879, attending the country schools. At that time his parents brought the boy to Pittsburg, and there he completed his education in the schools on the South Side. When eighteen years old, he left school and was for the next three years clerk in the Pittsburg office of the Rock Island railroad company. Before his election to his present position, he was for several years agent for a fire extinguisher. He was elected alderman in February, 1900, defeating S. T. Richards, who had previously held the office for fifteen years. Very few people thought Mr. Connor would be elected at that time, for his opponent's name was on three tickets, the republican, democratic and independent, while his own name appeared only in the citizens' column; but he won out by a safe majority after one of the most stubborn battles in the history of the ward. In the fulfillment of the duties of his office, Mr. Connor has won a host of friends by his affable and gentlemanly ways. He is a member of the Knights of Pythias and of the Episcopal church.

JOHN GROETZINGER, alderman for the third ward of Pittsburg, has long been active in Pittsburg politics. He was constable for Allegheny county from 1885 to 1897, and has been alderman since then. He was elected a member of the common council from the third ward in 1890, was re-elected in 1892, 1894 and 1896, and then resigned to undertake the duties of his present position. Alderman Groetzinger was born in Pittsburg in 1850, was educated there, but left school at an early age to work in a grocery. From this he went into a printing office, then into a wagon shop, where he learned the blacksmiths' trade. He worked at this trade until 1870, then joined the Pittsburg volunteer fire department. When the pay fire department was organized he became driver of the hook and ladder company, holding this position until 1882, when he was promoted to captain of the company. On April 22, 1885, while a member of the fire department, he was caught in the third story of a burning building which fell before he could escape, and received at that time injuries which led him to retire from the service. He was then made constable. Alderman Groetzinger is a member of the B. P. O. Elks, A. O. U. W. and several other organizations, and belongs to the German Lutheran church. He was married, in 1871, to Sarah C. McKain, daughter of Samuel McKain, of Allegheny, and has two sons: Samuel C. G. and Thomas G. E. Alderman Groetzinger has been for over twenty years an important factor in local political movements, and the various positions to which he has been elected give evidence of the esteem in which he is held by the public.

JAMES H. REED, one of the leading attorneys of Pittsburg and a former partner of Attorney-General P. C. Knox, was born in Allegheny city, Pa., Sept. 10, 1853, and is a son of Dr. J. A. and Elizabeth H. Reed. He attended the public schools and then pursued his studies at the Western university, Pittsburg, graduating from that institution in 1872. After graduation he studied law with his uncle, David Reed, a practitioner of considerable distinction, was admitted to the bar in 1875, and in 1877 formed with P. C. Knox the partnership which lasted until 1901. As a member of this firm, Mr. Reed soon acquired a high reputation, especially in the pleading of large corporation cases. In 1891, when Judge Acheson was appointed to Judge McKennan's place on the bench of the circuit court, leaving the district bench vacant, Judge Reed was practically the unanimous choice of the Pittsburg bar for the position, and was appointed to the place by President Harrison. His health failing somewhat, he resigned his office on Jan. 15, 1892, and after a period of needed rest, returned to his old place in the firm of Knox & Reed. Judge Reed is a member of the Masonic order. He is a member of the Presbyterian church, of which he is a trustee.

LOUIS BEINHAUSER has been for over forty years a prominent funeral director of Pittsburg. He was born in Hamberg, Germany, Feb. 12, 1837, and came to America in May, 1854. After spending about five months in New York, he went to the coal region of Pennsylvania, where he was engaged for a time as a journeyman cabinet-maker. He came to Pittsburg in 1858, and in 1860 went into the undertaking business, in which he has been successfully engaged since that time. Although he has never taken an active interest in politics, he holds in political matters to the tenets of the republican party. Mr. Beinhauser is a member of the I. O. O. F. and A. O. U. W., and in religious belief is a Lutheran. He is a man whose life has been one of long and useful service, unstained by corruption, and he enjoys the confidence of a host of friends. Mr. Beinhauser was married, in 1858, and has three children: Conrad F., Anna and Lulu.

WILLIAM LANG, a member of the board of aldermen of Allegheny city, Pa., is a native of that city, where he was born in February, 1852. As a boy he lived with his parents, John H. and Caroline Lang, in the fourth ward, where he attended the public schools. After leaving the old fourth ward school, he took a course at the Iron City commercial college, and for about a year worked with his father at the trade of tinsmith. He then learned the trade of iron-molder and went west, stopping first at Chicago. Not liking it there, he went to Milwaukee, Wis., where for four years he was in the foundry of E. B. Ellis. He returned to Allegheny city, and in 1886 was appointed letter-carrier. His next position was that of market constable at the city market, where he remained for ten years, to the entire satisfaction of the city officials and the patrons of the market. At the expiration of his ten years of service as market constable he was elected alderman on the republican ticket, having always affiliated with that party and taken an active part in its operations as a political organization. His offices are at No. 406 Ohio St. In 1881 he was married to Miss Emma Schatzman, of Canton, Ohio, and one son has been born to the union. Mr. Lang was one of the charter members of Allegheny lodge, No. 339, B. P. O. Elks, and still holds his membership in the lodge he helped to organize. He is also a member of Providence Presbyterian church.

NICHOLAS G. KLAUS, councilman for the borough of East Pittsburg, was born in Baldwin township, Allegheny county, Nov. 7, 1867. His parents, John and Mary Klaus, were born in Germany and emigrated to the United States. Nicholas Klaus was educated in the public schools, and worked for a time as a coalminer in the Turtle creek valley, but has been for the past fifteen years successfully engaged in the hotel business in East Pittsburg. In politics he is a democrat, prominent in local party affairs and has been councilman for about a year. Mr. Klaus was married July 21, 1889, to Mary E., daughter of Peter and Helen (McDonald) Cusac. The Cusacs are a prominent old family of Pittsburg. Mr. and Mrs. Klaus have had nine children, of whom six are living, viz.: Helen, Clarence, Harry, Mildred, William and Gertrude.

JAMES G. HARPER, alderman of the fifteenth ward of Allegheny city, Pa., was born in Allegheny city, Oct. 11, 1855, and is a son of Thomas and Mary C. Harper, the former of whom died in 1902. James obtained his primary education in the public school of the sixth ward. He then took a classical course in a private institution and became associated with his father in the manufacture of wagons and carriages, continuing in that business until he was twenty-five years of age. Upon leaving the wagon-works, he was for two years associated with Painter & Sons as a millwright in the rolling mills, but left this position to become an engineer for Oliver Bros. After two years with this firm, he entered the employ of Trimble Bros., in a planing mill, and while in the mill he had the misfortune to lose an arm in the machinery. This accident compelled him to seek some other line of employment, and for nine years he was in the county court-house in various clerical positions. He was next for four years in the United States internal revenue service under Collectors S. D. Wormcastle and George A. Miller. On the last day of April, 1900, he was appointed alderman, and after serving one year on this appointment he was elected for a term of five years. Mr. Harper was married, in 1880, to Miss Jane McCoubrie, of Allegheny city, Pa., and three children—Bessie, Martin and Jean—have been born to them. He is an unswerving republican, and his face is a familiar one at the meetings of that party, especially in the fifteenth ward, where he resides. He and his family attend the United Presbyterian church.

JOHN I. WALLACE, of Pittsburg, Pa., for many years a highly successful farmer of Allegheny county, but now retired from active life, was born in Baldwin township, Allegheny Co., Pa., Jan. 8, 1845, his birthplace being the old family homestead of his grandfather and now owned by the subject of this review. His paternal grandparents were Samuel and Mary (Barton) Wallace, natives of County Antrim, Ireland, and of the same general family as Sir William Wallace, the Scottish hero. James Wallace, their son and the father of John I. Wallace, was born on the old homestead in Baldwin township, Jan. 1, 1806, and spent his entire life on the farm where he first saw the light of day, enjoying excellent health and a halcyon existence until his death, Sept. 14, 1894, at the ripe old age of eighty-eight years. James Wallace was married, on Sept. 15, 1838, to Jane, daughter of John Irwin, one of the early settlers of the state, who had many thrilling experiences with the Indians while blazing the way for civilization, on two occasions being compelled to abandon his settlement and retreat to the sheltering walls of the towns of the coast region. Jane (Irwin) Wallace was born on Aug. 29, 1810, and lived to be almost eighty-eight years of age, her death occurring on April 19, 1898. She was the mother of three children, viz.: Samuel, John I. and Elizabeth. John I. Wallace devoted his entire business career to conducting the farm on which he was born, and by dint of energy and faithful adherence to duty, succeeded in increasing the old homestead by a considerable number of acres, and amply demonstrated that he was a thorough and conservative business man. Early in life he formed those fine habits and traits which composed his splendid character and which made him honored and esteemed by all with whom he came in contact. The operation of the golden rule was manifested in his daily life, while the beatitudes of the sermon on the mount were constantly exemplified by his dealings with his fellow-men, and his whole life has indeed been a beautiful one. Mr. Wallace continued to live on his farm until a few years ago, when he removed to Pittsburg, and has since resided in that city. His chief object in making this change was to give his children the advantages of the superior school facilities for which the metropolis of western Pennsylvania is justly famous. He was married, on Oct. 5, 1869, to Jane Mary Rath, a most excellent woman, who was born on Sept. 11, 1852, and after a happy married life of above twenty-seven years, died on Jan. 27, 1897, leaving the following children, viz.: James Harvey, Lillie Bell, Melvin E., John Duff, Rachel Agnes and Ethel Marie. Mr. Wallace is now living quietly at his city residence and is reaping the benefits and rewards that come to those who live correct and worthy lives, and who do their full duty to themselves and their fellow-men.

HENRY LOHREY, a well-known pork-packer and member of the school board of Allegheny city, Pa., is one of the substantial and progressive business men of the city. He was born at Cincinnati, Ohio, in 1855, and was educated in the public schools. Later the family removed to a farm near the city, where his father, Henry Lohrey, died in 1873. After the death of his father he continued to manage the farm for his mother until he was about twenty-four years of age, when he returned to Cincinnati and was employed by his brother as city salesman in the meat business. During the nine years that he was thus employed he learned the packing business in all its details, and in 1887 went into that occupation for himself, selecting Allegheny city as a location. Mr. Lohrey was the first to introduce boiled hams as an article of commerce in Allegheny city. For about three years he made a specialty of this line of meats, which became so popular that other dealers took it up, and he was forced to carry on a general meat-packing trade to protect himself. He established his packing-house at No. 2234 East St., and soon had a capacity of 250 hogs weekly, and could now, with his present capacity, handle 1,000 per week. Since that time he has held his own against all his competitors, and to-day enjoys a patronage second to none in the city. He was married, in 1881, to Miss Barbara Pichter, of Cincinnati, and to them five children have been born, three of whom are living: Charles H., Joseph E. and Walter G. Mr. Lohrey takes a wide-awake interest in all matters pertaining to local government, as well as general politics, and is considered one of the leading republicans in the tenth ward, where he resides. For the last eight years he has represented his ward on the school board, where he has fully demonstrated that he is the right man for such a position. He is a member of the German Lutheran church, and is regarded as one of the representative men of Allegheny city.

ISAAC A. LEVY, who was elected in February, 1902, for a five-year term to succeed John Cahill as alderman from the eighth ward, Pittsburg, was born in Russia in 1863. He came to Pittsburg in 1874 with his mother, the father having come over about nine months before. In Pittsburg Mr. Levy worked for a time at various occupations, and then went to Leetonia, Ohio, where he acted for three years as bookkeeper and clerk for Julius Skiroll. Returning to Pittsburg, he was employed for a time as traveling salesman for the wholesale dry goods firm of H. Oppenheim, and later served in the same capacity for the now extinct firm of Rosenthal, Aronson & Co. In 1890 he formed a partnership with Samuel Gusky in the wholesale notion business, under the name of Gusky & Levy, Mr. Levy representing the firm on the road. Giving up this business in 1892, he opened a commission house, engaged in this business until 1896, and then was for three years employed in the office of Sheriff Harvey Lowry. After this he went into the life insurance business, and was thus engaged when elected to his present position. Mr. Levy is a prominent member of various secret orders. He is a member of Montefiore lodge, No. 794, and Encampment No. 307, I. O. O. F. He represented his lodge for ten years, was nine years its secretary, and served a year, beginning March, 1899, as deputy grand master of Pittsburg. He has been no less prominent in the encampment, and represented his encampment for several years in the grand encampment. Mr. Levy organized Benner lodge, No. 399, Knights of Pythias; was elected past chancellor of the organization, and represented the chapter in the grand lodge for several years. He also served three years as grand trustee of the grand lodge of Knights of Pythias, and had the distinction of being the first man outside of Philadelphia ever elected to this position. He assisted in organizing the White Star company, No. 16, uniform rank, Knights of Pythias, and is its present captain. In politics Mr. Levy is an ardent and hard-working republican, and is the present chairman of his ward.

JOSEPH MITCHELL, Jr., alderman of the seventeenth ward of the city of Pittsburg, was born in County Down, Ireland, in 1841. His father, also named Joseph, was a native of the same county, and in 1846 both father and son came to America, landing in New York in March of that year. The family came directly to Pittsburg, settled in the ninth ward, where they lived for about eighteen years, and then moved to the twelfth ward. Joseph, Jr., attended the public schools of the ninth ward, and afterwards took a course in bookkeeping at Duff's business college. His first position was with W. H. McClurg, a grocer, whose place of business was at the corner of Sixth and Wood streets. He remained with Mr. McClurg about one and a half years, when he became bookkeeper for W. & P. Siebert, grocers, on the corner of Penn and Market streets. After three years with this firm he entered the employ of Gillespie & Mitchell as bookkeeper for their planing mill and lumber yard, and in 1861 entered the retail grocery line for himself, locating in the seventeenth ward, where he was in business for about five years. In 1872 he was elected alderman of the seventeenth ward and served for four years. In 1876 he was elected to the Pennsylvania legislature, and was re-elected in 1878, serving four years in all. He was then appointed state tax collector by the Allegheny county commissioners and served five years in that capacity. Since 1883 Mr. Mitchell has been engaged in the real estate business, and, as stated in the beginning, he is at the present time alderman for the seventeenth ward, having his offices at the corner of Forty-second and Butler streets. Mr. Mitchell has traveled extensively through the central and western states, and in 1863 he returned to Ireland, visiting the old farm near Belfast where he was born. He is a member of Excelsior lodge, No. 36, Ancient Order of United Workmen; Sheaf lodge, No. 732, Knights of Honor, and is prominent in the Masonic order, being a thirty-second degree Mason and a member of Syria temple, Ancient and Accepted Nobles of the Mystic Shrine. He is also a member of the Seventh United Presbyterian church, located on Forty-fourth street, Pittsburg. In 1865 he was married to Miss Adelaide V. McKee, and to this marriage there have been born five children: H. W., a lawyer in Pittsburg; D. E., a clerk in Heyl & Patterson's machine shops; J. C., a roll turner; Frank, a clerk, and B. C., clerk in a bank. All the boys have been properly reared and educated, and, like their father, they are all leading lives of activity and usefulness.

JOHN BATTLES, superintendent of the bureau of highways and sewers, Pittsburg, was born in Mount Savage, Allegany Co., Md., in 1853. He came to Pittsburg with his parents in 1860, and was there reared and educated in the public schools. When sixteen years old, he left school and went to work in a glass factory. Later he was employed in a rolling mill, and continued in the mill for many years, leaving it for good in 1892, after attaining the position of roller. Mr. Battles became in that year assistant superintendent of highways and sewers, and served in that capacity until July, 1900, when he was given the deserved appointment as superintendent of the bureau. On June 30, 1901, he was thrown out of office by the provisions of the Ripper bill, but was reappointed on December 1st of that year by Recorder J. O. Brown.

CHARLES P. BERNHARD, member of the common council from the third ward of Allegheny city, Pa., was born in that ward in 1860, and received his first education in the public schools there, completing the course of study when he was thirteen years of age. He took a complete course in the Iron City business college, and ever since leaving school has been associated with his father, John Bernhard, in the furniture business at No. 114 East Ohio St., Allegheny city. His mother, Margaret Bernhard, died in 1902. Charles Bernhard is a member of several fraternal and benevolent societies, belonging to Darling council, No. 888, Royal Arcanum; Twin City council, No. 121, Junior Order of United American Mechanics; North Side council, No. 8, Sovereigns of Industry, and Allegheny lodge, No. 339, Benevolent and Protective Order of Elks. For twenty-five years he has been a member of the Allegheny city gymnastic club, and is also a member of the Allegheny Jacksonian club. In political matters, locally at least, he is somewhat independent, frequently acting without regard to party affiliations. This independence does not appear to have injured his political influence, however, for in February, 1903, he was elected to represent his ward in the council. On all matters relating to national politics he acts with the republican party. As a member of the council he was appointed on the finance and charity committees, both of which are committees of considerable importance. In 1890 he was married to Miss Louise Musgrave, of Allegheny city. To this marriage two children have been born: Elmer and Edward G. Bernhard, both bright boys, and the joy and pride of their parents.

JAMES P. MURPHY, assistant smoke inspector of Pittsburg, is a native of that city. He was born in 1869, and attended the common schools and night school until his eighteenth year, when he gave up his studies to accept a position in a rolling mill, where he remained for several years, and became assistant roller. He left the employ of the company in a strike in 1897 and never returned to work. In August, 1898, Recorder E. M. Bigelow appointed Mr. Murphy to the office which he now holds. He was discharged, Aug. 10, 1901, by the provisions of the famous Ripper bill, and was reappointed in December, 1901, by Dr. J. Guy McCandless, director of the department of public works. He was employed from September 1st until the time of his reappointment, in the county commissioner's office, as inspector of county roads. Mr. Murphy is one of the prominent young men of Pittsburg, well and favorably known in the city, and is a man of whom much may be expected. He is chairman of the republican committee of the thirty-fifth ward. He is a member of the Catholic church, belongs to the Americus club, and is president of the Oneida social club.

PHILIP DEMMEL, superintendent of detectives, of Pittsburg, was born in Germany in 1844. In 1856 he came to America with his parents, locating at Coal Hill (now Mount Washington), thirty-second ward, Pittsburg, and received a limited education in the public schools. At an early age he went to work in a glass factory, and when thirteen years old started to learn the lithographic printing trade in Pittsburg, and continued at this work until the outbreak of the Civil war. Although only seventeen years old, Mr. Demmel enlisted to fight for his country, and served with distinction throughout the war. His record during these troubled times is a most interesting one, and one of which any soldier might well be proud. He enlisted on July 10, 1861, as a private in Company L, 62d Pennsylvania volunteer infantry, for a three-year term of service. Six months before the expiration of this term he re-enlisted as a veteran and served until the close of the war, being transferred at the end of his first term to Company K, 91st Pennsylvania volunteer infantry. He was mustered out at Camp Cadwallader, at Philadelphia, in August, 1865, after having participated in the grand review at Washington, D. C. During the war he fought in the following engagements: Siege of Yorktown, second Bull Run, second Cold Harbor, Gaines' Mill, Malvern Hill, Frayser's farm, Antietam, Fredericksburg, Gettysburg, Chancellorsville, Spottsylvania Court House, Willow farm, North and South Anna river, siege of Petersburg, the Wilderness, and in all the fights in which his regiment took part. Mr. Demmel was slightly wounded in the Wilderness and on several other occasions, and was wounded at Gettysburg. He spent about six weeks in the hospital at Germantown, but was in active service during almost all of his long period as a soldier. Returning to Pittsburg after the war, he worked at lithographic printing until 1868. At that time he was elected high constable of the borough of Birmingham and served as such until 1872, when the borough was made a part of Pittsburg, and Mr. Demmel was transferred to the Pittsburg police force and made lieutenant of police. Soon afterwards he resigned and was made market constable, serving in this capacity two years, and was then, in 1875, appointed detective by Mayor William C. McCarthy. In 1877 Mr. Demmel was made chief of police and served one year, and then returned to the detective force. In June, 1879, he resigned his position and became a private detective in the employ of Jones & Laughlin (American iron works), and served this firm for ten years. Returning to the detective force, he served on the Pittsburg force until September, 1901, when he was appointed inspector of police. After two weeks as inspector, Mr. Demmel was appointed to the two-fold position of superintendent of police and chief of detectives, and in January, 1902, he received his present position. Mr. Demmel's long service for the city has been a most creditable one, and he is a man in every way fitted for his present responsible office.

ROBERT H. LINDSAY, general ordinance officer, Pittsburg, was born in the first ward, Pittsburg, June 11, 1851. He attended the Pittsburg public schools, graduating from the Pittsburg high school in 1869, and then supplemented his education by two years of study at the Western university. He then entered the public service as clerk in the office of the county commissioners, remaining in this position until 1876. In 1877 he became clerk in the city assessor's office, and continued to serve in this capacity until 1897, when his present office was created. Mr. Lindsay was first appointed to fill this office, for which his long experience had fitted him, by Mayor H. P. Ford, and was afterwards reappointed by Mayor William J. Diehl, and Recorders A. M. Brown and J. O. Brown. Mr. Lindsay is a member of the Heptasophs and the Fraternal Order of Eagles. In religious belief he is a Presbyterian.

WILLIAM T. MARSHALL, attorney in Pittsburg, was born in Allegheny city, Pa., in 1858. He received his early education in the schools of his native city, and afterwards attended the Western university at Pittsburg. Leaving school at the age of nineteen, he was employed for a time in his brother's grocery in Allegheny city, and then studied law in the office of Hon. T. M. Boyne. In 1881 he was appointed deputy collector of customs at Pittsburg, serving in this capacity until 1885, when he became connected with the People's gas company, with which company he is still actively identified. Mr. Marshall has long been prominent in state politics and has always been an ardent republican. In 1887 he was a delegate to the republican state convention. He was a member of the Pennsylvania house of representatives from 1889 to 1901, and served as speaker of the house in 1901. His public career has been an honorable one, stained by no hint of political corruption. Says a friend in speaking of Mr. Marshall: "He was one of the most influential members of the Pennsylvania legislature. He was for some time chairman of the appropriations committee, and thus secured large sums for Allegheny county institutions, and he has never had a thing brought up against his character, either in public or private life." Mr. Marshall belongs to no secret order. He is a member of the Methodist Episcopal church.

FRANK C. PEARSON, chief clerk to the director of the department of charities and corrections of Pittsburg, was born in the seventeenth ward of that city in 1871. His parents moved to Homewood, Beaver Co., Pa., in 1879, and Mr. Pearson attended the public schools there until he reached the age of fourteen, when his parents removed to Ingram, Allegheny county, and he completed his education in Pittsburg, graduating from Duff's business college in 1889. He then became chief clerk to the superintendent of the city farm, which was at that time located at Homestead, and in 1892 was transferred to the city office of the department of charities and corrections. He spent seven years as cashier of that department, and then became chief clerk to the director of the department. Mr. Pearson is a director of the Cash building and loan association of Pittsburg. He is an enthusiastic Mason, has attained the thirty-second degree, and is a Shriner. He is a member of the Presbyterian church. In politics Mr. Pearson is a republican, and takes an active and important part in party affairs.

HUMPHREY LYNCH, alderman of the ninth ward of Allegheny city, Pa., first saw the light of day in County Cork, Ireland, in 1844. His parents were Michael and Johanna Lynch, both of whom are now deceased. Humphrey was educated at the Christian Brothers' school at Cork, after which he learned the shoemakers' trade and worked at it until 1880, when he came to the United States. He took up his residence in the ninth ward of Allegheny city, though for about five years after coming to this country he operated a shoe store in Pittsburg. In 1885 he opened a shoe store in Allegheny city, on Preble avenue, and conducted it until 1897,

He was elected school director in 1895 for a term of three years, and in 1897 he was elected alderman of the ninth ward, which position he still holds, his office being located at No. 654 Preble Ave. Before leaving his native land he was married, in 1874, to Miss Nora Crowley, of Cork, and the following children have been born to them: Michael, Joseph, Murray, Nora, Jeremiah, James and Margaret. Mr. Lynch is a sterling democrat, and he is looked upon as one of the leaders of that party in the ninth ward. He and his family are members and constant attendants at St. Andrew's Roman Catholic church.

GEORGE W. WILSON, director of the department of charities and corrections of Pittsburg, was born in Pittsburg in 1846, and was reared there, attending first the public schools and then the Western university, from which he graduated. Upon graduation he became a clerk in the wholesale grocery of his father, John Wilson, and in 1869 was made a member of the firm, which was thenceforth known as John Wilson & Son. John Wilson died in 1895, and the son sold out the business and spent three years in closing up the estate. Mr. Wilson has been long before the public eye and has held many public positions of trust and responsibility. In April, 1898, he was appointed assistant postmaster of Pittsburg, served in this capacity until Feb. 1, 1900, when he was elected director of the department of public charities. This place he resigned in June, 1900, was for a year director of the department of public works, resigning June 11, 1901, and on Nov. 26, 1901, was appointed to his present responsible position by Hon. J. O. Brown. Besides these offices, Mr. Wilson was fire commissioner of Pittsburg from 1868 to 1877, member of the common council from the twenty-second ward from 1888 to 1898, and for three years chairman of the committee of public works. He was also formerly for eight years school director, being a member of the central board of education. Mr. Wilson is a thirty-second degree Mason, a Shriner and Knight Templar, and belongs to the First Methodist Episcopal church, in which he holds the honorary position of trustee.

WILLIAM R. BROWNE, superintendent of surveys, Pittsburg, has been for many years a prominent engineer. A native of Greensburg, Pa., he has lived almost all his life in Pittsburg, where he attended school and received a good education. He began to study engineering in his youth and has followed this vocation ever since. Mr. Browne was appointed to his present position in 1882, and has fulfilled the duties of that office satisfactorily for over twenty years. In religious belief he is a United Presbyterian.

WILLIAM W. MURRAY, county commissioner of Allegheny county, was born on a farm in Washington county, Pa., Oct. 14, 1856. His parents moved to Allegheny county the following year, and there Mr. Murray was reared and received his education. In 1882 he came to Pittsburg as a clerk in the office of the county commissioner, and served in that capacity for fifteen years. In April, 1897, he was elected superintendent of the county poor farm, but served only three weeks, being then appointed county commissioner to fill a vacancy. In 1899 he was elected to the same office for a three-year term. Besides holding these positions, Mr. Murray was for twelve years a member of the Knoxville, Pa., council, and served one year as burgess, resigning at the end of that time. He also served three years as justice of the peace. Mr. Murray has business as well as political interests, being a director of the Chartiers Valley water company and the Bridgeville lumber and supply company. He is a member of the Masonic fraternity, the Heptasophs and the Knights of the Golden Eagle. In religious belief he is a Presbyterian.

JOHN A. MARTIN, alderman from the sixth ward, Pittsburg, was born in Pittsburg in 1870. His father, John Martin, was born in County Donegal, Ireland, and died in Pittsburg in 1899, at the age of fifty-eight. John A. Martin was reared and educated in Pittsburg, graduating from Duff's business college in 1887. He also studied law for a little over a year in the office of Blakeley, McElroy & Smith. Mr. Martin was for three years assistant agent of the Pennsylvania railroad company, at Homestead, and, returning to the sixth ward, he opened a small cigar and confectionery store. This store he kept for about a year and a half and has since that time devoted his attention entirely to politics. In 1896 he was candidate for councilman on the democratic ticket and was defeated by only seventeen votes. The following year he was again a candidate for the same office, and was this time elected with a plurality of 236. His first five-year term over, Mr. Martin became a candidate for re-election, and in February, 1902, received a handsome plurality of over 600 as a testimonial to his faithful services in the past. Mr. Martin belongs to the Heptasophs and is a member of the Catholic church.

GEORGE M. FOSTER, cashier in the office of the treasurer of Allegheny county, was born on a farm in Scott township, Allegheny Co., Pa., in February, 1854. He attended the schools of Scott township and the Dickson-Dunbar academy in Carnegie, and upon leaving school, at the age of twenty, learned the carpenters' trade and was a contracting carpenter until 1884. He then accepted a clerkship under David McGunnegle, at that time clerk of courts, where he remained two years, and then entered the treasurer's office, where he rose to the position of cashier, an office which he has held eight years. That Mr. Foster has for twelve years been a member of the school board of his township is evidence of his interest in public affairs. He is a member of the Junior Order of United American Mechanics, Knights of Pythias, Knights of the Golden Eagle, Royal Arcanum, and belongs to the Presbyterian church. Mr. Foster was married, in 1883, to Lizzie J. Collins, daughter of Samuel Collins (deceased), and to them have been born five children, as follows: Jean Ross, Bessie Collins, Louise Glenn, Harriet Bilmore and Matilda Georgia.

E. N. RANDOLPH, chief clerk in the office of the controller of Allegheny county, was born in Versailles township, Allegheny Co., Pa., in 1856, and was reared in Allegheny county and educated in the public schools, where he received a common education. He came to Pittsburg in 1868 and quit school the following year. He was first employed as an errand boy, and then became a florist, in which capacity his diligence and native ability won him the confidence of his employers, so that at the age of twenty he became superintendent of one of the largest commercial florist concerns in Pittsburg. He continued at this vocation until 1885, when he became one of the force in the controller's office, and now holds the position of chief clerk. Mr. Randolph has for years taken an active part in republican politics and has been prominently identified with the political campaigns of his party. In 1891 he was elected secretary of the republican state league clubs, and four times re-elected to the same position. He was also at one time secretary of the Allegheny county republican committee, and was in 1895-96 journal clerk of the Pennsylvania house of representatives. He was also formerly for two years president of the Pittsburg athletic club, at that time an important organization. Mr. Randolph is a member of the Independent Order of Odd Fellows, and in religion affiliates with the Presbyterian church.

JAMES D. CALLERY, president of the Pittsburg railway company, is widely known as one of the most successful business men of Western Pennsylvania. He was born in Pittsburg in 1857, and received his primary education in the Pittsburg schools, afterwards attending Notre Dame college, near South Bend, Ind., from which noted institution he graduated in 1874. School days being over, he at once entered upon his business career, working for his father, a large leather dealer. Mr. Callery has always been interested in this firm, which was incorporated in 1900 as the James Callery company. The elder Mr. Callery was also president of the Pittsburg & Western railroad company, whose line is now owned by the Baltimore & Ohio. He died in 1889. James D. Callery, the subject of this sketch, became president of the Second Avenue railway of Pittsburg in 1888. This line, at that time a horse-car line, was afterwards merged into the United Traction company, of which Mr. Callery became president in 1896. In January, 1902, the Pittsburg railway company was organized, taking in the United Traction company and also the street railway lines in Allegheny county, except the Pittsburg and Connellsville line, which terminated at McKeesport. Mr. Callery is a member of the Roman Catholic church and a republican in politics.

WILLIAM D. KING, M. D., one of the leading physicians of Pittsburg, was born in that city, Sept. 9, 1861, and is a son of Calvin and Rachel (Chambers) King. Dr. Calvin King has been for over half a century a prominent Pittsburg dentist. Dr. William D. King's family came originally from England. His great-grandfather, Courtland King, crossed the Monongahela river at Elizabeth, and settled on a farm near Library, where he spent the remainder of his days, dying at the age of sixty-two. Among his children were: John, grandfather of William D.; Elijah, who resided at Indianapolis, and Isaac, who made his home at Library. John King came to Library in infancy, and resided with his parents until he became twenty-eight years old, married Jane Stewart and settled on a farm near the old homestead. In 1836 he moved to Forward, where he purchased the farm of John Stoner, lived there until 1873, and then took up his residence in Central block. His life of ninety-two years was one of constant usefulness. In religion he was a rigid Baptist, although cherishing at the same time a broad Christian charity, while in politics he was a whig, and afterwards an abolitionist. He was a man of wide culture, a reader and a thinker. John King was the father of the following children: Dr. James L., of Pittsburg; Mary L., who died in 1877; Dr. William H., of Monongahela; John, of Spring Valley, Minn.; Dr. Courtland, of Pittsburg; Jane, wife of James Morn, who died in 1854; Dr. Calvin, of Pittsburg; Samuel J., of Forward township; Robert; Harvey, an infant child; Dr. Milton S., of Pittsburg, and Allie M., now Mrs. Devore. Dr. William H. King, third child of John and Jane King, was born in Allegheny county, April 17, 1823; graduated from Ohio college of dentistry, and practiced for some years in Lancaster, Ohio. On Aug. 22, 1862, he enlisted in Company F, 155th Pennsylvania volunteer infantry, under Capt. John Markell; was twice promoted for bravery in the service, and was mustered out as first lieutenant. He was a republican in politics, and in religious belief a Baptist. He was married, May 4, 1871, to Jane Carpenter. Dr. William D. King, subject of this article, graduated from Hahnemann medical college, Philadelphia, in 1884, and has been engaged in the practice of his profession in Pittsburg since then. Here his native ability, coupled with a studious disposition and faithful attention to his practice, has won him distinction as a homœopathic physician. There is possibly no physician in Allegheny county who has the distinction of having so large a general practice as Dr. King. He is obstetrician of the city hospital and chief of the dispensary staff, is a member of the State homœopathic society and of the American institute of homœopathy. He is a Baptist in religion, and in politics a republican. Dr. King was married, in 1891, to Nancy Tripp, daughter of Col. Alonzo Tripp, superintendent of a South Carolina railroad.

WILLIAM ROBINSON, alderman from the thirty-seventh ward, Pittsburg, was born in Allegheny city, Pa., Aug. 27, 1864, and came to the thirty-seventh ward when seven years old. Here he was raised and was given a limited education in the public schools, which ended in his fifteenth year. After this he worked at various employments until he became of age, when he became agent and ward correspondent for a number of Pittsburg papers. Thus he spent about ten years of his life and in the meantime, about 1887, he became interested in the real estate business, in which he has since been successfully engaged. In 1887 he was elected alderman from the thirty-seventh ward, and served one five-year term. He then devoted himself for several years to his business interests, and in September, 1898, was appointed alderman to fill a vacancy. At the regular election, in February, 1899, he was elected to the position on the republican ticket. In 1890 and 1892 he was a candidate for legislative honors, but failed to obtain the nomination. Mr. Robinson is known as a man temperate in habits, methodical and energetic in business affairs. He is charitable in word as well as in deed and has won the respect of all those who have had the pleasure of coming into close touch with him in a business or social way. He is a prominent member of the Masonic fraternity, a Knight Templar and Shriner.

CHARLES J. RUHLANDT, register of deeds, Pittsburg, was born in Pittsburg, on the South Side, July 27, 1860, and there reared and educated in the common schools. When nine years old he worked two months in a glass factory, and returning to school, continued until 1873, when he left for good to work in a glass factory on the South Side. From 1880 to 1885 he was associated with his brother, J. W. Ruhlandt, in a hotel on the South Side, and from 1885 to 1896 was engaged in the café business. During this time, from 1886 to 1888, he was also employed in the prothonotary's office. In 1896 Mr. Ruhlandt was appointed street inspector, serving in this capacity a year, and was then for two years otherwise engaged in the city service. In February, 1899, he was appointed assistant superintendent of streets, serving in this position five months, and was then appointed to his present office, in which he has given good satisfaction. In November, 1901, after being out of office two months, Mr. Ruhlandt was reappointed, and is now serving under this appointment. Mr. Ruhlandt is a member of the B. P. O. E., Junior Order of United American Mechanics and the Maccabees.

HENRY CHARLES EVERT, of Pittsburg, Pa., a prominent lawyer and senior member of the firm of H. C. Evert & Co., patent attorneys, of Pittsburg and Washington, D. C., was born in Pittsburg, Sept. 13, 1869, son of Henry and Marie (Nahmacher) Evert. His father was born on Nov. 1, 1825, came to Pittsburg at an early age and there was well known as a wholesale liquor dealer and an importer of wines. He was prominently identified with the commercial interests of the city and died on Jan. 9, 1871. Henry C. Evert was educated in the rudimentary courses in the public schools of Pittsburg, and Holy Ghost college and later attended the Western university. He then matriculated at the law department of Georgetown university, where he was graduated in 1890 with the degree of bachelor of laws. He continued his studies there, devoting his time to post-graduate work, and in 1891 received the degree of master of laws. He was admitted to the bar on June 21, 1891, and to the supreme court of Pennsylvania on Jan. 5, 1895, being at that time the youngest man to achieve that honor. Mr. Evert practices in the superior court, the supreme court of the District of Columbia, the court of appeals and many other high tribunals. His present firm was established at Washington in 1890, and later extended to Pittsburg. His associate in this firm is Mr. A. M. Wilson, of Washington, D. C., a well-known solicitor of patents of the national capital, with offices at No. 616 Ninth St., opposite the patent office. Mr. Evert is a member of the Odd Fellows, the chamber of commerce and the Second Presbyterian church and resides in the twentieth ward.

WILLIAM B. ARMSTRONG, alderman from the twenty-third ward, Pittsburg, was born in Pittsburg, July 12, 1854. He moved with his parents to Chicago when six years old, and remained there ten years, attending the public schools. Returning to Pittsburg, Mr. Armstrong went to work in a tan-yard and followed this vocation successfully for about twenty years, part of the time running a tan-yard of his own. He gave up this business in 1888, and spent two years in the grocery business at Scottdale, Westmoreland county. Returning to Pittsburg, Mr. Armstrong became assistant superintendent of the Second Avenue traction company, and was so engaged until 1900, when he was elected alderman for a five-year term, on the republican ticket. Alderman Armstrong is a prominent member of the Masonic fraternity, and is a member of the Maccabees, Woodmen of the World, Royal Arcanum, I. O. O. F. and its Encampment branch. In religious belief he affiliates with the United Presbyterian church.

FRANK ORBIN, superintendent of the bureau of electricity of the city of Pittsburg, was born in Butler county, Pa., in 1871. His father being a Methodist minister, and thus transferred from place to place, Mr. Orbin spent his youth at various points in western Pennsylvania. After the usual preparation, he entered the Pennsylvania state college, graduating from the mechanical engineering department in 1893, and then gained a year's practical experience in the Westinghouse plant at Pittsburg. After this he took a post-graduate course in physics and electricity at Johns Hopkins university. Thus thoroughly prepared, he entered the employ of the city of Pittsburg in 1895 as an inspector in the bureau of electricity, his duty being to inspect all electrical work done in the city. Mr. Orbin was advanced from this position in 1901 to be chief inspector, and in May, 1902, was made superintendent of the bureau. Mr. Orbin is a member of the Engineers' society of western Pennsylvania, and the American institute of electrical engineers. In religious belief he is a Methodist and in politics a republican. He resides in the nineteenth ward, Pittsburg.

JAMES V. McMASTERS, alderman of the city of Pittsburg and police magistrate, was born in Pittsburg, Dec. 24, 1854, and there raised and educated. When eighteen years old he entered the office of the county prothonotary, and remained there three years. Mr. McMasters was after this employed, up to 1877, in the office of his father, who was at that time alderman from the fifth ward. He next entered the employ of James Getty, a wholesale liquor dealer, and remained there eight years. In February, 1885, Mr. McMasters was elected alderman from the second ward and has since been three times re-elected. He is a member of the Jr. O. U. A. M., B. P. O. E. and American Eagles.

NICHOLAS H. VOEGTLY.

JACOB JOHN VOEGTLY, of Pittsburg, Pa., a prominent young attorney, with offices in the Syndicate block at No. 518 Fourth Ave., was born in Allegheny city, Jan. 1, 1875, son of Nicholas H. and Mary (Steiner) Voegtly. The Voegtly family is one of the most prominent in Allegheny county and is of Swiss origin. Nicholas Voegtly, Jr., the grandfather of Jacob John, having settled in Pittsburg in 1822, was the first member of the family to locate in America. He owned a large tract of land in Allegheny county, fronting on the Allegheny river, which is now included in the fourth, eighth, third and seventh wards of Allegheny city. He was a member of the legislature and also served as councilman of Allegheny city. He married Maria Rickenbach and their children were: Mary, widow of Henry Gerwig, now residing in Allegheny city; Henrietta (deceased); Elizabeth (deceased), who married Jacob Kopp; Susan (deceased), who married John Habermehl, and Nicholas H. Nicholas H. Voegtly was born in Allegheny city, Nov. 23, 1834, and spent his entire life in that city. He was an active citizen of that corporation and for thirty-five years was engaged in the lumber business. He represented the third ward of Allegheny city in the council for sixteen years, served several terms in the legislature and was mayor of Allegheny city for a short period immediately preceding his death. He was a director in the German National and the Third National banks and was also financially interested in other banking institutions. He was a director of three bridge companies and was secretary and treasurer of the Sixteenth Street bridge company. He was closely identified with the Voegtly Presbyterian church of Allegheny city, the building site of which was donated by his father. Nicholas H. Voegtly was married to Mary Steiner and they had the following children: William N., Charles, Frank L., Edwin B., Annie, wife of Edward E. Eggers; Helen S., Robert, Florence R., Emma M., Nicholas H., Jr., Jacob J., Flora E., Gertrude O. and Oscar, who died in childhood. Jacob J. Voegtly was educated in the public schools of Allegheny city, entering the high school in 1891, later attended the Park institute and in September, 1893, matriculated at the the Washington and Jefferson college, where he was graduated in June, 1897. He then entered the law department of the University of Pennsylvania, where he remained for two years, later read law in the offices of W. B. Rodgers and J. H. Johnston, and in December, 1900, was admitted to the bar. Since then he has engaged in the practice of law at Pittsburg, where he is a member of all courts and stands well among the younger element of the legal fraternity.

ROBERT DUNN LAYTON, immigrant inspector, post of Pittsburg, was born in Butler county, Pa., in 1847, and when two years old moved with his parents to West End, Pittsburg. Five years later the family moved to the city, and there Mr. Layton was reared, and attended the public schools. Later he continued his studies at Westminster college, New Wilmington, Pa., but left that institution in February, 1864, to enter the Union army, enlisting as a private in Company E, 13th Pennsylvania cavalry. He served with this regiment until mustered out in the early summer of 1865, and was honorably discharged in Philadelphia some time later. During the war Mr. Layton took part in all the principal battles and arduous campaigns in which his company was engaged. He was never wounded, never in the hospital, never had a furlough, and never asked for a pension. Just before the surrender of Joe Johnston, in April, 1865, Mr. Layton was captured and held prisoner for four days in a barn, and then, with twenty-five others, escaped and rejoined his regiment. After receiving his discharge at Philadelphia, he returned to Pittsburg and learned the toolmakers' trade, which had been his father's trade. He worked at this until 1882, when he was elected secretary and treasurer of the national organization of the Knights of Labor. He was twice re-elected to this position, and then, at the convention held at Cincinnati in 1885, resigned and went into the insurance business in Pittsburg, in which he was engaged for three years. At the suggestion of Senator Quay, Mr. Layton was sent to Indiana to assist the state republican committee in arranging for speakers and planning the republican campaign. He was occupied thus until the succeeding election in November, 1888. He returned to Pittsburg, closed up his insurance business, and in June, 1889, was appointed by President Harrison as immigrant inspector at the post of Pittsburg, he being the first to hold that office at Pittsburg. In June, 1893, Mr. Layton was removed by President Cleveland, returning to the insurance business for several years. In February, 1898, he was again appointed to office, stationed at New York for a time as boarding officer, and in May, 1898, was appointed to his old place as immigrant inspector at Pittsburg. In performance of the duties of this office, Mr. Layton acts as Chinese inspector, and as such has transported more people than all the other interior posts put together, a record which testifies to exceptional watchfulness and attention to duty. Mr. Layton is a member of Post No. 3, G. A. R., and belongs to no church.

FRANCIS J. TORRANCE. Among the "Captains of Industry," whose commanding ability and eminent success have made their names familiar wherever the English tongue is spoken, Francis John Torrance, first vice-president of the Standard sanitary manufacturing company, president of the Western Pennsylvania exposition society, president of the select council, and connected in many ways with numerous other positions of honor, trust and responsibility, stands out as one of the most remarkable men of this great industrial metropolis of America. He was born in the third ward, city of Allegheny, on June 27, 1859, and is still a resident of the city of his birth. Mr. Torrance is of Scotch-Irish ancestry, the son of Francis Torrance, one of the earlier and best-known of the business men of Allegheny county, who came to America from the north of Ireland in 1850, when thirty years of age, and located in Allegheny county. He was one of the large family of Francis Torrance, grandfather of the subject of this sketch, who was a well-to-do farmer of County Donegal, in the north of Ireland. The father of Francis J. was a man of sterling worth and honesty, and soon took a leading part in the development of his adopted county. He was one of the founders of the Standard manufacturing company, of which he was president many years, and was the manager of the Schenley estate for over thirty years. He held many positions of local importance, which shows the confidence and respect of his fellow-citizens. He was a member of the Allegheny city select council and of the school board for eighteen years, a trustee of the Baptist church of Allegheny and president of the board. Francis J. was given a good education. He attended the public schools of Allegheny city and graduated from the third ward school in 1874. He took a course at Newell institute and completed his school education at the Western University of Pennsylvania. He entered upon his remarkable business career in connection with his father, first as a clerk and then as superintendent of the Standard manufacturing company, which position he held until the death of his father, at the age of seventy years, in 1886. After his father's death, the son was appointed treasurer and general manager of the company in Pittsburg, and is at present the first vice-president, with offices in the Arrott building. This company has one of the finest and most extensive enameling works in the world, located in Allegheny city. Over 1,000 men are employed, and branch offices are located in New York, Philadelphia, Pittsburg, Chicago, Buffalo, San Francisco and Montreal. Mr. Torrance is also president of the Washington street railway company, president of the Riverside land company, president of the Pittsburg natatorium company, and president of the Western Pennsylvania exposition society, whose latest and most successful session (1902) closed in a blaze of musical glory under Sousa, Creatore and Damrosch. Few men have risen to such prominence at such an early age as Mr. Torrance. Genial, kind, easily approached, courteous to old and young, rich and poor alike, he is first and foremost in every good work, whether of business, social, religious, benevolent, educational or civic importance. He is a steam engine so far as the accomplishment of hard work is concerned, but does it so easily and good-naturedly that the cares and struggles of business have failed to furrow his ruddy, almost boyish face, and he bids fair to grow younger instead of older-looking with the advancing years. Mr. Torrance married Miss Mary R. Dibert, daughter of David and Lydia (Griffith) Dibert, of Johnstown, Nov. 6, 1884. They have but one child, a daughter, Jane. Mr. Torrance is a member of the Americus club, Pittsburg, and was its president for two years. He is also a member of the

Duquesne club, of the Press club and of the Fulton club, New York city; also the Stollers and the Pennsylvania society, New York city. He is president of the Allegheny select council, and is chairman ex-officio of all the standing committees of said council. In 1895 he was appointed by Governor Hastings commissioner of public charities of Pennsylvania, and was elected president of the State board of charities in 1902. Mr. Torrance has been prominently mentioned for governor of Pennsylvania. Commanding the confidence and respect of all classes of his fellow-citizens as he does, he could be elected to any office of trust and honor to which he might aspire.

HENRY HULL NEGLEY, of Pittsburg, Pa., a leading attorney-at-law, with offices at No. 413 Grant St., was born in Pittsburg, Nov. 12, 1868, son of Maj. Felix C. and Margaret A. (Dickson) Negley, his father having died on Oct. 5, 1901. Maj. Felix C. Negley was a son of John and Elizabeth (Patterson) Negley, the former having been born in East Liberty, then known as Libertytown, where his father owned the tract of land extending from Penn avenue to the Allegheny river, and from Black Horse hill, now Rebecca street, to Negley's Run, and included all of the present Highland park. John Negley for many years owned and operated a stage-coach line from Pittsburg to Buffalo, and was also extensively engaged in agriculture, quarrying stone and granite and the manufacture of brick. He was a prominent member of the state legislature and at one time was tendered the nomination for governor by the democratic party. He had a long and useful career and died at the ripe old age of ninety-four years. Maj. Felix C. Negley was born in Butler, Pa., Feb. 28, 1825, and was a civil engineer by profession. At the commencement of the Civil war, he organized and equipped, at a personal cost of over $60,000, a battalion of cavalry, known as the Negley scouts, of which command he was major. This battalion saw active service during the threatened invasion of Pennsylvania and was the nucleus from which was formed the 1st Pennsylvania volunteer cavalry, of which organization Major Negley was lieutenant-colonel. He was also commissioned as major in the recruiting service by Governor

Curtin, and performed his work well, which was that of enlisting negroes in Georgia and Alabama for the northern army. While in this latter service, he was twice drafted but on each occasion paid a substitute and continued in the recruiting branch of the army. At the close of the Civil war he returned to his home in the north and engaged in his customary pursuits. He was prominent in political affairs and was closely identified with the republican party. He held the office of school director in the second and fifth wards of Pittsburg for many years, was a member and president of the Pittsburg central board of education for twenty-one years and represented the various districts as school director for over forty years. He amassed considerable wealth but lost heavily in the panic of 1873-74. Henry H. Negley acquired his elementary training in the public and high schools of Pittsburg, and later spent two years at the United States military academy at West Point, which he was compelled to leave on account of his failing health. Subsequently he entered the Ohio Northern university and there was graduated with the degree of bachelor of arts. He then matriculated at the Ohio college of law and was graduated in the class of 1898, with the bachelor of laws degree. He was admitted to the bar of Ohio in October, 1898, and to practice in Allegheny county, in March, 1902, the intervening time having been devoted to traveling in Ohio. Mr. Negley is a member of all courts, has a fine practice and enjoys a splendid standing among his brother attorneys. He is a member of the Masonic order and an active and enthusiastic republican, taking considerable interest in political matters but never seeking office. He is also prominently identified with Company E, 3d regiment, United Boys' Brigades of America, and holds a commission in that organization.

WILLIAM J. GLENN, clerk in the prothonotary's office, Pittsburg, has a military record equaled by few men. He served with distinction in the Civil war, during riots and other difficulties in Pennsylvania after the war, and finally in the late Spanish-American war. Colonel Glenn was born on a farm in Scott township, Allegheny county, in 1840, and was educated in the country schools and at an academy at Mansfield, now Carnegie. In August, 1861, he enlisted as a private in Company E, 61st regiment, Pennsylvania volunteer infantry, and served until mustered out in September, 1864. He was promoted to sergeant-major in September, 1861, and to second lieutenant in May, 1862. He had charge of his company at Fredericksburg, Dec. 13, 1862, was recommended for promotion on account of gallant service in that battle, and in January, 1863, was made captain. Colonel Glenn fought at Williamsburg, Va., and then at Fair Oaks, where, on May 31, 1862, he was severely wounded and disabled for sixty days, so that he missed the seven days' fight at Richmond. After this he took part in the engagements at Chantilly, at second Bull Run, at Antietam, where he was acting adjutant, and at Fredericksburg, Va. His regiment took a leading part in the battle of Mary's Heights, making the first charge over the bridge, taking the heights; then marching on to Salem church, where another fierce conflict took place, and then returning across the river. The gallant 61st arrived at Gettysburg on the second day of July, 1863, after a march of forty-three miles without stopping for coffee, one of the hardest marches in the history of the war. After Gettysburg, Colonel Glenn fought with his regiment at Mine Run, the Wilderness, and on the James river, being wounded in the arm in the last-named fight, and later took part in engagements near Petersburg and Harper's Ferry. At Harper's Ferry, where he had charge of the regiment, he was wounded in the leg. After a few minor skirmishes, Colonel Glenn was mustered out of the service, spent several years in the oil region of Pennsylvania, and then returned to Mansfield, where, in 1874, he was made justice of the peace. He served ten years in this capacity and in 1884 became superintendent of the Allegheny county home, holding this position until 1897, when he resigned to go into the county commissioners' office. In April, 1898, Colonel Glenn again took up arms for his country in the Spanish-American war, as colonel of the 14th Pennsylvania national guard. He went with the regiment to South Carolina and remained there until mustered out in March, 1899. Returning then to civil life, he was employed in the coroner's office until April, 1902, when he entered upon his duties as clerk in the prothonotary's office. Besides his careers in two wars, Colonel Glenn can be proud of his record in the national guard. In August, 1874, he organized Company K, 14th regiment, Pennsylvania national guard, and was elected its captain. In 1885 he became major of the regiment, was made lieutenant-colonel in 1889 and colonel in 1895. He served as such until September, 1899, when, his time having expired, he was mustered out. He served with his regiment at the railroad riot in Pittsburg in 1877, and shortly afterwards at the coal riots in Luzerne county. He also distinguished himself for gallantry during the Johnstown flood, and at the Homestead riots in 1892.

Colonel Glenn attended the inauguration of every president from Garfield to McKinley. He is a member of Post No. 153, G. A. R., of which he was the first commander, and belongs to the Union Veteran Legion, No. 1, of Pittsburg, and the Pennsylvania Loyal Legion. As a great-grandson of James Glenn, a Revolutionary war soldier who served at Valley Forge, he is a member of the Sons of the American Revolution. He is also a member of the Masonic fraternity and the Presbyterian church.

WILLIAM HUGH FRANCIES, fourth-ward member of the common council of Allegheny city, Pa., is one of the younger members of that body. He was born in the ward he now represents, Dec. 31, 1874, and is of Scotch-Irish extraction, his parents being Samuel and Prudence Francies, long-time residents of Allegheny city. William received his primary instruction in the public schools of the fourth ward. In 1890 he completed the course of study in the ward school, and soon after entered the engineering department of the Western University of Pennsylvania, graduating as a civil engineer in 1896. For three years he was associated with A. G. Shaw in the engineering business, and was then for two years in the same line of work with the Monongahela street railroad company. In 1901 he accepted a position in the engineering department of the American bridge company, of Allegheny city, which position he still holds. Mr. Francies is a young man of high moral ideals. He is a member of the United Presbyterian church and has been a teacher in the Sunday-school. He is also a member of the Central Young Men's Christian Association, of Pittsburg, and of the Americus club of the same city. In politics he represents the younger element of the republican party, which in recent years has wielded such a powerful influence in shaping the destinies of that organization. He was elected, in February, 1903, to the common council, where his technical knowledge of engineering was recognized by an appointment on the committee on public works. He is also a member of the library and water committees. In the exercise of his official functions, he is actuated by the same conscientiousness that has distinguished his conduct in his private affairs, and to which is due his high standing in the community.

JOHN CAHILL, a prominent Pittsburg real estate man and formerly alderman from the eighth ward, was born in Pittsburg in 1854. When a boy he attended the city schools, but received only a limited education, being compelled to leave school at the age of twelve. He learned the trade of glass-blower and followed this vocation until 1891, when he was appointed by Governor Pattison to serve as alderman from the eighth ward. In 1892 he was elected to the position for a five-year term and re-elected in 1897. In 1902 he was again a candidate, but was defeated by Isaac Levy. Mr. Cahill has been for years an influential democrat and still takes an active interest in party matters. While engaged at his trade as a glass-blower, he acted as delegate to several conventions, notably the one in 1878 which organized the American flint glass workers' association. Since that time he has served as secretary of the association. Mr. Cahill belongs to no secret orders. He is a member of the Catholic church.

GEORGE L. HOUSE, superintendent of masonry at the Duquesne furnaces, but a resident of Braddock, was born in Pittsburg, Dec. 18, 1852. He is a son of Daniel and Margaret (Horton) House, the father a native of Lancaster, Pa., and a son of George House, who came to America from Baden-Baden, Germany, in the eighteenth century. Margaret (Horton) House, the mother of the subject of this sketch, was the daughter of James and Mabel (McCune) Horton, of Minersville, Pitt township, Pa., now the thirteenth ward of the city of Pittsburg. George L. House received his education in the common schools of his native city, in Wheeling, W. Va., whither he had moved with his parents in 1865, and in Sciotoville, Ohio, which became his home three years after leaving Pennsylvania. Upon finishing his school work, Mr. House learned the brick-layers' trade, and has since devoted the greater part of his time to that line of business. In early manhood he returned to Pittsburg, his native city, and worked for a time at the rolls in the Carnegie mills, on Thirty-ninth street. In 1876 he became a street-car conductor for a time, but on March 6, 1878, entered the employ of the Edgar Thompson steel company, working at his trade, and at the end of a year was made foreman. This responsible position Mr. House held for ten years, and then embarked in the contracting business with William Porter under the firm name of House & Porter. This firm has been very successful and has earned a just reputation for first-class and expert workmanship. July 20, 1895, Mr. House became superintendent of masonry at the Duquesne steel works and blast furnaces, where he has had entire charge of all the brick-work in the construction of the four large furnaces, from each of which about 500 tons of pig iron is turned out daily. His industry, skill and faithful attention to business has gained for him the complete confidence of his employers and the good-will of his fellow-citizens. Mr. House is a member of Braddock Field lodge, No. 510, Ancient Free and Accepted Masons; Shiloh chapter, No. 257, Royal Arch Masons, and Braddock Field lodge, No. 180, Ancient Order of United Workmen. He is a stanch republican, and is now serving as school director in the borough of Braddock. He is also a past member of the borough council.

JOHN J. WALKER, justice of the peace of Allegheny county, with headquarters at No. 911 Wood St., Wilkinsburg, has held that position since 1871, and is the oldest justice in continuous commission in Allegheny county. He was born in the third ward, Allegheny city, Pa., Feb. 1, 1841, was reared there and attended its schools, studying also at Mercer academy, Mercer, Pa., and at the Western university. He left school when sixteen years old, working as a painter in Allegheny city and Philadelphia. On April 17, 1861, he enlisted as a private in Company E, 7th Pennsylvania volunteer infantry and was one of the first to take up arms for his country against the rebels. Mr. Walker served his three months with this regiment, then returned to Allegheny city and engaged for a short time in the painting business. In September, 1861, he began to raise a company of artillery, which afterwards became Company C, 2d Pennsylvania heavy artillery. Mr. Walker was first lieutenant of the company until March, 1862, when he resigned and returned for a time to his business. Unable to remain away from duty, he re-enlisted in August, 1862, as a private in Company G, 139th regiment, Pennsylvania volunteer infantry. He served until Dec. 15, 1864, rising to the position of corporal. He then was commissioned captain of artillery in the regular army and served by order of Mr. Stanton, secretary of war, on detailed duty in Georgia and Tennessee until Dec. 9, 1866, when he resigned and came home. During the war Mr. Walker fought at second

Bull Run, Fredericksburg, Chancellorsville, Mary's Heights, second Chancellorsville, Gettysburg (three days), Mine Run, Savage Station, the Wilderness, Winchester, Petersburg and Sailor's Creek. In the Wilderness he was wounded and for six weeks prevented from active service. He was at Petersburg from July, 1864, to February, 1865. The war over, Mr. Walker resumed his painting business in Wilkinsburg and was thus engaged until 1879, when he became assistant in the office of the clerk of courts, in Pittsburg. He remained there until 1885, then became clerk in the office of the county treasurer for one year, and in 1888 was elected jury commissioner, serving three years. Mr. Walker has since that time devoted his attention to his business as justice of the peace and has not held other offices, although still taking an active part in republican politics. He is a member of Post No. 548, G. A. R.; B. P. O. E., I. O. O. F., K. of P., and Jr. O. U. A. M. He is past grand master of the Odd Fellows and Knights of Pythias, and is a member of the Methodist Episcopal church.

WILLIAM H. SARVER, the twelfth-ward member of the Allegheny city common council, was born in Allegheny city, Pa., in 1864, and is the son of William J. and Helena Sarver. His father is one of the oldest jewelry merchants in the city, his store on Federal street having been a landmark for the last forty years. After attending a private school for some time and the public schools of the first ward until he completed all the grades, Mr. Sarver went into the jewelry store with his father, with whom he is still associated, having an interest in the business. As a member of the council, he is on some of the most important standing committees, among which are the committees on public works and corporations. He is also a member of a sub-committee on public parks and property. His appointment to these committees is a fitting recognition of his public spirit, his executive ability and his business integrity. In politics he is a republican and he is always ready to defend his political opinions. He has frequently been called upon to serve his party in the capacity of a delegate to the nominating conventions. On such occasions he has invariably given his support to the candidates who had nothing in their records which they might be called upon to explain or for which they might have to apologize, believing with the late President Hayes that "He serves his party best who serves his country best," and believing also that defeat with a clean ticket is better in the end than victory with a corrupt one. Mr. Sarver is well known in church and Masonic work, being a member of Perrysville Avenue Methodist Episcopal church and Stuckrath lodge, No. 430, Free and Accepted Masons. He was married, in 1887, to Miss Lydie R. Osborn, of Allegheny city, and two bright boys, Earl F. and William J., Jr., have been born to them. In business, in his official position and in his church and lodge relations, Mr. Sarver sustains an irreproachable character, due to his genial disposition and his inherent good qualities.

FREDERICK RUOFF, pastor of the First German Evangelical Protestant church, of Pittsburg, was born in Balingen, Würtemberg, Germany, June 16, 1851, and raised and educated in Germany. Rev. Ruoff received an unusually complete education in the schools of his native country. He first attended the Latin school in his home town, and then went to a high school in Tübingen, from which he graduated in 1865. After this he attended the theological seminary in Blaubeuren, graduating in 1868, and in May, 1870, graduated from the University of Tübingen. He then joined the German army and fought throughout the Franco-Prussian war. Entering as a private in the 13th flying artillery, he was promoted to ensign after the battle of Woerth, and was made second lieutenant after the battle of Sedan. In the battles of Villiers and Champigny he was twice wounded and captured by the enemy. He was sent a captive to Paris and there held for two months. On being released, he spent six weeks in the hospital at Lagny and then joined his battery near Paris and served until the end of the war. Besides the battles already mentioned, he took a creditable part in many minor battles and skirmishes. After the war, Mr. Ruoff was selected to go to the government riding school at Hanover, where he remained six months and then served a year and a half with his regiment. In 1873 he left the army and the following year became pastor of the church of Mount Auburn, at Cincinnati. Here he remained until 1879, when he came to Pittsburg and assumed his present charge. During his long service in Pittsburg, Rev. Ruoff has fulfilled his duties as pastor to the satisfaction of his congregation and has made friends among all classes. He is a member of the F. and A. M., and A. O. U. W.

ISAAC NEWTON PATTERSON, of Pittsburg, Pa., a prominent attorney-at-law, with offices at No. 413 Fourth Ave., was born in Allegheny city, July 2, 1851, son of Abraham and Elizabeth (Young) Patterson, the former born in County Down, Ireland, in 1808, and when two years of age accompanied his parents to America and located in Mercer county, Pa. Abraham Patterson removed to Allegheny city in 1825, there spent the remainder of his life, and was engaged in building and timber manufacturing. He served in the councils of Allegheny city and Manchester, and was prominently identified with the progress of the city until his death, July 13, 1865. Elizabeth Young, mother of the subject, was born in Scotland and came to America with her parents in 1819, located in Allegheny city, where she was married, on Nov. 20, 1837, and died in November, 1895. Abraham and Elizabeth (Young) Patterson had the following children: Alexander (deceased), David Leslie, Elizabeth Y., wife of the late J. G. Stephenson, who was a prominent dry goods merchant of Pittsburg and president of the Arbuthnat-Stephenson company; Abram, better known as Abe (deceased); Agnes P., wife of Alexander McClure, president of the Alexander McClure timber company; Isaac Newton, Thomas Howe, Lillian B., Frank P., and four others that died in infancy. Isaac Newton Patterson was educated in the rudimentary courses in the public schools of Allegheny city, later attended the Pennsylvania military academy, and was graduated from the Western university, in the class of 1871, with the degree of bachelor of arts, and three years later his alma mater conferred upon him the degree of master of arts. In 1871 he registered as a student of law in the office of Stoner & Patterson, and in 1874 was admitted to the bar of Allegheny county, and since has successfully practiced in Pittsburg, where he is a member of all courts and of the Allegheny county bar association. Mr. Patterson has served as councilman and as a member of the board of education of the fifth ward of Allegheny city, and is a prominent figure in the public affairs of that corporation. He was married in Pittsburg, March 25, 1880, to Sadie J., daughter of J. Adolphus and Jane J. You, and though they have no children, their married life is a happy one. Mr. and Mrs. Patterson attend the Sixth United Presbyterian church, and reside in the fifth ward of Allegheny city. Alexander Patterson (deceased), oldest brother of our subject, was a prominent citizen of Allegheny city, where he was identified with the lumber business and was a leader of the republican side in political matters. He served in the Manchester council, was one of the first councilmen from that party of Allegheny city, and died in February, 1895. Abram Patterson, known to his friends as Abe, was born in Allegheny city in August, 1843; succeeded his father in the contracting business, and was a progressive and prosperous citizen. When eighteen years of age he enlisted in the 13th Pennsylvania volunteer infantry, served three years in the Civil war, and participated in many important engagements, being severely wounded in the seven days' fights around Richmond. He was a member of Post No. 88, Grand Army of the Republic, which is now called the Abe Patterson post, after him. He served seven terms as post commander, and was occupying that position at the time of his death, February, 1882. David Leslie Patterson, another brother, was born Feb. 2, 1840, and has spent his entire life in Allegheny city, where he is engaged in the manufacture and sale of lumber. He has served as councilman from the sixth ward for seven years, and for a number of years was school director for the fifth ward. He is president of the Standard building and loan association, and a member of the Sixth United Presbyterian church, of which organization he has been a member of the board of trustees for twenty-one years. He was married in Allegheny city, Sept. 26, 1866, to Duney E. Dean, a cousin of William Dean Howells, the novelist, and they have the following children: Alexander A., an attorney; May S., wife of Alexander Marion; David Leslie, who has served as city editor of the Pittsburg Chronicle-Telegraph; Edna V., wife of Preston C. Farrar; Agnes L., and Stuart Young.

JOHN C. HENRY, chief clerk to the bureau of health, Pittsburg, has been for years a leader in republican politics and active in local party affairs. He was born in the third ward, Pittsburg, in 1864, and was reared and educated there, graduating from the high school in 1881. He finished his education by attending night school, being employed during the day by John Paul, the hatter. After this he was for some time purchasing agent for the North American construction company and then became general traveling agent for R. D. Mettell & Co., dealers in electrical street railway material. For a time also, he worked as city salesman for the Electrical supply and construction company, now Doubleday, Hill

& Co., and then, in 1897, was appointed assistant clerk to the mayor of Pittsburg, at that time H. P. Ford. In the third year of Mayor Ford's term, Mr. Henry was appointed chief clerk and succeeded to the same position under Mayor William J. Diehl. When the new charter went into effect, in June, 1901, Mr. Henry was made chief clerk to the recorder, Hon. A. M. Brown, and in the same year obtained his present position. Mr. Henry was secretary of the fourteenth ward republican association for fourteen years, and has been secretary of the Young Men's republican tariff club, of Pittsburg, for ten years. In 1900 he was secretary of the League of republican clubs of Pennsylvania, and in 1901 acted as vice-president of the same organization. He is a member of the I. O. O. F., Jr. O. U. A. M., A. O. U. W. and Royal Arcanum and belongs to the Episcopal church.

CHARLES LUDLOW LIVINGSTON, attorney-at-law, with offices at No. 1102 Frick building, Pittsburg, Pa., is a native of New York city, having been born there June 10, 1870. The Livingston family is one of the oldest in the state of New York and adjoining states. Robert Livingston, the founder of the family in this country, coming to New York in 1672, where he acquired a vast tract of land on the Hudson river and founded Livingston manor. William Livingston, the great-great-grandfather of the subject of this sketch, and grandson of Robert, was the famous Revolutionary governor of New Jersey, while his great-grandfather, Brockholst Livingston, was a prominent attorney of New York, a judge of the supreme court of New York, and at the time of his death was a justice of the United States supreme court. He was also a colonel in the Revolutionary war and a general in the War of 1812. Through his paternal grandmother, Mr. Livingston is descended from William Allen, who was chief justice of Pennsylvania before the Revolution. Charles Ludlow Livingston is the son of Ludlow and Mary (Kieft) Livingston and the grandson of Anson Livingston. He was educated at Fordham college and New York university, graduating in 1891. Upon leaving college, he came to Pittsburg and perfected himself in the science of steel manufacture and electricity. Perceiving the immense advantages of his previous technical education if applied to the field of patent law, in 1899 he took up the study of law at the Western University of Pennsylvania, completed the course and commenced practice in January, 1903, devoting his entire attention to patent causes, for which his previous mechanical and electrical experience had eminently fitted him, and in which line he has built up a lucrative clientage. He was married, on Nov. 12, 1891, to Miss Mary E. Keating, daughter of A. F. and Emily Keating, and three children have been born to them. They are: Dorothy, Philip Anson and Carroll Ludlow. They reside at Oakmont, a suburb of Pittsburg. Mr. Livingston is just approaching the age when men accomplish their greatest achievements, and as his thorough knowledge of patent law, combined with his practical electrical and mechanical experience, brings him into close touch with ingenious and inventive minds and great industrial corporations, it is safe to predict for him a brilliant future and a career as illustrious as that of any of his historic ancestors.

ROBERT E. CLULEY, cashier in the Pittsburg postoffice, was born in Pittsburg in 1866. He was reared and educated in Pittsburg, graduating from the high school in 1884. Since that time he has had a successful career in the public service, being employed in several city offices before he obtained his present position. Mr. Cluley's first position was that of clerk in the office of the assessors of Pittsburg, where he remained four years. In 1888 he became bookkeeper in the department of charities, and was five years later promoted to the position of chief clerk, in which capacity he served seven years. Mr. Cluley then became chief clerk in the office of the director of public works, and was employed there until June, 1902, when he was made cashier of the Pittsburg postoffice.

ANDREW J. PITCAIRN, superintendent of the bureau of health, Pittsburg, was born in that city in July, 1853. He was reared in Pittsburg, attended school until he reached the age of twelve, and afterwards studied in a night school. Mr. Pitcairn's first occupation was in a tobacco factory, where he remained about a year. He entered the employ of the Pennsylvania railroad, working in the dispatcher's office, and while there learned telegraphy. He afterwards spent seven years of his life as a telegraph operator. In 1875 he gave up this business and was for three years deputy in the sheriff's office. After this he became a passenger brakeman for the Pennsylvania company, and after two years in this position, his ability and attention to duty won him promotion, and for the next twenty-one years, until September, 1901, he was a railroad conductor. He received the appointment to his present position Oct. 1, 1901, and has proved a capable and faithful official. Mr. Pitcairn has always taken great interest in public affairs. He served in the city council of Pittsburg from 1884 to 1896, representing the eighth ward, and was in 1897 member of the state legislature from the third legislative district. Mr. Pitcairn is a Knight Templar and Mystic Shriner. He is a member of the First Presbyterian church.

SAMUEL COULTER, chief of police of East Pittsburg, was born in England, at Newcastle-upon-Tyne, Aug. 18, 1868, son of James William and Elizabeth Coulter. His mother died when Samuel Coulter was three years old. His father left England to try his fortunes in America, and secured work in the coal mines of Ohio, sending for his children later. Samuel Coulter was educated in the schools of Perry county, Ohio, and learned the plumbing and pipe-fitting trade, at which vocation he was engaged for a number of years. Hearing of the rapid rise of East Pittsburg as a manufacturing town, he moved there in 1899, and secured a position as patrolman. After three years' service, he was made head of the force in March, 1902, and has proved an able and efficient chief. The police force of East Pittsburg consists of only three patrolman, besides the chief, yet so effective is the service that this small number is able to keep the peace in a town of 8,000 workmen. Mr. Coulter was married, July 4, 1889, to Ella, daughter of Edward and Elizabeth Duffy, early settlers of Perry county. Mr. and Mrs. Coulter have four children: James William, born July 2, 1890; Agnes, born April 25, 1893; Laurettie, born Dec. 22, 1899, and Clara, born Aug. 17, 1902. Chief Coulter is a member of Turtle Creek lodge, No. 777, I. O. O. F.; past chancellor of Oak Hill Knights of Pythias; member of Court Pride of the Union and Foresters of Braddock. In religious belief he is a Methodist. He has been prominent in democratic politics, holds the position of inspector, and is also a member of the county committee.

WILLIAM MARSHALL STEVENSON, librarian of the Carnegie free library, of Allegheny, was born in Johnstown, Pa., Nov. 30, 1855. He is of Scotch-Irish ancestry, and can trace his family history back to Robert Stevenson, who emigrated from Scotland to Ireland in 1677, and was a very prominent man in his day. He is the son of Ross and Martha Ann (Harbison) Stevenson, the father born in Strabane, Ireland, Nov. 12, 1814, and died in Washington, Pa., Jan. 10, 1893, and the mother born at West Lebanon, Pa., in 1831, and is still living. The family consisted of six sons and one daughter: Lizzie Hurst, now Mrs. Jerome W. Potts; Matthew Harbison, a practicing attorney of the Pittsburg bar; Thomas John, pastor of the First Presbyterian church, Hannibal, Mo.; Robert Francis, a prominent business man of Washington, Pa.; Joseph Ross, pastor of the Fifth Avenue Presbyterian church, New York city; Henry Patterson, who died in May, 1892, and William Marshall, the subject of this sketch. Mr. Stevenson was graduated with honors from Washington and Jefferson college in 1876, having acted as tutor in mathematics in his alma mater during his senior year. For two years after his graduation he was instructor in ancient and modern languages in the Placerville academy, California, and for the next two years studied music and languages at the leading institutions of the continent, chiefly at the University of Leipsic, the conservatory at Dresden, and at the College de France, Paris. While there he was under the instruction of some of the noted scholars, among them being Breal, the philologist, and Renan, the great French critic. Upon his return to the United States, Mr. Stevenson was called to the chair of Greek and Latin in the Pittsburg central high school, which position he held for four years, resigning to take up the study of law. He entered the office of John D. Schafer, was admitted to the bar one year later, and from 1885 to 1890 spent his time equally in the practice of law and in journalism, in the latter case on the staff of the New York Tribune, and later, a writer for the Chicago Mail, the Chronicle-Telegraph, the Times, and the Commercial Gazette, of Pittsburg. His connection with the Pittsburg newspapers was in the capacity of musical and dramatic editor and special reporter on legal topics. In 1889 he again visited Europe, this time in the study of the Spanish language and literature, and shortly after his return, was elected librarian of the Carnegie free library, of Allegheny, the first public, tax-supported library founded by Mr. Carnegie. Mr. Stevenson came to his position when the library had not one volume on its shelves, with no one to help him in his task of organization, and now it contains 50,000 volumes catalogued, and 10,000 pamphlets, documents and duplicates not catalogued. In 1899 he secured from Mr. Carnegie an additional gift of $25,000 for additions and improvements. Mr. Stevenson was a delegate to the international conference of librarians held in London in 1897, is a member of the American and the Keystone state library associations, the Pennsylvania free library commission, was first president of the West Pennsylvania library club, an honorary member of the Western Pennsylvania historical society and of the Deutscher Lese Verein. Mr. Stevenson is very versatile in his attainments, speaks German, French, Italian, Spanish and Russian fluently, reads Dutch, Danish, Swedish, Norwegian, Portuguese, modern Greek and Polish, with the aid of a dictionary, and has studied Sanskrit, Gothic, Turkish, Finnish, Arabic and Chinese. His literary work has been mostly contributions to periodicals and local histories, and in 1899 he published a sketch, "Mr. Carnegie and His Libraries," which met with very favorable and enthusiastic reception. In politics he is a republican, and in religion a Presbyterian. He has never married, but, as he expresses it, "is wedded to his work."

LINFORD L. DILWORTH, chief clerk of the department of public works, Pittsburg, was born in the fourteenth ward of that city in 1855. He was reared there and attended the public schools, and afterwards became a student at the West Philadelphia academy, from which he graduated in 1874. He then spent eight years as clerk for his father, John S. Dilworth, in the grocery of Dilworth & Co., being also for three years of the time engaged in the produce business for himself. In 1884 he embarked in the brokerage business, in which he was engaged until 1892, when he entered the employ of the Carnegie steel corporation. He remained with this concern three years, and then, in 1895, began his career in the city service as inspector in the bureau of water supply. After two years in this position, Mr. Dilworth was transferred to the board of viewers as clerk, was made chief clerk the same year, and served as such until June, 1902, when he was given his present office. Mr. Dilworth is a Presbyterian in religious belief, and in politics an influential republican.

SAMUEL G. BAILEY, attorney-at-law, whose office is at No. 807 People's savings bank building, Pittsburg, was born in Bavington, Pa., July 21, 1874. His parents were William S. and Esther Ann (Galbraith) Bailey, both of whom are living and respected residents of Washington county. The former is an ardent republican, and has acceptably filled the office of county commissioner of Washington county for two terms. Samuel G. Bailey received his education at the Ingleside academy and at Westminster college, at Lawrence, Pa., and also at Princeton university. He began reading law in the office of O'Brien & Ashley, then took the full law course in the Western University of Pennsylvania, graduating in 1897. He was at once admitted to the bar and began his practice in Pittsburg, and is now a member of all the courts. He is a tireless worker in his profession and is rapidly forging to the front in his practice. Politically, he is a republican, but has affiliated to some extent with the citizens' movement in its fight for cleaner and better local and state government. He was a candidate for the legislature on the citizens' and democratic tickets from the eighth legislative district in 1902, and although defeated by a small margin, he demonstrated his popularity. Mr. Bailey is chairman of the citizens' organization in the thirty-seventh ward, and is alert to its welfare. He is a member of Oakland lodge, No. 535, F. and A. M.

EDWARD MEYER, funeral director at No. 4705 Liberty Ave., Pittsburg, was born in Pittsburg, in the ninth ward, in 1858, and was there reared and educated in a parochial school. Leaving school in 1870, he became associated in business with his father, Anthony Meyer, who, prior to his death in 1887, conducted a retail furniture store and undertaking business in the ninth ward. Mr. Meyer remained in the employ of his father until 1880, and then started for himself in the undertaking business in the sixteenth ward. He moved to his present pleasant quarters in 1894. Mr. Meyer is an independent in politics. He is an earnest member of St. Joseph's Catholic church. He is a man of unblemished character, as honest in his business as he is proficient, and enjoys the respect of all who know him.

JESSE H. WRIGHT, of Stonedale, Pa., closely identified with the industrial interests of that section, was born April 18, 1866, son of Robert and Sarah Wright, the former a successful farmer and the son of Irish parents who came to the United States and settled in Franklin township, Allegheny county, Pa. His parents were both born in Franklin township and had thirteen children, four of them dying in infancy, Baxter B. in 1898, and the others are: Mary E., John F., James E., Robert M., Minnie E., Jesse H., Harry R. and Luella M. Jesse H. Wright has been engaged in industrial lines the greater part of his business career and is now in the employ of the South Pennsylvania company, of Oil City. He was married, on Oct. 21, 1894, to Ida Downing, and they have had three children: Sarah Eliza May, the eldest, born March 14, 1896; Raymond Percy Wilson, born May 28, 1897, and a son born February 13 and died March 2, 1901. Mr. Wright is well and favorably known in the community in which he resides and enjoys the confidence and respect of his neighbors and acquaintances. Mrs. Wright is the daughter of Archibald Downing, both father and mother being natives of Clarion county, the former born July 3, 1826, and the latter in 1829. They were married in 1851 in Venango county, removing in 1866 to Allegheny county, where they have since resided.

THOMAS EDGAR, alderman from the twenty-ninth ward, Pittsburg, was born in Pittsburg, in the thirty-third ward, in 1862. In 1866 he moved with his parents to the twenty-ninth ward, where he was reared and educated in the public schools. Upon leaving school he was employed for three years in the office of Lewis, Oliver & Co., now Oliver Bros., as office boy. He obtained a position with the Lewis foundry and machine company, where he learned the machinists' trade, remaining with this firm three and a half years. After this he was employed for about three years in the Westinghouse foundry and machine works, and for a year at Beaver Falls, Pa., in the Hartman steel works. Returning to Pittsburg, he was employed by Oliver Bros. for three years, and by Jones & Laughlin about two years. In 1892 Mr. Edgar engaged to work for Mr. F. O. Wolff, a civil engineer, remaining at this employment until his election as alderman from the twenty-ninth ward in 1895. In the council, Mr. Edgar performed his duties in a manner so satisfactory to his constituents that they re-elected him in February, 1902. Before this time, from 1894 to 1897, he had served as school director. Mr. Edgar is a member of the United Presbyterian church. In politics he is an active republican.

THOMAS RENSHAW, a prominent mine superintendent, residing in Carnegie, was born in Nottinghamshire, England, Nov. 26, 1850, son of Severn and Sarah (Burton) Renshaw. Severn Renshaw was a farmer in England. He and his wife were members of the Established church. They both died in England. Thomas Renshaw, the subject of this sketch, is the third of four children. Of the other three, John died in England in 1892, when fifty-eight years old; Edward is living in England, and Mary, also a resident of England, is the wife of James Lawrence. Thomas Renshaw came to America in 1869, locating in Pittsburg, and immediately commenced work in the coal mines, and has been engaged in coal-mining ever since that time. Commencing at the bottom, he has worked his way up and is now one of the best-known men in his business in Allegheny county. He formerly owned a quarter interest in the Nottingham coal mines, which was sold to Henry Floshheim and disposed of by him to the Pittsburg coal company. After the Nottingham mine was sold, Mr. Renshaw was employed by the Oak Ridge coal company for about six months, and then entered the employ of the Essen coal company, where he has for the past ten years been superintendent, with full charge of the mine. The Essen coal company has now been sold to the Pittsburg coal company, but Mr. Renshaw still has charge of the mine, where his ability and faithful attention to duty have made him a valuable superintendent. In politics Mr. Renshaw is a republican, and served three years as auditor of Union township, Allegheny county, resigning at the end of that time because of a change in residence. On May 30, 1875, Mr. Renshaw married Miss Elizabeth Hepplewhite, daughter of Ralph Hepplewhite, who was born in England, and Elizabeth (Marshall) Hepplewhite, a native of Banksville, Allegheny Co., Pa. Mrs.

Renshaw is the second of three children. An older sister, Mary J., married Ernest Salt, and resides at Millville, Allegheny county, and a younger sister, Isabella, lives at home with her mother. Mr. and Mrs. Thomas Renshaw have had six children. The first-born, Sarah B., died when two years old, and the youngest, Alvarine, born Aug. 16, 1896, died Oct. 26, 1899. Of the four living, Margaret married J. B. Davis, and has one child, Ralph S.; Ralph Marshall is a machinist; Lizzie Vietta and John D. are younger children at home. Mr. Renshaw and family attend the Episcopal church. Mr. Renshaw is a prominent and influential Mason and a member of the Knights of the Golden Eagle.

WILLIS A. BOOTHE, of Pittsburg, Pa., a prominent attorney, with offices at No. 413 Fourth Ave., was born in Pittsburg, in that part of the city now included in the thirteenth ward but formerly called Minersville, Aug. 6, 1851, son of Willis and Mary Ann (Pusey) Boothe, the former having died in November, 1889, and the latter in April, 1891. His mother was a daughter of Nathan Pusey, one of the early residents of Washington county, Pa., and a well-known citizen of that part of Pennsylvania. His father, Willis Boothe, was born in Derby, Conn., in 1806, and in his boyhood removed to New York state, locating at Binghamton, where he was reared and educated. In 1828 he removed to Pittsburg and engaged in different mercantile pursuits, a large portion of his time being devoted to the lumber business. While in no sense of the word a politician, yet Mr. Boothe held several minor offices and was well known throughout the city. He was an active member of the Seventh Presbyterian church and for many years an elder of that organization. He was married to Mary Ann Pusey, in Washington county, in 1834, and they had the following children: Martha, who married John H. Claney and died in September, 1894; Julia, wife of Fred Dickinson, of Chicago; Mary E., who married H. A. Lavely and died Oct. 27, 1897; Willis A., and Nathan P., who married Ada Brandt, of Des Moines, Ia. Willis A. Boothe was educated in the splendid public schools of Pittsburg and later attended the Western university, which at that time was located in Pittsburg. He read law in the office of David Reed, was admitted to the bar in 1874 and since has continuously practiced in Pittsburg. Mr. Boothe is a member of all courts, has a fine practice and stands well among his legal brethren, as is evidenced by his election to the position of treasurer of the Allegheny county bar association, which office he still holds. He was married in Salem, Ohio, Sept. 14, 1876, to Sarah H., daughter of Dr. Clements and Emilia Baelz, and they have had four children: Emilia B., Willis, Clements, who died in childhood, and Sarah Hester. Mr. Boothe and his family are members of the Third Presbyterian church, of which Mr. Boothe is an elder. He is a republican in his political views and, while not a seeker for office, yet holds the position of president of the school board of the twenty-second ward. Mr. Boothe is an able and popular member of the Allegheny county bar, commands a splendid legal business and is highly esteemed throughout the city for his manly qualities and strict integrity.

WILLIAM H. LINSLEY, mine superintendent, was born in Durhamshire, England, Jan. 25, 1856, son of William and Margaret Linsley. The father was a locomotive engineer in England and was killed in a wreck when twenty-seven years old, in 1858. In 1862 his widow married William Robinson, and shortly after this came to America, bringing with her her only child, William. On coming to America, William Robinson followed for a time his vocation as a blacksmith in Temperanceville, now West End, Pittsburg. He now resides in Carnegie, where he kept a grocery store. His wife died July 21, 1902, at the age of sixty-four. She was a daughter of William and Anna (Bell) Henderson, both now deceased, and was one of eight children, five of whom are still living: Thomas, a resident of Spring Valley, Ill.; Mrs. John Byers, of Mount Washington; John, who lives at Finleyville, Washington county; Mrs. David Fulton, of Castle Shannon, Pa., and Launcelot, also a resident of Castle Shannon. William H. Linsley, the subject of this sketch, was educated in the public schools. He has also recently completed a course in mining at the International correspondence school, Scranton, Pa. When a young man Mr. Linsley worked five years in a coal mine and then learned the blacksmith trade, which he followed for twelve years, about a year of that time being located in Carnegie. In 1884 he returned to the mines and was for five years engaged in weighing coal at the Nixon mine, Chartiers Valley coal company, and then became mine superintendent and foreman at the same mine, remaining there until 1899. At this time the mine was bought by the Pittsburg coal company and Mr. Linsley remained as superintendent and still holds that position. Besides this he is superintendent at the Harrison mine and the Esser coal mine, making three mines in all under his management. Mr. Linsley is widely and favorably known as a miner of exceptional ability and the importance of the trusts which he holds gives evidence of the confidence in which he is held by his employers. On Christmas day, 1877, he was married to Miss Elizabeth Boden, daughter of David and Helen (Cook) Boden, who are mentioned on another page of this work, and has eight children, viz.: Mabel Irene, graduate of the Duquesne business college, Pittsburg, class of 1897, now employed as clerk in the delinquent tax office, county court house, Pittsburg; Nellie V., graduate of Curry college, Pittsburg, class of 1898, for the past three years clerk in her father's office; William F., an electrician, employed in one of the mines of which his father is superintendent; Richard E., student at Duff's business college, Pittsburg; Robert Cook, attending graded schools; Clara I., Leile M. and Emma Eugene. Mr. Linsley takes an active interest in republican politics. He has for the past three years been school director in his township. He is an enthusiastic Mason, being a member of Centennial lodge, No. 544; Cyrus chapter, No. 280, and Chartiers commandery, No. 78.

FRANK F. SNEATHEN, of Pittsburg, Pa., a prominent attorney, with offices at No. 413 Fourth Ave., was born in Pittsburg, Oct. 24, 1857, son of John B. and Mary A. (Kiefer) Sneathen. John B. Sneathen was born in Dauphin county, Pa., in 1832, of Scotch ancestry, his parents having come from Scotland at an early date and settled in eastern Pennsylvania. John B. Sneathen came to Allegheny county when a mere boy, there acquired a thorough education, and when manhood was reached, engaged in the business of a commission merchant and coal shipper on the Ohio river. He was a prominent and progressive citizen, served as a councilman from the twenty-second ward for sixteen years, a school director for about twelve years, and died on June 10, 1896. His wife died on June 17, 1877. Frank F. Sneathen attended the schools of the second and twenty-second wards of Pittsburg, and spent the years from 1870 to 1873 at the Western University of Pennsylvania. Later he attended the Pennsylvania military academy at Chester, Pa., where he was captain of Company A, of the academy corps of cadets. He was graduated from that institution on June 21, 1877, and spent the next two years in attending a special law course at Harvard college. He returned to Pittsburg and registered as a student in the office of Hon. M. W. Atcheson, in July, 1879, where he remained until December, 1880, when he was admitted to the bar of Allegheny county. Mr. Sneathen is a member of all courts and has a fine practice. He is prominently connected with the Odd Fellows and the Royal Arcanum. His military record is a splendid one, having served as captain of Company F, 18th regiment, Pennsylvania volunteer infantry, from 1879 to 1881; major of that regiment from 1881 to 1884; lieutenant-colonel from 1884 to 1887, when he was retired with that rank. He was married in Pittsburg, Jan. 12, 1886, to Emma C., daughter of George A. Kim, and they have one daughter, Cora Marie.

GUSTAVUS B. OBEY, superintendent of the Youghiogheny and Monongahela division of the Pittsburg & Lake Erie railroad, with offices in Pittsburg, was born in the city of Pittsburg, Pa., May 23, 1865. He is the elder of the two children born to his parents, William H. and Rachael R. (Shaffer) Obey, his younger brother, Jared E. Obey, being a resident of Pittsburg. His father, who has been deceased for several years, was for a long time an officer in the service of the United States government, and during the Civil war was captain of Company F, 6th Pennsylvania artillery. Among the thousands of men in the service of the great railway systems of the country, there are many who began in humble positions and worked their way up to places of trust and responsibility. Such a man is Gustavus B. Obey. After receiving his education in the common schools of his native city and Westminster college, located at New Wilmington, Pa., he began his career as a railroad man in 1882 as assistant agent for the Pittsburg & Western, at Zelienople, Pa. About a year later he went to Callery Junction as telegraph operator, and from there to Allegheny city, where he remained until the great Johnstown flood, which cut off railroad and telegraph communication. Mr. Obey was sent to Foxburg, Clarion county, to assume the management of the division from that point until communication could be reopened. His work was so well done that after his return to Allegheny city, he was appointed chief train dispatcher and was again located at Foxburg, that place being decided on as a more advantageous point for the handling of trains than Allegheny city. During the succeeding years he was stationed at various points on the lines belonging to the Pittsburg & Western system. Leaving Foxburg he went to New Castle, Pa., then he was sent to Painesville, Ohio, where he remained for about two years. He then returned to New Castle as the chief train dispatcher for the main line of the road. Later he left the Pittsburg & Western and accepted a position with the Pittsburg & Lake Erie. This brought him to Pittsburg, where he has ever since been located. In a short time he became the chief train dispatcher for that railroad company, and in November, 1901, he was promoted to his present position, with headquarters in Pittsburg. Mr. Obey is prominent in the Masonic circles of Pittsburg, being a member of all the different bodies of that order. He is also a member of the Monongahela club and the Pittsburg railway club. In 1892, he led to the altar Miss Matie Lee Hart, a highly accomplished young lady of Foxburg, Pa. The wedded life of Mr. and Mrs. Obey has been a happy one. He resides at Coraopolis in a cozy suburban home, where he and his estimable wife are surrounded by a large circle of friends.

ALONZO N. McCANN, accountant in the department of public safety, Pittsburg, was born in Flemington, N. J., Sept. 29, 1843, was reared there and educated in the common schools of that city. He then engaged in business and in September, 1862, left a clerkship to enlist in the Union army as a private in Company F, 22d New Jersey volunteer infantry. Here he served nine months, fighting in the battles of Fredericksburg and Chancellorsville, and was then given an honorable discharge. Later, in August, 1864, he enlisted in the navy and served until the close of the war as ship's writer on the receiving ship "Vermont," at the Brooklyn navy yard. After the war he was employed for about two years as clerk in a dry goods store at Flemington, and then went to Brooklyn and was engaged as a dry goods salesman in Brooklyn and New York until 1892, when he came to Pittsburg. In 1896 Mr. McCann entered the service of the city under J. O. Brown, at that time director of public safety and now recorder, and has been accountant in the department of public safety ever since. Mr. McCann resides in the twentieth ward, Pittsburg. He is a member of the Baptist church.

FRANK B. DAVIS, of Stone township, Pa., a popular railroad conductor, is a native of Stone township and the son of David and Margaret (Burns) Davis. His father was a saddler by trade but during the latter years of his life devoted his attention to gardening, and died several years since. His mother is now sixty-two years of age and had nine children, eight of whom are now living. His paternal ancestors came from Wales and his mother's progenitors were from the Emerald Isle. Frank B. Davis attended the public schools of Stone township until he was sixteen years of age and then began to earn his own living, working at various occupations until he became a clerk for the Pittsburg & Lake Erie railroad. He continued in that position for two years and a half and for the next five years was connected with the operating department in the capacity of brakeman. In 1898 Mr. Davis was promoted to his present position of conductor and is now on the through freight of the York division of the Pittsburg & Lake Erie railroad. Mr. Davis was happily married to Helen, daughter of James O'Day, of McKee's Rocks, and they have three children. Mr. Davis is a republican in his political convictions, and in February, 1903, was elected a justice of the peace of Stone township, in which position he is making a fine record. Mr. Davis is a member of the Order of Railway Conductors, the Brotherhood of Railway Trainmen and the Alfaretta lodge of Knights of Pythias of McKee's Rocks. He has a pretty home in Stone township and is one of the substantial citizens of that community.

CHARLES E. MARTIN, of Pittsburg, Pa., a rising young attorney, with offices in the Park building, was born at Pittsburg, Jan. 13, 1881, son of James and Jennie (Scott) Martin, both natives of Allegheny county and residents of Pittsburg. Charles Martin was educated in the graded and high schools of Pittsburg, graduating from the latter institution in 1899. Subsequently he read law in the office of Lyon, McKee & Mitchell, of Pittsburg, and then attended the Pittsburg law school, graduating with the class of 1902. He was admitted to the bar on Oct. 4, 1902; at once entered on the practice of his profession, and has met with great encouragement in his vocation. His father was born in Lawrenceville, Pa., and has spent his life in Allegheny county, where he is an expert accountant for the Bessemer & Lake Erie railroad. His mother was born in Millville, Pa., and had four children, viz.: Walton W., M. D.; Charles E., Nellie, and Ralph (deceased). Walton W. Martin, a physician and surgeon, with offices at No. 4230 Sherman St., Pittsburg, was born in that city and educated in the splendid schools of his native town, graduating from the high school in 1896. He studied medicine at the Western University of Pennsylvania, graduated in 1900, and for the next year was resident physician for that institution. In 1901 Dr. Martin began the practice of his profession in Pittsburg, and has secured a splendid standing among the younger physicians of that city. He is a member of the Austin Flint medical society, the Hallman lodge of Masons, and the Order of Heptasophs.

R. H. RAMAGE, who was a well-known physician and surgeon of Carnegie, was a native of Pennsylvania, born Jan. 16, 1843. His parents, William and Sarah (Wilson) Ramage, were born in Washington county, and were prominent members of the Methodist church. Mr. Ramage was a farmer by occupation, was for twenty-five years justice of the peace, was a school director, and held several other public offices. He and his wife had seven children born to them, and all are living: Margaret; Benjamin F., a Westmoreland county farmer; R. H., the subject of this sketch; Rebecca J., now Mrs. Goshorn, of Allegheny; William, a mill worker of Allegheny; Mary, and John W., a farmer in Missouri. After receiving a common-school education, Dr. R. H. Ramage read medicine under Dr. White, a prominent physician of his time, and then attended the Hahnemann medical college, of Philadelphia. He next pursued his studies at the Hospital medical college, at Cleveland, Ohio, graduating from that institution in the class of 1872. After two years of hospital experience, he began to practice in Allegheny, and in December, 1877, came to Mansfield (now Carnegie), where he devoted his time to a steadily increasing practice until his death. Dr. Ramage was of the homœopathic school, and was a well-read man, informed on all the new discoveries in his profession, and thoroughly abreast of the times.

He had been an occasional contributor to medical journals. He took an active interest in the welfare of Carnegie, and at the time of his death owned several properties in that flourishing city. Dr. Ramage was married, Oct. 20, 1880, to Miss Sarah E. Belton, daughter of E. J. Belton, of Pittsburg. Mrs. Ramage died in August, 1901, at the age of fifty-five. She was a graduate of Pleasant Hill seminary, and taught school several years before her marriage to Dr. Ramage. An influential member of the Presbyterian church and a student of rare attainments, her life was an inspiration to the many who knew her, and her death brought sorrow to their hearts. Dr. Ramage was a prominent member of the Masonic fraternity, having been a member of Centennial lodge, No. 504, and Cyrus chapter, No. 280, R. A. M. He was also a member of Chartiers commandery, No. 78, Knights Templars. In politics Dr. Ramage was a republican.

HENRY L. KING, of Pittsburg, Pa., a prominent attorney, was born in that city, Sept. 20, 1858, son of Henry A. and Annie E. (Wenzel) King, both surviving and now residing near Greensburg, Westmoreland Co., Pa. The King family is of English origin, but later settled in Rhine province, Germany, this settlement having been made by the great-grandfather of Henry L., Job King, of Wolverhampton, England. The Wenzel family is of German origin, both of Mr. King's parents being born in that country and accompanying their respective parents to the United States, settling at Pittsburg in 1846. There his father learned the trade of glass-blowing and was so engaged until 1876, when he removed to his present home and since has devoted his attention to agricultural pursuits. Henry L. King was educated in the splendid public schools of Pittsburg, and at the branch normal school at Greensburg, taught school for five years in Westmoreland county, attended the law department of the University of Michigan and was there graduated in the class of 1885. He was admitted to the bar of Michigan in the spring of 1885, came to Pittsburg and was admitted to the bar of that city on Dec. 23, 1885. Since then Mr. King has been in continuous practice, is a member of all courts and devotes his attention to civil, building and loan and corporation business. He has met with unusual success and stands high among his confreres. Mr. King was married, in October, 1891, to Rose S. King, and they have three children: Sylvia A., Mignonette L. and Ruth E. He intends to remain in Pittsburg, Pa., which is the industrial center of the United States.

JOHN A. McCLARIN, of Tarentum, Pa., a successful truck farmer, was born in Beaver county, Oct. 27, 1825, son of William and Jane (Cork) McClarin, both natives of Ireland, who emigrated to Canada in 1815, later located in Beaver county, Pa., and in 1840 settled in Allegheny county, where they resided until their deaths in 1886 and 1882, respectively. They were the parents of seven children, two of whom are now living and are: John A. and Sarah J. William McClarin was a prosperous farmer, a leading democrat, and held the positions of supervisor, assessor and school director. John A. McClarin was reared on his father's farm, received his educational training in the common schools, and has lived on the farm he owns for seven years. He makes a specialty of truck and small fruits, and his labors and industry have been crowned with much success. In political matters he is a democrat, though in local matters he looks more to the man than to the party. He served as a school director for four years, and is well known and popular in the community in which he resides. Sarah J., the only surviving sister of John A. McClarin, was born in 1835, and subsequently married Amos Boyd, a glass-worker, who met his death in 1862 at Ball's Bluff, while serving in the Union army. Mr. and Mrs. Boyd had three children: James, of Beaver county; William, of Westmoreland county, and Mary J., who was educated in the common schools, married Walter Grove, of Venango county, and is the mother of the following children: Elmer E. (deceased), Earl and Edwin J.

SYLVESTER J. SNEE, of Pittsburg, Pa., a well-known attorney-at-law, was born in Jefferson township, Allegheny Co., Pa., July 8, 1876, son of John W. and Margaret (Huffman) Snee, both natives of Jefferson township, where they have spent their entire lives, with the exception of two years. His father was a successful farmer for many years, but has now retired from active participation in agricultural matters, and is spending the declining years of his life in comfort and ease at his home in Jefferson township. Mr. Snee's ancestors are of Irish extraction, and were among the earliest settlers of Jefferson township, where they enjoyed the respect and esteem due to honorable and upright people. Sylvester J. Snee was educated in the Duquesne college, Pittsburg, and the Washington and Jefferson college, Washington, Pa.; is a graduate of both institutions, and received the degree of bachelor of science from Washington and Jefferson college. Mr. Snee then read law in the office of George B. Guffy, of Pittsburg; later entered the law department of the Western University of Pennsylvania, and there was graduated with the class of 1902. He was admitted to the bar in September of that year, entered on the practice at once, and has since met with much encouragement in his professional career. Mr. Snee is a young man of ability and integrity, well-read in the law, and has a bright future before him as an advocate and counselor.

WILLIAM A. ARNOLD, M. D., of Tarentum, Pa., a well-known physician and surgeon, was born in that city, March 28, 1869. He is a son of George and Elizabeth (Mahaffey) Arnold, the former a native of Germany, and the latter born in Allegheny city, Pa. The parents of George Arnold were John and Katherine (Whiting) Arnold, both natives of Germany, who came to America in 1838, settling in Butler county, where they resided the remainder of their lives. The maternal grandparents of Dr. Arnold were James and Catherine Mahaffey, who were among the early settlers of Allegheny county. James Mahaffey was born in 1793; Catherine, his wife, in 1794, and both died in West Deer township in 1851. The maternal great-grandfather of Dr. Arnold, James Burns, was an early settler in Philadelphia, and was an officer in the Revolution. George Arnold, the father of Dr. Arnold, was born Feb. 2, 1824, reared on a farm, and educated in the common schools. In 1842 he came to Tarentum, where he resided until his death in May, 1889. He was a whig, and later a republican, and he and his wife were both members of the Methodist church. They were the parents of ten children, eight of whom are now living. Dr. Arnold was reared in Tarentum, graduated from the schools of that city, and in 1901 was graduated from the medical department of the Western university, and has since practiced medicine with much success in his native city. Prior to studying medicine, he was employed by the Flocus glass company, of Tarentum; rose to be general manager of that concern, and occupied that position when he retired from commercial life to study for his professional career. Dr. Arnold has taken a prominent stand among the physicians of Tarentum, and is a member of the Allegheny county medical society and of the Allegheny valley medical association. He is a member of the Odd Fellows and the Junior Order of United American Mechanics. He was married, on Dec. 8, 1897, to Julia E. Enrich, daughter of a prominent merchant, now deceased, and to them were born two daughters: Amarillo and Elizabeth. Dr. and Mrs. Arnold are members of the Methodist church, and prominent in social and religious circles of Tarentum.

WILLIAM MORGAN WATSON, of Pittsburg, Pa., a distinguished attorney-at-law, was born in Washington, Pa., April 3, 1855, son of James and Maria Woodbridge (Morgan) Watson. His mother was a daughter of George and Elizabeth (Aldrich) Morgan and her father a son of Col. George Morgan, who was Indian agent at Pittsburg at the beginning of the Revolutionary war and the builder of the first shingle-roof house in the city of Pittsburg, and who later removed to what is now Morganza, Washington Co., Pa., where he spent the remaining days of his life. It was at the old homestead at Morganza that Aaron Burr called to visit the great-grandfather of William M. Watson in 1803 or 1804, Burr being an old acquaintance of the Morgans in Philadelphia and Princeton, and while on this visit disclosed enough of his scheme to convince Colonel Morgan that he was guilty of treason and contemplated serious harm to the government. Acting on this information, Colonel Morgan despatched his two sons to Washington city to inform President Jefferson of Burr's intentions, which was the first information the president had of this contemplated action. The rest of the Burr case is too well known to be repeated here and Colonel Morgan's part in the affair is fully described in James Parton's life of Burr. Colonel Morgan was a brother of Dr. John Morgan, of Philadelphia, who was a famous physician and the first surgeon-general of the United States, holding that position under Washington's administration. Mr. Watson's father was a son of John and Mary (Miller) Watson and his great-grandfather, James Watson, is said by family tradition to have been a colonel in the patriot army during the American Revolution. Mr. Watson's father was a prominent attorney-at-law and was in continuous practice at Washington, Pa., from 1831 to 1875, a period of forty-four years. He was appointed judge of the court of common pleas for Washington and Greene counties but refused to serve, much to the regret of the attorneys of that section. His parents had ten children, two of whom died in infancy, George Morgan, a banker of Pittsburg, died in 1882, and the others are: Elizabeth T.; Mary B., widow of Rev. Alexander Reed; Jane G.; David T.; Matilda W., wife of Maj. Andrew G. Happer; James, a prominent lawyer of New York city, and William Morgan. William Morgan Watson was graduated from the Washington and Jefferson college in 1875; later was graduated from Harvard law school and in 1879 admitted to the bar. Since that time he has practiced his profession with unvarying success and is a member of all the local courts and of the supreme court of the United States. Mr. Watson was married in Pittsburg, in April, 1884, to Sarah Ormsby, daughter of William and Sarah (Ormsby) McKnight, and a member of a prominent colonial family. They have two children: Ormsby Morgan and Maria Morgan. Mr. Watson has always been a republican but is in no sense an office-seeker, preferring to devote his entire time to the profession in which he has made such a success. Mr. and Mrs. Watson are members of the Presbyterian church and reside at Swissvale.

GEORGE H. QUAILL, the great-grandson of Robert Quaill, an ancestor who is mentioned on page 358, Vol. II, of this work, is a prominent lawyer of the city of Pittsburg, and resides in the borough of Bellevue. He was born in the old ancestral homestead on the farm in Ross township, on Feb. 23, 1855. His father was David R. Quaill, who is still living at the advanced age of seventy-five years, and his mother was Sarah J. Shafer, a sister of Noah W. Shafer, a well-known and distinguished member of the Pittsburg bar. For several generations George seems to have been a favorite name in the Quaill family. This George obtained his education, until he was twelve years of age, in the public schools of the township where he was born, then spent two years at a business college in the city of Pittsburg, after which he finished his education at the Pennsylvania state normal school, at Millersville, Lancaster Co., Pa., where he graduated in 1873. Always a good student, he stood among the best in his classes and graduated with distinction. He taught school two years, then read law with his uncle above mentioned and was admitted to the Pittsburg bar on Feb. 23, 1878, where he at once took a prominent place as a general practitioner. As an indefatigable worker he has no peer, and his genial manners and strict adherence to business, coupled with his unswerving fidelity to his clients' interests, have secured for him a permanent and substantial clientage. This busy attorney, however, finds time for making himself useful in the community in which he lives. He has always been prominent in church circles. As a member of the Bellevue Methodist Episcopal church he has been honored in turn with every office the church had at its disposal. He has been president of the board of trustees for more than twenty years. He is also an active worker in the Sunday-school and is at his best when he is standing in the presence of a large Bible class. He is also prominent in lodge circles, being a past master of Bellevue lodge, No. 530, Free and Accepted Masons. For ten years he was an instructor in the Pittsburg school of Masonic instruction, and in 1900, as a reward for his services to the craft, he was honored with the appointment as district deputy grand master for this Masonic district, a position which he still holds. He is famous as an after-dinner speaker, and his responses to toasts at Masonic banquets have won for him applause on many occasions and caused his brethren to speak of him as the Chauncey Depew of Bellevue lodge. But the place where this man is seen at his best is in his home, which he has enriched with the literature of the world and embellished with the beauties of art. He has gathered together, year after year, from the standard authors and recent productions, as they have appeared, history, biography, theology, fiction, poetry, science and general literature, until he has now the finest private library in the town. He believes that the refining and educating influence of books and pictures in the home amply repays for all the expenditures made in this direction. His love of learning he gets from his mother, who was a gentle, ambitious and delicately-organized woman of culture and refinement, but who did not live to see the professional, social and business triumphs of her son, of which she had so fondly dreamed, and to fit and prepare him to accomplish which, she had made so many sacrifices. In 1881 the subject of this sketch was married to Miss Mattie L. Bruce, of Beaver county, Pa., who, with his three children—Roberta, David Harper and Martha V. Quaill—enjoys with him the luxuries of a beautiful home on Howard avenue, Bellevue.

ROBERT STEPHEN MARTIN, of Pittsburg, Pa., prominently identified with the legal profession of that city, with offices at No. 426 Diamond St., was born in Wayne township, Armstrong Co., Pa., Nov. 9, 1854, and is descended from Scotch-Irish ancestors, who settled in Pennsylvania shortly after 1820. Mr. Martin was educated in the common schools and the Dayton academy, then entered the law department of the Eastern University of Pennsylvania, where he was graduated with the class of 1878. He was admitted to the bar of Armstrong county, Pa., in January, 1879, and served as district attorney of that county from 1883 to 1886. Mr. Martin was admitted to the bar of Allegheny county in July, 1888, and since that time has been successfully engaged in a general practice at Pittsburg.

WILLIAM HILL, superintendent of the Allegheny workhouse and president of the First National bank of Carnegie, was born in County Down, Ireland, Dec. 3, 1837. His parents, David and Elizabeth (Dixon) Hill, came to America in 1841, and located in Allegheny county, near Carnegie, where Mr. Hill, who had been a schoolmaster in Ireland, continued his occupation as school-teacher for a time. Later he devoted his attention to farming and continued at that occupation until he moved to Carnegie, where he died a year afterwards at the age of sixty-three. William Hill, the subject of this sketch, is the oldest of four children. Margaret died in February, 1902, when about sixty-two years old; Elizabeth, now living in Carnegie, married David Given, who died in 1885, and Ellen is the wife of A. W. Ewing, and lives in Los Angeles, Cal. William Hill received a common-school education and then spent several years as a farmer. In 1876 he gave up agricultural pursuits and started the first brick and lumber business at Carnegie, and was engaged in this business for several years. He was justice of the peace for fifteen years, and resigned in 1876, when he became a member of the state legislature, serving in this capacity in the sessions between 1876 and 1879. After this he was mercantile appraiser for a year, and later served one three-year term as county treasurer. In 1886 Mr. Hill first became connected with the county workhouse, and has for the past sixteen years been an influential member of the workhouse board. Since 1891 he has been superintendent of the workhouse, and his long and efficient service has been an important factor in the success and usefulness of that institution. He has served several terms as school director, and was the first burgess of Carnegie, serving in that capacity three terms. He is now chairman of the Carnegie library commission. Mr. Hill was a director of the old Mechanics' National bank of Pittsburg for several years, before that institution was superseded by the First National bank of Pittsburg, and has been president of the First National bank of Carnegie since 1895. Before coming to Carnegie in 1896, Mr. Hill resided for several years in Clermont, Pa. He is now one of the most prominent and influential citizens of Carnegie, and is universally respected by all who know him. On June 15, 1887, Mr. Hill married Miss Elizabeth Boyd, daughter of William and Jane (Walker) Boyd, of Walker's Mills, both of whom are now dead. His youngest child, Boyd D., died in 1895, when three years old, and two others are living: Jane Boyd and William D. Mr. and Mrs. Hill are members of the United Presbyterian church, in which Mr. Hill has been actively interested for thirty years. During this time he has held many offices of responsibility, serving as trustee, church treasurer, superintendent of the Sunday-school and in other capacities. He has been active in the construction of three churches, and was a member of the committee which had charge of the erection of the last church.

JAMES R. TREACY, bottler, was born in the first ward, Pittsburg, Nov. 12, 1863, and has spent the greater part of his life in that city. After receiving a primary education in Pittsburg, he spent two years, 1880-82, at St. Francis' college at Loretto, Pa., and then became clerk in a queensware store in Pittsburg, remaining in this position about seven years. After this he spent a year in the employ of a Pittsburg brokerage firm, and in 1895 was appointed Chinese inspector, by John G. Carlisle. In the performance of the duties of this position he spent six months in Minneapolis and a similar period in Grand Forks, N. D., and then, on Nov. 1, 1896, resigned and returned to Pittsburg, where he has since engaged successfully in the bottle business. Although not actively interested in politics, Mr. Treacy believes in the principles advocated by the democratic party, and formerly served for four years as school director from the first ward. He is a member of the Elks and in religious belief is a Catholic.

 THOMAS McDERMOTT, of Glenfield, Pa., a prominent citizen and for years a skilled engineer, was born in the city of Pittsburg, Pa., Feb. 15, 1846, son of Patrick and Mary (Hanlon) McDermott, both natives of Ireland, his father having been born in the parish of Kallala, County Mayo, and his mother in the parish of Kellavey, County Armagh. His father was a son of Paul and Mary McDermott and came to the United States in 1845, settled in Pittsburg and there worked as a laborer. Subsequently he drifted into the scrap-iron business, beginning on a small scale, and by thrift, energy and economy built up the largest business of that nature in Pittsburg. He died when only fifty-three years of age and left a fortune of more than $100,000, a splendid tribute to his successful methods and financial ability. The mother of the subject was a daughter of Thomas Hanlon, of Kellavey, County Armagh, Ireland, who was a prominent citizen of that community, in which both he and his wife spent their entire lives. Thomas McDermott was educated in the Catholic schools of his native city, baptized at St. Paul's cathedral and for more than twenty years was a prominent engineer, but is now living quietly at Glenfield, where he has a magnificent residence overlooking the beautiful Ohio river.

JOHN M. RUSSELL, of Pittsburg, Pa., a practicing attorney, was born in Washington county, Pa., Dec. 7, 1872, son of William S. and Mary (McBride) Russell. He was educated in the rudimentary courses in the public schools, later attended the Union academy, of Burgettstown, and other educational institutions in Washington county, graduating from the Washington and Jefferson college in 1899. He then devoted his attention to reading law in the offices of Davidson & Galbraith, well-known attorneys of Pittsburg, and subsequently matriculated at the Pittsburg law school, where he was graduated with the class of 1902. He was admitted to the bar at Pittsburg in the December after his graduation, immediately entered on the practice, and is meeting with much encouragement and success in his vocation. Mr. Russell is a young man of fine parts, with good mental equipment and in many ways qualified to make a complete success of his professional career.

JOSEPH E. McCABE, secretary and treasurer of the Pennsylvania silica brick manufacturing company, at Latrobe, was born in Woodville, Allegheny Co., Pa., Sept. 17, 1861, in the house in which he now resides. His parents, Thompson F. and Mary J. (Richardson) McCabe, were natives and old residents of Allegheny county, where the father was an extensive farmer and prominent in educational affairs, being a school director many years. He was also a charter member of the Carnegie Presbyterian church and afterwards one of its trustees. He was a son of Joseph E. and Margaret (Fife) McCabe. Three of the sisters of Thompson F. McCabe are now living, all over eighty years old, and all widows. They are: Mrs. John Anderson, of Ohio; Mrs. Levi Brenniman, of St. Louis, and Mrs. Dr. Coulter, of Pittsburg. Mr. McCabe's wife, Mary Jane (Richardson) McCabe, was a daughter of James and Nancy Richardson, both of whom died in 1851, when Mary Jane was about sixteen years old. Of the ten children born to James and Nancy Richardson, only two survive. Henry Richardson, an old soldier who fought all through the Civil war, is now a prominent farmer in Kansas and owns about 800 acres of land, devoted to wheat, and Nancy A. is now the wife of William T. Easton, of East End, Pittsburg. Joseph McCabe, the subject of this article, is one of five children. The others are: L. Howard, of Allegheny, who married Alice J. Hultz and has two children, Alice Gertrude and Howard; Margaret M., now Mrs. J. Cubbage; Jennie M., who was born Sept. 25, 1857, and died Oct. 3, 1898, and Elizabeth, now Mrs. Andrew S. Hogan, of Green Tree borough, who has twins, Norman R. and Dorothy S. Joseph E. McCabe was educated in the public schools and then farmed the family farm until the property was sold in 1901. He owns considerable desirable property in Heidelberg, and the old McCabe homestead of about twenty-five acres, which will, with the growth of Carnegie, soon be within the city limits and be very valuable. The brick company, in which he is a stockholder, is an enterprising concern and the business bids fair to be most successful. Mr. McCabe has been for ten years a member of the school board and is now serving his second term as justice of the peace. He was married, on March 27, 1892, to Miss Bessie Holland, a native of this county, and daughter of Enoch and

Harriet Holland. Mr. Holland, a veteran of the Civil war, is now employed as a bookkeeper at the county home. Mrs. McCabe is one of eight children. Of the others, Anna is now Mrs. Frank Osborne, of Allegheny county; Izetta died when twenty-one years old; Harriet married E. G. Ott, a druggist in Carnegie; Reed lives in St. Louis; Adda died when two years old; Roberta is at home, and Florence died when a year and a half old. Mr. and Mrs. McCabe are the parents of four children: Marguerite, Walter Holland, Richard Fife and Joseph Ellsworth. Mr. McCabe is a member of the Knights of Malta. He and his wife are members of the Presbyterian church.

JOHN N. RADCLIFFE, of Pittsburg, Pa., a prosperous lawyer, with offices at No. 413 Grant St., was born in Banks township, Indiana Co., Pa., March 8, 1867, son of James and Annie (Nealen) Radcliffe, the former born in County Down, Ireland, Nov. 21, 1831, and the latter in County Kerry, Ireland, in 1844. His father came to America in 1847, and has since been a continuous resident of Indiana county, Pa., where he has prospered as a farmer. During the Civil war James Radcliffe served the federal government as a superintendent of transportation, having experienced former service as a wagon-master. Both parents of the subject are now living, reside on their farm in Indiana county, and have the following children: Samuel D., a grocery merchant of Kansas; John N.; Mary B., wife of Henry Gorman, of Banks township, Indiana county; Margaret J., Edith E.; James L., with the Santa Fe railroad at Los Angeles, Cal.; Cora, Olive and Ralph (twins), William H., Lola D., Valier G. and Glenn D. John N. Radcliffe was educated in the common schools of his native county and at the Indiana normal school, where he was graduated in 1890, with the degree of bachelor of arts. Prior to this, Mr. Radcliffe had engaged in teaching in Banks township, and in 1890 was elected principal of West Elizabeth schools, in Allegheny county, and for four years filled that position to the satisfaction of the entire community. In 1894 he registered as a student of law in the office of the late Judge Fetterman, of Pittsburg, and in March, 1896, was admitted to the bar at Pittsburg, where he is now a member of all courts and has a fine practice. He is a school director and member of the school board of West Elizabeth, where he resides, and takes an active interest in the bettering of educational methods. He was married in Pittsburg, March 20, 1892, to Emma Snee, and to them have been born two children: Leona M., on June 17, 1893, and

John N., Jr., on Feb. 12, 1895. Mr. Radcliffe and family attend the Presbyterian church of West Elizabeth. Ralph Radcliffe, a brother of the subject, was born and reared in Banks township, Indiana county, and was educated in the public schools and at the Indiana normal school. He began teaching when only seventeen years of age, and has since been successfully engaged in that profession. During the years of 1902-03 he taught in the Blairsville, Pa., public school, and in June, 1903, was elected principal of the Elliott school of the West End of Pittsburg, a decided compliment and one well deserved by this worthy young man.

GEORGE W. BEALE, a successful farmer and prominent citizen of Natrona, was born in Harrison township, Allegheny county, on April 18, 1855, on the farm he now owns. He is a son of Washington Beale, Jr., and Rosanna (McCune) Beale. The grandfather, Washington Beale, Sr., and two brothers, John and Albion, came from Tuscarora valley, Juniata county, in the year 1801, and were among the early settlers of Allegheny county. They located first on Jack's island, and then after a time moved over the river on a farm near Bull creek, buying in the following year the farm known as the Sam C. Alter farm. To Washington and Jane (Given) Beale were born the following children: Elizabeth, Margaret, James, Priscilla, Sarah, Washington, Alexandra, Thomas, Hannah and Nancy. To Washington Beale, Jr., and Rosanna (McCune) Beale, of Greensburg, were born the following children: Joseph G., Jane E., Mary J., James B., Margaret M., George W. and Sarah Agnes. Mr. Beale was a very successful farmer, and conducted the occupation on large scale. In 1857 he made his first trip to England after horses, and was the first importer of heavy draft horses in Pennsylvania. Of the four head with which he started for America, two were lost in a storm, but though unfortunate in his first venture, he did not give up, but made three trips afterwards with better success. At the time of his death, in 1885, he owned several large farms, was a stockholder in the Leechburg steel mills, and a stockholder in the Freeport National bank, of which he was also a director. He and his wife were members of the Freeport Presbyterian church. George W.

Beale was reared on the farm, educated in the common schools, and has followed the vocation of farming all of his active life. He is also engaged in the raising of fine horses and cattle, making a specialty of imported English horses and Alderney cattle. Mr. Beale owns the old homestead of 133 acres, and has forty acres on the bank of the Allegheny river, where he resides in one of the finest residences in Harrison township. Mr. Beale was born and raised a republican, imbibed the tenets of that party early in life, and is an active and ardent worker for the advancement of its principles. He has been school director for eight years, and is president of the board of commissioners for Harrison township, in which latter position he is serving his second term. Mr. Beale is also interested in stone-quarrying, and owns and operates a fine quarry which is situated about one mile from Natrona. He was married, on Nov. 22, 1877, to Zelia E. Harrison, of East End, Pittsburg, and they have one daughter, Martha E., a graduate of the public schools and Blairsville academy. Mr. Beale is a man of sterling worth and unimpeachable integrity, and is regarded with the highest esteem by all who have the honor of his acquaintance.

JOHN A. WILSON, of Pittsburg, Pa., long identified with the practice of law in that city, was born at New Brighton, Beaver Co., Pa., Nov. 2, 1843, son of James Perry and Nancy W. (Sullivan) Wilson. His father was a son of John and Effie (Bryan) Wilson, the former a native of Ireland, who, when three years of age, accompanied his parents to America and settled in Allegheny county, where his parents engaged in agricultural pursuits, as did their son, John, in later years. Effie Bryan, the grandmother of John A. Wilson, was born in Allegheny county and there spent her entire life. James Perry Wilson, the father of the subject of this sketch, was born at the corner of Penn avenue and Third street, Pittsburg, June 12, 1820; was a successful carriage-builder of Pittsburg, where he spent his entire life and there died on Nov. 11, 1886. His wife, Nancy W. Sullivan, was born on Eleventh street, South Side, Pittsburg, Dec. 1, 1822, and now resides at Avalon, Allegheny Co., Pa. John A. Wilson acquired his rudimentary education in the schools of Pittsburg, and completed his classical training at the Western university, from which he was graduated on June 24, 1864. In November, 1865, he registered as a law student with Marcus A. Woodward, a prominent attorney of Pittsburg; was admitted to the bar on Nov. 6, 1867, and has since continuously practiced in Pittsburg, where he is a member of all courts and has a fair practice. Mr. Wilson was married in the Fourth Avenue Baptist church of Pittsburg, April 2, 1868, to Bella J., daughter of ex-Mayor George Wilson and his wife, Mary F. (Howey) Wilson, and to them have been born the following children: George P., on June 8, 1870; John A., on April 27, 1874, and Ruth, on Nov. 2, 1882. Mr. Wilson's family are members of the Shady Side Presbyterian church of Pittsburg. George P. Wilson, his eldest son, a rising attorney, was born in Pittsburg, and educated in the rudimentary courses in the fourteenth ward and the high schools of his native city, and later attended Harvard university, where he was graduated in 1893, with the degree of bachelor of arts. He then read law in the office of his father, was admitted to the bar March 19, 1898, and has since practiced with much success.

FINLEY ROSS CUNNINGHAM, a substantial and worthy tiller of the soil, resides on a farm in West Deer township which has been in possession of his family for fully a hundred years. The first owner was his grandfather, Hughey Cunningham, who came there from Ireland at a very remote period and took up his abode on raw land in a sparsely settled neighborhood. The wife of this old emigrant, whom he married in Ireland, bore the name of Nancy, and the couple passed all their years cultivating the land and improving it for the benefit of their descendants. Their son, Robert, who was born in 1806, married Eliza Ross, of Westmoreland county, and they inherited and carried on the homestead place after the death of the original owners. Robert Cunningham became a successful farmer and was much esteemed in his community, holding the office of road commissioner for some years and otherwise sharing in the public life of the community. Originally a democrat, he joined the republican party at its organization, and both himself and wife were members of the United Presbyterian church. He died in 1893 and his wife some years later, after becoming the parents of seven children, of whom three daughters and one son survive. Two sons, Hugh and Robert, gave up their lives for their country during the terrible days of the Civil war. Finley Ross Cunningham, the only son now surviving of the above-mentioned family, was born in West Deer township, Allegheny county, Pa., Jan. 23, 1846. He was reared on the farm of his father, and after the latter's death inherited the place, to which he has since added forty-four acres, making his entire holdings 176 acres of excellent farming land. He has not only preserved his inheritance, but has cultivated the patrimonial acres with such skill and judgment as to greatly improve them in every respect. He carries on general farming and stock-raising and keeps many cows from which he markets milk and butter. Like his father, he has adhered to the fortunes of the republican party and for a number of years has held the office of assessor. Mr. Cunningham is the father of seven children: Mary E., Lida, Harley R., Courtland K., Hughey M., Geneva and Edna A. The parents were members of the United Presbyterian church. Mrs. Cunningham died Jan. 14, 1901.

JOSEPH P. FIFE, of Pittsburg, Pa., a prosperous attorney-at-law, with offices at No. 1219 Frick building, was born at Sterling, Ill., June 15, 1875, son of W. H. G. and Mary E. Fife, both natives of Pennsylvania. Mr. Fife acquired his classical education at the Leland Stanford, Jr., university and was graduated from the Harvard law school in the class of 1900. Mr. Fife is a man of splendid natural abilities and these, combined with the excellent literary and legal education which he has received, well prepared him for the arduous duties of the exacting profession that he espoused. He was admitted to the bar in March, 1901, and since has practiced his profession with much success and has achieved a respectable position among the attorneys of Pittsburg.

ANTHONY STAAB, of the firm of Yunker & Co., funeral directors at No. 110 South Main St., thirty-sixth ward, Pittsburg, was born in the thirty-fourth ward, Pittsburg, in 1866. When three years old his parents moved with him to Elliott, Allegheny county, and there Mr. Staab attended school until he reached the age of thirteen. He then went to work in the iron mill of Painter & Son, was employed there for seven years, and then engaged for a year in the general hauling business. In 1892 Mr. Staab went into the livery and undertaking business, in which he has since been engaged. He is a prominent man in his profession and a member of the Funeral Directors' association of Allegheny county. Mr. Staab is a member of the German Catholic church. In political belief he is a democrat.

ROBERT KENNEDY, a well-known citizen of Tarentum, Pa., was born in East Deer township, Allegheny county, April 23, 1842. He was just upon the threshold of his manhood when the great Civil war broke upon the country. On Aug. 27, 1861, he enlisted from Wood county, W. Va., as a private in Capt. Ansel B. Denton's company, afterwards Company C, 18th United States infantry, Col. Henry B. Carrington, commanding, and Oliver Shepherd, lieutenant-colonel. The 18th was one of the three battalion regiments organized under President Lincoln's proclamation of May 31st, ordering an increase in the regular army. The regiment took the field in December, 1861, and from that time until mustered out it was on the firing line, sustaining the heaviest losses of any regiment in the regular army. It participated in the siege of Corinth, Miss., during the entire month of May, 1862; was at Perryville, Ky., in the following October; at Stone River and Murfreesboro during the last days of 1862 and the first days of 1863; at Hoover's Gap in June, 1863, and in all the battles and skirmishes of the Chickamauga campaign. Mr. Kennedy was captured at Chickamauga, Ga., on Sept. 20, 1863, and remained a prisoner for nearly fifteen months. In that time he saw the inside of some of the most noted prisons of the Confederacy. For eleven days immediately following his capture he was confined at Belle Island, Va.; then for the next two months in Smith's building, Richmond, Va.; then at Danville, Va., until April 6, 1864, when he was removed to the famous prison at Andersonville, Ga. He remained at Andersonville until about the middle of September, when he was transferred to the race-track prison, Charleston, S. C., held there for about three weeks, and then taken to Florence, S. C., where he was exchanged on Dec. 15, 1864. Up to the time of his capture, Mr. Kennedy had been with his command, obedient to the orders of his superiors, and always at his post of duty. In recognition of his meritorious services he was promoted to the rank of corporal in May, 1863. He was in all the engagements in which the regiment took part, and was in a number of expeditions involving skirmishes and dangerous situations. As instances of the valor of the 18th regiment, it is worthy of mention that at the battle of Stone River it lost 102 officers and men, and at Chicka-

mauga forty-eight were either killed or mortally wounded. Corporal Kennedy received his honorable discharge, and was mustered out with his regiment at Camp Thomas, Ohio, Feb. 10, 1865, having served four months and fourteen days more than the three years for which he enlisted. On Nov. 11, 1869, he was married to Miss Maria Crawford, at Hites, Allegheny county. After a few years of happy wedded life, she passed away, and on July 6, 1892, he was united in marriage to Idaletta M. Dickey, of Tarentum. To this union two sons have been born: Robert Dickey, born May 13, 1898; and George Russell, born April 7, 1901. Mr. Kennedy is a member of Eli Hemphill post, No. 135, department of Pennsylvania, Grand Army of the Republic, of which he served one term as commander. He is also a past master of his Masonic lodge, has served twelve years as a school director and one year as road supervisor. In all these positions he acquitted himself with credit and acquired a reputation for that conscientious discharge of his duties which marked his career as a soldier in the army of his country.

SILAS AUSTIN WILL, a well-known attorney of Pittsburg, was born July 28, 1846, in Milford township, Somerset Co., Pa. His parents, Silas and Harriet (Chorpenning) Will, were both natives of Somerset county. During his boyhood the subject of this sketch attended the common schools of Somerset county, but in August, 1862, he enlisted as a private in Company C, 142d Pennsylvania volunteer infantry, and served with that regiment until January, 1864. In August, 1864, he enlisted in Company K, 5th heavy artillery, and served in that regiment until the close of the war, when he was mustered out with the rank of corporal. While in the infantry service he participated in the famous battles of Antietam, Fredericksburg, Chancellorsville and Gettysburg, and while in the artillery he was chiefly engaged in guerrilla warfare. After the war was over he set to work to complete his education, and graduated from the Millersville normal school, near Lancaster, Pa. For the next six years he taught in the public schools, and on April 1, 1875, was duly registered and began the study of law in the offices of Gazzam & Cochran, of Pittsburg. On April 14, 1877, he was admitted to the bar, and since that time he has been in continuous practice. He is a member of the bar association, and practices in all the state and federal courts. His home is in the thirteenth ward of the city of Pittsburg, and for nine years he represented that ward as the member of the board of school directors. In politics Mr. Will is an uncompromising republican, and he takes an active interest in all political matters. He is a member of Hays post, No. 3, Grand Army of the Republic; the Royal Arcanum, the Knights of the Maccabees, and a life member of the National Fraternal Congress as past president; also a member of the Improved Order of Heptasophs, having served eight years as the head of the order in the capacity of supreme archon; also a member of the Americus club. His wife died Sept. 6, 1901, leaving no children. On Sept. 2, 1903, he was married to Sarah H. Brant.

A. J. KELLY, Jr., vice-president of the Commonwealth real estate and trust company, has been for many years prominent in Pittsburg business life. He was born on a farm in Washington county, Pa., in 1856, and lived there until his eighteenth year. He went to Jefferson academy, at Cannonsburg, in order to continue his education. Leaving school in 1877, Mr. Kelly went to Canton, Ohio, was employed for a while as clerk and later studied law in the offices of Lynch & Day. He returned to Pittsburg in 1879, and in 1880 became clerk in the United States pension agency. The following year he began his long career as a real estate man, in the office of W. A. Herron & Sons, remaining with this concern until 1902, when the business was merged into the Commonwealth real estate and trust company. He then became vice-president of the new concern. In politics Mr. Kelly is a republican. He is a member of the Presbyterian church.

CARROLL P. DAVIS, of Pittsburg, Pa., a prominent attorney-at-law, with offices in the Park building, was born in that city, Feb. 1, 1868, son of Charles C. and Westanna (Preston) Davis. Mr. Davis acquired his classical education at the Phillips academy, Andover, Mass., and at Yale college, being graduated at the latter institution in 1891. Mr. Davis then read law in the office of D. T. Watson, a well-known attorney of Pittsburg, and was admitted to the bar in December, 1892. Since then he has practiced with much success, is a member of all courts and stands high among the attorneys of Allegheny county.

WILLIAM SCOTT, the well-known marble-cutter of Bakerstown, bears a name that is highly honored in Allegheny county, both on account of his own merits and the distinguished services of his father during the Civil war. His grandfather, John Scott, who is mentioned in another part of this work, was a native of Ireland who came to Allegheny county in 1822 and settled in West Deer township with his family. Included in the latter was an infant son named William, whose birth occurred in Ireland, Dec. 22, 1821. He grew up on the farm, but afterwards engaged in merchandising, which was the principal occupation of his life, though he also did some farming. He affiliated with the democratic party, served as justice of the peace and altogether became one of the most prominent and popular men in his community. When the Civil war began, he lost no time in offering his services to the government, and in August, 1861, became a member of Company B, 61st regiment, Pennsylvania volunteer infantry. He served without injury until the battle of Fair Oaks, fought in June, 1862, when he was killed in action. He had already been promoted for meritorious conduct and gave promise of a brilliant career in the army, had not his life been cut short by the fortunes of war. His surviving comrades honored him by giving his name to the local Grand Army post, established in his honor in West Deer township, and the Woman's Auxiliary of the G. A. R. at Tarentum is also called by his name. This gallant soldier, whose fame is so tenderly cherished at his old home, was married Nov. 20, 1845, to Mary J., daughter of Michael and Jane (Wilson) Carlisle. The latter couple were natives of Ireland, who emigrated to Allegheny county in 1817 and settled on a farm in West Deer township, where the father died July 10, 1850, and his widow March 12, 1862. They had six children, but Mrs. William Scott, who was born Aug. 12, 1821, is the only survivor of the family. This venerable lady, now in the eighty-third year of her age, resides at Bakerstown with her son, who is the subject of this sketch. Since sixteen years old, she has been a member of the Deer Creek United Presbyterian church, to which her parents also belonged. William Scott, son of the deceased veteran and the lady above described, was born in Bakerstown, Pa., Dec. 9, 1859, and consequently was still a mere lad when his father was killed in battle. He was reared on a farm, educated in the neighborhood schools and when nineteen years old went to Brownsdale to learn the trade of marble-cutting. After acquiring the necessary skill, he worked at this trade for a while in Allegheny county and in 1882 began business on his own account at Bakerstown, which he has since continued with success. Mr. Scott is a democrat in politics, has held the offices of assessor and constable and is now serving as justice of the peace. He is president of the Bakerstown creamery company, secretary of the Bakerstown mutual fire insurance company and secretary of the Bakerstown cemetery association. He is a member of Hampton lodge, No. 1004, I. O. O. F., and of the Junior Order of United American Mechanics. On May 10, 1882, Mr. Scott was united in marriage with Miss Martha J. S., daughter of W. S. Marshall, elsewhere mentioned in this work. She is a native of West Deer township and was born Nov. 17, 1860. Leon Vernon, the only son of Mr. and Mrs. Scott, was born April 13, 1883, was educated in the Bakerstown schools and the Actual business college, and is a young man of bright promise.

RALPH CARTER DAVIS, of Pittsburg, Pa., a well and favorably known young attorney, with offices in the Bakewell building, was born in Erie county, Pa., Sept. 22, 1881, son of Livingston L. and Anna (Carter) Davis, his father a native of Crawford county, his mother of Erie county, and both now residing at Homestead, Pa. Ralph C. Davis was educated in the graded and high schools of Homestead, read law in his father's office, and later attended the Pittsburg law school. He was admitted to the bar in September, 1902, immediately began the practice in Pittsburg, and at that time was the youngest attorney engaged in practice in Allegheny county. Mr. Davis is a young man of fine natural abilities, has been well grounded in the principles of law, and is making a decided success of his professional career.

JACOB W. KRAUS, of Pittsburg, Pa., one of the most successful of the younger members of the bar of that city, with offices in the Hampton law building, was born in Pittsburg, Oct. 9, 1874, son of Martin and Elizabeth (Engle) Kraus, both natives of Germany, who came to Pittsburg in childhood and have since resided in that city. His father has been in the real estate business at Mount Oliver for thirty-five years, has served as burgess of that borough and as a school director of the twenty-seventh ward, being one of the first to fill that position in that ward. Mr. Kraus was educated at the Duquesne college and the Pittsburg college, and was graduated from the latter institution in 1900 with the degree of bachelor of arts. He then matriculated at the Notre Dame university, Indiana, where he devoted his attention to law. On graduation he returned to Pittsburg, was admitted to the bar on June 9, 1901, and has since met with much success in the practice of his profession. Mr. Kraus is borough solicitor of Mount Oliver borough, and practices in all the courts. He is highly regarded by the attorneys of Pittsburg, and is fast winning a place of prominence at the bar. He possesses ability, integrity and energy, and with such endowments a successful career is assured.

WILLIAM A. GRISCOM, a resident of Avalon borough, son of John S. Griscom, was born in Philadelphia, May 29, 1863; was educated in the Quaker schools, and graduated from the high school in 1881. At the age of eighteen years he accepted a position in the transportation department of the Pennsylvania lines west of Pittsburg, and has served continuously in this department for the last twenty-two years. Mr. Griscom was married, Oct. 20, 1887, to Bessie Taylor, of Sewickley, Pa., and to them have been born two sons: John Lloyd and Walter. His father, John S. Griscom, was born in Philadelphia. After finishing grade and high schools in that city, he became an engineer in the coast survey for the United States, and at the breaking out of the Civil war was on the coast of Mexico. At the call to arms he returned home and enlisted in the United States navy, being assigned to the gunboat "Mackinaw." At the time of his death, Dec. 25, 1864, he was acting as lieutenant in the defense of Fort Fisher. Mr. Griscom was a member of the Masonic order and of St. John's commandery, Philadelphia. William A. Griscom, the subject of this sketch, has also a record in the annals of war. He enlisted as a private in Company E, 14th regiment, at the age of twenty-one, in which he served five years, going through the various non-commissioned offices. In 1888 he enlisted in Battery B, where he served three years. He then left the national guard till the breaking out of the Spanish war, when he became one of the chief promoters in the organization of Company K, 17th regiment, national guards of Pennsylvania. On the return of the old regiment from the Spanish war, Company K, which Mr. Griscom represents as captain, was made Company H, 14th regiment, national guards. In August, 1898, he was elected second lieutenant; in October of the same year, first lieutenant, and in February, 1899, he was elected captain, which position he now holds. Mr. Griscom saw service in the anthracite coal strike of 1902. This company was located for some time at Mahanoy City, Schuylkill county. In politics Mr. Griscom is a republican, and has always taken an active part in the politics of his county and district. Having been appointed justice of the peace for Avalon borough by Gov. Robert Pattison to fill an unexpired term, he was elected by the people for a term of five years. In February, 1903, he was elected to the highest position in Avalon borough, that of burgess. Mr Griscom's record from a business standpoint speaks for itself, having been in the employ of one company during his entire career. In religious faith he is a Presbyterian.

JOHN A. STALEY, broker of Pittsburg, was born in Sidney, Ohio, in 1861. He came to Pittsburg with his parents in 1866, and there received his education in school and under private tutors. When about seventeen or eighteen years old, he began to read law in the office of Thomas M. Marshall, and spent four years in this manner, but never practiced, preferring to devote himself to mercantile pursuits. Mr. Staley was for a number of years engaged in the hotel business on Penn avenue, and then, in 1894, bought a café which he ran for five and a half years. In 1902 he became a member of the firm of J. B. Eisaman & Co., prominent stock brokers of Pittsburg. Mr. Staley is a member of no secret orders. He belongs to the Roman Catholic church. While not taking an active interest in party matters, in political belief he is a democrat, with independent tendencies.

WILLIAM H. HARVEY, contractor of general painting and member of the Allegheny city common council from the fourth ward, is a native of Butler county, where he was born in 1872. His parents are John and Margaret Harvey, well-known residents of Butler county. Until he was seventeen years of age, William attended the common schools, thus securing a good, practical education. He then went to Allegheny city and learned the painting trade with Robert Jamison, serving an apprenticeship of five years.

When he was about twenty-two years old he started in business for himself as a contractor, in which he still continues, his present offices being located at No. 605 Sandusky St. Politically, Mr. Harvey is an uncompromising republican, and is always ready to do battle for his political opinions. Still he is not offensive in pressing his views, and numbers among his personal friends many who are his political opponents. In February, 1903, he was elected to the common council, where he has been honored with appointment upon the grade crossing, public works and library committees. Mr. Harvey is a member of Allegheny lodge, No. 339, Benevolent and Protective Order of Elks, which is the only fraternal organization to claim his affiliation.

DANIEL BODEN, superintendent of the Mansfield coal and coke company, Carnegie, was born in Staffordshire, England, son of Thomas and Elizabeth Boden. Thomas Boden was interested in the coal business in England, but came to America for his health and did not engage actively in business. He and his wife were residents of Pittsburg and members of the Methodist Episcopal church. Mr. Boden died in 1864, when about seventy years old, and his wife died the next year at about the same age. Of the fifteen children born to Mr. and Mrs. Thomas Boden, four survive: Eliza, now Mrs. Thomas Tramford, who lives in England; Samuel, for many years a resident of Scott township, Allegheny county, also now in England; Mary, who married George Green, of Allegheny county, and Daniel, the subject of this sketch. Daniel Boden attended the public and select schools, and after completing his education went to work in the mines, and has been a miner ever since, with the exception of less than a year, which he spent as mail agent in the United States civil service. Mr. Boden has held his present responsible position for the past seventeen years, and is a man well acquainted with all the details of mining. The Mansfield coal and coke company is a prosperous concern which gets out about 1,800 tons of coal a day. Mr. Boden has served as a member of the city council and held several other public positions, but does not now take so great an interest in politics as formerly. He has been for the past six years a member of the school board of Carnegie, is a trustee of the Carnegie library, and treasurer of the Miners' accidental association. He was married, in 1871, to Miss Sarah McVay, daughter of Timothy McVay, of Allegheny county, now deceased. Mr. and Mrs. Boden have had three children, all of whom died when young. Mr. Boden and wife are members of the Methodist Episcopal church, of which Mr. Boden is treasurer and one of the committee on publishing. He is a member of various secret organizations.

ADDISON MURRAY IMBRIE, of Pittsburg, Pa., a successful general practitioner of law, was born near New Galilee, Beaver Co., Pa., July 29, 1853, son of James M. and Clorinda (Jackson) Imbrie, the former dying on April 12, 1889, and his mother on April 18, 1899. Both parents were natives of Beaver county, where his father was engaged in agricultural pursuits for many years and was a prominent factor in the development of that section. The Imbrie family is of Scotch origin, and James Imbrie, the great-grandfather of Addison M., settled in Moon township (then Allegheny county, where his will is filed) in 1790, there died in March, 1803, and is buried in the old Service graveyard, near his home. His son, Rev. David Imbrie, was born in Philadelphia on Aug. 22, 1777, and studied divinity under Dr. John Anderson, of Moon township, and in 1803 was licensed to preach at the Seceder church. He married Jean, daughter of John and Annie (Atchison) Reed, who were both natives of Lancaster county, and settled in Washington county in 1777. David and Jean Imbrie had the following children: Ann Reed, born March 29, 1805, married Joseph Sharp, and died Sept. 11, 1881; Maria Smart, born Sept 1, 1807, married Dr. J. W. Calvin, and died in August, 1851; Jean, born July 1, 1809, and died unmarried in October, 1857; David Reed, born Jan. 24, 1812, and died Jan. 29, 1872; John Reed, born April 13, 1815, and died March 28, 1860, and with two of his sons is interred in the cemetery at Washington, Pa.; James Milton, born March 9, 1816, and died April 12, 1889; Elmira Emily, born March 2, 1819, married John M. Buchanan, and died Oct. 15, 1895. David Imbrie died June 12, 1842, and his wife on March 18, 1825, and both are buried in the Seceders' graveyard, near Darlington. The mother of Addison M. Imbrie was a descendant of Samuel Jackson, who settled in Chester county, Pa., about 1729, and was prominently identified with that section of the state. Addison M. Imbrie acquired his educational training in the public and private schools, having attended the Darlington academy and the Mt.

Pleasant academy, of Westmoreland county, and was graduated from Washington and Jefferson college in the class of 1876. He read law in the office of Samuel B. Wilson, of Beaver, Pa., and in April, 1878, registered as a student in the office of Thomas M. Marshall, a prominent attorney of Pittsburg. He was admitted to the bar in July, 1880, for the next ten years was associated in the practice with his former preceptor, Thomas M. Marshall, and since that time has maintained independent offices. He is a member of all courts, the Allegheny county and the Pennsylvania state bar associations, and enjoys a lucrative practice. Mr. Imbrie was married in Allegheny city, Pa., Oct. 2, 1884, to Hattie Silliman, and they have had two children: Addison M., Jr., who died in childhood, and Boyd Vincent. Mr. Imbrie is a member of the Duquesne, Monongahela and Country clubs, of the Episcopal church and the Sons of the Revolution.

ROBERT PALMER, a resident of Haysville borough, was born in Manchester, Allegheny county, and is a son of Alexander and Sarah Palmer. He received his education in the public schools of Allegheny city. Mr. Palmer, being of a very ambitious nature, began work at an early age, being employed by the firm of Ritchey & Feinkbine, known as Old Point saw-mill, of Allegheny city, when he was but fourteen years of age. Following his inclination toward mechanics, he next sought employment in the shops of the Fort Wayne railroad in January, 1878, and it was not long before his superior ability was recognized, and he was promoted to the position of fireman, Sept. 16, 1879. Mr. Palmer worked in this position five years, when a second promotion made him engineer. On Jan. 1, 1900, he was appointed to the responsible position of assistant road foreman of engines of the eastern division of the P., F. W. & C. railroad. Three years later he was again promoted, this time to the position of road foreman of engines on the T., W. V. & O. railroad, a position which requires great presence of mind and prompt action. Mr. Palmer was married, June 10, 1886, to Ada V. Ballard, of Emsworth, Pa., and to them have been born two children: Robert B. and Sarah Maria.

GEORGE ELLIOTT PEEBLES, of Pittsburg, Pa., a rising young attorney, was born in Allegheny city, Pa., Nov. 26, 1877, son of William and Margaret J. (McKelvy) Peebles, both natives of Pittsburg, where his father has spent his entire life. His parents had three children, the others being William McKelvy and Jane McCully. George E. Peebles was educated in the rudimentary branches at the Liberty public school and the Shady Side academy, graduating from the latter institution in 1895. Subsequently he matriculated at Princeton university and was graduated from that famous seat of learning in 1899. Mr. Peebles then studied law in the office of J. E. McKelvy, a prominent attorney of Pittsburg, later attending the Pittsburg law school, from which institution he was graduated in 1902. He was admitted to the bar on June 21, 1902, at once began the practice, and has since continued quite successfully. Mr. Peebles is well endowed by nature and training for the arduous profession which he has espoused, and the future is bright with promise of a long and prosperous career at the bar.

HON. JOHN F. COX, a prominent member of the Allegheny county bar, is a native of Mifflin township, Allegheny county, Pa. He is the son of William and Anna (Dellenbaugh) Cox, the former a native of Northamptonshire, England, and the latter of Switzerland. His paternal grandparents were Thomas and Catherine Cox and his maternal grandparents were Christian and Anna Dellenbaugh. His father was twice married, his first wife being a Miss Hannah Ford, whom he married in England, in 1828. Soon after this marriage he emigrated to America and settled in Allegheny county. He located opposite what is now the borough of Homestead, where for many years he was engaged in the manufacture of salt. Later he removed to Mifflin township and engaged in farming. He retired from active business in 1878 and spent the remaining days of his life in Homestead, enjoying the fruits of his labors of earlier years. John F. Cox was born Oct. 6, 1852, on the farm in Mifflin township, where, until he was eighteen years of age, he assisted with the work of the farm and attended the common schools. He then entered Westminster college, at

New Wilmington, Pa., and studied in that institution for three years, after which he went to Union college, located at Alliance, Ohio, and graduated from that college in 1876. He then taught in the schools of Camden and Homestead for three years, then read law with Maj. W. C. Moreland and John H. Kerr, of Pittsburg, and in 1880 he was admitted to the bar. He soon acquired a high standing at the bar, and his practice now extends to all the state and federal courts. In politics Mr. Cox is an enthusiastic republican and is generally identified with all movements touching the welfare of that party. In 1884 he was elected to the state legislature and in 1886 he was re-elected. He has been borough solicitor for Homestead, where he resides, for fifteen years.

JOSEPH JENNINGS KINTNER, of Pittsburg, Pa., a prominent practitioner of law, was born in Wyoming county, Pa., Sept. 4, 1870, son of Col. J. C. and Mary A. (Jennings) Kintner. His father was a prominent merchant of that section of the state and an important factor in its political affairs, having served on the staff of Gov. Henry M. Hoyt and also occupied the position of collector of internal revenue. His mother was a woman of fine character and urged upon her son the advantages to be derived from a full educational training, all of which sank deep into the mind of Mr. Kintner. His father died when Joseph J. was but fifteen years of age, and his mother died in 1889, just a few months after her son had entered college. Joseph J. Kintner received his primary education in the public schools, then prepared for a college course at the Wyoming seminary, Kingston, Pa., and later entered the Pennsylvania state college. On the completion of the course at that institution, Mr. Kintner commenced the study of law in the office of W. H. Spender, completed his legal studies under Charles H. Smiley, and was admitted to the bar of Perry county in 1894. The following year Mr. Kintner removed to Clinton county, remained until the fall of 1898, and then located at Pittsburg, where he now enjoys a splendid practice. He was married to Florence Kindig, March 24, 1898, and they have three children: Elizabeth, born June 2, 1899; Joseph Richard, born Feb. 10, 1901, and Louise, born Sept. 28, 1902. Mr. Kintner has always taken an active part in politics, and when only twenty-two years of age was burgess of Bloomfield; he also served as deputy register and recorder and clerk of Perry county. At the time of his removal to Pittsburg he was the republican candidate for district attorney of Clinton county, but withdrew from the ticket to enter the larger field. Shortly after his removal to Allegheny county, he located in the borough of Aspinwall, has since taken an active interest in local affairs, and for a time was a member of the school board of that borough. Mr. Kintner is in great demand as a campaign speaker, and has been prominently identified with the republican side of all political contests since 1892. Mr. Kintner is also closely associated with a number of business enterprises, being a director in the American insurance company, the Negley & Clark company, the Duquesne roach powder company and the Pennsylvania novelty company, and has valuable holdings of real estate.

ARTHUR JAMES KUHN, a prominent real estate man of Homestead and secretary of the Homestead realty company, was born at Broad Fording, Westmoreland Co., Pa., Feb. 2, 1853, son of Andrew James and Margaret (McGough) Kuhn, both natives of Pennsylvania. His paternal grandfather, George Kuhn, a native of Berks county, Pa., moved to Westmoreland county in early life and died there. He was a farmer. He married a Miss Topper. Andrew J. Kuhn, son of George Kuhn, was a merchant at Broad Fording, Westmoreland county. He also ran a line of boats on the canal, and had a line of transportation freight wagons between Pittsburg and Philadelphia, before the Pennsylvania railroad was built. In 1852 he located in Latrobe, and when the Pennsylvania railroad was being built he furnished materials and supplies for the contractors. He died in Latrobe in 1857. He married Margaret McGough, daughter of Arthur McGough. Arthur McGough, a native of Wilmington, Del., was a pioneer farmer of Westmoreland county, where he died. Andrew J. Kuhn and wife had three children: George, Arthur J. and Jennie. Arthur J. Kuhn, the subject of this sketch, was reared in Latrobe, Pa., and educated at St. Vincent's college. In 1868 he started in to learn the drug business and was a druggist for almost twenty years, at first a member of the firm of Kuhn Bros., Latrobe, and later at Meyersdale, Pa., and Oakland, Md. In May, 1887, he located in Homestead, continuing in the drug business until 1892. Since that time he has been successfully engaged in the real estate and insurance business. In February, 1901, when several real estate firms were consolidated as the Homestead realty company, with a capital of $100,000, Mr. Kuhn was made secretary of the new corporation, and still holds that position. He is also president of the Homestead land investment company, of Homestead, a director and member of the executive committee of the Duquesne library land company, director of the Beaver terrace land company, and director of the Beaver terrace railway company. Mr. Kuhn was married, Jan. 29, 1876, to Mary H., daughter of Francis and Margaret (Honan) McCollum, of Chester, Pa., and has one daughter, Margaret Hilda. He is a member of the Roman Catholic church, K. of C., C. M. B. A. and Y. M. I. He is also a member of the B. P. O. E. Mr. Kuhn is a popular and enterprising citizen of Homestead, and enjoys the confidence of its best people. He has served his borough as school director for one term, and was for two terms justice of the peace. Politically, he is a democrat.

JOHN MOORE PETTY, of Pittsburg, Pa., a prominent attorney-at-law, with offices in the Frick building, was born near Fort Scott, Kan., Aug. 28, 1869, son of George M. and Elizabeth J. (Brown) Petty, the former a native of Connecticut, and his mother of Allegheny county, Pa. The maternal grandfather of John M. Petty was one of the early settlers of Pittsburg, where he was engaged in the real estate business and was a prominent and influential citizen. The Brown family has been closely identified with the growth and advancement of Pittsburg for many years, and many of its members have occupied positions of honor and trust in that city. George M. Petty was a member of the 15th Pennsylvania volunteer cavalry, enlisted in 1861, and served for three years. After receiving his discharge he returned to Pittsburg, where he remained until 1880, except for a three years' residence in Kansas. He served as cashier of the Diamond bank during its existence. John M. Petty removed with his parents to Pittsburg when only two years of age, and after a nine years' residence there accompanied his parents to a farm in Nebraska, where they now reside. Mr. Petty was educated in the common schools of Nebraska and at the high school at Ord, Neb., and during all of this time worked on his father's farm. After reaching manhood, Mr. Petty secured a position in a general store at Ord, and six months later went into the county clerk's office, where he remained for one year. Mr. Petty then removed to Chicago, became assistant bookkeeper for Alexander Revell, and one year later was given a position in another department. In the spring of 1892 he came to Pittsburg to study law in the office of his uncle, Robert B. Petty, and in 1895 was admitted to the bar of Allegheny county. Mr. Petty is a member of all courts in Pennsylvania, and also the United States district and circuit courts, but confines his practice almost entirely to civil business. He is a well-known citizen, member of the Presbyterian church, and resides in the thirteenth ward of Pittsburg.

JESSE MAINHART HOUSE, of Homestead, Pa., a well-known contractor and builder, was born at Lycippus, Westmoreland Co., Pa., May 26, 1871, son of Allen W. and Martha (Mainhart) House. His paternal grandfather was Daniel House, a native of Schuylkill county, Pa., of German descent, who married Eliza Crimmel, of Juniata county, also of German descent, and they had a family of five sons: Jesse, Joseph, Allen W., William H. and Daniel N. The elder House was a farmer by occupation and settled in Mount Pleasant township, Westmoreland Co., Pa., about 1838, and there resided until his death. His sons, Jesse and Joseph, served in the Union army during the Civil war, the former dying in the service, and his remains are now buried at Culpeper Court House, Va. Allen W. House, father of the subject, was born in Mount Pleasant township, Westmoreland county, Dec. 18, 1844, and there was reared and educated in the common schools. When fourteen years of age he was apprenticed to the blacksmiths' trade, and later served an apprenticeship at the carpenters' trade, which he followed as a joiner for three years. Then he engaged in the business of contracting and building, and followed that vocation in Somerset, Westmoreland and Allegheny counties until 1902, residing at Homestead since 1888. He was married, on July 4, 1867, to Martha, daughter of Jacob and Savilla (Blyholder) Mainhart, of Pennsylvania township, Westmoreland Co., Pa., but formerly of Germany, and they have eight children: Lawrence L., Jesse M., Harry, Jacob; Della, wife of Edward Rorneck; Viola, wife of Arthur Woodhall; Jennie and Cleveland. Jesse M. House was reared in his native town, educated in the public schools and at Curry institute, at Pittsburg, and then learned the carpenters'

trade under his father. In 1888 he located at Homestead, where he at once commenced contracting and building, and has since successfully continued. He has a well-established business and has accumulated a nice competency. He was married, on Feb. 23, 1891, to Mary A., daughter of Nicholas and Anna Walker, formerly of Germany, but now of Homestead, and they have four children: Marie, Jesse, Russell and Kenneth. He is a member of the Lutheran church, the Elks and the Knights of Malta, and his political affiliations are with the democratic party.

DENNIS Æ. BEHEN, of Pittsburg, Pa., a well-known attorney, with offices in the Bakewell building, was born in Little Rock, Ark., July 7, 1871, son of Dennis and Mary (Watterson) Behen, the former a native of Ireland, who died in Pittsburg, Aug. 1, 1896, and the latter born in Indiana county, Pa., and died on June 18, 1903. Mr. Behen was graduated from Mount St. Mary's college, of Emmittsburg, Md., in the class of 1894, with the degree of master of arts, then read law in the offices of Watterson & Reid, of Pittsburg, and was admitted to the bar of Allegheny county, March 13, 1897. He is a member of all courts and the Allegheny county bar association and makes a specialty of real estate law and orphans' court practice, in which he has been very successful. He is a charter member of Duquesne council of Knights of Columbus, member of the Keystone bicycle club and the Pittsburg lodge of Elks, and resides in the twenty-first ward.

JAMES ELDER BARNETT, of Pittsburg, Pa., attorney-at-law, was born at Elder's Ridge, Indiana Co., Pa., Aug. 1, 1856, and was graduated from Washington and Jefferson college in 1882. He studied law at the Columbia law school of New York city, taking the municipal law course, and was then admitted to the bar of Washington county, and in 1900 to the Allegheny county bar. He was appointed deputy secretary of the commonwealth by Gen. Frank Reeder and served in that capacity from July 1, 1895, to Oct. 19, 1897, when he resigned that office to return to his practice. He enlisted in the national guard of Pennsylvania in 1884 and rose through the various military grades to that of the lieutenant-colonelcy, to which he was elected in 1897. He volunteered with his regiment for service in the Spanish-American war and saw active campaigning in the Philippines, participating in all the engagements of his regiment during that insurrection, which continued until the capture of Malolos. When Col. A. L. Hawkins was appointed to the command of the district of Cavite, P. I., on April 14, 1899, Lieutenant-Colonel Barnett was placed in command of the regiment and served in that capacity until the regiment was mustered out at San Francisco, Aug. 22, 1899. He succeeded Colonel Hawkins to the command of the district of Cavite, when the latter became incapacitated by illness, and served in that position from May 10, 1899, until the regiment embarked for the United States, July 1, 1899. Colonel Barnett was nominated for state treasurer by the republican state convention, Aug. 24, 1899, and elected to that important position at the general election in the succeeding November.

ADOLPH HERMAN SCHROEDER, whose shaving parlors at Homestead are among the finest in Allegheny county, is a native of Schulitz, Germany, where he was born April 11, 1875, and is the son of Emil and Julia (Cromrey) Schroeder. Until he was about fourteen years of age he attended the schools of his native town, graduating from the high school in 1889. He then served one year as bookkeeper in the mayor's office at Schulitz, and in 1890 came to America. The first three years of his residence in this country was spent as a barbers' apprentice in one of the best shops of the city of Pittsburg, Pa. He then worked as a journeyman barber in several cities of the country, among them Baltimore, Boston and New York. When the call for volunteers was made in the spring of 1898, to serve in the war with Spain, Mr. Schroeder enlisted as a private in Company A, 47th New York volunteer infantry, and served nearly eighteen months in Porto Rico. In the fall of 1899 he was mustered out with the rank of second lieutenant. Returning to Pittsburg in 1900 he opened his present place of business, which is one of the finest establishments of its kind in Homestead. On June 1, 1902, he was married to Miss Julia, daughter of Amos and Annie (Davis) Kurtz, of Somerset county, Pa., and one little daughter, Emma, has come to bless the union. Mr. Schroeder is a republican in politics, a member of the Lutheran church and of Homestead lodge, No. 1049, Independent Order of Odd Fellows. He is master of his trade and his shaving parlors are patronized by the best people in Homestead.

WILLIAM A. HOPE, a well-known attorney of Pittsburg, with offices at No. 415 Fourth St., was born July 11, 1856, on what was known at that time as the Whitaker farm—now the borough of Whitaker—in Mifflin township, Allegheny Co., Pa. He is the son of Thomas and Martha A. (Whitaker) Hope. His father is the son of James and Jane Hope and was born in England, Feb. 8, 1828, but came with his parents to America while he was still in his infancy. They settled in Allegheny county near what is now the borough of Carnegie. Here the family has ever since resided, Thomas being engaged in various occupations, such as coal-mining, farming and tool-dressing. He is still living and is engaged in farming on the Mercer road near the town of Franklin. The Whitaker family is also of English extraction. James Whitaker (at that time spelled Whiteacre), came over with Lord Baltimore on his last voyage and settled in Maryland. Shortly after the Revolutionary war the family removed to Pennsylvania and settled upon a 600-acre tract of land extending from Green Springs to the Homestead borough line. Upon the death of James Whitaker, his son, Aaron, the great-grandfather of William A. Hope, succeeded to 200 acres of this land and cultivated it until he passed away, when it descended to his son of the same name. Aaron, the second, built the old American furnace in Clarion county, one of the first in western Pennsylvania. In addition to the 200 acres inherited from his father's estate, he became the possessor of about 800 acres of iron-ore lands near Sligo Junction, Clarion Co., Pa. He died in 1847, after a brief illness, and was buried in the old cemetery adjoining his farm. During his life he took an active interest in the welfare of the county and was regarded one of the most progressive men in the community. His wife was Anna Dellenbach, a native of Switzerland, who died at the advanced age of eighty-eight, at Homestead, Pa. Their children were: Martha A. (Mrs. Hope), Christopher D., Elijah A. and Eliza (twins), the latter the wife of Charles K. West, of Ohio; Fannie, wife of J. W. Adams, of Braddock, Pa.; Wilbur F. and Aquilla T., who died in his infancy. Mrs. Hope died July 28, 1881; Christopher and Wilbur are farmers, the former in Iowa and the latter in Kansas; Elijah is a retired capitalist, living in Oakland, Cal. The children of Thomas and Martha A. Hope were: Jennie A., the wife of M. P. Schooley; William A., the subject of this sketch, and Christopher W., who died in 1862 at the age of four years. He and his mother rest side by side in the cemetery at Franklin. William A. Hope received his first schooling in what was known as the old

Scrubgrass schoolhouse in Scott township. He next attended the common school of Franklin and graduated from the Forbes school, in the sixth ward of the city of Pittsburg, when he was thirteen years of age. He was then admitted to the Pittsburg central high school for a time, but at an early age he began life for himself. He taught music, worked as an accountant, held various other positions and learned the trade of a stair-builder. He was also for two years editor of the Braddock Herald. From boyhood his desire was to be a lawyer, and while employed in the different avocations mentioned, he devoted most of his spare time to reading such law books as he could get hold of until 1875, when he entered the office of Hon. John H. Kerr, of Pittsburg, and began the study of law in a regular way. For three years he remained in the office of Mr. Kerr, when his health failed and he went west, where he found employment as a teacher in the public schools. In the fall of 1880 he returned to Pittsburg and renewed his studies, and in the following spring was admitted to practice in the courts of Allegheny county. In October, 1883, he was admitted to practice in the Pennsylvania supreme court. During his twenty-one years of practice in the city of Pittsburg, he has attained a high standing at the bar and has acquired a large clientage. Most of his time is devoted to the examination of titles, though he does a general business as attorney and counselor-at-law. He was married at Kansas City, Mo., Feb. 4, 1886, to Miss Katie E. Goldman, a daughter of the late Jonathan and Marie Goldman, both of whom were of Swiss descent, but were natives of Berks county, Pa. Mr. Hope is a member of Guysuta lodge, No. 513, Free and Accepted Masons, and he resides in the borough of Knoxville, where he is well known and universally respected.

WILLIAM E. BEST, of Pittsburg, Pa., an able lawyer, with offices in the Bank for Savings building, was born in that city, Jan. 11, 1873, son of Richard and Clara (Fritch) Best, both natives and life-residents of Pittsburg. The Best family were among the early settlers of Pittsburg and since that time have been closely identified with its advancement and progress. William E. Best received his rudimentary educational training in the graded and high schools of Pittsburg and later matriculated at Cornell university, where he was graduated in 1894. Subsequently he read law in the offices of Clarence Burleigh, a prominent attorney of Pittsburg, and was admitted to the bar of Allegheny county in March, 1895. Since that period, Mr. Best has prosecuted his professional duties with much success and now stands well at the bar of Pittsburg, where he is a member of all courts and of the Allegheny county bar association. Mr. Best is prominently connected with the leading fraternal orders and holds membership in the Masons, Odd Fellows, Junior Order of United American Mechanics, Royal Arcanum, Foresters of America and the Independent Order of Foresters. He was married in Pittsburg, Jan. 12, 1900, to Grace, daughter of Henry and Hannah Atkinson, the former having been a prominent citizen and the first manufacturer of brick in Allegheny county. Mr. Best resides in the thirty-first ward and his home life is an ideal one.

JACOB TRAUTMAN, president of the First National bank of Homestead, was born in the town of Higch, Bavaria, Germany, Feb. 18, 1843. His parents, Adam and Margaret (Redhair) Trautman, came to America in 1845. On coming to America, Adam Trautman engaged in the hotel business and continued at this vocation until he died, at the age of sixty-two, in 1878. Of the eight children born to Mr. and Mrs. Adam Trautman, Margaret, wife of Adam Idle, died of cholera in 1849; Susan married John Miller, now deceased; Daniel died in St. Clair township, Allegheny county, in 1876; John died in 1899 at Columbus, Ohio; Peter is a resident of Mount Oliver, Allegheny county; Frederick died in Homestead in November, 1901; Jacob is the subject of this sketch, and Henry died in Columbus, Ohio, in 1891. Jacob Trautman was reared in Columbus, Ohio. After obtaining a common-school education, he learned the trade of a painter and paper-hanger and then followed this vocation in Columbus for eleven years. In 1879 he located in Homestead and started in for himself, being successfully engaged in business up to 1889, when he retired from active life, although he has since then been more or less actively interested in real estate. Mr. Trautman's first wife, Celia (Barker) Trautman, of Columbus, Ohio, died in 1878, and he later married Mrs. Elizabeth Redhair, a native of Germany. Mr. Trautman had no children of his own, but his present wife, by a previous marriage, has six children, all of whom are now married. Mr. Trautman was one of the organizers of the First National bank of Homestead, and since the organization he has been a director and stockholder and since 1895, president of the bank. He is also a stockholder in the Mifflin Park land company and the Mifflin street railway company, and is one of the foremost business men of Homestead. He is a member of the F. and A. M., Royal Arcanum and Heptasophs. In politics he is a republican.

FRED GERDTS, of Duquesne, Pa., a prominent real estate dealer, was born in London, England, May 3, 1863, son of Frederick and Anna (Schumaker) Gerdts, natives of Germany who landed in America, July 11, 1873, locating in Mifflin township of Allegheny county, opposite to McKeesport. The elder Gerdts was employed in the mines of that vicinity for eight years and then went with the National tube works, at McKeesport, with which concern he continued until his death, Nov. 7, 1902, having resided in McKeesport for nearly twenty years. Fred Gerdts, the only son of his parents, was reared from ten years of age in Pennsylvania, attended the public schools of Mifflin township and McKeesport, and began his business career as a clerk in a grocery store at the latter place. He was engaged in that capacity for ten years and in 1889 went to Duquesne, commenced the grocery business on his own account and for six years prospered in that venture. He was unfortunate enough to have his establishment destroyed by fire, and in 1895 began his present real estate business, in which he has met with much success. He was happily married, Oct. 12, 1888, to Susie B., daughter of Robert and Elizabeth Mills, of McKeesport, and they have three children, viz.: Raymond F., Robert B. and Anna Elizabeth. Mr. Gerdts is closely connected with a number of leading fraternal orders, holding membership in the Elks, the Odd Fellows and the Masons, and is thoroughly in sympathy with them in their great works for the brotherhood of man. He is a stanch republican in his political affiliations and opinions, and has served as auditor of the borough for three years, borough clerk for one year and is now filling his second term as tax collector. Mr. Gerdts is also a notary public and is one of the best-known and most popular citizens of Duquesne.

EDWARD SCHREINER, of Pittsburg, Pa., a well-known attorney, with offices at No. 718 Frick building, was born at Allegheny city, Dec. 8, 1875, and is a son of John and Mary (Ziegler) Schreiner. His father, born in Germany, resided there until nineteen years of age, when he came to Allegheny city, where he has since followed the occupation of a contractor with much success. Mr. Schreiner was educated in the schools of his native city and at Cascadilla preparatory school, and in the fall of 1895 matriculated at Cornell university, where he remained for one year. Subsequently Mr. Schreiner entered the law department of the University of Michigan and was graduated from that famous seat of learning in 1899, with the degree of bachelor of laws. He was admitted to the bar of Michigan, and later came to Pittsburg, read law in the office of J. S. Ferguson, and was admitted to the bar of Allegheny county, where he is a member of all courts and has a fine clientage. Mr. Schreiner was married at Steubenville, Ohio, Dec. 15, 1902, to Ruth Foster. He resides in the twentieth ward and is widely known throughout the city. He is a member of the Delta Upsilon fraternity.

THOMAS GRAHAM, retail shoe dealer in Verona, was born in Scotland, March 1, 1847. His father, Thomas Graham, was a blacksmith. He died in Scotland in 1849 and his wife, Isabella (Christy) Graham, in 1860. They had one son and five daughters, of whom four are now living in Scotland. Thomas Graham, whose name appears at the head of this sketch, was reared and educated in Scotland and came to America in 1872. He located first in Pittsburg, then came a year later to Sandy Creek, in Penn township, where for several years he followed the vocation of a shoemaker. Coming to Verona in 1886, he engaged in the retail shoe trade, in which he has been most successful. In politics he is a republican, although never an aspirant for office. He attends the United Presbyterian church. Before coming to America, Mr. Thomas was married to Miss Annie Dobie and has one son, Henry D., who was born in Scotland, in October, 1867. He was married in 1901 and has one child, Thomas C., named for his grandfather.

CHAUNCEY LOBINGIER, of Pittsburg, Pa., a successful general practitioner of law, with offices in the Park building, was born at Mount Pleasant, Westmoreland Co., Pa., July 30, 1873, son of J. Smith and Mary J. (Cochran) Lobingier, both surviving and residing at Mount Pleasant, Pa. Chauncey Lobingier was educated at Mount Pleasant institute, where he was graduated in June, 1892, and later attended Lafayette college, where he was graduated in June, 1896. Then Mr. Lobingier read law in the office of Murphy & Hosack, of Pittsburg; was admitted to the bar on March 23, 1900, and has since practiced with much success. He is a member of all county and state courts, of the Allegheny county bar association, and has a fine practice. Mr. Lobingier is a member of Duquesne lodge, No. 546, Ancient Free and Accepted Masons, and is a member and secretary of the Theta Delta Phi association of western Pennsylvania, member of the East End board of trade, and resides in the twentieth ward. He was married in Easton, Pa., Oct. 31, 1900, to Isabella Allderdice, daughter of George and Frances (Houston) Danby. Mr. Lobingier is a member of the East Liberty Presbyterian church, and has served that organization in a number of official capacities.

HUGH S. CRAIG, attorney-at-law, is the son of William B. and Catherine H. (Singer) Craig, both of whom are natives of the Keystone state. The father was born in Cumberland county and his wife in Pittsburg. William B. Craig is a Presbyterian minister, though he has retired from the active work of the pulpit and is living, with his wife, a retired life at Shippensburg, Pa., happy in the reflections consequent upon a well-spent life. Hugh S. Craig was born at Duncannon, Pa., July 19, 1864. After attending the common schools and the Cumberland valley state normal school, at Shippensburg, Pa., he graduated from the Croton military institute of Croton, N. Y. He read law in the office of Kennedy & Doty, and on Dec. 24, 1887, was admitted to the Allegheny county bar. He at once entered upon the general practice of his profession and during the sixteen years that have followed his admission, he has established a good business. He is a member of all the state courts, practices in the circuit and district courts of the United States and is a member of the Allegheny county bar association. In October, 1898, he was married to Miss Harriet J., daughter of Rev. John F. and Margaret (Guthrie) Hill, of Cannonsburg, Pa., at Germantown (Philadelphia), Pa. Two children have been born to this union, Thomas S. and William Boyd. For the last twenty-five years Mr. Craig has been a resident of Pittsburg, or in the immediate vicinity of the city, and he is well known in legal, church and Masonic circles. He and his family attend Calvary Protestant Episcopal church, he is a member of Hailman lodge, No. 321, Free and Accepted Masons, located at Pittsburg, and of the Pennsylvania consistory, S. P. R. S. He takes an active interest in church and lodge affairs, though his greatest energies are devoted to the demands of his noble profession.

JOHN K. LOWRY, wholesale liquor dealer of Homestead and councilman from the third ward, is a son of John Lowry, and grandson of Thomas Lowry, who came to America from Ireland in 1830, and located in Pittsburg, where he followed his vocation as a weaver up to the time of his death, in 1849. He married Mary Bowman, and had six children: Thomas, Samuel, William, Joseph, John and Mary A. (Mrs. Samuel Maxwell). John Lowry, father of the subject of this sketch, was born in Ireland, but came to America when an infant, and was reared and educated in Pittsburg. He learned the saddlers' trade, and has followed this vocation all his life. He has been a resident of Homestead since 1872, and served two years as a member of the first council of the borough. He married Matilda Francis and reared four children: Belle, wife of George Munhall; Mary (deceased), John K., the subject of this sketch, and William (deceased). John K. Lowry was born July 26, 1860, in Allegheny city, Pa., and has lived in Homestead since 1872. After a common-school education, he served a three-year apprenticeship as a saddler and was engaged at this occupation for twenty years. Since 1898 he has been a wholesale liquor dealer at Homestead, and does an extensive and profitable business. On Feb. 18, 1881, Mr. Lowry married Jeanette, daughter of Levi and Hester (Snowden) Farquahar, of Pittsburg. Mr. and Mrs. Lowry have four children: Frank, Alice E., Blanche M. and Florence V. Mr. Lowry takes an active interest in public affairs, and is serving his third term as a member of the council of Homestead borough. In politics he is a republican. He is a member of Homestead lodge, No. 1049, I. O. O. F.

ROBERT OLIVER YOUNG, of Homestead, Pa., an old and highly-respected citizen, was born in Pittsburg, Pa., April 24, 1847, son of Robert and Elizabeth (Ewart) Young, both natives of Pittsburg. His paternal grandfather was William Young, born in the north of Ireland, and was a pioneer merchant and teacher of Pittsburg. His father was also a merchant and teacher of Pittsburg and died in that city in 1848. Robert Oliver Young was the only child of his parents and was reared and educated in his native city, where, in 1864, he began his apprenticeship at the brick-layers' trade, which vocation he followed until 1902, when he embarked in the wholesale liquor business at Clairton, Allegheny county, and is meeting with much success in that venture. Mr. Young has been a resident of Homestead since 1881 and is well and favorably known in that borough. He was married, on Sept. 17, 1878, to Eliza J., daughter of William J. and Rose A. (Coshy) Johnson, of Pittsburg, and they have three children, viz.: Olivet V., Harry L. and Robert O. J. Mr. Young and family are members of the Episcopal church and he is a member of the Ancient Order of United Workmen, the Knights of Pythias and the Elks. Mr. Young was a soldier in the Civil war, enlisting in August, 1864, in Company F, 193d Pennsylvania volunteer infantry, and after a term of three months was honorably discharged from the service. Mr. Young is prominent in the public affairs of Homestead, for seven years was a member of the council and is a stanch republican in his political views and affiliations.

LAWRENCE B. COOK, of Pittsburg, Pa., a successful lawyer and a prominent member of the Pennsylvania legislature, with offices at No. 422 Fifth Ave., was born in Indiana county, Pa., Sept. 27, 1870, son of Jeremiah and Lena A. (Wagoner) Cook, both natives of Indiana county, Pa., and both now residing at Pittsburg. Mr. Cook was educated in the preliminary courses in the public schools of Pittsburg, later attended a private academy at Washington, and completed his classical training at Curry institute. Mr. Cook then, like many of the great Americans who have achieved success by their personal efforts, engaged in teaching school, and at the same time studied law during his leisure hours. He was admitted to the bar of Allegheny county, December, 1892, and has since taken a prominent stand among the leading attorneys of Pittsburg. Mr. Cook enjoys a large and lucrative practice and is a member of all state and federal courts. He is well and favorably known throughout the county, and the esteem in which he is held was demonstrated by his election to the state legislature in November, 1902, a position which he is now filling to the entire satisfaction of his constituents. He resides in the sixth ward of Pittsburg, and is easily one of the most popular young men of the city.

JACOB ELICKER, of Homestead, Pa., for many years a leading florist of that borough and still prospering in that vocation, was born in Baldwin township, Allegheny county, April 3, 1858, son of Peter and Catherine (Rothar) Elicker, both natives of Germany. His father came to America in the early fifties, settled in Baldwin township and was employed as a miner along the Monongahela river for many years, and in later life purchased a farm in Mifflin township, where he lived for fifteen years. He was a supervisor of Mifflin township for several years, was a member of the Lutheran church and was the father of the following children, viz.: John; Caroline, wife of Adam Snyder; Jacob; Margaret, wife of Robert Wolff; Adam; Lizzie, wife of Robert Snyder; Henry, William, Peter, and Kate, wife of O. P. Antos. Jacob Elicker was reared in Allegheny county, educated in the common schools and remained under the parental roof until his twenty-fourth year, having worked in the mines since seventeen years of age. Then he followed carpentering for four years in Baldwin township, engaged in gardening for several years and in 1891 embarked in the florist business on a small scale in Mifflin township, and now has eight fine greenhouses and supplies the leading families of Homestead and vicinity. Since April, 1900, he has maintained a retail store on Eighth avenue and does a large business in cut flowers. He was married, on Sept. 23, 1879, to Sophia, daughter of Frederick and Wilhelmina (Rebke) Drewes, of Baldwin township, and they have four children, viz.: Harry, Ida, Edna and William. Mr. Elicker is a member of the Junior Order of United American Mechanics, the Knights of Pythias, the

Foresters of America, the Red Men and the Woodmen of the World. His political affiliations are with the republicans and he is an active and ardent advocate of the tenets of that great organization.

CHARLES A. LEWIS, of Pittsburg, Pa., a prominent and progressive young attorney, was born in Monongahela borough, Washington Co., Pa., May 12, 1871, son of Albert G. and Hattie L. (McCurdy) Lewis, both now residing at Elizabethville, Pa. Mr. Lewis secured his education in the graded and high schools of Elizabeth and then studied pharmacy in the Western university, where he was graduated in 1893, with the degree of graduate of pharmacy. Subsequently he studied law in the offices of Crumrine & Patterson and also of E. J. Kent, and was admitted to the bar in December, 1900, and is a member of all courts. Mr. Lewis has one of the best practices of any of the younger members of the Pittsburg bar and has fast gained a place of honor and respectability among the leading lawyers of Allegheny county. He was married at Elizabeth, Aug. 23, 1901, to Lillian P. Pollock, and they have one son, Charles P., born Sept. 27, 1902. Mr. Lewis is a member of Stephen Barrett lodge, No. 526, Ancient Free and Accepted Masons, of Elizabeth, and is prominently identified with that great fraternity. He is also solicitor of the borough of Elizabeth and an honored citizen of that community.

WILLIAM G. GUILER, attorney-at-law, located at No. 432 Diamond St., Pittsburg, Pa., is a descendant of one of the oldest families of Pennsylvania. In fact, his ancestry can be traced back to the time when some of the Guilers went from Holland to Scotland with King William of Orange. From Scotland one branch of the family emigrated to Ireland, settling in County Derry about the year 1796 Near the close of the eighteenth century Alexander Guiler, the great-great-grandfather of the subject of this sketch, came to America and settled in what is now Fayette county, Pa. There he purchased land and engaged in farming until his death. His wife was a Miss Greer, a native of Ireland. William Guiler, a son of Alexander, was born in Fayette county in 1801 and died there in 1865. Like his father, he was a tiller of the soil. His wife was Nancy Carr. They had five children, viz.: Absalom, Andrew, Alexander, Joseph and Mary. Of these, the second son, Andrew, is the only one now living. He was an officer in the Civil war and a breveted captain by reason of his bravery in the battle before Petersburg in 1865. Absalom Guiler was born in 1819. He learned the tailors' trade, and upon arriving at man's estate, became a merchant tailor. During the Mexican war he served as first sergeant of Company H, 2d Pennsylvania volunteers, participating in the bombardment of Vera Cruz, the battle of Cerro Gordo mountain, in which he was slightly wounded, in the storming of the castle of Chapultepec, and the battle of Bealan gate, his regiment being the first to enter the city of Mexico. His colonel recommended his appointment to a lieutenancy in the regular army, but he declined and returned to his home and business. In the autumn of 1861 he helped to organize the 85th Pennsylvania volunteer infantry, and was elected major of the regiment. With his regiment he took part in all the battles of the Peninsular campaign until the hardships and exposures of war compelled him to resign his commission and retire from the army. He died April 29, 1873, as the result of a fall from his horse a short time before. His wife was Elizabeth Jeffries, a native of Fayette county, Pa., born in 1820, and died in May, 1887. The children of Absalom and Elizabeth Guiler were: Caleb J., Virginia, William G., Joseph and Dr. A. G. Guiler. All are living except the daughter, Virginia. William G. Guiler was born July 20, 1847. After such a primary education as the common schools of his native town afforded, he attended the Madison institute, of Uniontown, Pa., and for the next two years taught in the public schools of Fayette county. While thus employed he spent his leisure time in reading good books and perfecting himself in his classical studies. He read law in the office of the late G. W. K. Minor, one of the most prominent lawyers at the Fayette county bar, and was admitted to practice in the courts of Fayette county in September, 1868. In 1870 he was admitted to the bar in Allegheny county, and for some time immediately following his admission there he practiced in Pittsburg, but on account of failing health returned to Fayette county, where he remained until 1895, returning then to Pittsburg. While in Fayette county he held the office of county attorney and was prominently mentioned as a candidate for judge. Both in Fayette county and since coming to Pittsburg, Mr. Guiler has confined his practice to civil cases. He practices in all the local, state and federal courts, is a member of the county bar association, and has a large clientage, among which are a number of large and important corporations. Mr. Guiler has been twice married. His first wife was Laura J. Lenhart, to whom he was married Dec. 22, 1870. She was the daughter of Leonard Lenhart, a steamboat builder of Brownsville, Pa. Her death occurred Oct. 10, 1884. To his first marriage four children were born, three of whom are still living. They are Carrie, Leonard K., who is a graduate of Princeton university and a law student, and Mary M. In August, 1886, he was married to his present wife, who was Miss Emma B. Newton, a daughter of Dr. O. E. Newton (deceased), a prominent physician of Cincinnati, Ohio. One daughter, Margaret Grace, has been born to this second marriage.

HOWARD LINHART BLACK, of Duquesne, Pa., a prominent real estate dealer, was born at Braddock, Pa., June 1, 1859, son of Eslie P. and Elizabeth J. (Porter) Black, natives of Allegheny county and of Irish and English descent, respectively. His paternal great-grandfather Black was a native of Ireland, emigrated to America, and was a farmer by occupation. Here his son, Francis Black, grandfather of the subject, was born. Francis Black was also a farmer, and in early manhood located in Iowa, later went to Colorado and California, and died in the last-named state in the eighties at the age of ninety-nine years. The maternal grandfather of Mr. Black was Francis Porter, a native of England, who came to America about 1829, located at Braddock, Allegheny county, Pa., and there worked in the coal mines until his death. The father of the subject was reared in Allegheny county, was a well-known pilot and captain on the Monongahela, Ohio and Mississippi rivers, following the river for over forty years, and dying in 1896, at the age of seventy-four years. He had a family of nine children, six of whom grew to maturity, viz.: Jennie, wife of S. W. Hare; James, Howard L., Frank, Annie, wife of E. B. Williams, and Samuel. Howard L. Black was reared in Braddock and Pittsburg, educated in the public schools and at Curry institute, and in 1877 began his business career as bookkeeper for S. W. Hare & Co., plumbers of Pittsburg. He continued in that line of employment until 1889, when he embarked in the real estate and insurance business at Duquesne, where he had previously located in 1886. He has successfully continued in that business to the present time and handled some large deals in that part of the county. He was appointed postmaster of Duquesne by President Harrison in 1889 and satisfactorily filled that office for five years, being the second man to fill that position in the borough. He was married, on Jan. 21, 1883, to Annie M., daughter of Joseph and Priscilla (Barchfield) Kennedy, of Pittsburg, and they have six children: Fannie P., F. Norman, Bessie L., Joseph K., Howard E. and Priscilla J. Mr. Black and his family are members of the Methodist Episcopal church, and he is a member of the Knights of Pythias and Royal Arcanum, is vice-president of the Duquesne land company, and a stockholder in the Duquesne trust company, of which latter institution he was one of the promoters and organizers. Mr. Black is prominently identified with the republican party, served three years as auditor of Mifflin township, and is one of the progressive and substantial citizens of Duquesne.

WILLIAM VOKOLEK, a Pittsburg attorney, with offices at No. 424 Fourth Ave., is a native of Bohemia. His parents came to this country in 1873, and since that time his father has been a resident of New York city. His mother died in New York in 1888. William Vokolek was born April 19, 1868, and was therefore but five years old when he came with his parents to America. He was educated in the public schools of New York city, after which he took a business college course and worked three years as an accountant. He entered the academic department of the German theological seminary of Bloomfield, N. J., and graduated from that institution in 1892. He next attended the McCormick theological seminary, Chicago, for one year, then took a course of law, and graduated from the Kent college of law, Chicago, in 1895, with the degree of bachelor of laws. The same year he was admitted to practice in the courts of Cook county and the supreme court of the state of Illinois. In the autumn of 1895 he removed to Scranton, Pa., and early in 1896 was admitted to the bar of Lackawanna county, in which Scranton is located. He continued in practice at Scranton until November, 1902, and during that time he was counsel for the Greek Catholic union of the United States and the National Slavonic society. In November, 1902, he removed to Pittsburg, and at the fall term of court was admitted to the Allegheny county bar. Since that time he has practiced his profession in Pittsburg. He is the attorney for the National Slavonic society, of which he is a member. He is also a member of the Knights of Malta; the Union Masonic lodge, No. 291, of Scranton; the Slavonic Presbyterian union and the Slavonic benevolent union of the United States of America; the Bohemian gymnastic association, of Allegheny city, and the Elmhurst country club. He has been twice married, his first wife being Miss Josephine Chvatal, of Chicago. In 1896 he was married a second time to Miss Emily Kriz, also of Chicago. By his first wife he has one daughter, Josephine. To his second marriage there have been born four children: Agnes M., born at Scranton; Emily, Lillian and Annie. Mr. Vokolek resides at McKeesport, where he and his wife both belong to the Presbyterian church. He is an accomplished linguist, speaking Bohemian, Russian, Polish, German and English, and is deeply interested in the Americanizing of the Slavonic races of the United States.

CHARLES HENRY VONDERA, a well-to-do citizen of Mifflin township, Allegheny county, is a son of Henry and Christina Wilhelmina (Heisterburg) Vondera, and is of Holland Dutch ancestry. His paternal grandfather, Frank Vondera, was a native of Hesse Darmstadt and a shoemaker by trade, who came to America in 1849 and located in Baldwin township, Allegheny county, where he followed his trade of shoemaking until 1863, when he removed to Mifflin township, and there lived until his death. The maternal grandfather of the subject was Christian Heisterburg, a native of Germany, and also a shoemaker by trade, who came to America in 1848 and resided in Mifflin township until his death. Henry Vondera, father of subject, came to America in 1847, and to Mifflin township in 1863, where he resided on his farm, about one and a half miles from Homestead, until his death in 1897, at the age of seventy-three years. He had a family of six children, viz.: Christian F., Frank H.; Lena, wife of Frank Bost; Charles H.; Mary, wife of Peter Sorg, and Louisa, wife of William J. Hall. Charles H. Vondera was born in Mifflin township, July 5, 1865, and there was reared to manhood and educated in the common schools of his native township. He has followed gardening and farming all of his business career, has made a success of these vocations, and has a good competency. He was married, on Sept. 22, 1898, to Estella, daughter of Frank Daniels, of West Virginia, and they have one daughter, M. Luella. Mr.

Vondera is a member of the Lutheran church, and his political affiliations are with the republican party. He is prominently identified with the public affairs of the township, in the spring of 1903 being elected township tax collector for a three-year term, an evidence of his popularity.

EVAN JONES, general contractor, has been for many years actively engaged in the construction of large public and private works, and although born in Wales, has been a resident of Pittsburg since he was five years old. He was born in Cardiganshire, Wales. Mr. Jones attended the Pittsburg schools until he reached the age of eighteen, and then learned the plasterers' trade, at which he was engaged for some ten years. His career as a general contractor dates from 1874, his first work being in heavy grading and sewerage for the city of Pittsburg. Since that time he has done an extensive business in tunneling, sewerage and street paving, and in the building of heavy retaining walls. Among other works which he has built might be mentioned the construction of the Thirty-third street sewer, the foundation for the Carnegie building on Fifth avenue, and the foundations for the great trip-hammers at the Latrobe works. In politics Mr. Jones is a republican. He served for six years in the common council of Pittsburg from the sixth and fourteenth wards, was for some five years member of the poll boards of the city, and is now serving his third term on the Forbes street school board, of which he is president.

THOMAS C. GABLER, attorney-at-law, whose offices are located at No. 307 Bakewell building, is a native of Monongahela township, Greene Co., Pa., where he was born Nov. 13, 1855. He is the son of Allen K. and Maria (Jones) Gabler, both of whom were natives of Greene county and spent their entire lives there, the father dying Jan. 5, 1896, and the mother in January, 1879. Mr. Gabler was educated in the public schools of Greene county, Waynesburg college and Bethany college, located at Bethany, W. Va., from which institution he was graduated in 1876. He took a scientific course in the same institution, after which he began the study of law in the offices of Wyly & Buchanan, at Waynesburg. In October, 1877, he was admitted to the Greene county bar and practiced his profession there until the spring of 1880, when he removed to Cincinnati, Ohio. For four years he practiced in the Ohio courts with constantly increasing success, when failing health compelled him to seek a change of climate and he went to Colorado. A residence of a year and a half among the mountains restored his health and he returned to Greene county, Pa., where he practiced until 1894, when he was admitted to the bar of Allegheny county and took up his residence in the borough of Sheridan, for which he is the solicitor at the present time. Mr. Gabler was married, on Oct 9, 1899, to Elizabeth, daughter of Hon. A. A. Purman, of Waynesburg. He is a member of Lodge No. 11, B. P. O. Elks, of the city of Pittsburg, which is the only secret order or civic organization to claim him as a member. He practices in all the courts of the county, state and United States.

WILLIAM EVANS, who is now serving his fifth successive term as street commissioner of Homestead, was born in Allegheny county, Pa., May 13, 1850, son of David and Mary (Evans) Evans, natives of Wales, who came to America in 1840 and located at Sugarloaf, Luzerne Co., Pa. Here David Evans was employed for several years in the anthracite coal mines, and about 1849 came to the Monongahela river valley, Allegheny county, where he was employed in the bituminous coal mines until his death, which occurred in 1863. He reared a family of four sons: Reese, Evan, David and William. William Evans, the subject of this article, was reared in Allegheny county and received a limited education in the public schools. When twelve years old he began to work about the coal mines, and at the age of fourteen started his apprenticeship at the blacksmiths' trade, and followed that vocation for thirty-four years. He was employed by Jones & Laughlin from 1879 to 1887, by the Carnegie steel company from 1887 to 1892, and from 1892 to 1896 had charge of the blacksmith department of the National tube works, Riverton. Since 1880 he has resided in Homestead, where he has valuable property interests, accumulated by his own thrift and industry. On Aug. 25, 1875, Mr. Evans married Miss Annie Oxley, daughter of Thomas and Elizabeth Oxley, of Redman Mills, Allegheny Co., Pa., and has two children living: Thomas H. and Mary. Mr. Evans is a progressive and influential citizen of Homestead, and his long service as street commissioner is an evidence of the esteem in which he is held in the community. In politics he is a republican.

EMIL SPARR, member of the board of assessors of Allegheny county, is a prominent resident of the thirteenth ward, Pittsburg, and formerly represented his ward in the common council. He was born in Berlin, Germany, in 1850; came to Rochester, N. Y., with his parents in 1852; lived there until 1868, and then came to Pittsburg, where he has since resided. Mr. Sparr received his education in Rochester, and then learned the lithographing business, and was engaged in this business in Pittsburg until 1877. After this he was for ten years fireman in the Pittsburg paid fire department, and then was from 1887 to 1896 employed as inspector on the city board of survey. He was elected to the Pittsburg common council in 1896, and was twice re-elected, serving, in all, six years. While in the council, in 1897, he became foreman for Keeling & Ridge, general contractors, and remained with this firm until April, 1902, when he was appointed to his present responsible position by Recorder Brown. Mr. Sparr is a member of the I. O. O. F. and the Encampment, and belongs to the German Protestant Evangelical church.

HENRY A. MILLER has been a practicing attorney in the courts of Allegheny county for more than a quarter of a century. At the present time his offices are located at No. 86 St. Nicholas building, Pittsburg, Pa. He is a native of the Keystone state, was born in Butler county, Feb. 28, 1841, and is the son of William H. and Charlotta (Weisenstein) Miller. Both parents were natives of Germany, the father of Prussia, and the mother of Würtemburg. William Miller was a cabinet-maker by trade; he came to America in his early manhood, and spent the remainder of his life in Butler county. His wife survived him and died in November, 1902, at the advanced age of eighty-nine years. Henry A. Miller received his education in the common schools, the Butler county academy and the Weatherspoon institute. In September, 1861, he enlisted in the 78th Pennsylvania volunteer infantry as a private, and remained in the service until 1865, when he was discharged with the rank of sergeant-major. At the close of the war he located in Franklin, Venango Co., Pa., and read law in the office of Archibald Blakeley for about two years, when he was admitted to the Venango county bar. That was in 1867, and he practiced in that county until 1875, when he was admitted to the bar of Allegheny county. Since then he has been engaged in the practice of his profession in Pittsburg, being a member of the county bar association and of all the courts. He was married at

Pleasantville, Pa., to Miss Frances S. Merrick. To this union two daughters have been born: Charlotta and Mary S. Mr. Miller is well known in Masonic circles, being a member of Dallas lodge, No. 508, of Pittsburg, and a member of Pittsburg consistory of the Ancient and Accepted Scottish Rite. He resides in the twenty-first ward of the city of Pittsburg.

WILLIAM JOSEPH LEADER, of Duquesne, Pa., a successful merchant and a well-known citizen, was born in Bedford county, Pa., Jan. 13, 1866, son of George C. and Sarah (Manspeaker) Leader, both natives of Bedford county and of German and Scotch descent, respectively. His paternal grandfather, Daniel Leader, was a native of Pennsylvania and a lifelong farmer of Bedford county, and his maternal grandfather, George Manspeaker, was a shoemaker by trade and spent most of his life in Bedford, where he died at a ripe old age. George C. Leader, father of the subject, was a brick and stone mason and a life-resident of Bedford county, where he died, Dec. 5, 1902, at the age of seventy-three years. He was a veteran of the Mexican war, in which he served about eighteen months, and was the father of fourteen children, ten of whom grew to maturity, viz.: Lottie, wife of William Shook; Mary, wife of Frank Yarnell; Sallie, Daniel, Clayton, George, William J.; Belle, wife of John Foor; John G. and Lavinia. William J. Leader was reared in Bedford, Pa.; attended the public schools of that place, and there learned the brick-layers' trade under his father, which he successfully followed until September, 1897, six years of which time was devoted to contracting at Duquesne and Homestead. Among the many fine structures erected by him may be mentioned the high school of Homestead, a similar building at Munhall, and many of the principal business blocks and dwellings of Homestead and vicinity. He came to Allegheny county in 1886; has been a resident of Duquesne since 1891, where he engaged in the wholesale liquor business in 1897, which he has successfully continued to the present time. He was married, on Jan. 12, 1893, to Mary, daughter of Christian Dierstein, of Duquesne, and has three children, viz.: Joseph K., Elizabeth and Frederick. Mr. Leader is a member of Vesta lodge,

No. 352, Knights of Pythias, of which he held the office of financial secretary for two years; member of the Duquesne lodge, No. 64, uniform rank, Knights of Pythias, in which he served as lieutenant for two years and as captain for three years; Eclipse lodge, No. 892, Independent Order of Odd Fellows; Foresters of America, and the Benevolent and Protective Order of Elks. While engaged in the business of contracting, Mr. Leader built the main sewer for Duquesne, did the first street paving, built the retaining wall for the Pennsylvania railroad along Duquesne avenue, between Grant street and Oliver station, and erected many of the principal buildings of the borough. Mr. Leader's political affiliations are with the republican party, and he takes great interest in the public affairs of his section of the country.

HAROLD A. MILLER, M. D., of Pittsburg, Pa., a successful general practitioner of medicine, was born in Alliance, Ohio, Sept. 20, 1873, son of Addison Miller, now a resident of Pennsylvania, and of his wife, K. H. (Thompson) Miller. He is a member of the Allegheny county, the Pennsylvania state, the Fort Pitt and the West Pennsylvania medical societies, the Pittsburg pathological society, the medical staff of the West Pennsylvania hospital, and is the medical director of the Pittsburg life and trust company.

DR. ROBERT W. McCLELLAND, a prominent homœopathic physician, residing in the city of Pittsburg, Pa., was born in that city, June 22, 1857. He is of Scotch-Irish ancestry, his father a native of Ireland, coming to this country in 1816, and settling in Pittsburg. He was an architect and contractor, and was the designer and builder of some of the finest buildings erected in the city of Pittsburg during the active period of his chosen life-work. He was also postmaster of Pittsburg from 1867 to 1871. Dr. McClelland, after attending the public schools of his native city, spent two years at Lafayette college, preparatory to the study of medicine, followed by a course of study at Cornell university, from which institution he graduated in 1882 with the degree of bachelor of science. He further pursued the study of medicine at the Hahnemann medical college, of Philadelphia, from which he was graduated with honors in 1884. After graduation he went abroad from time to time to secure the advantage of special work in foreign hospitals, a part of this work being a special course in orthopedics under Professor Wolff, of Berlin, and later a clinical course under Dr. Lorenz, of Vienna. Returning to Pittsburg, he began the practice of general medicine and surgery, in connection with his two brothers, Drs. J. H. and J. B. McClelland, with whom he is still associated. He is a member of the orthopedic staff in the Homœopathic hospital of Pittsburg, and is the lecturer on anatomy and physiology to the training school for nurses, which is carried on in connection with the hospital; is a member of the Allegheny county homœopathic medical society, the Pennsylvania state medical society, the American institute of homœopathy, the East End doctors' club, the University club, the Pittsburg golf club, and was the first president of the Cornell club of western Pennsylvania. He is a thirty-second degree Mason, being a member of Franklin lodge, No. 221, and the Pennsylvania consistory, A. and A. Scottish Rite. He is also a member of the Third Presbyterian church of the city of Pittsburg. In politics he is a republican, and while taking no active part in political work, has been at all times interested in matters of public welfare. His brother, Dr. James H. McClelland, with whom he is associated, is well known over the country as a leading surgeon. After graduation in 1867 from the Hahnemann medical college, of Philadelphia, Dr. J. H. established himself in general practice in Pittsburg, where he is now associated with his two brothers. He is a member of the board of trustees of the Pittsburg homœopathic hospital, a member of the surgical staff of the same institution, and was actively interested in the erection of the buildings now occupied by the hospital. He was instrumental in founding the first training school for nurses in this city. He has been successively president of the following organizations: the Allegheny county homœopathic medical society, the Pennsylvania state homœopathic medical society, the American institute of homœopathy, which office he held in 1892, and the East End doctors' club. He is ex-vice-president of the Association of health authorities, of which the governor of the state is president; a member of the Pennsylvania state board of health, the Sanitary commission of Allegheny county, the American public health association, the Pittsburg golf club, the University club, and was vice-president of the Hospital Staff association of western Pennsylvania. From 1876 to 1878 he was professor of surgery in the Hahnemann medical college, of Philadelphia, and subsequently lectured on operative surgery in the Boston university school of medicine. In conclusion, it may be said that the firm of the Drs. McClelland is highly respected, and has always occupied a prominent position in the community.

WILLIAM ALVAH STEWART, M. D., of Pittsburg, Pa., was born in Tioga county, Pa., June 14, 1862. Dr. Stewart was educated in the high schools of western New York, then entered the State normal school of Geneseo, N. Y., and graduated from that institution in 1885. The six years following his graduation were devoted to teaching. In 1891 he matriculated at the New York homœopathic medical college and hospital, from which institution he graduated in 1894. After serving two years as interne in Flower hospital, he went to Washington, D. C., where he engaged in practice until 1901. Since that time he has been located in Pittsburg. His specialty is gynecology and general surgery. He is a member of the surgical staff of the department of gynecology of the Pittsburg homœopathic hospital. Dr. Stewart is a member of the Allegheny county and Pennsylvania state medical societies, the American institute of homœopathy, the New York state homœopathic medical society, and the Homœopathic medical society of Washington, D. C. He is also a member of the Duquesne club and the East End doctors' club. He is a fourteenth-degree Mason and a Mystic Shriner.

LEWIS E. DAVIS, M. D., of Pittsburg, Pa., a leading physician, was born on Davis island, Allegheny county, Oct. 6, 1855, son of James and Nancy (Burns) Davis, his father having been a gardener and fruit-grower and died in 1896. His mother was born in West End, Pittsburg. Her father came from Scotland and her mother from Wales. Dr. Davis' paternal grandfather was a native of Wales, came to the United States in 1796 and after living at different places settled on an island which he named "Davis" after himself, and where Mr. Davis' father, two sisters and three brothers were born. The paternal grandmother of Dr. Davis was also from Wales and was a descendant of Lord Llewellyn, a noted man of that country. Dr. Davis was educated in the elementary branches in the public schools of Robinson township, received special courses from Dr. John D. Davis, of Marshall township, with whom he read medicine for five years, entered Jefferson medical college and was graduated from that famous institution in 1881. He began the practice of his profession under his former preceptor, Dr. Davis, where he remained for one year and then went to Wisconsin. After practicing in the Badger state for some time, he went to Pittsburg and practiced in the twenty-third ward until 1899, when he removed to his present location, No. 317 South Craig St. Dr. Davis enjoys a large general practice but devotes the greater part of his time to the rectum. He attended special post-graduate courses at the Post-Graduate college, of New York city, in 1899 and 1901-02, giving his attention to diseases of the rectum and to surgery. He is on the medical staff of Passavant hospital, examiner for the Royal Arcanum and was surgeon for the Baltimore & Ohio railroad for five years. He is a member of the Allegheny county, the Pennsylvania state and the American medical associations and is also a member of the Knight Templar Masons, the republican party and the Christian church of Alder street. He was married, in 1887, to Sarah D., daughter of Thomas and Elizabeth (Berry) Figley, of Pittsburg, and they have four children: Marion Elizabeth, Lewis Elwood, Clark Bane and John Duff.

ROBERT W. CLARK, M. D., of Pittsburg, Pa., a successful general practitioner of medicine, was born near Lancaster, in Lancaster county, Pa., Aug. 2, 1848, son of Alexander Scott and Isabelle Jane (Neeper) Clark, his father having been a prosperous farmer and his ancestors on both sides having come to America prior to the Revolutionary war. His paternal great-grandfather, Thomas Clark, was a native of County Tyrone, Ireland, and when three years of age accompanied his parents to America, settling in Lancaster county, Pa., where the family have since lived, the original farm being now in the hands of his descendants. Dr. Clark was educated in the public schools and at the academy of Lancaster and then spent one year at the University of Pennsylvania, one year at the University of Michigan, and then returned to the University of Pennsylvania, where he was graduated from the medical department in 1871. For the next year he was resident physician of the Philadelphia hospital, then went to Tuscarawas county, Ohio, where he practiced for one and a half years. He next removed to Dunbar, Fayette Co., Pa., and for seventeen years met with much success in the practice of his profession in that city. For the next eight years Dr. Clark was engaged in the practice at Uniontown, Fayette Co., Pa., and in 1898 came to Pittsburg and now has a splendid standing among the physicians of that city. He is medical examiner for the Penn mutual life and other insurance companies and is a member of the Allegheny county and Pennsylvania state medical associations, member and ex-president of the Fayette county medical society, and was surgeon for the Baltimore & Ohio railroad from 1875 to 1887. He is prominently identified with the Masons, being a Knight Templar and Shriner, and is an ardent member of the republican party. Dr. Clark was married, in 1886, to Ella, daughter of J. J. and Roseanna (Ankeny) Schell, her father being president of the banks at Somerset and Berlin, Pa., and a prominent figure in the financial world. Her ancestors are among the earliest settlers of Somerset county, founded the town of Somerset and are still prominent in its affairs. Dr. and Mrs. Clark have two children: Robert W., Jr., and Eleanor Schell, students of the schools of Pittsburg and vicinity.

LEWIS W. WILSON, real estate and insurance agent at No. 3741 Boquet St., Pittsburg, was born May 15, 1847, son of William and Eliza (Harris) Wilson. William Wilson was a native of Fayette county, Pa., and son of Frederick Wilson. Lewis W. Wilson was educated in the schools of Fayette county, and when twenty-one years old began dealing in real estate. When a young man, he was also interested in manufacturing in Fayette county, but moved to McKeesport in the early seventies, and later to Pittsburg, where he is still in business. When East Pittsburg became a place of importance, he opened an office on Cable avenue, near Braddock avenue, where he conducts a flourishing business in insurance and real estate. Mr. Wilson is agent for the New York life insurance company, and writes for several fire insurance companies. On Jan. 22, 1872, Mr. Wilson married Melinda, daughter of Henry and Jane (Campbell) Schnatterly, old settlers of Fayette county. Of the children born of this union, Pleassie is the wife of W. G. Roden, a jeweler in Pittsburg; Emma is married to H. H. Howard, and lives in Pittsburg, and William Wood is manager of the Bell telephone exchange at Charleroi. Mr. Wilson and family are members of the Uniontown Baptist church.

DR. GEORGE C. JOHNSTON, a prominent Pittsburg physician and X-ray specialist, was born in New Lisbon, Ohio, April 3, 1869. He is the son of George N. and Emma (Coffin) Johnston. His father is a well-known Presbyterian minister, holding the degree of doctor of divinity, and is now the pastor of the Presbyterian church at Shields, Allegheny Co., Pa., but his mother died in 1899. Dr. Johnston received his early education in the public schools of Steubenville, Ohio. After a three years' course in the Washington and Jefferson college, at Washington, Pa., he took a special course in chemistry in the Western University of Pennsylvania preparatory to the study of medicine, and graduated from the Western Pennsylvania college of medicine in 1896. Immediately after his graduation he began the general practice of medicine in the city of Pittsburg and continued in that line until 1900, since which time he has been devoting his time and attention to X-ray work. He holds the position of radiographer to the St. John's and Children's hospitals in the city of Pittsburg and is professor of electro-physics in the Western Pennsylvania medical college. He is a member of the medical societies of Allegheny county and the state of Pennsylvania, the American medical association, the American society of electro-therapeutics, the Western Pennsylvania medical society, the alumni association of the Western Pennsylvania college, Alpha chapter of the Phi Beta Pi, and an honorary member of the Tri-State medical society. He is also a member of the Masonic fraternity, holding his membership in Pittsburg lodge, No. 484. Dr. Johnston is a contributor to the Pennsylvania State Medical Journal, American Medicine, Advanced Therapeutics, and various other medical and scientific journals, and is regarded as an authority upon all questions touching his specialty. He was married, in 1898, to Miss Ida B. Davis, of Pittsburg, a daughter of Gustavus C. and Lottie (Caskey) Davis, whose ancestors were among the early settlers of the country. They have one little daughter, Dorothy Davis Johnston. Dr. Johnston and his wife are both members of the First Presbyterian church of Pittsburg. In connection with a sketch of Dr. Johnston, it is worthy of remark that his maternal ancestors were among the pilgrims who came over on the "Mayflower" in the winter of 1620.

EDWARD R. GREGG, M. D., of Pittsburg, Pa., a prominent physician and surgeon, was born in Buffalo, N. Y., Feb. 24, 1870, son of R. R. and Hattie (Williams) Gregg, his father having been a prominent physician of Buffalo until his death in 1886, and his mother is now residing in Pittsburg. Dr. Gregg was educated in the public schools of his native city, graduated at the Buffalo high school in 1889 and then entered Hahnemann medical college at Philadelphia, were he was graduated in 1892. Later he attended a post-graduate course at the Philadelphia polyclinic and was surgeon to the Hahnemann medical college dispensary during that year. Then he went to Pittsburg as house surgeon of the Homœopathic hospital and served for two years in that capacity. The next year was devoted to taking special courses in Berlin, and Dr. Gregg returned to Pittsburg in 1895 to resume general practice. He was appointed staff surgeon in the Homœopathic hospital, which position he now holds in connection with the secretaryship of the medical board of that institution. He is a member of the Allegheny county and the Pennsylvania state homœopathic medical societies, the American institute of homœopathy, the surgical and gynecological department of the foregoing, honorary member of the Dunham medical society, of Chicago; member of the East End doctors' club and surgeon for the Pittsburg & Lake Erie railroad and Pittsburg railway company. He is also a member of the Masonic fraternity and the Arctic Brotherhood of Alaska. In December, 1897, he started for Alaska with two companions, sailing around South America and experiencing a shipwreck on the coast of Patagonia. Then they sailed around Cape Horn to Seattle, where one of the party remained, Dr. Gregg going to Alaska, where he spent two years, and one year in Rampart city, where he was surgeon of the town hospital. Next he went to Nome, and there was municipal and United States health officer, and surgeon to the city hospital. He remained at Nome until November, 1900, when he returned to Pittsburg and resumed his practice of general surgery and gynecology. While in Nome he took an active part in the organization of a civil government and helped to form a well-ordered city out of chaos. Dr. Gregg's ancestors came to America from Scotland early in the eighteenth century and his great-great-grandfather, Capt. James Gregg, was a militia officer in the patriot army during the struggle of the colonies to wrest independence from the mother country.

J. C. DUNN, M. D., of Pittsburg, Pa., a prominent physician and dermatologist, was born in Pictou county, Nova Scotia, in December, 1847, son of William and Catherine C. (McIntosh) Dunn, both natives of Nova Scotia and descendants from Scotch ancestry. His father was a millwright and farmer, and was a soldier of Great Britain who came to America during the Revolutionary war and later settled in Nova Scotia. Dr. Dunn was educated in the scientific and classical courses of the public schools of his native town and at the Pictou academy. He taught school in Nova Scotia for three years and was principal of the schools at Stellartown when he withdrew from that avocation. He entered the Jefferson medical college at Philadelphia, was graduated in 1871 and immediately began a general practice in Pittsburg. Dr. Dunn continued as a general practitioner until 1886, when he confined his practice to dermatology, and since has achieved unusual success in that specialty. He was physician and surgeon to the St. Francis hospital for several years, is dermatologist and physician to West Pennsylvania hospital, dermatologist to St. Francis hospital, consulting obstetrician at Rheineman hospital, consulting dermatologist at Pittsburg free dispensary, in charge of the dermatological work at the West Pennsylvania college dispensary, professor of clinical dermatology, materia medica and therapeutics at the Western Pennsylvania medical college. Dr. Dunn is a member and ex-president of the Allegheny county medical society, member of the Pennsylvania state and the American medical associations, the Pittsburg academy of medicine, the American association of obstetricians and gynecologists, ex-member of the American public health association, honorary member and ex-president of the West Pennsylvania hospital staff, and also a member of the Austin Flint medical society of East End, Pittsburg. Dr. Dunn is identified with a number of the prominent fraternal orders, holding membership in the Ancient Order of United Workmen, the Royal Arcanum, the Protected Home Circle and the Odd Fellows. He was a member and president of the board of health of Pittsburg for several years and is a member of the republican party. Dr. Dunn is a member of the Fourth Presbyterian church of Pittsburg, has been a member of its sessions for thirty years, was superintendent of the Sabbath-school and delegate to the general assembly which met at Washington, D. C. He was married, in 1872, to Juliette Thalia, daughter of Edward G. and Wilhelmina DuBarry, who died June 22, 1903, after a protracted illness. Her father was born in Philadelphia and was a machinist and her mother was a native of Germany, who came to America in early life, settled at Economy, Allegheny county, and subsequently removed to Pittsburg. Dr. and Mrs. Dunn are the parents of six children, two of whom are living, viz.: John Sidney, a student at Westminster college, and George DuBarry, a student at East Liberty academy. Dr. Dunn has made an unqualified success of his career and stands high as a physician and as a man.

GEORGE HOGG, contractor and builder, who resides at No. 514 Fourth St., Braddock, is a progressive Scotchman who was born in Carnoustie, May 7, 1851, son of George and Isabel (Matthenson) Hogg. He was educated in Dundee, Scotland, and learned the stone-masons' trade, and served for many years with Brown & Sons, extensive contractors of that place. Mr. Hogg was married, Dec. 31, 1873, to Jessie, daughter of William and Agnes (Eadie) Latto, of St. Andrews, Scotland, and resided in Dundee until 1880, when he came to America and located in Braddock. He has secured an extensive patronage as a lumber dealer, contractor and builder during his long residence in that city. Most of the schoolhouses in Braddock and nearby boroughs were erected by Mr. Hogg, as were many other public buildings. He also built the Westinghouse electrical works at East Pittsburg, which are the largest of their kind in the world, with a ground space 1,000 by 430 feet. The children of Mr. and Mrs. Hogg are: William M., mentioned below; Georgiana, who died in infancy; David M., in the class of 1903, Western university; Agnes, at home; Isabelle, in the class of 1904, Braddock high school; George, Jr., a student at Shady Side academy; Charles and Jessie, attending the Braddock schools. Mr. Hogg is a member of Braddock Field lodge, No. 510, F. and A. M.; Shiloh chapter, No. 257, R. A. M.; Tancred commandery, No. 48, Knights Templars; Pennsylvania consistory, of the Scottish Rite; Syria temple, A. A. O. N. of M. S.; Braddock Field lodge, No. 529, I. O. O. F., and B. P. O. Elks of Pittsburg. He is also a member of the Monongahela club, of Pittsburg, and is generally recognized as one of the most prominent and progressive citizens of Braddock. William M. Hogg, son of George Hogg, was born in Dundee, Scotland, May 19, 1875. He came to America with his parents in 1880, and received a grammar-school education in the Braddock schools. He then learned the brick-laying trade with his father, and worked at the trade four years. He has since been employed in the counting-room and other departments, and on Jan. 1, 1902, became a partner in the firm of the George Hogg company. He belongs to the same lodges as his father, except that he is a member of the Wilkinsburg Elks, No. 577, and is also a member of several other secret societies. He was married, Jan. 1, 1898, to Amelia Jane, daughter of Frank and Lucy Bridges, who were formerly residents of Johnstown. Mr. and Mrs. William M. Hogg have two children: Lucile, born Nov. 23, 1898, and Wallace Bruce, born Jan. 1, 1901.

PROF. W. E. EICKEMEYER, principal of the Bethlehem German Lutheran Evangelical school, in the eastern district of the Ohio synod, thirty-first ward of Pittsburg, was born Oct. 25, 1881, in Bornholm, Ontario, Canada. He is a son of Henry and Emma Eickemeyer, natives of Canada and of German descent. To them were born eight children, of whom the subject of this sketch is the eldest. Professor Eickemeyer was educated in the Lutheran parish schools of Marysville, Ohio, and in the Woodville seminary, where he took a course in languages. He devoted many hours a day to the study of music, in which he became proficient both as a teacher and as a chorister, and is at present the organist and chorister in the Lutheran church in Allentown, as well as a teacher of music in the city. His parents live at Marysville, Ohio, where his father is one of the leading merchants and manufacturers of that town. Mr. Eickemeyer came to Pittsburg in September, 1901, and assumed the position of principal in the parochial school. He is recognized as an accomplished young man, a thorough teacher, and has already done much for his church, his school and the community.

HENRY B. NAYLOR, son of Harry and Annie M. (Baldwin) Naylor, was born in Pittsburg, April 19, 1864. His father was born in Manchester, England, in March, 1836, and came to America in 1859, locating in Pittsburg, where he engaged in the oil-refining business. Later he removed to Oil City, where he died March 15, 1903. The mother, Annie M. Baldwin, was born in Boston, Mass., in 1840, and went with her parents to Pittsburg. Mr. Naylor received his education in the public schools of Oil City, and later prepared himself for his remarkably successful business career through the correspondence school of the Scranton engineering college. Mr. Naylor's first work was that of machinist, a trade he had learned in Oil City and followed for twelve years, the learning and mastering of the trade in Oil City occupying three years. He then was with the Westinghouse company, of Pittsburg, three years, and four years with the McIntosh-Hemphill company, of Pittsburg. Later he became superintendent of the Second National bank building, and in 1900 he became superintendent of all the property of Henry Phipps, the millionaire capitalist and philanthropist, in Pittsburg and Allegheny. Mr. Naylor has charge of all buildings, erection of new ones, rents and contracts, hiring, and the like. He is now erecting for Mr. Phipps the thirteen-story Bessemer building, on the corner of Sixth street and Duquesne way, and the Phipps power house, Pittsburg. Mr. Naylor was president of the board of school control for the first ward, Allegheny, where he has resided since 1898. He was the prime mover in the establishment, by the first ward board in 1900, of the Allegheny training school, of which Mr. Hoyt is principal. This is one of the finest schools of its kind in the state connected with the public schools, and Mr. Naylor has given it much attention and has shown the greatest interest in its success, not only in its establishment, but in all its work since. In 1902 Mr. Phipps erected a fine two-story brick building, known as the Phipps gymnasium and playground, and in this institution also Mr. Naylor has taken an important part. It is a public institution containing free baths and reading-rooms open to all. Mr. Naylor has taken up the cause of the children of the ward, and to him more than to any other man in the ward are due the excellent advantages enjoyed by young and old. Mr. Naylor is a republican in politics, is a member of the citizens' party, interested in party reform in the county, and in favor of good, clean administration in public offices. Mr. Naylor is a Mason, belonging to Allegheny lodge, No. 223; Allegheny chapter, No. 217; No. 35, Knights Templars, and to Syria temple, A. A. O. N. M. S., of Pittsburg; also to No. 25, A. O. U. W., Allegheny, of which he is past master workman. Mr. Naylor was married, on Dec. 2, 1882, to Mary Ada Wolf, the youngest daughter of King Wolf, of Armstrong county, a farmer and blacksmith. They were married by Rev. Dr. Sloan, of the Presbyterian church, and now reside in the fifteenth ward, Allegheny. They are members of the Central Presbyterian church, of which he is also a trustee. The parents of Mr. Naylor were married April 20, 1863, and have seven children, of whom the subject of this sketch is the oldest, the others being: Mazie, a teacher in the public schools of Oil City; Della Baldwin, married to Fred M. Morgan, living in Denver, Col.; James D., of Pittsburg; Annie M., at home; John A., of Uniontown, Pa., and Bernice U., living with Mr. Naylor in Allegheny. Mr. Naylor is a splendid example of physical manhood, and shows his English lineage in his sturdy physique. He makes stanch friends and some enemies. His progress has been rapid, and he has climbed the ladder of success by hard work and faithful, conscientious attention to duty.

THOMAS PROSSER, general contractor in Carnegie, with an extensive business in street-paving, building sewers and excavating, was born in Staffordshire, England, March 24, 1846. His father, Thomas Prosser, came to America in 1871, and died in 1881 at the age of seventy. His wife, Mary Ann Prosser, died in England, March 8, 1867, at the age of sixty-one. Thomas Prosser, Sr., was a miner in England, and continued to work in the mines after coming to America. Mr. and Mrs. Thomas Prosser had ten children, of whom Thomas, Jr., the subject of this sketch, and two others are living: James, a miner, who resides in Carnegie, and Jane, who married George Betz. The subject of this sketch was educated in England, and followed coal-mining there. Coming to America in 1868, he settled near Sharon, Pa., where he was engaged in mining for fifteen years, and then turned his attention to the contracting business, in which he has met with marked success. His contracts amount to between $40,000 and $50,000 yearly, and he employs from thirty-five to forty men most of the time. Mr. Prosser has done much valuable work in Carnegie and nearby towns, but most of his contracts are for improvements in Pittsburg and Allegheny. Prior to his coming to Pennsylvania, Mr. Prosser was married to Miss Catherine Cox, of Staffordshire, their marriage occurring on June 7, 1867. She was the daughter of Thomas and Hannah Cox, both of whom lived and died in England. Mr. and Mrs. Prosser have had ten children born to them, viz.: Thomas, a resident of Carnegie, who married Miss Musgrave, and has six children: Kate, Lillie, Jennie, Edna, Thomas and George; Jennie M., who married William Tatterdale, a steel-worker, and has one child, Ethel; James, an assistant in his father's business, living at home; Katie, who died in 1890 in her seventeenth year; William H., a resident of Carnegie, who married Miss Berdella Bell, and has one child, Berdella; Hannah J., who married Samuel Sarner, a farmer, and has one child, Harold; George H., at home, a civil engineer employed by the National mining company; Laura H., at home; Albert E., a plumber, and Edith, in school. Mr. Prosser and family are members of the United Presbyterian church. Mr. Prosser is a member of the I. O. O. F., and also a member of the Sons of St. George. In politics he is a republican, and cast his first vote for President U. S. Grant.

PROF. R. M. SHERRARD, principal of the No. 2 eleventh ward public school of Allegheny city, was born in Bucyrus, Ohio, Oct. 1, 1869. The Sherrard family is an old and respected one in Ohio, John Sherrard being the great-grandfather of the subject of this sketch, Robert A. Sherrard the grandfather, and John Hindman Sherrard the father. Mr. Sherrard, the father, was born on Sugar Hill farm, near Steubenville, Ohio, March 24, 1830. His mother was Keziah Neulon Fulton, daughter of Abram Fulton, of West Newton, Pa. The Sherrards and Fultons came from the north of Ireland in a very early day, the former coming in 1770, and the latter in about 1768. The father attended Washington college, graduating in 1857, and in the fall of the same year was married. He graduated from the Western theological seminary in 1861, and located in Rimersburg, Clarion county, remaining there from 1861 to 1867. During the Civil war he was in the Christian commission at Chattanooga as a missionary among the soldiers.

From 1867 to 1878 he was pastor of the Presbyterian church of Bucyrus, Ohio, and going from there to Washington, Pa., he became a member of the faculty of the Washington female seminary, at the same time holding the pastorate at Prosperity. In 1882 he moved to Delphos, Ohio, remaining until 1888, when he went to Rockville, Ind., then to Thorntown in 1896, retiring in 1900 on account of ill-health. He moved to Wilkinsburg, Pa., where he now resides. Professor Sherrard was educated in the schools of the towns in which his father was pastor, entered the preparatory department of the Washington and Jefferson college in 1886, graduating in 1891. From 1891 to 1894 he attended the academy at Chambersburg, then spent a year at private study, and in 1895 took charge of the department of Latin and Greek in Indiana state normal school. In September, 1899, he was elected to the eleventh ward public schools, his present position, with 600 children and thirteen teachers under his charge. Professor Sherrard has made his own way to the front, and stands to-day as one of the leading young principals in the city. He was married, Nov. 25, 1903, to Lyda Reid, daughter of Charles W. Cochran, of Pittsburg. Professor and Mrs. Sherrard are now living at No. 307 Neville St., Pittsburg.

WILLIAM VOGT, pastor of St. Joseph's Roman Catholic church, Carnegie, was born in Germany, near Cologne, June 13, 1870. His parents, Francis and Elizabeth (Goebel) Vogt, are still living, his father being now seventy-three years old, and his mother sixty-nine. Francis Vogt, now a farmer in Germany, served in the German army five years in the fifties. He and his wife are loyal members of the Roman Catholic church. They had six children born to them, as follows: Frank, a farmer in Europe; Joseph J., a priest, residing in Verona, Pa.; Sophia, at home with her parents; William, the subject of this sketch; Herman, who died in 1882, when ten years old, and August, also a priest, located at Mount Oliver, Allegheny county. Rev. William Vogt received his early education in Germany, and studied three years in a gymnasium in his native land. Coming to America in 1886, he resumed his studies, and, completing his education in 1895, was ordained to the priesthood at St. Vincent's, Beatty, Pa., and at once began his life-work as a priest, his first position being that of assistant pastor of St. Martin's Roman Catholic church, Pittsburg. After five years' faithful service in Pittsburg, Father Vogt took up his present charge, in June, 1900, where his application and attention to duty have made him popular with his congregation and strengthened and enlarged his church. St. Joseph's church has in connection a parochial school of some 200 pupils, taught by four of the sisters of St. Agnes, and the Sunday-school has an attendance of about 300. Father Vogt is an enthusiastic church worker, a diligent student, and his church is prosperous and well equipped.

JARED B. FIFE, real estate, loan and insurance agent at Carnegie, Pa., was born in Allegheny county, Pa. His parents, Nathaniel and Eleanor B. Fife, were natives of Pennsylvania, where Mr. Fife farmed a part of an estate in Allegheny county, which was bought in 1766 and is still in possession of the Fife family. Jared B. Fife attended the public school, and later Bethel academy, and on July 4, 1861, enlisted in the Union army as a private in Company H, 62d Pennsylvania volunteers; served three years, taking part in the battles of Yorktown, Gaines' Mill, Malvern hill, Antietam, Fredericksburg, Gettysburg, Petersburg, and in numerous other engagements, coming out with the rank of corporal. After the war he spent several years in mercantile pursuits, keeping a general store for a time, and afterwards a hardware business in Mansfield (now Carnegie). He sold out in 1874, when he became superintendent of Chartiers cemetery for nine years, being engaged in his present business since 1885. In the fall of 1888 he was elected tax collector of the borough, which position he has held ever since. In 1869 he married Mary A. Marshall, daughter of the late Rev. George Marshall, D. D., and Mary Lee Marshall. Mr. Fife's eldest child, George M., died Feb. 25, 1893; his daughter, Agnes Genevieve, is now at home. In religion the family are Presbyterians. J. B. Fife is a prominent Mason, and a member of Espy post, No. 153, G. A. R., of which he was the second commander. In politics he is a stanch republican.

W. H. ERSKINE, superintendent of the Rosslyn brick company, Carnegie, was born in Hancock county, W. Va., Jan. 28, 1867. His father, John Erskine, came to America in 1848, settling in Steubenville, Ohio, but is now living in Carnegie, at the age of sixty-seven. His wife, Eleanor (Eaton) Erskine, is also living. She is sixty-one years old. Mr. and Mrs. John Erskine had five children, of which the subject of this sketch was the second born. The others are: Eva, now Mrs. S. Steadman, of Baltimore, Md.; Nora E., now Mrs. William Bindley, and a resident of Cincinnati, Ohio; Louise, at home, and Hannah, who died when three years old. W. H. Erskine attended the public schools, and later studied two years at Mount Union, Ohio. After completing his education he started at once to learn the brick business and became a molder. His next position was that of foreman, which he followed for several years in Pennsylvania and at Saginaw, Mich., remaining four years at the latter place. In April, 1897, he came to Carnegie, and was for four years superintendent at the Fort Pitt brick-yard. Since 1891 Mr. Erskine has been superintendent of the Rosslyn brick company. This company is doing so flourishing a business that it is unable to keep up with its orders, although it employs about forty-five men, and produces 40,000 bricks a day. On Oct. 20, 1894, Mr. Erskine married Miss Laura Hunt, daughter of William and Julia (Hood) Hunt. Mr. and Mrs. Hunt had two other children besides Mrs. Erskine. They are: Charles, an engineer, married to Rose O. Wesley, and George, who married Stella Crawford. William Hunt is an engineer, and has followed this vocation all his life. His wife died in February, 1901. Mr. and Mrs. W. H. Erskine have two children: Earl Roy and Mildred. Mr. Erskine and wife are members of the Presbyterian church. Mr. Erskine is a prominent member of the I. O. O. F. He is not actively interested in politics, but votes the republican ticket.

WILLIAM HEISEL, glass-worker, residing on Beechwood avenue, Carnegie, was born in Pittling, Prussia, Dec. 17, 1846. His parents, John and Gertrude (Baker) Heisel, came to America in 1848, and settled at first near Homestead, Allegheny Co., Pa., and four years later moved to South Side, Pittsburg. The father was a coal-miner all his active life, and met his death in an accident while working in a coal mine, leaving a widow and four young children to mourn his loss. In all, six children were born to Mr. and Mrs. John Heisel, and of these only two survive, William, the subject of this sketch, and Anna, now Mrs. Adam Epp, residing in West End, Pittsburg. The mother died of apoplexy, in her eighty-fourth year. William Heisel attended St. Michael's school, on Pine street, South Side, Pittsburg, and at an early age went to work in the glass-works. He has been a glass-worker continuously since 1857. Mr. Heisel has always been a skillful workman, and, beginning at the bottom, has worked up through all the departments of the glass trade. He spent six years of his life at his trade at Elwood, Ind., and four years at Muncie, Ind., but has been a resident of Pennsylvania most of the time, and is now working at McDonald. On May 11, 1870, Mr. Heisel married Mary Marion, a native of Pennsylvania. Of the children born of this marriage, Gertrude is a stenographer and typewriter, Edward died when fifteen months old, Amelia is a bookkeeper in Carnegie, Elmer died in 1878 when four years old, Lillian is a stenographer in Pittsburg, Olivia, Alice and William are younger children in school. Mr. Heisel and family are members of the Roman Catholic church, as were Mr. Heisel's parents before him. Mr. Heisel is a member of the Knights of Maccabees and of the American bottle-blowers of the United States and Canada. He takes an interest in politics, and has been a delegate to political conventions on several occasions, but has never cared to hold office. He and his family occupy a residence which he purchased in 1898 on Beechwood avenue, one of the most sightly residence localities in Carnegie.

WILLIAM H. McKELVY, one of the foremost physicians of Allegheny county, was born Sept. 21, 1843, near Wilkinsburg, Pa. He is a son of James McKelvy, a native of County Down, Ireland, who came to Allegheny county when five years old, settling in Wilkinsburg and living there until his death at eighty-eight years. His wife, Rosanna Swisshelm, was born in Lancaster county, Pa., and was a daughter of Lieutenant Swisshelm, an officer in the Revolution. They were the parents of six children: James, circuit judge in the seventh judicial district of Minnesota, 1866-83, and died in St. Cloud in 1884; Elizabeth Hagen, who died in Lamar, Mo., where her husband, Rev. Mr. Hagen, was a Presbyterian minister; John S., Martha J., Wilbur F. and William H., the subject of this sketch. Mr. McKelvy was educated in Wilkinsburg academy and at Allegheny college, in Meadville, Pa. He was graduated from the College of physicians and surgeons in New York city in 1866, and opened an office in Pittsburg in 1867. In 1868 he was elected physician to the county jail, a position he held for thirteen years. Mr. McKelvy is interested in educational matters, being a member of the central school board for twenty-seven years and president of the same for twenty years. He is a member of the library association, and was one of the trustees of the Carnegie library for six years. Mr. McKelvy is a member of the Allegheny county medical society of Pittsburg and of the American medical association. He is a Mason and Knight Templar, and active in promoting the good of the order in the state. He is a republican and a stanch supporter of his party. He was married, March 23, 1897, to Margaret Youngson, of Pittsburg.

GEORGE W. BODEN, mine foreman of the Bower Hill coal mine, was born in Mercer county, Pa., June 23, 1869, a son of David and Ellen (Cook) Boden, both natives of England. The father was a mill worker in England and also worked in the mines there, and on coming to America, in 1859, continued to follow his vocation as a miner. He located first at Pottsville, Pa., and later at Banksville, where he opened up a mine of his own but discontinued it after about a year, and became a mine foreman in the same place. He next spent a year prospecting for coal in Mahoning county, Ohio, and then, returning to Pennsylvania, was a mine foreman in Mercer county. In 1876 he opened up the Nixon mine and was foreman and stockholder in this mine until about a year before his death. He died Jan. 6, 1888, when fifty-six years old. His wife is still living at the age of sixty-six, a member of the Free Methodist church and an honored resident of Carnegie. Of the children of Mr. and Mrs. David Boden, Mary A. and Nellie both died when young and William David died when seventeen years old. William was a boy of unusual promise and his death was a sad blow to many. Of the others, Elizabeth A. married William Lindsley, superintendent of mines for the Pittsburg coal company; Lina E. is the wife of James M. Sloan, also a mine superintendent; George W. is the subject of this sketch; Chauncey C. is conductor on the Great Northern railway and David J. is an engineer on the Wabash railway. George W. Boden was educated in the public schools of Carnegie, and then went to work in a mine under his father, remaining there four years. After this he spent a year as an employe at the Schultz bridge works at McKeesport, and was for eighteen months fireman on the Pittsburg & Lake Erie railway. The next five years of his life he was weighmaster in a coal mine and then became shipping clerk for his uncle, David Boden, at the Mansfield coal mine. After this he was for four years employed by the Alexander Black coal company and when the company sold out, he remained as weighmaster at the mine until June, 1902, when he obtained his present position. The Bower Hill coal mine, situated two miles west of Carnegie, on the Pan Handle railway, is a valuable property and employs 125 men. Mr. Boden has a certificate from the state of Pennsylvania to act as mine foreman in any bituminous coal mine in the state. This certificate is a valuable testimonial to the experience and ability of its owner. On June 26, 1894, Mr. Boden was married to Miss Leila T. McMillen, a native of Allegheny county and daughter of Alexander J. and Matilda (Brown) McMillen. Mr. McMillen is a farmer in Upper St. Clair township and is prominent in educational affairs, having held the position of school director in his township. His wife died when forty-five years old. A son of Mr. and Mrs. McMillen, Ellis B., is a railroad man and makes his home with Mr. Boden, and a daughter, Maud B., also lives at the Boden home. Mr. Boden and wife have had three children: James A., Harold R. and George W. George W. died July 23, 1900, when six months old. Mrs. Boden died July 28, 1900. She was born Oct. 25, 1871. She was a faithful wife and mother and esteemed by her family and friends. Mr. Boden is a prominent citizen of Carnegie, takes an active interest in the welfare of the city and is a stockholder in the Building and Loan association. He is a member of the Knights of the Golden Eagle, a past commander and present member of the Knights of Malta and a member of the Royal Arcanum. In politics he is a republican.

JOHN PHILIP BOHLANDER, of Elizabeth, Pa., a successful and prosperous carpenter, was born at Dravosburg, Allegheny Co., Pa., March 8, 1859, son of Philip and Catherine (Miller) Bohlander, both natives of Germany. His father came to America in 1852, located at Dravosburg, and there was engaged in mining coal for John F. Dravo until about 1866. He then removed to Armstrong, Westmoreland county, where he worked as a butcher for a year, thence to Shaner Station of that county and there followed the trade of butchering for two years. In 1869 the elder Bohlander located at Elizabeth, where he conducted the leading meat-market of that borough until his retirement in 1902. He has some valuable real estate in Elizabeth and is reckoned one of the solid and progressive citizens of that borough. He was born in Germany in 1832, and, in 1854, married Catherine Miller, also a native of Germany, who died in 1867, leaving three children: Leonard, John P. and George. Philip Bohlander was again married in 1874 and on that occasion espoused Susan Messersmith, also a native of the Fatherland, who bore him three children: Christian, Alexander and Catherine, the latter deceased. Philip Bohlander is now enjoying the fruits of a well-spent career and is a member of the Presbyterian church, the Knights of Pythias and the Odd Fellows. John Philip Bohlander was reared in Elizabeth and educated in the public schools of that borough, completing his course in 1877. He then devoted his attention to the carpenters' trade, served an apprenticeship of four years and since has successfully followed that vocation. He resided in Homestead from 1897 until 1903, when he moved to Elizabeth, where he has valuable property interests. He was married, on Nov. 29, 1883, to Caroline F., daughter of Peter and Anna (Altmeyer) Yellig, and they have three sons: John P., George L. and William H. Mr. Bohlander and his wife are members of the Methodist Episcopal church and he is a member of Elizabeth lodge, No. 444, Knights of Pythias; Old Monongahela lodge, No. 209, Odd Fellows; Boaz council, No. 814, Royal Arcanum; Homestead council, No. 21, Order of Americus, and the Junior Order of United American Mechanics. His political affiliations are with the republican party and he is an active worker for its advancement and success.

JAMES M. SCHOULTS, a prominent contractor and builder, of Carnegie, was born in Allegheny county, Pa., Dec. 25, 1843. His parents, James and Sarah A. Schoults, both died of small-pox when the subject of this sketch was about a year and half old, and Mr. Schoults was reared by William McElhany on a farm in Indiana township, now called Richland township. As a boy he worked on the farm and attended the district school, and, when less than eighteen years old, began to learn the carpenters' trade. He has followed that vocation continuously since that time and has met with marked success. He has built many houses in Crafton and other places in Allegheny county and erected, in 1896, the Hustler building, which was the first tall building to be built in Carnegie. In former years, when a contractor was expected to understand architecture, he planned all his buildings, but has not given any attention to architecture for several years past. Mr. Schoults has won for himself a reputation for excellent work and enjoys the confidence of all who know him. On April 21, 1859, he married Miss Elizabeth Crummy, a native of Allegheny county, and daughter of David Crummy. The children born of this marriage were: Nancy Jane, who married John Leslie and has five children living: Pearl, Margaret, Edna, John and May; Margaret, who married John Hall of Allegheny, and has two children: Fern and Albert; and Mary F., now married to Adam Frederick of Allegheny, who has five children: Roy, Norman, Wilmer, Verna and Milford James. Mrs. Schoults died Aug. 10, 1881. She was a member of the Methodist Episcopal church. On May 1, 1883, Mr. Schoults married as his second wife, Miss Emma J. McClelland, daughter of William and Mary (Anderson) McClelland, and granddaughter of James and Sarah (Peebles) Anderson. Mr. and Mrs. McClelland were born on the same day, Aug. 14, 1836. Mr.

McClelland died Feb. 2, 1897, and his wife Jan. 12, 1894. Mr. and Mrs. McClelland were the parents of eight children, of whom Mrs. Schoults is the only one now living. The others were: Mrs. Steven Large, James E., Mrs. John Culbert, George Elmer, William John, Joseph S. and David Henry. By his second marriage Mr. Schoults is the father of two children, Minnie Myrtle and Earl Milford. Mr. Schoults belongs to no secret organizations. In political belief he is a republican, but takes no active interest in party politics. Mrs. Schoults, Minnie and Earl are members of the First Methodist Episcopal church of Carnegie.

GEORGE T. KIRKBRIDE, of the firm of Kirkbride & Sanford, dealers in general dry goods, Carnegie, is one of the most prominent business men in Carnegie. He is secretary, treasurer and general manager of the Fort Pitt stone and brick company, Carnegie, and a member of the Carnegie board of trade. He was born Oct. 15, 1861, in Mansfield, now Carnegie, in the historic Davis house, which he has recently purchased. Mr. Kirkbride's parents were Capt. Thomas E. and Annie E. (Moreland) Kirkbride. They were married in 1857 and came to Carnegie, then called Mansfield. At the first call for men to fight in the Civil war, Mr. Kirkbride volunteered and was made captain of a company recruited in the West End, Pittsburg. The company was one of those which composed the 13th Pennsylvania volunteer infantry and afterwards was merged into the 102d volunteer infantry, Army of the Potomac. The intrepid Captain Kirkbride fought in all the battles of his command until, on May 5, 1864, he received a mortal wound while fighting in the Wilderness. He was taken to a hospital at Washington, where he died sixteen days later. His young wife was at his bedside when the end came. Captain Kirkbride and wife were members of the Methodist Episcopal church of Mansfield. They had two other children besides the subject of this sketch. Of these, the daughter, Ida M., afterwards Mrs. J. M. Belleville, of Philadelphia, died when thirty-seven years old; and the son, Charles E. Kirkbride, is a machinist of Allegheny. George T. Kirkbride, the subject of this sketch, attended the public schools of Carnegie, and when twelve years old was employed by the late W. J. Ford, who was then a banker and postmaster of Carnegie. He remained with Mr. Ford for two years and then learned telegraphy and was a telegraph operator until 1887. Then, in company with Mr. Sanford, he bought out the dry goods business of A. W. Waldie, and has since been engaged in the dry goods business with good success. The store, which is large and commodious, carries a full line of dry goods, notions, millinery, wall paper and house furnishings, and does a steadily increasing business. Besides this, the firm also owns, in the second ward, Carnegie, the dry goods store formerly kept by McCracken & Co., where they have a good trade. In 1898 Mr. Kirkbride organized the Fort Pitt stone and brick company, of which he is secretary, treasurer and general manager, and H. J. Verner, president. This business, by means of good management and the addition of improved machinery, has grown to be one of the leading industries in Carnegie. The concern produces 40,000 bricks a day and employs fifty men, with a pay roll amounting to $30,000 per year. Mr. Kirkbride was married, Nov. 10, 1890, to Miss Jennie Waldie, a native of Carnegie, and daughter of James and Jane Waldie, old and respected residents of that city, and sister of the late A. W. Waldie. Mr. and Mrs. Kirkbride have two daughters, Ida J. and Elizabeth Lucile. Mr. Kirkbride and wife are members of the United Presbyterian church. In politics Mr. Kirkbride is a republican, but has been too busy with other matters to take great interest in party questions. He served three years as a member of the Carnegie school board, however, and during that time the Carnegie high school was erected. He is an enthusiastic member of the Masonic fraternity, being a past master of Centennial lodge, No. 544, A. F. and A. M.; member of Cyrus chapter, No. 280, and Tancred commandery, Knights Templars.

WILLIAM BORGMANN was born in Westfalen, Germany, March 16, 1856, son of William and Maria (Hanefeld) Borgmann, natives of Germany. William Borgmann, Sr., a son of Ebehard Borgmann, was a hotel-keeper in Germany and ran a grocery in connection. He retired from business seven years before his death, which occurred in 1894. His wife died when sixty-six years old, in August, 1902. Both were members of the Roman Catholic church. Besides this son, William, the subject of this sketch, they had one daughter, Emma, who married Dr. Otto Plange, a resident of Muenster, Germany. Dr. Plange and wife have four children; Julius, Margaret, Paul and Otto. William Borgmann was educated in a gymnasium at Bochum, Germany, and after completing his education spent several years as a banker. He was married in Germany, Oct. 18, 1884, to Miss Hedwig Plange, a sister of Dr. Otto Plange, who married Mr. Borgmann's sister. Mrs. Borgmann is a daughter of Theodore and Theresa Plange. Her mother died in 1898, at the age of seventy-nine, and her father a year later, when eighty-two years old. Mr. Borgmann came to America in 1890, locating first in Pittsburg, where he remained three years, and then in Carnegie, where he has since resided. During his residence in Carnegie he worked first for Emil Grimm, and later for Julius Gottfried and then engaged in the wholesale liquor business for himself. Now he is general manager for the Chartiers Valley brewing company. Mr. and Mrs. Borgmann have four children: Hedwig, William, Ingelborg and Erich. Mrs. Borgmann and children came to America in 1899, and have since resided in Carnegie. The family are members of the St. Joseph Roman Catholic church. Mr. Borgmann, although for most of his life a citizen of Germany, is an ardent admirer of the energy and progress of the United States, and a loyal citizen of his new country.

ALBERT FREDERICK LEUSCHNER, of West Homestead, Pa., a prosperous wagon-builder, was born at Radeberg, in Saxony, Germany, Sept. 24, 1874, son of Edward Frederick and Pauline (Rehn) Leuschner, who were natives of Germany. His parents came to the United States in 1883, located at Homestead, where his father embarked in the business of wagon-making, having learned that trade in the old country. He established the business now conducted by his son and successfully ran the same until his retirement in 1900, when he disposed of the stock and good-will to the subject of this sketch, which establishment the latter has since conducted with skill and ability. Prior to the purchase of his father's interests, Albert F. had been identified with the business for a number of years, under the firm name of Leuschner & Son, and was in active charge of the blacksmith department. His father, who died on March 17, 1902, had been twice married, first to a Miss Eisel, who bore him three children: Max, Richard and Herman; and on the second occasion to Pauline Rehn, by whom he had two children: Albert F. and Mary A. Albert F. Leuschner was reared in Homestead from nine years of age, attended the public schools of that borough and when thirteen years of age became an apprentice at the wagon-makers' trade, which he completed when nineteen years old. He then turned his attention to learning the blacksmith trade, which he finished in 1895, and two years later embarked in business with his father, as previously stated, and became sole proprietor in 1900. He was married, on Oct. 17, 1896, to Ida Clare Mitchell, of New Castle, Pa., and they have one son, Edward Robert. Mr. Leuschner is a member of the

Lutheran church, the Masons, the Elks, the German Haragin lodge of Homestead and the Homestead Eintracd singing and turnverein society. He is a stanch republican in his political views and associations, has twice served as a delegate to county conventions and since 1900 has been prominently identified with the school board of West Homestead borough, being president of the school board. He is a member of the republican county committee.

ROBERT LEWIS WATSON, of Duquesne, Pa., superintendent of the Duquesne water-works, was born near Bellefonte, Pa., June 8, 1864, son of James and Elizabeth (Hess) Watson, both natives of Centre county, Pa. His paternal grandfather, Robert Lewis Watson, was also a native of Centre county and the son of James Riddle Watson, a native of Scotland and a pioneer farmer of Centre county, Pa. His paternal grandmother was a Miss Williams, of Welsh descent, and a woman of many fine traits of character. The maternal grandfather of the subject, Lewis Hess, was a native of Pennsylvania, of German descent, a farmer and lumberman, who married Elizabeth Shirck. James Watson, father of the subject, was a prominent farmer of Centre county, where he died, and his remains are buried in the Bellefonte cemetery. He reared a family of three children, viz.: Andrew J.; Anna B., wife of Weisel E. Turner, and Robert L. Robert L. Watson was reared in the county where so many of his relatives have lived, educated in the common schools, and when sixteen years of age removed to Joliet, Ill., where he was employed for nine years as engineer at the plant of the Illinois steel works. In 1889 Mr. Watson came to Duquesne, Pa., where he served as engineer for the Carnegie steel works until 1896, when he went to the Pacific coast and was employed in the capacity of an engineer at Everett, Wash., for two years. In 1898 he returned to Duquesne and became engineer at the plant of the American tin plate company, which position he ably filled until 1900, when he was appointed to his present position of superintendent of the Duquesne water-works, which office he has filled to the entire satisfaction of the borough. He was married, on Aug. 8, 1891, to Jennie, daughter of James and Margaret (O'Neill) Bready, of Duquesne, and they have five children, viz.: Belle, Robert L., Jr., Ralph O., William A. and Margaret. Mr. Watson and his wife are members of the Presbyterian church, and his political affiliations are with the republican party.

ROBERT E. SMALLEY, foreman of the docks in the shipyards at Elizabeth, was born Oct. 14, 1861, in Washington county, Pa., and is the son of Andrew J. and Annie (Roher) Smalley, both natives of that county. His education was obtained in the common schools, which he left at an early age to accept employment in a planing mill at West Brownsville, where he remained for six years. About 1881 he began work on the river as a ship carpenter, and has continued in that business ever since. For the last four years he has held his present position as foreman of the docks in the Elizabeth yards. Mr. Smalley was married, in 1896, to Miss Lydia Lambert, a daughter of Henry and Jane Lambert, of Elizabeth, and one son, Andrew J., has come to bless this union. Politically, Mr. Smalley is a democrat. He served on the Elizabeth school board for two years, and is now serving his second term, having been re-elected in 1903, in which office he discharges the duties of the position with intelligence and fidelity. He is a member of the Masonic fraternity, the Knights of Pythias, the Royal Arcanum, the Modern Woodmen of America, and the Methodist Episcopal church. In all these organizations he is a respected member, and takes an active interest in their growth and usefulness.

EDWARD MORTON, a well-known farmer of Scott township, Allegheny county, Pa., has lived all his life in that township. He was born on Nov. 30, 1873, and is the only son of Margaret Morton, who was for many years one of the best-known and most generally loved women in Scott township. She was born in Ireland, in 1836. In 1869 she came to this country. Upon landing in America, she came directly to Allegheny county. After living a short time in Pittsburg, she moved upon the farm in Scott township now owned and operated by her son and daughter. This farm consists of sixty acres and is one of the best in the township. During the last thirty years of her life she conducted a dairy. In this work she was ably assisted by her children, Edward, the subject of this sketch, and a daughter, Ann Jane, who was born in December, 1870. Mrs. Morton met with a tragic death on May 19, 1903. While riding with her daughter in a buggy, the vehicle broke down and she was thrown out with such force that her skull was fractured. She lived but a short time after the accident, her death being universally mourned by the people of the surrounding neighborhood. For many years preceding her death, she had been a consistent member of the United Presbyterian church and she died steadfast in the faith. Both her children are members of the same denomination. Edward Morton received a good education in the common schools, and he has kept up with the march of events by reading and study since he left the schoolroom. He takes a keen interest in political matters and is one of the acknowledged leaders of the republican party of Scott township. He is a member of West Liberty council, No. 273, Junior Order of United American Mechanics, and of Washington camp, No. 2, Patriotic Order Sons of America. There is something both noble and pathetic in the love of Edward Morton and his sister for their honored mother and for each other. During her life their highest ambition was to please her and lighten her burdens.

GEORGE HAYDEN BAIRD, one of the leading merchants of the town of Bridgeville, Pa., was born in Fayette county of that state, Aug. 21, 1870, and is the son of Jeremiah and Margery M. Baird. Both his parents were natives of Pennsylvania and were of Scotch-Irish descent. The father was born on Oct. 9, 1828, and died on May 29, 1901. During his life he was a prosperous farmer of Fayette county. The mother was born on Oct. 25, 1825, and died on March 26, 1902. She was a daughter of Robert Finley. To this couple were born eleven children: Winona C.; Margaret, now the wife of Dr. William McClure; Robert, William F., Moses A., Mary M.; George H., the subject of this sketch; Edward J., James F., Anna Florence and Benjamin B. Until he was twenty-two years of age, George lived at home with his parents, assisting with the farm work and attending the common schools. Later he took a partial course in the Kiskiminetas institute at Saltsburg, after which he finished his education in Duff's business college in the city of Pittsburg, graduating in the class of 1891. In the spring of 1899 he established his present place of business in Bridgeville, and owing to his genial disposition and his correct business methods, he has prospered from the outset. Mr. Baird is a member of Bridgeville lodge, No. 396, Independent Order of Odd Fellows, and Centennial lodge, No. 544, Free and Accepted Masons. On all political questions touching state or national problems, he affiliates with the republican party, but in local matters he is not a partisan in any sense of the term, believing in the election of the best men to local offices. On Sept. 14, 1899, he was married to Miss Ella M., daughter of the late John H. and Rebecca H. Morgan. Mrs. Baird's father was born in Allegheny county, Pa., Sept. 16, 1839, and died there March 18, 1874. Her mother was born on April 11, 1841, and is still living at the age of sixty-two years, but she is so well preserved that she has the appearance of being much younger. John H. and Rebecca Morgan were married on Feb. 22, 1866, and their daughter, Ella, was born on Dec. 27, 1869. Like her husband, she is of Scotch-Irish lineage. She graduated from the Washington seminary with the class of 1894, and for four years after leaving school, she was a teacher in the public schools of Bridgeville, most of the time in the second grade. Mr. and Mrs. Baird are members of and regular attendants at the Presbyterian church. They have no children. He has recently completed one of the cosiest homes in the Bridgeville borough, a handsome two-story house which, with the lot upon which it stands, cost him nearly $5,000.

LEONARD RIEHL, farmer and justice of the peace of Scott township, Allegheny Co., Pa., is a son of Peter and Rebecca (Heldman) Riehl, both of whom were natives of Germany. Rebecca Heldman came to America in 1858. Two years later Peter Riehl came, and the couple were married in Allegheny county, Pa., in 1862. They had two sons: Leonard, the subject of this sketch, who was born Feb. 5, 1864, and Peter, born May 3, 1866. Leonard Riehl was brought up on his father's farm, attended the common schools, and later took several terms at Duff's business college in Pittsburg, thus securing a good, practical education. He owns a farm of seventy-eight acres—one of the best in Scott township—and manages it in the most approved manner. He takes an active interest in everything that has a tendency to promote the welfare of the community in which he lives, and is regarded as one of the most public-spirited men in the township. Early in 1902 he was nominated by the republican party for the office of justice of the peace, and at the election on February 17th of that year, he was triumphantly elected for a term of five years, many of his political opponents voting for him because of the confidence they had in him as a man and a neighbor. In 1891 Leonard Riehl and Paulina Fischer were made man and wife. She is a daughter of John and Doretta Fischer, both natives of Germany and well-known residents of Allegheny county, and was born March 27, 1868. Mr. and Mrs. Riehl are the parents of five children, viz.: Arthur Otto, Walter Waldorf, Laura, George Dewey and Sylvia Doretta. Both parents are members of the German Lutheran church, and consistently practice the tenets of their religion in their daily conduct.

HENRY DAUBE, a prosperous and well-known farmer of Scott township, Allegheny Co., Pa., is a lifelong resident of the county, having been born there Sept. 7, 1857. His father, Henry J. Daube, was born in Germany in 1814, and died in Allegheny county in 1886. His mother was Catharine (Chisler) Daube. She, too, was a native of Germany, and is still living with her son, John H. Daube, in Scott township. Henry Daube was reared on a farm. As a boy he attended the common schools during the winter months, thus securing a fair education, to which he has added by reading and observation. Ever since reaching manhood he has followed the vocation of a farmer, and few men can show a better-managed farm than his. He has always been a democrat in politics and keeps himself well informed on the political topics of the times. In 1873 he was married to Miss Barbara Snyder, a daughter of Anthony and Mary (Portman) Snyder. Mrs. Daube was born in Allegheny county in 1859. She and her husband are the parents of five children: Mary, aged eighteen years; Joseph, sixteen; Tillie, thirteen; Harry, eleven, and Lucy, eight. Mr. Daube and his wife are both members of the Roman Catholic church, and are regular attendants upon the church rites.

WILLIAM ALDERSON, who owns one of the largest farms in Scott township, Allegheny Co., Pa., was born in that county, April 3, 1837. He is a son of Thomas and Jane (Parker) Alderson, both of whom were natives of England, the former being born March 6, 1808, and the latter, Aug. 17, 1810. They were married in England, but came to America in the early thirties and located at Pittsburg, Pa., where for about fifteen years Thomas Alderson followed the business of a coal operator. At the end of that time he became a farmer and remained in that occupation until his death, which occurred on Jan. 30, 1888, his wife having died some ten years before—Dec. 25, 1878. They were the parents of eleven children, the oldest of whom, Mary, was born in England, April 3, 1830, and came with her parents to America when she was a babe. The others were all born in Allegheny county, Pa., at the dates given: Jane, Feb. 27, 1832; Sarah Ann, Oct. 30, 1835; William, our subject, April 3, 1837; Elizabeth, March 12, 1839; Margaret, March 20, 1841; John, Nov. 8, 1843; Sarah, Oct. 9, 1845; Emma, Sept. 26, 1847; Annie, Oct. 13, 1849, and Hattie, March 26, 1851. John and Sarah are deceased, but the others are still living. William Alderson received a common-school education and began life as a farmer on a small scale. He now owns three tracts of land in Scott township, aggregating 115 acres, all of which is in a fine state of cultivation. For the last twenty-five years he has continuously held some of the township offices, which shows the esteem in which he is held by his neighbors. Until about ten years ago he always worked and voted with the democratic party, but since that time he has been an enthusiastic republican. In 1876 he was married to Miss Annie Vero, the daughter of Joseph and Phœbe Elizabeth (Thomas) Vero. Mrs. Alderson is a native of Staffordshire, England, but came with her parents to this country when she was about seven years of age. They settled at Pittsburg, where she obtained a good education in the city schools. To William and Annie Alderson have been born the following children: James William, Jane Lizzie (now the wife of Alvah Sharlton), Margaret, Thomas Parker, Harry Lawrence, Anna (deceased), Edith Mabel, Emma Bockstoce, Phœbe Eleanor, Raymond Russell, William Henry, Annie Roberta, Walter Howard and John Albert. Mrs. Alderson is a member of the United Presbyterian church. William Alderson, although not a member of any religious denomination, is a man of sound morals and an unimpeachable integrity. He is a member of Castle Shannon lodge, No. 108, Independent Order of Odd Fellows, and finds in the precepts of that order excellent rules for the government of his actions in all his relations with mankind.

ALBERT WEIR, liveryman and undertaker in the town of Imperial, North Fayette township, is one of the enterprising young business men of Allegheny county. He was born in the county, Dec. 1, 1874. His parents, Andrew and Margaret (Metzker) Weir, were both natives of Germany, the former being born in 1821, and the latter in the same year. When Andrew Weir was thirty-five years of age he came to America and settled in Allegheny county, where he passed the remainder of his life as a farmer. He died in 1891 at the age of seventy years. About the time that he came to this country, Margaret Metzker also came over with her parents, and they located in Allegheny county. She was married to Andrew Weir at Pittsburg, in 1857. Albert Weir is one of a family of several children and was brought up on his father's farm, receiving such an education as the common schools afforded. He followed agricultural pursuits until about 1898, when he learned undertaking, and later embarked in the business for himself, connecting with it a well-equipped livery stable. On Jan. 19, 1899, he was married to Miss Lucy, a daughter of Jabez and Susie Dore. She was born at Youngstown, Ohio, April 12, 1878. Her father was of English descent on the paternal side, and his mother was of Welsh lineage. Mrs. Weir's mother was of Scotch-Irish extraction. Both her parents were natives of Ohio. Mr. and Mrs. Weir have one child, Jabez, who was born Dec. 11, 1899. Both husband and wife are members of the United Presbyterian church. Politically, he is a republican.

REV. M. J. ORZECHOWSKI, pastor of St. Adelbert's church, Pittsburg, Pa., has been a resident of the United States since June, 1888. He was born in Warsaw, Poland, March 19, 1879, and attended the parochial schools there until he was nine years of age. Upon coming to America he went to Detroit, Mich., where for seven years he was a student in the Polish Seminary of St. Cyril and Methodius, taking the philosophical and classical courses. He then spent one year in Cincinnati, Ohio, in a theological course, after which he went to Overbrook, Pa., where a three-year theological course completed his education. On July 6, 1902, he was ordained by Bishop John Foley, of Detroit, for the Harrisburg diocese. Father Orzechowski said his first mass in the Polish Church of St. Hedwijs, in Chicago, where he spent one month as a priest immediately after his ordination. From St. Hedwijs he was sent to Lebanon, Pa., as an assistant for three weeks, when he was transferred to Lancaster, Pa., as an assistant at the Church of St. Anthony. He remained here but one month, when he was appointed pastor of Our Lady of the Consolation, a Polish church at Mt. Carmel, Pa. After eight months he resigned his charge, the parish being too small to support a priest. He then came to St. Adelbert's, on Fifteenth street, South Side, Pittsburg, where he is at present, and where his work is meeting with favorable results.

JOSEPH A. VERNON, who is one of the well-known contractors of the city of Homestead, is a son of John and Catherine (Mehan) Vernon, and was born in the city of Pittsburg, Nov. 3, 1870. He is one of a family of thirteen children, nine of whom are still living, viz.: Kate, wife of Thomas Hickey; Annie, wife of Antona Nestler; Ellen (deceased); Mary (deceased), who was the wife of Patrick Brennan; Arthur; Lizzie, wife of John Nestler; Jennie, wife of Dennis Byrne; William; Joseph A.; Alice (deceased), who was the wife of Frederick Mayo; John, Olivia and Ferguson (deceased). His father came to this country from Ireland about the year 1850. He is a native of Belfast. For a number of years he followed the business of a contractor in the cities of

Pittsburg and Homestead, in the latter of which he now lives retired. Catherine Mehan is a native of Londonderry, Ireland. She came to this country some years after her husband, and they were married in Philadelphia in 1856. Joseph A. Vernon was educated in the common schools, after which he learned the carpenters' trade in Homestead, and has been engaged at that occupation since 1887. In 1900 he began contracting for himself, and although there were a number of older contractors with whom he had to compete, he has been quite successful, some of the best buildings in the city being erected under his supervision. He is a member of the Catholic church. He takes an active interest in political affairs, always working with the republican party, to which he belongs.

GEORGE WASHINGTON RICHARDS, of Duquesne, Pa., a leading druggist, was born in Dravosburg, Allegheny county, Aug. 20, 1868, son of William and Mary (Williams) Richards, natives of Wales, who came to America in 1850, settled in Mifflin township, Allegheny county, where his father worked as a mining engineer for fifteen years, and later became an engineer in the mines of Dravosburg. He continued in that capacity until his death in 1890, at the age of sixty-five years, and was the father of nine children, all of whom are living, viz.: James; Charlotte, wife of Edward Morgan; William; Elizabeth, wife of David J. Lloyd; Thomas, John, Harry, George W. and Edward. George W. Richards was reared at Dravosburg, educated at the public schools and at the Dravosburg academy, where he was graduated in 1883, and subsequently completed a course at the Western university, at Pittsburg, graduating from that institution in 1892. From 1883 to 1892 he was employed as a clerk for the drug firm of J. R. McLain & Co., at Dravosburg, and in 1892 graduated from the Pittsburg college of pharmacy, received his certificate from the State pharmaceutical examining board, and also was licensed by the Ohio state board of examiners. Then he located at Duquesne, where he managed the drug establishment of W. J. E. McLain; in 1893 he became a partner of his former employer, under the firm name of McLain & Richards, which partnership has since continued. In 1902 they purchased the store of the Porter drug company, corner of Sixth street and Grant avenue, and now conduct this pharmacy as a branch, their main place being located at Grant and Duquesne avenues. Mr. Richards is a stockholder in the First National bank of Duquesne, of which he was a director for five years, and is also interested in and was one of the organizers of the Duquesne trust company, of which he is vice-president and which began operations on May 25, 1903. He is also a dealer in real estate, handling his own property, and is one of the most enterprising and progressive citizens of the borough. The religious belief of Mr. Richards is that of the Presbyterian faith, but he is liberal and broad-minded in his views, and is a supporter of all denominations. He is a member of Duquesne lodge, No. 751, B. P. O. Elks; Vesta lodge, Knights of Pythias, and is prominently identified with the operations of these orders. His political affiliations are with the republican party, and he has represented the first ward in the borough council, where he made a good record and there displayed the business acumen and sound judgment which have marked his private affairs.

STEPHEN S. CRUMP, of Dravosburg, Pa., president of the State bank, was born near Wheeling, W. Va., Nov. 6, 1830, and is the son of John and Ruth (Robinson) Crump, both natives of Virginia. His paternal grandfather, Stephen Crump, was, in later life, a farmer of Washington county, Pa., and married Nancy Sisson. His maternal grandfather, John Robinson, was a native of the north of Ireland and an early settler of Ohio county, W. Va., where he followed his occupation of farming. John Crump, the father of the subject of this sketch, was a wagon-maker by trade, and during the latter years of his life resided at Beaver, Pa., where he died. Stephen S. Crump was reared in Ohio county, W. Va., until his sixteenth year, attending the common schools of that county, and in 1847 located in Pittsburg, where he was employed as clerk in the oyster house of Holt & Maltby for two years. Then he went to McKeesport, where he clerked in a general store until 1852, when he went to Dravosburg, accepting a position in the store of John F. Dravos, in whose employ he remained until 1863. In that year he formed a partnership with his father-in-law, J. C. Risher, and began operating the Amity coal mines under the firm name of J. C. Risher & Co. By the death of Mr. Risher in 1899 the firm was dissolved, but the business was continued by Mr. Crump as S. S. Crump & Co. until 1899, when it was sold to the Monongahela River consolidated coal and coke company. While operating the Amity mines, Mr. Crump did an extensive and profitable business, mining some 2,500,000 bushels of coal annually, which he shipped to Cincinnati, Louisville and New Orleans. He also shipped a great deal of coal for other mines, and during this period conducted a general store at Dravosburg. In 1903 the State bank of Dravosburg was organized, with a capital of $75,000. Mr. Crump was elected president, and since that time has ably filled that position. He was married, on June 3, 1856, to Agnes, daughter of John C. and Nancy (McClure) Risher, of Dravosburg, and their home life is an ideal one. During his residence at Dravosburg he has served many years as postmaster under the different administrations, and when the borough of Dravosburg was incorporated in 1903, was elected its first burgess. He is exceedingly prominent in financial circles, being vice-president of the Tradesmen's National bank of Pittsburg, president of the Dravosburg bridge company, director in the McKeesport title and trust company, treasurer of the Richland cemetery company, and trustee of the J. C. Risher estate.

CHARLES WILLIAM ALLEBRAND, the pioneer funeral director of Duquesne, Pa., was born in McKeesport, Pa., June 26, 1862, son of John and Rachel (Nicholaus) Allebrand, both natives of Germany. His paternal grandparents were John and Margaret (Hach) Allebrand, who came to America in 1842, and shortly afterwards settled at McKeesport, where his grandfather engaged in butchering, an occupation at which he prospered until his death in 1864. His wife had died in 1861, leaving the following children, viz.: Nicholaus, John, Philip, and Elizabeth, the latter the wife of George Kinzenbach, a prominent citizen of McKeesport. Philip Allebrand was a soldier of the Civil war, enlisting as a private in Company I, 63d Pennsylvania volunteer infantry; was promoted to a corporalship, and served as such until his death in the fights around Petersburg in 1864. The maternal grandfather of the subject was William Nicholaus, who married a Miss Schoeller, both natives of Hesse Darmstadt, Germany, and they settled at McKeesport in the early forties, where his grandfather was engaged in the butchering business until his death. John Allebrand, father of Charles W., was born at Charhesen-Steinhau, Germany, May 11, 1833, and accompanied his parents to the United States in 1842. In 1854 he went to California, where he was engaged in the butchers' business, and also was part owner of a gold-producing mine, and in 1860 returned to McKeesport, where he married Rachel, daughter of William Nicholaus, of that city, and at once opened a meat-market. He conducted the market with much success until 1878, when he removed to his farm in North Versailles township and there engaged in agricultural pursuits until 1890, when he retired from active business, and now makes his home at McKeesport, though he spends much of his time in traveling. He had six children that grew to maturity, viz.: Charles W., Margaret (deceased), John N.; Louisa, wife of Frank Hoag; Fredericka, wife of Charles F. DeLong, and George A. Mr. Allebrand is a member of Aliquippa lodge, No. 375, Ancient Free and Accepted Masons; his religious affiliations are with the Presbyterian church, and in his political opinions and associations is a republican. Charles W. Allebrand was reared in McKeesport, educated in the public schools of that city and at Duff's business college, of Pittsburg. Then he spent two years in a mining venture in Colorado, and in 1889 located at Duquesne, where he embarked in his present business of undertaking, and has since continued in that line with much success, being the leading funeral director of that community. He was married, on Dec. 16, 1885, to Lida, daughter of James and Hetty (Carpenter) Michael, of North Versailles township, and a member of a prominent family of western Pennsylvania. Mr. and Mrs. Allebrand are the parents of four children, viz.: Henrietta, Carl F., J. George and J. Neeland. He and his wife are members of the First Presbyterian church of Duquesne, and Mr. Allebrand is a member of the Benevolent and Protective Order of Elks. Mr. Allebrand is a prominent republican, and has served as school director of the borough for two terms. He was one of the promoters and organizers of the Duquesne electric light company and president of that corporation for three years.

MRS. ANNA T. WINTERS, of Glenfield, Pa., a prominent woman of that borough, was born on Oct. 17, 1852, daughter of Hugh and Wealtly Annie Luster. She was married, on July 17, 1873, to Alexander Winters, and they are the parents of the following children: John W., who was born Aug. 29, 1874, and married Jennie Steward, Jan. 15, 1901; Blanche R., born Sept. 29, 1875, and married Charles Vaughn, Nov. 14, 1900; Minas T., born May 27, 1877, and married Nellie Walker, Aug. 20, 1902; Lula M., born July 17, 1880; Lily M., born July 17, 1880; Fern E., born Oct. 20, 1883; Olive L., born April 28, 1886, and Cuba H., born Nov. 25, 1888. Mrs. Winters' father, Hugh Luster, was the son of Arthur Luster, who was one of the first settlers of Allegheny county and a soldier in the patriot army during the struggles of the colonies to secure independence from the mother country. Hugh Luster was a soldier of the Civil war, first entering for a service of six months and later enlisting for three years, during which service he received a gunshot wound that entirely severed his thumb from his hand. This wound physically incapacitated him for service and he received an honorable discharge, returned to his home at Kilbuck, now known as Glenfield, where later he was accidentally killed by a moving train. Mrs. Winters had four sisters and an equal number of brothers, viz.: Mary, Mellie, Cordelia, Sarah, Charles, James, Amos and Arthur. Her husband, Alexander Winters, is the son of Robert Winters, and is a prosperous and successful plasterer and one of the most highly respected citizens of Glenfield, where he has made his home for a number of years. Mr. and Mrs. Winters have reared a family of intelligent and energetic children, supplied them with every necessity and given them all the advantages afforded by the educational institutions of that community.

HENRY D. THOMSON, superintendent of the Nixon, Leesdale and Summer Hill coal mines, resides with his family on School Hill avenue, Glendale, Woodville postoffice. He was born at McKeesport, Allegheny Co., Pa., Sept. 2, 1858. His parents, Joseph and Jane (Donaldson) Thomson, were born in Scotland, and married there, the father being engaged in sinking mine shafts. Mr. and Mrs. Joseph Thomson came to America in 1856, settling first in Allegheny, later at McKeesport, and moving thence to Westmoreland county. Joseph Thomson was an able mine foreman most of his active life. He died July 8, 1897, when seventy-one years old. His wife is still living at the age of seventy-five, a devout member of the Presbyterian church and a respected resident of North Huntington township, Westmoreland county. Mr. and Mrs. Joseph Thomson were the parents of ten children, of whom six are living, viz.: Grace, wife of John Shields, a bookkeeper at Robbins Station, Westmoreland county; Henry D., the subject of this sketch; Ellen, now Mrs. S. P. Radisbaugh, of Shaner Station; Mary, wife of Charles Thomas, of McKeesport; Jennie, now Mrs. Robert Morrison, of Etna, and Guy, an engineer in charge of the power plant at Woodville. Henry D. Thomson was educated in the public schools and in Curry institute, Pittsburg, graduating from that school in 1888. After graduation he was employed until 1897 as mine foreman for John Blyth & Co., and then came to Carnegie as mine foreman for the Pittsburg coal company. On Jan. 1, 1902, he was appointed superintendent of the company's interest as a reward for faithful and efficient services. Before coming to Carnegie, Mr. Thomson was school director in

Westmoreland county for six years. He was married, Dec. 29, 1889, to Miss Christina Torrence, a native of Scotland, but a resident of America since 1887. Mrs. Thomson is a daughter of William and Isabel Torrence, who reside in Braddock, where Mr. Torrence is a boiler-maker. She is the second of seven living children. The others are: Mrs. Alexander Kerr, of McKeesport; John, a foreman of the boiler-makers at Braddock; Mrs. C. P. Sanborn, of Huntington, W. Va.; William, employed as a scalper in the Homestead mills, residing in Braddock; Andrew, learning the machinists' trade at Huntington, W. Va., and James, employed at the Westinghouse plant at Wilmerding. Mr. and Mrs. Thomson have four children: Alexander, Isabel, Henry and William T. Mr. Thomson and wife are members of the Presbyterian church of Carnegie. Mr. Thomson is an enthusiastic member of the Knights of Pythias, in which he has passed through all the chairs. He is also a member of the Knights of Malta, Knights of the Golden Eagle, Junior Order of United American Mechanics, and is chief of the Order of Scottish Clans. In politics he has always been a republican.

JOHN SLOAN, conductor on the Pan Handle railway, residing with his family in Carnegie, was born in Westmoreland county, Dec. 5, 1838. His parents, Canada and Mary (Williamson) Sloan, were both born in Ireland and married there. They came to America before 1830, and after a year's residence in Quebec, where they landed, came to Pittsburg, and from there moved to Westmoreland county. The father farmed there in the summer, and in the winter went from house to house, plying his trade as a shoemaker. He died Feb. 10, 1861, when about fifty-one years old, and his wife died two years later at about the same age. They were worthy people, respected in the community where they lived. They were the parents of eleven children, six of whom are living, viz.: Joseph, a stone contractor of Johnstown; Sarah, widow of James Galbreath, residing in Johnstown; Mary, wife of Nathan Griffey, a farmer in Ligonier valley, Westmoreland county; John, the subject of this sketch; Matilda, now the wife of Amel Boucher, a member of the police force of Johnstown, and Frank, a passenger conductor, residing in Pittsburg. The others died in childhood. John Sloan was educated in the public schools of Ligonier township, Westmoreland county, and after school days learned to be a miller and followed this vocation ten years. In 1863 he became a railroad brakeman, and was ten months later given charge of a train as conductor. He has been on the pay-roll for thirty-eight years, always for the same company, with the exception of five months, when he came to Carnegie in 1870. He has been in many wrecks and accidents, but has escaped injury and is still hale and hearty, although one of the oldest conductors on the road. Mr. Sloan is a genial, pleasant gentleman, and his long service testifies to the esteem in which he is held by his employers. He was married on Dec. 5, 1860, his twenty-second birthday.

CHARLES AMER HAMILTON, one of the most popular young politicians of Allegheny county, is a descendant of one of the oldest families in western Pennsylvania. His paternal grandfather was for many years one of the best-known coal operators in the vicinity of Pine Run. He was also prominent in river navigation. Charles A. Hamilton was born in West Elizabeth, Jan. 17, 1874, and is a son of Denny P. and Sophia J. (Kelley) Hamilton. His father served with distinction in the Civil war, and is now residing at Braddock, Pa. His maternal grandfather, Jacob Amer Kelley, was also a soldier in the Civil war, and was killed in battle. Charles Hamilton has always lived in Allegheny county. He was educated in the public schools and entered upon his business career as a clerk. At the present time he holds a responsible position at Clairton. As a political worker he has few equals. He is an excellent mixer, a good judge of human nature, fertile in resources, and withal a young man of cool judgment. He is a republican, but during the campaign in Allegheny county in 1902 he took an active part in the citizens' movement. This shows that he places the public welfare above any mere question of party, and, with his superior ability, genial disposition and general popularity, there is certainly a brilliant future awaiting him.

CHARLES F. KNODERER (deceased), of Glenfield, Pa., for many years a prosperous and successful blacksmith of that borough, was born in Alsace, Germany, and when a young man came to America, settled at Kilbuck, now Glenfield, Pa., about 1844, and after a long and prominent career died on March 13, 1880. He was the son of Christian and Margaret Knoderer, the former of whom was a famous soldier, having been a captain under the great Napoleon for seventeen years and accompanying the emperor on the Russian campaign with 386 men, of which number only five returned with their captain to France. Christian Knoderer was an expert swordsman and fought many hand-to-hand fights, and on one occasion was severely wounded in a combat with three men, armed with sabers, whom he met single-handed. He came to the United States in 1844, purchased a farm of 106 acres in Ohio township, where his wife was born, in 1804, and remained on his farm until his death, at the age of eighty-five years. Charles F. Knoderer also upheld the family reputation for military prowess, participating in the Civil war and there rendering distinguished services to the Union army for two years and making a splendid reputation as a soldier. He was married, in 1868, to Amelia Lauderbaugh, and to them were born the following children: Albertiana, Clara, Christian, Emma and Sarah Elizabeth. Mrs. Knoderer was the daughter of Philip and Elizabeth Lauderbaugh, the former having been a soldier of the Civil war and a member of Company D, 63d regiment, Pennsylvania volunteers, and died while in the service. Charles F. Knoderer was a man of fine business ability and possessed a clear conception of his duty to his fellow-men, according to each one his rights and privileges and living according to the admonitions of the Golden Rule. He was very popular in Glenfield, where he was widely known, and enjoyed the respect and esteem of his entire acquaintanceship.

JOHN BERKENBUSH, of Haysville, Pa., a well-known citizen and a highly successful farmer, was born in Johnstown, Cambria Co., Pa., Jan. 25, 1860, son of George W. and Johanna (Bradour) Berkenbush, his father having been born in Germany, coming to America in 1844 and settling in Cumberland, Md., where he remained for several years and then removed to Johnstown, Pa., where he died in 1887. The elder Berkenbush was a baker and miller, and devoted the greater part of his career to the latter calling. His parents had ten children born to them, viz.: Elizabeth, Henry, Emma, Mary, Charles F., John, Anna, Catharine, Carrie and George W., of whom Elizabeth, Henry and Emma are deceased. John Berkenbush was educated in the public schools of Johnstown and was an employe of the Cambria steel company and the Pittsburg steel company (limited) during a number of years. He was a cupola foreman in the works of the Pittsburg steel company for four years; then for fourteen years was night superintendent of the Schoenberger works of Pittsburg, and now resides on his fine farm in Aleppo township, where he is pleasantly and profitably engaged in agricultural pursuits. Mr. Berkenbush was happily married to Margaret, daughter of Benjamin and Martha Murphy, Sept. 5, 1888, and they have had seven children, viz.: John B. (deceased), George W., Edna B., Mabel I., Charles F., Clarence and Kenneth. He is identified with two fraternal orders, holding membership in the Maccabees and the Masons and being in close sympathy with their high objects and purposes.

DAVID FRANKLIN BAIR, of Homestead, Pa., a prominent contractor and builder, was born near Greensburg, Pa., Feb. 27, 1844, son of Benjamin and Catherine (Shuey) Bair, both natives of Westmoreland county, Pa. His father was a prosperous farmer of that county, where he spent his entire life and there died in 1901, at the advanced age of eighty-seven years. He reared a family of eight children, viz.: Isaac, Jacob; Susannah, wife of George Smail; David Franklin, Hannah; Kate, wife of Jerry Congaware; Joseph and Emanuel. David F. Bair was reared in his native county and educated in its common schools. He served an apprenticeship as a carpenter, worked as a joiner for four years and for several years was engaged in contracting at Greensburg. In 1879 he came to Homestead as foreman in the McClean planing mill, where he remained for a number of years, and then became foreman of the carpenter department of the Homestead steel works. Since 1900 Mr. Bair has been following contracting and building with much success and has erected some of the handsomest structures in Homestead. He was married, in 1873, to Margaret, daughter of Abner and Mary A. (Kestler) Evans, of Greensburg, and they are consistent members of the Presbyterian church. Mr. Bair is also a member of the Knights of Honor, the B. P. O. Elks and of the republican party.

WILLIAM GRAY, tax collector of Homestead, and prominent real estate and insurance agent, is the son of John S. and Catherine (Jenkins) Gray, and was born at Banksville, Allegheny Co., Pa., Nov. 4, 1872. His father was a native of England and his mother of Wales. His maternal grandfather, William Jenkins, was for many years a resident of the South Side, Pittsburg, where he followed the occupation of a shoemaker. John S. Gray, the father of William, came from England in 1869 and settled in Allegheny county. For about fifteen years he was employed in the mines, but in 1885 he removed to Homestead and since that time has been connected with the Homestead steel works. He had twelve children, five of whom grew to maturity. They are: Isaac, William, Thomas, John and Anna. William Gray was educated in the public schools of Allegheny county and at the age of fifteen years he entered the Bryce glass works, where he remained as an employe for eight years. He then became interested in base-ball and for the next five years played with various clubs. From 1898 to 1903 he was employed in the Homestead steel works. In the spring of 1903 he was elected tax collector of Homestead by a decisive majority. Upon taking his office he also embarked in the real estate and insurance business. He was married, Nov. 19, 1896, to Estella L., daughter of Peter and Louisa (Wietz) Stemmler, of Homestead, and they have four children: Naomi A., Ruth L., Ella C. and Charles S. He and his wife are both members of the First Baptist church of Homestead. He is also a member of Homestead lodge, No. 479, Knights of Pythias, and the uniform rank of the same order. In politics he is a republican and as such was elected tax collector.

THOMAS MERRIMAN, of Glenfield, Pa., a successful and prosperous farmer, was born on Jan. 2, 1842, and has devoted the major part of his life to agricultural pursuits. He was a soldier of the Civil war, first enlisting for three years in Company C, 61st regiment, Pennsylvania infantry, and at the expiration of that service re-enlisting for the remainder of the war in Company E of the same regiment. He was in many of the leading battles, participating in the fights of Williamsburg, Fair Oaks, White Oak Swamps, seven days around Richmond, Antietam, Fredericksburg, Gettysburg, the Wilderness, Cold Harbor and Petersburg, and also served under Sheridan in the Shenandoah valley and with Grant at the capture of Richmond. At the close of the war he was honorably discharged, returned to his home, and on Nov. 14, 1873, married Mary Eckerman, and they had the following children: Pansy (deceased), Frank, Albert, Josephine, Perry, Catharine, Mary, Jacob, Thomas and Archie. Mrs. Merriman died on April 21, 1893, and is sincerely mourned by a large circle of friends and admirers. The paternal grandfather of the subject, Samuel Merriman, was one of the first settlers of Allegheny county and owned a large tract of land in what is now Aleppo township. He was a soldier of the patriot army during the struggles of the colonies for independent government, and his remains are buried in the family cemetery on the Merriman farm, which is one of the oldest burying-grounds in Allegheny county and in which all of Mr. Merriman's grandparents are interred.

www.ingramcontent.com/pod-product-compliance
Lightning Source LLC
Chambersburg PA
CBHW081212170426
43198CB00017B/2596